P9-DDD-079

Paris
Eating & Drinking

timeout.com

Published by Time Out Guides Ltd, a wholly owned subsidiary of Time Out Group Ltd.
Time Out and the Time Out logo are trademarks of Time Out Group Ltd.

© Time Out Group Ltd 2007
Previous editions 1996, 1997, 1999, 2000, 2002, 2003, 2005.

10 9 8 7 6 5 4 3 2 1

This edition first published in Great Britain in 2007 by Ebury Publishing
Ebury Publishing is a division of The Random House Group Ltd,
20 Vauxhall Bridge Road, London SW1V 2SA

Random House Australia Pty Limited 20 Alfred Street, Milsons Point, Sydney, New South Wales 2061, Australia
Random House New Zealand Limited 18 Poland Road, Glenfield, Auckland 10, New Zealand
Random House South Africa (Pty) Limited Isle of Houghton, Corner Boundary
Road & Carse O'Gowrie, Houghton 2198, South Africa

Random House UK Limited Reg. No. 954009

Distributed in USA by Publishers Group West
1700 Fourth Street, Berkeley, California 94710

Distributed in Canada by Publishers Group Canada
250A Carlton Street, Toronto, Ontario M5A 2L1

For further distribution details, see www.timeout.com

ISBN 10: 1-904978-95-9
ISBN 13: 9781904978954

A CIP catalogue record for this book is available from the British Library

Colour reprographics by Wyndeham Icon, 3 & 4 Maverton Road, London E3 2JE

Printed and bound in Germany by Appl

Papers used by Ebury Publishing are natural, recyclable products made from wood grown in sustainable forests

Time Out Guides Limited
Universal House
251 Tottenham Court Road
London W1T 7AB
Tel + 44 (0)20 7813 3000
Fax + 44 (0)20 7813 6001
Email guides@timeout.com
www.timeout.com

Editorial

Editor Rosa Jackson
Deputy Editor Lesley McCave
Editorial Assistant Hannah Sztumpf
Researcher Phillipe Landry
Proofreader Tamsin Shelton

Editorial/Managing Director Peter Fiennes
Series Editor Sarah Guy
Deputy Series Editor Cath Phillips
Business Manager Gareth Garner
Guides Co-ordinator Holly Pick
Accountant Kemi Olufuwa

Design

Art Director Scott Moore
Art Editor Pinelope Kourmouzoglou
Senior Designer Josephine Spencer
Graphic Designer Henry Elphick
Digital Imaging Dan Conway
Ad Make-up Jenni Prichard

Picture Desk

Picture Editor Jael Marschner
Deputy Picture Editor Tracey Kerrigan
Picture Researcher Helen McFarland

Advertising

Sales Director Mark Phillips
International Sales Manager Ross Canadé
International Sales Executive Simon Davies
Advertising Sales (Paris) Matt Tembe
Advertising Assistant Kate Staddon

Marketing

Group Marketing Director John Luck
Marketing Manager Yvonne Poon
Marketing & Publicity Manager, US Rosella Albanese

Production

Group Production Director Mark Lamond
Production Manager Brendan McKeown
Production Coordinator Caroline Bradford

Time Out Group

Chairman Tony Elliott
Managing Director Mike Hardwick
Financial Director Richard Waterlow
TO Magazine Ltd MD David Pepper
Group General Manager/Director Nichola Coulthard
TO Communications Ltd MD David Pepper
Group Art Director John Oakey
Group IT Director Simon Chappell

Written and researched by:
Marie-Noëlle Bauer, Anna Brooke, Lise Charlebois, Alison Culliford, Greg Delaney, Trish Deseine, Natasha Edwards, Duncan Fairgrieve, Phyllis Flick, Helen Harding, Rosa Jackson, John Laurenson, Jennifer Joan Lee, Alexander Lobrano, Steve Ludot, Olivier Magny, Nicola McDonald, Adrian Moore, Stephen Mudge, Ariadne Plaitakis, Louise Rogers, Katherine Spenley, John Talbott, Kathryn Tomasetti, Alice Quillet.

Additional contributions by:
Julianna Barnaby, Jemma Birrell, Maryanne Blacker, Peterjon Cresswell, Ethan Gilsdorf, Hannah Goldberg, Catherine Rowles, Sharon Sutcliffe; Natalie Whittle.

Special thanks to Samuel Landry.

Area maps Philippe Landry.

Other maps JS Graphics (john@jsgraphics.co.uk).

Cover photography by Chris Tubbs taken at Maison Blanche (see page 110 for contact details)
Page 3 photography by Chris Tubbs taken at Café de l'Homme (see page 112 for contact details)
Photography: pages 5, 13, 21, 25, 30, 70, 73, 74, 79, 92, 93, 100, 105, 109, 111, 113, 121, 123, 133, 134, 145, 167, 168, 181, 188, 190, 206, 210, 211, 215 Jean-Christophe Godet; pages 12, 19, 35, 39, 40, 45, 50, 51, 52, 57, 61, 66, 67, 82, 83, 85, 89, 114, 115, 119, 125, 130, 139, 142, 149, 151, 155, 157, 161, 163, 165, 171, 172, 175, 176, 177, 179, 186, 187, 191, 192, 194, 198, 199, 203 Karl Blackwell; pages 14, 156 Britta Jaschinski; page 184 Ed Marshall.

Contents

About the guide 9
Small wonders 12
A la carte 15

FRENCH CUISINE

French 20
Fashion 108
Le Snacking 113
Vegetarian 117

INTERNATIONAL

African & Indian Ocean 122
The Americas 124
Caribbean 129
Eastern Mediterranean 130
Far Eastern 132
Indian 141
Italian 144
Japanese 150

Jewish 154
North African 156
Spanish 160
Other International 162

ON THE TOWN

Cafés, Bars & Pubs 166
Tea Rooms 191
Wine Bars 196
Eating with Entertainment 203
Shopping & Cooking 205

INDEX & MAPS

Index 216
Lexicon 234
Arrondissement Map 240
Street Maps 242
Métro Map 256

bumpy boat ride at the seaport where you lost your wallet: $45
(not feeling queasy: priceless)

©2006 MasterCard International Incorporated

Don't worry. MasterCard Global Service™ is available wherever you travel, in any language you speak. So just call the local toll-free number and we'll rush you a new card most anywhere in the world. For a complete list of toll-free numbers, go to www.mastercard.com.

AUSTRALIA	1800-120-113	ITALY	800-870-866
BRAZIL	0800-891-3294	MEXICO	001-800-307-7309
CANADA	1-800-307-7309	PUERTO RICO	1-800-307-7309
FRANCE	0-800-90-1387	SPAIN	900-97-1231
GERMANY	0800-819-1040	UK	0800-96-4767
HONG KONG	800-966677	USA	1-800-307-7309

From all other countries call collect:
1-636-722-7111

there are some things money can't buy. for peace of mind there's MasterCard.

About the Guide

How the guide was produced

The contents of the guide were originated by journalists living in Paris – most of them long-term residents – and based on real experiences in restaurants, cafés and bars. Venues are tested anonymously, with *Time Out* paying the bill.

For this eighth edition, we have re-tested most of the establishments listed in the seventh edition, while adding plenty of new entries that reflect the changing Paris restaurant scene. Places that disappointed were removed from the guide unless they are especially well known. This time round, we have grouped all French restaurants together.

Every review, as well as addresses, prices and opening details, has been double-checked for accuracy. But details can change (particularly for annual holidays), so it's a good idea to ring ahead.

How to use the listings

Restaurants are divided into sections denoting the type of establishment and style of food. Within each section, they are listed in order of arrondissement (area), then alphabetically. We also provide two indexes (*see p216*), one by area and type of restaurant, the other alphabetical.

Critics' picks

A star – ★ – after the restaurant's name indicates that it is a critics' favourite, one of the best in its category. Stars are awarded not only for great food (or drinks, in **Cafés, Bars & Pubs**), but also for a particularly fun atmosphere.

Telephones

Paris and Ile de France numbers begin with 01. From abroad, leave off the 0 at the start of the ten-digit number. The country code is 33.

Opening hours

Times stated for restaurants apply to service hours, when you can order food, rather than opening and closing times. Those given for bars and cafés are opening and closing hours, with food service hours if relevant.

Credit cards & currency

The following abbreviations are used: AmEx: American Express; DC: Diners' Club; MC: MasterCard; V: Visa. A €15 minimum spend usually applies to credit card transactions. Most Paris restaurants do not accept payment by travellers' cheques.

Prices & prix fixe menus

'Average' means the average cost for a three-course à la carte meal without drinks. If no average price is listed, the only option is the prix fixe. In our listings, 'Prix fixe' indicates the price for the restaurant's set-price menu at lunch and dinner. If served only at lunch, the fixed-price menu is listed separately under 'Lunch menu'.

Within reviews, we make a distinction between set menus and the 'carte', which allows you to order items individually. Set menus, or prix fixes, are the most popular way of eating in Paris restaurants and often represent the best value. A 'formule' is a type of prix fixe, but often with a more limited choice of dishes.

Service & tipping

Prices on restaurant menus (and listed in this guide) must by law include a 12-15 per cent service charge. A small tip of €1-€5 euros (or small change in a café) is a nice, though entirely optional, gesture.

Wheelchair access

In general, only new or renovated restaurants offer full wheelchair access, including disabled toilets. Where we have listed 'Wheelchair access', the dining room is easily accessible and the owners have shown a willingness to help the disabled. It's worth ringing ahead to check if an establishment can cater for you as sometimes only one or two tables are wheelchair accessible.

In the heart of the Marais.....

STOLLY'S
stone-bar

16, rue Cloche-Perce
75004 Paris
m Saint-Paul
Happy Hour
16h30-20h00
www.cheapblonde.com

Smoking

Restaurants are required by French law to have a non-smoking section. However, most either allocate one or two tables near the loo to non-smokers or ignore the law altogether. In our listings, 'Non-smoking room' means that the restaurant has a separate room for non-smokers. 'Non-smoking' means that the entire restaurant is smoke-free. That said, at the time of writing, the French government was planning to abolish smoking in public places from January 2007, although this had yet to be confirmed. If the law goes through, only tabacs (cafés that sell cigarettes) and nightclubs will allow people to light up.

Maps

Each restaurant, café and bar in this guide has a map reference that corresponds to the street maps starting on page 242. We also provide detailed area maps for five neighbourhoods: the Marais, the Champs-Elysées, St-Germain-des-Prés, Oberkampf and Bastille. Restaurants, cafés and bars are located on these maps by name. The same grid is used for all the maps.

Savoir faire

Learn to saunter into Paris restaurants with a certain insouciance.

Restaurants are busiest at lunch between 1pm and 2pm, at dinner between 9pm and 11pm. Popular restaurants sometimes have two sittings, around 7.30pm (aimed at tourists) and 9.30pm. Check Le Snacking chapter (*pp113-116*) for mid-afternoon possibilities.

Aperitifs, wine, water & digestifs As well as standard 75cl bottles, wine comes in half-bottles (37.5cl) and carafes or pichets, usually 25cl (un quart), 46cl (un pot lyonnais) and 50cl (un demi-litre, or une fillette if served in a tall carafe). You're entitled to ask for 'une carafe d'eau', which is tap water, though most waiters will try to sell you mineral water. Be warned that restaurants now commonly charge €4-€5 for a litre bottle of mineral water (or sometimes even a half-litre). Digestifs offer the opportunity to discover potent drinks such as vintage Armagnac or a flaming prune eau-de-vie.

A matter of course French meals usually consist of three courses – entrée (starter), plat (main course) and dessert or cheese – although at more formal restaurants, there may be an additional amuse-bouche or amuse-gueule (appetiser or hors d'oeuvre), a fish course before the main course, cheese (before dessert), and petits

fours served at the end with the coffee. This is invariably black (un expresso or un express) – if you ask for a café au lait after dinner, expect a strange look.

Loafing Bread is served free with any café or restaurant meal and you're entitled to as much as you can eat – don't be afraid to ask for more.

Dress You are what you wear in Paris. Restaurant-goers on the whole opt for the 'smart-casual' look, so while you won't need a tie, leave the bermuda shorts and tracksuits behind. Haute cuisine restaurants normally expect a jacket and tie in the evening.

Reservations It's always a good idea to book at popular restaurants – the first question you are likely to be greeted with is a gruff 'Avez-vous réservé?' Famous haute cuisine establishments take bookings months in advance. For bistros, plan a few days ahead (though a handful are booked up weeks or months ahead). However, it's also worth trying at the last minute to see if there's room. Note that some tables are much more accessible at lunch.

Bar & café customs Drinks prices often vary in a café: they're cheapest at the bar, more at a table and even more sitting outside. There will often be a further increase (majoration), generally about 50 cents, after 10pm.

Small
wonders

A restaurant's size is no measure of the chef's talent, as bistros grow increasingly compact. Rosa Jackson squeezes in to investigate.

La Cerisaie. *See p14.*

Le Temps au Temps

Every day Sylvain Endra puts a 'complet' ('fully booked') sign in front of his restaurant. He started this ritual only a few weeks after taking over an eccentric little bistro in an out-of-the-way street east of place de la Bastille. Endra did away with the antique clocks that cluttered the walls, keeping just one big clock as a reminder that from now on Le Temps au Temps would run like a state-of-the-art Swiss watch. Within days word had spread that this chef from Lyon – who looks barely old enough to have fuzz on his chin – was turning out contemporary bistro food worthy of a much more expensive restaurant.

The chef's bistro – often referred to as the neo-bistro – is nothing new in Paris, dating back to the early 1990s, when Yves Camdeborde created a sensation with La Régalade on the outer edge of the 14th arrondissement. Several other chefs followed suit, many of them alumni of Le Crillon's kitchens under chef Christian Constant (who now runs his own bistro, Le Café Constant, along with the more formal Le Violon d'Ingres and the fish restaurant Les Fables de la Fontaine). But what is changing is the size of their establishments. The bigger the chef's talent, it seems, the smaller the space he tries to squeeze it into. Thus, several of the city's best new bistros seat no more than 30 and have just one (young) cook.

Again, Camdeborde has led the way, by selling La Régalade to ambitious young chef Bruno Doucet and opening a 30-seat bistro in the hotel Le Relais St-Germain, which he now runs with his wife. Exhausted by the three-sittings-per-night

pace he had set himself at La Régalade, Camdeborde now offers a no-reservations brasserie service during the day and at weekends, and a single-sitting five-course dinner that changes every night. By May 2006 his prix-fixe dinner was booked up until Christmas, except for the tiny pavement tables (each big enough for one person) that come out in good weather.

Now in his late 30s, Camdeborde is old enough to have spawned protégés

> Wright's haute cuisine-trained friends joined him every Saturday until he had mastered a style of French bistro cooking.

who have gone off to open their own, smaller versions of La Régalade. In a sleepy part of the 13th arrondissement, Sylvain Danière runs L'Ourcine, a bistro with plain wooden tables and a compact open kitchen in the back. With so little emphasis on decor, Danière is free to focus on his menu, whose creations might include strips of John Dory with white beans and red onion, pork cheeks with lentils and foie gras and lime cream with an orange tuile for dessert.

Le Pamphlet

More recently, Camdeborde protégée Nadège Varigny – who worked in La Régalade's dining room for 12 years – took over a narrow yellow dining room near Notre Dame. Going one step further than Camdeborde, whose fondness for offcuts showed up in dishes such as sheep's testicles, chef Guy Bommefront serves an extensive offal menu: look for salads of groin de cochon (the tip of the muzzle) or tétine de vache (cow's udder), or slightly more standard dishes such as sheep's brain meunière (in lemon and butter), tongue and veal kidneys. Almost as unusual is the fluffy sheep's milk ice-cream he serves for dessert.

Toiling alone in the tiny open kitchen of Le Timbre, whose name ('the postage stamp') says it all, Manchester-born Chris Wright never set out to be a chef. He originally manned the front of house, but when his chef moved on he found himself taking over. Fortunately, Wright had help from haute cuisine-trained friends, who joined him every Saturday until he had mastered a simple yet precise style of French bistro cooking. His short, market-inspired menu draws on the finest ingredients – such as the day's catch from Le Dôme's celebrated fishmonger – and includes a nod to his native land with cheese from Neal's Yard Dairy.

Working in the shadow of the hideous Montparnasse tower, Cyril Lalanne has quietly made a rather big name for himself at La Cerisaie. The size of his restaurant – a mere 25 seats – didn't prevent him from winning the prestigious Jacquart prize in 2005 for best Paris chef under 30. As in so many neo-bistros, the south-western French slant proves irresistible – on the short menu, you'll find foie gras in various guises, while a choice of Armagnacs provides the finishing touch. Lalanne does have plans to move – not to accommodate more diners, but to give them and the food a little more breathing space.

And therein lies the rub with neo-bistros: in a bid to make their cooking accessible, with the average price of a meal around €30 without drinks, chefs often sacrifice the customer's comfort. A perfect example is L'Epi Dupin, which has drawn the foodie hordes for two nightly dinner sittings since it became known in the mid 1990s. With barely room for the waiters to squeeze between the closely packed tables, a meal here can prove stressful no matter how good the food.

In fact, only a handful of bistros have focused on comfort – Le Pamphlet and Le Dôme du Marais could both rival some haute cuisine restaurants, although in keeping with current trends Le Pamphlet recently opened an annex.

Interestingly, too, not all pint-sized bistros try to cram in as many sittings as possible. When we visited Le Temps au Temps, the chef looked remarkably relaxed in the kitchen as he listened to the radio while whipping up dishes such as spiced mackerel fillets on marrow bone. His wife was due to have a baby in a few days, and the dining room was packed, as usual, but he smiled and said, 'I'm taking it easy tonight. I've booked only one sitting.'

A la carte

Where to go...

...to eat after midnight
L'Atmosphère, Cafés, Bars & Pubs
Bar des Théâtres, Cafés, Bars & Pubs
A la Bière, French
Black Calvados, Fashion
Le Boeuf sur le Toit, French
Bofinger, French
Brasserie Flo, French
Café de Flore, Cafés, Bars & Pubs
Café de l'Industrie, Cafés, Bars & Pubs
Café Marly, Cafés, Bars & Pubs
En Colimaçon, French
Chez Gladines, French
A la Cloche d'Or, French
La Coupole, French
Curieux Spaghetti Bar, Fashion
Au Dernier Métro, Cafés, Bars & Pubs
Les Deux Magots, Cafés, Bars & Pubs
L'Etoile Manquante, Cafés, Bars & Pubs
Le Flore en l'Isle, Cafés, Bars & Pubs
Général Lafayette, Cafés, Bars & Pubs
Le Georges, Fashion
La Gueuze, Cafés, Bars & Pubs
Hôtel Costes, Fashion
Julien, French
Ma Bourgogne, French
Le Petit Fer à Cheval, Cafés, Bars & Pubs
Au Pied de Cochon, French
Le Stella, French
Le Tambour, Cafés, Bars & Pubs
Terminus Nord, French
La Tour de Montlhéry (Chez Denise), French
Le Vaudeville, French
Le Wepler, French
Le Zéphyr, French

...to drink after 2am
Le Bréguet, Cafés, Bars & Pubs
Le Crocodile, Cafés, Bars & Pubs
Harry's Bar, Cafés, Bars & Pubs
Le Purgatoire, Cafés, Bars & Pubs
Le Tambour, Cafés, Bars & Pubs
Viaduc Café, Cafés, Bars & Pubs

...to eat al fresco
Café Marly, Cafés, Bars & Pubs
La Cagouille, French
Le Châlet des Iles, French
Contre-Allée, French
Café Delmas, Cafés, Bars & Pubs
L'Espadon, French
Le Georges, Fashion
La Grande Cascade, French
Le Parc aux Cerfs, French
Pitchi Poï, Jewish
Le Pré Catelan, French
Restaurant du Palais-Royal, French

Rouge Saint-Honoré, Le Snacking
Le Square Trousseau, French
Le Zéphyr, French

...for ancient walls
Allard, French
L'Ami Louis, French
Anahi, The Americas
Chez Marianne, Jewish
L'Ecurie, French
Mon Vieil Ami, French
Perraudin, French

...for the artworks
Chez Corto, French
La Coupole, French
Guy Savoy, French
Juvénile's, Wine Bars
Le Méditerranée, French
Pétrelle, French
La Table Dancourt, French
Taillevent, French
Wadja, French
Willi's Wine Bar, French
Ze Kitchen Galerie, French

...for unusual beers
Le Bouillon Racine, French
Le Ch'ti Catalan, French
The Frog & Rosbif, Cafés, Bars & Pubs
Le Général Lafayette, Cafés, Bars & Pubs
Graindorge, French
La Gueuze, Cafés, Bars & Pubs

...for a business lunch
Alain Ducasse au Plaza Athénée, French
L'Arpège, French
L'Astrance, French
Benoît, French
Le Bristol, French
Le Carré des Feuillants, French
Chez la Vieille, French
D'Chez Eux, French
Drouant, French
Gaya Rive Gauche, French
Le Grand Véfour, French
Flora, French
Guy Savoy, French
Aux Lyonnais, French
Macéo, French
Le Meurice, French
Michel Rostang, French
Mori's Venice Bar, Italian
Le Pamphlet, French
Restaurant Hélène Darroze, French
Restaurant du Palais-Royal, French
Savy, French
La Taverna degli Amici, Italian
Ze Kitchen Galerie, French

...for a carnivorous feast

Le Bis de Severo, French
Au Boeuf Couronné, French
Boucherie Roulière, French
Le Bouclard, French
La Bourse ou la Vie, French
Chez Omar, North African
Le Duc de Richelieu, French
Georget, French
Le Nemrod, Cafés, Bars & Pubs
L'Opportun, French
Le Père Claude, French
Au Petit Marguery, French
Le Pied de Cochon, French
Le Plomb du Cantal, Cafés, Bars & Pubs
Savy, French
La Table Lauriston, French
La Tour de Montlhéry (Chez Denise), French

...to celebrity spot

Alain Ducasse au Plaza Athénée, French
Les Ambassadeurs, French
L'Ami Louis, French
Anahi, The Americas
L'Atelier de Joël Robuchon, French
Brasserie Lipp, French
Café de Flore, Cafés, Bars & Pubs
Café de la Mairie, Cafés, Bars & Pubs
Chez Arthur, French
Le V, French
L'Espadon, French
404, North African
Market, French
Le Père Claude, French
Le Voltaire, French
See also pp108-112 Fashion

...for the cheese course

Astier, French
Chez Michel, French
Chez René, French
Le Comptoir du Relais St-Germain, French
Flora, French
Le Graindorge, French
Le Timbre, French

...with children

Altitude 95, French
Berthillon, Tea Rooms
Brasserie Flo, French
La Coupole, French
Gli Angeli, Italian
Higuma, Japanese
New Nioullaville, Far Eastern
Le Président, Far Eastern
Scoop, Le Snacking
Le Troquet, French
Wadja, French

...for cocktails

Andy Wahloo, Cafés, Bars & Pubs
Café Le Passy, Cafés, Bars & Pubs
Calle 24, The Americas
Chez Richard, Cafés, Bars & Pubs
China Club, Cafés, Bars & Pubs
Le Crocodile, Cafés, Bars & Pubs
Harry's Bar, Cafés, Bars & Pubs
Hemingway Bar at the Ritz, Cafés, Bars & Pubs

Le Kiosque Flottant 2, Eating with Entertainment
The Lizard Lounge, Cafés, Bars & Pubs
Le Plaza Athénée, Cafés, Bars & Pubs
Le Train Bleu, French
Zéro Zéro, Cafés, Bars & Pubs

...for designer style

Alain Ducasse au Plaza Athénée, French
Alcazar, French
Andy Wahloo, Cafés, Bars & Pubs
Atelier Renault, Cafés, Bars & Pubs
Café Marly, Cafés, Bars & Pubs
De La Ville Café, Cafés, Bars & Pubs
Gaya Rive Gauche, French
Le Martel, Fashion
Mon Vieil Ami, French
Pétrelle, French
Senderens, French
La Table du Lancaster, French
See also pp108-112 Fashion

...for unusual desserts

Le 144 Petrossian, French
Les Ambassadeurs, French
Angl'Opéra, French
Le Chamarré, French
L'Epi Dupin, French
Flora, French
Gaya Rive Gauche, French
Jean, French
Pierre Gagnaire, French
Spoon, Food & Wine, Fashion
Ze Kitchen Galerie, French

...with your dog

Le Balzar, French
Le Clown Bar, Wine Bars
Khun Akorn, Far Eastern
Pétrelle, French
Le Suffren, French
Table d'Hôte du Palais-Royal, French

...before/after a film

Le Balzar, French
Le Boeuf sur le Toit, French
Chez Lili et Marcel, Cafés, Bars & Pubs
La Coupole, French
Les Editeurs, Cafés, Bars & Pubs
Fish, Wine Bars
Korean Barbecue, Far Eastern
Pause Café, Cafés, Bars & Pubs
Le Rendez-vous des Quais, Cafés, Bars & Pubs
Le Wepler, French

...with a foodie

Allard, French
L'Arpège, French
L'Astrance, French
L'Atelier de Joël Robuchon, French
Le Chamarré, French
Le Chateaubriand, French
Le Comptoir du Relais St-Germain, French
Drouant, French
Guy Savoy, French
Hiramatsu, French
Kinugawa, Japanese
Pierre Gagnaire, French
Le Pré Verre, French
Le Reminet, French

Ribouldingue, French
La Table du Lancaster, French
Taillevent, French

...on a first date
404, North African
Café Marly, Cafés, Bars & Pubs
Chez Dom, Caribbean
Chez Richard, Cafés, Bars & Pubs
China Club, Cafés, Bars & Pubs
La Charlotte en l'Ile, Tea Rooms
Le Clown Bar, Wine Bars
Le Fumoir, Cafés, Bars & Pubs
Julien, French
Le Kiosque Flottant 2, Eating with Entertainment
Martel, Fashion
Le Reminet, French

...for game
Astier, French
Auberge le Quincy, French
La Biche au Bois, French
Chez Casimir, French
Chez Michel, French
Chez Toinette, French
Michel Rostang, French
Au Petit Marguery, French
Le Repaire de Cartouche, French
Le Troquet, French

...with grandma
Angelina, Tea Rooms
Chez Jenny, French
La Coupole, French
Le Dôme, French
Josephine 'Chez Dumonet', French
Ladurée, Tea Rooms
Lasserre, French
La Méditérranée, French
Le Soufflé, French
Le Train Bleu, French

...with a group of friends
Alcazar, French
L'Ambassade d'Auvergne, French
Le Café du Commerce, French
Chez Gégène, Eating with Entertainment
Chez Michel, French
Entoto, African & Indian Ocean
La Famille, French
La Fresque, French
Likafo, Far Eastern
New Nioullaville, Far Eastern
Le Pacifique, Far Eastern
Table d'Hôte du Palais-Royal, French

...for kitsch
La Charlotte en l'Ile, Tea Rooms
Les Chineurs, French
La Madonnina, Italian
Au Pied de Cochon, French
Le Président, Far Eastern

...for a late lunch
L'Atelier de Joël Robuchon, French
L'As du Fallafel, Jewish
Café du Commerce, French

Café Marly, Cafés, Bars & Pubs
Camille, French
Curieux Spaghetti Bar, Fashion
Dong Huong, Far Eastern
La Grande Armée, French
Higuma, Japanese
Juvénile's, Wine Bars
Le Nemrod, Cafés, Bars & Pubs
New Pondichery, Indian
Polichinelle Café, Cafés, Bars & Pubs
Le Tambour, Cafés, Bars & Pubs

...to eat organic
Bioboa, Le Snacking
Bread & Roses, Le Snacking
Les 5 Saveurs d'Anada, Vegetarian
Le Potager du Marais, Vegetarian
Rose Bakery, Cafés, Bars & Pubs

...for a romantic meal
L'Astrance, French
Le Châlet des Iles, French
Le V, French
La Ferrandaise, French
Flora, French
Le Grand Véfour, French
Lapérouse, French
Le Pamphlet, French
Le Pré Catelan, French
Restaurant du Palais-Royal, French
Sardegna a Tavola, Italian
Le Temps au Temps, French
La Tour d'Argent, French
Le Train Bleu, French

...to talk about the rugby
L'Ami Jean, French
The Bowler, Cafés, Bars & Pubs
Brasserie de l'Isle St-Louis, French
The Frog & Rosbif, Cafés, Bars & Pubs
La Régalade, French

...for the soufflés
L'Atelier de Joël Robuchon, French
Flora, French
Josephine 'Chez Dumonet', French
Pierre Gagnaire, French
La Régalade, French
Le Soufflé, French
Le Troquet, French

...for rare spirits
Auberge le Quincy, French
La Cagouille, French
Le Carré des Feuillants, French
La Cerisaie, French
La Crypte Polska, Other International
Dominique, Other International
Michel Rostang, French
Pitchi Poï, Jewish
Restaurant Hélène Darroze, French
Au Trou Gascon, French

...for a bistro feed on a Sunday
L'Alivi, French
L'Ambassade d'Auvergne, French
L'Ami Louis, French
L'Ardoise, French

L'Assiette, French
L'Auberge du Clou, French
Benoît, French
A la Bière, French
Le Bistrot des Vignes, French
Boucherie Roulière, French
Camille, French
Aux Charpentiers, French
Chez Gladine, French
Chez Maître Paul, French
Chez Paul, French
Christophe, French
Le Comptoir du Relais St-Germain, French
Drouant, French
Le Kiosque, French
Ma Bourgogne, French
Le Mâchon d'Henri, French
Mon Vieil Ami, French
Le Parc aux Cerfs, French
Le Père Claude, French
Le Petit Marché, French
Le Petit Pontoise, French
Le Polidor, French
Le Réconfort, French
Le Reminet, French
La Rôtisserie du Beaujolais, French
Table d'Hôte du Palais-Royal, French
Thoumieux, French
La Tour de Montlhéry, French
Un Jour à Peyrassol, French
Le Zéphyr, French

...for a sunny café terrace
Café de Flore, Cafés, Bars & Pubs
Café de la Mairie, Cafés, Bars & Pubs
Café du Marché, Cafés, Bars & Pubs
Café Delmas, Cafés, Bars & Pubs
Caves de Bourgogne, Wine Bars
Chez Prune, Cafés, Bars & Pubs
Les Deux Magots, Cafés, Bars & Pubs
Le Flore en l'Isle, Cafés, Bars & Pubs
Grizzli Café, Cafés, Bars & Pubs
Le Jemmapes, Cafés, Bars & Pubs
La Palette, Cafés, Bars & Pubs
Pause Café, Cafés, Bars & Pubs
Le Rendez-vous des Quais, Cafés, Bars & Pubs
Le Rostand, Cafés, Bars & Pubs
Vavin Café, Cafés, Bars & Pubs

...for a timewarp
Allard, French
L'Ami Louis, French
Benoît, French
Chartier, French
Chez René, French
La Fermette Marbeuf, French
Georget, French
Julien, French
Aux Lyonnais, French
Perraudin, French
Savy, French
Le Train Bleu, French

...with a vegetarian friend
L'Arpège, French
L'As du Fallafel, Jewish
La Bastide Odéon, French
Bioboa, Le Snacking

Chez Marianne, Jewish
La Connivence, French
Kastoori, Indian
Macéo, French
Rose Bakery, Le Snacking
Spoon, Food & Wine, Fashion
La Voie Lactée, Eastern Mediterranean
See also pp117-119 Vegetarian and
pp144-149 Italian

...for the view
Altitude 95, French
Bar Panoramique, Cafés, Bars & Pubs
Le Café de l'Homme, Fashion
Le Georges, Fashion
Le Jules Verne, French
Le Rostand, Cafés, Bars & Pubs
La Tour d'Argent, French
Le Ziryab, North African

...for weekend brunch
404, North African
Alcazar, Fashion
Blue Bayou, The Americas
Breakfast in America, The Americas
Café Charbon, Cafés, Bars & Pubs
Chez Prune, Cafés, Bars & Pubs
E-Dune, Cafés, Bars & Pubs
Forêt Noire, Tea Rooms
The Lizard Lounge, Cafés, Bars & Pubs
Pitchi Poï, Jewish
A Priori Thé, Tea Rooms
Zebra Square, French

...for the wine list
Alain Ducasse au Plaza Athénée, French
Astier, French
Le Bistrot du Sommelier, French
Le Carré des Feuillants, French
A la Grange Batelière, French
Macéo, French
Le Passage des Carmagnoles, French
Le Repaire de Cartouche, French
Spoon, Food & Wine, Fashion
Taillevent, French
La Tour d'Argent, French
Wadja, French
Willi's Wine Bar, French
Yugaraj, Indian
See also pp196-201 Wine Bars

...with a writer
Café de Flore, Cafés, Bars & Pubs
Café des Lettres, Cafés, Bars & Pubs
Le Couvent, Cafés, Bars & Pubs
Les Editeurs, Cafés, Bars & Pubs
Le Fumoir, Cafés, Bars & Pubs

...on your own
L'As du Fallafel, Jewish
L'Atelier de Joël Robuchon, French
La Coupole, French
Fish, Wine Bars
Huîtrerie Régis, French
Mirama, Far Eastern
Le Temps au Temps, French
Willi's Wine Bar, French
See also pp150-153 Japanese
and pp113-116 Le Snacking

French Cuisine

FRENCH	20
FASHION	108
LE SNACKING	113
VEGETARIAN	117

French

French food has never been synonymous with fun. Yet things are changing in Paris. Some call it 'la jeune cuisine', others 'génération C' (for 'cuisines et cultures') or 'le fooding'. All of these aim to describe a new spirit that is sweeping through the capital and even provincial France – chefs care less about guidebook ratings and more about finding some personal satisfaction in their work. One might walk away from haute cuisine to open a tiny bistro off the beaten path, while another might amuse himself within a grand setting. At every level, chefs are growing more creative and daring. If bistros are still the major genre in Paris, there is a growing number of more ambitious restaurants where the price you pay for adventurous cooking still looks reasonable compared to haute cuisine (Ze Kitchen Galerie, Jean, Flora and Gaya Rive Gauche are a few examples). At the time of writing the haute cuisine world looked set for another round of musical chefs, which could affect Le Crillon, La Tour d'Argent, the George V and the Bristol. Brasseries, meanwhile, have little lustre left in the kitchen as so many are now run by chains – go for the historic settings, buzzy atmosphere and seafood platters.

1ST ARRONDISSEMENT

L'Ardoise ★

28 rue du Mont-Thabor, 1st (01.42.96.28.18). M° Concorde or Tuileries. **Open** noon-2.30pm, 6.30-11pm Tue-Sun. **Average** €35. **Prix fixe** €31. **Credit** MC, V. **Wheelchair access. Map** G5.

Considering this restaurant's location between the Louvre, place Vendôme, place de la Concorde and Tuilerie gardens, it's not surprising that the most of the customers here – in the evenings at least – introduce themselves with 'Bonjour. Er… do you speak English?' A few years ago it would have been 'Non' followed by some form of abuse. Financial if you were lucky. But Paris has changed. Foreigners are the lifeblood of restaurants like these and many have the grace to treat foreigners as if they've come from a sort of Outer France. Anyway, here's such a place and it's a great choice. OK, it has useless decor. The tables a bit too close together. But it's very, very good food for the price. Our langoustine ravioli with crustacean sauce and crème fraîche had us swooning from the outset. So did the scallops marinated in thyme and sweet garlic, even if they did taste as if they'd been marinated in lemon juice. And although our pan of pork cheeks with mashed potato was too rich to fully enjoy, our other main, a 'shoal' of sea bass, salmon and scallops with artichoke, was excellent. Puddings – including strawberry feuillantine and crème brûlée with tremendously strong-tasting blackcurrants – were also very good. The bill came as a pleasant surprise. In fact, we had just one slight disappointment: there are few wines by the glass.

Le Carré des Feuillants

14 rue de Castiglione, 1st (01.42.86.82.82/ www.carredesfeuillants.fr). M° Concorde or Tuileries. **Open** noon-2pm, 7.30-10pm Mon-Fri. Closed Aug. **Average** €175. **Prix fixe** €150. **Lunch menu** €65. **Credit** AmEx, DC, MC, V. **Map** G5.

It's kid gloves from the moment they open the front door at Alain Dutournier's long-running restaurant, and such impeccably well-drilled and cordial service is a rare treat. The decor is handsome, although perhaps too masculine, in tones of anthracite with rather cold lighting and chilly modern art. A first course of cep mushroom caps stuffed with warm pâté was a sensual contrast of earthy flavours and textures, while griddled squid with courgettes was spiked with Espelette pepper and garnished with a silky black leaf of squid's ink pasta and a gâteau of tomato and aubergine, a brilliant contemporary riff on Basque country cooking. Veal sweetbreads, crisply pan-fried and served in a version of sauce gribiche sharpened with oyster juice, was brilliant, while a thick slab of turbot was cooked to alabaster perfection and served with an inventive side of quinoa (the grain that seems to be all the rage in Paris at the moment), mixed with morel mushrooms. Desserts were magnificent as well – in a take on cherries jubilee, plump cherries were sautéed in flaming kirsch and served with tiny chocolate sponge pastries and a lemon verbena sauce. A good run of reasonably priced south-western French wines complement the food well and keep the bill down. All told, a magnificent meal that trounced any initial doubts about the vaguely sad, corporate decor.

Chez La Vieille

*1 rue Bailleul/37 rue de l'Arbre-Sec, 1st (01.42.60.
15.78). Mº Louvre Rivoli.* **Open** noon-2pm Mon-
Wed, Sun; noon-2pm, 7.30-9.30pm Thur. **Average**
€50. **Lunch menu** €27. **Credit** AmEx, MC, V.
Map J6.

Entering via the stairwell of an apartment building
into this tiny, friendly bistro full of mainly Corsican
regulars feels like being let in on a secret. The menu
also holds some surprises. Corsican specialities such
as the charcuterie, (excellent) spicy tripe or the ewe's
milk cheeses rub up against hearty French classics
such as calves' liver, veal kidneys or braised beef
with carrots. But the really extraordinary thing
happens when you order the 'chariot' of starters.
First, it's whole terrines of (homemade) pâté. Then
a tub of asparagus. Then a vat of marinated herring.
Then, just to tease your appetite a little further, a
plate of stuffed cabbage. The pudding (if you get
that far) obeys the same gargantuan principle (crème
caramel, chocolate mousse, apple tart and prunes in
wine, to name a few). We had some pleasantly
peppery Côtes du Rhône by the glass, but for those
who want to crack open a bottle, there are plenty of
fantastic-looking reds and whites from Corsica.

L'Espadon

*Hôtel Ritz, 15 pl Vendôme, 1st (01.43.16.30.80/
www.ritzparis.com). Mº Concorde or Madeleine.*
Open noon-2pm, 7.30-10pm daily. **Average** €225.
Prix fixe €180 (dinner only). **Lunch menu** €75.
Credit AmEx, DC, MC, V. **Wheelchair access**.
Map G4.

When a famous politician appeared out of nowhere
and left smiling and saying goodbye to people he
clearly didn't know we got to thinking there must
be a special table at the Ritz's restaurant where the
ultra-famous are hidden from the sort that slouches
in for the lunchtime prix fixe. Our lunch menu began
well with swooningly good warm foie gras amuses-
bouches and continued in the same vein with subtle
and refined mackerel with lobster and fennel, and
some beautiful green asparagus with langoustines
and champagne vinegar. 'Splendid cook, this Michel
Roth', we thought. Then everything went wrong.
First, we had to wait for absolutely ages. Then our
roast monkfish (marinated with herbs with saffron
froth and artichoke cream) arrived undercooked and
the veal (with capers, preserved lemon, spinach and
mushroom gratin) overcooked. Things recovered
with the arrival of the magnificent cheese trolley
(don't miss the 'trappiste' and the Ritz's own goat's
cheese.) We also loved our strawberry and hazelnut
meringue with Bourbon vanilla pudding. And while
we weren't bowled over by our sommelier's choice
of wine, at least he kept it coming, despite the fact
that we'd only ordered a couple of stingy glasses...
meaning that we too were able to leave the Ritz
waving goodbye to total strangers.

La Fresque

*100 rue Rambuteau, 1st (01.42.33.17.56). Mº Les
Halles.* **Open** noon-3.30pm, 7pm-midnight Mon-Sat.
Average €20. **Lunch menu** €13.50. **Credit** MC,
V. **Wheelchair access**. **Non-smoking room**.
Map K5.

A few years ago this good and very modestly priced
bistro would have been in the middle of the greatest
food market in the world. Les Halles was Zola's 'Belly
of Paris'. But since the Forum des Halles, one of the
city's grandest architectural mistakes, replaced that
spectacle, the throng of local regulars can at least
concentrate on the menu – which is a good one.
Choosing from the lunchtime prix fixe, we started
with a plate of deliciously garlicky prawns, boudin
blanc on a bed of salad and, best of all, mushroom
quiche. Our waiter (friendly, efficient and child-
tolerant) told us it was own-made and we believed

Chez la Vieille

him. Our pork fillet in grainy mustard sauce was tender and not dry as this dish too often is. Tender too (though a bit overcooked) was our beef flank steak in roquefort sauce, accompanied by potatoes roasted un-Frenchly in their jackets. Puddings (€4 extra), such as the very rummy rum baba with Chantilly and crushed strawberries with mascarpone froth, were excellent, as was the pleasantly rustic Côtes du Rhône included in the price of the meal.

Le Grand Véfour

17 rue de Beaujolais, 1st (01.42.96.56.27). M° Palais Royal. **Open** 12.30-1.30pm, 8-9.30pm Mon-Thur; 12.30-2pm Fri. Closed one week mid-Apr, late July-late Aug, ten days late Dec. **Average** €180. **Lunch menu** €78. **Credit** AmEx, DC, MC, V. **Map** H5.

Opened in 1784 as the Café de Chartres, this is one of Paris's oldest and most historically powered restaurants. Many of the greats of this world have feasted on this very spot, from Napoleon and Josephine to Simone de Beauvoir to Victor Hugo, who was a regular. We were seated at the table named after him, which affords a view over the majestic gardens of the Palais Royal and is also the perfect spot from which to admire the mirror-studded dining room, with its magnificent painted ceiling and wall panels. Another appreciable aspect of this gourmet experience is that the thrill is unmarred by the bombastic pomposity that is all too often typical of similar establishments. Each member of staff is perfectly charming, particularly the sommeliers and the dashing premier maître d', Christian David. From the beautifully presented amuses-bouches through the selection of salted or unsalted butter to the luscious petits fours, everything is a treat for the eye and the palate. We splashed out à la carte and were treated to a fantasia-style succession of delicacies beginning with miniature frogs' legs artistically arranged within a circle of sage juices and a 'special' first course of creamed Breton sea urchins served in their spiny shells with a quail egg and topped with caviar. Another stunningly presented starter was flash-fried langoustines served with a tangy mango sauce nestling inside a curled shell, tiny girolles and a swirl of coriander juice. We continued with turbot meunière in white truffle oil and fillet of sole with a Mediterranean-style compote of vegetables – both very slightly overcooked. Desserts comprised a tiramisu-style chestnut mousse with a flavoursome orange and pumpkin sorbet, and an adventurous but not quite so successful artichoke flan with sugar-preserved vegetables and a refreshing bitter almond sorbet. Increasingly reluctant to leave the beautiful cocoon, we extended the experience as long as possible with cups of Arabica coffee accompanied by blackcurrant and mango fruit jellies and ambrosial rose- and lemon-flavoured chocolates. The sommelier then recommended a superb, complex and aromatic Armagnac. All good things come to an end, but this particular pleasure trip had a truly spectacular finale.

Macéo

15 rue des Petits-Champs, 1st (01.42.97.53.85/ www.maceorestaurant.com). M° Bourse or Pyramides. **Open** noon-2.30pm, 7.30-11pm Mon-Fri; 7.30-11pm Sat. **Average** €45. **Prix fixe** €30, €36. **Credit** MC, V. **Wheelchair access. Map** H5.

This elegant former brothel with its high ceilings and clouds of Second Empire mouldings has to be one of the most pleasant dining rooms in Paris. It even has a 'salacious library' (this really was an elegant brothel) overlooking the Palais Royal. None of which prepares you for the shock of an all-vegetarian menu – a mad idea in a country where vegetarianism is seen as a perversion. The proprietor is English (he also owns Willi's Wine Bar a couple of doors down), which must explain it. There is, that said, a non-veggie menu too, but we were to be disappointed. From the over-salted asparagus cream amuse-gueule onwards there was something bleached and lifeless about the colours and tastes of what we were being served. Although the rabbit is a subtle-flavoured animal, 'potted rabbit with spicy red onions' should have tasted less vague. Our other starter of asparagus soup was the amuse-gueule, only bigger. We had one pretty good main: an accurately cooked duckling with peas and white beans. But even the pear and beetroot crumble on our panna cotta and a fine bottle of St-Chinian from the Languedoc didn't alter the impression that tough decisions need to be taken in the kitchen.

Le Meurice ★

Hôtel Meurice, 228 rue de Rivoli, 1st (01.44.58.10.10/www.lemeurice.fr). M° Tuileries. **Open** 7-10.30am, noon-2.30pm, 7.30-10pm Mon-Fri; 7.30-10pm Sat. Closed Aug. **Average** €200. **Prix fixe** €190 (dinner only). **Lunch menu** €75. **Credit** AmEx, DC, MC, V. **Wheelchair access. Map** G5.

There can be few more pleasant places to be than the Meurice when the sun is playing on the gilt-tipped railings of the Tuileries gardens and Yannick Alléno is working his magic in the kitchens. The dining room, built during the royal restoration that followed the fall of Napoleon, is perhaps the most beautiful in Paris. The floor is a mosaic of imperial olive leaves, the wall is fine-veined marble and the windows are hung with heavy velvet. The effect, however, like that of the well-rounded young ladies in the fresco on the ceiling, is of a gravity-defying lightness. There's something of that in the cooking too, even when you're choosing, as we were, from the more delicately priced lunch menu. The cream of potato and nutmeg with snail fricassée, for example. Normally, everything is heavy about the potato, but Alléno takes it and turns it into a Mediterranean wood nymph. He also knows how to draw all the flavour out of his ingredients, as he showed with a tremendous morel mushroom fricassée. For the mains, it was the sommelier's talents we appreciated most. He chose us a glass of regal Crozes-Hermitage for our veal kidney studded with rosemary and cooked in its own fat, accompanied by some little green broad beans, and a bewitching Puligny-Montrachet for our paella-style 'risetto' (pasta, not rice) with langoustines. For dessert, two wonderfully light Bourbon vanilla feuillantines with wild strawberries completed one of the finest lunches Paris has to offer.

Au Pied de Cochon

6 rue Coquillière, 1st (01.40.13.77.00/www.piedde cochon.com). M° Châtelet or Les Halles. **Open** 24hrs daily. **Average** €35. **Prix fixe** €18.50, €24. **Credit** AmEx, DC, MC, V. **Wheelchair access. Non-smoking room. Map** J5.

Mrs Chirac once mused, during an agricultural visit, that the pig is the animal that most resembles man. So it's fitting that, among the photos on the wall of famous customers, is one of her illustrious husband. Mr Chirac looks almost ecstatic to find himself in this 24-hour-a-day, seven-day-a-week temple to the trotter where the door handles are trotters made of brass and the table legs trotters made of wood. These days, of course, they make a big song and dance about the fact that they have lots of other things to eat and, on our last visit on a packed Sunday lunchtime, they had a fancy-pants menu that was entirely pig-free. We tried it. It was nice. But this really is the place to discover the superb French delicacy that is foot of pig; for the jaded, there is a collection of breaded tail, ear, brawn and trotter called St Anthony's Temptation. The tail is long and straight and can be eaten like corn-on-the-cob. The ear was more of a challenge – very cartilaginous. Overall, though, this restaurant is well worth a try if you're curious.

Restaurant du Palais-Royal ★

110 galerie Valois, 1st (01.40.20.00.27/ www.restaurantdupalaisroyal.com). M° Bourse or Palais Royal. **Open** noon-2.30pm, 7-10.30pm Mon-Sat. Closed 18 Dec-18 Jan. **Average** €60. **Credit** AmEx, DC, MC, V. **Wheelchair access. Non-smoking room. Map** H5.

This restaurant's terrace is of the most magical places to dine in Paris, especially late on a warm summer evening after the rest of this public garden has been shut off to the hoi polloi. The Palais-Royal is a perfect example of the French 'rationaliste' approach to gardens, full of the crunch of gravel and trees in lines. But even in the red and quietly trendy dining room there is something very special about dining under these splendid arcades alongside the elegant commissars of arts and letters who work at the Ministry of Culture a few doors down. We shared one of three hard-to-choose-between risottos as a starter. Ours, called Black, Black and Lobster, sounded like the sort of thing the men in flowery ties at the next table should be buying for the Pompidou Centre. It was tremendous. The rice was still firm in a wash of squid's ink where we found lumps of garlic and parmesan. On top, tender but fleshy pink lobster, sun-dried tomato, a slice of courgette, a couple of beans and a pea. Exquisite. Our mains were, inevitably, more restrained but good

nevertheless – a roasted sea bass with 'melted' leeks, and a hare stew that managed to be both heartily countrified and refined. We'd ordered two 50cl jugs of wine: a light and pleasant Bourgogne aligoté and a Bordeaux. We were particularly enthusiastic about the latter even after we noticed, on the bill, that they'd actually given us a Chilean cabernet sauvignon instead. The waiter practically forced us into having a baba au rhum for pudding, which turned out to be fabulous. We especially liked the little, clear bottle of alcohol he brought with it, just in case we thought the baba hadn't been sufficiently doused.

Le Soufflé

36 rue du Mont-Thabor, 1st (01.42.60.27.19). M° Concorde. **Open** noon-2.30pm, 7-10pm daily. Closed public holidays, two weeks in Feb, three weeks in Aug. **Average** €45. **Prix fixe** €29.50, €33. **Lunch menu** €23. **Credit** AmEx, DC, MC, V. **Wheelchair access. Non-smoking room. Map** G5.

When we first perused the menu here we laughed at what seemed like eggy overkill, the €29.50 all-soufflé menu; but after seeing a towering apple-Calvados version float by, only to be doused in a generous slosh of the apple liqueur (the bottle is left on the table for more sloshing), we decided to take the plunge. Of the starters, a fluffy spinach soufflé, with just the right balance of airy creaminess, stood out. For mains, alongside the traditional savoury options (such as cheese, shrimp, roquefort, morel mushroom), we tried an inventive escalope of salmon topped with its own mini salmon soufflé that was, despite another soufflé yet to come, irresistible. By the time we were tucking into dessert – chocolate with a dark chocolate sauce plus the apple-Calvados that had tempted us – we were swapping soufflé tips (ours only recently formed) with our neighbour, an impeccably dressed regular who advised us on seasonal specials. Many diners, especially at lunch, opt for a cheaper and lighter option – just two soufflés, a savoury and a sweet – and there are also excellent alternatives (like tender roast lamb with a gratin dauphinois) for the not-yet-converted. But, when a soufflé is this good, why have anything else?

Table d'Hôte du Palais Royal

8 rue de Beaujolais, 1st (01.42.61.25.30/ www.carollsinclair.com). M° Bourse. **Open** 11.30am-2.30pm, 6pm-midnight daily. **Average** €40. **Prix fixe** €28. **Credit** AmEx, MC, DC, V. **Map** H5.

Caroll Sinclair's new restaurant, in a gorgeous setting just outside the Palais-Royal garden, has a more informal atmosphere than her previous restaurant Le Safran, and is all the better for it. The idea of 'table d'hôte' is that diners should feel like guests in a private home. The large and merry birthday group with us on the ground floor certainly seemed at ease, while downstairs are more private salons including two lined in panelling from the Orient Express. Don't mind the rather formal welcome by the maître d' – the theatrical chef will soon come to say hello As for the food, prepare yourself for something quite delicious. Although there is a very good value prix fixe, which is pulling a younger crowd, we went à la carte with a wonderful crayfish bisque, smoked salmon served with small clumps of dill-sprinkled potato salad, an exceptional spicy boeuf tartare, and an interesting hybrid meat and fish dish of tuna steak served with warm foie gras and wild mushrooms. The latter was a success, although it was a strange sensation to eat fish with meat accoutrements. There is an alternative to the pricey but well-chosen wine list in the form of a perfectly quaffable carafe wine that gets served in beautiful antique decanters. We could only manage ice-creams for dessert, which change according to the day. Our visit coincided with superb coffee and chocolate flavours, drizzled with homemade caramel.

La Tour de Montlhéry (Chez Denise)

5 rue des Prouvaires, 1st (01.42.36.21.82).
RER Châtelet Les Halles. **Open** noon-3pm, 7.30pm-5.30am daily. Closed 14 July-15 Aug. **Average** €40.
Credit MC, V. **Wheelchair access. Map** J5.
At midnight, this place is packed, jovial and gruff. Book ahead at this venerable all-night den if you want to eat before 2am. Come hungry too for a feast of savoury traditional dishes, and thirsty for the house Brouilly, served by the litre. 'Water? Oh, we don't serve that here!' the waiter jokes to diners devouring simply towering rib steaks served with marrow and a heaping platter of fries, homemade and among the best in Paris. The Tour de Montlhéry dates back to when the Les Halles neighbourhood was still the city's wholesale market and this corner the meatpackers' district (a few wholesale butchers are still next door), and this accounts for the reverence given to game, beef and offal on the menu. Adventurous souls can try tripes au calvados, grilled andouillettes (chitterling sausages) or lamb's brain, or go for an interesting stewed venison, served with succulent celery root and own-made jam. There are a few fish dishes too. Tourists mingle with regulars in the intimate red-checked dining room. It's a friendly place and, like us, you could end up tasting a portion of the neighbour's roasted lamb or chatting by the barrels of wine stacked atop the bar.

Willi's Wine Bar ★

13 rue des Petits-Champs, 1st (01.42.61.05.09/
www.williswinebar.com). M° Pyramides. **Open** 9am-midnight, food served noon-3pm, 7-11pm Mon-Sat.
Closed two weeks in Aug. **Average** €35. **Prix fixe** €34 (dinner only). **Lunch menu** €25. **Credit** MC, V.
Wheelchair access. Non-smoking. Map H5.
This smart, buzzing, English-run wine bar and restaurant manages to do some very French things better than much of the local competition. The long bar at the entrance, for instance, serves as a bar rather than a bit of period decor, where local Anglos can crack open a bottle and drink as they've been brought up to drink, standing up (or, for the

Americans, sitting on stools). The cellar has been stocked extensively and with discernment so here, we think, is a chance to let go the budget a little in exchange for some oenological education. We very much enjoyed our complex, refined Côtes du Rhône (Domaine de la Clape 2004), which was the type of wine that can lull you into believing that it will make you a wiser, finer human being. Meanwhile, the cooking here is precise, daring, colourful and eclectic. Of our starters, we particularly liked a combination of just-seared scallops with leeks, wild mushrooms and a thread or two of hot chilli pepper. When it comes to the mains, chef François Yon is good at glazes on meats that can give a modern and aesthetic air even to traditional favourites like the Salers beef with gratin dauphinois. For pudding, the best was an intense chocolate terrine bathed in crème anglaise.

2ND ARRONDISSEMENT

Angl'Opéra

39 av de l'Opéra, 2nd (01.42.61.86.25/
www.anglopera.com). M° Opéra. **Open** noon-2.30pm, 7.30-11.30pm Mon-Fri. **Average** €38.
Lunch menu €17. **Credit** AmEx, MC, V. **Map** H4.
Giles Choukroun, who has a reputation as one of the more daring young chefs in the capital, is behind this hotel restaurant. Upmarket office types keep it busy at noon, but what happens at night? After hours, it turns out, this is a relaxed and very charming place for a meal in a stylish dining room with excellent service. Because it's written in the random style of Dadaist poetry, the short menu requires considerable explanation, which seems to have violently antagonised many French food critics. 'Hot bouillon, herbs, ginger, soft-boiled egg…and foie gras' turned out to be tiny cubes of raw foie gras garnished with fresh mint, tarragon and lemon verbena, which you douse with hot bouillon and eat with spoonfuls of scrambled egg with 'apéro-peanuts' (peanuts surrounded with a crunchy shell). Salmon with lemon risotto, a shot glass of hot coconut milk and mussel juice; Chinese soup spoons of oysters on fresh peanuts in a herby dressing; and steamed skate in a sauce of poppy seeds, fennel and citrus fruit were all superb. Deep-fried camembert wedges with a salad of celery root and apple in a soy dressing were lovely, but the best conclusion to a meal here, from a menu that changes often, were the poached lychees in a soup of Schweppes, lemon verbena and green and Mexican papaya. The wine list is wonderful too, including a surprisingly good petit syrah from Mexico for a bargain €20. A real treat.

La Bourse ou la Vie

12 rue Vivienne, 2nd (01.42.60.08.83). M° Bourse.
Open noon-3pm, 7-10pm Mon-Fri. **Average** €25.
Credit MC, V. **Wheelchair access. Map** H4.
After a career as an architect, the owner of La Bourse ou la Vie has a new mission in life – to revive the dying art of the perfect steak-frites. His vivid yellow

Un Jour à Peyrassol. *See p27.*

and red dining room, with chairs that must have belonged to an old theatre, makes a slightly unlikely setting for the meat fest that takes place here daily. Skipping all the usual French formalities, he referred to us (two women) throughout the meal as 'mes amours' and launched into the familiar 'tu' with even the most serious-looking businessmen. The only decision you'll need to make here is which cut of beef to order with your chips, unless you inexplicably choose the cod from the perfunctory, laminated menu. One of us had a thick strip of ultra-tender coeur de filet while the other opted for a huge, surprisingly un-chewy bavette. Rich, creamy pepper sauce is the speciality here and our neighbour's steak looked naked without it. The real surprise, however, is the frites, which gain a distinctly animal flavour and inimitably crunchy texture from the suet in which they are cooked. Polishing off the last of a Bordeaux cru bourgeois served by the carafe (€20 for 50cl), we skipped the own-made desserts that are temptingly displayed at the entrance.

Drouant

18 rue Gaillon, 2nd (01.42.65.15.16/www.drouant. com). M° Quatre Septembre. **Open** noon-2.30pm, 7pm-midnight daily. **Average** €67. **Lunch menu** €45. **Credit** AmEx, DC, MC, V. **Wheelchair access. Non-smoking room. Map** H4.
Star Alsatian chef Antoine Westermann, who runs the successful Ile St-Louis bistro Mon Vieil Ami, has whisked this landmark 1880 brasserie into the 21st century with bronze-upholstered banquettes and armchairs, a pale parquet floor and incongruous butter-yellow paint and fabrics. Young chef Antony Clémot has left Mon Vieil Ami to oversee the dining room here, although you'll still see him dressed in his chef's whites as he lingers by the entrance greeting customers. Black suits are de rigueur in a dining room heavy with testosterone (at least at lunch). Westermann has dedicated this restaurant to the art of the hors d'oeuvre, served in themed sets of four ranging from the global (a successful Thai beef salad with brightly coloured vegetables, coriander and a sweet and spicy sauce) to the nostalgic (silky leeks in vinaigrette). The bite-sized surprises continue with the main course accompaniments – four of them for each dish, to be shared. It took a little convincing, but the waiter allowed us to share an order of crisp-skinned pork belly, which left us just enough room to try the series of chocolate desserts the best of which was a lemon-chocolate 'satin'.

La Fontaine Gaillon

pl Gaillon, 2nd (01.47.42.63.22/www.la-fontaine-gaillon.com). M° Quatre Septembre. **Open** noon-2.30pm, 7-11.30pm Mon-Fri. **Average** €55. **Lunch menu** €38. **Credit** AmEx, DC, MC, V. **Wheelchair access. Non-smoking room. Map** H4.
A lovely Louis XIII fireplace, crystal chandeliers, wood panelling and soft velvet upholstery – not to mention the sheltered outdoor terrace with its ornately sculpted fountain – all imbue this restaurant, bought and relaunched by Gérard

Depardieu in 2003, with an undisputable touch of historic class. But it seems to suffer from an identity crisis: is it a smart restaurant or a rôtisserie? Is it formal or relaxed? Staff in their black trouser suits could have come straight out of a training academy, yet lacked any spark of enthusiasm, food was overpriced and dull, and the wine list, in particular, is pricey: our red Moulis from the Bordeaux region at €40 was one of the rare good deals to be unearthed. From the €38 lunch menu, our starters of whelks with garlic mayonnaise, curiously served warm, and melon with Parma ham both suggested brasserie rather than gastronomy. Of the three main course options – spit-roast suckling pig with herbs, steak tartare with rocket or fresh cod – the suckling pig had already run out fairly early into lunchtime. As neither of the others appealed, they did reluctantly offer us an alternative of lamb chops (reasonable) with artichoke hearts and potatoes, oddly accompanied by an additional bowl of potato purée. For dessert, a run-of-the-mill moelleux au chocolat with vanilla ice and a crème brûlée. The carte has many of the same options, plus tuna carpaccio, spit-roasted lamb and pigeon. The dressed-up business clientele is clearly prepared to pay, so make your mind up, Gérard, and give us food to match the setting.

Le Grand Colbert

2-4 rue Vivienne, 2nd (01.42.86.87.88). M° Bourse. **Open** noon-1am daily. **Average** €40. **Prix fixe** €34 (dinner only). **Lunch menu** €28. **Credit** AmEx, DC, MC, V. **Wheelchair access. Map** H4.
The lofty listed dining room, with its frescoes, green palms and globe lights that evoke older days, is presumably the main reason why this vintage brasserie continues to pack in an eclectic mix of tourists (the menu is cheerfully translated into English) and Bourse-side businessmen, for foodwise the emphasis is firmly on quantity. A huge bowl of lentil salad was enough to feed an army. Despite looking rather grey, it had nice firm Puy lentils with chopped shallots and a very mustardy dressing. A similarly mustardy dressing came on the salad that accompanied a rather squidgy steak tartare (clearly of the minced rather than chopped-with-a-knife ilk). We would have liked the option to mix it ourselves – as it was it had plenty of capers, a lot of mustard and too much egg, though the chips were chunky and good. A huge piece of salmon came with sorrel sauce, spinach and a grilled tomato, while crème caramel was a vast square wedge chopped off a block. Verdict? Come here if you're ravenous but not for culinary precision.

Aux Lyonnais

32 rue St-Marc, 2nd (01.42.96.65.04). M° Bourse or Richelieu Drouot. **Open** noon-2pm, 7.30-11pm Tue-Fri; 7.30-11pm Sat. Closed last week in July, first three weeks in Aug, one week at Christmas. **Average** €40. **Prix fixe** €28. **Credit** AmEx, MC, V. **Wheelchair access. Map** H4.

This Ducasse-run bistro has perfectly preserved the bouchon style and the pretty c1900 decor (though perhaps they could refresh the ceiling a bit), keeping the hearty spirit but revitalising the cuisine, including an update of that Lyonnais classic, quenelles and crayfish sauce Nantua. As is the wont of today's new-look, rustic-chic terroir cooking, most things arrive here in cast-iron casseroles or glass preserving jars, viz our delicious starters, a glass jar with a poached egg in an exceptional frothy sauce of morels and crayfish, and a little orange cocotte packed with spring vegetables, still just crunchy, in herb butter. Main courses featuring lots of simmering and stewing are a bit less exciting. Veal marengo – named after a Napoleonic battle – proved to be a hefty veal shank braised in wine with confit tomatoes, whole cloves of garlic and tiny potatoes. The navarin of lamb, involving a large chunk from the saddle, was rather fatty, but came with a superb accompaniment of green beans and carrots. Back to preserving jars for dessert, with a clever take on peach melba somewhere between deconstructed trifle and ice-cream sundae. Wines focus on Burgundy, Beaujolais and the Côtes du Rhône, plus the inevitable Coteaux du Lyonnais. Well advised by the very helpful sommelier, we treated ourselves to a pot of excellent Gevry Chambertin 1er Cru from the blackboard extras.

Le Mesturet

77 rue de Richelieu, 2nd (01.42.97.40.68/ www.mesturet.com). Mº Bourse. **Open** noon-3pm, 7-10pm Mon-Fri; 7-10pm Sat. **Average** €30. **Prix fixe** €19, €25. **Credit** AmEx, DC, MC, V. **Wheelchair access**. **Non-smoking room. Map** H4.

Alain Fontaine, former co-owner of La Baracane and L'Oulette, has created an exemplary bistro in this old café space not far from the old Paris Stock Exchange and the former Bibliothèque Nationale. If the tile floors and wooden chairs are standard issue, cloth napkins, paper tablemats with groovy graphics, low lighting and flea market-find decorative objects instantly make the point that this is a real bistro serving freshly prepared food. Here, for very modest prices, you'll find cooking that sincerely seeks to highlight the best of French produce, with Fontaine taking particular pride in ingredients he obtains from small producers in his native south-west. The menu is cleverly accented by a blackboard selection of dishes that change daily, making it even easier to become a regular at this thoroughly likeable place. Starters of free-range chicken terrine with vegetable chutney and an aubergine and cheese terrine with salad were excellent, as were mains of blanquette de veau and sea bream with vegetables. It's obvious there is a professionial in the kitchen, in this case a young chef who previously worked at L'Oulette. Finish up with a cheese such as a creamy, runny rocamadour or maybe a fruit crumble. From an outstanding wine list, the Marcillac was a treat at €15.

Un Jour à Peyrassol

13 rue Vivienne, 2nd (01.42.60.12.92/ www.peyrassol.com). Mº Bourse. **Open** noon-2pm, 8-10pm daily. **Average** €25. **Credit** MC, V. **Wheelchair access. Non-smoking. Map** H4.

As anyone who has travelled around Provence will know, come winter and restaurants there go truffle crazy, putting the black tuber into everything from soup to ice-cream. This casually chic little offshoot of the Commanderie de Peyrassol, a picturesque wine-producing castle in the Var, keeps up the game with its blackboard menu long on truffle treats. Other things are on the menu – such as cep soup, scallop salad, stewed veal, tagliatelle with salmon or the salade du domaine (mesclun, grilled vegetables, feta cheese, olives and sun-dried tomatoes), and the enjoyable if gimmicky 'sardinettes' (tiny sardines served in their tin, accompanied by salt and a boiled potato), but truffles take pride of place. They can be eaten on toast or atop a baked potato, but we chose scrambled eggs generously littered with truffle shavings (the milder and cheaper brumale rather than melanosporum variety), and plentiful nuggets of the precious fungus in a rich, creamy sauce enveloping fluffy gnocchi. Our food was served with two types of good bread: slices of a large country boule and dense, dark olive bread. Just as complementary was the Commanderie's wine – white, red and rosé AOC Côtes de Provence (also available at the shop two doors away). A small glass was offered as an aperitif, a good incentive to order more with the meal.

Le Vaudeville

29 rue Vivienne, 2nd (01.40.20.04.62/www.vaudeville paris.com). Mº Bourse. **Open** noon-3pm, 7pm-1am daily. **Average** €40. **Prix fixe** €19.90-€27.90. **Credit** AmEx, DC, MC, V. **Wheelchair access. Map** H4.

Unlike some Flo restaurants in more touristy locations, this Bourse-side brasserie still draws a largely Parisian clientele, who linger here over a leisurely late lunch. The service is affable and the interior art deco at its purest, with geometrical frosted glass lights, original chairs and loudly striped pink marble effects everywhere. The classic brasserie fare – think oysters, steaks, sole, plus a few variants (salmon with leek gratin, or a more adventurous-sounding salad of crayfish tails, green asparagus and citrus fruit) – is not expensive if you stick to the set menus (though prices shoot up once you go beyond). We began with six fines de claires oysters, then a decent rumpsteak with tiny sautéed potatoes and a Charolais steak tartare. The tartare was well seasoned, but the side of chips was dismal: regulation machine-cut with a strong taste of cooking oil. If the chefs can shuck an oyster, surely they can cut up a potato? Paris's brasseries could do with an update but, as with most of the Flo group, the strong point here is the shellfish. If you're after oysters and the timewarp brasserie experience, then this is still one of the better places to find them.

3RD ARRONDISSEMENT

L'Ambassade d'Auvergne
*22 rue du Grenier St-Lazare, 3rd (01.42.72.31.22/
www.ambassade-auvergne.com). M° Rambuteau.*
Open noon-2pm, 7.30-10pm daily. **Average** €42.50.
Prix fixe €28. **Lunch menu** €20. **Credit** AmEx,
MC, V. **Wheelchair access. Non-smoking room.**
Map K5.
The Auvergne is perhaps best known for one
ingredient: lentils. A bit ho-hum, perhaps, or so you
might think until you've tasted the Puy lentils tossed
with bacon and shallots and smothered in goose fat
at L'Ambassade d'Auvergne, a country inn on the
fringes of the Marais. The waiters charmingly refer
to this dish as a salad, and you can think of it this
way as you help yourself again and again from the
big earthenware bowl that will be left on your white
linen-draped table. The light eater of our twosome
unearthed a salad (green leaves this time) with
melting cabécou cheese and turbot with braised
fennel from the otherwise hearty menu, while the
guiltless gourmand tucked into the lentils, followed
by côtelettes de canard (duck breast with the bone
still attached) with sautéed oyster mushrooms. Often
bland, these mushrooms were imbued here with
meat jus to become wonderfully savoury; however,
too much salt overpowered the dish. An iced parfait
made with marc de prune, a regional eau-de-vie,
provided the perfect ending to a reasonably priced
meal (around €35 per person) made all the more
enjoyable by the quirky maître d'. A word about the
wines: there is a reason why the Auvergne is a little-
known wine region, so you might be better off with
something from elsewhere.

L'Ami Louis
*32 rue du Vertbois, 3rd (01.48.87.77.48). M° Arts
et Métiers.* **Open** 12.30-1.45pm, 7.30-11.30pm Wed-
Sun. Closed mid-July to mid-Aug. **Average** €125.
Credit MC, V. **Wheelchair access. Map** K4.
A strange place, this bistro that time forgot, where
wealthy clients – bankers, artists and intellectuals,
according to the owner, but mostly tourists during
our visit – tuck into expensive dishes such as poulet-
frites or côte de boeuf. The carefully preserved pre-
war interior, resplendent with stovepipe and red
gingham curtains, could have been the inspiration
for *'Allo 'Allo!*, but the food is pricey for the quality.
A large plate (enough for two) of decent, if too
thickly cut ham from the Ardennes and a côte de
boeuf (again for two) – nicely grilled on the outside,
but grey, stringy and flavourless on the inside –
notched up a whopping €117. In terms of redeeming
factors, the service is professional, unobtrusive
and genuinely warm (perhaps with the exception of
the proprietor, who seemed to be having an off day),
and although the wine list features plenty of grand
bottles at grand prices, producers are well chosen
– we drank a juicy St-Joseph 2000 from Bernard
Gripa at €52. But if our experience is anything to go
by, the food is unexceptional and you need an
expense account.

Camille
*24 rue des Francs-Bourgeois, 3rd (01.42.72.20.50).
M° St Paul.* **Open** noon-midnight daily. Closed
Christmas and New Year. **Average** €30. **Lunch
menu** €21. **Credit** AmEx, DC, MC, V. **Wheelchair
access. Map** L6.
Jazz faded into the background as Camille filled up
with the right mix of real people and thankfully
few of the Marais main drag fashionistas. The food
was just as welcome: expert classics executed with
flair and delivered by aproned waiters who ruled the
dining room with prompt efficiency. Indeed, we
were pleased with a buttery pumpkin velouté
made with a magical stock, plus a melt-in-your-
mouth warm herring salad with potatoes and
carrots. Contentment continued with a cod fillet,
olive oil and mash plate that looked and smelled
almost too good to eat, and creamy lentils with a
perfectly pink ham slice so tender it shredded under
the fork. Desserts are mostly old-fashioned tarts; we
bit into a mousse-like chocolate variation with a
shortbread crust. The menu is seasonal, with a few
plats du jour thrown in for good measure; otherwise,
no flairs. Come to Camille for consistency and
simple, fresh, flavourful dishes.

Chez Jenny
*39 bd du Temple, 3rd (01.44.54.39.00/www.chez-
jenny.com). M° République.* **Open** 11am-midnight
Mon-Thur, Sun; 11am-1am Fri, Sat. **Average** €35.
Prix fixe €19. **Credit** AmEx, DC, MC, V.
Wheelchair access. Map L5.
Having booked our table, we could happily bypass
the queue of waiting punters to enjoy an extended
family Sunday lunch in this popular Alsatian
brasserie. These events are always fraught with
problems. Will Granny enjoy the place? Will
everyone decide what to eat before the staff give up
on us? As it was, our charming waitress was
patience itself and allowed us time to enjoy an
aperitif maison, the royal griotte – kir with attitude.
Dressed in vaguely Alsatian costume, in keeping
with the superb marquetry by Charles Spindler, she
quickly guided our bewildered table towards
platters of mixed Brittany oysters, whose briny
freshness impressed all. This was followed by a
massive choucroute Jenny for most of the table.
Tension rose as Granny tucked in – choucroute, as
she had remarked several times, was one of her most
successful and revered specialities. But as she
suspiciously forked some of the preserved cabbage
into her mouth, a beatific smile came over her
face, bringing sighs of relief all around. 'Not bad,'
was what she actually said, but no praise could be
higher for Jenny's signature dish, laden with
sausages and pork produce of all sorts. A couple of
bottles of top-quality Altenberg riesling put us in
the mood for puddings. Crème brûlée seemed to have
been prepared too long ahead of time, but the
blueberry tart was a real Alsatian treat and
Granny's café liégeois was finished with a speed that
only pensioners can manage.

French Cuisine

Le Petit Marché – hip food with Asian flourishes.

Les Chineurs

55 rue de Bretagne, 3rd (01.42.78.64.50). M° Arts et Métiers. **Open** noon-2.30pm, 7.30-11.45pm Mon-Sat. **Average** €30. **Lunch menu** €28. **Credit** MC, V. **Map** L5.

A chineur is an antique bargain-hunter and one must assume that the vintage light fixtures, antique tables and mismatched chairs, glasses and plates are the planned result of someone's careful shopping in the Marais. The food is more sophisticated than the surroundings might suggest, as illustrated by starters such as white beans with strips of duck and grilled prawns with tabouleh. Just as exciting were mains of steak with mixed peppercorns, perch with a spring roll of shaved seasonal vegetables and a tasty slice of rolled milk-fed pork stuffed with ham and foie gras. Desserts run from ice-cream to a crème brûlée atop crushed rhubarb and halved strawberries or baba au rhum with an incongruous pot de chocolat on the side. The service is professional, there is a non-smoking section facing the street and even the bread and coffee are chosen and served with care.

Georget (Robert et Louise)

64 rue Vieille-du-Temple, 3rd (01.42.78.55.89). M° St Paul. **Open** noon-2.30pm, 7.30-11pm Tue-Sat. Closed Aug. **Average** €30. **Lunch menu** €12. **Credit** MC, V. **Map** L6.

The name game is complicated here: the family is called Georget, but the restaurant is also known as Robert et Louise. This anachronism is only the beginning of the charm offensive. As you enter the long, old-fashioned room, with its dusty artwork and distressed ceramics, your eye is immediately drawn to the blazing wood fire over which hunks of meat are being grilled. The scene could come from a Victor Hugo novel: an elderly matriarch encourages an obese poodle to come to her side. Desolately peeling a carrot, she is helped by a group of relaxed young waiters and cooks. The starters, which included a tasty herring on some warm potatoes, are just an excuse for the main event, a Desperate Dan-sized portion of côte de boeuf, a woody crust cutting into perfectly rare beef, accompanied by some classic pommes de terre sautées and a freshly dressed salad. Other choices include various omelettes for the less carnivorous. Puddings, including a reasonable chocolate Charlotte, are as ordinary as the grill is exceptional. As we drained a light, scented bottle of Chiroubles, we noticed that as the flames were dying down in the hearth, cast-iron cauldrons were being placed on the embers; a beef stew as a plat du jour for that very evening. This is where Madame's carrot had been destined and we were tempted to watch over the pot with her until suppertime.

Le Hangar

12 impasse Berthaud, 3rd (01.42.74.55.44). M° Rambuteau. **Open** noon-3pm, 6.30pm-midnight Tue-Sat. Closed Aug. **Average** €35. **No credit cards. Wheelchair access. Map** K5.

Unless you are visiting the doll museum, you are unlikely to find yourself in the impasse Berthaud, but it is worth making the effort to check out Le Hangar, a bistro near the Pompidou Centre with a pleasant traffic-free terrace and excellent cooking. The exposed stone walls and smartly set tables are immediately welcoming, and on a Friday lunchtime the light, long room was comfortably full with locals and a table of slightly baffled Americans. A bowl of tapenade and toast accompanied us as we chose from the fairly comprehensive carte. We picked some tasty and grease-free rillettes de lapereau (rabbit) alongside a perfectly balanced pumpkin and chestnut soup. Our main courses included a well-seasoned steak tartare, served with a crisp salad and some pommes dauphines, and a superb ris de veau on a bed of melting chicory. We were tempted by the puddings, particularly the chocolate soufflé and warm white wine tart with cinnamon, but resisted not through lack of appetite, but because the bistro refuses credit cards, and we were busy doing mental arithmetic. Fortunately, a nice plate of complimentary homemade petits fours managed to satisfy our sweet tooth.

Le Pamphlet ★

38 rue Debelleyme, 3rd (01.42.72.39.24). M° Filles du Calvaire. **Open** noon-2.30pm, 7.30-11pm Mon-Sat. Closed two weeks in Aug. **Average** €33. **Prix fixe** €50. **Credit** MC, V. **Non-smoking room. Map** L5.

Is Alain Carrère one of the most underrated of Paris chefs? Probably. In any case, on several visits, the cooking here has never disappointed us. If the service can be slightly officious, the good-value menu, complete with amuse-gueule and after-dinner nibbles, and well-spaced round tables make this Marais restaurant a highly civilised place to eat. Basque-Béarnaise touches reflect Carrère's south-west origins, though he draws on the Mediterranean as well, along with excellent fish delivered twice weekly from St-Malo. His style is a mix of rustic and refined. We began with a duo of chunkily chopped tuna tartare and smooth mackerel rillettes, served slightly warm on a bed of delicate Basque-style red peppers with mesclun and an expertly seasoned combination of lentils and lamb sweetbreads. Next, a rich classic of well-prepared veal kidneys. The meal's star turn, though, was delicious rack of lamb, cooked to just crisp on the edge, pink in the centre, and set off brilliantly by a tangy garnish of diced feta, cucumber, tomato and mint. The Mediterranean theme continued in an accompaniment of moist, grainy polenta with black olives. We finished with a slice of sheep's cheese and black cherry jam. Note that Carrère has recently opened a bistro offshoot, Le Petit Pamphlet, on nearby rue St-Gilles.

Le Petit Marché

9 rue de Béarn, 3rd (01.42.72.06.67). M° Chemin Vert. **Open** noon-3pm, 7.45pm-midnight daily. **Average** €30. **Lunch menu** €13 (weekdays only). **Credit** MC, V. **Wheelchair access. Map** L6.

Just a step away from the place des Vosges, the Petit Marché has become a hip Marais bistro, attracting a fashion-conscious, alternative local crowd. The woody interior is warm and welcoming, but on our last visit for Sunday lunch, we opted for a table on the heated terrace with an unprepossessing view of the gendarmerie opposite. The menu is short and modern, with Asian touches. Raw tuna was flash-fried in sesame seeds and served with a Thai sauce, making an original, refreshing starter, while crispy-coated deep-fried king prawns had a similar oriental lightness. The main course vegetarian risotto was rich in basil, coriander, cream and al dente green beans. Pan-fried scallops with lime were accurately cooked to avoid any hint of rubberiness, and accompanied by a good purée and more beans. Desserts tend to be more traditional, leading off with rice pudding, fruit crumble and orange mousse. From the short wine list we chose a carafe of the house red (a bargain at €9), which was unusually good. Service was exceptionally friendly, and what with the long opening hours, fair prices and easygoing nature of the place, an ongoing success looks assured.

Le Réconfort

37 rue de Poitou, 3rd (01.49.96.09.60). M° St-Sébastien Froissart. **Open** noon-2pm, 8-11pm Mon-Fri; 8-11pm Sat, Sun. Closed one week in Aug. **Average** €35. **Lunch menu** €13, €17. **Credit** MC, V. **Wheelchair access. Map** L5.

Votive candles, menus glued into kitschy novels, plenty of red velvet – Le Réconfort may be a 'boutique' restaurant, but the at-home ambience is wildly successful, with quality food and decent prices to match (though the clubby groove music is a tad too in-your-face). Chef Guilhem livens up French standards without taking too many risks, as in starters of marinated mushrooms stuffed with chèvre alongside a beetroot and rocket salad, or the sardine and sesame seed rillettes served with artichokes. Both the chicken breast with lemon-cream sauce and parmesan polenta, and the breaded monkfish with sun-dried tomato 'red pesto' and olive-laced mashed potatoes tasted comfortingly familiar, but innovated just enough to be fresh. Indian touches appear throughout: a little cumin here, a sari-clad waitress there. Desserts included ginger ice-cream and a whipped-up pistachio tiramisu. Bucking the bistro trend of overcharging for alcohol, Le Réconfort's list of very reasonably priced wines, including several at €3 a glass, was a welcome relief.

4TH ARRONDISSEMENT

L'Alivi

27 rue du Roi-de-Sicile, 4th (01.48.87.90.20/ www.restaurant-alivi.com). M° Hôtel de Ville. **Open** noon-2.30pm, 7-11.30pm Mon-Fri; noon-11.30pm Sat, Sun. **Average** €35. **Prix fixe** €22. **Credit** AmEx, MC, V. **Wheelchair access. Map** K6.

Amid the oak beams, stone walls and Corsican music, you could be forgiven for thinking you've stumbled upon a tavern hidden away in the mountains of the Ile de Beauté. Until, that is, you note the decidedly Parisian crowd tucking into the hearty dishes. Chef Franck Guglielmi uses only top-notch ingredients, many imported directly from Corsica, such as the generous offerings of charcuterie. Terrine de sansonnet aux myrtes (a pâté of starling and myrtle) sounded too intriguing to pass up, and we were not disappointed by its lovely woody flavour. The choice of mains is almost overwhelming but without hesitation the gourmand between us ordered the civet de sanglier, wild boar stew served in a rich red wine sauce. The meat was of an otherworldly tenderness and the presentation was simple and unpretentious. Make the experience complete with a selection of the island's cheeses or one of the desserts made with brocciu, a creamy ewe's milk cheese. The wine list offers an opportunity to try some of Corsica's best bottles. If your head isn't already swimming from all this goodness, sip a chestnut liqueur before heading back out into the bustle of Paris.

L'Ambroisie

9 pl des Vosges, 4th (01.42.78.51.45). M° Bastille or St Paul. **Open** noon-1.45pm, 8-9.45pm Tue-Sat. Closed two weeks in Feb, three weeks in Aug. **Average** €250. **Credit** AmEx, MC, V. **Wheelchair access. Non-smoking room. Map** L6.

Chef Bernard Pacaud never compromises on quality and always complies with the seasons. Autumn brings rosy-fleshed partridge accompanied by meaty ceps and chestnuts, lightly crumbed turbot with superlative celeriac purée and braised fresh celery stalks, aromatic crayfish soup chock-full of sweet-tasting tails, embellished with young celery leaves. This is serene, sophisticated food, high on tradition; Pacaud sees no need to innovate purely for the sake of it. Thus his signature dish of pearl-pink langoustines with a light curry sauce balanced between almost transparent sesame seed discs, a dish gorged with flavour, is still on the menu and always in demand. His foie gras flavoured with 12 herbs and served with tiny pickled fruit and veg is a wonderful contrast of soft and crunchy, technically perfect. For dessert, tarte fine sablée, a foamy, feathery chocolate tart with vanilla ice-cream, and a choc-coated igloo of crunchy hazelnut ice-cream. Sweets just don't come any better. On previous visits we've groaned about the service – frosty, overly serious – but this time it was charming, with waiters ever-attentive but displaying wit and warmth in equal parts. The wine list is remarkable, but as you'd expect in this 17th-century townhouse-cum-palazzo, replete with Aubusson tapestries, ample marble and gilt and a 400-year-old stone floor from an abbey (which have been worn wonky by many a monk's knee acrobatics, quipped the waiter), the price tags are majestic too.

Benoît

20 rue St-Martin, 4th (01.42.72.25.76/www.alain-ducasse.com). M° Châtelet or Hôtel de Ville. **Open** noon-2pm, 7.30-10pm daily. Closed Aug. **Average** €65. **Lunch menu** €38. **Credit** AmEx, MC, V. **Wheelchair access. Map** J6.

After Aux Lyonnais, this is the second Paris bistro Alain Ducasse has taken over with Thierry de la Brosse, the owner of L'Ami Louis. He has kept most of the kitchen staff but put David Rathgeber, the young former chef of Aux Lyonnais, in charge along with a charming young maître d'. Our autumn lunch started with some of the last ceps (fresh porcini mushrooms) of the season, fried to perfection in oil with little adornment – they didn't need it. Just as understated was the marinated salmon with a warm salad of ratte potatoes (a small yellow variety) a twist on the classic herring. A main dish of frogs' legs in cream sauce with trompettes de la mort mushrooms might not have been nouvelle cuisine, but it seemed light next to the cassoulet – a cast-iron pot brimming with succulent lamb, duck and beans. Baba au rhum, another Ducasse speciality, came with a choice of rums. Little Ducasse touches were visible everywhere, from the quality of the bread to the madeleines served with coffee, but he is wise enough to leave the decor – red velvet banquettes, etched glass, faux marble columns – untouched. This is still one of the most exclusive bistros in town, although the €38 lunch menu no longer seems an afterthought.

Bofinger

5-7 rue de la Bastille, 4th (01.42.72.87.82/ www.bofingerparis.com). M° Bastille. **Open** noon-3pm, 7pm-1am Mon-Fri; noon-1am Sat. **Average** €45. **Prix fixe** €29.90. **Credit** AmEx, DC, MC, V. **Wheelchair access. Non-smoking room. Map** M7.

Bofinger's proximity to the Bastille Opéra and convenience for the Marais art galleries are two good reasons to come here and it still draws queues waiting for a table on a Saturday night. The belle époque setting, with dark wood and glass partitions, long banquettes and white tablecloths, is part of the city's undying brasserie heritage, and the sight of waiters manipulating large trays as they climb the stairs to the upper dining room is all part of the spectacle. Yet we wish they would take a bit more care about their cooking and show a little more concern for their customers. The two diners next to us stared at their dismally frazzled morsels of unidentifiable fish, and pushed away the purée. 'Was there something wrong?' enquired the waiter. 'I didn't like it', said the girl, earning a shrug in response and thus absolving the restaurant of all fault, by casting doubt on her taste rather than the purée. Better to go for the choucroute, the shellfish or a daily special – we've had decent autumn game in the past. Our six fines de claires oysters and six spéciales Gillardeau were good if not exceptional; we noticed that other French diners were tucking into luxurious seafood platters. We finished with a millefeuille: the tasty if rubbery vanilla cream but decidedly soggy flaky pastry were a little like the whole experience – a dining hall conveyer belt that merits more effort.

Brasserie de l'Isle St Louis
*55 quai de Bourbon, 4th (01.43.54.02.59). M°
Pont Marie.* **Open** noon-midnight Mon, Tue,
Thur-Sun. Closed Aug, 23-25 Dec. **Average**
€27.50. **Credit** DC, MC, V. **Wheelchair access.**
Map K7.
The Ile St-Louis is one of the most visited sights in Paris, but island life does not include many down-to-earth restaurants. Happily, this old-fashioned brasserie soldiers on while exotic juice bars and fancy tea shops come and go. The terrace has one of the best summer views in Paris, and was packed with tourists on a sunny September lunchtime. We decided to sit in the dining room, whose shabby chic charm reminded us of our student days. Stuffed game and nicotine-stained walls make for a convivial Parisian experience, and our slightly gruff waiter had obviously served a good many choucroutes and tartares in his life. We began with a well-dressed frisée aux lardons and a slab of fairly ordinary terrine, followed by a greasy slice of foie de veau, prepared à l'anglaise with a rasher of bacon, and a more successful pan of warming tripe. Nothing was gastronomically exciting, and a tad more sophistication in the kitchen would transform this delightful place into something more exceptional. We dodged the very ordinary looking puddings and instead enjoyed a lesson on how to make a steak tartare from our waiter, who at one point almost raised a smile.

Café de la Poste
13 rue Castex, 4th (01.42.72.95.35). M° Bastille.
Open 11am-4pm, 6.45-10.30pm Mon-Fri; 6.45-
10.30pm Sat. Closed one week in Feb, two
weeks in Aug. **Average** €22.50. **Credit** MC, V.
Wheelchair access. Map L7.
This small, friendly restaurant is just the type of place that originally created the myth that you can't get a bad meal in Paris. Why? Because good, simple, affordable food is cooked and served with care and pride in a pleasant, original setting. Bare wood tables, a bar and walls covered in a sort of Dadaist mosaic of cracked tiles and shards of mirror create a homely setting that evokes the vanished Paris of photographers such as Edouard Boubat. Start with the salad of melted goat's cheese served on thin slices of pear with triangles of toasted country bread, or the delicious foie gras, homemade and generously served in two slices. Next, go with the daily special – lasagne, perhaps – or a not unpleasantly chewy rump steak in tangy roquefort sauce with excellent chips. These golden, twice-fried potato slices are absolutely delicious. Though the fruit tarts are a word-of-mouth favourite, we missed the last slice of a pretty fabulous-looking tarte Tatin when we came for a late lunch and settled for a textbook-perfect chocolate mousse instead. A friendly crowd and

attentive but unintrusive service – no mean trick in a space this small – make this a lovely place to come à deux or even on your own. Highly recommended.

Coconnas
*2 bis place des Vosges, 4th (01.42.78.58.16).
M° Chemin Vert or St Paul.* **Open** noon-2.15pm,
7.30-10.15pm Tue-Sun. **Average** €55. **Lunch
menu** €25, €32. **Credit** MC, V. **Wheelchair
access. Non-smoking room. Map** L6.
It would be hard to think of a finer setting than this bourgeois dining room on a corner of the place des Vosges – except perhaps that of La Tour d'Argent, which has the same owner. Come here for a romantic dinner and you will hardly care what's on your plate, which is something the restaurant had apparently been counting on for a while. Recently, however, the arrival of young Breton chef Aymeric Kräml has caused a buzz. We sensed a Breton influence in the cooking, particularly in roasted cod with beer sauce, served on a buckwheat galette with rounds of andouille (a potent tripe sausage). Even if it wouldn't appeal to everyone, this was the best dish in a meal that seemed a little too fussy – we wished that the chef would just let the sole meunière be its glorious self, instead of distracting us with capers, sun-dried tomatoes and diced lemon. Foie gras with warm toast was tasty, while quail galantine proved bland, apart from the accompanying salad. The prize for weirdest dish went to the strawberries served with a minty chocolate milkshake, complete with striped plastic straw. It's hard not to love this place for its ceremony – staff pull off the feat of acting formal yet relaxed – but the food still has some catching up to do.

Le Dôme du Marais ★
*53 bis rue des Francs-Bourgeois, 4th (01.42.74.54.17).
M° Rambuteau.* **Open** noon-2.30pm, 7-11pm Tue-
Sat. Closed three weeks in Aug. **Average** €40.
Prix fixe €32, €45. **Lunch menu** €17, €23.
Credit AmEx, MC, V. **Non-smoking room.
Map** K6.
Most people come here for the setting – and it's true that the glass-domed, circular former auction room of the Mont de Piété (a sort of municipal pawnbroker) is spectacular – but chef Pierre Lecoutre's surprisingly ambitious cooking lives up to the surroundings. Lecoutre alters his menu frequently with a seasonal carte and daily changing lunch menu, featuring some admirably adventurous combinations that reflect his modern take on terroir. A salade de bulots – whelks with lamb's lettuce, red onion and seaweed – was interesting, though the walnut oil dressing slightly overpowered the taste of the whelks; we also liked the hearty own-made black pudding, served warm with dandelion salad. Main courses included magret de canard and a fricassée of lamb's sweetbreads and oyster mushrooms, but the star turn was the pot-au-feu de pintade. The cast-iron casserole of guinea fowl pot-roasted with seasonal vegetables in an unusual and delicious creamy watercress sauce put a sophisticated edge on a rustic dish. Desserts were

satisfying too, a strudel-like pomme croustillante, and a dark-chocolate assortment, including bitter chocolate ice-cream, fondant and chocolate cake. With its formal service, this place draws a slightly older crowd than the usual Marais set, but it's definitely one of the better places to eat in the Marais.

Ma Bourgogne

19 pl des Vosges, 4th (01.42.78.44.64). M° Bastille or St Paul. **Open** noon-1am daily. Closed Feb. **Average** €40. **Prix fixe** €35. **No credit cards. Map** L6.

On an early summer afternoon the terrace of Ma Bourgogne, under the arcades of place des Vosges, can hardly be bettered. The passing tourist trade dominates and our waiter was happy to provide a flourish of English to welcome us. We were less reassured when his mastery of the electronic ordering pad seemed rudimentary. The food was acceptable if uninspiring; a plate of charcuterie was copious but lacked any star item, and the sarladaise salad was short on foie gras. The house speciality of steak tartare was well seasoned and excellent, but the accompanying frites squidged rather than crunched. Hot Lyonnais sausage would have been better without the rather insipid gravy. Hankering after a few more sips of our Brouilly, we ordered cheese, which wasn't exactly earth-shattering. Probably best to stick with a tartare and a bottle of wine and soak up the cosmopolitan atmosphere.

Mon Vieil Ami ★

69 rue St-Louis-en-l'Île, 4th (01.40.46.01.35). M° Pont Marie or St Paul. **Open** noon-2.30pm, 7-10.30pm Wed-Sun. **Average** €39. **Lunch menu** €15. **Credit** AmEx, DC, MC, V. **Wheelchair access. Non-smoking. Map** K7.

Antoine Westermann of the Buerehiesel in Strasbourg has created a true foodie destination on the Ile St-Louis. Although Westermann may be one of Alsace's greatest chefs, the modernised bistro cooking draws from all the regions of France – but, more unusually, pays as much attention to vegetables as to meat and fish. Starters of a 'tartare' of finely diced raw vegetables with sautéed baby squid on top, seasoned with Espelette pepper and coriander, and warm white asparagus with Bayonne ham, dressed with red onions, cress and lamb's lettuce, impressed us with their deft seasoning and accuracy of preparation. Then came a cast-iron casserole of roast duck with caramelised turnips and couscous and gleamingly fresh, chunky flakes of hake on a generous barigoule of stewed artichoke hearts and fennel, the only odd touch an unnecessary blob of tartare sauce. Desserts revisit bistro favourites – rum baba, chocolate tart or a light variation on the café liégeois in a cocktail glass layered with black coffee jelly, coffee ice-cream and a creamy froth laced with pine kernels. Service is pleasant and relaxed and the mix of chatty French bon vivants and a couple of English foodies imparted the undeniable good mood that comes from eating well. Even the classic high-ceilinged Ile St-Louis dining room has been successfully refreshed

with black beams, clever white perspex panels between wall timbers and a long black table d'hôte down one side. The wine list covers all of France, with plenty of interesting options.

Le Temps des Cerises

31 rue de la Cerisaie, 4th (01.42.72.08.63). M° Bastille or Sully Morland. **Open** 7.30am-8pm Mon-Fri. **Food served** 11.30am-2.30pm. Closed Aug. **Average** €18.50. **Lunch menu** €13.50. **No credit cards. Wheelchair access. Map** L7.

An old-fashioned corner bistro on the edge of the Marais with a €13 menu is an increasingly rare treat. Le Temps des Cerises fulfils many a Francophile dream. A curvy zinc bar, old-fashioned wrought-iron bistro tables and a sweet, caring patronne, aided by a waitress who has her favourites, all give the place an essential Parisian buzz. The cuisine is tasty and simple without any pretence of gastronomic sophistication. We began our meal with two wafers of innocuous terrine de sanglier (wild boar), nicely served with some cornichons and salad, which we followed with a well-beaten bavette coated in a blue cheese sauce and served with homely sauté potatoes. To finish, a crumble of apples, quinces and nuts was solid but comforting, while a selection of three cheeses cut at the bar accompanied the last of our fruity bottle of Coteaux de Quercy (a region to which the carte pays homage) gave just the right traditional feel. As we left, regulars were embracing the staff and tables of tourists were congratulating themselves on having found the real thing. The only minus point is the refusal of all credit cards.

Le Trumilou

84 quai de l'Hôtel de Ville, 4th (01.42.77.63.98). M° Hôtel de Ville or Pont Marie. **Open** noon-3pm, 7-11pm Mon-Sat; noon-3pm, 7-10.30pm Sun. Closed two weeks in Aug, one week at Christmas. **Average** €23. **Prix fixe** €15.50, €18.50. **Credit** MC, V. **Wheelchair access. Non-smoking room. Map** K6.

Ducking into this oddly named bistro from the windswept quai behind the Hôtel de Ville, we were greeted by the owner Alain Charven, champagne glass in one hand, Gauloise in the other. The food is dependable and copious, and by sticking to the traditional and eschewing adventurous dishes, you'll be treated to well-executed French classics such as magret de canard, hearty stews and generous steaks. From the starters, the cucumber salad was fresh but uninspiring, while the tarte au boudin noir turned out to be a more uplifting combination of slow-cooked apple segments with small slices of black pudding. The pot-au-feu, served in a steaming metal casserole, was clearly designed to provide natural protection from Parisian winters. Desserts, however, were below par, and the apple tart grand-mère was anything but grandmotherly. Not ideal for a tête-à-tête, with its cloud of smoke and alcohol fumes, punctuated by raucous laughter from the owner as well as the diners, the Trumilou is nonetheless deservedly popular.

Coconnas. *See p33.*

Mi Cayito

What better than candle light and a rocking chair to discover the multiple flavours of cuban cuisine with a modern twist?

Our dishes, such as fricasse of shrimps and sweet potato, beef fillet flavoured with cumin and lime as well as other savoury and sweet dishes and a Sunday brunch menu give you a real taste of cuba.

Mi cayito is about atmosphere and style and the welcoming smile of Reinaldo.

**OPEN DAILY
7pm-2am**

AVERAGE À LA CARTE € 25 - SUNDAY BRUNCH € 15 - € 2

**Cuban Restaurant in the Montorgueil Area
10, rue Marie Stuart 75002 PARIS**

**Tél: 01 42 21 98 8
www.mi-cayito.co**

Le Vieux Bistro

14 rue du Cloître-Notre-Dame, 4th (01.43.54.18.95/
www.lamaree.fr). M° Cité or St-Michel. **Open** noon-
10.30pm daily. **Average** €45. **Lunch menu** €26,
€30. **Credit** DC, MC, V. **Wheelchair access.**
Non-smoking room. Map J7.

Le Vieux Bistro has long got by on an enviable
reputation as the only decent place to eat on the Ile
de la Cité, and the quintessential bistro interior with
tiled floor, lacy curtains and wooden tables, framed
old Byrrh ads and vintage culinary prints of
grandiose gâteaux, and a dyed-in-the wool list of
age-old classics likes to keep up the game. The
message here is sturdy traditional cooking – think
potato salad and lyonnais sausage, pâté de tête,
boeuf bourguignon and tarte Tatin. We began
with a salad of frisée, bacon and poached egg
and leeks vinaigrette, which came atop a pile of
chopped lettuce under a massive dollop of what was
more mayonnaise than vinaigrette. A massive côte
de boeuf for two – almost jelly rare in the centre
under a thick crunchy crust – accompanied by an
uninspired gratin dauphinois was fine but utterly
predictable and decidedly overpriced. Wines favour
the Beaujolais. Come here if you're hungry, in pocket
and longing for a Paris that hasn't changed for
centuries, but don't come if you're after the slightest
touch of imagination.

5TH ARRONDISSEMENT

L'AOC ★

14 rue des Fossés-St-Bernard, 5th (01.43.54.22.52/
www.restoaoc.com). M° Cardinal Lemoine or Jussieu.
Open noon-2pm, 7.30-11pm Tue-Sat. **Average**
€30. **Credit** AmEx, MC, V. **Wheelchair access.**
Non-smoking room. Map K7.

Stepping in off the pavement on a wet night, we
immediately met Jean-Philippe Latron and his
charming wife Sophie, and the tone was set for the
rest of the meal. Latron, overseeing a wonderful
rôtisserie with a tumble of potatoes roasting at the
bottom in the dripping, vaunted the roast pork with
enthusiasm but no pressure, and then Sophie slipped
Nyons olives and sliced saucisson on to the table as
nibbles while we perused the menu. The idea here
is that everything is AOC, or Appellation d'Origine
Contrôlée – a French certification for produce
that meticulously respects the rules set down by
a governmental body appointed to determine
specifically authentic regional foodstuffs. And here
it's not only a clever idea to serve up pedigreed
produce, but one that really works, as the food is
simple, hearty and delicious. Marrow bones with
Guérande sea salt were a treat, as was delicious
terrine de foie gras de canard, and the pork roast and
roast lamb were both tender, full of flavour and
generously served. Further, this is a relaxed, happy
dining room filled with a savvy clientele, making for
a low-key atmosphere that is richly welcome in this
age of soulless fashion restaurants. We finished up
with a first-rate baba au rhum and a delightful crème

brûlée redolent of AOC vanilla from Réunion. A nice
wine list, comfortably spaced tables and low lighting
are further bonuses.

Le Balzar

49 rue des Ecoles, 5th (01.43.54.13.67/
www.groupflo.fr). M° Cluny La Sorbonne. **Open**
noon-midnight daily. **Average** €25. **Prix fixe**
€19.90 (from 10pm). **Credit** AmEx, DC, MC, V.
Wheelchair access. Map J7.

'Pink' and 'piggy' were our first impressions of this
famed haunt of artsies and intellectuals. The Italian
couple next to us squeezed in front of the picture
windows as we waited an hour for a table and ate
every scrap of their giant jarret de porc (a fat-
wrapped, fleshy hunk of pure pig) and surreally
meaty choucroute. But to our relief, the Balzar's
pleasures were not purely porcine. The excellent
house salad could've made a meal in itself: tender
baby spinach, crisp green beans and raw
mushrooms topped with slices of foie gras and
smoked goose breast. The pavé de boeuf was cooked
to rosy perfection, but we sent the undercooked
chips back to the frier. Our last lick of chocolatey
profiteroles, however, came with the rude reminder
that few Paris brasseries have retained their
independence. Now that it's a cog in the powerful
Flo wheel, quick turnover of clients and cash is now
the order of the Balzar day. A magnificently
moustachioed maître d' offered us complimentary
coffee back in the tight-squeeze front window in
exchange for our table. An evening of serious
discussion, once a vibrant Left Bank custom, is not
really an option.

Chez Léna et Mimile

32 rue Tournefort, 5th (01.47.07.72.47/
www.chezlenaetmimile.com). M° Place Monge.
Open noon-2.30pm, 7-11pm Tue-Thur; noon-
2.30pm, 7-11.30pm Fri, Sat. **Average** €30. **Prix
fixe** €39. **Lunch menu** €21. **Credit** MC, V.
Non-smoking room. Map J9.

A sweeping perched terrace, quiet street and rare
patch of greenery give Léna and Mimile an al fresco
edge. The food tries, if a little too hard, to compete.
The prominent vegetables are from trendy producer
Joël Thiébault, bread hails from Poujauran, and
there's a menu inspired by culinary-chemist Hervé
This (artichokes in ascorbic acid, anyone?). At €39,
the basic menu is pricey, but it does include a half-
bottle of wine and coffee. We kicked off with velvety
homemade foie gras and a layered, tongue-teasing
tartare of salmon and tuna zapped with gingery soya
sauce. The anchovy-buttered scorpion fish on a bed
of mesclun and tiny grenaille potatoes was
refreshing but uninspired. Less successful were two
thin slices of (not very) caramelised roast lamb,
reheated and doused in ginger sauce. Our eager
waiter mistakenly identified the dessert du jour as
crumble (it proved to be a fab-looking croustillant
of rhubarb and fresh strawberries), so we went
instead with chocolate mousse overkill and a
delicious, caramel-crisp almond tuile laden with

vanilla cream and fresh raspberries. Starry terraces invite lingering. Stay a while as you debate whether to take home a slab of the splendid foie gras.

Chez René

14 bd St-Germain, 5th (01.43.54.30.23). Mº Maubert Mutualité. **Open** 12.15-2.15pm, 7.45-10.30pm Tue-Sat. **Average** €50. **Prix fixe** €43 (dinner only). **Lunch menu** €32. **Credit** MC, V. **Wheelchair access. Non-smoking room. Map** K7.

Entering this calm, Beaujolais-hued bistro is a little like going back to 1957, the year it opened. No muzak, no mobile phones. Just the muted manoeuvres of seasoned staff and murmured miam-miams of contented regulars. Behind us, a portly lady, vieille France incarnate, tucked into a vast plate of boeuf gros sel. Opposite, a ruddy businessman impressed a Japanese client with his stamina for rare steak and robust red. René is best known for traditional meats, but we opted for fish and came up trumps. A warm salade de rascasse (scorpion fish) was simple and refreshing. But the langoustines fraîches were unbeatable. Ten delicate halves, pincers intact, were intricately woven into an eye-catching crown. Doused in a creamy tarragon and cognac sauce and lightly grilled, they deserved every last crunch, poke and lick. Classic desserts were spot on. Own-made gâteau de riz came with the best vanilla-rich crème anglaise we've ever had. And the plate of petits fours secs (hazelnut meringues, chocolate, pink sugar and almond tuiles, pistachio and almond financiers, all direct from Mâcon) was so generous that we took some home, licking our lips all the way.

Christophe

8 rue Descartes, 5th (01.43.26.72.49). Mº Cardinal Lemoine or Maubert Mutualité. **Open** noon-3pm, 7-11.30pm daily. **Average** €30. **Lunch menu** €19. **Credit** MC, V. **Map** J8.

It offers little in the way of decor – white walls and black-lacquered tables – but Christophe has won the hearts of Latin Quarter locals by opening every day of the week and serving uncompromising French cuisine. Unfortunately, the pricier carte holds the more interesting choices: sautéed langoustines in filo pastry or tuna tartare and cockles in a fluffy cream sauce to start, followed by mains such as a superb cut of lamb atop white beans or a trio of Basque pork (black pudding, pig's trotter with prunes and a huge slice of perfectly cooked meat). Simple desserts follow, such as an apple tart or a below-average moelleux au chocolat. Wines start at €14, with plenty by the glass and some by the carafe. Service was great until the end, when it ground to a halt.

Le Cosi

9 rue Cujas, 5th (01.43.29.20.20). Mº Cluny La Sorbonne/RER Luxembourg. **Open** noon-2.30pm, 7.45-11pm Mon-Sat. Closed Aug. **Average** €40. **Lunch menu** €15.50, €20 (Mon-Fri). **Credit** MC, V. **Wheelchair access. Map** J8.

Russet-coloured, Latin Quarter Cosi soon makes you want to head for the Ile de Beauté, with its tempting bottles of olive oil, photos and a bookshelf of coffee table guides to the island, but it does its regionalism without overkill, meaning that you don't feel you have to be Corsican to come here. The food reflects both mountain peasant food and Mediterranean vegetable and fish preparations, varying from rustic – and sometimes rather heavy – to sophisticated. A sustaining soupe au figatelli, made with white beans and slices of figatelli, the pungent, near-black, smoked liver sausage that is the most distinctive of all Corsican charcuterie, and a lighter, warm herby tomato tart, were typical of these contrasts. Main courses showed a similar range with medallions of monkfish, rigatoni pasta with aubergines (Corsica was long under Genoese rule) and a copious tianu stew of white beans, tomatoes and pork served in a terracotta dish, a sort of Corsican cassoulet. Follow advice on the unfamiliar wines – we enjoyed an excellent red Clos Reginu E Prove from near Calvi.

L'Ecurie

2 rue Laplace, 5th (01.46.33.68.49). Mº Maubert Mutualité. **Open** noon-2.30pm, 7pm-midnight daily. **Average** €20. **Prix fixe** €15 (dinner only). **Lunch menu** €11.50. **No credit cards. Map** J8.

Cash-strapped carnivores need look no further. This former stable – dimly lit, decked out with horsey paraphernalia and sporting what must be one of the city's last Turkish loos – is a magnet for hungry students, plus a few of their grey-haired profs. The bargain €15 menu is what it's all about: start with a generous salad (topped with walnuts or a mound of slightly bizarre grated blue cheese); go straight for the flame-grilled bavette (a moist and smoky flank steak, which, for an extra €2.40, is smothered in mustard, pepper or a rich roquefort sauce) and super-crispy frites; and save room for a pot of sturdy crème caramel. No culinary surprises here (the open kitchen lets you eyeball the whole process from start to finish), but the added value is in the convivial patron (a ready extra for *'Allo 'Allo!'*), who pops sangria on the table when you arrive and brings a cognac chaser with your bill.

L'Equitable

1 rue des Fossés-St-Marcel, 5th (01.43.31.69.20). Mº Censier Daubenton or St-Marcel. **Open** noon-2.30pm, 7.30-10.30pm Tue-Sat. Closed three weeks in Aug. **Average** €30.50. **Lunch menu** €22. **Credit** AmEx, MC, V. **Wheelchair access. Non-smoking room. Map** K9.

At Yves Mutin's bistro, first impressions are deceptive. With the stable-like entrance, auberge trimmings and starchy ambience, we braced ourselves for a stolid meal of country-style fare, but the setting belied an inventive cuisine that made the prix fixe menu stunning value for this part of town. The lower-priced option featured starters of crispy pig's trotters or duck terrine followed by mains of magret de canard and a knuckle of pork stew. From the more intricate, pricier menu, we chose a generous

L'AOC. *See p37*.

Le Pré Verre. See p42.

portion of marbled foie gras, guillotined by a wafer-thin slice of pain d'épice and deliciously set off with apple compote sprinkled with balsamic vinegar, as well as a superb dish of langoustines in a savoury lentil broth. The wide choice of mains included a tenderly cooked sea bass in a truly Gallic garlic and parsley sauce, and a winter dish of roasted calves' kidneys, which was a little over-roasted, but well matched with the salty pancetta and braised endives. To round off this feast, we enjoyed two impressive desserts of crème brûlée with pistachios and morello cherries, and a thick, caramelised chunk of pineapple in a rich rum sauce flambéed by the waiter.

Moissonnier

28 rue des Fossés-St-Bernard, 5th (01.43.29.87.65). M° Cardinal Lemoine. **Open** noon-2pm, 7.30-10pm Tue-Sat. Closed 24, 25 Dec. **Average** €40. **Lunch menu** €24. **Credit** MC, V. **Wheelchair access. Map** K8.

Moissonnier, with its red leather banquettes and bright interior, has for many years stylishly upheld the cooking of Lyon. At lunchtime a mixture of informed tourists and seriously greedy academics from the Jussieu university campus were sitting down to enjoy a gastronomic experience that leaves any afternoon activity seriously compromised. Begin your exploration of this region's cooking with the saladiers lyonnais. Twelve bowls will be wheeled towards you, but put aside any idea that salads are a low-calorie option, for this feast includes not only mushrooms, lentils and celeriac, but also tripe, pied de porc and various sausages, not to mention some meaty, well-seasoned rillettes that winning soused herrings. By this time your appetite should be well and truly open for a tablier de sapeur, a rare dish that is to tripe what wiener schnitzel is to veal, only here served with a rich sauce gribiche; or you could try the puffy expanse of quenelles de brochet floating in a torrid pool of seafood sauce. Bypassing Lyon, you could also enjoy a simple grilled fish or steak, accompanied by the richest of potato gratins, oozing cream and garlic. By now, even buoyed by a carafe of light Coteaux du Lyonnais, your body should reject the idea of a traditional but carefully prepared pudding in favour of a long walk in the nearby Jardin des Plantes.

Le Moulin à Vent

20 rue des Fossés-St-Bernard, 5th (01.43.54.99.37/ www.au-moulinavent.com). M° Jussieu. **Open** noon-2pm, 7.30-11pm Tue-Fri; 7.30-11pm Sat. Closed Aug, 24, 25 Dec. **Average** €50. **Lunch menu** €35. **Credit** MC, V. **Wheelchair access. Map** K8.

Long linen-clad tables line the two walls of this old-fashioned bistro, and with two packed services you're guaranteed to get intimate with your neighbours. Ours brandished €500 notes and meaningless pleasantries, but boy did they know their chateaubriand. Topped with shallots is good, but the tang of almost lemony, tarragon-filled béarnaise is unmatched. Everyone comes here for the sublime

beef (only Salers, direct from the Auvergne) and whether you like it thick and bloody or melting in a rich bourguignon sauce you won't be disappointed. If you can't choose, get one each and swap halfway through as we did. These pricey meats come only with potatoes, pan-fried and scrumptious, so start with a salad. Laden with roquefort, our frisée easily fed two. Desserts can also be shared: half a rummy rice pudding with crème anglaise is all you'll have room for. The only low note was the wine. We ordered a 2004 Moulin à Vent, only to be served up a cold bottle of 2005. Our amiable waiter, after a bill muddle, sought to make amends, but the complimentary digestifs didn't quite do it.

Perraudin

157 rue St-Jacques, 5th (01.46.33.15.75). M° Cluny La Sorbonne/RER Luxembourg. **Open** noon-2.30pm, 7-10.30pm Mon-Sat. Closed Aug. **Average** €40. **Prix fixe** €28 (dinner only). **Lunch menu** €18. **Credit** DC, MC, V. **Wheelchair access. Non-smoking room. Map** J6.

This ever-popular Latin Quarter eaterie has the quintessential Parisian bistro look, except that here it is c1910. Its shabby dark red interior, red-checked tablecloths and frayed posters on dulled mirrors don't look immediately inviting. Nonetheless, at lunch, local bohemians and academics crowd into Perraudin for no-nonsense, hearty bistro food. From the starters, the snails were excellent and thankfully avoided the common bistro vice of over-butteriness. We were also pleased with the Flemish tarte au maroilles, a tasty cheese and onion quiche. We resisted the waiter's exhortations to try the tête de veau, opting for the more sedate boeuf bourguignon, an acceptable rendition of the Burgundy classic, and the gigot d'agneau, parsimonious slices of lamb bolstered by an overflowing earthenware dish of gratin dauphinois – all washed down with a decent 1999 Bordeaux. Desserts covered familiar territory of heavy-duty profiteroles or dense chocolate mousse, but the more unusual tarte au sucre, another Flemish speciality, was enjoyable, though a little weighty at this stage of a copious meal. Overall, the food is solid and unpretentious, the service efficient and we were charmed by Mr Rameau, the owner, boasting with pride of his wife's bistro recipes.

Le Petit Pontoise

9 rue de Pontoise, 5th (01.43.29.25.20). M° Maubert Mutualité. **Open** noon-2pm, 7.30-10.15pm daily. Closed 25 Dec, 1 Jan. **Average** €35. **Credit** AmEx, DC, MC, V. **Map** K7.

As soon as we walked into this lemon-hued, blackboard-festooned bistro, the dessert menu perched above our heads caught our eye. Having resolved beforehand to forgo the sweets, we suddenly struggled to limit ourselves to three. The old-fashioned, too-rare sabayon (a teasing concoction of frothy champagne custard and ice-cream) was sublime; the decadent, grandmotherly chocolate cake came a close second; and the too-sugary, pink-praline-topped île flottante was hands down the prettiest. We ordered the rest of our meal with this end in sight. A circle of homemade foie gras and fig terrine made a perfect shared starter, and mains didn't disappoint. The duck parmentier (a shredded melt of confit, topped with mash and pan-fried foie gras) gave new meaning to comfort food. Likewise, pots of saucy pig cheeks and boeuf gros sel, lentils and bone marrow were reassuringly earthy. Wine regions get a blackboard each, as does the tempting fish, which we missed this time. But that's just another reason to come back. Be sure to book.

Le Pré Verre

8 rue Thénard, 5th (01.43.54.59.47). M° Maubert Mutualité. **Open** noon-2pm, 7.30-10.30pm Tue-Sat. Closed first two weeks in Aug. **Average** €30. **Prix fixe** €25.50 (dinner only). **Lunch menu** €12.50. **Credit** MC, V. **Wheelchair access. Non-smoking room. Map** J7.

Beetroot has insinuated itself into the strangest places – these days all of the capital's trendy spots squeeze it in somewhere – but in ice-cream, served alongside other garden-variety desserts such as parsley-marinated strawberries, it's still a rare find. The bold (read: brisk service) Pré Verre stakes its reputation on the innovative (read: in-your-face) collision of continents and culinary cultures: roast cod spiked with cassia bark is paired with smoked potato purée, lemon-zested lamb with a side of azuki beans, a cumin-laced rabbit thigh with grilled aubergine. At its best (the melt-in-the-mouth cod and mash or the crisply smooth lentil and pork galette to start), the taste-bud challenge is sensational. At its worst (the rabbit and, dare we admit it, iced beetroot), it's not just banal but irritating. We went with our testy waiter's enthusiastic recommendation of 2004 Cheverny and weren't totally convinced; but at €17, and with a €25.50 menu, we didn't feel the pinch. Seating is tight and the noise level is high, but the main dining room is blessedly non-smoking.

Le Reminet ★

3 rue des Grands-Degrés, 5th (01.44.07.04.24). M° Maubert Mutualité or St-Michel. **Open** noon-2.15pm, 7.30-11pm Mon, Thur-Sun. Closed three weeks in Aug. **Average** €35. **Lunch menu** €13 (Mon, Thur, Fri). **Credit** MC, V. **Map** J7.

Hugues Gournay's tiny bistro, now extended into its vaulted cellar, is a diner's dream. Open on weekends (as inventive one-man spots so rarely are), and thankfully resistant to the two-sitting trend, this is somewhere you'll want to savour. Expect creative, fresh cooking made with top-quality ingredients from the charming, personable chef. Delicate herring fillets interleafed with fine strips of green apple rivalled the panache of a cognac jelly, pickle purée-crowned duck terrine. Taste buds on alert, we were soon swapping bites of roast pigeon in a zingy cranberry and prune sauce and the thickest, most melting and divine lamb steak imaginable. Aubergine and mozzarella, enlivened with confit tomatoes, garlic and olives, gave the lamb a refined Mediterranean edge, while the pigeon was paired

with tender, moreish cabbage. Desserts kept the stakes high. Both the aniseed tuile topped with pastis mousse and orgeat (barley syrup) and an inventive mocha confection (coffee meringue, bitter chocolate mousse, espresso jelly) demand a return visit. Gourmands take note: the €50 tasting menu, with two starters, two mains, cheese and assortment of desserts, guarantees double the pleasure.

Restaurant Marty

20 av des Gobelins, 5th (01.43.31.39.51/www.marty-restaurant.com). M° Les Gobelins. **Open** noon-3pm, 7-11pm Mon-Thur, Sun; noon-3pm, noon-midnight Fri, Sat. **Average** €50. **Prix fixe** €30. **Lunch menu** €29. **Credit** DC, MC, V. **Wheelchair access. Non-smoking room. Map** K10.

While most Parisian brasseries sport belle époque gilded and mirrored luxury, Marty is pure art deco. Sumptuous curves, leopard-print wooden chairs, and period chandeliers and murals adorn the spacious split-level dining areas. Were it not for the food and efficient staff (one monsieur sports a classic handlebar moustache), you might think this was a Prohibition-era jazz club. We found the starter of crabmeat and avocado purée rich and thoroughly rewarding. Likewise, an Asian-inspired starter of cold root veg and mangetout stuffed into a blossom-shaped crispy crêpe. Mains of salmon and cod brochette with corn cake, and a mixed grill of tuna, sea bream and salmon were competently prepared, if a little over-salted. But a fresh fruit-topped rice pudding, creamy and big enough to share, was thoroughly beyond reproach. All in all, the prix fixe is a steal, the covered terrace provides a fine refuge from foul weather, and the downstairs room would host a memorable reception. Afterwards, take a stroll up nearby rue Mouffetard to walk off this classy brasserie experience.

Ribouldingue

10 rue St Julien le Pauvre, 5th (01.46.33.98.80). M° St-Michel. **Open** noon-2pm, 7-11pm Mon-Fri; 7-11pm Sat. **Average** €35. **Prix fixe** €25. **Credit** MC, V. **Map** J7.

Ribouldingue means 'binge', and the outside lettering appears to be the work of a happy but drunken artist, while the drawings decorating the interior are of crazy, gleeful dancing figures. It is the joyous creation of Nadège Varigny, who spent 12 years working in La Régalade's dining room before opening this restaurant with Guy Bommefront (formerly of Le Troquet) in the kitchen. Full of eager diners, including critics and chefs, who love Camdeborde's type of food – simple, honest, gutsy bistro fare, in some part based on innards, mixed with terrines, salads and fish — it's the darling of the moment among adventurous eaters. You can get lighter food, but rather go for the sautéed brains with divine new potatoes or veal kidneys with a perfectly prepared potato gratin. Or try the groin de cochon (the tip of the muzzle) or tétines de vache (thin, fried slices of the udder). Just don't miss the fluffed-up ewe's cheese with bitter honey or tarte Tatin.

La Rôtisserie de Beaujolais

19 quai de la Tournelle, 5th (01.43.54.17.47).
Mº Jussieu. **Open** noon-2.15pm, 7.30-10.15pm
Tue-Sun. Closed four days at Christmas. **Average**
€40. **Credit** MC, V. **Wheelchair access.**
Map K7.
Little sibling to La Tour d'Argent across the street,
La Rôtisserie de Beaujolais is another ball game
altogether, but an entertaining one. Wooden tables
covered with checked cloths set the unpretentious
tone, and the menu of solid bistro classics attracts a
clientele that has lived through at least one World
War, sometimes two. We happily ate our way
through the autumn menu, which was peppered with
game dishes. Scrambled eggs with truffle lacked the
punch one might hope for, but made up for it with a
nice, creamy texture, while the compote de lapereau,
a rillette-like spread, was generous enough to share.
The rest of the poor bunny presumably went into one
of the seasonal picks, lapereau with lemon, whole
garlic cloves and spoon-soft polenta – a successful
southern-influenced dish. Crisp-skinned roasted
pigeon came on a slightly soggy bed of paillasson
potatoes, but by now the Beaujolais for which
this bistro is named was working its magic and
we were willing to overlook small flaws. Desserts
are wonderfully classic, including a coffee-flavoured
parfait glacé and, for the devil in anyone, the alcoholic
cherry and chocolate concoction that's dubbed
'le petit diable'.

La Table de Fabrice

13 quai de la Tournelle, 5th (01.44.07.17.57/
www.latabledefabrice.fr). Mº Cardinal Lemoine,
Maubert Mutualité or Pont Marie. **Open** noon-
2.30pm, 7-11pm Mon-Fri; 7-11pm Sat. Closed Aug.
Average €30. **Prix fixe** €40. **Credit** AmEx,
MC, V. **Wheelchair access. Non-smoking**
room. Map K7.
Fifteen years in some of the best Paris kitchens –
Lasserre, Joël Robuchon, Alain Senderens – have
given Fabrice Deverly style and some substance,
along with square plates and a light Italian accent
in his cooking. With a few tables spilling on to the
Seine-side pavement, his enchanting spot is bold
and uneven. Shards of brik-like pastry dominated
our dinner. Two paper-thin circles produced a
crab millefeuille; wrapped around goat's cheese it
was a croustillant. And that was just to start. A
too-thick tuna steak, its herb 'crust' a mass of fresh
dill, was likewise trapped in a papery parcel. All
three dishes came with lashings of balsamic vinegar.
But Deverly's promise came to the fore with his
signature risotto. At €36, the summer truffle special
looked too pricey so we opted for the lentins de chêne
(similar to shiitake) version included in the €40
menu. Every mouthful of rich, creamy rice, the
earthy edge of mushroom neatly set off by shaved
parmesan, was sublime. With truffles it was surely
stupendous. And there's the rub: the most exciting
courses – like a carrot moelleux with carrot jam,
cream and strips of sweet, al dente veg – are strictly
à la carte. Substance costs, it seems.

La Tour d'Argent

15-17 quai de la Tournelle, 5th (01.43.54.23.31/
www.tourdargent.com). Mº Cardinal Lemoine or
Pont Marie. **Open** 7.30-10pm Tue; noon-2pm,
7.30-10pm Wed-Sun. **Average** €200. **Lunch**
menu €70. **Credit** AmEx, DC, MC, V. **Wheelchair**
access. Non-smoking room. Map K7.
There is something inescapably mummified about
the silver tower, and it's not just that the gilt is
starting to peel. Stripped of its third Michelin star in
1996, it experienced a second tumble in 2006 that
sent its 89-year-old owner to hospital with a stroke
and his head chef packing. Stéphane Haissant boldly
stepped into the breech, but, as the mausoleum effect
of the main floor hall of fame confirms, the
restaurant is immune to change. The Tour's
reputation is its main draw. Camera-toters snap
lunchtime mementos, there's a souvenir shop and if
you choose any of the ducks you'll get a postcard
with Donald's number inscribed. But unlike the
Queen – who ate the 185,397th specimen in 1948 –
your name won't make it into the archive. The €70
lunch menu provides a glimpse at this history
without breaking the bank. Stupendous views of
Notre Dame and consistently royal service ensure
value for money. Prettily pink, swimming in orange
sauce, the caneton rôti was a much better choice than
the Mediterranean-inspired lamb with a flaccid
veggie-stuffed crêpe. Starters were suitably refined
– a dill-infused millefeuille of eel, plus airy pike
quenelles – and the fruit laden, lime-zapped financier
was one good pud. Ultimately, the Tour is more
interested in itself than your palate. If history is what
you're looking for, pleasure is guaranteed.

6TH ARRONDISSEMENT

Alcazar

62 rue Mazarine, 6th (01.53.10.19.99/
www.alcazar.fr). Mº Odéon. **Open** noon-2.45pm,
7pm-12.45am Mon, Tue, Thur-Sun; noon-2.45,
7pm-12.15am Wed. **Average** €50. **Prix fixe** €39.
Credit AmEx, DC, MC, V. **Wheelchair access.**
Map H7.
Alcazar was transformed into a gastrodrome by Sir
Terence Conran in 1998. Despite some anti-Brit
teasing, it has proved as popular as his food outlets
in London. The clean anonymous lines of the former
cabaret have a distinctly late '90s feel, home to many
a booming English voice. On a quiet Sunday evening
it took a while to be offered an aperitif, but the food,
which aims to be a notch above the average seafood-
strong brasserie, was consistently fine. We began
with deeply flavoured crab bisque and, to establish
our Gallic street cred, a dish of buttery escargots.
The famous fish and chips would win no prizes in
Yorkshire, but succeeds through its tempura-like
lightness to lure unsuspecting Frenchmen into a
British culinary trap. Giving it a miss this time, we
opted for scallops on a bed of orange-tinted chicory,
and a wedge of macho boudin noir (black pudding),
accompanied by exceptional creamed potatoes.

There are no half bottles on the long wine list, but a good choice available by the glass. Traditional puddings are well prepared, but there are some lighter options too.

Allard

41 rue St-André-des-Arts, 6th (01.43.26.48.23/
www.allard-restaurant.com). M° Odéon or St-Michel.
Open noon-2pm, 7-10.30pm Mon-Sat. Closed three weeks in Aug, 25 Dec. **Average** €60. **Prix fixe** €32. **Lunch menu** €24. **Credit** AmEx, DC, MC, V. **Wheelchair access. Map** H7.

If St-Germain seems to be turning into a suburb of Milan with its proliferation of Italian restaurants, it's reassuring to come across an excellent example of a traditional bistro. With its vanilla-coloured walls and a coat rack in the narrow hall connecting the two small dining rooms (the front one has more atmosphere), Allard has a delicious pre-war feel, a first impression that is confirmed by the kitchen itself (though not the rather steep prices). It sends out glorious Gallic grub that's exactly what everyone dreams of finding in Paris. Winter is the perfect time of year for this place – start with sliced Lyonnais sausage studded with pistachios and served with potato salad in delicious vinaigrette, or maybe a sauté of wild mushrooms, and then choose between one of the three classics: roast shoulder of lamb, roast Bresse chicken with sautéed ceps or roast duck with olives. All three are superb, but be warned that portions are enormous. If you have any space left, finish up with the tarte fine aux pommes and go with one of the good, if slightly pricey, Bordeaux.

La Bastide Odéon ★

7 rue Corneille, 6th (01.43.26.03.65/www.bastide-
odeon.com). M° Odéon. **Open** 12.30-2pm, 7.30-10.30pm Tue-Sat. Closed Aug, 24, 25 Dec, 1 Jan. **Average** €40. **Lunch menu** €26.

It's not just its position – tucked neatly beside the Odéon theatre and seconds from the Jardins du Luxembourg – that draws well-dressed Parisians and international visitors to the Bastide Odéon. It has also discreetly become one of the most consistently reliable addresses in the area, with its pleasant service and modern spin on terroir. Although the name and yellow and russet decor suggest Provence, chef Gilles Ajuelos's cooking is full of southern inspiration rather than southern cliché. He spreads his net right along the Mediterranean seaboard (ingredients include feta, dates and polenta) and beyond – the Bastide Odéon is one of the rare places in France where you can eat British Hereford beef – as he mixes stalwarts like pieds et paquets with some more unusual combinations, and ever-present herbs. Ibérico ham with grilled peppers and artichokes, and a millefeuille of tomato and ricotta, were pleasant starters before a successfully tangy grey mullet with wild capers, lemon, olives and tomato in a veal jus reduction, and our long-time favourite of roast farm chicken with whole cloves of preserved garlic and new potatoes – simple but delicious. The attractively presented desserts were good too, among them a millefeuille with bourbon vanilla and a saffron-tinted poached pear with fromage blanc ice-cream.

Au Bon Saint-Pourçain

10 bis rue Servandoni, 6th (01.43.54.93.63).
M° Mabillon or St-Sulpice. **Open** noon-2pm, 7.30-10.30pm Mon-Sat. Closed Aug. **Average** €30. **No credit cards. Wheelchair access. Map** H7.

This corner bistro just behind St-Sulpice is atmospheric and almost claustrophobically intimate. The patron has a reputation for being a character whom customers either love or fear. On our last lunchtime visit the boss was absent and a charming young waitress was in charge, but one thing is sure: you are going to overhear your neighbours in the tiny room, which feels more like a farm kitchen than an urban bistro. Our fellow guests included a couple of supremely elegant French ladies-who-lunch and a funky Home Counties family from England. Our meal of comforting old-fashioned bistro cuisine began with a generous fromage de tête with a perky caper relish and a compote de lapereau, a little cold but accompanied by a well-dressed salad with walnuts. For our main courses we chose a gorgeously gelatinous tête de veau, sauce gribiche, and a well-cooked quality entrecôte with a pot of potent marchand de vin sauce. The steak was accompanied by a dried-up gratin dauphinois, but the waitress sweetly replaced it with a pile of French beans. Homely puddings complete a reassuringly traditional meal, but don't order the horrid reheated filter coffee – better to stick with the rough but drinkable St-Pourçain red wine. Despite a reasonable bill, remember that this is a technology-free zone: credit cards aren't accepted and the cash machine is not next door.

Boucherie Roulière

24 rue des Canettes, 6th (01.43.26.25.70).
M° Mabillon. **Open** noon-2.30pm, 7-11.30pm Tue-Thur, Sun; noon-2.30pm, 7pm-midnight Fri, Sat. **Average** €30. **Credit** MC, V. **Wheelchair access. Map** H7.

This is not somewhere to take your vegetarian friends, as the long, narrow Boucherie Roulière glorifies the profession of meat preparation. The blackboard menu offers a simple collection of grilled meat and fish, accompanied by traditional bistro favourites to begin and end your meal. Our guest found the ravioles aux truffes an irresistible first course. Despite the fear that these might not live up to their billing, they managed to have a real perfume of the earthy luxury, and were richly creamy as well. A terrine de canard was a fine, meaty homemade pâté, setting us up for our main courses, which include a perfectly grilled rognon de veau (veal kidney) with a separate pot of sauce and some seriously good mash. The thick tuna steak was pink and moist, showing that the fishmonger's art is taken seriously here too. Drinking the excellent house red, it was hard to resist the single cheese on offer,

Boucherie Roulière.

a carefully chosen, ripe camembert followed by some alcohol-soaked baby cherries served with a scoop of first-class vanilla ice-cream. Service is of the boisterous macho Parisian style but friendly enough.

Bouillon Racine

3 rue Racine, 6th (01.44.32.15.60/www.bouillon-racine.com). M° Cluny La Sorbonne. **Open** noon-2.30pm, 7-11pm daily. **Average** €35. **Prix fixe** €26. **Lunch menu** €15.50. **Credit** AmEx, DC, MC, V. **Wheelchair access. Non-smoking room.** **Map** J7.

The Bouillon Racine has a long history and one of the most spectacular art nouveau settings in Paris. It began life as a workers' soup kitchen, but has now been restored as a popular Latin Quarter bistro with a Belgian accent – a good list of Belgian beers is on tap, plus classic dishes of waterzooi and carbonnade. Soups are still served as starters, but on a quiet early summer evening we plumped for an oeuf poché au vin rouge et champignons, and a tuna tartare with the unusual addition of coconut milk. As with much of the food, it was pleasant but somehow lacked a freshly cooked zing (the speed of the arrival of the poached egg was a giveaway). Main courses of sea bream fillet served on a bed of spinach, and a compact slice of spit-roasted, overstuffed suckling pig on homemade purée were decent, but lacked culinary buzz. Nursed by the gentle jazz that incongruously fills the restaurant, we enjoyed a comforting chestnut 'velvet' dessert, and good room-temperature cheese.

Les Bouquinistes

53 quai des Grands-Augustins, 6th (01.43.25.45.94/www.lesbouquinistes.com). M° Odéon or St-Michel. **Open** noon-2.30pm, 7-11pm Mon-Sat. **Average** €42. **Lunch menu** €25, €28. **Credit** AmEx, DC, MC, V. **Wheelchair access. Map** J6.

This sleek modern outlet of the Guy Savoy group has an unbeatable position on the banks of the Seine, and very quickly the restaurant packs out with a tourist-led crowd eager to enjoy this bistro take on haute cuisine. We were disappointed not to be automatically presented with the 'retour du marché' lunch menu. After we plucked up courage and asked for it, it was politely brought to the table, but by then we had been left too long with the carte, which seemed far more appealing. A dish of warm oysters with fennel was frothed in the modern manner and served with some seaweed bread. Initially, this seemed an exquisite dish, but it failed to sustain interest to the last spoonful. Our main courses were both up to standard, with a perfectly cooked thick slice of pan-fried foie gras accompanied by a sweet apple and celery compote, and musky wild mushrooms with light gnocchi. We dodged the good-looking puddings in favour of an economic 'café et l'addition'. The golden white Quincy was well chosen as at all Guy Savoy restaurants, but the service cuts corners on numbers, and obtaining the bill in a full restaurant took too long, even with a Seine view.

Brasserie Lipp ★

151 bd St-Germain, 6th (01.45.48.53.91/www.brasserielipp.com). M° St-Germain-des-Prés. **Open** 11.45-12.45am daily. Closed 24, 25 Dec. **Average** €50. **Credit** AmEx, DC, MC, V. **Wheelchair access. Non-smoking room.** **Map** H7.

When somewhere as old and stylish as the Lipp – fuelling Paris politicos and Left Bank intellects in art nouveau grandeur for more than a century – lets plebby newcomers sit at the coveted ground-floor tables, you know that something revolutionary is afoot. But the democratic urge was short-lived. We were tucked comfortably into the back room where we ogled not presidential hopefuls but an army of starched, black-tied waiters (all surely contemporaries of the eponymous Léonard) as they strove, amid the swirl of gargantuan, tender côtes de boeuf, surreally pink platters of piggy choucroute, and some of the zingiest steak tartare we've ever eaten, to tame the barbarian invasion. But when our neighbours asked to have their raspberry-hued Gevrey-Chambertin put on ice, the staff simply and heroically refused. Competition may have made Lipp relax some of its time-honoured snooty standards, but there has been no accompanying compromise of culinary rigour. After succulent, meaty mains – all spot-on, bloody or blue as required – we opted for a barrage of classic desserts: chilly profiteroles swimming in thick chocolate, a slab of beautiful tarte Tatin and the famous wedge-like millefeuille, courtesy of Dalloyau (for something different try the praliné '2,000 feuilles'). As the revolving door whirled us back on to the street, we felt the ghost of Mitterrand wish us good night.

Aux Charpentiers

10 rue Mabillon, 6th (01.43.26.30.05). M° Mabillon or St-Germain-des-Prés. **Open** noon-3pm, 7-11.30pm daily. Closed 25 Dec, 1 May. **Average** €32. **Prix fixe** €26 (dinner only). **Lunch menu** €19. **Credit** AmEx, DC, MC, V. **Wheelchair access. Non-smoking room.** **Map** H7.

It was 25 years since we had last eaten at Aux Charpentiers, when it was a cheap and cheerful student haunt overlooking the marché St-Germain. Now, with unchanged vintage decor, it has become a serious Parisian bistro, where simple hearty dishes are prepared with unusual care and served by a friendly team, which knows how to welcome tourists and regulars alike. We began our meal with a salad of crisply fried sweetbreads and a compote de lapereau – a highly seasoned rabbit terrine with an earthenware jar of crunchy gherkins on the side. We chose the plat du jour of stuffed cabbage (the ultimate comfort food) and a more elaborate duck with olives and port, which was well cooked but with just a touch of tourist blandness. Resisting the great-looking rum babas, we plumped for a slice of well-aged brie. Looking around at the splendid zinc bar and happy St-Germain crowd, we vowed not to wait another quarter of a century before returning.

Chez Maître Paul

12 rue Monsieur-le-Prince, 6th (01.43.54.74.59/ www.chezmaitrepaul.com). M° Odéon. **Open** 12.15-2.30pm, 7.15-10.30pm daily. Closed three days at Christmas, Mon and Sun in July and Aug. **Average** €40. **Prix fixe** €29, €35. **Lunch menu** €22. **Credit** AmEx, DC, MC, V. **Wheelchair access. Map** H7.

There is something comfortingly homely about Maître Paul in a street where globalisation is attempting a gastronomic takeover. The welcome is consistently warm and the room is a reassuringly design- and concept-free zone. Perhaps this accounts for the restaurant's popularity with both tourists and locals in search of rib-sticking tradition in a cosy atmosphere. The menu never strays far from the Franche-Comté region near the Swiss border, and after a glass of mac-vin, a mixture of grape juice and eau-de-vie from the Jura, we cut into the best-quality Monbéliard sausage possible served on a bed of warm potatoes, and hummed happily over a creamy dish of escargots, which made a change from the usual butter, garlic and parsley fix. Cream also played a big role in a tender Jura-style fricassée de veau, and the cheese-topped poulette. Pungent regional cheeses and an unchangingly satisfying gâteau aux noix completed our meal, which included half a bottle of light, drinkable red. Forget the diet and enjoy some genuine mountain man cuisine here.

Chez Marcel

7 rue Stanislas, 6th (01.45.48.29.94). M° Notre-Dame-des-Champs. **Open** noon-2pm, 7.30-10pm Mon-Fri. Closed Aug. **Average** €35. **Lunch menu** €16. **Credit** MC, V. **Wheelchair access. Map** G8.

It is comforting when a restaurant appears unchanged since World War I. Banquettes and bric-a-brac, a long zinc counter, charming old-school waiters, Marcel has it all. Does the trad food still do the trick for a lunchtime crowd of the predominantly portly? Well, if you're in the mood for cutting-edge fusion, this is not the place for you, as the menu of Marcel's egg mayo and pig's ears followed by Lyonnaise specialities such as quenelles and gras double is likely to leave you nonplussed. We began with a wedge of rillettes de canard, tastier than the usual pork version, and an egg mayo that was totally at home, though the piped mayonnaise seemed a suspicious frill. Trump card from the carte was a groaning plateful of perfectly pink medaillons de veau with a delicate basil sauce and some good sauté potatoes. A feuilleté de volaille forestière was a less successful choice from the €16 lunch menu, with too much flake and not enough fowl. We finished up our carafe of reasonably priced rosé de Provence with a passable plate of cheese, and some cherry sorbet. For gently priced tradition with a smile, look no further.

La Closerie des Lilas

171 bd du Montparnasse, 6th (01.40.51.34.50/ www.closeriedeslilas.fr). M° Port-Royal. **Open** noon-2.30pm, 7.30-11.30pm daily. **Average** €85. **Lunch menu** €45. **Credit** AmEx, DC, MC, V. **Wheelchair access. Map** H9.

Once, at the end of a long evening at the Closerie bar, we found to our horror that we didn't have enough money to pay the bill. The barman took what we had with a big smile and a magnanimous 'Don't worry about it'. Elegance abounds at this Montparnasse institution that has, at one time or another, counted Ingres and Chateaubriand, Trotsky and Lenin, Apollinaire, Picasso and (bien sûr) Hemingway among its regulars. On our last visit we spotted one of the leaders of the Parti Socialiste and a legend of French rock. The restaurant has recently recovered a good, fine-eating reputation, but we (and the French rock legend as well, apparently) prefer the simpler and cheaper brasserie, because there you can sit closer to the piano and the dark, velvety atmosphere of the bar. We ate well from an unpretentious menu that is strong on seafood (tremendous oysters and a fine clam soup). Our mains of poached pike dumplings and a fish panaché, though nothing outstanding, were carefully cooked and nicely presented. Chocolate profiteroles were, as always when done right, that sublime meeting of crisp and creamy, hot and cold. Staff were efficient, discreet and friendly – obviously forgetting that we owed them money.

Le Comptoir du Relais

9 carrefour de l'Odéon, 6th (01.44.27.07.50). M° Odéon. **Open** *Brasserie* noon-10.30pm Mon-Fri; noon-6pm, Sat, Sun. *Restaurant* 8.30-10.30pm Mon-Fri. **Prix fixe** €40. **Credit** AmEx, DC, MC, V. **Map** H7.

For a few blissful months after it opened, it was easy to get a dinner reservation at Yves Camdeborde's bistro in the Relais St-Germain hotel. Now word has got out in a big way and the tiny art deco dining room is booked up several months in advance for the single dinner sitting. The good news is that you can show up anytime between noon and 6pm (10.30pm on weekends) and choose from a simpler bistro menu that includes typically Camdebordian dishes such as deboned, breaded pig's trotter. We were able to reserve one of the tiny pavement tables for an early summer dinner and so indulged in the full five-course feast, which changes daily. Our meal started with velvety chicken soup spiked with vin jaune from the Jura region and poured into a martini glass over girolle mushrooms – light and appetite-whetting. Less successful was a gelée made with crabmeat and veal trotter and flavoured with piquillo pepper and basil, the gelatinous veal trotter seeming a little out of place. We could find no flaw with the main event, roasted saddle of lamb from the Pyrénées served with an intense thyme-flavoured jus and ravioles du Pays Basque, whose tender wrappers contained deliciously spiced summer vegetables. It would be worth coming here for the cheese course alone – a giant wicker basket of oozing specimens is plunked on the table for diners to help themselves. Dessert was perfect for a hot day: prosaic-sounding melon balls livened up with honey, plenty of lime juice, ginger and crushed nougatine.

L'Epi Dupin

11 rue Dupin, 6th (01.42.22.64.56). M° Sèvres Babylone. **Open** 7-9pm Mon; noon-2.30pm, 7-9pm Tue-Fri. Closed Aug, one week in Feb. **Prix fixe** €31. **Lunch menu** €22-€31. **Credit** MC, V. **Wheelchair access. Non-smoking. Map** G8.

With an impressive following of locals and informed foreign foodies, François Pasteau's €31 menu produces some of the most sophisticated value in town. There has been no let-up in the quality of the cooking, as recent starters of tempura-style langoustines sitting on pineapple chutney and a dish of pig's ears and veal tails with a stunning mustard ice-cream showed. Mignon de porc in a crisp pastry shell and honey-basted filet de canard served on some creamy polenta were both classy creations, and we mopped up the sauce with crusty own-made bread. An excellent take on the oozing chocolate pudding recipe and some mango and pineapple slivers with white chocolate ice-cream finished off our meal. The wine list was disappointing, with four bottles unavailable, but a red Pic St-Loup was a sturdy oaked choice. This lapse shows the restaurant's main downside – its popularity. A booking for 1pm found us still standing on the pavement 15 minutes later. Once you're seated the meal moves along quickly, and tables are too close to avoid noise overkill. Cooking as fine as this needs more breathing space than this tightly packed wheatsheaf (épi du pain) provides.

La Ferrandaise

8 rue de Vaugirard, 6th (01.43.26.36.36). M° Odéon/RER Luxembourg. **Open** noon-2.30pm, 7-10.30pm Tue-Thur; noon-2.30pm, 7pm-midnight Fri; 7pm-midnight Sat. **Prix fixe** €30, €38. **Credit** AmEx, MC, V. **Map** H7.

This newly opened bistro with stone walls, giant chandelier and portraits of cows on the walls has quickly established a faithful clientele that seems to be dominated by local business people rather than academics from the nearby Sorbonne. In the modern bistro tradition, the young, northern French chef serves solid, classic food with surprising new twists. Before ordering we nibbled on a platter of excellent ham, sausage and terrine, accompanied by crisp-crusted, thickly sliced sourdough. Almost every dish from the blackboard menu has a variation on standards: we started with potato stuffed with escargots in a camembert sauce and a fricassée of mushrooms with two poached eggs, followed by a huge slice of milk-fed pork with salsify and truffle sauce and a wonderfully flavoured, slightly rosé slice of veal. Dessert was a cold soup of intense chocolate with rum-soaked bananas and a layered glass of minced mango and meringue.

Huîtrerie Régis

3 rue de Montfaucon, 6th (01.44.41.10.07). M° Mabillon. **Open** 11am-midnight Tue-Sun. Closed mid-July to end Sept. **Average** €35. **Prix fixe** €21.50-€30. **Credit** MC, V. **Non-smoking. Wheelchair access. Map** H7.

Parisian oyster fans are often obliged to use one of the city's big brasseries to get their fix of shellfish, but what if you just want to eat a reasonably priced platter of oysters? Enter Régis and his 14-seat oyster bar in the heart of St-Germain. The tiny white room feels pristine, and the tables are properly laid. Here, you can enjoy the freshest oysters from the Marenne for around €25 a dozen. We joyously plunged into the briny spéciales and a dozen prawns, which came with tip-top bread and butter. In just 18 months Régis seems to have attracted an enviable crowd of fans who have discovered that oysters make a sexy prelude or postlude to an evening at the cinema. Hungry souls can supplement their feast with a rather ordinary scallop terrine or more happily enjoy a slice of rustic own-made apple tart or the cheese of the day. Régis can wax lyrical about his oysters, and the welcome could not be warmer.

Josephine 'Chez Dumonet'

117 rue du Cherche-Midi, 6th (01.45.48.52.40). M° Duroc. **Open** 12.30-2.30pm, 7.30-10.30pm Mon-Fri. **Average** €55. **Credit** AmEx, MC, V. **Wheelchair access. Map** F8.

This bastion of classic bistro cooking, where the use of luxury ingredients brings a splash of glamour, is guaranteed to please the faithful, well-heeled local clientele. The room with its nicotine-coloured walls and massive cast-iron radiators looks comfortingly old-fashioned, while the formal staff reinforce the impression of serious Parisian eating. The good news is that several dishes are available as half portions, opening up the possibility of exploring some classy numbers without your credit card melting. We were tempted by a salad of lamb's lettuce, warm potatoes and truffle shavings in its €31 half-portion version. This was a sexy dish, with the musky perfume of black truffles gloriously present. After a slab of excellent homemade terrine, we tried the often-abused tournedos Rossini. Here, the fresh truffles and slice of foie gras on a tender fillet might have found favour with the great musician, whose incitement to an impatient chef to 'tournez le dos' if he did not want advice gave a name to this star dish. Delicious sautéed potatoes, rich in goose fat and a touch of garlic, accompanied both this and a top-quality andouillette. After finishing our bottle of Côtes du Rhône, we resisted the sumptuous-looking puddings and settled for some excellent petits fours and a digestif from the traditional bar.

Lapérouse

51 quai des Grands-Augustins, 6th (01.43.26.68.04). M° St-Michel. **Open** noon-3pm, 7.30-10.30pm Mon-Fri; 7.30-10.30pm Sat. Closed Aug. **Average** €100. **Lunch menu** €30, €45. **Credit** AmEx, DC, MC, V. **Wheelchair access. Non-smoking room. Map** J6.

Writers from Victor Hugo to Proust once enjoyed dining at this 17th-century Seine-side restaurant. The famous private dining rooms used to lock from the inside for between-course hanky panky.

La Ferrandaise. See p49.

However, the main dining room is also as romantic as you could wish for, and on Monday lunchtime we had the place almost to ourselves. The other surprise was the price of the lunch menu, which comes in at €30 for two courses or €45 for three courses (in the main dining room only), both served with a complimentary glass of wine. Alain Hacquard's menu cuts no corners and exquisite grand restaurant trimmings were all deliciously present, even if the cuisine is not quite on a level with the decor. A creamy cauliflower soup with slivers of scallops was slightly too white in taste as well as appearance, while the home-smoked fillet of beef was an original, if not entirely successful, idea. However, classic veal kidney bathed in Madeira sauce and served with a pot of creamy pasta was perfect. As we tucked into crispy millefeuilles and finished the last drops of house wine, we felt privileged to relax in such civilised surroundings.

Le Mâchon d'Henri

8 rue Guisarde, 6th (01.43.29.08.70). M° Mabillon. **Open** noon-2.30pm, 7-11pm daily. **Average** €24. **Credit** MC, V. **Map** H7.
This bistro in the heart of St-Germain immediately put us in a good mood – firstly, it was open for Sunday lunch, an increasingly rare phenomenon, and secondly, we were given a plate of outstanding saucisson sec while we looked at the menu. In an area where tourist tat wins out over gastronomic excellence, this tiny bistro provides a reasonably priced selection of traditional rustic dishes. We began with a ramekin of escargots, doused in garlic butter and served with potatoes, and a huge plate of marrow bones, accompanied by wholemeal

toast and coarse salt. Main courses were equally authentic, with a generous, well-seasoned bowl of Caen-style tripe, and a superbly cooked magret de canard, served whole. The gratin dauphinois was wholesome rather than inspiring, but by then we were already on good terms with the charming waiter and the couple opposite, something which is inevitable in such intimate surroundings. Rather than attack a homely pudding, we plumped for a serious vieille prune digestif.

La Maison de la Lozère

4 rue Hautefeuille, 6th (01.43.54.26.64/www.lozere-a-paris.com). M° St-Michel. **Open** noon-2pm, 7.30-9.45pm Tue-Sat. **Average** €26. **Prix fixe** €21.80, €25.50. **Lunch menu** €14.50, €16. **Credit** MC, V. **Wheelchair access**. **Map** J7.
The sparsely populated Lozère, a region of craggy stone houses on the southern slopes of the Massif Central, hides culinary secrets that its little Paris embassy (there's a regional cultural centre just next door) is bursting to reveal. Cheese aficionados, in particular, need look no further. Our roquefort salad starter was a cavernous bowl of crisp leaves weighed down with moist, crumbly slices of unadulterated blue heaven; a ripe, tangy zap to wake up our taste buds and a bold advertisement of things to come. After succulent mains of garlic-roasted lamb (be sure to eat the melting cloves that clutter the plate) and a lean pork fillet topped with black pudding and caramelised apples, we settled for an unmatchable dessert of more cheese. The day's selection of gently aged goat and ewe (smoothly fresh to nutty, hard crottins), cantal and blue (six in all) was come-hitherishly laid out on

Le Parc aux Cerfs

50 rue Vavin, 6th (01.43.54.87.83). M° Notre-Dame-des-Champs or Vavin. **Open** noon-2pm, 7.45-10.30pm daily. Closed Aug. **Prix fixe** €30-€35 (dinner only). **Lunch menu** €23.50-€29. **Credit** MC, V. **Wheelchair access**. **Non-smoking room. Map** G8.

Aside from a lamentable policy of linguistic segregation – lumping all the anglophones into the bar area up front – this stylish Montparnasse bistro is a delight for its worldly crowd and excellent modern bistro cooking. In a neighbourhood that's known around the world for hackneyed myths of la vie de bohème past, this place surprises by actually serving up a lot of atmosphere with just enough of that odd but appealing edge that comes from a lot of creative types gathered in one place. We were a happy sixsome who ate our way through the menu with tremendous pleasure on a surprisingly busy weekday night. Starters of foie gras, and smoked salmon and chèvre terrine, tomme cheese and black cherry relish were excellent, and a fricassée of free-range chicken with coriander and olives, a daily special, was the star of the main courses. Salers steak in port sauce came with a wonderful pile of creamy potato gratin, and sea bream in a light sauce of preserved lemon and white wine was accompanied by couscous. Desserts such as apple crumble with salted caramel ice-cream were splendid, and the wine list lavish. Note that there's a charming interior courtyard for summer dining too.

a heaving board that was left at our table long enough to encourage the full taste test; ditto the big loaf of country bread. Be sure to keep some of the robust Cévennes (the good-value house red) to ensure that the cheeses achieve maximum flavour. Like the Lozère, this is an understated, welcoming spot guaranteed to surprise the picky palate while satisfying even the most prodigious appetite. Be prepared to leave addicted.

La Méditérranée

2 pl de l'Odéon, 6th (01.43.26.02.30/www.la-mediterranee.com). M° Odéon. **Open** noon-11pm daily. **Average** €55. **Prix fixe** €29, €32. **Credit** AmEx, MC, V. **Wheelchair access**. **Non-smoking room. Map** H7.

The frescoes by Bérard and Vertès, with plates copying Cocteau's personal doodlings, give this long-established fish restaurant undeniable artistic street cred. It's a delightful place to enjoy a meal, and a number of Left Bank intellectuals still hang out in the shadow of the newly restored Théâtre de l'Odéon. Expectations run high, but a recent lunch had too many disappointing moments. The cooking had neither the charm of a bistro nor the finesse of haute cuisine. A standard fish soup was satisfying enough, but a pastilla de légumes (vegetables wrapped in crisp pastry) was indifferent, and we couldn't finish it. Thankfully, a white sun-infused Cassis wine got the seal of approval. A pink wedge of tuna with split peas was perfectly cooked, but a piece of cod was overcooked, only saved by a tasty accompanying aubergine purée. A pudding consisting of a base of apples topped with a crème brûlée managed to hit the high notes at the end.

Le Petit Saint-Benoît

4 rue St-Benoît, 6th (01.42.60.27.92). M° St-Germain-des-Prés. **Open** noon-2.30pm, 7-10.30pm Mon-Sat. Closed Aug. **Average** €20. **No credit cards. Map** H6.

Could it be, hidden behind a veil of blue smoke and red-checked tablecloth, Marguerite Duras? Er, no – just a photo of her hanging out here 40 years ago. The robust Côtes du Rhône wine served with lunch may have clouded our vision, but this resolute throwback to an earlier generation of bistros is definitely haunted by the old ghosts of St-Germain-des-Prés intellectuals. In a moneyed district taken over by fashion, it's authentically crotchety in all the ways you love to complain about – snappy maternal waitresses who scrawl your order on the paper tablecloth; walls yellowed by the puff of tobacco clouds; no reservations, no credit cards and no modern toilet. Most of the food has likewise made few concessions to modernity. This is welcome in a stewed rabbit in foie gras sauce, less so in desserts, especially the house speciality 'Benoît aux pommes' – a clafoutis heavy enough to serve as light weaponry. The basic starters are what you might imagine for €3, while the beef and petit salé – salt pork with lentils – are reliable standards. The no-fuss vibe is what draws the regular crowd, mostly middle-aged, past the rotating door and into the rabbit's den of a room; and that is what you'll remember long after the budget meal has faded from memory.

Huîtrerie Régis, serving simple shellfish in St-Germain. *See p49.*

Le Polidor

41 rue Monsieur-le-Prince, 6th (01.43.26.95.34).
M° Odéon. **Open** noon-2.30pm, 7pm-midnight daily.
Average €22. **Prix fixe** €20-€30. **Lunch menu**
€12 (Mon-Fri). **No credit cards. Wheelchair**
access. Map H7.

Le Polidor is one of the rare bona fide bistros to have
survived in St-Germain, a part of the city that seems
more inclined to pasta and salad these days than the
slow-simmered carnivorous dishes that are the heart
of any real Gallic menu. On a cold night, the foggy
windows were a promise of conviviality, the room
was packed, and the big zinc bar run by a big blonde
hostess, scrubbed sideboard, nicotine-stained walls
and worn tile floors created an appetising funk of
pre-war Paris. Then we locked horns with said
waitress as we attempted to squeeze into a wobbly
table in a far corner of the main dining room. 'What
do you think you're doing?!' she bellowed, almost a
perfect caricature of the nasty shop clerks and foul-
tempered concierges who were once deemed to be a
classic element of the Parisian landscape. Shrugging
off her temper, we studied the menu, ordered
and continued our conversation. Our first surprise
came with the wine, a red from the Béarn at €12 –
it was good, even surprisingly good at this price.
Then, a basket of bread that was excellent, as were
first courses of oeufs mayonnaise, crudités (fresh

vegetables with a creamy vinaigrette) and even
a terrine de brochet (pike-perch). Was it possible
that we were going to have a good meal at a budget
restaurant? Then a delicious guinea hen braised
with cabbage and bacon, and a very respectable
steak-frites arrived and a quiet wonderment
overtook us. OK, the fruit tarts were disappointing,
but a cheese plate was well chosen, the crème
caramel was good, and so was the coffee. Snarly
service aside, we'll definitely be back.

Restaurant Hélène Darroze

4 rue d'Assas, 6th (01.42.22.00.11). M° Sèvres
Babylone. **Open** 12.30-2pm, 7.30-10.15pm Tue-Sat.
Prix fixe €168. **Credit** AmEx, DC, MC, V.
Wheelchair access. Map G7.

With its hip decor in tones of orange and plum,
Hélène Darroze's restaurant is one very serious
establishment, with legions of knowledgeable
waiters, well-spaced tables, glistening glasses and a
trolley groaning with aged Armagnacs. Darroze
hails from the south-west so there are some regional
classics on her menu, but in her creative hand
everything old seems new again. Foie gras appears
in various guises, including a luscious terrine
layered with chunks of farm-raised chicken and
black truffles. Duck liver mousse comes with a
sugared crème brûlée coating, topped with apple
sorbet. And while a spring vegetable salad might

sound ho-hum, Darroze's version, with gem-coloured peas in their shells, tiny fennel, onions, carrots and artichokes draped with ruby red Bellota ham and shaved parmesan, was alive with flavour. Out came milk-fed lamb encased in an anchovy and manchego cheese crust, deftly cooked scallops, squid and clams resting on a bed of al dente pasta, and line-caught sole, deboned tableside and served with a shellfish sauce flecked with tiny scallops. Inventive pairings and classy flavours that confirm the Ducasse-trained Darroze's sure touch. Desserts were just as impressive: wild Andalucian strawberries with a nougat parfait, and delicious pineapple Victoria – tiny pieces of fruit in a froth of vanilla, piña colada, lemon and curry. And to finish, a trolley laden with macaroons, chocolate truffles and stacks of other sugary morsels.

Restaurant Wadja

10 rue de la Grande-Chaumière, 6th (01.46.33.02.02). Mº Vavin. **Open** noon-2pm, 7-11pm Mon-Sat. **Average** €30. **Prix fixe** €14. **Credit** MC, V. **Map** G9.

Despite its Polish name, Wadja is the epitome of the French neighbourhood bistro. On our last lunchtime visit the place was not so much humming as vibrating to the animated chatter of the regulars. Gentle banter from the patronne and a charming if overstretched waiter add to the fun of the old-fashioned room, decorated with some unusually attractive artwork. The cooking follows the modern trend for 'improved' classic bistro dishes. Starters included a cassolette d'escargots in a rich wine and shallot sauce or some home-smoked salmon over a fish tartare, both of which were first-rate. A gigot de sept heures, which is one of the place's signature dishes, lived up to its reputation, with spoon-tender meat and a rich, well-reduced sauce. The plat du jour of a crispy rissole of pied de porc was creamy, but a little cloying after a while, saved by a well-dressed accompanying salad. We resisted a moelleux au chocolat, but the tarte aux mirabelles looked tempting and homemade. With a bottle of fruity Chiroubles, the bill was reasonable and the cooking justified the chattering crowd's enthusiasm.

Salon Hélène Darroze

4 rue d'Assas, 6th (01.42.22.00.11). Mº Sèvres Babylone. **Open** 7.30-10.15pm Tue; 12.30-2.30pm, 7.30-10.15pm Wed-Sat. **Average** €75. **Credit** AmEx, DC, MC, V. **Map** G7.

The ground floor of Hélène Darroze's celebrated restaurant is given over to the Salon, which serves expensive tapas-sized portions of her sophisticated take on south-western French specialities. In sleek modern style, the windowless space centres attention on the kitchen. The charming head waitress explained the principle of choosing four or five dishes from whatever part of the menu we wanted. Despite this total freedom, we constructed a conventional four-course meal, but you could concentrate on starters or plunge into a pudding feast. The results abounded in memorable creations;

an escaoutoun from les Landes was a glorious saucer of polenta generously topped with black truffles, while a glass slipper filled with aïoli and lobster was topped with piping hot fish stock to produce a sublime result. Baby chops of suckling lamb from the Pays Basque were plump and juicy, rice with calamari ink was just as in a Spanish port, and the foie gras was predictably outstanding. Star of the puddings was the baba, which featured wild strawberries, an Armagnac-soaked sponge, topped off with a vanilla mousse. We drank a sublime golden Pacherenc du Vic Bilh (€45). Hélène Darroze can have us back in her salon whenever she likes.

Aux Saveurs de Claude

12 rue Stanislas, 6th (01.45.44.41.74/ www.auxsaveursdeclaude.fr). Mº Vavin. **Open** noon-2.30pm, 7.15-11.30pm Mon-Sat. Closed three weeks in Aug, ten days at Christmas, one week at Easter. **Average** €30. **Lunch menu** €15, €20. **Credit** AmEx, MC, V. **Non-smoking room**. **Map** G8.

Run by a charming and talented young couple who sincerely want you to have a good meal (and you will), this sweet mini bistro in Montparnasse is worth wending your way to the neighbourhood for. With parquet floors, soft lighting, vanilla-painted wainscotting and mirrors, the intimate room is a relaxing and pleasant place to dine. Recent starters on the blackboard have included a fine fricassée of ceps and other wild mushrooms, and ravioles de Royans (tiny ravioli stuffed with cheese) with yellow chanterelles. Typical main courses are the entrecôte with bordelaise sauce and puréed potato, veal kidneys sautéed with wild mushrooms and chestnuts, and salmon with an unusual 'gâteau' of rice mixed with fromage blanc. Desserts include first-rate tartes Tatin and chocolate tarts. Book ahead.

Le Timbre

3 rue Ste-Beuve, 6th (01.45.49.10.40). Mº Vavin. **Open** 7-10.30pm Mon; noon-2pm, 7-10.30pm Tue-Sat. Closed first two weeks in Aug. **Average** €30. **Prix fixe** €30 (Sat dinner only). **Lunch menu** €22-€26. **Credit** MC, V. **Wheelchair access**. **Map** G8.

It may only be the size of a postage stamp, but this Timbre will take you to the heart of France and even across the channel to Britain, courtesy of Mancunian chef/owner Chris Wright. We were cheered by the simple but tasty cuisine that owes more to pastoral France than northern mills. Tender bundles of chopped calamari were wrapped in ham and a flaky-based tart of caramelised onions topped with anchovies had a real kick. Mains included a perfectly cooked magret de canard on a bed of broccoli and olives, and a giant rissole of spicy black pudding served with Puy lentils. The wine list is short, but our Languedoc red was an oaky treat that needed cheese. Here, Wright plays the national card with a plate of great crumbly mature cheddar from Neal's Yard in London. We watched as the chef prepared the melt-in-your-mouth millefeuilles in his galley kitchen, and a bubble of patriotism rose at our table.

Ze Kitchen Galerie

4 rue des Grands-Augustins, 6th (01.44.32.00.32/ www.zekitchengalerie.fr). M° St-Michel. **Open** noon-2.30pm, 7.30-10.45pm Mon-Fri; 7.30-11.45pm Sat. **Average** €50. **Lunch menu** €23, €34. **Credit** AmEx, DC, MC, V. **Wheelchair access**. **Map** H6.

It's not easy to write in English about this trendy restaurant without making a joke about ze silly name. Once past the play on words, the clean lines and austere style of the restaurant make one fear a fusion stitch-up. The good news is that despite a menu rich in modern conceits, the food on a recent lunchtime visit was outstanding. The menu is built around meat or – more frequently – fish, simply grilled. Chef William Ledeuil is influenced by Thai spicing and Asian cooking techniques. A pale seafood soup was finely balanced and subtly spiced, and a complex starter of delicate prawn stacks proved that the chef has absorbed Eastern influences and come up with something refreshingly original. Best of the main courses were some tender grilled calamari, topped with a mound of tempura-style soft shell crabs, as fine as you would eat in Singapore. Beautifully presented puddings combined similarly diverse elements, but relied for their success on top-quality fruit and ice-cream to round off our contemporary lunch, which we accompanied with a well-chosen bottle of white Pacherenc du Vic Bilh.

7TH ARRONDISSEMENT

Le 144 Petrossian

18 bd de La Tour-Maubourg, 7th (01.44.11.32.32). M° La Tour Maubourg. **Open** noon-2.30pm, 7.30-10.30pm Tue-Sat. **Average** €80. **Prix fixe** €45. **Lunch menu** €35. **Credit** AmEx, DC, MC, V. **Map** E6.

Since early 2006 Rougui Dia, a young Senegalese-French chef, has directed the kitchen in which she was sous-chef for several years, with intriguing results. As before, you'll find Russian specialities such as blinis, salmon and caviar (at €39 an ounce) from the Petrossian boutique downstairs but Dia has thrown in preparations and spices from all over the world. We started with the 'tsar's cup' of three different slices of marinated salmon on a bed of artichoke hearts with cumin, and a divine risotto with codfish caviar and crisp parmesan. Similarly Med-meets-Russia were main courses of lamb 'cooked for eleven hours' on a raisin-filled blini, and roast sea bream with a terrific lemon-vodka sauce, accompanied by tasty kasha. A cool runny-centred chocolate cake with ice-cream and jellied quince finished things off in modern French style. A caution: while at lunch they offer glasses of wine for €5, at dinner bottles start at €40.

Altitude 95

1st level, Eiffel Tower, Champ de Mars, 7th (01.45.55.20.04/www.altitude-95eleor.com). M° Bir-Hakeim/RER Champ de Mars. **Open** noon-2.30pm, 7-9.30pm daily. **Average** €50.

Lunch menu €22.50, €28.50 (Mon-Sat). **Prix fixe** €52 (dinner and Sun lunch). **Credit** AmEx, DC, MC, V. **Wheelchair access**. **Map** C6.

There is a certain thrill in eating on the first floor of the Eiffel Tower, especially if one manages to exercise enough charm to gain a window seat. Mimicking the Jules Verne theme captured by the haute cuisine establishment one floor up, Altitude 95 is supposed to resemble an airship, although with its quantity of nuts and bolts, and its rather sombre aspect, the decor is closer to *20,000 Leagues Under the Sea*. On the whole, the cuisine is not as uplifting as the view. The à la carte option is pricey and unadventurous; the two-course lunch menu is better value, but offers very limited choice. The rabbit terrine starter interlaced with figs was enjoyable, despite the disconcerting jelly base covering the entire plate. The main course of pike-perch with Swiss chard was satisfying if a little bland, while the seared tuna was served on an unappetising purple bed of mashed kidney beans. Despite the rather average food, this is a novel lunch location, and a handy method for bypassing the tourists queuing to ascend the metallic monster the orthodox way.

L'Arpège

84 rue de Varenne, 7th (01.45.51.47.33/www. alain-passard.com). M° Varenne. **Open** noon-2pm, 8-10.30pm Mon-Fri. **Average** €250. **Credit** AmEx, DC, MC, V. **Wheelchair access**. **Map** F6.

Assuming you can swallow a brazenly high bill – we're talking €42 for a starter of potatoes here – and forsake the normal full-dress drill of an haute cuisine meal, odds are good that you'll have a spectacular time at chef Alain Passard's Left Bank table. Chrome-armed chairs in the already minimalist dining room look like something you would have found in the private lunch room of the East German Communist party, and the only decorative element in the room aside from Lalique glass inserts in the panelling are bound bunches of trimmed twigs on each table. But then something edible comes to the table – superb sourdough bread with bright yellow Breton butter so good you want to eat it by the spoonful. Next, the signature amuse-bouche of an eggshell filled with a raw yolk, cream and smoky maple syrup, a winning combination, and then the brilliant first courses. Tiny potatoes are smoked in oat straw and served with a horseradish mousseline: the sweet taste of the potatoes is amplified and framed by the sharp horseradish and the smoke enobles the dish, giving it perfect balance. In contrast, delicate vegetable-stuffed ravioli in lobster bouillon were quietly sexy, but nowhere near as satisfying, especially at €58. A main course of free-range chicken slowly sautéed with pan juices was the apotheosis of comfort food, while plump scallops from Normandy wore bay leaf collars and sat on tiny beds of baby leeks aside a smoky tomato relish and a slightly bitter yellow Thai curry. Desserts are similarly elegant and edgy, including the famous tomato roasted with 12 flavours, a

Christmas pudding spectrum of tastes that includes whole almonds and raisins, and a brilliant avocado soufflé with pistachios and a stoned yellow plum inserted into its folds. Service is impeccable, and the atmosphere surprisingly low-key – the chef himself appeared several times in Converse All-Stars and many of the male diners were tieless. The one terrible drawback to a meal here, however, is the hideously expensive wine list.

L'Atelier de Joël Robuchon ★

5 rue de Montalembert, 7th (01.42.22.56.56).
M° Rue du Bac. **Open** 11.30am-3.30pm, 6.30pm-midnight daily. **Average** €70. **Prix fixe** €58-€122. **Credit** MC, V. **Non-smoking. Map** G6.
Several years after it opened, L'Atelier's bento box decor still looks fresh and innovative – bright displays of red peppers and green apples prevent the mix of black lacquer, dark wood and red stools from looking too sombre. 'Small plates' range from about €12 to €30 – and, given their minimalist size (when the menu says 'the langoustine' it means just one), it would take quite a few to fill anyone up. That said, the food is pretty fabulous. Our first round of dishes all had a Mediterranean slant: a plate of silky Spanish ham with tomato toasts; a little tower of roasted aubergine, courgette and tomato layered with buffalo mozzarella; and marinated anchovy fillets alternated with strips of roasted red pepper. Next, three takes on French classics: three frogs' legs fritters flavoured with parsley and served with garlic cream; a poached egg atop parsley purée and bathed in mushroom cream; and a single scallop in its shell topped with truffle shavings (€18). In a signature main dish of merlan Colbert, the stunningly fresh whiting was served with a herb butter alongside the chef's legendary potato purée. The carbonara, made with Alsatian bacon and crème fraîche, proved a worthy interpretation of this Italian classic. Chartreuse soufflé was dramatically pierced at the table with a spoon and topped with a dollop of sorbet. Reservations are taken only for the 11.30am and 6.30pm sittings.

Au Bon Accueil

14 rue Monttessuy, 7th (01.47.05.46.11). M° Alma Marceau or Ecole Militaire. **Open** noon-2.30pm, 7.30-10.30pm Mon-Fri. **Average** €65. **Prix fixe** €31 (dinner only). **Lunch menu** €27. **Credit** AmEx, MC, V. **Wheelchair access. Map** D6.
Ever since Jacques Lacipière opened this bistro in 1990 it has been one of the good deals of the 7th arrondissement, and local residents' loyalty is still well merited. The pleasantly redone dining room, with big windows, well-designed lighting and a stone satyr beaming down from a pilaster, provides the setting for excellent updating of French classics. We started with a chaud-froid combination of raw marinated sardines sandwiched between tiny, new spring leeks and a frazzle of deep-fried onion and chervil, and a tomato stuffed with petits gris snails, which was tasty, although the tomato sat oddly between cooked and raw. To follow, rosé veal

kidneys were attractively presented pyramid-style on a bed of fresh spinach, while a rich braised beef cheek in deep red wine sauce, cleverly offset by the tart flavours of stewed rhubarb, showed how Lacipière injects tradition with a few surprising touches. A well-ripened assortment of cheeses from Marie-Anne Cantin, and a chewy macaroon with raspberries and vanilla ice-cream completed the €27 lunch menu, as we finished off an excellent 1998 Graves chosen from the good-value suggestions at the front of the wine list. A relaxed atmosphere and courteous, conscientious staff make this an address to cherish only a few metres from the Eiffel Tower.

Le Café Constant ★

139 rue St-Dominique, 7th (01.47.53.73.34).
M° Ecole Militaire/RER Pont de l'Alma. **Open** noon-2.30pm, 7-10.30pm Tue-Sat. **Average** €27. **Credit** DC, MC, V. **Wheelchair access. Map** D6.
Curiously, it's at this winsomely simple and very brightly lit neighbourhood bistro that we've again discovered why we were once so impressed by chef Christian Constant, who worked at the exalted Crillon before setting up shop at Le Violon d'Ingres. Try as we might, we've always found Constant's Violon squeaky, while this café purrs with good times, good food and good value, as an appealingly diverse crowd of locals and Constant fans have quickly sussed out. The blackboard menu changes frequently, but it offers a good range of dishes that allow you to design a satisfying meal. If you're very hungry, start with the peppery pâté de campagne or maybe the salmon-wrapped poached eggs in gelatin, and follow with the steak, grilled steak tartare or calf's liver, all of which come with a generous choice of side dishes, such as pommes dauphinoises or green beans. Finish up with the peach melba, a real treat made with fresh peach. All the food is spectacularly fresh and flavourful, portions are more than fair and the wine list is a true gift, with a lovely Cahors going for a mere €14. No booking, but if you come early or late, there is rarely a wait.

Le Chamarré

13 bd de la Tour-Maubourg, 7th (01.47.05.50.18/ www.lechamarre.com). M° Invalides. **Open** noon-2.30pm, 7-10.30pm Tue-Fri; 7-10.30pm Sat. **Average** €60. **Prix fixe** €28. **Lunch menu** €40. **Credit** AmEx, DC, MC, V. **Wheelchair access. Non-smoking room. Map** E6.
In a relaxed dining room furnished with banquettes scattered with tiny chocolate and orange velvet cushions and softly lit by coloured glass lights, Jérome Bodereau and Antoine Heerah serve a menu where the mainstay of each dish is European (Scottish grouse, Breton lobster, cochon de lait), overlaid with nuances of Mauritian cuisine that concentrate on the fruity rather than the spicy. Tiny blobs of chutneys and dribbles of molasses are presented on the plate as on a painter's palette. The 'carte blanche' menu has the extra frisson of surprise – you don't know what you are going to get until it arrives in front of you. The procession of plates

began with two variations on octopus: one side smoked, the other macerated in ginger, accompanied by mango, guava and tomato chutneys. Vegetables 'from here and elsewhere', including chestnut, nestled in a subtle sorrel-flavoured foam set off by Mauritian pesto (spicier than the Italian version). King prawns dressed in crispy jackets of angel hair were ideal for dipping in the various condiments; the lobster, caught off Brittany, was roasted with a seasoning of crevettes and coloquinte, and served with a risotto of lentils, roe and bouillabaisse jus. The main dish, cochon de lait, with a wonderfully crispy skin that reminded us that there is a Chinese as well as Indian influence on Mauritian cooking, was accompanied by a little cake of belly and trotters, and simply served in its cooking juices. Then two desserts: an orange, which had been preserved with its bitter skin then fried with crispy sugar cane, accompanied by a divine pêche de vignes sorbet; and an unusual savarin. This meal was like a memorable piece of theatre, ably animated by the maître d' and waiters who deliver their descriptions of each dish with aplomb.

Chez l'Ami Jean

27 rue Malar, 7th (01.47.05.86.89). M° Invalides. **Open** noon-2pm, 7pm-midnight Tue-Sat. Closed Aug. **Average** €50. **Prix fixe** €30. **Credit** MC, V. **Wheelchair access** (reservation recommended). **Map** D6.

There are few places in Paris that will attract four raucous rugby players from Biarritz in town for a Six Nations match and a distinguished elderly American couple on a romantic city break. This is one of them. The laid-back atmosphere and unpretentious food make everyone feel instantly at home. The man responsible is chef Stéphane Jégo who, after more than ten years at La Régalade, took over the oldest Basque restaurant in Paris. While the food here isn't entirely Basque, it's strongly influenced by south-west France. Wild boar, game, duck and foie gras appear on the seasonal menu. If it's chilly outside opt for the hearty petit salé, a satisfying salted pork and lentil stew, and in summer sit at the bar with a plate of cured Bayonne ham. The three-course, €30 set menu is great value and jam-packed with quality ingredients. The wine selection is good and contains interesting Basque options such as Irouléguy, made with the distinctive tannat grape. Although there are two sittings, booking is essential as it's a popular place.

Chez les Anges

54 bd La Tour-Maubourg, 7th (01.47.05.89.86/ www.chezlesanges.com). M° La Tour Maubourg. **Open** noon-3pm, 7.30-11pm Mon-Sat. **Average** €50. **Prix fixe** €40. **Wheelchair access. Map** E6.

Jacques Lacipière of the bistro Au Bon Accueil is behind the revival of this restaurant, which was known for its superb Burgundian cooking in the 1960s and '70s. It has been through a few incarnations since, including a stint as the Paul Minchelli fish restaurant, but Lacipière has brought back the original name (now written in frosted glass across the transparent façade) and the focus on Burgundy wines. You can order à la carte, with main dishes priced at around €20 to €30, but we opted for the good-value 'menu surprise'. This takes a tapas-style approach, with each course arriving in sets of two or three tiny portions. Although the cooking wasn't on the level of, say, L'Atelier de Joël Robuchon, the chef was clearly making an effort and our waiter was full of good will, not even frowning when we chose to drink a glass of wine each rather than ordering a bottle off the impressive wine list. Among the highlights of our meal were a cauliflower bavarois – an original way of preparing this underdog vegetable – and little frogs' leg fritters. Veal sweetbreads with 'wild asparagus' (actually hops) were also prepared with skill, and the dessert trio of cherries jubilee, a tiny chocolate cake and mint sorbet proved perfectly complementary.

D'Chez Eux

2 av de Lowendal, 7th (01.47.05.52.55/ www.chezeux.com). M° Ecole Militaire. **Open** noon-2.30pm, 7.30-10.30pm Mon-Sat. Closed three weeks in Aug. **Average** €60. **Lunch menu** €34-€40. **Credit** AmEx, DC, MC, V. **Wheelchair access. Non-smoking room. Map** E7.

The warm welcome from the manager, who handed out complimentary kirs, a hunk of saucisson each and a large basket of bread and butter as soon as we sat down, was a sign of how well we'd be treated during the course of the meal. We opted for the €40 lunch menu and started with salads from a selection on a trolley, including pearl onions in a sweet tomato sauce, fresh anchovies and cold pot-au-feu in a mustard sauce, as well as a plate of charcuterie. This was followed by poule-au-pot, a boiling hen cooked with leeks and carrots, served with rice and an individual bowl of the cooking broth, and an enormous plate of boudin noir (black pudding) with sautéed apples. Finally, we dug into a selection of desserts placed before us in large, help-yourself bowls. Generous as the portions are, we couldn't help but feel that the food was too straightforward to merit the rather steep price.

Chez Germaine

30 rue Pierre-Leroux, 7th (01.42.73.28.34). M° Duroc or Vaneau. **Open** noon-2.15pm, 7-10pm Mon-Fri; noon-2.15pm Sat. Closed Aug. **Average** €25. **Prix fixe** €14. **Lunch menu** €12 (weekdays only). **No credit cards. Non-smoking. Map** F8.

The new owner of Chez Germaine knows better than to change a winning formula. You still have the distinct impression of being at your grandmother's house, and the furniture hasn't changed since 1952. Over the years, people have mainly come to enjoy simple food in this slightly kitsch environment and luckily it's still possible today. The menu may have been slightly updated to cater to 21st-century diners but it remains traditional. Start with cold herring and boiled potatoes, coddled eggs with cream and bacon, a green salad with ewe's milk cheese and figs,

Chez les Anges

French Cuisine

or leeks vinaigrette. For mains, try the sea bass with an aubergine gratin and the steak with bone marrow or – if you're not on a hot date – with epoisse, an incredibly stinky cheese from Burgundy that's melted on the meat. Everything here seems to be prepared with loving care and the owner was very attentive. For many regulars, though, Chez Germaine's selling point is the fact that it is entirely non-smoking – and has been since 1968.

Cinq Mars

51 rue de Verneuil, 7th (01.45.44.69.13). M° Alma Marceau. **Open** noon-2.30pm, 7.30-11pm Tue-Fri; 12.30-3pm Sat. Closed three weeks in Aug. **Average** €35. **Lunch menu** €17, €21. **Credit** MC, V. **Wheelchair access**. **Map** G6.

With its mix of bistro chic and minimalist concrete, it's easy to see why Cinq Mars has become a big hit with a hip local crowd in this not-so-hip area. Despite the stylish surroundings, the atmosphere is laid-back and the menu down-to-earth. From a list of French basics, we chose cucumber with goat's cheese and a slice of foie gras – both fine but unmemorable. Rich and satisfying veal kidneys in a wholegrain mustard sauce and a too-chewy duck breast each came with a generous portion of mashed potatoes, rather heavy food for a warm spring night. A Corbières 2003 stood up to our mains and we finished off with a good-quality chocolate mousse. As is now customary in cool Paris bistros, it came in a large communal bowl from which we helped ourselves, until the waitress started looking alarmed at the rapidly vanishing mousse. Service was discreet and friendly.

Le Clos des Gourmets

16 av Rapp, 7th (01.45.51.75.61/www.closdes gourmets.com). M° Alma Marceau/RER Pont de l'Alma. **Open** 12.15-2pm, 7.15-10.15pm Tue-Sat. **Prix fixe** €29, €33 (dinner only). **Lunch menu** €25, €29. **Credit** MC, V. **Wheelchair access**. **Map** D5.

As its name suggests, this small, elegant address three minutes from the Eiffel Tower takes its food very seriously. Pompous it isn't, however. Arnaud and Christel Pitrois offer a genuinely warm welcome, happy to explain the ins and outs of a menu that's always inventive and, at €29 for a three-course lunch, excellent value. Roast mackerel, fresh market salad tossed in walnut oil, a lentil 'cappuccino' and hare terrine all sounded appetising as starters, but we opted for a superb cream of sweet chestnut soup, served with tiny chicken gnocchi and croûtons. Main courses lived up to the same standard. Roast sea bass came on a bed of puréed potatoes and black truffles, set off by a delicate wild rocket sauce. Spring chicken came topped with pine nuts, mushrooms and crunchy roast potatoes, served in a rich jus. We deliberated long and hard over the mandarin soufflé, poached fennel and warm chocolate tart, before eventually opting for a sublime – and highly unusual – avocado millefeuille in a tangy orange sauce. A couple of glasses of Sancerre from a good list rounded things off nicely. Book in advance.

Les Fables de la Fontaine

131 rue St-Dominique, 7th (01.44.18.37.55). M° Ecole Militaire. **Open** noon-2.30pm, 7-10.30pm Tue-Sat. **Average** €40. **Credit** DC, MC, V. **Wheelchair access**. **Map** D6.

When a star chef owns several restaurants, it can sometimes mean that his talent isn't fully focused on the smaller establishments. This is not the case at Christian Constant's fish and seafood restaurant. In this tiny 20-seater, his team does an excellent job. As we sat down, we were offered bread with a delicious buttery sardine spread to go with our glasses of inexpensive and good Touraine and muscadet wines. The lobster ravioli and crisp red snapper on creamy aubergine that followed were heavenly and, as a result, a tough act to follow. We enjoyed the sea bass fillet served with a morel mushroom risotto, despite the slightly bizarre parmesan foam. Hake was perfectly cooked but the piquillos (sweet red Basque peppers) and asparagus mix that came with it left us uninspired. A perfect slice of gâteau Basque and a bowl of strawberries and cream topped it all off. The restaurant was quiet at lunch, but it's best to book in the evening. A great place for an intimate meal with friends.

Gaya Rive Gauche

44 rue du Bac, 7th (01.45.44.73.73). M° Rue du Bac. **Open** 12.15-2.30pm, 7.15-10.45pm Mon-Fri; 7.15-10.45pm Sat. **Average** €80. **Credit** AmEx, MC, V. **Wheelchair access**. **Non-smoking**. **Map** G6.

Pierre Gagnaire, a chef known for his individuality, recently took over this Left Bank seafood restaurant, redecorating with a fish-scale wall and cloth-less white tables. The line is blurred between starters and main courses with menu titles such as 'insolites' (unexpected) and 'essentiel'. What a relief, though, to see starters at less than €20 and main courses at less than €30, even if the great man himself is not in the kitchen. Served in a martini glass, flakes of cod with soba noodles, mango, grapefruit and wasabi was a good idea that didn't quite work as it was overwhelmed by the taste of sesame oil. Also typical of Gagnaire's style was a seafood jelly with neatly arranged coco de Paimpol white beans and Spanish ham. To continue, we chose strips of wild sea bass simply sautéed and deglazed with manzanilla sherry – exactly as advertised. As so often happens with Pierre Gagnaire, not everything works and yet it's exciting to experience his unique take on French cuisine. The new Gaya is refreshing in a city where most seafood restaurants have fallen into a minimalist rut.

Le Jules Verne

2nd level, Eiffel Tower, Champ de Mars, 7th (01.45.55.61.44). M° Bir-Hakeim/RER Champ de Mars. **Open** 12.15-1.45pm, 7.15-9.45pm daily. **Average** €170. **Prix fixe** €128 (dinner only). **Lunch menu** €57 (Mon-Fri). **Credit** AmEx, DC, MC, V. **Wheelchair access** (reservation recommended). **Non-smoking**. **Map** C6.

From the unbeatable view and attentive service right down to the compartmentalised china, a meal at the Jules Verne, 125 metres up on the second level of the Eiffel Tower, offers an experience not unlike a first-class airline flight. Like the first-class cabin, the decor is handsome enough, if a little stale; a modernist symphony in grey and black. As on most flights, lunchtime diners here covered the gamut from grey flannel to plaid flannel, and the food, though respectable and fancy, felt a bit soulless. Our starters, an aspic of crabmeat garnished with celery rémoulade (with a surfeit of white pepper) and slices of a dark, gamey venison and foie gras terrine with quenelles of apple-quince compote and onion jam, all afloat in a pool of gossamer apple-quince jelly, were technically impressive, though not stirring. Saddle of rabbit was a mixed bag, with a perfectly textured, luminescent reduction sauce accenting desperately overcooked meat, and stewed veal shank suffered from a common pitfall of that cut – it was tender to the point of being mushy. The meal took a sharp upswing with dessert, a deeply flavoured chocolate mousse accompanying an imaginative terrine of pain d'épices and chocolate ganache. Even though we didn't swoon over most of the food, the combined forces of elegant service, spectacular location and dazzling view made lunch at this institution into a singular and very satisfying (if expensive) experience. A word of warning, however: when we called in November to make a dinner reservation, the first opening was in late March.

Nabuchodonosor

6 av Bosquet, 7th (01.45.56.97.26/ www.nabuchodonosor.net). M° Alma Marceau. **Open** noon-2.30pm, 7.30-11pm Mon-Fri. Closed 1-15 Aug. **Average** €42.50. **Prix fixe** €31 (dinner only). **Lunch menu** €21. **Credit** MC, V. **Wheelchair access. Map** D6.

Given its plush leather chairs, soft lighting and wine-coloured walls, this place could easily be mistaken for the dining room of an exclusive gentlemen's club. During the week, at both lunch and dinner, it's packed with businessmen sealing deals with a good meal and a digestif, and the general atmosphere is subtly masculine. The food is not for the faint-hearted, either. We were tempted by the pot-au-feu de paleron, melt-in-the-mouth boiled beef and vegetables served with a slice of pan-fried foie gras, and the honey-and-ginger-glazed duck breast. The duck was slightly tough but the dish entirely redeemed by the accompanying potato gratin – absolutely sinfully rich but delicious. All the portions are very generous, even the cheese plate, which we were too full to finish. The friendly, attentive all-male staff offer good advice concerning the wine list. Perfect for wooing business clients or impressing your future in-laws.

Thoumieux

79 rue St-Dominique, 7th (01.47.05.49.75/ www.thoumieux.com). M° Invalides or La Tour-Maubourg. **Open** noon-3pm, 6.45-11pm Mon-Sat;

noon-11pm Sun. **Average** €40. **Lunch menu** €33, €20 (Mon-Sat). **Credit** AmEx, MC, V. **Wheelchair access. Non-smoking room. Map** E6.

Thoumieux sprawls along the rue St-Dominique, undisturbed since 1923. Run by the same family since it opened, this big, popular bistro groans with tradition, from its stern, black-jacketed waiters to its red velvet banquettes. The menu presents every bistro standard you can think of: sole meunière, tripes, foie de veau, côte de boeuf, pied de porc and coq au vin are all correctly made with high-quality products. Don't be surprised, however, if the crust on your onion soup is a bit blackened. Even so, you won't feel compelled to complain to your weary waiter when he comes to collect your plate, as this detail seems unimportant. Move on, instead, to well-cooked beef from the Limousin region, or take on the enormous cassoulet, loaded with confit duck and the famed white beans from Tarbes. We paired ours with an outstanding Cahors, one of the less expensive choices on an expensive list. Indeed, prices have crept up here over the last several years, but it is nonetheless a pleasure to sit back and watch this juggernaut roll on.

Le Violon d'Ingres

135 rue St-Dominique, 7th (01.45.55.15.05/ www.leviolondingres.com). M° Ecole Militaire/RER Pont de l'Alma. **Open** noon-2.30pm, 7-10.30pm Tue-Sat. Closed three weeks in Aug. **Average** €80. **Prix fixe** €100. **Lunch menu** €50. **Credit** AmEx, DC, MC, V. **Wheelchair access. Map** D6.

Chef Christian Constant greeted us at the door when we came for lunch. He stopped by our table to make sure everything was going well, and bid us a solicitous farewell when we staggered out after a generous and beautifully executed lunch. Even when Constant was not physically surveying the elegant dining room, his attention could be felt in every detail. Constant spent eight years running the vast kitchens at the Hôtel de Crillon, training a generation of very successful young chefs, before leaving to open a place of his own. Our lunch menu, featuring polenta perfumed with black truffle, plump scallops bathing in butter and a refined parfait of bitter coffee, mascarpone and chestnut cream, provided us with more than we had expected, in terms of both quantity and quality. The standard menu does not veer off on experimental paths, but it does what it does very, very well. Some have complained that the chef has lost his spirit for innovation. And while it is true that Constant is not reinventing the wheel, we come here for another, rarer experience. Seated at a table here, we can watch while one of Paris's great chefs indulges in a personal pleasure, just as the famous Ingres took time out from his painting to privately play his beloved violin.

Le Voltaire

27 quai Voltaire, 7th (01.42.61.17.49). M° Rue du Bac. **Open** 12.15-2.30pm, 7.30-10pm Tue-Sat. Closed Aug, one week at Christmas. **Average** €80. **Credit** MC, V. **Wheelchair access. Map** G6.

With its perfect riverside setting, the Voltaire might be just another tourist-led Parisian bistro, but past the velvet curtains, after maître d' Antoine has escorted you to one of the cosy tables, you realise that this is a genuinely chic spot whose regulars treat it like a private club – at lunch many of the ladies were greeted with a kiss on the hand. From a delicate nibble to a serious feed, Le Voltaire caters to everyone. Our guest kept us waiting, slightly too intimidated to enter after Jean-Paul Belmondo popped in for a spot of lunch. Full marks to the staff who took the presence of a screen legend in their stride, indulging his celebrity lap dog. A vast bowl of lamb's lettuce and beetroot salad was exemplary, while a golden feuilleté encased fresh and tangy goat's cheese. Lobster omelette was just the sort of luxury (€41) nursery food that Le Voltaire does so well: creamy and thick with firm morsels of shellfish. A tasty sauté de lapin was a real country treat and the plate of well-cooked fresh vegetables and crisp fries were exemplary. A bowl of intense chocolate mousse and a blackcurrant sorbet completed an expensive but exquisite lunch, accompanied by raspberry-scented, chilled Chinon (€29.50). Monsieur Belmondo seemed happy too.

8TH ARRONDISSEMENT

Alain Ducasse au Plaza Athénée

Hôtel Plaza Athénée, 25 av Montaigne, 8th (01.53.67.65.00/www.alain-ducasse.com). M° Alma Marceau. **Open** 7.45-10.15pm Mon-Wed; 12.45-2.15pm, 7.45-10.15pm Thur, Fri. Closed last two weeks in Dec, mid-July to mid-Aug. **Average** €250. **Prix fixe** €300. **Lunch menu** €200. **Credit** AmEx, DC, MC, V. **Wheelchair access**. **Non-smoking room**. **Map** D5.

The sheer glamour factor would be enough to recommend this restaurant, Alain Ducasse's most lofty Paris undertaking (though he is only rarely in the kitchen). Once a muted grey space, the dining room now glitters with thousands of crystals. Because of its layout, the many waiters are a conspicuous presence, but they are also personable with none of the stiffness sometimes encountered in this style of restaurant. We opted for the €200 menu, which allowed us each to try three half-portions from the 'Plaisirs de table' part of the carte – the dishes without truffles or caviar. The meal started beautifully with an amuse-bouche of a single langoustine in a lemon cream with a touch of Iranian caviar. A raw-cooked salad of autumn fruits and vegetables proved an odd mish-mash, however, surrounded by a red, Chinese-style sweet and sour sauce. We lapped up a crayfish velouté with a poultry-liver royale (flan), but found the turbot in a stock of shellfish and 'bouquet' prawn sauce strangely characterless, while Breton lobster came in a rather overwhelming sauce of apple, quince and spiced wine. Then a good half-hour went by before we were served a delicious breast of pigeon and royale-style hare in a sauce so strong that the small portion became difficult to finish. Cheese was

predictably delicious, as was the rum baba with a choice of the finest rums for dousing. A grapefruit and quince tart was interesting rather than hedonistic.

Les Ambassadeurs

Hôtel de Crillon, 10 pl de la Concorde, 8th (01.44.71.16.17/www.crillon.com). M° Concorde. **Open** 7.30-10pm Mon; 12.30-2pm, 7.30-10pm Tue-Sat; Sun brunch noon-3pm. Closed Aug. **Average** €185. **Prix fixe** €200 (dinner only). **Lunch menu** €70. **Credit** AmEx, DC, MC, V. **Wheelchair access**. **Map** F5.

The 18th-century butterscotch marble decor by Jacques-Ange Gabriel is unlikely to put anyone at ease (the tables are miles apart), but the service is so enthusiastic, warm and polished that even before you've ordered you'll feel very, very special (although still not entirely at ease). Since the arrival of chef Jean-François Piège, the experience of eating at Les Ambassadeurs has become sublime. He describes his cuisine as 'permissive traditional' and we had, indeed, been staggered at his permissiveness at dinner here some months before. Back then we had sampled one of the signature dishes, a clever deconstructed spaghetti carbonara that was what the reinterpretation of classics is all about. Now we wondered whether lunch would be as good. At €70 per person, it may sound absurd to say that the lunch menu is excellent value, but compared to almost anywhere serving haute cuisine it is. Amuses-bouches were in a class of their own: beetroot lemonade, an ambrosian foie gras and crayfish concoction, a ball of pea purée that exploded in the mouth, a ham and cheese cigarillo and a bonbon of truffle butter that we ate with excellent bread were… well, we're stuck for words. Starters were a reconstituted poached egg with crayfish and asparagus, and duck foie gras prepared two ways (warm in a duck bouillon and cold in a layered rectangle). In a main of Rossini-style blue-fin tuna, a tube of foie gras was magically embedded in the tuna's raw centre. Crunchy-soft veal sweetbreads came with fresh morel mushrooms and tiny roasted potatoes. At Les Ambassadeurs it's a succession of bright ideas that make the meal memorable: bite-sized ice-creams arrive straight after the mains followed by tiny citrus-flavoured madeleines and pineapple macaroons. This could have been our dessert, but it was just a prelude to the chocolate, banana and lime gâteau, and gariguette strawberries and basil enveloped in a feather-light meringue cage studded with gold leaf – looking like an elaborate stage set by Cecil Beaton. Coffee was perfect and the chocolates fab. Sommelier David Biraud presides over a staggering list of top-class and top-priced wines, and though we opted for just a gin and tonic, a glass of wine and a bottle of water between us, we left feeling drunk from having eaten so well. The bill for two was €200, but for dinner you won't get away with spending less than €400 – and that's not counting wine. All the same, this is currently one of the very best places anywhere.

Celebs and mere plebs are treated equally at **Le Voltaire**. *See p59.*

L'Angle du Faubourg

195 rue du Fbg-St-Honoré, 8th (01.40.74.20.20/ www.taillevent.com). Mº Charles de Gaulle Etoile, George V or Ternes. **Open** noon-2.30pm, 7-10.15pm Mon-Fri. Closed Aug, public holidays. **Average** €85. **Prix fixe** €70 (dinner only). **Lunch menu** €35. **Credit** AmEx, DC, MC, V. **Wheelchair access**. **Map** D3.

If a place can be this busy in a dead part of town on a strike day when there is sleet blowing, you know it's doing something right. Perhaps not the decor, but the food and wine, definitely. The wine list is extensive yet clear, with plenty of well-priced bottles, and a whole page of options by the glass. Once we'd decided to take that route, the sommelier became our accomplice for the evening, choosing a wine to compliment each dish we ordered. After a false start with a flat glass of Montlouis that we quickly sent back from whence it came, we particularly loved the elegant Meursault 2001 that we drank with our langoustines with Avruga (herring) caviar and a strange but wonderful Irouléguy from the Basque country, whose citrus notes went fabulously with our simpler starter of vegetables with orange. Our best main was a superbly full-flavoured beef jowl 'daube', which, our waiter announced impressively, had been stewed for five hours. A full-bodied Montcalmes from the Languedoc accompanied it perfectly. For pudding, the lemon 'cannelloni' was an utter delight.

Le Bistro de Marius

6 av George V, 8th (01.40.70.11.76). Mº Alma Marceau. **Open** noon-2.30pm, 7-11pm Mon-Thur, Sun; noon-2.30pm, 7-11.30pm Fri, Sat. **Average** €40. **Lunch menu** €28, €32. **Credit** AmEx, DC, MC, V. **Wheelchair access**. **Map** D5.

Next door to the posh restaurant Marius et Janette, this annex attracts those in search of the day's catch in a more relaxed atmosphere. At first glance, it has all the ingredients of a memorable Paris meal – a wood-panelled dining room, cheerful checked tablecloths, a lovely summer terrace and unfailingly polite waiters. Our initial surprise was to see the menu written in fashion-speak: pdt for potatoes and HO for olive oil. Much more of a rude shock were our starters – what was described as mini tartares of tuna and salmon came as one large tartare with a strangely gelatinous consistency and tomato taste, while an avocado and crab salad consisted of three measly slices of avocado atop crabmeat that we suspected could only have come from a tin. Sole meunière, at €35, had a strangely deep-fried quality rather than the buttery taste we had been craving, and 'salt and pepper prawns' came with an oily garlic and tomato sauce. Even the crème caramel was odd, with crunchy, sugary shards atop the liquid caramel. Only a full bottle of Viognier between the two of us helped us stomach a shockingly high bill of €140.

Le Bistrot du Sommelier

97 bd Haussmann, 8th (01.42.65.24.85/
www.bistrotdusommelier.com). M° St-Augustin.
Open noon-2.30pm, 7.30-10.30pm Mon-Fri. Closed
end July to end Aug. **Average** €65. **Prix fixe** €60-
€100 (dinner only). **Lunch menu** €39. **Credit**
AmEx, MC, V. **Wheelchair access. Map** F3.

How does personal service from one of the world's
best sommeliers grab you? This is precisely what
you'll get at title-holder Philippe Faure-Brac's mecca
for wine lovers, where the list naturally includes not
only France's most prestigious crus and vintages, but
a marvellous selection of insiders' wines from Corsica
(Philippe's wife hails from the Ile de Beauté) and the
Rhône (he was born there). Despite the eye-popping
bottle list and the interesting à la carte dishes, we
think the best idea is to go for one of the blind
discovery options. Our five-course, €75 'menu
tentation', presented as a 'voyage through classicism
and originality', lived up to its description. Dinky,
comté-stuffed ravioles de Royan with a parsley and
tomato dressing went down a treat with a glass of
Montravel. Next came an alliance of textures via the
slab of sea bass in a tart vinaigrette with a wonderful
wine from the quality-conscious Corsican Canarelli.
A Pomerol reflected the earthy taste of the wild
mushrooms that accompanied the chicken stuffed
with goat's cheese. However, the best match of the
evening came courtesy of the cheese course: a warm
ste-maure goat's cheese on fig bread with a sprinkling
of olive purée that was the perfect partner for the
truffly, spicy flavour of a Jurançon Clos Lapeyre. All
in all, a marvellous, good-value experience.

Le Boeuf sur le Toit

34 rue du Colisée, 8th (01.53.93.65.55/
www.boeufsurletoit.com). M° Franklin D Roosevelt
or St-Philippe-du-Roule. **Open** noon-3pm, 7pm-1am
daily. **Average** €30. **Prix fixe** €19.90, €29.90.
Credit AmEx, DC, MC, V. **Wheelchair access.**
Non-smoking room. Map E4.

Some of Paris's most extraordinary brasseries are
hidden away in unlikely corners of the city behind
unprepossessing exteriors. Tucked up a side street
in the officey 8th, a short stroll from the Champs-
Elysées, this is one of them. Even once inside, this
former cabaret doesn't reveal itself straight away.
As you walk towards the back, its splendour looms
like a stage set. This is the Paris of Josephine Baker
and Jean Cocteau, all palm trees and elegant art deco
geometry (it's everywhere from the mirrors to the
knife and fork on your table). The smart, suity diners
often start with the reliably good oysters. We settled
down to a platter of 12 briney Brittany belons
with rye bread, salted butter and tangy shallot-
laced mignonette sauce. A good bottle of white
Sancerre accompanied them nicely, even if it was a
bit too expensive at €37. Butter overwhelmed our
plancha-fried salmon with saffron butter and
crushed potato, but the deep brown langoustine
sauce on our crisp-skinned perch was a treat. The
tangerine gratin with sabayon froth added to a
general feeling of well-being.

Le Bristol ★

Hôtel Bristol, 112 rue du Fbg-St-Honoré,
8th (01.53.43.43.00/www.lebristolparis.com).
M° Miromesnil. **Open** noon-2.30pm, 7.30-10.30pm
daily. **Average** €170. **Prix fixe** €175. **Lunch**
menu €80. **Credit** AmEx, DC, MC, V. **Wheelchair**
access. Map E4.

The Bristol is one of the most romantic of Parisian
palace hotels. In a city that sometimes lacks green
credentials, the hotel's central garden is a jewel. The
summer dining room, which spills out on to a
terrace, feels gloriously airy and, as we waited for
our guest, we had plenty of time to appreciate the
atmosphere and the delicious amuses-bouches. Like
all luxury venues the world over, chic has been
replaced by platinum credit cards, and as our fellow
guests set up tripods to photograph their pumped-
up poulet en vessie (an old-fashioned Lyonnais dish),
the primitive and the sophisticated mingled
uncomfortably. Star chef Eric Fréchon is a name that
the sleek maître d'hôtel slipped frequently into his
description of the dishes, and of course we nodded
knowingly. The lunch menu for €80, while nobody's
idea of a bargain, is surprisingly reasonable for this
quality of cooking. Three little eggs sitting in a
serried rank were filled with a delicious cep and egg
mixture, and accompanied by a crispy mushroom
toast. The raw langoustine bathed and cooked in
piping hot seafood bouillon at the table was just the
sort of dish at which top chefs and professional
service excel. None of us could resist the ris de veau,
écrevisses and ceps, a dish of stunning simplicity,
perfectly timed, with firm mushrooms, melting
sweetbreads and plump crayfish. We plucked a
flambéed dish of mirabelles and ice-cream from the
menu, while wily clients tucked into the splendid
cheese board.

Chez Cecile:
La Ferme des Mathurins

17 rue Vignon, 8th (01.42.66.46.39). M° Madeleine.
Open noon-2.30pm, 7-10.30pm Mon-Fri; 7-10.30pm
Sat. **Average** €30. **Prix fixe** €35 (dinner only).
Lunch menu €32. **Credit** AmEx, DC, MC, V.
Map G4.

Decorated with photos of plump nude early 20th-
century women, this newly opened, long and narrow
bistro presents straightforward contemporary
cooking that chef Stéphane Pitre picked up during
previous stints at the Ritz in London and in
Martinique. The clientele, as befits a place around the
corner from Fauchon, is all suits and ties. Starters
include winners such as prawn fritters and sautéed
foie gras with just the right amount of diced beetroot.
Similarly well balanced was a huge kidney in
Corsican wine sauce with classy smashed potatoes,
and an upmarket 'burger' with truffle sauce and
tiny fish. Original desserts included bananas
prepared several ways and a Grand Marnier soufflé
accompanied by a lemongrass and Grand Marnier
infusion in a tiny shot glass. Another plus is the huge
choice of wines, with plenty by the glass and carafe.

Le V

*Hôtel Four Seasons George V, 31 av George V, 8th (01.49.52.70.00/www.fourseasons.com). M°
George V.* **Open** noon-2.30pm, 6.30-11pm daily.
Average €250. **Prix fixe** €120. **Lunch menu**
€75. **Credit** AmEx, DC, MC, V. **Wheelchair
access.** **Map** D4.

Everything you've heard about the wonders of Le
Cinq and chef Philippe Legendre is true, judging by
our autumnal meal here. Like the staidly beautiful
surroundings – grey walls, gilt flourishes and
soaring flower arrangements – the food is lush but
never overworked. Lobster, sevruga caviar, truffles,
foie gras, milky veal and turbot are handled with
exacting respect and imagination. The maître d'
confided that some diners return habitually for
Legendre's leeks stuffed with black Périgord truffles;
beneath the silky poached leeks and copious truffles,
hidden by the sieved plate, lurks the finale, a clear,
addictive broth. Velvety foie gras comes paired with
tiny columns of earthy truffle and fruity jam. Roasted
pigeon is teamed simply with steamed green cabbage
and rich pan juices, veal shares a plate with a squirt
of capers and parmesan and tiny braised winter
vegetables – all made heady in this chef's hands.
Dessert, while delightful, was less superlative –
roasted pineapple with mango, paw-paw and a ten-
flavour exotic sorbet – but the suggested dessert
wine, South Africa's Klein Constantia, was a
transcendent indulgence at €30 a shot. Service was
seamless. Worth a blow-out any day.

Le Cou de la Girafe

*7 rue Paul Baudry, 8th (01.56.88.29.55). M° St
Philippe-du-Roule.* **Open** noon-2.30pm, 7.30-11pm
Mon-Sat. **Average** €50. **Lunch menu** €24-€35.
Credit AmEx, MC, V. **Wheelchair access.**
Map E4.

At first there seems to be something a bit banal
about this beige and brown restaurant, which is far
enough from the Champs-Elysées to attract more
locals than tourists. Since changing hands in 2005,
it has a freshly revamped dining room with a
vaguely safari feel that comes from discreet leopard
print – we sank into big cushions on the banquette
at the back of a nearly empty dining room on a May
bank holiday. Frédéric Claudel took over the kitchen
in March 2006 and, though the menu doesn't make
a particularly original read, we were surprised at the
impeccable food. The assiette de saumon presented
salmon in all its guises – smoked, raw, cooked,
potted – keeping one of us busy while the other ate
her way through a starter of herrings with warm
potato salad and a spring rabbit stew presented in
an iron cocotte. Thin, crunchy slices of red onion and
plenty of fresh herbs made the herrings seem a
modern dish rather than a bistro classic, while the
little black casserole burst with chunks of juicy meat
and tiny spring vegetables that had preserved all
their colour and texture. A panna cotta didn't make
any waves, but this is an address to keep in mind
for its combination of style and substance.

Fermette Marbeuf 1900

*5 rue Marbeuf, 8th (01.53.23.08.00/www.fermette
marbeuf.com). M° Alma Marceau or Franklin
D Roosevelt.* **Open** noon-3pm, 7-11pm daily.
Average €50. **Prix fixe** €30. **Lunch menu**
€19.50, €24.50. **Credit** AmEx, DC, MC, V.
Wheelchair access. **Non-smoking room.**
Map D4.

Looking like an ersatz belle époque interior, this
is actually the genuine article. Every detail of this
old restaurant has been painstakingly restored
and a conservatory bought at auction has been
reassembled and positioned off the main dining
room. The whole experience is like being inside a
poster by Mucha or an operetta by Offenbach. Part
of Les Frères Blanc chain, La Fermette initially comes
across as a place that doesn't need to try, but to
our surprise everything was fine. We stuck to the
set menus and were surprised by the chicken liver
terrine, which was fresh and nicely spiced (although
the accompanying onion jam was only OK).
The mussel and saffron soup was, again, fresh and
light. Magret de canard à l'orange came with a purée
of caramelised turnip and was deftly executed
(although by the time it hit the table the sauce had
developed a skin). Tournedos of Scottish salmon with
bacon and cream was tasty, and for dessert the pain
perdu with ice-cream and sticky butterscotch sauce
was excellent. The wine list is comprehensive and
competitively priced and service was professional,
although increasingly strained as the place filled up
with a mostly business clientele. In the evening the
restaurant is touristy, although French theatre-goers
arrive after ten. Only one caveat, the music, including
mawkish palm court tunes.

Flora ★

36 av George V, 8th (01.40.70.10.49). M° George V.
Open noon-2.30pm, 7-11pm Mon-Fri; 7-11pm Sat.
Closed three weeks in Aug. **Average** €75. **Prix fixe**
€36. **Credit** AmEx, MC, V. **Wheelchair access.**
Map D4.

With her flaxen hair, Polish fairytale name and hip,
Mediterranean-tinged cuisine, star chef Flora Mikula
is a welcome female presence in the testosterone-
soaked Parisian galaxy. The decor of her softly
sexy restaurant belongs somewhere between a
department store bridal boudoir and a Palais Royal
antiques shoppette. The luxuriously local, mainly
French, clientele kindly dresses to match the
cushions. It would also be entirely restful if it weren't
for the disconcerting way the stressed and at times
brash staff attempt to look as though they are
neither. As we were deeply, plushly seated before a
generous glass (rare) of Cuvée Flora champagne
(nice touch), our waitress, teeth gritted, would come
speeding from the kitchen. Approaching our table,
her lips would widen to somewhere near a smile and
she would suddenly slow down, arriving smoothly
before us as if passing by the headmaster's office in
a school corridor. Disastrous impact between plates
and silky tablecloth thus avoided, we could
concentrate on the deconstructed tarte niçoise, the

frogs' legs brochettes with a Thai dip and 'tapas de la mer' of scallops, mussels, razor clams and oysters, all perfectly cooked in different ways. We finished with a chocolate platter. And very, very pleasant it all was, if a little finicky ('feminine' is how other critics tend to describe it). Prices are very sensible given the quartier.

Fouquet's

99 av des Champs-Elysées, 8th (01.47.23.70.60/ www.lucienbarriere.com). M° George V. **Open** noon-3pm, 7pm-midnight daily. **Average** €90. **Prix fixe** €70. **Credit** AmEx, DC, MC, V. **Wheelchair access. Non-smoking room. Map** D4.

Chef Jean-Yves Leuranguer, formerly of the Martinez in Cannes, has made dining at Fouquet's a real, if expensive, delight. We adored our five-course menu dégustation. A starter scallop salad with fresh mango and sautéed leeks – very light and modern – was followed by a rich and rustic risotto of wild mushrooms and warm foie gras. This was definitely the high point of our dinner, but the turbot with squid sauce, tomatoes, courgette flowers and aubergines was good too, with strong Mediterranean colours and flavours. With the Chablis going slightly to our heads, the desserts (yes, plural) went by in a flurry of sorbets, chocolate, praline and petits fours. The service was impeccable, even after we asked to be moved away from a table of noisy trade unionists. As for the decor of the place, although the textured, red wallpaper is rather more reminiscent of a British city pub than a Parisian café, the overall effect is pleasantly old-style, creating a kind of 1950s French charm.

Garnier

111 rue St-Lazare, 8th (01.43.87.50.40). M° St-Lazare. **Open** noon-3pm, 7-11.30pm daily. Closed last week in July, two weeks in Aug. **Average** €50. **Prix fixe** €29.50. **Credit** AmEx, DC, MC, V. **Wheelchair access. Non-smoking room. Map** G3.

It's hard to work out whose favourite restaurant this might be, but you get the sense that the clientele is made up of regulars – ancient out-of-towners mostly. One of the few brasseries in Paris not owned by the Flo or Frères Blanc group, this two-floor space is all curtained windows, brass railings, dark wood floors, glass and mirror partitions and Lalique-like light fittings. It's neither charmingly old-fashioned nor contemporary, and consequently misses being anything. The service is smooth and the menu offers all the usual oyster and shellfish options along with classic fish mains. One of us opted for the lunch menu at €29.50 (for three courses) and the other chose six spéciales de Normandie Utah Beach oysters and a main from the carte. From the menu, smoked salmon rectangles with sweet dill and cucumber salad was fine if unspectacular, and the sea bream with glazed carrots in an orange reduction with cumin seeds was well executed, although the portion was somewhat mean. The oysters were top-notch, while main course scallops were juicy and the pan-fried spinach a good if unsurprising accompaniment.

Everything here is served on lovely china, but it all comes at an inflated price. It's impossible to say why Garnier is so busy – no occasion we can think of would be enhanced here – but seafood and fish lovers will undoubtedly leave sated.

Lasserre

17 av Franklin D Roosevelt, 8th (01.43.59.53.43/ www.lasserre.com). M° Franklin D Roosevelt. **Open** 7-10.30pm Mon-Wed, Sat; 12.30-2pm, 7-10.30pm Thur, Fri. Closed Aug. **Average** €220. **Prix fixe** €185. **Lunch menu** €75. **Credit** AmEx, DC, MC, V. **Wheelchair access. Map** E4.

Distinguished founder René Lasserre died in 2006 aged 93, but his restaurant lives on. The dining room is reached by a padded lift controlled by uniformed staff, and the first impression takes you back to a 1950s dream of upmarket living. Quaintly old-fashioned chandeliers frame the famous opening roof, which even in relatively inclement weather will perform its magical open sky effect to please the child in all but the most hard-hearted diner. After amuses-bouches of delicate foie gras toasts and a tasty parcel of fish we were impressed by our first courses. Seared foie gras accompanied by preserved fruits managed to be firm and free of any excess fat, while a timbale of black truffle and foie gras macaroni was intensely flavoured. Main courses included one of the house specialities, pigeon André Malraux, which was exceptionally moist, plump and tender, accompanied by melting spears of salsify. Some pungent slivers of black truffle and a side dish of perfect pommes de terre soufflées crowned fork-tender fillet steak into which slivers of foie gras had been artfully introduced. It was hard to resist the pudding of the day, sensational crêpes suzette, prepared at the table with all the swish professionalism that can only be found at this sort of French establishment. We could have lived without the tinkling pianist's repertoire of muzak, but others seemed to be lapping it up.

Ledoyen ★

1 av Dutuit, 8th (01.53.05.10.01). M° Champs Elysées Clemenceau. **Open** 8-9.30pm Mon; noon-2pm, 7.30-10pm Tue-Fri. Closed Aug, 24-26 Dec. **Average** €180. **Prix fixe** €168. **Lunch menu** €73. **Credit** AmEx, DC, MC, V. **Wheelchair access. Map** F5.

Lunch at Ledoyen, with the autumn foliage glistening gold outside the opulent, window-wrapped dining room, is paradise incarnate. Christian Le Squer is a culinary deity with a provocative sense of humour: who else would pair a liquid peanut butter tart with a slice of foie gras, both doll-sized, for their opening flourish or serve tiny lemon mousse marshmallows and candy apples – minute tongue teasers of bright red candy filled with apple sorbet and surmounted by a sphere of green-topped Granny Smith – as pre-dessert mignardises? It's not the chance to witness a truffle ceremony (big wooden box, respectful sniffs, white gloves and a goodly grate of magic mushroom) performed for moneyed regulars, or the seductive elegance of the spacious Second Empire salon, that makes eating here a truly divine experience – it's the celestial quality of the cooking. Smoked eel perched on a lie-de-vin-glazed canapé of toast; peppery hare terrine with a side of gold-leafed meat jelly; delicate strips of red mullet floating in a vivifying sauce of its own very fishy liver; melting breasts of herb-encrusted poule faisane, wrapped around a just-cooked liver and paired with juice-quenched roasted roots and a single sprout farci. Desserts, likewise, had us in raptures (try the chocolate millefeuille: paper-thin slivers of crunchy chocolate layered with sweet mascarpone cream and an oomphy scoop of bitter coffee sorbet). As far as heavens go, lunch at Ledoyen has a reassuringly democratic spirit: the set menu is a mere (compared with the carte) €73, and excellent wine comes by the glass (€15 a shot). And, if you can splurge a bit more, invest €22 in the potent allure of the superbly heaving cheese trolley.

La Marée

1 rue Daru, 8th (01.43.80.20.00/www.lamaree.fr). M° Ternes. **Open** 12.30-2.30pm, 7.30-10.15pm Mon-Fri; 7.30-10.15pm Sat. **Average** €120. **Prix fixe** €120. **Lunch menu** €70. **Credit** AmEx, DC, MC, V. **Wheelchair access. Map** D3.

There is, it must be said, something staid, boring and sad about La Marée. The quiet, the extraordinary number of uniformed staff, the dreary decor are all a bit pre-sexual revolution. But the splendid amuses-gueules soon wiped the sneer off our faces. The tangy anchovy with dill, crabmeat with cucumber purée, spicy fish mousse and miniature prawn cocktail were all tremendous. Lobsters are a big feature in this restaurant. There is even an 'all lobster' menu for €84. But, already aware of a large bill looming, we shared a silver soupière of lobster bisque in order to get at least a taste of the big crustacean. After this delicious French classic, the mains were more modern. John Dory fillet with Provençal-style squid was packed with flavour. Even more memorable was the superb Puligny-Montrachet from the Côte d'Or in Burgundy. For pudding we shared a millefeuille that had the shape and even a bit of the scale of a tower-block. A fine supper in dull surroundings. Better, at least, than the other way round.

Pierre Gagnaire

6 rue Balzac, 8th (01.58.36.12.50/www.pierre-gagnaire.com). M° Charles de Gaulle Etoile or George V. **Open** noon-1.30pm, 7.30-9.30pm Mon, Tue, Thur, Fri; 7.30-9.30pm Wed; 7.30-10pm Sun. Closed first two weeks in Aug. **Average** €200. **Prix fixe** €235. **Lunch menu** €90. **Credit** AmEx, MC, V. **Wheelchair access. Map** D3.

Pierre Gagnaire's cool grey and polished wood dining room felt a little deserted on our lunch visit, with no more than four tables occupied. Could it be that his culinary acrobatics combined with stiff prices are starting to put off even the very rich (who, we have noticed, appreciate value for money as

much as anyone)? Most starters now cost more than €100, which seems to be the price of culinary experimentation (Gagnaire is something of a scientist, often working with 'molecular gastronomy' specialist Hervé This). One of us ordered the €90 lunch menu to compare it with the à la carte offerings, and it was far from the same experience. The menu's starter and main course – caramelised onion with salsify and diced carrot, then venison flavoured with juniper and served with parsnip cream – were both conventionally presented on single plates, while each à la carte dish involved four or five plates. Even the shared amuses-bouches filled the table: an egg 'raviole' (interesting technically but jarring to the palate), crisp-like waffled potatoes with chilli, ricotta with green apple, fish in a cauliflower 'jelly', and glazed monkfish. Langoustine, at €122, came in four variations – raw, skewered, grilled and in a creamy sauce – making a grand total of five langoustines. The most spectacular of our dishes was the seafood main course, which included an enormous, 25-year-old oyster grilled tableside in goose fat (in the end, it tasted much like a cooked oyster) and John Dory with a delicious spice mix, along with scallop and sea urchin concoctions. The best thing about the lunch menu is that it brings you four desserts (half 'le grand dessert'), which the waiter kindly replicated for the à la carte meal. These clementine, raspberry and vanilla, chocolate and passion fruit puddings offered the kind of indulgence you crave at this type of restaurant. Coffee is shockingly priced at €8.50, but if you care you shouldn't be here. Remarkably, though, if you don't finish your wine, staff will let you take it home – and what could be more chic than a Pierre Gagnaire doggy bag?

Pomze

109 bd Haussman, 8th (01.42.65.65.83/ www.pomze.com). M° Miromesnil. **Open** 8am-11pm Mon-Fri; 9.30-11pm Sat. **Average** €38. **Prix fixe** €32. **Credit** AmEx, MC, V. **Wheelchair access. Non-smoking room. Map** F3.

Ever since that little scandal back in the Garden of Eden, the humble apple has been crying out for a funky image makeover. 'C'est chose faite', as they say, with this fabulous three-level apple emporium encompassing a ground-floor boutique (selling cakes, preserves, ciders and brandies), a tea salon in the basement and a smart restaurant on the first floor. With the help of our lovely waiter, we kicked our meal off with a bang by picking a sumptuous champagne-like Royal Kiev Guillet from the extensive cider list. More apple-tinged delights soon followed as we were dazzled by a smoked salmon starter topped with a tiny manzana verde Bavarian pyramid filled with wasabi, as well as an equally winning main course of vanilla-infused steamed sea bass served with a side mix of ceps and apples. The only small pit of disappointment was the blackberry trifle with candied apple bits – which, compared to the rest, was dull and predictable.

L'Angle du Faubourg. *See p61.*

Restaurant Cap Vernet

82 av Marceau, 8th (01.47.20.20.40). Mº Charles de Gaulle Etoile. **Open** noon-2.30pm, 7-11pm Mon-Fri; 7-11pm Sat. **Tapas served** 10pm-3am. Closed 24, 25, 31 Dec, 1 May. **Average** €55. **Credit** AmEx, DC, MC, V. **Wheelchair access**. **Non-smoking room**. **Map** D4.

We popped in for a late evening meal to this former Guy Savoy outlet, which enjoys a fine reputation for shellfish and modern fish cookery. The interior has recently been redone in plum and exotic wood and there is a 50-seat terrace in warm weather. The short carte has an impressive range of speciality oysters, but from the bank of seafood we chose some langoustines, which were firm and especially fresh. Plump crab ravioli were impressively refined, bathing in a subtle shellfish jus, which had been frothed in the modern manner. A pavé of Scottish salmon was seared on the outside with a rare interior, as requested, and accompanied by a pungent ginger butter and some basmati rice, while steamed half-salted cod featured melting flakes of fish sitting astride some potatoes roughly crushed in olive oil, the whole dish scattered with a few slivers of olives. A Picpoul de Pinet was an unusual and reasonably priced white wine from the Languedoc to accompany the seafood. The pudding list looked tempting, including an original pain d'épices with a compote of dried fruits, the perfect ending to a light, highly professional meal.

Savy

23 rue Bayard, 8th (01.47.23.46.98). Mº Franklin D Roosevelt. **Open** noon-2.30pm, 7.30-11pm Mon-Fri. Closed Aug, bank holidays. **Average** €40. **Prix fixe** €28.50. **Lunch menu** €23.50. **Credit** MC, V. **Map** E4.

This Auvergnat brasserie, on a quiet street in one of the city's most exclusive areas, was founded in 1923 and the decor (mirrors, brass and stuffed animals) hasn't changed since. It has a pair of long, narrow dining rooms, the first of which is very bright and resembles an art deco railway dining car. We launched into a farçou aveyronnais, a blackened crêpe containing minced spinach and leeks, and slices of tomme de Cantal (a fresh cheese) with tomato. Both were OK, but the problem with regional cuisine is that one is never quite sure how the food is supposed to be (was the farçou actually burnt?). The slow-cooked shoulder of lamb was delicious (€45.50 for two – including a mountain of frites), but frankly there was enough meat for four, so for the first time ever in Paris we asked for a doggy bag. Cheeses such as camembert and roquefort came in separate portions. Other desserts appeared to be made on the premises and a chocolate marquise and chocolate/caramel ice-creams rounded off a pleasant dinner on a warm spring night. Fortifying rather than refined (and bear in mind that the menu becomes even heartier between September and March).

Senderens

9 pl de la Madeleine, 8th (01.42.65.22.90).
M° Alma Marceau. **Open** 12.30-2.30pm, 7.30-
11.30pm daily. **Average** €85. **Credit** AmEx,
DC, MC, V. **Wheelchair access**. **Non-smoking
room**. **Map** F4.

Lucas Carton is dead, long live Alain Senderens.
This retirement-age chef has reinvented his art
nouveau institution with a *Star Trek* interior and a
mind-boggling fusion menu. Instead of his famed
canard à l'Apicius, Senderens now serves roast
duck foie gras with a warm salad of black figs
and liquorice powder, or monkfish steak with
Spanish mussels and green curry sauce. Each dish
comes with a suggested wine, whisky, sherry or
even punch (to accompany a rum-doused savarin
with slivers of ten-flavour pear), and while these are
perfectly matched, the mix of flavours and alcohols
can prove a little overwhelming by the end of a meal
– ours started with whisky to accompany semi-
smoked salmon with Thai spices and iced cucumber,
then continued with white wine and a sparkling rosé.
Senderens still seems to be coming to grips with his
new style – a sole tempura was not as crisp as it
might have been – but even a slightly flawed meal
here is a fascinating experience, as much for the
eclectic clientele as the adventurous food. If you can't
get a reservation in the main dining room, consider
the tapas bar upstairs.

Stella Maris

4 rue Arsène-Houssaye, 8th (01.42.89.16.22/
www.stellamarisparis.com). M° Charles de Gaulle
Etoile. **Open** noon-2.30pm, 7.30-10.30pm Mon-Fri;
7.30-10.30pm Sat. Closed two weeks in Aug, 25 Dec.
Average €80. **Prix fixe** €85, €130. **Lunch menu**
€43, €53. **Credit** AmEx, DC, MC, V. **Wheelchair
access**. **Map** D3.

Tateru Yoshino has divided his life between Paris and
Tokyo for many years. Trained by Joël Robuchon and
Michel Troisgros, he turns out food that is resolutely
French. A certain Japanese understatement and
demureness pervade, however, and every element of
each dish has its own strong identity yet sits
harmoniously with all the others. No chasing around
the plate trying to build the perfect mouthful. It's the
edible equivalent of a voyage concocted by an
experienced luxury tour operator, each part intense
yet balanced, surprising but not disorienting. The
service was at times faltering, but charmingly so and
the space is beautiful. The elderly Japanese man with
a gravelly voice at the next table provided a soothing
background hum as we floated our way through
foie gras with carrots, truffles and pistachio oil, pan-
fried sea bass with saffron risotto and a Grand
Marnier soufflé that instantly disappeared upon
hitting our tongues in a sugary breeze. The exquisite
tasting-menu-going-home-present cake aux marrons
glacés brought it all dreamily back next morning at
breakfast. Expensive, but wonderful.

La Table du Lancaster

Hôtel Lancaster, 7 rue de Berri, 8th (01.40.76.40.18/ www.hotel-lancaster.fr). M° George V. **Open** 12.30-1.45pm, 7.30-10pm Mon-Fri; 7.30-10pm Sat, Sun. Closed mid-July to mid-Aug. **Average** €135. **Prix fixe** €120 (dinner only). **Lunch menu** €60 (Mon-Fri). **Credit** AmEx, DC, MC, V. **Wheelchair access. Non-smoking. Map** D4.

The restaurant in this gorgeous hotel, where Marlene Dietrich once lived, is all the things you would expect from a place that today attracts *Hello!*-shy celebs. Indeed, the Lancaster has been described as the new Ritz, and the dining room, a beautifully appointed, unshowy space that on a summer day spills out onto a lovely terrace, is an oasis of luxury and calm. The first time we lunched here, Isabelle Adjani sat next to us – this time it was only Suzy Menkes, the *Herald Tribune*'s fashionista. Legendary chef Michel Troisgros (of La Maison Troisgros in Roanne) is in charge, although he is seldom in the kitchen. His influence is pervasive, though, and he has arranged starters and mains around several favourite themes – Tomatoes, Citrus, Spices, Greens and Dairy – that sound much more appealing in French. One of us opted for the set menu while the other chose from the carte. Amuses-bouches of Japanese radish brushed with an astringent citrus glaze arrived on delicate parmesan biscuits. The set menu included wonderful seared tuna in a cold, soupy Thai-tasting sauce with delicately flavoured short grain japonica rice. A dessert of summer fruit and ice-cream was light and beautifully presented. A la carte, we had steamed poached eggs with sea urchin coral, which was heavenly, followed by a surprisingly bland sole in carrot sauce that was not sufficiently cooked. Two glasses of Côtes de Provence rosé, a bottle of Evian and two espressos brought the bill to €149 – which is fair enough for this class of dining. The service, which was previously more formal, has warmed up. All told, the cooking here is creative, precise, and very, very elegant.

Taillevent ★

15 rue Lamennais, 8th (01.44.95.15.01/ www.taillevent.com). M° Charles de Gaulle Etoile or George V. **Open** 12.15-1.30pm, 7.15-9.30pm Mon-Fri. Closed Aug. **Average** €195. **Lunch menu** €70. **Credit** AmEx, DC, MC, V. **Wheelchair access. Non-smoking room. Map** D3.

Like La Tour d'Argent, Taillevent owes much of its ongoing success to the personality of its owner, Jean-Claude Vrinat. Change (including a recent refurbishment) always seems to occur seamlessly here, yet Vrinat is not afraid to hire young chefs with caractère. One of his most brilliant recent decisions was to put Alain Solivérès in charge of the kitchen, which on the day we visited was turning out truly flawless food. We were led through the spacious and rather subdued front room to the livelier, almost brasserie-like second room, where we were seated conspiratorially side by side. Prices here are not as shocking as in some restaurants at this level – with

a bottle of wine at €64, some mineral water and two coffees, our bill came to €300 à la carte. However, we found out only after this meal, upon consulting the website, that a €70 lunch menu is available – a shame that none of the staff mentioned it. One of our starters, the rémoulade de coquilles St-Jacques, had been introduced only the previous day, and the gallant, good-humoured waiters were eager to see our reaction. It was quite a technical feat, with slices of raw, marinated scallop wrapped in a tube shape around a finely diced apple filling, all of it encircled by a mayonnaise-like rémoulade sauce. An earthier – and lip-smackingly good – dish was the chef's trademark épeautre – known in English as spelt – cooked with bone marrow, black truffle, whipped cream and parmesan cheese, and topped with sautéed frogs' legs. Whole pan-fried red mullet was again typical of Solivérès's southern-influenced cooking: the fish had been completely deboned and stuffed with a delicate spider crab filling. We couldn't resist the chef's re-creation of a medieval dish by Guillaume Tirel: the caillette de porcelet aux épices et raisins de Málaga, a spicy round sausage alongside two beautifully juicy little pork chops, all perched atop a mound of caramelised cabbage and Puy lentils. To follow, ravioli au chocolat araguani was perhaps the most surprising and wonderful dessert we had tasted this year: pillowy pockets of soft chocolate pasta that explode in the mouth, releasing liquid bitter chocolate. The young sommelier's suggestion was equally spot-on.

9TH ARRONDISSEMENT

L'Auberge du Clou

30 av Trudaine, 9th (01.48.78.22.48/www.auberge duclou.wanadoo.fr). M° Anvers or Pigalle. **Open** noon-3pm, 7-11pm daily. **Average** €35. **Prix fixe** €38. **Credit** MC, V. **Wheelchair access. Non-smoking room. Map** H2.

With its real log fire upstairs, beamed ceiling and sash windows, the Auberge du Clou resembles a comfortable private house and makes a lovely setting for a winter meal. The inventive cuisine injects a whirl of cosmopolitan ideas on to classic foundations, and while the two- or three-course weekly menu is superb value, it's the à la carte that features the most interesting dishes, including accomplished creations such as crunchy, warm oyster tempura with beansprouts; and sea bream sandwiched with daikin, wasabi and rocket, making a pretty study in green and white with flaky fish punctuated by bursts of spice. There are also more classic dishes, such as a delicious combination of artichokes and warm foie gras, and a generous serving of monkfish with girolles and a gratin of ratte potatoes. We finished with an original take on crème brûlée made with fromage blanc and passion fruit. The wine list is pleasantly global. We had a gently perfumed Argentinian white – or on Monday evenings (when upstairs is closed) you can bring your own.

Casa Olympe

48 rue St-Georges, 9th (01.42.85.26.01). M° St-Georges. **Open** noon-2pm, 8-11pm Mon-Fri. Closed one week at Christmas, one week in May, first three weeks in Aug. **Prix fixe** €38. **Credit** AmEx, MC, V. **Map** H3.

Chef Dominique 'Olympe' Versini used to preside over an ever-so-fashionable 15th arrondissement restaurant before de-camping to this location just off the place St-Georges. An esoteric decor of mustard-coloured walls, glitzy Murano chandeliers and rather dark oil paintings of ostensibly happy seaside scenes lent a rather melancholy aura to the premises, a gloom that seemed to have overtaken Olympe's minions, all bearing identical stern expressions and humourless demeanour. Thankfully, redemption came in the form of the food, with an array of colourful and elegantly presented dishes from the short menu. We started with the fulsome, calorie-enhancing crispy black pudding served in dainty pastry and another enjoyable starter of small aubergines cooked Italian style, accompanied by tomatoes and fromage frais. The mains were even better, including a truly glorious dish of langoustine-stuffed ravioli swimming in a seafood-infused light cream sauce, bursting with flavour. The other main course was a similarly good rendition of red mullet, served with a flan of cebettes (spring onions) and offset by a sauce of piquillo peppers. Adjusting belts after this feast in preparation for the heavier desserts, reason prevailed and we opted for the in-season red fruit salads, one accompanied by olive sorbet and the other by almond blancmange. An attractive wine list rounded off a good meal – just a shame the service didn't match the quality of the cuisine.

Charlot, Roi des Coquillages

81 bd de Clichy, 9th (01.53.20.48.00/www.charlot_paris.com). M° Place de Clichy. **Open** noon-3pm, 7pm-midnight Mon-Fri, Sun; noon-3pm, 7pm-1am Sat. **Average** €60. **Prix fixe** €25. **Credit** AmEx, DC, MC, V. **Wheelchair access**. **Non-smoking room**. **Map** G2.

Aside from its endearing, campy glamour – apricot velvet banquettes and peculiar laminated lithographs of shellfish – the main reason that this long-running fish-house is so popular is its flawless catch-of-the-day menu. A curious but buzzy mix of tourists, night people, arty locals, executive couples and good-humoured folks in from the provinces patronise this place and, given such an eclectic clientele, staff are to be commended for their outstanding professional service. Depending on the season, the seafood platters are what the regulars opt for, and even in the middle of summer – off-season many shellfish – the prawns, sea urchins and lobster are impeccable. Otherwise, start with the excellent fish soup, followed by a classic such as grilled sea bass or superb aïoli (boiled salt cod with vegetables and lashings of garlic mayonnaise), and finish off with crêpe suzette or the delicious tarte Tatin with cinnamon.

Chartier

7 rue du Fbg-Montmartre, 9th (01.47.70.86.29/www.restaurant.chartier.com). M° Grands Boulevards. **Open** 11.30am-3pm, 6-10pm daily. **Average** €19. **Prix fixe** €18.20. **Credit** DC, MC, V. **Wheelchair access**. **Non-smoking room**. **Map** J4.

We had not been to Chartier for a while, and it was good to see the vast 19th-century soup kitchen with its mirrored interior, complete with napkin drawers for the regulars, retaining its quintessential Parisian buzz. We began with some plump escargots and a salty rollmop herring accompanied by a very cold potato salad. Main courses were a mixed bag: a do-it-yourself steak tartare was fine and served with crunchy frites, but the lapin sauce à la moutarde was disappointing, with a cloyingly sweet mustard sauce and some woefully overcooked pasta. A complaint to the waiter brought a visit from an accusatory manager. First he claimed that perhaps we didn't know what rabbit tasted like, followed by a comment that it was the moutarde à l'ancienne that gave the sauce its 'special' taste. In the end our unflappable old-school waiter changed the dish for an excellent andouillette and some more of the crispy fries. Some well-chosen cantal and brie accompanied the last of our bottle of Bordeaux and restored our spirits. The place used to be famous as an incredible bargain, which is no longer the case, but it remains competitively priced.

Chez Corto

47 rue Rodier, 9th (01.49.95.96.80). M° Anvers. **Open** noon-2.30pm, 7.30-11pm Mon-Fri; 7.30-11pm Sat. **Average** €36. **Lunch menu** €28. **Credit** MC, V **Map** J2.

This bistro run by young chef David Bruminaud is one of the best value restaurants to have opened in Paris recently, and a must if you're staying in the area. Interesting rather than distracting contemporary art lines the white stone walls and a maître d' in a black fedora welcomed us warmly. The clientele is exclusively local even here in the heart of Pigalle. Starters included a cold carrot soup, hot chèvre with walnuts and a splendid Mediterranean quiche made with black olives, tomatoes, broccoli and cheese and served with crisp salad greens. Just as good were main dishes of cod rolled in spices, lamb orientale and tender-as-can-be, crunchy-skinned duck breast served with citrus sauce and potatoes. We found no flaw with a strawberry pastry and well-made panna cotta with caramel. Even the bread and coffee were excellent. Fairly priced wines cost from €14 by the bottle.

Le Ch'ti Catalan

4 rue Navarin, 9th (01.44.63.04.33). M° St Georges. **Open** noon-3pm, 6-11pm Mon-Fri; 6-11pm Sat. **Average** €28. **Lunch menu** €13.50. **Credit** MC, V. **Wheelchair access**. **Map** H2.

It's rather unconventional, to say the least, to pair ingredients such as endives, bacon and eel, commonly found in the north of France, with the sunny flavours of French Catalan cooking. But that's what two friends of different origins have done in this ochre-painted bistro with an unprepossessing façade, just off the *Amélie*-like rue des Martyrs. The amazing thing is, it works. The waiter explained the blackboard menu to us in great detail – some of the dishes are completely northern, some are Catalan, and others are a combination of the two. Anchoïade – red peppers with tangy anchovies – was not only fresh and tasty, but the presentation could have rivalled that of a luxury restaurant. Tender pork cheeks served in a casserole with melting white beans were succulent though unfinishably generous. We finished with gueule noir (black jaw) – crushed spice biscuits with crème fraîche and egg – which refers to the slang for miners in northern France, who made a snack of speculoos biscuits crushed in milk. Le Ch'ti Catalan does a cheap lunch menu too, but it's well worth ordering à la carte to try some of the more intriguing dishes.

A la Cloche d'Or

3 rue Mansart, 9th (01.48.74.48.88/www.alacloche dor.com). Mº Blanche. **Open** noon-2.30pm, 7pm-1am Mon; noon-2.30pm, 7pm-4am Tue-Fri; 7pm-4am Sat. Closed Aug. **Average** €30. **Prix fixe** €27, €30. **Lunch menu** €17-€29. **Credit** AmEx, MC, V. **Map** G2.

The golden bell has not only been tolling good times in Pigalle ever since it was opened by actress Jeanne Moreau's parents in 1928, but it's an endearingly campy Gallic retort to the theatre-district restaurant traditions of New York and London. The mock medieval decor here, including a big ersatz hearth with spit, may have you waiting for Catherine Deneuve as the character she played in that 1970s classic *Peau d'Ane*, but it's far more likely you'll share your meal with an edgy mix of off-duty go-go girls and boys, bouncers, club owners, tourists, neighbourhood regulars and the occasional real-life actor or actress. The soundtrack that plays here is pure Cage aux Folles, while service is friendly, flirtatious and English-speaking. If the kitchen is unlikely to leave you with lasting memories, the general quality of the trad French grub it sends out is considerably better than what you find in the other late-night option – Paris brasseries – these days. The house terrine with onion jam was quite good, the steak tartare better than average and the accompanying frites bliss. Less successful was a very bony slice of lamb roast with ratatouille, but the cheese tray was tempting and offered a good excuse to order a bit more of the eminently drinkable (and affordable) Cahors. This winsomely eccentric quartier, which has blessedly survived the furious tides of fashion, is well worth discovering.

Georgette

29 rue St-Georges, 9th (01.42.80.39.13). Mº Notre-Dame-de-Lorette. **Open** noon-2.45pm, 7.30-11pm Tue-Fri. Closed first three weeks in Aug. **Average** €32.50. **Credit** AmEx, MC, V. **Wheelchair access**. **Map** H3.

A mix of 1950s vintage formica tables (with matching bar) and ancient wooden beams provides the external charm, but what has won this bistro a loyal following since it opened three years ago is the female chef's loving use of seasonal ingredients. Forget pallid supermarket tomatoes – here, in late summer, they were orange, yellow and green, layered in a multicoloured salad or whizzed in a flavour-

Le Ch'ti Catalan. *See p69.*

packed gazpacho. Another winning starter was the rocket salad with buffalo mozzarella, saved from banality by top-notch ingredients. Rib-sticking meat dishes satisfy the local business crowd, while lighter options might include sea bream (slightly bony) with Provençal vegetables, a charlotte of juicy lamb chunks and aubergine, and even an unsweetened prune and pear compote (though the creamy Fontainebleau fromage blanc with raspberry coulis takes some beating). We've found it's unwise to order fish on a Monday here (when the wholesale market is closed), but otherwise Georgette is one of those charmed bistros where it's hard to go wrong – even the bread is delicious.

A la Grange Batelière

16 rue de la Grange Batelière, 9th (01.47.70.85.15). Mº Richelieu Drouot. **Open** noon-3pm Mon-Fri; in the evening the 1st and 3rd Wed of the month. Closed two weeks in Aug. **Average** €55. **Lunch menu** €25-€30. **Credit** AmEx, MC, V. **Wheelchair access**. **Map** H3.

For decades an unreconstructed, old-fashioned Parisian brasserie, la Grange Batelière has been dragged into the 21st century due to a revamp by new owners, comic Mimie Mathy and her partner chef Benoist Gérard. Spruced up with theatrical-mauve banquettes and Provençal yellow, the new decor is attractive, and from the blackboard menu, the cuisine is similarly colourful and elegant. Celebrity ownership inevitably means celebrity prices, and €40 per head is steep for a bistro lunch. This has not deterred the crowds, however. On the lunchtime we visited, it was bursting at the seams and bustling with expense-account diners, gossip journalists and local well-heeled trendies. We started with a pleasant gazpacho garlanded with olive oil and – an original twist – topped by a floating island of celeriac rémoulade, as well as the unusual carpaccio of pineapple and grilled gambas. Mains were pleasant, though a little bland, including an ample chateaubriand steak served with a potato gratin and a rather ordinary calf's liver. Desserts of pâtisseries, ice-creams and sorbets were decidedly middle-of-the-road. However, service is friendly and atmosphere lively, so this place is worth a visit if you can find someone to fund the meal.

Jean

8 rue St-Lazare, 9th (01.48.78.62.73). Mº Notre-Dame-de-Lorette. **Open** 11am-3pm, 5-10.15pm Mon-Fri. Closed Aug. **Average** €60. **Prix fixe** €56-€75 (dinner only). **Lunch menu** €36. **Credit** AmEx, DC, MC, V. **Wheelchair access**. **Map** H3.

An odd place, this. The wood-panelled walls and banquettes make it feel like a family-run brasserie from the 1950s, while owner and host Jean-Frédéric Guidoni brings a serious dose of class (with just the right touch of humour) having worked at Taillevent for 20 years. In this context, the rather wacky food from chef Benoît Bordier is all the more surprising. After considering the expensive carte (mains cost

€28-€35), we settled on the just-as-adventurous sounding set menu for €37, which changes every week and offers two choices for each course. The île flottante, a quenelle of mousse made with the blue cheese fourme d'ambert in a tomato-watermelon soup, made a refreshing starter for a summer night. Less successful was pork knuckle with langoustine jelly, with its gelatinous texture and conflicting flavours. Histoire Simple, as its name implied, was a simple dish of veal liver with sautéed spring vegetables, while black cod topped with two strips of rhubarb and served with a spinach mousse wowed us with its perfect balance. Desserts were just as whimsical – cherries with white beer sorbet and a semolina-lemon biscuit, and little churros with vanilla ice-cream and chocolate sauce. Glasses of Alsatian Riesling made a refreshing accompaniment to this food, and we stayed long after the meal savouring a conversation with the chatty owner.

Pétrelle

34 rue Pétrelle, 9th (01.42.82 11.02). Mº Anvers. **Open** 8-10pm Tue-Sat. **Average** €57.50. **Prix fixe** €25. **Credit** MC, V. **Wheelchair access**. **Map** J2.

Jean-Luc André is as inspired a decorator as he is a cook, and the quirky charm of his dining room has made it popular with fashion designers and film stars. A faded series of turn-of-the-century tableaux is his latest flea-market find, while summer holidays were spent revamping the loos. Behind all this style is some serious substance – André seeks out the very best ingredients from local producers such as market gardener Joël Thiébault, who grows 1,400 varieties of vegetables. As André now runs the épicerie and stylish café Les Vivres next door, Pétrelle is open in the evenings only – but the €25 set menu, formerly only available at lunch, is now offered at dinner (and the restaurant no longer opens for lunch). This no-choice three-course meal is stunning value (on our last visit, marinated sardines with tomato relish, rosemary-scented rabbit with roasted vegetables, deep purple poached figs). It's tempting, however, to splash out on the more extravagant à la carte dishes such as the tournedos Rossini or one of many game concoctions in winter.

Velly

52 rue Lamartine, 9th (01.48.78.60.05). Mº Notre-Dame-de-Lorette. **Open** noon-3pm, 8-11pm Mon-Fri. Closed three weeks in Aug. **Average** €30. **Lunch menu** €23. **Credit** MC, V. **Wheelchair access**. **Non-smoking room**. **Map** H3.

The setting is modest – old tiled floors, an art deco bar, bare wood tables – but the atmosphere is the real thing, that of a timeless neighbourhood bistro. Although it has only been open for a few years, Velly has the well-oiled feeling of a restaurant that has found its groove: the two dining rooms fill with office workers at lunch, locals and a fair number of well-informed tourists in the evening. The blackboard menu changes according to what's available at the wholesale Rungis market, offering a limited but tempting selection of classic dishes with a modern pirouette. Our meal started with an avocado and crab 'mosaïque' that in a lesser bistro could have been an iffy choice, but here it was zingy and fresh, with proper chunks of toothsome crabmeat. Ravioles d'escargots put a light spin on snails, with paper-thin pasta and a delicate herb sauce that needed a bit of an extra kick (black pepper did the trick). Technically, the risotto with scallops and mousseron mushrooms was not a risotto at all – it was rice in a mushroom cream sauce, presented in a cute little white bowl – but the flavours worked perfectly together. Onglet de veau proved to be red, juicy and easier on the jaw than most entrecôtes. The real surprise, though, was the salsify fritters, an original take on this hard-to-prepare root vegetable. Things went a tiny bit downhill with dessert – an average crème brûlée, and a banane créole that didn't taste of the promised rum – but we lingered happily over the last drops of our wine from the Pays Roannais, a little-known part of Burgundy.

10TH ARRONDISSEMENT

Brasserie Flo

7 rue des Petites-Ecuries, 10th (01.47.70.13.59/ www.floparis.com). M° Château d'Eau or Strasbourg St-Denis. **Open** noon-3pm, 7pm-1am daily. **Average** €30. **Prix fixe** €19.90 (after 10.30pm), €22.90, €29.90. **Credit** AmEx, DC, MC, V. **Map** K3.
The first in what went on to become a brasserie empire for Jean-Paul Bucher (who has now sold his shares in the Flo Group), this art nouveau Alsatian brasserie, located on a surprisingly charming and tranquil passage just off the rather seedy rue du Fbg-St-Denis, dates from the late 19th century. The young Bucher took over in 1968 and, for all of the criticism the Flo Group receives, managed to preserve much of its original identity. Join the contented mix of tourists and Parisians who come as much for the handsome surroundings of intricate carved dark wood, ornate light fixtures and faded frescoes as for the platters of shellfish, sole meunière, hearty portions of choucroute, steak tartare and a taste of old-time Paris. Don't expect culinary magic – the food is basic, but definitely satisfying.

Chez Arthur

25 rue du Fbg-St-Martin, 10th (01.42.08.34.33). M° Château d'Eau or Strasbourg St-Denis. **Open** noon-2.30pm, 7-11.30pm Tue-Sat. Closed Aug. **Prix fixe** €22, €27. **Lunch menu** €15. **Credit** AmEx, MC, V. **Map** K4.
Smack in the middle of a shabby part of the 10th arrondissement that's heavily populated with theatres is Chez Arthur, a restaurant said to be a favourite of the actors and actresses performing nearby. At 8pm, we had come too early to star gaze, but were still looking forward to some well-prepared traditional French cuisine in what seemed to be a faded but charming bistro. The welcome and service were more than friendly, but the food was a bit of a let-down. The salmon in our tartare was fresh, but

a dull cream sauce failed to add excitement. Scallops with endive weren't much better. Things improved with our plate of gambas, whose creamy, rich sauce was good enough to make us overlook the rather dry accompanying rice. Magret de canard was so-so and the accompanying Sarlat-style potatoes were a mixed bag – some crisp, others soggy. Expect predictable desserts such as moelleux au chocolat, crème brûlée and apple crumble.

Chez Casimir

6 rue du Belzunce, 10th (01.48.78.28.80). M° Gare du Nord. **Open** noon-3pm, 7-11pm Mon-Fri. Closed three weeks in Aug. **Average** €30. **Credit** DC, MC, V. **Wheelchair access**. **Map** K2.
Thierry Breton's charming bistro is something of an oasis in this part of the 10th arrondissement. On this lovely street, it's hard to imagine that you're only two minutes away from the seedy neighbourhood that surrounds the Gare du Nord. The simple but cheery decor and warm welcome add to the provincial feel. The blackboard menu changes daily and offers modern bistro cooking based on fresh market produce. Our first courses included a well-made rabbit terrine and delicious cured salmon, both served in antique glass jars with thick slices of freshly toasted bread. Main courses were equally good, with a plate of four perfectly cooked scallops served over an outstanding celery root purée and an ample monkfish pot-au-feu, a nice combination of braised fish with carrots, onion and potatoes served in its own miniature cast-iron pot. Dessert was a tasty, warm peach crumble. A great meal, happily washed down with an inexpensive vin natural from Thierry Puzelat.

Chez Michel

10 rue de Belzunce, 10th (01.44.53.06.20). M° Gare du Nord. **Open** 7pm-midnight Mon; noon-2pm, 7pm-midnight Tue-Fri. Closed three weeks in Aug. **Average** €30. **Prix fixe** €30. **Credit** MC, V. **Wheelchair access**. **Map** K2.
Thierry Breton is from Brittany and proud of it. His menu is stacked with hearty regional offerings and he sports the Breton flag on his chef's whites. Chez Michel, with its old-style red velvet banquettes and woody interior, is just behind the imposing St-Vincent-de-Paul church and a few minutes' walk from the Gare du Nord, and while the area isn't particularly classy, the food is. Marinated salmon with purple potatoes served in a preserving jar, pickled herring-style, was melt-in-the-mouth tender. So too fresh abalone, while the rabbit braised with rosemary and Swiss chard might just be the best bunny in town. Blackboard specials, which carry a €5-€15 supplement, follow the seasons. Game lovers are spoilt in the cooler months with wood pigeon, wild boar and venison, and there are usually some juicy fat, fresh scallops on offer too. Breton's Paris-Brest, choux pastry filled with hazelnut butter cream, is simply too good to miss. Staff can be excruciatingly slow and adept at not catching your eye, but they're good-natured enough.

Velly. See p71.

L'Hermitage

5 bd de Denain, 10th (01.48.78.77.09). M° Gare du Nord. **Open** noon-3pm, 6-11pm Mon-Sat. **Average** €25. **Prix fixe** €12.50, €21.50. **Credit** MC, V. **Wheelchair access. Non-smoking room.** **Map** K2.

Whether travelling for business or pleasure, the first and last reflex of many is the solace of a good Gallic meal. Leaving aside the woeful quality of what's served aboard the trains these days, it's also much too easy to go wrong with restaurants in this busy part of town. Happily, however, this excellent restaurant is just a few steps from the front doors of the Gare du Nord, and boasts a stunningly good-value menu, a pretty dining room done up in cherrywood parquet and mahogany panelling and a team of talented cooks in the kitchen. This place is very popular with the throngs who live or work in the neighbourhood, so if you want to tuck into a feast here, you should book ahead. The menu changes regularly, but a sauté of ceps with garlic and parsley, wild mushroom terrine, and oysters on the half-shell were all first-rate starters. Similarly, real care has been taken in the preparation of delicious main courses such as sautéed scallops surrounding a mousseline of sweet potato, roast pheasant with apples and buttered cabbage, and veal medallions with tomato relish and tagliatelle dressed with basil oil and lemon juice. We admire the obvious commitment to quality at L'Hermitage, but two caveats to bear in mind are the fact that they are not particularly attentive to solitary diners, and that service can be very slow (which is useful to know if you're catching a train).

Julien

16 rue du Fbg-St-Denis, 10th (01.47.70.12.06/ www.julienparis.com). M° Strasbourg St-Denis. **Open** noon-3pm, 7pm-1am daily. **Average** €30. **Prix fixe** €19.90 (after 10.30pm), €22.90, €29.90. **Credit** AmEx, DC, MC, V. **Wheelchair access.** **Map** K4.

Plunked down among the kebab shops that fill this rather seedy faubourg is this spectacular art nouveau brasserie, which has been standing for more than 100 years. Red velvet curtains, sinuous wood, exquisite stained glass, belle époque lamps and brightly coloured peacocks make for a dramatic setting, and are a stark contrast to the grime of the streetlife just outside Julien's front doors. While most come for the elegant decor, the food is more than passable. You can't go wrong with oysters, foie gras or properly seasoned steak tartare. Less successful was the duck magret, accompanied by tasteless wild mushrooms that we suspected had been frozen. For dessert we dug into a satisfying plateful of profiteroles with Valrhona chocolate. As might be expected, the crowd on Easter Sunday was predominantly French and of a certain age, but come after 10pm and you'll find a younger, more varied coterie of diners, here to take advantage of the late-night dining at bargain prices.

Rôtisserie Ste-Marthe

4 rue Ste-Marthe, 10th (01.40.03.08.30). M° Belleville or Colonel Fabien. **Open** noon-2pm, 8-11pm Mon-Fri; 8-11pm Sat, Sun. Closed at lunchtime in Aug. **Average** €10. **No credit cards. Map** M3.

There is more to ethical eating than animal welfare, bio-produce and fair-trade economics. In a

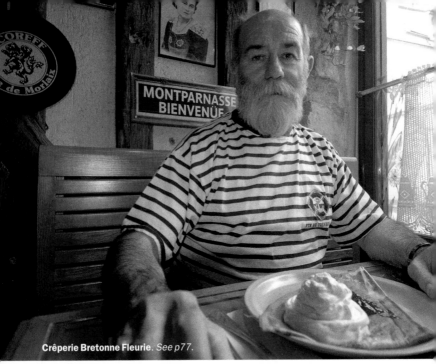

Crêperie Bretonne Fleurie. *See p77.*

downmarket but buzzing spot in north-east Paris – filled with wobbly chairs, vinyl tablecloths and lots of babas (hippies) and bobos (bourgeois bohemians) – the 'social good' value of your euro will shoot sky high with every bite. Run by the Association Rôtisserie Ste-Marthe (who use the space for a community restaurant at lunch), the tiny kitchen is manned – or rather womanned – nightly by a different neighbourhood organisation that cooks to raise money for humanitarian projects. Given Belleville's ethnic mix, you'll be treated to traditional menus from Brazil to Morocco. When we last visited, three diminutive Ecuadorian ladies were in charge of our dinner. Their labour of love – steaming plates of Quito's famous creamy potato, pork and avocado soup, spicy empanadas and salad, and thick slices of banana cake with coconut ice-cream – were in aid of a family of Ecuadorians seeking to open a canteen near Quito. There's nothing gourmet here (even wine is €1 a glass), but if you want every bite to go further than your stomach, the rôtisserie, oozing warmth and spirit, is irresistible.

Terminus Nord

23 rue de Dunkerque, 10th (01.42.85.05.15/ www.terminusnord.com). M° Gare du Nord. **Open** 11am-1am daily. **Average** €30. **Prix fixe** €19.90 (after 10.30pm), €22.90, €29.90. **Credit** AmEx, DC, MC, V. **Map** K2.

The Terminus Nord, one of the ubiquitous Flo Group brasseries, sits directly across from the Gare du Nord along a strip lined with a number of other establishments offering sustenance for hurried travellers. The Terminus, however, is clearly one of the brighter places on the block. Visitors will know they are in Paris the moment they step into this immense brasserie, with its brusque, white-apron clad waiters and cosmopolitan clientele. The impressive decor is art deco, with high ceilings, towering mirrors, sleek lines and banquettes. The food is typical Flo fare, with a heavy leaning towards fish and shellfish. During a recent visit we saw several tables happily feasting on gigantic ice-lined seafood platters. We started with freshly shucked oysters, a delicious rémoulade of cod, and a generous portion of fish soup, served in its own tureen with the traditional toppings of shredded cheese, toasted baguette and an intense, garlicky rouille. The choucroute was a bit ordinary and too much for one, with mounds of sauerkraut topped with a thick slice of pork and at least three different sausages. For something lighter try the assiette nordique, with a variety of smoked fish, or the more classic sole meunière. No surprises for dessert, with offerings such as tarte Tatin, crème brûlée and profiteroles.

11TH ARRONDISSEMENT

Astier

44 rue Jean-Pierre-Timbaud, 11th (01.43.57.16.35/ www.restaurant-astier.com). M° Parmentier. **Open** noon-2pm, 8-10.15pm Mon-Fri. Closed eight days at Easter, Aug, eight days at Christmas. **Prix fixe** €28. **Lunch menu** €23. **Credit** MC, V. **Map** M4.

Astier is a local institution, famous for its generous cheese platter and unbeatably priced bistro staples. In summer the 'terrasse' (the pavement) feels like an in-between world. Not really in the street, not really in the restaurant. The waiters engage passers-by, balance knives and chairs on their foreheads and generally keep everyone fed, watered and happy with their charming and quirky service. The wine list is extensive and well explained. A shame, then, that the food felt slightly soulless following a change of owner in summer 2006. Rather bland starters of vichyssoise and pressed sweetbreads were outstripped by spanking fresh John Dory with a moist and smoky aubergine confit and pesto. The cheese platter lived up to its reputation with at least ten choices of perfectly ripe varieties, from delicate ash-dusted goat's cheese to a pungent and fruity pont l'evêque. The only dessert we reckoned we could manage afterwards was a watermelon soup with fromage frais sorbet and mint – it sounded promising, but quickly fizzled out. The wonderful value for money prix fixe and effortless welcome made up for all the little quibbles. We'll be back.

Le Bistrot Paul Bert

18 rue Paul Bert, 11th (01.43.72.24.01). M° Faidherbe Chaligny. **Open** noon-2pm, 7.30-11pm Tue-Thur; noon-2pm, 7.30-11.30pm Fri, Sat. Closed Aug. **Average** €35. **Prix fixe** €30. **Lunch menu** €16. **Credit** MC, V. **Wheelchair access**. **Map** N7.

This heart-warming bistro gets it right almost down to the last crumb. What they do really well here is the très Parisien and vaguely snobbish concept of simple gastronomy: high-quality seasonal produce, very simply prepared. A starter salad of ris de veau illustrates the point, as the lightly browned veal sweetbreads were perched on a bed of green beans and baby carrots and lightly nipped with a sauce of sherry vinegar and deglazed cooking juices. In a similar vein, two fried eggs came in a stout terracotta dish with a generous scattering of fresh morels and swirl of cream seasoned with the mushroom cooking juices. This is the way that many Parisians prefer to eat these days, eschewing elaborate dishes for straightforward preparations that highlight the natural taste of the produce. Though this approach is appealing, there are times when it can be too plain. Cod steak with a fan of roasted carrots and white asparagus was perfectly cooked but needed a sprinkling of grey sea salt and a squirt of lemon juice to become interesting. Tuna steak was likewise impeccable but a bit dull, a trickle of good olive oil notwithstanding. Carnivores seem to fare better under this minimalist regime, as a roasted shoulder of suckling pig and a thick steak with a raft of golden, clearly homemade thick-cut frites looked inviting indeed on our neighbour's table. This is one of the rare bistros that still offers a help-yourself cheese tray, with nicely aged, seasonal specimens. Desserts are superb too, including what may be the best île flottante in Paris and a truly top-notch

Paris Brest (choux pastry filled with mocha-hazelnut cream). The extensive and regularly evolving wine list is a vinophile's dream, with plenty of fairly priced bottles.

Le Chateaubriand ★

129 av Parmentier, 11th (01.43.57.45.95). M° Goncourt. **Open** noon-2pm, 8-11pm Tue-Fri; 8-11pm Sat. Closed three weeks in Aug. **Prix fixe** €30-€36 (dinner only). **Lunch menu** €13. **Credit** MC, V. **Wheelchair access**. **Map** M4.

After a smash hit debut at La Famille in Montmartre, self-taught Basque chef Iñaki Aizpitarte has taken over this very stylish bistro. His menu displays the same nervy set of gastronomic balls that made La Famille a hit too – to try the cooking at its most adventurous, come at dinner, as a much simpler menu is served at lunch. Think dishes that have been profoundly deconstructed down to their very essence and then put back together again. This may sound like a load of food-ranter's nonsense, but you'll understand immediately if you try his starters such as chunky steak tartare garnished with a quail's egg, Vietnamese-style dipping sauce with whole peanuts, asparagus with a sublime tahini foam and little splinters of sesame-seed brittle; or tuna belly with smoked eel, a combination that's as odd as it is successful. Mains from the debut menu were similarly sassy, including crusty fatback with grated celeriac vinaigrette and a liquorice syrup. It's nearly impossible to explain the intricate but perfect balance of texture and taste in this dish, but suffice to say that after the initial shock wore off – liquorice is a strong taste – it was one of the most interesting compositions we've come across in a long time. The chef doesn't always need to be cerebral to make you wildly happy either – his Spanish goat's cheese with stewed apple jam is brilliant, for example, as is his chocolate custard with Espelette pepper. A fantastic list of easy drinking wines, a sassy bunch of waiters and one of the coolest crowds to be found anywhere in Paris at the moment make this place a slam-dunk, but book a few days ahead if you want to join the party.

Chez Ramulaud

269 rue du Fbg-St-Antoine, 11th (01.43.72.23.29). M° Faidherbe Chaligny or Nation. **Open** noon-2.30pm, 8pm-midnight Mon-Thur; noon-2.30pm, 8pm-12.30am Fri; 8pm-12.30am Sat. Closed at lunchtime for the first three weeks in Aug. **Average** €28. **Prix fixe** €29. **Lunch menu** €16. **Credit** MC, V. **Wheelchair access**. **Map** N7.

At the far end of the faubourg, in an area formerly immune to fashion, a few interesting modern bistros are cropping up. Leading the bunch is Ramulaud, a relaxed neighbourhood place with wooden tables and a subtle retro decor. Our lunchtime visit found the room humming with a local crowd, who appreciate the care of the cooking and the reasonable prices. The blackboard offerings initially looked rather tame, but simplicity and clear, uncluttered tastes are always a winner. We began our meal with

+ tv's, football, rugby & darts...

Lush Bar 16 rue des Dames,
Paris 17 métro: Place Clichy

+ pool table, big screens, lunch...

Rush Bar 32 rue St Sebastien
Paris 11 métro: St Sebastien

bubar

a special wine bar
loved by:
vogue, cosmopolitan, elle,
time out, paris dernière...

open every day from 7pm
3 rue des tournelles
paris 4°   métro bastille

an olive and mushroom clafoutis. The main courses included perfectly cooked red mullet on a bed of aromatic fennel and other vegetables, and a chicken breast with pommes allumettes. Fearing industrial fried chicken, we were thrilled to find a magical golden parcel of moist, tasty meat, which was truly memorable. Turning our backs on the tempting dessert list, we opted for the à la carte cheese trolley, which we were left in charge of long enough to indulge in a tasty tour of well-aged varieties. In the evenings the menu is slightly more sophisticated and on occasional Sundays there is a guinguette – a retro-style French dinner-dance.

Crêperie Bretonne Fleurie

67 rue de Charonne, 11th (01.43.55.62.29).
M° Ledru-Rollin or Charonne. **Open** noon-3pm,
7pm-midnight Mon-Fri; 7pm-midnight Sat. Closed
Aug. **Average** €15. **Credit** MC, V. **Wheelchair
access. Map** M7.
We went to lunch the day after returning from l'Île d'Ouessant, the island off the westernmost tip of Brittany, and arriving at this regional outpost it was a cinch to pretend we hadn't come back to Paris. Although the capital's regional restaurants are somewhat in decline, this place remains a charmingly feisty and very authentic little bit of Brittany near the Bastille, a neighbourhood more commonly associated with the Auvergne. We sipped excellent Rance valley cider while waiting for our galettes (buckwheat crêpes), and they were delicious. As a crêpe master had explained to us on Ouessant, the art of crêpe making is to create crispy edges without burning it. On this basis, the crêpe maker here deserves a medal of sorts, since our complète (filled with ham, gruyère and an egg) and galette with lardons (chunky bacon), egg, onion, gruyère and mushroom had a bit of brown lace at the edges but were perfectly done in the centre, where the deep yellow egg yolk peers out from behind four folds. A simple dessert crêpe (made with wheat flour) with butter and sugar was excellent, while Ar Gwella, a galette with a pool of hot chocolate sauce and a ball of vanilla ice-cream, was superb. A perfect place for a light bite, especially if you're on your own, as between the schoolroom map of Brittany and a puppet-theatre-like model of a sinking ship, there is plenty to look at while you eat.

Juan et Juanita

82 rue Jean-Pierre Timbaud, 11th (01.43.57.60.15).
M° Couronnes. **Open** noon-midnight Tue-Sat;
noon-5pm Sun. **Average** €25. **Lunch menu** €12.
Sunday brunch €19, €21. **Credit** AmEx, MC, V.
Wheelchair access. Map N4.
This eccentric little bistro is no longer the bargain it once was. Still, the shopfront dining room with embossed black wall covering, a ribbon of diamond-shaped mirrored wainscotting and bubblegum pink tables was packed out with a diverse but happy crowd on a late spring night, and owner Carine Francart waited on the throng with charm and efficiency. Starters were variable: fresh goat's cheese

whipped with chopped fresh vegetables and a side salad of rocket was delicious, while a millefeuille of leathery aubergine, a few shreds of roasted pepper, hunks of mozzarella and whipped goat's cheese was poorly composed and underseasoned. Both of our mains were delicious, however. The signature lamb shank didn't taste of the mint mentioned on the menu, but rich, tender meat was accompanied by well-made gravy and delicious olive oil mash. Braised duck with mash went down a treat as well. Though we might have preferred some cheese to accompany the rest of our superb Château Richard Bergerac, an organic wine made in the Dordogne by Englishman Richard Doughty, apple and berry crumble and panna cotta with an apricot coulis were nice finishers.

Le Marsangy

*73 av Parmentier, 11th (01.47.00.94.25). M°
Parmentier.* **Open** noon-2pm, 8-10.30pm Mon-
Fri; 8-10.30pm Sat. Closed two weeks at Christmas,
first two weeks in Aug. **Average** €28. **Prix fixe**
€22. **Credit** MC, V. **Wheelchair access.
Map** M5.
Although the menu had barely changed since our last visit, and prices have crept up, Le Marsangy continues to offer a great, easygoing bistro buy in one of the more animated neighbourhoods of eastern Paris. This is an old slipper of a place, just the sort of friendly, easy-going bistro you want at the end of the day. The ox-blood walls and low lighting create a stylish but laid-back atmosphere, and the wine list offers some of the best deals in the city, including a flinty Chablis for €18 and the alluringly named Côtes du Rhône La Sagesse Gramenon for €25. If first courses of rabbit terrine and layered avocado and crayfish seemed sparingly served, mains delighted with their generosity. An order of scallops grilled in their shells garnished with finely chopped endive, bacon and a little cream brought six juicy alabaster crustaceans on the half-shell to the table, a remarkably good buy even with a price supplement. A veal chop was served in a pleasant sauce of deglazed pan juices, but tepid, overcooked penne stood in for the promised tagliatelle, a disappointing and sloppy substitution, even if the restaurant was quiet due to school holidays. Similarly, aside from a big wedge of vivid orange mimolette, the cheese tray had been in and out of the fridge too many times, so that most of the specimens were rather sorry looking. Salted-butter caramel ice-cream was superb, however, and the service from Mathilde couldn't have been friendlier, which is why we'll be back in the hope that the several tatty details of this meal were just the result of an off night.

Paris Main d'Or

133 rue du Fbg-St-Antoine, 11th (01.44.68.04.68).
M° Ledru-Rollin. **Open** noon-3pm, 8-11pm Mon-
Sat. Closed one week at Christmas, Mon in Aug.
Average €25. **Lunch menu** €12. **Credit** MC,
V. **Wheelchair access. Non-smoking room.
Map** M7.

The Paris Main d'Or, named after a diminutive adjacent street, not a gold-fingered gangster, is a jam-packed temple to everything that's good about Corsican cuisine: fabulous charcuterie, gamey roast meats, robust fish and lots of brocciu, a soft white cheese that features liberally in both starters and mains. We arrived just after 10pm, but still had to wait half an hour for a table; just enough time, in other words, to digest the full allure of the menu. After a copious plate of tasty saucisson and cured ham and a richly fishy suppa di pesci, we opted for intense and meaty mains: a daube de boeuf, melting in a sauce of sturdy Corsican red and served without pretension in a brimful stoneware pot, plus an incomparable version of the island's justly famous cabri – three generous slices of juicy yet crisply roasted kid paired with a hearty portion of roast potatoes. Vegetarians are likewise well served by the brocciu-stuffed courgettes. For dessert, try the local version of tiramisu. Despite the uninspired decor and recent expansion, the place exudes an overwhelming Mediterranean charm and, even at the end of a long night, an engaging, southern-accented hospitality. After a few glasses of local wine (yet another of Corsica's enviable exports) you'll feel right at home – if home ever tasted this good, that is.

Le Passage des Carmagnoles

18 passage de la Bonne-Graine, 11th (01.47.00. 73.30). M° Ledru-Rollin. **Open** noon-3pm, 7-11.30pm Mon-Sat. **Average** €20. **Credit** AmEx, MC, V. **Wheelchair access. Non-smoking room. Map** N7.

The song of the Carmagnoles was a revolutionary song of the sans-culottes (emblematic figures of the French Revolution), and this friendly beamed bistro with a crowd of regulars is in one of the last passages of the Bastille still dominated by furniture makers. The former emphasis on andouillette seems to have shifted slightly, with only a couple of dishes featuring the famous tripe sausage. The boss claimed to have the best Beaujolais nouveau in town, not a big boast but we enjoyed a glass with our first courses, which included a tasty croustade d'escargots, and a salade du verger – a wholesome mix of beans, tomatoes, cervelas sausage and gizzards. Main courses included a tender autumn civet of ostrich bathing in pinot noir, and we couldn't resist the fricassée of andouillette with white wine, mushrooms and bacon; both dishes were accompanied by herby potatoes. The andouillette was of excellent quality and the wine of the month, an oaky Gaillac, was outstanding. Our appetites flagged before the traditional puddings or tempting cheese board, so we opted instead for a digestif, and a chat with the boss, who proudly promoted his philosophical dinners. Sartre's quotation 'hell is other people' was to be up for discussion; the accompanying good food and wine could sway the argument.

Le Repaire de Cartouche

99 rue Amelot/8 bd des Filles-du-Calvaire, 11th (01.47.00.25.86). M° St-Sébastien Froissart. **Open** noon-2pm, 7.30-11pm Tue-Thur; noon-2pm, 7.30-11.30pm Fri, Sat. Closed last week in July and first three weeks in Aug. **Average** €40. **Lunch menu** €13-€25. **Credit** MC, V. **Wheelchair access. Map** M5.

'Cartouche's Hideaway' honours Paris's answer to Dick Turpin, Robin Hood and Fagin rolled into one. On an icy January night, the dark panelling, impeccable white napery and leaded windows provided a civilised retreat from the bleak boulevards north of the Bastille, and the food was exceptional. After flavoursome goose rillettes and rustic bread, we enjoyed a perfect timbale of firm, fresh whelks with tiny ratte potatoes in a creamy herb dressing, and a generous portion of foie gras, pan-fried and served in a rich, meaty glaze. To follow, the pink-roasted Pyrenean suckling lamb with plump haricots blancs was exemplary. A slab of seasonal venison, with its accompanying pile of finely diced, thoughtfully herbed wild mushrooms, melted in the mouth. Desserts included a sorely tempting cranberry and chocolate-chip clafoutis (cooked to order, in advance) but we plumped instead for a millefeuille of feather-light chestnut mousse between slivers of dark bitter chocolate, and a chocolate mousse pavé given plentiful zing by the addition of fresh ginger extract. The wine list is exhaustive and well presented, but look no further than the special selections accompanying each week's new menu: a golden-delicious white Burgundy from Vézelay (served by the glass) went down well with the whelks and foie gras, followed by a smooth, good-value Vin de Pays de la Principauté d'Orange. Rodolphe Paquin is a chef of stature (in every sense, as seen on his frequent sorties into the dining room), and a tireless communicator of his enthusiasm for fine ingredients and inventive takes on traditional French fare.

Le Temps au Temps

13 rue Paul Bert, 11th (01.43.79.63.40). M° Faidherbe Chaligny. **Open** noon-2pm, 8-10.30pm Tue-Sat. Closed Aug. **Average** €32. **Prix fixe** €27. **Lunch menu** €11-€16. **Credit** MC, V. **Non-smoking. Map** N7.

Sylvain Endra looks barely old enough to shave, let alone single-handedly wield a knife in the kitchen of a successful neighbourhood bistro. Yet, ever since he and his wife took over Le Temps au Temps a couple of years ago, they have put a 'complet' sign outside every night. The secret is a combination of boundless creativity and genuine enthusiasm. A big clock, huge bouquet of flowers and whimsical butterfly chandelier over the bar dress up the buzzy little dining room. The chef's dramatic style shone through immediately in a starter of mackerel fillets perched atop an os à moelle. The marrow itself turned out to be too fatty to eat, but the mackerel was beautifully spiced with turmeric, ginger and coriander. Meanwhile, we lapped up a cream of asparagus soup topped with chunks of confit pork cheek and tiny courgette dice. A main course of pork belly a la plancha, served with a daring frothy seafood sauce, was again not quite perfect – the pork was a little too chewy – but such flaws are easy to forgive considering the chef's admirable willingness to take risks and the price of the set dinner menu, a mere €27. Pollack with creamed artichokes and exceptionally moist chestnuts was spot on. We shared a chocolate terrine for dessert, which had a wonderful, almost chewy texture and came with honey sorbet that was obviously own-made. A bottle of Côtes de Nuits Village for €27 went down a treat with this sophisticated bistro fare, served in a blessedly non-smoking environment.

Au Vieux Chêne ★

7 rue du Dahomey, 11th (01.43.71.67.69). Mº Faidherbe Chaligny. **Open** noon-2pm, 8-10.30pm Mon-Fri; 8-10.30pm Sat. Closed one week in July, two weeks in Aug. **Average** €35. **Prix fixe** €29 (dinner only). **Lunch menu** €13. **Credit** MC, V. **Wheelchair access**. **Non-smoking room**. **Map** N7.

Not only has the rest of the world discovered one of our favourite bistros, but alas, Au Vieux Chêne looks set to become fashionable not just with the sort of arty liberal types who keep France's art galleries humming and its movie industry reeling, but also big wallets travelling here from other parts of town. Happily, despite the signs of incipient gentrification, this place remains a treat that's larger than the sum of its parts. If everyone loves the fly-in-amber atmosphere of old enamelled advertisements, the zinc-capped bar by the door when you come in and the tile floor, what makes this spot so special is the earnestness of their desire to please – everyone here wants you to eat and drink to your heart's content. And we did indeed, as chef Stéphane Chevassus just gets better and better. A starter of langoustines encased in fine crunchy angel hair and garnished with slices of fresh mango was delicious and refreshing, while chilled tomato soup was garnished with mint, a ball of tomato sorbet and a drizzle of olive oil, a charming study in Mediterranean ton sur ton. Chevassus is a gifted game cook too – we loved the pigeon sautéed with Chinese cabbage and its accompaniment of mushrooms cooked with galangal root, which brought out the sweetness of the bird. Cod with potatoes dressed with chives, olive oil and preserved lemons was excellent, and the Faugères the friendly waiter suggested went down a treat with a shared plate of perfectly ripened cheeses from Alléosse.

12TH ARRONDISSEMENT

Auberge le Quincy

28 av Ledru-Rollin, 12th (01.46.28.46.76/ www.lequincy.fr). Mº Gare de Lyon. **Open** noon-2.30pm, 8-9.30pm Tue-Fri. Closed mid-Aug to mid-Sept. **Average** €60. **No credit cards. Wheelchair access. Map** M8.

Anybody seeking a massive feast of trad French cooking will be in gastro-heaven here. Our host, Bobosse, proposed a cornucopian selection of starters, including fine foie gras, well-aged wafer-thin country ham, delicious warm caillettes (pork and chard patties) on a bed of mesclun, and a hunk

Le Temps au Temps

of homemade terrine accompanied by a garlicky cabbage salad. The main courses kept up the quality with a creamy, succulent côte de veau aux morilles presented in a copper pan, and scallops that were untrimmed, quickly fried and served on a bed of pasta. Not sophisticated cuisine, but perfectly timed and irresistibly fresh. Our appetites were waning now and we resisted a serious-looking chocolate mousse, plumping instead for glasses of vieille prune served from a traditional wooden watering can and flambéed at the table by Bobosse with well-rehearsed theatricality. The bill, which included a handsome quantity of Brouilly, was substantial but worth every penny. Remember that the cackling patronne does not have any truck with credit cards, so a totter to the cash machine is involved, which might just give you a thirst for that final nightcap.

A la Biche au Bois

45 av Ledru Rollin, 12th (01.43.43.34.38). M° Gare de Lyon. **Open** 7-11pm Mon; noon-2.30pm, 7-11pm Tue-Fri. Closed last week in July, first three weeks in Aug, one week at Christmas. **Average** €23.20. **Prix fixe** €23.20. **Credit** AmEx, DC, MC, V. **Wheelchair access. Map** M8.

Anywhere else, we might be complaining about being jammed in so tightly, but however crowded it gets here, it doesn't seem to matter because everyone always seems so happy with the food and the convivial atmosphere. Unusually, fellow diners even say hello as you squeeze into your seat. It's impossible not to be enthusiastic about the more-than-generous portions offered with the €23.20 prix fixe menu, one of the very few in town to include a selection of game in season. The night we visited, there was even Scottish grouse, incredible when you consider that only the top restaurants offer it as a main course, at three times the price. We began with a massive salade niçoise, replete with fat chunks of tuna, Christmas-red tomatoes and plenty of olives, and a hearty slab of game terrine with the requisite jar of gherkins, both of which were virtually a meal in themselves. Mains included tasty portions of wild duck in blackcurrant sauce, traditional partridge with cabbage, and a filling wild venison stew, which, like the coq au vin and the boeuf bourguignon, was served in the Biche's signature cast-iron casserole dishes. All came in gargantuan portions. Lingering too long over your choice of the many perfectly ripe cheeses incurs the risk of getting served automatically with half a dozen of them, doled out by the friendly waiters ever eager to ensure no one waddles home still hungry. If you can still do dessert, go for one of the own-made tarts laden with seasonal fruits or, for something lighter, one of the sorbets liberally drenched in vodka, Calvados or liqueur according to flavour. As for the wine list, it too has a reputation as one of the best-value selections in town – particularly the Rhône section – and we can see why. Be sure to book in advance, but expect to wait anyway – trust us, it's a small price to pay for a blissful if unsophisticated experience.

Comme Cochons ★

135 rue Charenton, 12th (01.43.42.43.36). M° Reuilly-Diderot. **Open** noon-2.30pm, 8-11pm daily. **Average** €30. **Credit** MC, V. **Wheelchair access. Non-smoking room. Map** N8.

Pigs get a bad rap in Anglo-American culinary lore where they conjure images of indiscriminate gobbling, but for the French, more sensibly, they're a symbol of friendly mingling ('être amis comme cochons'). At this popular bistro in the growingly trendy 12th, friendly exchange is dominated by the audible yum yums ('miam miam' in French) of near-ecstatic diners spurred on by the dynamic and quirky waiters, eccentric photos of whom adorn the walls. Saturday lunch, in particular, functions like a drop-in centre with groups genially expanding as yet another chair is haphazardly added to a packed table. Some starters are only seasonal: the magnificent fricassée de girolles (a mass of grilled yellow mushrooms on a bed of tart leaves) is available in autumn only. Likewise the wine-rich civet de biche (a melt-in-the-mouth stew of baby venison) and duo de canard (a scrumptious pairing of confit thigh and slices of rosé breast served on a bed of saucy white beans) are predominantly winter courses. But, with inspiration the chef's speciality, it's no wonder that each season brings new fuel for kitchen fantasies. Dinners are more resolutely gourmet, while the excellent-value lunch menu is mindful that you may have to go back to work. The good selection of wines is well priced, with lots of southern finds. On our last visit, we couldn't decide between the own-made tarte Tatin or perfectly runny moelleux au chocolat, so we greedily had both.

La Connivence

1 rue de Cotte, 12th (01.46.28.46.17). M° Ledru-Rollin. **Open** noon-2.30pm, 8-11.30pm Tue-Sat. Closed two weeks in Aug. **Prix fixe** €20-€25. **Lunch menu** €14-€17. **Credit** MC, V. **Wheelchair access. Non-smoking room. Map** N8.

Southern French cooking with an unusual Madagascan spin works brilliantly in this ochre-painted bistro near the place d'Aligre market in summer. Chef Pascal Kosmala presents a thoughtful menu with several wholly vegetarian options, a bonus for Paris, based on seasonal ingredients enlivened by an original use of spices. We began with a light vegetable feuilleté flavoured with anise and cumin, and the star dish, a delicate crab galette refreshingly combined with citrus and cinnamon flavours. The duckling cooked three ways – confit, sautéed magret and parmentier – was delicious, with none of the greasiness sometimes found in traditional duck dishes, and the second main course, pâté d'oie, was equally good. Presented beneath a dome of brioche, a rich stew of goose and vegetables was balanced by the vinegary sharpness of marinated veal. Both dishes were hearty without being cloying, leaving plenty of room for iced nougatine in a berry coulis and an intriguing parfait of white chocolate and coconut on a juniper biscuit. The wine list favours youngish, southern wines, including increasingly fashionable Madiran; we were pleased with a chilled Brouilly at €22.50. Although we had booked late, there were still a few tables of youngish, well-groomed locals lingering with a glass of wine and listening to gentle jazz.

Le Duc de Richelieu ★

5 rue Parrot, 12th (01.43.43.05.64). Mº Gare de Lyon. **Open** 7am-2am Mon-Sat; hot food served from 11.45am. Closed Aug. **Average** €22. **Prix fixe** €14.50. **Credit** MC, V. **Wheelchair access. Non-smoking room. Map** M8.

Not only a wonderful exception to the rule that most restaurants within easy walking distance of any Paris train station will be mediocre at best, this jolly, bawdy bistro is well worth a meal even if you're not catching a train at the Gare de Lyon. Proprietor Stéphane Derre, formerly at the popular Le Gavroche, is a proud and generous restaurateur, which shows in the quality of the house Beaujolais (the Morgon is the best bet) and the excellent produce with which the kitchen works. Come here hungry, as portions are generous. The menu, which changes daily, has an appealingly Cro-Magnon tilt to it, including excellent jambon persillé, the Burgundian classic of big chunks of ham in parsleyed ham-bone aspic, along with superb steaks. Another good starter is a plate of saucisson and an order of oeufs mayonnaise, hard-cooked eggs glossed with ivory-coloured mayonnaise, the sure sign of a bona-fide old-fashioned bistro. A huge plate of deliciously crisp golden chips accompanied a perfectly grilled pavé de boeuf, while an excellent blanquette de veau, a real granny's treat of simmered veal in lemon-spiked cream sauce, came with rice. Cheeses included a st-marcellin that was so perfectly ripened it had to be eaten with a spoon: bliss. Desserts are good too, including classics such as baba au rhum, millefeuille and a lovely tarte Tatin. Booking is always advised, especially on Wednesday and Thursday nights, when a pianist adds to the party-like atmosphere in this from-the-provinces-style dining room with raspberry red walls and hand-painted lampshades.

L'Encrier

55 rue Traversière, 12th (01.44.68.08.16). Mº Bastille or Gare de Lyon. **Open** noon-2pm, 7.30-11pm Mon-Fri; 7.30-11pm Sat. Closed Aug. **Average** €30. **Prix fixe** €22. **Lunch menu** €13. **Credit** MC, V. **Wheelchair access. Map** M8.

Through the door and past the velvet curtain, you find yourself face-to-face with the kitchen of L'Encrier, which was in full swing on a weekday evening with a crowd of locals, many of whom seemed to know the charming boss personally. Value is tremendous here, with a €13 lunch menu and a €22 menu in the evening, as well as a few à la carte choices. We began with fried rabbit kidneys on a bed of salad dressed with raspberry vinegar, an original and wholly successful combination. A spiced homemade terrine was more banal, but main

course goose magret with honey was a welcome change from the usual duck version and served, like the andouillette we also ordered, with crunchy, thinly sliced sautéed potatoes. Our bottle of fruity Chinon was a classy red at a rather steep €24, but worth every cent. To finish our meal we shared a chocolate cake that had a nice spongy texture but was a little low on cocoa punch; the popular profiteroles looked better. The attractive space and friendly service attract a hip Bastille crowd.

L'Oulette ★

15 pl Lachambeaudie, 12th (01.40.02.02.12/ www.l-oulette.com). Mº Cour St-Emilion. **Open** noon-2.15pm, 7.45-10.30pm Mon-Fri. **Average** €60. **Prix fixe** €39 (dinner only), €48-€82. **Lunch menu** €25-€32. **Credit** AmEx, DC, MC, V. **Wheelchair access. Map** P10.

As the Bercy neighbourhood has grown up over the last decade, L'Oulette has deservedly become a local institution. Busy at noon with bigwigs from the Ministry of Finance, it's considerably quieter in the evening when it pulls a crowd of boho couples who have bought flats in this still-evolving area. A table for one was perfect: on the banquette, no direct sightlines, and the comfort of being half-hidden from most of the room by a flower-topped divider. From this vantage point, a starter 'club sandwich' of foie gras poached in Muscat wine and served on small squares of corn bread with sweet onion compote was a brilliantly festive creation, offering a sexy range of tastes and textures and impressing with the precision of its execution. Tiny squid cooked with cumin and anise and served on warm potatoes was also an outstanding dish. The main course – sole on a bed of quinoa with fried courgettes and a tomato bouillon with Lucques olives – was superb and a fascinating reflection of how chef Marcel Baudis's creativity continues to broaden and deepen (his original forte was the cooking of south-western France). Desserts are similarly sophisticated and adult, including a wonderful composition of warm pink grapefruit in pomegranate juice and lemon verbena cream with citrus cake. All told, an excellent meal, and a place that would also be ideal for a tête-à-tête or perhaps a business meal.

Le Square Trousseau

1 rue Antoine-Vollon, 12th (01.43.43.06.00). Mº Ledru-Rollin. **Open** noon-2.30pm, 8-11.30pm Tue-Sat. **Average** €35. **Lunch menu** €20, €25. **Credit** MC, V. **Wheelchair access. Non-smoking room. Map** N7.

After a long absence we were happy to be heading to a restaurant that had not only been the setting for many good times, but once channelled the buzz of the up-and-coming Bastille. In those days, about a decade or so ago, this area of eastern Paris had a real edge and was the subject of endless breathless reportages in lifestyle glossies the world over. On a wintery Tuesday night, however, the crowd was decidedly lacking in supermodels, fashion designers or any of the other fauna that once made this place

L'Avant-Goût

so much fun. Instead, large tables of businessmen stared at Xeroxed charts between courses, and in the non-smoking room a parsimonious table of North Americans worked a calculator to keep costs down. The most delicious aspect of the evening was the amber belle époque mouldings that give this place its personality. The food was just fine, but it came too quickly and lacked passion. Scallops marinated in their shells were generously served – there were four – but a starter of basil-stuffed ravioli in a taupe-coloured cream sauce was dull indeed. A good bottle of Bandol and excellent bread from organic baker Moisan kept spirits up until the main courses arrived, but again they were just passable. A thick tuna steak came with a springtime bonnet of finely diced vegetables and a drizzle of vinaigrette, while a good steak was accompanied by a mixture of haricot verts and button mushrooms and a portion of thickly sliced chips. Absent-minded service and a really mediocre rice pudding led us to conclude that, though this is a fine spot if you happen to be in the area, it no longer casts a spell.

Le Train Bleu

Gare de Lyon, pl Louis-Armand, 12th (01.43.43. 09.06/www.le-train-bleu.com). M° Gare de Lyon. **Open** 11.30am-3pm, 7-11pm daily. **Average** €65. **Prix fixe** €45. **Credit** AmEx, DC, MC, V. **Wheelchair access. Non-smoking room. Map** M8.
This has to be the most glamorous station buffet in the world, complete with 19th-century frescoes to welcome travellers from the famous train bleu, which used to link Paris with Ventimiglia. The

cooking is classic but a cut above the average brasserie, and we began with a saucisson de Lyon served on warm ratte potatoes, which set us up nicely for main courses, including a long-cooked, crisply breaded pied de porc; a tartare to which a slug of Cognac gave an added punch; and the most sophisticated dish, a plump and juicy veal chop served with creamy wild mushroom lasagne. The evening ended on a high note with a scrumptious vacherin, a chocolate sortilège – an upright cone of mousse-filled dark chocolate accompanied by pistachio ice-cream – and a rum baba, with a whole bottle of rum temptingly left on the table for extra dousing. Service throughout was particularly efficient and charming. The only caveat is the expensive wine list, from which we chose a perfumed red Beaune, the suggestion of the month but hardly a bargain at €48 a bottle.

Au Trou Gascon ★

40 rue Taine, 12th (01.43.44.34.26/www.autrou gascon.fr). M° Daumesnil. **Open** noon-2pm, 7.30-10pm Mon-Fri. Closed Aug. **Average** €56. **Prix fixe** €50 (dinner only). **Lunch menu** €36. **Credit** AmEx, DC, MC, V. **Wheelchair access. Map** P9.
The grey lacquered chairs and modern artworks are sleek and contemporary – although glorious ceiling mouldings add an old-world touch – and the cooking is a very classy take on the food of Gascony. But you'd expect nothing less from founder Alain Dutournier, who also runs the high-class Carré des Feuillants. All that is good about the south-west is celebrated, including foie gras, lamb, duck, ham and Madiran wines. Succulent Chalosse chicken came

crammed with slices of pungent black truffle balanced by a delicate celeriac purée, while a steaming plate of cassoulet uniting lamb, pork sausage, duck and those peerless Tarbais beans was light years away from the heavy stew that so often bears the name. Starters, including a tart topped with peppery sour cream and scallop carpaccio, and just-cooked Scottish salmon confirmed that chef Jean-François Godiard is expert at highlighting natural flavours. Don't miss the baba landais with sticky vieux garçon liqueur sauce; it's a feathery-light sensation. All this, plus first-rate service and an encyclopaedic wine list, means that an excursion into the less tourist-travelled 12th is well warranted.

Les Zygomates
7 rue de Capri, 12th (01.40.19.93.04). M° Daumesnil. **Open** noon-2pm, 7.30-10.30pm Tue-Thur; noon-2pm, 7.30-10.30pm Fri, Sat. Closed Aug. **Average** €30. **Lunch menu** €14.50. **Credit** MC, V. **Wheelchair access. Non-smoking room. Map** Q10.
For a long time this friendly bistro was just about the only reason to employ your zygomates (the facial muscles used to smile) in this rather vague, mostly modern corner of Paris. These days new pedestrian streets and a prettier pavement are giving the area a little more allure and, as this is one of the last bona-fide cheap-rent zones in Paris, it's starting to attract a younger, more urban crowd. The dining room is snug – be forewarned that the non-smoking zone is a claustrophobic alcove – but winsomely pretty, with the old marble sideboard, painted glass ceiling and etched glass partitions that were fixtures of the butcher shop that originally occupied this space.

This carnivore's heritage comes through amply on the menu, with dishes such as a foie gras and duck salad – a nice mix of leaves generously garnished with meat and liver – and an enormous and delicious pièce du boucher, or large slab of flavourful beef, which came with a disc of creamy pommes dauphinoises, spinach and wild mushrooms. The starter of lobster and wheat berries au gratin was rich and delicious, with a surprising amount of crustacean for the money, and cod steak with tapenade was pleasant too. The only choice for dessert is l'assiette des Zygomates, a wonderful miniature buffet of pastries and sorbets. Delicious cooking, a nice wine list and engaging service make this place well worth recommending, but don't expect much elbow room.

13TH ARRONDISSEMENT

L'Avant-Goût
26 rue Bobillot, 13th (01.53.80.24.00). M° Place d'Italie. **Open** 12.15-2pm, 7.45-10.45pm Tue-Fri. Closed two weeks in Aug, one week in Sept. **Average** €31. **Prix fixe** €31. **Lunch menu** €14. **Credit** MC, V. **Wheelchair access** (reservation recommended).
Self-taught chef Christophe Beaufront has turned this non-descript street on the edge of the villagey Butte-aux-Cailles into a foodie destination. The dining room is brightly coloured and comfortable, and we were seated at a convivial round table with plenty of space around us. Staff didn't turn a hair when half our party of four arrived 45 minutes late for lunch, leaving us to sip a warming winter

aperitif. Despite a little eye-rolling from the waitress, they even did their best to cater to the vegan in our group, presenting her with a beautiful plate of vegetable accompaniments (though the waitress drew the line at serving the parsley soup without its accompanying oysters). Most representative of Beaufront's cooking is his pot-au-feu de cochon aux épices, a much-written-about dish that has been on his menu for years. He got bored of serving it in a cast-iron pot, so now presents the pork, sweet potato and fennel garnished with deep-fried ginger on a plate with a glass of bouillon to drink on the side. It was very good, not earth-shaking, and we were a little let down by the very ordinary moelleux au chocolat – however, a starter of piquillo pepper stuffed with smoked haddock rillettes illustrated his talent, as did the slow-cooked lamb shank. Reluctant cooks will be interested to know that Beaufront's food is available to take away across the street.

Chez Gladines

30 rue des Cinq Diamants, 13th (01.45.80.70.10). M° Corvisart or Place d'Italie. **Open** noon-3pm, 7pm-1am daily. **Average** €18. **Lunch menu** €10. **No credit cards. Wheelchair access.**

Tucked behind place d'Italie in the hip Butte-aux-Cailles neighbourhood, this is where the local students come on a Friday night for some good nosh at honest prices. Reservations aren't possible in a place like this, but, never mind, have a drink at the bar, or outside on the cobbled street in summer, and wait for the genial barman to call out your name. Squeezed into tables fused together like one long communal board, you'll be sharing more than just the conversation as bread baskets and carafes of water get passed along by your fellow diners. Those on tight budgets come for the salads, which, considering their sheer size, will leave even the hungriest of the cash-poor sated. Still, it would be a shame to miss some of the Basque specialities on offer, such as the satisfying chipirons biscaïna, squid served in a thick vegetable and tomato stew. Wash it all down with one of the rustic reds, like the Madiran, a good match for this simple but gratifying fare. Come for the boisterous atmosphere and a filling meal before heading off for a bit of bar-hopping nearby.

Chez Paul

22 rue de la Butte-aux-Cailles, 13th (01.45.89.22.11). M° Corvisart or Place d'Italie. **Open** noon-2.30pm, 7.30pm-midnight daily. **Average** €33. **Credit** MC, V. **Wheelchair access.**

On a quiet Sunday night, the Butte-aux-Cailles still had a happy buzz, with a young crowd making its way from bar to bar. Against this backdrop, Chez Paul plays the quietly self-important, grown-up restaurant in relation to the many other livelier ones nearby. A bit of folklore – the sea salt in a little wooden basket, a proper pepper mill, flea-market carafes for water – is meant to link this place to its surroundings, and it would likely work were it not for the servers wearing uniforms and prices that are

rather stiff for the neighbourhood. The food itself is just fine. Starters included provocative rustic grub such as tablier de sapeur ('fireman's apron', which is breaded tripe as eaten in Lyon), along with marrow bones, country terrine, oysters, and delicious ham braised in hay, sliced thin and served with salad dressed with mixed peppercorns and cumin seeds. Mains are classic with no deviating flourish whatsoever, including boudin noir, onglet (flank steak), prime rib, suckling pig and sea bass fillet, all served with curiously boring potato purée. The quality of the meat here is very good, however, and aside from some rather dull desserts – a short list runs to cherry clafoutis and apple tart – and a similarly uninteresting wine list, this place makes for a pleasant if pricey meal.

L'Ourcine ★

92 rue Broca, 13th (01.47.07.13.65). M° Gobelins. **Open** noon-2.30pm, 7-11.30pm daily. Closed Mon, Sun, Aug. **Lunch menu** €19.50. **Prix fixe** €29 (dinner only). **Credit** MC, V. **Map** J10.

The French love their food, and they love to talk about it. It seems that everywhere you go, people are mentioning this little bistro headed by Sylvain Danière, formerly of La Régalade under Yves Camdeborde. And the talk isn't for nothing. The dining room, with its cream walls and wooden tables, is decidedly plain, perhaps to avoid competing with the beautifully presented fare. Indeed, as the waitress set down a complimentary amuse-bouche of airy mushroom mousse topped with tiny golden croutons, we knew we were in for a treat. What followed was a veritable parade of traditional French dishes reworked into contemporary inspirations. The procession started with spider-crab-stuffed ravioli, the sweetness of the meat wonderfully offset by the bed of slightly bitter endives meunières. The delicately flavoured seafood bisque was quite perfect. A main of filet mignon de porc was wisely and expertly served in its simplest form, accompanied by roasted garlic cloves and grenailles, little whole potatoes. Just when it seemed the meal had reached its highest point, dessert arrived: egg-sized chocolate quenelles served in a saffron-infused crème anglaise. Need any more reason to go and see what all the talk is about?

Au Petit Marguery

9 bd du Port-Royal, 13th (01.43.31.58.59/ www.petitmarguery.fr). M° Gobelins. **Open** noon-2.15pm, 7.30-10.15pm Tue-Sat. Closed Aug. **Prix fixe** €35. **Lunch menu** €26.20. **Credit** AmEx, MC, V. **Wheelchair access. Map** J9.

'We really should go back in the game season,' is a comment often made about the attractively old-world Petit Marguery, and so it was with something of a sense of triumph that we entered the restaurant to have lunch in the first week of October. The three-course prix fixe (€35, plus rather too many supplements) is a game lover's fantasy and we plunged straight in with a grouse purée, and a pheasant and foie gras terrine. The purée was a real

Forget the location – it's the cuisine that counts at **La Cerisaie**. *See p86.*

winner, a mousse-like paste with a rich game and juniper flavour. The terrine was well made but there was disappointingly no perceptible taste of pheasant. Warming to our task, we continued with that most classic of French game dishes, lièvre à la royale, a long-marinated wine-infused hare dish. This was a joyful autumn dish, as was the wonderfully moist partridge served plainly on liver-spread croûtons. Our strong Crozes Hermitage red (€24) held up well to the game assault, and to finish our meal we indulged in soufflés au Grand Marnier, which, although spectacular in appearance and making, lacked enough punch to crown our hunter's feast. The downside of the meal was the rather sullen service; perhaps our waiter hadn't bagged his bird.

14TH ARRONDISSEMENT

Apollo

3 pl Denfert-Rochereau, 14th (01.45.38.76.77/ www.restaurant-apollo.com). M° Denfert-Rochereau. **Open** noon-3pm, 7-11pm daily. **Average** €35. **Lunch menu** €15-€18 (Mon-Fri). **Credit** AmEx,

MC, V. **Wheelchair access. Non-smoking room. Map** H10.

Parisian RER stations may not be synonymous with suave dining, but the brains behind Quai Ouest have transformed Denfert-Rochereau's cavernous railwaymen's offices into a bold and brash new restaurant. With starfish suspended from the high ceilings, and a backdrop of Damien Hirst-inspired encased monochrome junk, the Apollo caters well to its clientele of local trendies. Ubiquitous porthole convex mirrors promote mid-dinner preening, and stark '70s shiny white banquettes are perfect for showing off the latest Gucci purchase. The menu covers a familiar range of fashionistas' comfort food – Caesar salad, shepherd's pie, the ever-present club sandwiches – as well as venturing into more daring territory with caramelised braised endives in a rich balsamic sauce, and the less-successful neige of Puy lentils, literally sunk by a dishwater-style insipid soup. With a '70s soundtrack and stylish surroundings, there is ambience aplenty at the Apollo, even if culinary aspirations are resolutely earthbound.

L'Assiette

181 rue du Château, 14th (01.43.22.64.86/
www.chezlulu.fr). M° Mouton Duvernet. **Open** 7-11pm
Mon-Fri; noon-4pm, 7-11pm Sat, Sun. **Average** €50.
Prix fixe €50 (weekdays only). **Credit** AmEx, MC,
V. **Wheelchair access. Map** G10.
Eccentric, hands-on chef Lulu, still sporting her
trademark beret, continues to pull celebrity crowds
to her deluxe bistro. The stripped-wood floor and
wipe-off laminated veneer tables make this an
unusually relaxed and lively room for what is actually
one of the capital's most expensive bistros. The
exceptional freshness and quality of the products,
coupled with the simple precision of the cooking,
almost justify the price. Refreshingly free of frilly
appetisers, our autumn meal began with a pheasant
and foie gras terrine that retained a taste of game, and
a mound of the plumpest imaginable cockles bathed
in a frothy lemon butter. A simply roasted wild duck
with a punchy jus was served with a preserved pear,
which may have come from the tree that harboured
our other dish of moist partridge. This was
accompanied by gravy-infused cabbage, which had
been cooked to melting point without sacrificing
colour or texture. Lulu makes an apology on the menu
for the nursery puddings such as crème caramel and
marquise au chocolat, claiming disingenuously that
these are the only ones she knows how to make. They
seemed the part, but we opted for a pile of thinly
shaved cheese from the Pyrenees, which brought the
meal to a memorable close. The wine list features
many regional choices, and our tannic red from the
Roussillon region (€36) perfectly complemented the
game. We will save up for a return visit to sample
some fish, which looked tempting.

Le Bis de Severo

16 rue des Plantes, 14th (01.40.44.73.09).
M° Alesia or Mouton Duvernet. **Open** noon-
2.30pm, 7.30-10.30pm Tue-Sat. **Average** €30.
Prix fixe €22. **Credit** MC, V. **Map** G10.
This newly opened branch of the bistro Severo down
the street looks like 1,000 others in the deepest 14th,
but what a difference. Chock-full of locals, it has a
huge meat-focused menu and, on our visit, just one
waiter, one young Japanese chef and a dishwasher.
The signature dish is a pricey but worth it (€70 for
two, €80 for three) côte de boeuf from the Limousin,
that can be prepared crunchy on the outside and
nearly raw on the inside, if you ask nicely. To start,
try the boudin noir (black pudding) shaped into a
timbale or grilled goat's cheese, both served with
beautiful salads. Desserts include a perfect crème
caramel. There is quite a strong wine list, with the
lowest priced bottle a fine Cahors at €13. The only
flaw was the tired bread from the baker Poujauran.

La Cagouille

10 pl Constantin Brancusi, 14th (01.43.22.09.01/
www.la-cagouille.fr). M° Gaîté. **Open** noon-2.30pm,
7.30-10.30pm daily. **Average** €45. **Prix fixe** €26,
€42. **Credit** AmEx, MC, V. **Wheelchair access**.
Map F9.

La Cagouille is a very pleasant destination on warm
summer nights, perfect for enjoying the tree-sheltered
terrace on this otherwise rather characterless corner.
The night we visited the weather was less than
co-operative, but the sleek, marine-themed interior is
also welcoming. The menu changes daily, according
to the market and chef Gérard Allemandou's
mood, but make no mistake: this is a temple to all
things fishy. Everything on offer is as fresh as if
you'd caught it yourself, and the array of dishes is
impressive. Having trouble deciding? The prix fixe,
good value at €42 for three courses plus coffee and
wine, is a great way to sample some of the more
classic choices on the blackboard. After gobbling
up the complimentary dish of cockles in butter, move
on to a warm salad of tender, melt-in-your-mouth
scallop coral served on a bed of greens, or perhaps
crispy fried anchovies, deliciously salty. The main
courses are served in their simplest incarnations,
such as red mullet fillet punctuated by a delicate
butter sauce. The wine list is exhaustive, and the
knowledgeable staff will steer you in the right
direction. After such light fare, it's easy to find room
for the enormous crème caramel, or perhaps a digestif
in the cosy Cognac bar.

La Cerisaie ★

70 bd Edgar Quinet, 14th (01.43.20.98.98). M° Edgar
Quinet or Montparnasse. **Open** noon-2pm, 7-10pm
Mon-Fri. Closed end July to end Aug, one week
at Christmas. **Average** €30. **Credit** MC, V.
Non-smoking. Map F9.
Nothing about La Cerisaie's unprepossessing red
façade in the shadow of the hideous Montparnasse
tower hints at the talent that lurks inside. The chef's
wife quickly made us feel welcome in the minuscule
ochre and red room. It took only one spoonful of the
'bouillon de pot-au-feu, raviole de foie gras' for us to
understand this was no ordinary bistro. Deeply
flavoured and perfectly seasoned, it contained
almost microscopic dices of raw vegetable and a
single raviole, the coolness of its foie gras filling
contrasting with the hot bouillon. With a simple
starter of white asparagus served with preserved
lemon and drizzled with bright green parsley oil,
chef Cyril Lalanne proved his ability to choose and
prepare the finest produce. Bourride de maquereau,
a thrifty housewives' take on a southern French
classic, combined big mackerel fillets, perfectly
cooked potato and a garlicky mayonnaise sauce.
Another main of cochon noir de Bigorre, an ancient
breed of pig, made us feel we had never really tasted
pork before. The juicy pink meat came atop a bed of
very thinly sliced rounds of carrot, turnip and
asparagus in a succulent jus. Baba à l'Armagnac,
an interesting variation on the usual rum cake, was
a touch too dry but came with the best Chantilly
cream we had tasted in years, which was almost
as dense as ice-cream. There is a good selection
of wines from small producers, many of them
affordable – look for Armagnacs and other alcohols
from the south-west too.

La Contre-Allée ★

83 av Denfert-Rochereau, 14th (01.43.54.99.86).
M° Denfert-Rochereau. **Open** noon-3pm,
7-11pm Mon-Sat. Closed Aug. **Average** €45.
Prix fixe €35 (dinner only). **Lunch menu** €25.
Credit AmEx, MC, V. **Non-smoking room.**
Map H10.

Ushered into this bistro by a cold wind on an April evening, we were enchanted at once by the genuine welcome, as well as by the soft lighting and warm tones of this contemporary and chic setting. Seated in the cosy dining room at linen-covered tables set well apart from one another, you immediately get the sense that this is a place of refinement and quiet discretion. The service was impeccable, and our elegant waitress guided us through the menu choices with descriptions that had us wanting to sample everything. Chef Sylvain Pinault, who previously worked at the Crillon, changes the offerings frequently, and the night we visited his cooking left us speechless. The feuilleté d'escargots in beurre blanc was flawless, the pastry light and flaky while the rich sauce enveloped the meaty little morsels beautifully. Salmon carpaccio was of the highest quality. What guaranteed that we would be back, however, was the piccata de veau (veal escalope) over a parmesan risotto enhanced with meat jus. The risotto was of an otherworldly creaminess and the meat was cooked to perfection. Our bottle of Mont Baziac brought everything together seamlessly. Highly recommended.

La Coupole

102 bd du Montparnasse, 14th (01.43.20.14.20/
www.flobrasseries.com/coupoleparis). M° Vavin.
Open 8.30-10.30am, noon-2.30pm, 6.30pm-1am
daily. **Average** €45. **Prix fixe** €29.90 (dinner
only), €22.90 (after 10.30pm). **Lunch menu**
€22.50 (Mon-Sat). **Credit** AmEx, DC, MC, V.
Non-smoking. Map G9.

Josephine Baker, Ernest Hemingway, Simone de Beauvoir – everyone who was anyone during les années folles flocked to this elegant brasserie to drink champagne, cut a rug in the downstairs dance hall, and, of course, to see and be seen. Today Montparnasse is no longer the hip hangout it once was and the artists, writers and intelligentsia have migrated to other corners of the capital, but La Coupole still hangs on to some of its magic. A combination of nostalgia, reasonable prices and supreme people-watching make it hugely popular with Parisians and tourists alike. Classed as a historic monument, La Coupole opened in 1927 and has been serving its famous lamb curry ever since. In light of its popularity, a savvy option for soaking up the atmosphere of the enormous art deco dining room is a late-night dinner – a good-value prix fixe is available after 10.30pm. You may still have to wait, but it's easy to while away the time in the bar américain sipping a cocktail. Once seated, it would be a shame to forgo one of the platters of oysters on offer, a true delight in such lovely surroundings, but the meatier dishes, such as fillet of duck with Sichuan pepper or sauerkraut cooked in riesling, are just as tempting if a little inconsistent in quality. Complete your La Coupole experience with one of the iced desserts, such as the parfait glacé au café. Amazingly, the entire restaurant is now non-smoking.

Le Dôme

108 bd du Montparnasse, 14th (01.43.35.25.81).
M° Vavin. **Open** noon-3pm, 7pm-12.30am daily.
Closed Sun and Mon in July and Aug. **Average**
€70. **Credit** AmEx, DC, MC, V. **Wheelchair**
access. Non-smoking room. Map G9.

At a time when many Parisian brasseries seem to be on their uppers, this venerable old boat of a place continues to abide not only by its own myths but those of a livelier and more glittering Montparnasse. A mix of artists, editors, politicos, tourists and celebrating locals swan by for superb platters of shellfish, including some of the best oysters in the city, and other fabled marine pleasures such as an immaculate sole meunière, prepared with gorgeous fish caught off the Ile d'Yeu off the Vendée coastline, or salt cod aïoli made with cod they salt themselves. The bouillabaisse is also very good, although this dish just never tastes quite the same overlooking a ribbon of tarmac as it does facing the Med. This is a fine place to experience the best of classical French fish cookery – revolving around simple sauces such as hollandaise, garlic mayonnaise, melted butter, beurre blanc and olive oil – as the ingredients and preparation are first-rate. Finish up with some of the fine Auvergnat cheeses that the Bras family bring to the capital from the land of their ancestors, and don't hesitate to order from the lower echelons of the wine list, since it offers good value at all price points. Expensive, but worth it.

Natacha

17 bis rue Campagne-Première, 14th (01.43.20.
79.27). M° Raspail. **Open** noon-2.30pm, 7.45-11pm
Tue-Fri; 7.45-11pm Sat. Closed three weeks in Aug.
Average €35. **Lunch menu** €16-€26. **Credit** MC,
V. **Wheelchair access** (reservation recommended).
Map G9.

Though the hipsters, most notably Mick Jagger, who once made this Montparnasse bistro a legend have moved on, it maintains a quiet chic that pleases a polite but self-satisfied crowd of publishing, showbiz, media and political types, many of whom would secretly like to find themselves as fodder for the sort of people-press magazines you flick through at the hairdresser's. Rich and successful, perhaps, but not famous, even if their eyes dart hopefully around in the room. But this low-lit, high-ceilinged Pompeian red-painted room with cushioned banquettes still has a worldly charm whether you decide to play games with the regulars or not. The food is good too, running to a roster of Gallic treats such as langoustine bisque, artichoke with poached egg or sautéed langoustines with salad in a delicious peppery dressing to start, followed by braised veal shank with vegetables, hachis parmentier (the French version of shepherd's pie) or fish. Don't bother with the côte de boeuf, which is disappointingly dainty, and be prepared for rather patronising if efficient service.

L'Opportun ★

*64 bd Edgar Quinet, 14th (01.43.20.26.29).
Mº Edgar Quinet.* **Open** noon-3pm, 7-11.30pm
Mon-Sat. Closed Aug. **Average** €35. **Prix fixe**
€21 (until 10pm). **Credit** AmEx, DC, MC, V.
Wheelchair access. Non-smoking room.
Map G9.

Corpulent owner-chef Serge Alzérat is passionate about Beaujolais, dubbing his convivial cream and yellow restaurant a centre of 'beaujolaistherapy' and a place for 'the prevention of thirst'. He's also an advocate for good, honest Lyonnais food. Thus his menu is littered with the likes of sabodet (thick pork sausage) with a purée of split peas, duck skin salad, tête de veau (a favourite of President Chirac, whose photo graces the walls) and meat, lots of it. There's a lightweight 250g veal or beef onglet or, if you need a heftier protein fix, there's a 400g version, both served with mounds of savoury cabbage dotted with bacon and crusty, baked potatoes. Starters are just as generous: a salad of dandelion leaves with roasted tomatoes, bacon chunks and a runny poached egg, and rounds of lightly toasted chèvre, accompanied by thick slices of ham and apple. Fromage fans should skip dessert and try the st-marcellin by Roanne's master cheesemaker Hervé Mons.

La Régalade

*49 av Jean-Moulin, 14th (01.45.45.68.58).
Mº Alésia.* **Open** 7-11pm Mon; noon-2.30pm,
7-11pm Tue-Fri. Closed Aug. **Prix fixe** €30.
Credit MC, V.

There is much debate as to whether La Régalade still lives up to its reputation after chef Yves Camdeborde left in search of new culinary adventures at Le Comptoir du Relais St-Germain a few years ago. Judging by the packed house on the Friday night we visited, this spot doesn't seem to be taking much notice of all the nay-sayers. Indeed, the waiters were evidently so confident that the crowds would be forever queued up outside that the service was dismissive at best, despite a friendly welcome. No matter, we were there for the food. While the offerings on the menu had our mouths watering, the final outcome was somewhat lacking, such as a starter of foie gras in an asparagus bouillon that was so salty a carafe of water was required. The brandade de morue proved a good choice, however, its creamy garlic packing a punch. A main of caramelised pork was unexceptional, though charmingly served with a generous portion of mashed potatoes in a cast-iron pot, echoing the homely spirit of the terrine plopped on the table at the start of our meal, to be enjoyed at will with hearty country bread. Though La Régalade's reputation may be hanging on by a nostalgic thread, it's still hard to beat for generous portions at reasonable prices.

15TH ARRONDISSEMENT

Bistro d'Hubert

*41 bd Pasteur, 15th (01.47.34.15.50/www.bistro
dhubert.com). Mº Pasteur.* **Open** 7.30-10.15pm
Mon, Sat; 12.30-2.15pm, 7.30-10.15pm Tue-Fri.
Average €50. **Prix fixe** €26, €34. **Credit** AmEx,
DC, MC, V. **Wheelchair access. Non-smoking**
room. Map E9.

The decor of this friendly bistro, like its location near where the Métro comes hurtling out of the ground, is unassuming and gives little indication of the more adventurous traits of the cooking. After an appetiser of homemade duck pâté, we tucked into our starters – a beef carpaccio that had been livened up with powdered hazelnuts, and the fraîcheur de crabe, a crabmeat salad sandwiched between wafer-thin biscuits and dressed with a pastis and star anise sauce. Often vegetables fade into the background of the food they are served with. Here, they don't just accompany the cooking, they underpin it. The tender wok-fried chicken was served with a pile of sautéed mushrooms, and the juicy and perfectly prepared slice of veal came with fried chayotte squash, a delicately flavoured vegetable. Both dishes arrived at the table with their little bowl of fluffy mashed potato. We had planned on ending the dinner at this point, but when we came upon the dessert menu this idea was quickly abandoned and we brought our meal to a sticky and gooey close with the gâteau de caramel, a salted-caramel concoction served with apple mousse and elderflower syrup.

Café du Commerce

*51 rue du Commerce, 15th (01.45.75.03.27/
www.lecafeducommerce.com). Mº Emile Zola.*
Open noon-midnight daily. **Average** €27.
Prix fixe €26.90 (dinner only). **Lunch menu**
€14. **Children's menu** €8.50. **Credit** AmEx,
DC, MC, V. **Wheelchair access. Non-smoking**
room. Map C8.

Starting life in the 1920s as a car workers' canteen, this three-level brasserie situated on the 15th arrondissement's bustling rue du Commerce offers traditional, no-nonsense cuisine to a varied clientele of retail-fatigued shoppers, retirees enjoying the long opening hours and the odd travelling salesman squeezing in a meal on a tight budget. With the pleasant art deco interior, trompe l'oeil murals and horticultural excesses draped from balconies in the central atrium, the surroundings have always been more memorable than the cuisine. Wise diners general eschew the more complex offerings (the tête de veau is a little risky), and focus on reliable basic brasserie fare. Although we were disappointed by the onion soup, a flavourless broth with limp croutons, things looked up with the red meat specials doused in thick sauces and accompanied by chubby slabs of golden frites, some of the best in Paris. Desserts covered typical territory – chocolate mousse, crème caramel et al – and, like the rest of the carte, were somewhat hit or miss. The bill is always a little steeper than expected, but we left satisfied.

Every oyster's a pearl at seafood shack **L'Uitr**. *See p91.*

L'Os à Moelle

3 rue Vasco-de-Gama, 15th (01.45.57.27.27).
Mº Lourmel. **Open** noon-2pm, 7-10.30pm Tue-
Thur; noon-2pm, 7-11.30pm Fri, Sat. Closed last
week in July, first three weeks in Aug. **Prix fixe**
€38 (dinner only). **Lunch menu** €32. **Credit** MC,
V. **Wheelchair access** (reservation recommended).
Map B9.

The early dinner sitting at L'Os à Moelle on a
weeknight attracted a room full of American, British
and Japanese diners who looked pleased to have
trekked to the outer edge of the 15th for a genuine,
albeit tourist-friendly, bistro experience (the waiters
automatically spoke to us in English). With just two
choices for each course, decision-making is kept to
a minimum. A red pepper mousse with Espelette
pepper and fresh fava beans whetted our appetites
before a thin yet rich-tasting mushroom and
asparagus soup with hazelnut oil, served from a big
white tureen. So far, so good, but our bottle of
Lalande de Pomerol had yet to appear and, when
it did, no one asked us to taste it. Next up, three
Normandy oysters served warm with herb butter
– the liquid had lost its vivid flavour in the heating
– and a round slice of unexceptional foie gras
mi-cuit with grated beetroot salad. Neither of us
could find fault with our fish courses, monkfish in a
cream sauce flavoured with mousseron mushrooms,
cockles and tarragon, and snow-white cod with
asparagus and morels. Meats were similarly
satisfying – a pigeon leg and slices of slow-cooked

shoulder of beef, both served with fava beans, peas
and spring onions – but things fell apart slightly
after this with bitter-tasting fresh goat's cheese
and a melon 'mousse' that was really just a frothy
fruit salad. There was little time to breathe between
courses and we left feeling that chef Thierry
Faucher, along with the dining room staff,
could benefit from slowing down a bit. The casual
sister establishment La Cave de l'Os à Moelle,
just opposite, serves robust food buffet-style, in a
cellar-like setting.

Le Père Claude

51 av de la Motte-Picquet, 15th (01.47.34.03.05).
Mº La Motte Picquet Grenelle. **Open** noon-2.30pm,
7-11pm daily. **Average** €40. **Credit** AmEx, MC, V.
Wheelchair access (reservation recommended).
Non-smoking room. Map D7.

Recent renovations have made this bistro as neat
and unfussy as the lobby of a modern luxury hotel
– beige carpeting, Scandinavian-style furniture,
and pleasant, professional waiters. But the sleekness
belies the basic if well-executed bistro food, some of
it roasted right behind the zinc-and-marquetry bar.
A chèvre croustillant with salad was just the right
combination of creamy and crisp, while the cold
fish terrine cleverly came with garlicky tomato salsa.
For mains, we couldn't resist that sizzling rôtisserie
meat, ordering a mixed grill of chicken, beef, pork
and boudin, and a poulet rôti moelleux, both
accompanied by silky mashed potatoes that added

to the home-cooked, comfort-food feeling. For dessert, we enjoyed an apple clafoutis and an assortment of sorbets, including green apple not unlike an Italian gelato. Surprisingly, the light-filled, glassed-in terrace jutting on to the pavement is reserved for non-smokers, a real plus. On the afternoon we visited, the crowd was mostly middle-aged couples and business bods (we were the sole English speakers) and, seeing the photo near the entrance of a smiling Chirac with Gregory Peck, we wondered how often heads of state and Hollywooders really eat here. Just then Lionel Jospin and his entourage arrived, proving that even ousted party leaders appreciate a humble lunch in an executive setting.

Restaurant Stéphane Martin

67 rue des Entrepreneurs, 15th (01.45.79.03.31).
M° Charles Michel or Commerce. **Open** noon-2.15pm, 7.30-10.30pm Tue-Sat. Closed three weeks in Aug. **Prix fixe** €32. **Lunch menu** €15. **Credit** MC, V. **Map** C8.
We were initially struck by the rather starchy atmosphere at Stéphane Martin's eponymous restaurant, with a decor of mauve theatre-style drapes, heavy pile carpet and dimmed lights reminding us of an antechamber to the Comédie-Française rather than a restaurant. Things warmed up as other diners arrived and the chef emerged from the kitchen to joke and chat with the many regulars. Martin's cuisine is original and inventive, with dishes combining fine, fresh ingredients and intricate sauces such as honey-braised knuckle of pork served with red cabbage, sea bass with tabouleh and pollack with creamed cauliflower. Starters were attractively presented, albeit somewhat parsimonious, with one dish of three lonely-looking scallops served with steamed fennel, and another of spindly frogs' legs, saved by an accompaniment of delicately prepared parmesan and garlic ravioli. A main course of veal kidney with Swiss chard and chorizo was delicious, as was the excellent mi-cuit foie gras, sprinkled with caramelised balsamic vinegar and papaya, and served with a herb salad. Original takes on classic desserts – pineapple tarte Tatin and strawberry tiramisu – rounded off an enjoyable and theatrically presented meal.

Restaurant Thierry Burlot ★

8 rue Nicolas-Charlet, 15th (01.42.19.08.59).
M° Pasteur. **Open** noon-2.30pm, 7.30-10.30pm Mon-Fri; 7.30-11.30pm Sat. Closed ten days in Aug. **Average** €32. **Lunch menu** €26. **Credit** AmEx, MC, V. **Wheelchair access. Non-smoking room. Map** E9.
Thierry Burlot's modern bistro continues to succeed in drawing in crowds with an enticing menu of artistically prepared food served in stylish and upbeat surroundings. Produced with fresh ingredients, the offerings vary from earthy truffle-laden dishes to lighter fish and seafood numbers, including the quite exquisite langoustines grilled with vanilla, served as a starter or main course. Our

meal started with the excellent lightly poached egg topped with shards of truffles and framed by fresh leeks, contrasting with the less successful starter of an insipid mélange of ice-cold tomato gazpacho and chopped raw mackerel. From the mains, the oven-cooked sea bass came in a delightful herb and mushroom sauce, and the homely looking risotto transpired to be a creamy, savoury delight, topped with the ever-present truffles. Original desserts included a refreshing fromage blanc ice-cream, as well as intricate chocolate dishes and homemade caramel ice-cream (with old-style salted-butter caramel). Service was undertaken by an efficient, if rather charmless, coterie of black-clad Parisian twentysomethings, but we ended our meal satisfied.

Le Sept/Quinze

29 av Lowendal, 15th (01.43.06.23.06). M°
Cambronne. **Open** noon-2.30pm, 8-11pm Mon-Fri; 8-11pm Sat. Closed two weeks in Aug, one week at Christmas. **Prix fixe** €30 (dinner only). **Lunch menu** €18. **Credit** MC, V. **Wheelchair access. Map** D8.
There is a lot to like about this convivial Mediterranean bistro, stranded on a rather lonesome strip between the 7th and 15th arrondissements. Considering the quiet neighbourhood, we were surprised to find the place absolutely packed with a young, professional, mostly French crowd when we visited on a Saturday night. The mood inside was deafeningly festive. No one seemed to mind that their elbows brushed their neighbours' as they sliced into crispy brik pastry packages of beef topped with black olive tapenade. Gently priced, modern and sunny, this food is a refreshing change from heavier, standard bistro fare. A rewarding combination was a shallow dish of warm Jerusalem artichokes in cream sauce, topped by a glistening heap of salty salmon roe and garnished with a cool wedge of lemon. Not all the dishes were so well balanced. A rocket, apple and walnut salad with an oversweet vinaigrette was mounted on a tuile of asiago cheese that was chewy where it should have been crispy, and tender little squid grilled a la plancha with oranges and almonds just tipped the flavour scale over into bitter. Still, this light and elegant fare hits more than it misses. The short wine list was augmented by specials that included, unusually, both a Californian red zinfandel and an Argentinian sauvignon. Their sweet, bold notes are just right for this cuisine, and their presence on the blackboard shows that someone here is paying attention. Judging by the crowd, it's paying off. The same team runs the very likeable Bistro d'en Face (24 rue du Docteur-Finlay, 15th, 01.45.77.14.59), which is popular with editors from the nearby Hachette publishing house.

Le Suffren

84 av de Suffren, 15th (01.45.66.97.86). M° La
Motte Picquet Grenelle. **Open** 7am-midnight daily. **Average** €25. **Credit** AmEx, MC, V. **Wheelchair access. Non-smoking room. Map** D7.

Despite the recent revamp of this erstwhile traditional brasserie, which nestles in the shadow of the Eiffel Tower, some things have escaped unscathed, with the cuisine unmodified and the waiters gloriously unreconstructed. Our rather portly septuagenarian waiter, in a figure-hugging T-shirt, spent most of our lunch castigating his female colleagues in a foghorn voice, leaving us desperately trying to attract his attention for the next course. His successor strived to look industrious, busily sorting out receipts and assorted paperwork, but proved to be as inefficient in serving as her predecessor. None of this, however, seriously detracted from our meal. The menu is peppered with traditional brasserie offerings, from vertiginously stacked seafood platters to a choice of every imaginable cut of beef, the latter accompanied by potatoes in their various guises: long fat chips, browned gratin dauphinois or creamy purée. There have been reports in the past of some unreliable cuisine, and our chateaubriand was slightly over-charred, but otherwise the snails for starters were plump and tasty, the seafood fresh and copious, and desserts hearty and plentiful. The eccentric service has not deterred the clientele, with a lively lunchtime crowd of tourists, loafers and a group of exhausted regulars in running kit joking with the patron about refuelling with steak-frites after having completed the Paris marathon.

Le Troquet

21 rue François-Bonvin, 15th (01.45.66.89.00). M° Sèvres-Lecourbe. **Open** noon-2pm, 7.30-11.30pm Tue-Sat. Closed three weeks in Aug, one week at Christmas. **Prix fixe** (dinner only) €30, €38. **Lunch menu** €24, €28. **Credit** MC, V. **Map** D8.

Crowds of gleeful foodies gather nightly at chef Christian Etchebest's shrine to Basque country cuisine to enjoy a modern take on traditional south-west specialities such as chipirons (small squid), piquillo peppers and ossau-iraty, a ewe's milk cheese set off with cherry jam. The €30 three-course blackboard menu is excellent value, but we plumped for the six-course menu dégustation, which may be verging on gluttony. We sailed with ease, however, through the modest-sized portions of attractively presented and delicately prepared food, including a double serving of desserts. An excellent debut of enticing chorizo-laced chickpea soup served with generous slices of foie gras was followed with a series of memorable offerings, among them ris de veau (sweetbreads), lightly cooked with trademark squid, then a seafood-inspired dish of delicate scallops on a bed of aubergines, and a final savoury of tenderly cooked magret de canard served with traditional white haricot beans. While not as sensational as the savouries, desserts were nonetheless satisfying. Good-humoured and efficient service and a cheerful Friday night crowd combined with the delicacies to make this a memorable meal in a friendly Basque enclave located deep in the 15th arrondissement.

L'Uitr ★

1 pl Falguière, 15th (01.47.34.12.24). M° Falguière. **Open** noon-2.30pm, 7.30-10.30pm daily. **Average** €30. **Prix fixe** €15, €19. **Credit** MC, V. **Wheelchair access. Non-smoking room. Map** F8.

Tucked away behind the botched urban renewal of the neighbourhood surrounding the Gare Montparnasse, this swell little sea shack is a great spot for anyone who can't get down to the shore for oysters, fish and other shellfish. As the name would indicate, oysters star on the blackboard catch of the day menu here, and they offer an admirable selection of varied sizes and provenances identified according to the individual producer. Yvon Madec's plump, briny Breton spéciales went down a treat with a bottle of muscadet, and a side of prawns came with delicious fresh mayonnaise. Even the bread and butter are good here, and the relaxed service at bare wood tables set with Basque linens evokes relaxed holiday dining a long way from city streets. If most of the many regulars come to feast on oysters at very reasonable prices, main courses are appealing too, including a very generous bowl of coques (cockles) lashed with lemony butter sauce and accompanied by a side of parsleyed potatoes, tuna steak or sardines. The wine list is brief but well compiled, including a good all-purpose muscadet for €13 and a luscious Irancy (a light Burgundian red) for €22.

16TH ARRONDISSEMENT

Astrance ★

4 rue Beethoven, 16th (01.40.50.84.40). M° Passy. **Open** 12.30-1.45pm, 8.15-9.45pm Tue-Fri. Closed Aug. **Average** €100. **Prix fixe** €150. **Lunch menu** €70, €115. **Credit** AmEx, DC, MC, V. **Map** B6.

When Pascal Barbot opened Astrance, he was praised for creating a new style of Parisian restaurant – refined, yet casual and affordable. Three years later, this small, slate-grey dining room feels exactly like an haute cuisine restaurant, with seemingly as many staff as there are customers and prices comparable to Taillevent's. A mysterious reservations system makes it nearly impossible to book for dinner, even several weeks in advance, while lunch is slightly easier. We hesitated over the three-course lunch menu at €70 before settling on the more extravagant menu automne – most of those around us chose the menu Astrance at €150, giving free rein to the chef. We resisted the aperitif trolley being wheeled around and then had to wait 40 minutes, sustained by mineral water and an amuse-bouche, before our first courses arrived. From then on it was smooth sailing through the six courses. A celeriac velouté layered in a shot glass with lime yoghurt and juniper cream piqued our appetites, before foie gras interspersed with thin slices of white mushrooms, its delicate flavours lifted by a lemon condiment. Next up, the sweetness of a slice of (ever so slightly chewy) lobster was played off by the bitterness of candied grapefruit peel, a grapefruit

Le Kiosque. *See p95.*

and rosemary sorbet, and raw baby spinach leaves. Textures came to the fore in a dish of warm salmon served with chips of dried chestnut, tiny chanterelle mushrooms and mushroom vinegar. The meat course, crisp-skinned pigeon with bilberry chutney and quince confit, offered a beautiful contrast of tart, sweet and earthy. After a light sorbet of chilli pepper and lemongrass, we amazingly still had an appetite for dessert – a sign that Barbot keeps fats to a minimum. A thin, meringue-like coconut case contained a light, milky ice-cream, served with carefully selected exotic fruits – more of the fruits came with coffee and little madeleines flavoured with chestnut honey. Beautiful as this food was, it didn't send us into ecstasies – rather, the experience was quietly pleasurable, the only flaw being the (albeit reasonably priced) wines by the glass that weren't elegant enough to stand up to the food.

Le Bistrot des Vignes

1 rue Jean-Bologne, 16th (01.45.27.76.64/ www.bistrotdesvignes.fr). M° La Muette or Passy. **Open** noon-2.30pm, 7-10.30pm daily. Closed three weeks in Aug. **Average** €27. **Prix fixe** €28 (dinner only). **Lunch menu** €25.50. **Credit** AmEx, MC, V. **Wheelchair access. Map** A6.

Tucked away on a quiet corner in the 16th, just down from Passy Plaza shopping central, the Bistrot des Vignes pulls in a crowd of locals. Such is their loyalty that many even have their own table constantly set aside, just in case they drop by. Just try bagging a table, unannounced, for Sunday lunch. Impossible! A relaxed, friendly vibe prevails with butter-yellow walls garnished with black and white photos of vineyards and grape pickers, and tangy-coloured chairs (red, blue, green and yellow) adding a capricious country touch. Food follows the seasons, with starters running from salads (spinach leaf and fresh parmesan, red peppers marinated in pesto) to feathery red mullet 'doughnuts' with a sweet chilli dipping sauce or a marinated salmon and broccoli tart. Mains in the form of duck breast coated in honey, served sliced on triangles of toasted gingerbread, and John Dory fillets baked with spicy aubergine and peppers with a watercress sauce showed a chef adept at turning out likeable, nicely balanced food. The île flottante is a dessert delight.

Brasserie de la Poste

54 rue de Longchamp, 16th (01.47.55.01.31). M° Trocadéro. **Open** noon-2pm, 7-10pm Mon-Sat. Closed three weeks in Aug. **Average** €26. **Prix fixe** €24, €29. **Lunch menu** €15. **Credit** AmEx, DC, MC, V. **Map** C5.

The name, which refers to the post office across the street, is nondescript. The restaurant itself – the warm decor is more café than brasserie – is equally unremarkable, though tasteful. What keeps regulars streaming into this neighbourhood haunt is the food – sophisticated, solid and surprisingly good value, even at dinner. A generous starter of foie gras and beef tongue millefeuille was hearty, delicious and intelligent, served with a sticky demi glace, fig compote and savoury financier cake. Velvety scrambled eggs with foie gras, presented inside a trio of emptied egg shells and served with toast soldiers, elevated the humble staple to the sublime. Mains were even more impressive: the sage-roasted

rack of lamb was just the way lamb should be: perfumed, plump, pink, tender and juicy. Veal liver with wild berries was proclaimed as 'the best ever' by one very contented diner, who raved about its crispy, char-grilled exterior, the quivering, melt-in-the-mouth interior, and the lip-smacking balsamic glaze crowned with fresh, wild berries. The portions were generous to a fault – we had no room left for dessert. Given the reasonable prices, though, we could easily afford to go back again to try them.

Le Chalet des Iles
carrefour des Cascades, Lac Inférieur du Bois de Boulogne, 16th (01.42.88.04.69/www.lechalet desiles.net). M° La Muette/RER Henri Martin. **Open** noon-2.30pm, 8-10.30pm daily. **Average** €45. **Credit** AmEx, DC, MC, V. **Wheelchair access.**
Even the most blasé Parisians can't help but revel in the idyllic island setting of Le Chalet des Iles. After a short, soothing boat ride across the Bois de Boulogne's Lac Inférieur, Le Chalet rewards with a light and airy room, elegant, ever-so-slightly formal French country decor (in soft greens, yellows and rusts actually found in nature... unlike the large arrangements of artificial flowers), solicitous service and menus in English, on request. By and large, we were also rewarded by lunch, starting with an unusual rendition of classic oeufs en cocotte with earthy girolle mushrooms and sweet chestnuts, a salad of firm green lentils with toothsome quail confit, and a velvet-textured crème de lentilles with parmesan (and a surfeit of salt). For main courses we dodged tourist-friendly offerings of macaroni and cheese gratin and sauté de poulet 'shop suey au

wok' in favour of a winey risotto with six beautifully seared sweet scallops; sea bream with a mirin-laced Asian glaze; and a thick chunk of seared, well-cooked cod in brown butter accompanied by rich and chunky mashed potatoes. The desserts we sampled – brioche perdue (a variation on French toast); a trio of small, lightly flavoured chocolate, coconut and pistachio panna cotte; and profiteroles with a small pitcher of warm bittersweet chocolate sauce for pour-it-yourself fun – were rendered with somewhat less skill. Better to simply order a digestif and savour a few extra moments in this unexpected slice of Parisian countryside before the boat returns you to the bustling city.

La Gare
19 chaussée de la Muette, 16th (01.42.15.15.31). M° La Muette. **Open** noon-3pm, 7.30-10.30pm Mon, Sat; noon-3pm, 7-11.30pm Tue-Fri, Sun. Closed 25 Dec. **Average** €35. **Lunch menu** €15. **Prix fixe** €27, €32. **Credit** AmEx, MC, V. **Wheelchair access. Non-smoking room. Map** A6.
This was once a train station on the Petite Ceinture, the railway circling Paris built by Napoleon III. The ticket office is now the bar and the platforms downstairs have become a colossal dining area. After pushing the train theme hard, however, it seems the restaurant is now taking itself more seriously. The menu, while still dominated by the rôtisserie specialities, has been refined. We were seduced by the pince de tourteau (crab claw) with an avocado mousseline, and the black truffle risotto. Stuck awkwardly into the middle of the rice was a grilled wafer of comté cheese: unexpected and

delicious. The no-nonsense mains were excellent: the gigot d'agneau, accompanied by a jus so concentrated that it is served in a shot glass, was very tender and cooked exactly as requested. The portions seemed undersized until the giant bucket of accompanying purée was dropped off – salty but divine. La Gare is in the heart of the posh 16th – if you ask for water, staff will assume you want it from a bottle – but prices are varied and reasonable. Evenings are generally calm, but lunch is often packed with locals with coiffed pooches in tow and an international crowd from the OECD, just around the corner.

La Grande Armée

3 av de la Grande-Armée, 16th (01.45.00.24.77). M° Charles de Gaulle Etoile. **Open** noon-2am daily. **Average** €45. **Credit** AmEx, MC, V. **Wheelchair access. Non-smoking room. Map** C3.

A brasserie dedicated to the Napoleonic Grande Armée might not seem the obvious place for a Brit to turn to for lunch, but decoration is by trendsetting interior designer Jacques Garcia, who jointly owns the place with the Costes brothers. Jingoism is therefore limited to a few hussar prints and cut-outs; otherwise the room is pure Garcia, with lots of deep red contrasting elegantly with powder blue, while each seat is covered with a velvet stole, like a discarded papal vestment. Designed to please successful young professionals for whom their parents' choice of restaurant would be too stuffy, but for whom straying far from the 16th would be unthinkable, the menu confirms this 'cool' formula, with expensive caviar listed among the starters and a cheeseburger among the main courses. We kicked off with a parmesan soufflé – a baby ramekin, nicely puffed and served with a well-dressed salad – plus a more interesting sea bass carpaccio with lime. Steak tartare was well seasoned and accompanied by outstanding thin frites, but it looked humble next to the parmentier de canard, which was luxuriously crowned with two slices of fried foie gras. Finishing our fruity Brouilly, we resisted the puddings, which include the delicious pom pom pomme, a mixture of apple crumble, pie and ice-cream. We were as conquered as Napoleon's all-powerful army – and didn't even mention Waterloo.

La Grande Cascade

Pavillon de la Grande Cascade, allée de Longchamp, Bois de Boulogne, 16th (01.45.27.33.51/ www.lagrandecascade.com). M° Porte Maillot, then taxi or 244 bus. **Open** 12.30-2.30pm, 7.30-10.30pm daily. Closed two weeks in Dec and Feb. **Average** €150. **Prix fixe** €70, €165. **Lunch menu** €70. **Credit** AmEx, DC, MC, V. **Wheelchair access.**

Originally Napoléon III's hunting lodge, this Bois de Boulogne pavilion was transformed into an upmarket eaterie for the 1900 Great Exhibition. The sumptuous dining room features stunning frescoes and chandeliers, and on a summery lunchtime we were seated on the terrace under the belle époque

porte-cochère. An army of be-suited waiting staff, relaxed and unperturbed despite the searing heat, catered for the whims of the clientele of captains of industry and indolent Neuilly types. Chef Richard Mebkhout's inventive cooking was immediately revealed by a series of exquisite summer-themed tasters, which set our taste buds running. From the menu du marché, the enticing starter consisted of fine ingredients of crab and langoustine, but was somewhat spoiled by an overly intricate preparation mixing too many conflicting flavours: jellied tomatoes, fennel mousse and sprinklings of caviar. The mains were simpler and ultimately more successful: seared pollack, served on top of just-cooked summer vegetables in a garlic-perfumed cream sauce, garnished with deep-fried parsley, and a succulent roasted veal served with oven-cooked shallots and dried fruit. Simple, summery berry pastries rounded off the meal. Service was flawless, the food elegant and, handily, you can procure the big winnings needed to finance a meal here at the Longchamp racetrack just opposite.

Hiramatsu ★

52 rue de Longchamp, 16th (01.56.81.08.80/ www.hiramatsu.co.jp). M° Boissière or Trocadéro. **Open** noon-2pm, 7.30-9.30pm Mon-Fri. Closed Aug. **Average** €150. **Prix fixe** €95, €130. **Lunch menu** €48. **Credit** AmEx, DC, MC, V. **Wheelchair access. Non-smoking room. Map** K7.

From the moment you arrive at Hiramatsu's new quarters, which occupy the premises of the former Faugeron restaurant, you know you're in for a first-class experience. Glide through the three doors leading into the restaurant, opened successively by doormen who have magically anticipated your arrival, and enter a hushed, well-appointed dining room accentuated with the finest luxuries: vases and water glasses by Baccarat, champagne flutes by Riedel, cutlery by Christofle, porcelain from Limoges. The heavy, leather-bound tome of a wine list is, of course, de rigueur. The room breathes light and space, a much-needed commodity when you consider the sizeable team of sommeliers and waiters skilfully performing their roles with orchestrated moves and balletic grace. As for the cuisine, let's just say that it soars well beyond the expectations created by the sumptuous surroundings. The menu découverte was a culinary tour de force: every one of the ten courses delighted the eye and astounded the palate. Even an amuse-bouche of spiced crab with apple mousse was stunning in its clarity of flavours and aesthetic simplicity: the ambrosial spoonful was served on top of a shiny red apple presented like a Magritte painting. Each dish that followed was refined, light and imaginative, such as a starter of barely cooked Breton lobster in jelly, green pea and chestnut purée, and vanilla coulis. Flavours that shouldn't go together? Take another bite. A main course of smoked Challans duck, dusted with pain d'épices and served with an intense violet-flavoured sauce, was another revelation. The choice of desserts concluded the experience with a bang – go for the caramelised homespun cotton candy on poire William jelly with champagne: a very grown-up concoction that would bring out the awestruck child in anyone.

Le Kiosque

1 pl de Mexico, 16th (01.47.27.96.98). M° Trocadéro. **Open** 12.15-3pm, 7.30-11pm daily. **Average** €35. **Prix fixe** €24.90, €29.90. **Lunch menu** €26, €29. **Credit** AmEx, MC, V. **Map** B5.

This little restaurant, located not far from the Trocadéro on the tranquil place de Mexico in the tony 16th, is a cheerful place for lunch or dinner in what is an all-too-often overpriced neighbourhood. Decorated in bright shades of green, red and purple, this 'concept' eaterie, owned by a former magazine editor, offers a broad selection of French papers, accompanied by food and wine that draw inspiration from a different region of France every week. The starter of a giant shrimp-filled samosa with Espelette pepper and a sweet dipping sauce was delicious, although the following courses of grilled tuna brochette with ratatouille and free-range Normandy chicken with preserved lemon, Picholine olives and coriander were both a little overcooked. The dessert and cheese were, however, superb: a deconstructed, creamy strawberry tiramisu layered in a glass, and savoury baked camembert with green salad and a little pot of honey for drizzling on to the hot cheese.

Le Passiflore ★

33 rue de Longchamp, 16th (01.47.04.96.81/ www.restaurantpassiflore.com). M° Iéna or Trocadéro. **Open** noon-2.30pm, 7.30-10pm Mon-Fri; 8-10pm Sat. **Prix fixe** (dinner only) €38, €54. **Lunch menu** €35. **Credit** AmEx, MC, V. **Wheelchair access. Map** C5.

Roland Durand's 30-year career has included the haut bourgeois heights of the Pré Catelan and the more prosaic challenge of bashing out 23,000 lunches at a sitting during the '98 World Cup, but it's his passionate exploration of Asian cuisine that informs the brilliance of his first solo venture. After our first sip of a sweet, spicy beetroot gazpacho, we abandoned the prix fixe and ate practically the whole menu, highlights of which included a fresh foie gras sautéed with pineapple and violets; a deep, fragrant wild boar and tamarind curry; and a ravioli of foie gras in a frothy truffle broth of pagan decadence. The masterpieces are the sorbets – some more familiar flavours like basil, bitter chocolate and lychee, others teasing with unfamiliar herbs, but all combining astonishing aromas in their creamy coldness. The wine list is as serious as the menu is whimsical, with a connoisseur's selection of Bordeaux as well as regional curiosities from Corsica and Savoie. The crowd is not 'les pipol' (celebrities) but the food is some of the most original, ambitious and exciting in Paris, with none of the pomposity of better-known gastro-shrines.

Le Pré Catelan

rte de Suresnes, Bois de Boulogne, 16th (01.44.14.41.14/www.lenotre.fr). M° Porte Maillot, then 244 bus. **Open** Nov-Apr noon-1.30pm, 7.30-9.30pm Tue-Sat. May-Oct noon-1.30pm, 7.30-9.30pm Tue-Sat; noon-1.30pm Sun. **Average** €175. **Prix fixe** €140, €180. **Credit** AmEx, DC, MC, V. **Wheelchair access.**

This grand French restaurant in the Bois de Boulogne is known as an ideal spot for a leisurely Sunday lunch during the summer, but it does wonders for the soul any time of the year. On a brisk day in November, we stopped in for lunch, longing for a mid-week break from the city grind. A short taxi ride later, we were seated beside a roaring fireplace in this welcoming belle époque mansion, perusing the business lunch menu and nibbling complimentary scallops served on the half-shell. Frédéric Anton's cooking is simple yet inventive. For starters, we chose the lightly fried langoustine with a caviar-laced sauce and drizzle of avocado cream, and the slice of silky foie gras encrusted with coriander and fennel seeds. Our main courses included the ultra-fresh cod simply presented with onions and confit tomatoes, and a house speciality – tender pigeon breast cooked in bouillon and served on a bed of broccoli-flecked couscous with bite-size merguez. The outstanding cheese trolley is one of the best in Paris, with an extensive selection delivered fresh daily from the famed Alléosse cheese shop. For dessert, don't miss the tower of millefeuille. Service is remarkably efficient, cheerful and accommodating. The impressive selection of wines includes an assortment of half-bottles priced at a très palatable €14.

Restaurant GR5

19 rue Gustave Courbet, 16th (01.47.27.09.84). M° Trocadéro. **Open** noon-2pm, 7-10pm Mon-Sat. **Average** €25. **Prix fixe** €16 (dinner only). **Lunch menu** €14. **Credit** AmEx, MC, V. **Wheelchair access. Map** B4.

Named after the famous hiking trail winding through the Jura to the Alps, this little refuge among the area's chic boutiques serves hearty cheese and potato-based Alpine cuisine. Red-and-white checked tablecloths and wood-panelled walls hung with dried flowers, cowbells and ski posters make convincing surroundings. The queyrassienne (€35 for two people) is an addictive take on traditional fondue: this bubbling pot of three cheeses contains chunks of smoky bacon and sweet onion confit, accompanied by bread cubes and potatoes. Absolutely divine. Tartiflette (potato, cheese and bacon gratin) with walnut salad is an equally rib-sticking option for €17. A €16 prix fixe menu offers traditional French fare, but no fondue. The wine of choice is the delicate Crépy – a crisp regional white wine that makes the perfect partner for the hearty cuisine. Though happily stuffed with cheese and potatoes, we couldn't resist ending our meal with chocolate fondue. The tiny pot of chocolate was served with mixed fruit, marshmallows and ladyfingers. Good, but not quite worth €13. Fortified for the walk home, we headed into the chilly night air, straining our ears for the crunch of snow.

Le Stella

133 av Victor Hugo, 16th (01.56.90.56.00).
M° Victor Hugo. **Open** noon-3pm, 7pm-1am
Mon-Fri; noon-midnight Sat, Sun. **Average** €45.
Credit AmEx, MC, V. **Wheelchair access**.
Map B4.
Deep in the velvet-lined precincts of the well-mannered, discreetly vieille France part of the 16th arrondissement, this long-running brasserie deserves kudos for an elegant updating that hasn't diminished its charm. This is a tweedy sort of place, since the Parisian bourgeoisie loves to affect a sort of off-to-the-hunt look, even if the plaids are Chanel for the ladies and cashmere for the gents. If you get the local codes, fine; if not, you won't be condescended to – there is real hospitality from the moment you step through the front door. The waiters are prompt and professional for a change, and miraculously enough – it's not a given in Parisian brasseries – the simple food is quite good. Start with oysters or maybe some prawns in their shells with a good lashing of own-made mayonnaise, and then eat well from a classic register that runs to dishes such as an impeccably prepared sole meunière or steak with béarnaise sauce and frites. The baba au rhum is the signature grown-up Parisian pudding, and the wines by the carafe are good and fairly priced. Ideal for a relaxed meal that offers a nuanced portrait of Parisian life.

La Table de Lauriston ★

129 rue de Lauriston, 16th (01.47.27.00.07).
M° Trocadéro. **Open** noon-2.30pm, 7-10.30pm
Mon-Fri; 7-10.30pm Sat. Closed last three weeks
in Aug. **Average** €45. **Lunch menu** €25.
Credit AmEx, DC, MC, V. **Wheelchair access**.
Serge Barbey's dining room has a refreshingly feminine touch: stripes of pink, orange and silver paint, with velvety chairs in indigo and gold, patterned banquettes and whimsical paintings. In keeping with this, the restaurant seems to attract local foodies rather than the type of business diner who seems unaware of what he (or she) is eating. At the next table we spotted TV personality Jean-Pierre Coffe, an outspoken opponent of 'la malbouffe' (junky eating). To start, a few stalks of asparagus from the Landes had been expertly peeled and trimmed to avoid any stringiness, and were served with the simplest vinaigrette d'herbes. More extravagant was the foie gras cuit au torchon, in which the duck liver was wrapped in a cloth and poached in a bouillon. It proved extraordinarily flavourful, though the toasted bread could have been fresher. A main course blanquette de lotte au safran cost a rather steep €22.50 as we had failed to order it as part of the prix fixe. We were pleased, however, with the lobster-like chunks of fish in a creamy saffron sauce, with lightly cooked baby vegetables adding colour contrast. Onglet de veau (hangar

steak) turned out to be two generous steaks spiced with Sichuan pepper and served with sautéed ratte potatoes. Skip the crème brûlée and the moelleux au chocolat, and order a dessert with attitude: the giant baba au rhum.

La Table de Robuchon

16 av Bugeaud, 16th (01.56.28.16.16). M° Victor
Hugo. **Open** noon-2.30pm, 7-10.30pm daily.
Average €80. **Prix fixe** €150. **Credit** MC,
V. **Non-smoking. Map** B4.
We had high hopes for this place, a follow-up to the deservedly popular Atelier de Joël Robuchon in the 6th. Sitting at real tables rather than counters, customers here can order from a menu that mimics the Atelier's winning formula of haute cuisine served in tapas-sized portions or as regular starters and main courses. Yet, while the menu at the two establishments is nearly identical, the overall experience here was a let-down. The decor, for one, hardly whet the appetite: blue patterned carpeting, dark gold-leaf walls and faux-looking wood veneer tables (sans tablecloth) recall a three-star hotel lobby more than an innovative restaurant. The food, though beautifully presented and expertly prepared, also lacked excitement. A promising amuse-bouche of foie gras mousse, port reduction and parmesan foam, which stunned our palates with pleasure, quickly gave way to anticlimax. Oeuf cocotte in mushroom cream was very good, but too subtle; frogs' legs croquettes, though dainty and delightful, still tasted like a high-end version of something from a deep-fried seafood basket. A main course of foie gras-stuffed quail with truffle-studded purée, however, epitomised culinary perfection. But not the clumsy dish of braised eel proffered as a substitute for sold-out tuna belly – it was pierced with small bones that took the pleasure out of every flavourful bite. Desserts were scrumptious and fun, but despite a chocolate garnish resembling the ring of Saturn, they were hardly out of this world either.

Zébra Square

3 pl Clément Ader, 16th (01.44.14.91.91/
www.zebrasquare.com). M° Passy/RER Kennedy-
Radio France. **Open** noon-3pm, 7.30-11pm Mon-Fri;
noon-3pm, 7pm-midnight Sat; noon-4pm, 7-11.30pm
Sun. **Average** €39. **Lunch menu** €25 (Mon-Fri).
Sunday brunch €26. **Credit** AmEx, MC, V.
Wheelchair access. **Map** A7.
Zébra Square is next door to the centre of French radio and television, which despite its nickname 'Le Grand Camembert', is a culinary blackspot. So when this stylish and modern restaurant with branches in Monte Carlo and Moscow opened a few years ago, Parisian TV and radio folk tossed their hats in the air with glee. Lunch is what it's all about, with a very good-value prix fixe: €25 including a glass of wine, plus a supplement for pudding. We picked the well-chosen and well-priced house Touraine as our aperitif and kept them coming by the glass for the fishier parts of our lunch: marinated salmon with a window box of dill and the plat du jour sea bream

with orange butter sauce. Risotto was surprisingly fabulous, as was the steak tartare with well-cut chips. For pud we shared a millefeuille, which came with a small earthenware pot of caramel sauce that you can pour over your dessert or knock back in one, depending on how you've been brought up. This isn't really a tourist address, but there are plenty of worse places you could end up after a visit to the Eiffel Tower.

17TH ARRONDISSEMENT

Ballon & Coquillages
71 bd Gouvion-St-Cyr, 17th (01.45.74.17.98).
Mº Porte Maillot. **Open** noon-3.30pm, 7pm-midnight daily. Closed first three weeks in Aug. **Average** €40. **Credit** AmEx, MC, V. **Wheelchair access. Map** B2.
Hardly any bigger than an oyster itself, this charming little raw bar is a really great addition to the neighbourhood around the Porte Maillot and Palais des Congrès. Not only is it open daily until midnight, but the round mosaic-topped counter is a haven of conviviality in decidedly corporate precincts. Take one of the red leather-covered stools and design your own feast. The oysters – Gillardeau, spéciales de Normandie, Utah Beach and plates de Bretagne, among others – are sold by threes and your first order should comprise a minimum of nine. Otherwise, garnish your tray with bigorneaux (sea snails), red prawns, grey shrimp, langoustines (rather pricey), clams, cockles and mussels, or opt for one of the suggested platters, including a tempting oyster sampler with four different types of oyster. If you're still hungry afterwards, you can order a plate of tarama served with hot toast, smoked salmon, smoked eel and herring, or a Scandinavian plate of smoked salmon, herring and tarama. Save a little space, though, as you don't want to miss out on the delicious own-made crème caramel, served in a big wedge. From a curious and rather expensive wine list with almost twice as many reds as whites, an excellent pick is the Château Theullet Bergerac, a dry white that goes well with shellfish.

Le Bistral
80 rue Lemercier, 17th (01.42.63.59.61).
Mº Brochant. **Open** noon-2.15pm, 8pm-midnight Tue-Sat. **Average** €40. **Credit** DC, MC, V. **Map** F1.
The unassuming exterior of this cosy bistro hides a new mecca for food and wine lovers. The emphasis here is as much on the eclectic wine list as the blackboard menu and dishes vary according to what is available at the nearby Marché des Moines. Many of the wines are available by the glass and each of the enthusiastic waiter/sommelier's suggestions went perfectly with our courses. Our starter of choucroute with pan-fried foie gras was a melt-in-the mouth combination of two Alsatian classics. We continued with a main course of juicy guinea fowl

accompanied by vegetable gratin, and a hearty bourguignon of venison with celeriac mash. The raspberry and red pepper tart with honey and chilli sauce made a sublime finale. The warm and friendly atmosphere adds to the pleasure of dining here. The dining room is very small, so booking is a must.

Le Bistrot d'à Côté Flaubert ★
10 rue Gustave-Flaubert, 17th (01.42.67.05.81/ www.michelrostang.com). Mº Pereire or Ternes. **Open** noon-2.30pm, 6-11.30pm Tue-Fri; 6-11.30pm Sat. Closed one week in Aug. **Average** €50. **Lunch menu** €29. **Credit** AmEx, DC, MC, V. **Wheelchair access. Map** D2.
Michel Rostang has his finger in so many pies now that you might not expect a visit to one of his offshoot bistros to be so special. But this meal proved thoroughly enjoyable. Le Bistro d'à Côté Flaubert was the original baby bistro when it opened in 1987, and the food continues to please. Rostang's formula is so right – not dressing up bistro food with faux haute cuisine presentation, but elevating it with great ingredients and spot-on cooking. The dining room, a former belle époque épicerie, is fun and charming with its tongue-in-cheek decor of toby jugs and old Michelin guides and an elegant portrait of Rostang's grandmother on the burgundy-coloured walls. Waiters and waitresses slide between the tightly arranged tables in bright red ties. They seemed rather inexperienced, but were certainly good-humoured and enthusiastic. Most diners were talking loudly in English; they included a typically 17th mix of big hair and leopardskin, one old lady who kept her fur coat on throughout the meal, and bourgeois parents taking out their sullen children. A lobster salad was a fresh and appetising pyramid of mesclun, coriander, the most succulent lobster flesh and tiny ravioli; the wild duck and foie gras pâté en croute was deliciously moist with its taste-enhancing jelly, and the crusty bread is wonderful. The same could be said of the flavoursome tendrons de veau stuffed with mushrooms and the daily special of sea bass in a Thai-style sauce. Glazed cubed carrot and turnip and the lemongrass-spiced risotto that came with the fish were served in mini cast-iron casseroles that keep their heat. We didn't realise until it came to looking at the desserts that you have to order the fondant au chocolat before the meal starts. But after a little bit of banter with the waitress this extra-bitter version of the moelleux arrived and melted like magma when we cut into it. The pain perdu with marmalade sorbet was equally good. And though it took consultations with three waiters to get a genuine wine recommendation, we were pleased with the excellent Saumur Champigny Vielles Vignes that we finally drank.

La Braisière
54 rue Cardinet, 17th (01.47.63.40.37).
Mº Malesherbes. **Open** noon-2.30pm, 7.30-10.30pm Mon-Fri; 7.30-10.30pm Sat. Closed Aug. **Average** €54. **Lunch menu** €33. **Credit** AmEx, DC, MC, V. **Wheelchair access. Map** E2.

A few doors down from the house where Claude Debussy wrote *Pelléas et Mélisande*, this rather staid patrician restaurant is very in tune with the image of the 17th arrondissement – elegant, buttoned-up and understated. On a recent lunchtime visit the warm, cosseting room was full of local couples and knowing businessmen. The saucisson and crispy biscuits immediately alerted us to the fact that someone serious was in charge of the kitchen, confirmed by two pots of meaty and highly seasoned rillettes d'oie as a pre-starter to the €33 menu. Before our first courses arrived, chef Jacques Fausset passed through the restaurant shaking hands, a nice personal touch that set us up perfectly for a rich and delicious gâteau de pommes de terre au foie gras bathing in girolle-perfumed cream, and a venaison de Colbert au foie gras – a duck terrine enriched with chunks of liver. By now we were settling down to this life of bourgeois comfort and our pleasure was confirmed by the tender pink rognons de veau served on a circle of crushed potatoes with a layer of spinach, which we enjoyed with one of the white wines of the month, a rich and vibrant St-Joseph. To finish this fine meal we opted for cheese, a plate of perfectly ripe st-nectaire accompanied by two glasses of fruity Bordeaux. If Fausset had been around in Debussy's time, the composer might not have found the will to leave the table and finish his masterpiece.

Chez Fred

190 bis bd Pereire, 17th (01.45.74.20.48). Mº Pereire or Porte Maillot. **Open** noon-2.30pm, 7-11pm Mon-Sat. Closed Christmas and New Year. **Average** €40. **Prix fixe** €30. **Credit** AmEx, MC, V. **Wheelchair access**. **Map** C2.

Chez Fred has an unprepossessing ring to it in English, but this bouchon lyonnais near the Porte Maillot is well worth a visit. The room smells inviting with a table of hors d'oeuvres, cheese and puddings to greet you on entering. There is a warm, informal atmosphere to match, with marble-topped tables and lively attentive service, obviously much appreciated by a regular business crowd at lunchtime. After some tasty saucisson, we began our meal with a classic jambon persillé, which was moist and vibrant, with fresh parsley strewn on top for extra herby effect. The homemade terrine was also a real winner, moist and rich with just the right fat content. For one of our main courses we went for the plat du jour, a petit salé aux lentilles, with a generous helping of different joints of ham on a tender yet still shapely bed of lentils. The menu lists a number of lyonnais specialities and we couldn't resist the quenelle de brochet, a giant pike-perch dumpling gently absorbing a lake of lobster sauce. It's not a light dish, but here it was unusually flavoursome and comforting. Hitting our gastronomic stride, we waddled slowly off home with a melting slice of freshly baked fig tart, and a selection of perfectly matured cheese to finish up our delightfully fruity bottle of Beaujolais.

Chez Léon

32 rue Legendre, 17th (01.42.27.06.82). Mº Villiers. **Open** noon-2pm, 7.30-10pm Mon-Fri. Closed Aug, Christmas and New Year. **Average** €35. **Prix fixe** €26. **Credit** AmEx, MC, V. **Wheelchair access**. **Non-smoking room**. **Map** E2.

From the outside this place looks rather impressive, intimidating even, with all its brass and starched napkins. Inside, you find yourself in a simple and un self-consciously old-fashioned Parisian bistro full of pullover-wearing pillars of the local community. All very untrendy and rather pleasant, especially as, exceptionally enough in the age of the euro, the prix fixe has again gone down in price. The menu includes some of the middle-class heroes of French cuisine. The homemade ham in parsley aspic, for example, was an extraordinarily savoury (if slightly rich) starter. We drank a big Languedoc red with it. It needed something lighter – a Touraine, for example – but still, it was a happy reunion with this fine Burgundian classic. Andouillette with Dijon mustard sauce and an impeccable steak-frites were the sort of thing you think you must be able to do as well at home but can't. Puddings of banana tart and apple pie were similarly irreproachable. A good place to celebrate a special occasion such as an important wedding anniversary.

Le Clou

132 rue Cardinet, 17th (01.42.27.36.78/ www.restaurant-leclou.fr). Mº Malesherbes. **Open** noon-2.30pm, 7.30-11pm Mon-Fri. Closed two weeks mid-Aug, one week at Christmas. **Average** €42.50. **Prix fixe** €30 (dinner only). **Lunch menu** €21. **Credit** AmEx, DC, MC, V. **Wheelchair access**. **Map** E1.

Though 'le clou' means 'the nail', there is nothing cobbled together about this bistro, named after its chef, Christian Leclou. It seems he has a sense of humour as he has hung his diplomas in the gents, and another proclaiming him a knight of the Rabelaisians of Chinon hidden away in the corner. Otherwise the decor is that of a good old-fashioned bistro, with lace curtains, wood and posters, and we were surprised to see a valet parking service at such an unpretentious place. On a Tuesday night after a bank holiday there weren't many people in but those who were formed fine 17th-arrondissement museum-pieces. Later, friends popped in for a drink at the bar and a group of four distinguished businessmen settled in for some wine tasting and nibbles from the mouth-watering cheeseboard. There is some wonderful food to be had here: we tasted fabulous, firm, rosy pink foie gras with thin slices of dried fig, and a black pudding and chestnut terrine, artfully presented. The dish of the day, veal in thyme jus, was a chunky cut, perfectly seared and pink in the middle, with crisp sauté potatoes and two types of mushroom. Cod on diced courgettes was disappointingly watery, however. All food products proudly bear their place of origin. Desserts lived up to the rest of the meal, with the superb combination of raspberry sorbet and chocolate moelleux, and a grandma's dessert of 'lait de la mère Lili' on a prune compote with a warm madeleine.

Goupil le Bistro
4 rue Claude Debussy, 17th (01.45.75.83.25). M° Porte Champerret. **Open** noon-2.30pm, 8-10pm Mon-Fri. Closed first three weeks in Aug. **Average** €35. **Credit** AmEx, MC, V. **Wheelchair access.** **Map** C2.
On the outer edge of the 17th, Goupil is everything you imagine a traditional French bistro to be, with its burgundy and cream colour scheme, wooden tables and chairs, bunches of flowers and scribbled blackboard menu. You picture a curly-moustached owner – yet the man behind this restaurant is a twentysomething chef who toils in an open kitchen that would look at home in a space shuttle. The short selection of dishes reflected the autumn season, with plenty of wild mushrooms and warming dishes to combat the chill in the air. The tarte fine aux maquereaux comprised fish fillets layered on buttery puff pastry topped with taste bud-tingling mustard sauce. Beetroot carpaccio with lamb's lettuce and egg mimosa again elevated its humble ingredients thanks to elegant presentation and a perfectly balanced dressing. Just as impressive was the more luxurious monkfish meunière (cooked in butter) with sautéed artichokes and chanterelles, and rounds of pork tenderloin with more chanterelles and a tiny quantity of rich potato purée. We indulged in a shared île flottante more out of curiosity than hunger, and a French school dinner staple rose to new heights.

Graindorge
15 rue de l'Arc de Triomphe, 17th (01.47.54.99.28/ www.legraindorge.free.fr). M° Charles de Gaulle Etoile. **Open** noon-2pm, 7-11pm Mon-Fri; 7-11pm Sat. Closed 1-25 Aug. **Average** €50. **Prix fixe** €32. **Lunch menu** €28. **Credit** AmEx, MC, V. **Wheelchair access. Map** C3.
This timewarp address takes a wee bit of finding. Its untrendiness is one of the best things about it, considering that chef Broux hit upon his style 15 years ago and the local clientele has remained faithful ever since. His winning combo of unflinching value, a passionate commitment to using seasonal produce and a good sprinkling of northern French and Flemish fare (waterzooï, chicory, speculoos biscuits) is irresistible. The interior is airy art deco, white doilies abundant, the silver sugar bowls overflowing and the velvet banquettes comfortable and cloisonned off for added intimacy. Although that day the Burgundy-fuelled booming voices of two local barristers caressing each others' egos were impossible to shut out, the food kept our concentration where it belonged: in our plates. The generous, just-warm asparagus was flooded with a rich, herby, eggy, buttery sauce à la flamande. The red mullet with spring vegetables was well seasoned, tender and firm and the café liégeois nicely hyped up with a foamy coffee sabayon, own-made coffee ice-

cream and caramelised rice krispies that provided a welcome crunch. Mme Broux's angelic countenance made up for the at-times detached service from the rest of the staff.

Guy Savoy
18 rue Troyon, 17th (01.43.80.40.61/ www.guysavoy.com). M° Charles de Gaulle Etoile. **Open** noon-2.30pm, 7-10.30pm Tue-Fri; 7-10.30pm Sat. **Average** €170. **Prix fixe** €230, €285. **Credit** AmEx, DC, MC, V. **Wheelchair access. Map** C3.
Be prepared to blow your salary and opt for one of the dégustation menus that allow you to try a selection of both Guy Savoy's seasonal inspirations and his personal classics. Thankfully, the sober Jean-Michel Wilmotte-designed dining rooms create a calm setting for the flurry of activity – a whirlwind of staff wielding trays, pushing trolleys and spooning sauces – though slightly brighter lighting would flatter the food more. Some of the greatest pleasures come from some of the simplest-sounding ideas, brilliantly executed, such as the tiny potato stuffed with a mushroom in a buttery froth that began the menu d'automne. We continued with a land-sea combination of mousseron mushrooms and mussels, then a pyramid of raw duck foie gras with huge shards of black truffle around a pile of leeks, bathed in truffle juice – the perforated dish subsequently lifted up to reveal the second, more robust aroma of leeks bathed in duck stock. Red mullet with barely cooked spinach and a mini aubergine followed, though it was the wafer-thin circle of buttery potato to accompany it that was a crowning moment. Another was the artichoke soup with more black truffle (a Savoy classic). Only the meat course disappointed: gamey pigeon served so rare (or, in fact, raw) that they took it back and cooked it a little more, on pumpkin dribbled with cress purée, and a spoonful of truffled mash (a gift from the 'truffle menu'). Everything comes with appropriate different breads, made by Maison Kayser in the 5th, wielded by an enthusiastic young waiter who coaxed us into sampling the colossal cheese trolley too, before another trolley intervened, laden with marshmallows, sorbets and chocolate mouse, as a prelude to the clementine in various guises – warm and spicy, jellied, caramelised and frozen in a sorbet. With the coffee and plate of tiny madeleines, we thought we had finished. Not so. An Earl Grey sorbet was so good that just when we thought we really could not eat any more… we did.

L'Huîtrier
16 rue Saussier-Leroy, 17th (01.40.54.83.44). M° Ternes. **Open** noon-2.30pm, 7-11pm Tue-Sun. Closed July, Aug, Sun in May, June and Sept. **Average** €40. **Credit** AmEx, DC, MC, V. **Map** C2.
As you'd suppose, it's oysters a go-go in this little restaurant. The narrow, nautical dining room could feel cramped were it not for its blond wood and brightly lit cream decor. The friendly staff will describe the available oysters, most of which are

La Famille. *See p103.*

from the Marennes-Oléron region, and if you think you don't like yours raw, try the poached or oven-browned versions. A dozen small fines de claires cost €16 and the spéciales are priced from €24. Our choice of six medium fines de claires cost €12 and all of them retracted when the cilia was pricked – a sure sign of freshness. You can follow these with any of several daily fish specials, such as grilled sardines or monkfish depending on the season. The wine list is decent and cheeses are from nearby Alléosse. Favoured by management types at lunchtime and local residents looking for an iodine fix at night.

Michel Rostang

20 rue Rennequin, 17th (01.47.63.40.77/
www.michelrostang.com). M° Pereire or Ternes.
Open 7.30-10.30pm Mon, Sat; 12.30-2.30pm, 7.30-10.30pm Tue-Fri. Closed first three weeks in Aug.
Average €150. **Prix fixe** €175, €275 (late Dec-late Mar truffle menu). **Lunch menu** €70.
Credit AmEx, DC, MC, V. **Wheelchair access.**
Non-smoking room. Map D2.

This is not a restaurant. It is a 'maison', a historic establishment, the flagship of the Michel Rostang fleet. And, like many French chefs of his generation, Michel Rostang needs to cling to past glory as much as he needs to leave it behind. The four dining rooms are themed according to the art or artefacts adorning their wood-encased walls. You pass by softly lit, glass-fronted, wine cellar scenes on your way to the loo and the whole place begins to feel faintly like an antechamber to Santa's grotto, a throwback to the days when eating in such restaurants was almost a holistic experience. Our starters of lobster gratin ('a family recipe') and foie gras rolled and roasted in a sesame crust, with rhubarb and Banyuls foam, exemplified how the food seems to sway between the overportioned and provincially bourgeois (aimed certainly at safeguarding a traditional clientele) and simply breathtaking. The signature poulet de Bresse had done a little too much Pilates for our taste, but puddings were glorious. They are sculptural affairs where six chocolate preparations, impossibly balanced upon each other, are described somewhat minimalistically as 'a bar', and puff pastry layers hide caramelised apple purée and the lightest ever, intensely lemony, crème pâtissière. The service is effortlessly masterful. The wines are just as they should be – prices also. Go there quickly before it all disappears.

Restaurant L'Entredgeu ★
83 rue Laugier, 17th (01.40.54.97.24). Mº Porte de Champerret. **Open** noon-2pm, 7.30-11pm Tue-Sat. Closed first three weeks in Aug. **Average** €30. **Prix fixe** €30. **Lunch menu** €22. **Credit** DC, MC, V. **Wheelchair access. Non-smoking room. Map** C2.

Warning. Reading the menu will make you doubt your capacity for pudding. Choosing between the robust dishes will have you wishing you'd gone elasticated. Have no fear. The announced heartiness belies refined, perfectly gauged cooking served in civilised portions at all three courses. We had heard reports that this neo-bistro, one of the current Parisian stars of the booming genre, was prone to overcrowding and long waits between sittings. Not on our visit. True, the service was at times bordering on clinically efficient, but at L'Entredgeu the fabulous, excellent value food is the thing. The place is brisk, well lit and full of chattering locals rejoicing in what Paris does best. It is not for lingering smoochily over barely visible plates. Anyway, you will be too busy marvelling at the sharp gribiche sauce cutting through your milky crisp battered oysters, the depth and aroma of the saffrony fish soup, the perfect layered execution of the caramelised pork belly, and the delicate desugaredness of whichever dessert you will not resist. The wine list is creative and assured. Before it arrives (and you won't wait for long), try the Alain Renardat Cerdon du Bugey, a sparkling rosé wine with hints of raspberry.

Ripaille
69 rue des Dames, 17th (01.45.22.03.03). Mº Rome. **Open** noon-2.30pm, 7.30-11pm Mon-Fri; 7-11.30pm Sat; 7.30-10.30pm Sun. **Average** €30. **Prix fixe** €23, €29. **Lunch menu** €11-€23. **Credit** AmEx, MC, V. **Wheelchair access. Map** F2.

We usually love restaurants with high ceilings and dubious art. Pocket-sized dining rooms we love also, but here the cramped tables had us handing dishes to neighbours our waiter couldn't reach. Overstretched also seemed to describe the chef, whose complicated menu had us at first disbelieving, then intrigued but ultimately disappointed. Our starter was so stodgily nondescript that we had to recheck the menu to remind ourselves what we were supposed to be eating. Frogs' legs? In a croustade? Are you sure? The fish special was fresh and properly cooked, but accompanied by the same roast white asparagus (only green asparagus roasts well) that had appeared in a starter, plus weird crunchy, greasy,

cheddary bits like those that fall from your toasted cheese and cook at the bottom of the oven. (We usually like those too.) The worst was yet to come in the form of a white chocolate ganache in carrot juice with pink grapefruit segments that was simply inedible. Perhaps it's the cheerful, chummy service, the large helpings and the truly excellent wine list, which was wonderfully explained, that keep this place completely full. Whatever it was, we just didn't understand it.

La Soupière
154 av de Wagram, 17th (01.42.27.00.73). Mº Wagram. **Open** noon-2pm, 7-11.30pm daily. **Average** €50. **Prix fixe** €31. **Credit** AmEx, DC, MC, V. **Wheelchair access. Map** D1.

For 20 years chef Christian Thuillart and his wife, Camille (who works front-of-house), have been quietly serving great food in this very bourgeois quartier. Christian's speciality is mushrooms cooked every which way (he also has a knack with black and white truffles). The restaurant's decor, however, is unremarkable. Seating just 30, its individuality comes from bland murals and a ceiling of painted clouds. In summer a few tables are set out on the shaded pavement. The set menu is not cheap: at €31 for lunch, you might expect fireworks. But we're happy to report that this is almost what we got. The warm supion salad (an infant squid) was cooked to perfection, the squid lying beneath baby salad leaves and a thick tomato coulis with slivers of fried garlic. The fricassée of wild mushrooms was similarly executed – a simple, no-nonsense presentation and totally delicious – topped with a fennel flower (there was a €6 supplement, however). The suprême de pigonneu (squab breasts) with a crust of gingerbread, baby leeks and crushed herby potatoes was, again, outstanding; and the daurade (sea bream) served with a courgette and carrot mousse, a splash of pesto, roasted mini tomatoes and baby rocket screamed 'fresh'. For dessert we had a selection of sorbets; mango, apple and lemon, and a baba with fennel ice-cream and candied fennel strips. This was an unusual tour-de-force. Our chilled red wine – a Domaine St Nicolas Reflets – was a good fruity biodynamic wine from the Vendée. Service is enthusiastic and knowledgeable, if somewhat on the garrulous side.

18TH ARRONDISSEMENT

Le Bouclard
1 rue Cavalotti, 18th (01.45.22.60.01/ www.bouclard.com). Mº Place de Clichy. **Open** noon-2.30pm, 7-10.30pm Tue-Sat. Closed Aug, Sat in July. **Average** €45. **Prix fixe** €45. **Lunch menu** €17, €20. **Credit** AmEx, MC, V. **Wheelchair access. Non-smoking room** (reservation recommended). **Map** G1.

The lardy great-grandmother of chef Michel Bonnemort lolls by her Aga in a sepia photograph, mascot of this purveyor of 'cuisine grand-mère'. The chef, when he emerges from the underground regions, is the spitting image, with a personality to match. For our money this is the perfect old-style bistro, with its tiled floor, art nouveau mirrors, wine posters, red curtains, oil lamps and a host of other assorted bric-a-brac, its buxom waitress and thin young waiter, and its fabulously calorific food. This kind of grande bouffe doesn't come cheap, and dare we say even Michel's great-gran probably didn't serve up foie gras every day, but the menu baptême offers the very pinnacles of Le Bouclard's fare including the foie gras, which would set you back €25 à la carte. Why is the latter so special? Well, it's strong-flavoured, pink and marbly and accompanied by a huge bowl of garlicky potatoes in truffle juice. The gratin d'écrevisses, equally luxurious, has lots of fleshy crayfish nestling in Mâcon blanc-laced cream. The magret de canard is a whole big breast of duck that you carve yourself, cooked to perfection with foie gras on top. But nothing could beat our rapture on tasting the saltimbocca of guinea fowl, melting with the flavours of Parma ham and garlic. Desserts, from the 'seven deadly sins', are perfect to finish a meal here as they combine cholesterol-slicing alcohols and ices. Seated in the stage-like upper enclave, we had a grand view of local bohemians carousing below and lingered until past 1am.

Café Burq

6 rue Burq, 18th (01.42.52.81.27). M° Abbesses or Blanche. **Open** 8-11.30pm Mon-Sat. **Prix fixe** €25, €29. **Credit** MC, V. **Wheelchair access** (reservation strongly recommended). **Map** H1.

An architect and an actor run this compact two-level café with no decor to speak of beyond several lighting fixtures made from orange Plexiglas. They've made it such a febrile success that the good-natured waiters always seem perilously close to letting the whole place slip completely out of control. Not ideal for a tranquil tête-à-tête, but very much a happy, happening pre-club launch pad with a group of friends, this place is all about a bawdy, smoky good time. Surprisingly, given such anarchic circumstances, the food is quite good and very reasonably priced (though if you arrive too late there is a chance it will have completely run out). From the blackboard menu, go with starters such as baked camembert with salad or a delicious chicken breast salad in a ginger-and-soy sauce vinaigrette, and then opt for an onglet with red onion-and-balsamic sauce or maybe the lamb shoulder or roast salmon. All mains come with delicious mash. The wine list is intelligent, if veering towards rather high-octane bottles; the Beaumes de Venise clocked in at a hefty 14%. Desserts are excellent too – try the chocolate quenelles. A great snapshot of the new energy in Montmartre.

Chez Toinette ★

20 rue Germain-Pilon, 18th (01.42.54.44.36/ www.chez-toinette.com). M° Abbesses. **Open** 7.15-11pm Mon-Sat. Closed Aug. **Average** €26. **Credit** MC, V. **Wheelchair access.** **Map** H2.

This stalwart purveyor of bistro fare in a side street behind the Théâtre de Montmartre has increased its prices in line with its burgeoning success. The blackboard menu is still, however, good value in an area notorious for tourist rip-offs. Squeezing into the seats at our table, we were immediately set at ease by the amiable waiter, who described each dish with pride, and then presented us with an appetiser of olives, ripe cherry tomatoes and crisp radishes. From the starters, try the red-blooded wild boar terrine, the pleasing chèvre chaud with a glorious creamy st-marcellin on a bed of roquette and lettuce, or the soufflé-like asparagus quiche. This is something of a red meat emporium with a string of toothy carnivorous mains including mignon de porc, spring lamb and assorted steaks, with only the occasional fish dish. We opted for one of each; the lamb seared in rosemary was a delicious lean morsel, while the simple and elegant John Dory was accompanied by an effective combination of fluffy mash and steamed vegetables. Desserts mainly cover standard ground of crème brûlée and chocolate mousse, so instead we rounded with the alcoholic option of Armagnac-steeped prunes.

L'Entracte

44 rue d'Orsel, 18th (01.46.06.93.41). M° Abbesses or Anvers. **Open** noon-2pm, 7-10.30pm Wed-Sat; noon-2pm Sun. Closed Aug, one week at Christmas. **Average** €30. **Credit** AmEx, MC, V. **Map** J2.

In a road filled with trendy boutiques, how nice it is to find a restaurant that retains an atmosphere of old Montmartre. Owner Gilles Chiriaux is proud to be the second generation to run this cosy bistro, with the most enormous bouquet of flowers on the bar. The names of Carlos and Sonia, his parents, still adorn the plates, and the walls are filled with paintings and framed photos of local celebrities such as the drag queen Michou. The welcome from Gilles and his assistant Alain could not have been warmer, although they seemed surprised that newcomers such as us should walk through the door. 'All these people are our friends,' they said, indicating the convivial group of 15 or so people crammed into the front section. The food is old-fashioned, but lovingly prepared, consisting of mainly meat dishes with a special of skate with capers that our neighbours, a glamorous lady in a fur coat and her date, urged us to try. The delicious-sounding mackerel marinated in white wine was off the menu so we contented ourselves with fresh sardines and oeufs en meurette. The skate wing was indeed dramatic and we tried to imagine the size of the whole fish that this fleshy morsel came from. Both it and the veal in the style of Michou were in an overwhelmingly buttery sauce that was tempered somewhat by the hand-cut frites, a true pleasure. Desserts are unremarkable, though Spanish strawberries in March were surprisingly flavourful, and our St-Joseph served chilled proved to be a supremely good choice.

La Famille

41 rue des Trois-Frères, 18th (01.42.52.11.12).
M° Abbesses. **Open** 8-11.30pm Tue-Sat. **Average**
€35. **Prix fixe** €29, €35. **Credit** AmEx, DC, MC, V.
Map H1.

Inaki Aizpitarte's successor, Bruno Viala, is
continuing the tradition of food with attitude in his
own tongue-in-cheek style at this hip Montmartre
neo-bistro. This results in some hits and some
misses. The amuse-bouche of green fish roe with a
shot glass of watery jus was far from appetising, but
soon the polished starters arrived. Homemade foie
gras terrine fell into sublime chunks, accompanied
by apple sorbet, apple slices and dabs of balsamic
reduction, while raw salmon coated in thyme and
rosemary was served, as on a palette, with spicy
tomato sorbet, red pepper slivers and tiny bunches
of basil. The special of roasted whole sea bass in
black olive tapenade tasted delicious though the
bones made eating fiddly (the result of too long in
the oven or inexpert dissection by the waiter?).
Ginger-coated cod 'nuggets' went well with their
crisp fennel salad, but the joke of serving them in
polystyrene boxes didn't seem that funny when we
thought about the ozone layer. We'd still come back,
though, as the ambience is great. We loved sitting
up at the bar, next to the owner and his cousin,
and the pretty, minimalist decor and attractive
staff add to its appeal. Girls: if you like to watch a
man potter around in the kitchen, you'll love the
sexy waiter who flambées bananas on a small red
table in a pastiche of brasserie pomp. This and the
'sweet sushi' that came with dabs of ginger paste
were a success.

Histoire De

14 rue Ferdinand Flocon, 18th (01.42.52.24.60).
M° Jules Joffrin. **Open** noon-2pm, 7.30-11pm
Mon-Sat. **Average** €32. **Lunch menu** €29.
Credit MC, V.

For the past two years, a new fusion-influenced chef
has been reviving the tired cuisine at this once-
fabulous place behind Sacré Coeur. The clientele
is a mix of locals and folks from nearby hotels and
the food is also a mix, from classics such as huge
mackerel fillets on a bed of carrots to a 'trio' of duck
preparations (confit, forcemeat-stuffed with cabbage
and rare, crisp-skinned breast, seeing as you ask) as
well as plenty of beef, veal and fish dishes. Wines
are affordable – another bonus. This is an ideal
safe harbour as you descend from the upper end
of Montmartre, with its charming vineyard, towards
the Métro station.

La Mascotte

52 rue des Abbesses, 18th (01.46.06.28.15/
www.la-mascotte-montmartre.com). M° Abbesses.
Open noon-3pm, 7pm-midnight Mon-Fri; noon-
midnight Sat; 11am-midnight Sun. **Credit** AmEx,
DC, MC, V. **Map** H1.

The food at this Montmartre brasserie is quite
unremarkable; the atmosphere, on the other hand,
offers a real slice of old Paris in an area that is
increasingly trendy and faddish. Gnarl-faced
drinkers, chain-smoking ladies wearing vintage
Sonia Rykiel, cigar-chomping gents and eccentrics
of all kinds people the brown and cream art deco
interior at all hours. Lobsters await their fate on
death row in a tank. The waiters are antiques, with
manners to match, bustling around a wooden
dresser with napkin compartments. Out front, in
season, is the oyster stand, and a few of these
bivalves with a glass of chilled Sancerre makes a
good winter cheerer. Otherwise, there is a limited-
choice prix fixe and an à la carte list of everything
you'd expect from a brasserie. Our starters of lobster
bisque and courgette risotto were rather tasteless.
Scorpion fish was better, accompanied by spicy
chorizo and red peppers. A nice Pouilly Fumé
was good value at €25. They do a strong line in
alcoholic puddings – flambéed crêpes, vodka-
drenched sorbets and, in our case, Cognac-poached
strawberries that even a notorious boozer declared
to be 'a bit much'. On Sundays from 11am the street
market invades the bar with an accordionist and
local characters such as drag queen Michou.

Aux Négociants

27 rue Lambert, 18th (01.46.06.15.11). M° Château
Rouge. **Open** noon-2.30pm, 8-10.30pm Mon-Fri.
Closed Aug. **Average** €24. **Credit** AmEx, MC, V.
Map J1.

Ah, now you know why you came to Paris! Little
bistros like this, like the superb papeterie next door,
are getting rarer by the year, but at the Négociants
the ceiling just gets a little browner, the patron a
little balder and the menu a little porkier as time goes
by. This restaurant not only boasts a handsome,
horseshoe-shaped bar, but people actually stand
there, drink wine and read the newspaper while
you're eating. How authentic is that? And the food
is absolutely worthy of the place. We enjoyed
a couple of faultless starters: pork rillettes, and
herring fillets with onion, juniper berries and warm
potatoes. Although the cooking leans towards Lyon,
the blackboard wine menu is quite ecumenical,
with what looked like considered and dependable
choices from all around France. As we forked our
way happily through the day's specials of stuffed
cabbage and sabodet dauphinois (a big sausage with
pistachio nuts), we sloshed down a bottle and a bit
of light, fresh and gently priced Côte Roannaise
(Loire Valley). It was getting towards siesta time as
we ambled towards afters and there was nothing left
but chocolate mousse. As disappointments go, this
we could cope with.

La Table Dancourt

4 rue Dancourt, 18th (01.42.52.03.98). M° Anvers
or Pigalle. **Open** noon-2.30pm, 7.15-11pm Tue-Sat;
noon-2.30pm Sun. **Average** €38. **Lunch menu** €25.
Credit MC, V. **Map** J2.

Located on one of Montmartre's busiest tourist
streets, this bistro doubling as a contemporary art
gallery provides a surprising haven amid the T-shirt
and bag shops. But its clients are hardly tired

backpackers – the dining room attracts locals who live or work nearby and know good food when it appears in their quartier. Choose from a wide selection of terrines or foie gras as starters and a variety of winning mains, such as perfectly cooked suckling pig served with an aubergine timbale, and what was called beef tartare but in reality was beef carpaccio atop a mound of shoestring potatoes. Service is unhurried, pleasant and welcoming. The wine list (a work in progress) is, even at this point, bold and comprehensive.

Le Wepler

14 pl de Clichy, 18th (01.45.22.53.24/www. wepler.com). M° Place de Clichy. **Open** 8am-1am daily. **Average** €40. **Prix fixe** €25. **Lunch menu** €16. **Credit** AmEx, DC, MC, V. **Non-smoking room. Map** G2.
Among the fast food joints on place de Clichy stands the brasserie Le Wepler. A Paris institution, it started serving oysters to the likes of Picasso, Modigliani and Apollinaire in 1892, and some old photographs on the walls give an idea of what the place would have been like in its heyday. The food, apart from the super-fresh seafood, is unremarkable. We started with a shared plate of voluptuous assorted oysters. A nicely cooked swordfish steak on a bed of cabbage, and a crispy pig's trotter with béarnaise sauce followed. But the chips, described on the menu as 'frites fraîches', were soggy. The wine, a white Burgundy, was reasonably priced at €8.80 for a 50cl carafe. For dessert the crêpes Suzette were zesty, while the assiette piña colada did not live up to its exotic name. Although the people-watching was a little disappointing on a Saturday lunchtime, the waiters were friendly, and this would be the perfect place for anyone suffering from an attack of the midnight oyster munchies.

19TH ARRONDISSEMENT

A la Bière

103 av Simon Bolivar, 19th (01.42.39.83.25). M° Colonel Fabien. **Open** 7am-3pm, 5pm-12.30am daily. **Prix fixe** €12.30. **Credit** DC, MC, V. **Map** M3.
In the previous edition of this guide we wrote 'This is one of the few bargains left in Paris – let's hope it stays that way'. So far, so good. Keeping pace with inflation, the prix fixe has gone up by 50 cents for the same quality. On a hill leading up to the Buttes Chaumont, it's always filled with locals, with some particularly eccentric characters to be found at the bar. The young son of the family that runs it was training a new waitress the day we visited, and he's a fine example to follow. When our cack-handedness with the snail tool caused a mollusc to fly across the room, spraying garlic sauce over people's heads, he mimicked a goalie and laughed, 'Last time that happened, I caught it!' Later on, he told the waitress not to start packing away as it was only midnight. Our other homely starter of warm herring with

boiled potatoes was satisfying, followed by escalope de veau sauce normande and saumon à l'oseille. The veal was served in a not-too-creamy mushroom sauce, with lots of hand-cut chips and green beans; the salmon equally complemented by its sorrel sauce and fresh parsley, though disappointingly served with tagliatelle rather than vegetables. Crusty country baguette accompanies every meal. The own-made desserts are well worth having – a rich crème brûlée with caramel sauce at the bottom, and a lovely slice of tarte Tatin. The pinot noir wine of the month went down very smoothly with this traditional fare. On Fridays and Saturdays there is live music.

Au Boeuf Couronné ★

188 av Jean-Jaurès, 19th (01.42.39.54.54/www.au-boeuf-couronne.com). M° Porte de Pantin. **Open** noon-3pm, 7pm-midnight daily. **Average** €50. **Prix fixe** €32. **Credit** AmEx, DC, MC, V. **Wheelchair access.**
The crowned king of meaty brasseries pulls in an old-school crowd that would be at home in a Claude Chabrol film: wealthy businessmen, ladies of a certain age (these two had a whole bottle of whisky on their table as they sat conspiratorially side by side), an aristocratic-looking man with his daughter. What are they doing in the working-class 19th arrondissement? These dedicated carnivores must be in the know, because the Boeuf Couronné is the last vestige of the old meat district that all but disappeared when La Villette became the science and music complex it is today (keep your autograph book handy as performers from the latter often eat here). Everything is authentic about this brasserie, from the oak dresser with its baguette compartment to the prettily uniformed waitresses and the menu, which features such bygone specialities as tête de veau vieille France and os à moelle. Like most of the diners, we went for the latter as a starter and it was gargantuan: three marrowbones whose squelchy contents were enhanced by the sel de Guérande and black pepper served on the side. The snails were prime specimens too: large, garlicky and meaty. Give yourself a good three or four hours here – the steaks are beyond belief. The 340g Irish entrecôte was pure heaven, served with pommes soufflées (like little Yorkshire puddings) and thankfully some refreshing watercress, while the chunks of tête de veau were incredibly fresh with their ravigote sauce (a vinaigrette of onions, capers, shallots and parsley). A half-bottle of 1999 Château Rose du Pont Médoc is a good choice if you're going for wine in moderation. Then we stumbled on the pudding zenith of our Paris eating days: a soufflé glacé flavoured with Grand Marnier, with a crème brûlée top and biscuit crust, surrounded by raspberry coulis and accompanied by a 'verre Nicole', a tiny glass of the orange liqueur. It's a shame, however, that cigar smokers aren't encouraged to retire to the dedicated fumoir as the pungent stink may spoil your meal.

La Boulangerie. *See p106.*

La Cave Gourmande

10 rue du Général Brunet, 19th (01.40.40.03.30).
M° Botzaris. **Open** noon-2pm, 7-11pm Mon-Fri.
Prix fixe €36. **Lunch menu** €31. **No credit
cards. Wheelchair access. Non-smoking**.
Mark Singer doesn't take credit cards and English
speakers sometimes get a frosty reception. For
all that, it's worth making the trip to the Buttes
Chaumont to try his sublime food. The deal is
a three-course seasonal menu with changing plats
du jour and an optional cheese course. You can't
have fewer than three courses and dessert must be
ordered at the outset. Singer has a talent to make
even dishes that sound heavy turn out to be light.
Foie gras and oreille de cochon metamorphosed into
a heavenly mini soufflé with tiny crackling of the
pig's ear; a 'croquant' of prawns in a Thai-inspired
broth came with the unnecessary embellishment of
a bouillon served in an eggshell with a straw.
Sauvageon (the issue of a farmed duck impregnated
in a flying swoop by a wild one) came as a leg stuffed
with foie gras and as a pink magret, with tiny cubed
apple pieces and spring onion. The 'bonbon' is one
of Singer's trademarks: a Christmas cracker of flaky
pastry filled sometimes with beef, sometimes with
lamb. Of the desserts, the banana number was quite
the best thing we'd seen done with this everyday
fruit: wrapped, again, in pastry, with almonds, coffee
ice-cream and a small pot of melted, creamed
Carambar. The Sierra du Sud Côtes du Rhône was
a real discovery, though as on a previous visit we
were left to pour our own wine. The clients tend to
be older, or foodie couples with babysitters booked
for the night. English-speaking gourmands should
not be put off – sooner or later Singer will realise
that some of us do appreciate good food.

Restaurant L'Hermès

23 rue Mélingue, 19th (01.42.39.94.70).
M° Pyrénées. **Open** noon-2pm, 7.30-10.30pm
Tue, Thur-Sat; 7.30-10.30pm Wed. Closed Aug.
Average €33. **Prix fixe** €28. **Lunch menu**
€14.50. **Credit** MC, V. **Wheelchair access**.
Non-smoking room. Map D3.
Just north of the Pyrenees, literally and in terms of
its cuisine (it is hidden between the Buttes Chaumont
and Pyrénées Métro), is this neighbourhood secret
worth discovering. Yellow walls, Mediterranean
checked tablecloths and oil paintings of vegetables
make for a welcoming atmosphere, and the friendly
staff are passionate about south-western cuisine.
The prix fixe changes weekly and the à la carte
fortnightly, so seasonal produce is much in evidence,
such as the reinette apples and wild mushrooms of
our early autumn visit. There is also a luxury plat
on offer for gourmands – on that day a civet de lièvre
à la royale (stuffed with foie gras) for the princely
sum of €35, and a cassoulet. From the €28 prix
fixe, all three daily specials proved good – a salad
of marinated squid with a hint of aniseed came
with unusual green lentil quenelles; the 'jolie gigue
de lapereau' with prunes and a jus de grenache

was delicious, and the strawberry cake was perfect
with its kiwi coulis. From the carte, the starter of
aumônière de langoustines au foie gras de canard
et Noilly Prat was almost haute cuisine, tenderly
wrapped in its brik parcel with fabulous flavours
within. The main dish of Gascon porc à la paysanne
(topped with grilled cheese) was rather mundane,
though we liked the omelette aux fines herbes,
pommes dauphines and carrot purée that
accompanied it, and rejoiced in the choice of a honey-
and cinnamon-drizzled croustillant de reines de
reinette to finish. Wines are chosen with equal care
– our half-bottle of Domaine Lerys Fitou (€12) was
robust and flavoursome, and the house aperitif of
citrus-spiked wine is a real taste of the country. Be
sure to book as there is a policy of one sitting of
diners per table per night.

20TH ARRONDISSEMENT

Le Baratin

3 rue Jouye Rouve, 20th (01.43.49.39.70).
M° Pyrénées. **Open** 12.15-3pm, 8-11pm Tue-
Fri; 8-11pm Sat. **Average** €30. **Lunch menu** €14.
Credit DC, MC, V. **Map** N3.
This bistro wins the best-value-for-money prize for
a place few people will ever venture to. Way up the
Belleville hill, it's been here for 20 years, run by
a warm Portuguese-born cook and her wine-
obsessed partner. At lunch, the unprepossessing
menu with starters of soup, salad and terrines looks
standard – until you sample the exquisite quality of
the raw wild salmon and chicken. Then we had
carefully sourced, perfectly cooked and plated
monkfish and lamb, each with intense sauces that
we sopped up with bread. Last came a well-matured
brie and prunes in red wine, which we combined
for a successful 'one plus one equals ten' result.
Beware, though: Le Baratin has suddenly become
the darling of the French press, with the result that
it's always crowded.

La Boulangerie

15 rue des Panoyaux, 20th (01.43.58.45.45).
M° Ménilmontant. **Open** noon-2pm, 8-11pm
Mon-Sat. **Average** €34. **Prix fixe** €28.
Credit AmEx, DC, MC, V. **Map** P4.
On the face of it, there were many faults with
our meal here: three fish dishes were off the menu;
our wine tasted odd; and the hampe de boeuf was
distinctly tough. Yet, we left feeling fulfilled and
happy, and will probably return. It's the service
that does it. When we asked for a second opinion
on the Philippe Jambon Baltailles Beaujolais we
had ordered the jolly and charming manager
explained this small producer wine was an acquired
taste, that the waitress should have warned us, and
immediately offered to change it simply because we
didn't like it. In the end we opted to have it decanted.
Certain wines are offered 'au compteur' (you pay for
only what you drink), and homemade rabbit rillettes
came to the table while we awaited our food. The

dried goose magret on just-cooked spring vegetables was a success, the healthiness of crisp slivers of carrots and courgettes providing carte blanche to enjoy the cholesterol-filled magret. In place of the papaya and seafood salad they provided cod rillettes topped with slices of waxy new potatoes with pesto, which was actually very good. A duck cassoulet that we'd reluctantly ordered as the fish dishes were off turned out to be pleasantly light as it didn't include beans but was stewed with Chinese cabbage and galangal. The beef, a difficult cut, was nevertheless enhanced by its topping of red onion confit and delicious potato cake. The own-made macaroons are always a good bet, and the tarte Tatin, served cold, was moist and citrussy. If there are risks in the wine and food, one always has the impression that what is served up is done with care, and you'll pass a very pleasant evening in picture-postcard bistro surroundings with a relaxed crowd of bon vivants.

Le Casque d'Or

pl Maurice Chevalier, 20th (01.43.58.37.09).
M° Couronnes or Ménilmontant. **Open** 8pm-
midnight Wed-Fri; noon-midnight Sat, Sun.
Average €28. **Credit** AmEx, DC, MC, V. **Map** P4.
This restaurant dedicated to the Auvergne region of central France has moved to a pretty address on place Maurice Chevalier, beneath the immense neo-Gothic pile of Notre-Dame-de-la-Croix: birdsong, greenery and a tiny, warm-hearted neighbourhood bistro, just off boulevard de Ménilmontant. Our hearty Sunday lunch of Auvergnat specialities included the unappetisingly named sac d'os ('bag o'bones'), a rare speciality that's handmade by one Monsieur Mas in the village of Le Rouget. Knuckles of salt pork were tightly bundled into a haggis-like caul, pot-roasted and served in an earthenware terrine dish (for two people). The result was moist, melting and richly flavoured, with just a hint of tripe, but disappointingly served with dryish plain boiled potatoes (no butter). We couldn't help but eye our companions' aligot (a superb amalgam of smooth mashed potato and Auvergnat cheese) with envy, and relished a taste of their meats: delicious honey-roast ribs of suckling pig, and succulent chunks of lean beef. A bottle of organic Gamay from noted Vendée winemaker Thierry Michon went down a treat, and the desserts were unexceptionable: a fine apple tart, slabs of chocolate fondant, and an iron pot of fromage blanc with golden plum coulis.

En Colimaçon (Ma Pomme)

107 rue de Ménilmontant, 20th (01.40.33.10.40/
www.encolimacon.com). M° Ménilmontant. **Open**
5pm-2am Mon, Sat; noon-2pm, 5pm-2am Tue-Fri;
some Sun with music. Closed mid-July to mid-Aug.
Average €25. **Prix fixe** €21. **Lunch menu** €10.
Credit DC, MC, V. **Map** P4.
Pierre has given up trying to convince people his restaurant is called En Colimaçon – they just kept on referring to is as Ma Pomme and the business

card now surreally translates as 'the spiralling apple'. The spiral staircase in the corner is indeed handsome, as is the spacious room, with its red velvet seats, contemporary wrought-iron chandeliers and changing art on the walls. After four years this café-bistro has now hit its stride and the three-course prix fixe is great value. The room was empty at 9.30pm, full an hour later with groups and couples in their 30s, bobo (bohemian bourgeois) to the core but not pretentious. Everything is good and there is plenty of choice for vegetarians, fish and meat eaters with a Basque slant to the cuisine. The scallops in an orange sauce with black rice, adorned with rose petals, was well worth splashing out on à la carte, and squid baked with sausage was also tasty. A perfectly pink magret de canard was served in a black cherry sauce that did not overwhelm the duck, and vegetable ravioli, just a tad overcooked but with lashings of sliced parmesan, was a noble effort on the veggie front. The tarte Tatin reminded us how wonderful this pudding can be. There's a flambée version à la carte, as well as alcoholic sorbets, while the prix fixe includes interesting variants on standards such as a tarte au chocolat flavoured with Espelette pepper and ginger. It's always worth lingering in the bar area at the front, where an arty Ménilmontant crowd hangs out, for a digestif.

Le Zéphyr ★

1 rue du Jourdain, 20th (01.46.36.65.81).
M° Jourdain. **Open** 10am-2am daily. **Average**
€50. **Credit** AmEx, DC, MC, V. **Map** P3.
With drop-dead gorgeous decor, staff and clientele, the Zéphyr is the pinnacle of 20th arrondissement style in a quartier that is fast becoming a very in place to live. You will swoon over the art deco surroundings, with painted panels, mirrors and engraved glass, candlelit in the evenings and with a sweet zinc bar and terrace for an aperitif. On the night that we visited a sophisticated 'Cointreaupolitan' was the cocktail maison, which gave us time to peruse the blackboard. Foie gras is a speciality, and between the foie gras mi-cuit served with mango chutney in a preserving jar and the foie gras du jour, marbled with asparagus and heightened by dabs of piquant sauce, the former was the tastier. As we ate, delicious aromas wafted across from the burning sprig of thyme that accompanied the souris d'agneau in its flavoursome reduction. The contrasting seafood salad was a gargantuan plate filled with luscious gambas, moules, roast vegetables with real flavour and leaves, topped with a skewer of grilled prawns. We decided to eschew the joint plate 'tout chocolaté' in favour of a moelleux each, accompanied by slim glasses of Cognac granita, which ably cut through the rich and unadulterated chocolate. It is hard to get out of here for less than €100 not including the pricey drinks (a trolley of aged Cognacs was hard to resist), but, believe us, it really was a fabulous meal in a glamorous and sexy atmosphere.

Fashion

The Costes brothers have set the standard for cool in Paris with ever-fashionable haunts such as Hôtel Costes, Le Georges, Café Marly (*see p166* **Cafés, Bars & Pubs**) and La Grande Armée (*see p94* **French**). Expect stunning-looking staff, enviable locations (the top of the Pompidou Centre is hard to beat) and food that doesn't take itself too seriously. Costes aside, the area around the Champs-Elysées is the place to see pumped-up lips and St-Tropez tans, with Black Calvados being the latest new restaurant to attract a glam Parisian crowd. The opening of the furiously trendy Hôtel Amour in a sleepy part of the 9th arrondissement and the Kube (*see p189* **Cafés, Bars & Pubs**) in the far reaches of the 18th suggests that fashion no longer knows any boundaries in Paris.

Hôtel Costes

239 rue St-Honoré, 1st (01.42.44.50.25/ www.hotelcostes.com). M° Concorde or Tuileries. **Open** 11.30am-1am daily. **Average** €80. **Credit** AmEx, DC, MC, V. **Non-smoking room. Map** G5.
Doing dinner at Hôtel Costes is almost a cliché. This place has defined cool chic for so long that if you've ever been before you know exactly what to expect, and if you haven't you can probably imagine. Posse of scary looking doormen? Check. Snippy maître d'? Check. Sulky coat girl? Check. Unutterably sexy interior? Check. For us familiarity breeds content, which is why we don't mind that Costes' menu never seems to change. Tomates mozza, club sandwiches, signature penne and, for the serious abstainers, a plate of steamed veg. Not subscribing to that school of thought, we went for the chicken nems and carpaccio as starters. Working on the principle that food in a Costes restaurant is generally perfectly acceptable – no more, no less – we were shocked by the sauce on the carpaccio. We could make out ginger, shallot, garlic, coriander, lemongrass and parmesan, but mostly it tasted like spicy mothballs. We fared better with the mains: the grilled chicken with potato purée was exactly what we expected and the burger better than average. Fortunately, we speak fluent Costese so were able to translate aller-retour PP9 to rare burger and chips. The point about the food here is that it's not the point. The Hôtel Costes continues to offer glamour in spades, so if you're looking for a little bit of fabulous, get dressed up, book a terrace table and gawk at the gorgeous people.

Le Murano

13 bd du Temple, 3rd (01.42.71.20.00/www. muranoresort.com). M° Filles du Calvaire. **Open** noon-3pm, 8-10.30pm Mon-Thur, Sun; noon-3pm, 8pm-midnight Fri, Sat. **Average** €60. **Lunch menu** €26-€33. **Credit** AmEx, DC, MC, V. **Wheelchair access. Non-smoking room.** Non-smoking for Sunday brunch. **Map** L5.

The real surprise at this ultra-fashionable restaurant in the pompously named Murano Urban Resort is the quality of the contemporary French cooking by a team of young chefs. Cranberry velvet upholstered chairs and banquettes punctuate an all-white space, and a DJ spins bouncy lounge music. As we eyed up the menu, we ogled the *Ab Fab* crowd, which often seemed a parody of itself. The menu, which changes regularly, runs from calorie-conscious dishes such as quinoa salad to more sophisticated choices, such as roast sea bass with sweet Cévennes onions and three-pepper mousse. Herb risotto with sesame-coated prawns was delicious, as was a generous sauté of girolles. Mains were excellent too, including a smoked salmon steak with potato waffles and an interesting cranberry crème fraîche garnish. We decided to live large and pay €7 for a side of 'hay-cooked potatoes', which turned out to be a good but stingily served mash in a potato-shaped vessel of hardened hay. Reine claude plums in a salted caramel sauce were a superb dessert and, aside from the high-attitude service and a miserably overpriced wine list, the Murano offers a fun night out.

Curieux Spaghetti Bar

14 rue St-Merri, 4th (01.42.72.75.97/www. curieuxspag.com). M° Hôtel de Ville or Rambuteau. **Open** noon-midnight daily. Closed 25 Dec. **Average** €20. **Lunch menu** €12. **Credit** AmEx, MC, V. **Wheelchair access. Non-smoking room** (lunchtimes only). **Map** K6.
Curious, perhaps, but very clever, this restaurant with a strategic location between Les Halles and Le Marais is pulling hungry young hordes, including a pre-clubbing crowd, with its amusing decor, easy prices and tasty high-carb menu. The walls are papered with Michelin maps of Italy, crystal chandeliers illuminate the crowd at the long red bar, and waiters with low-riding jeans swivel around the room serving a mostly but not exclusively male crowd. A nice mix of lounge and house music puts

everyone in a good-time groove, and the cheap house wines and generously served spaghetti do the rest. The namesake pasta comes in two portion sizes: assiette (plate) or marmite (casserole), and for an idea of how generously served the latter is, the menu also notes that you can request a 'spaghetti bag' to take home your leftovers. If you're ravenous, start with bruschetta such as mortadella with capers or the pleasant mozzarella with pesto sauce, and then bag your spag as a classic with marinara sauce and deliciously garlicky meatballs. For something lighter, try the popular grilled chicken breast strips with lemon-herb sauce. If you're feeling sloppy or are wearing a white shirt, you can don a paper bib.

Georges

Centre Pompidou, 6th floor, rue Rambuteau, 4th (01.44.78.47.99). M° Rambuteau. **Open** noon-1am Mon, Wed-Sun. **Average** €70. **Credit** AmEx, DC, MC, V. **Wheelchair access. Map** K5.
The first thing you need to know about Georges is how to actually get there. There's no point seeking out the special lift at the front of the Centre Pompidou – find the escalator on the left and enjoy the ride through the transparent tube. The second thing to know about Georges is that the service can be somewhat glacial. Be prepared and go with it, because – maybe because of that froideur – this place is still seriously cool. And if that's not what grabs you, then think location, location, location. The food is the same-old same-old Costes brothers fare that's hard to get excited about. But the view over Paris is equally hard to ignore. Despite the designer interior (complete with weird aluminium pods), Georges is really all about the terrace. Book a table at sunset, drink cocktails (including a very good Cosmopolitan), tuck into California rolls, tuna tartare or avocado and crab salad to start and enjoy the snob value in ordering le tigre qui pleure as a main. We've never yet got a convincing explanation as to why anyone would want to call a steak a crying tiger, so we have to assume that it's simply to fox outsiders. A stunning address.

Black Calvados ★

40 av Pierre 1er de Serbie, 8th (01.47.20.77.77/ www.bc-paris.fr). M° Iéna. **Open** 8pm-3.30am Mon-Sat. Closed 6-20 Aug. **Average** €60. **Credit** AmEx, MC, V. **Map** D4.
Strangely named for anyone who doesn't know the Serge Gainsbourg song *On va a la Calvados ce soir* (1960), from which the phrase was borrowed, this black-lacquered dining room with many mirrors has become the new haunt for the city's fashion crowd. Aside from its strategic location in the heart of the Golden Triangle, where many of the fashion houses have their headquarters, the creator of this sizzling new address is Alexandre de Betak, who has decorated and directed runway shows for Dior, Viktor & Rolf and various other designers, working with Soundgarden frontman Chris Cornell. So yes, that probably is John Galliano sitting across the room, and that's doubtless Carine Roitfeld (editor of

Café de l'Homme. *See p112.*

French *Vogue*, darling) next to them. Oh, and the food – think modish fashion fodder, including the inevitable rocket salad, steaks and sole, plus a few original twists such as Kobe beef mini burgers, truffle-laced macaroni and cheese and lobster rolls. It's all very twee – and quite tasty – just don't forget to ditch the jeans and dress in black if you want to get past wardrobe patrol at the door.

Le Buddha Bar

8 rue Boissy d'Anglas, 8th (01.53.05.90.00/ www.buddha-bar.com). M° Concorde. **Open** noon-3pm, 7pm-12.30am Mon-Thur, Sun; noon-3pm, 7pm-midnight Fri, Sat. Closed at lunch first three weeks in Aug. **Average** €60. **Prix fixe** €60-€80. **Credit** AmEx, MC, V. **Wheelchair access. Map** F4.
You may want to invest in a pair of night-vision goggles before dinner at Buddha Bar. We're all in favour of low lighting, and we would like to be able to say that practically pitch-black makes for easy seduction, but the truth is that squinting is not a good look. Once our eyes adjusted, though, we were reminded just how stunning this place is. The giant shiny Buddha, the beautiful (if inefficient) red velvet chandeliers, the dramatic staircase, dark wood and whole exotic Asia vibe really is magnificent. The room was full of business diners and second daters

and it's easy to see why. Buddha Bar impresses. From a menu full of fusion we chose sushi and a salad to start and seared tuna and curried prawns as mains. And here's the surprise – the food was very good. The Buddha Bar rolls – a combo of spicy tuna, salmon, avocado and cucumber – were deliciously zingy and a salad of calamari and noodles surprisingly hearty. The sesame-crusted tuna was perfectly cooked and the plump gambas came with a delicious creamy sauce. All in all, a winner. Our only gripe was with the barmaid, who waltzed off with our change and avoided all attempts at eye contact thereafter.

Maison Blanche

15 av Montaigne, 8th (01.47.23.55.99/www.maison-blanche.fr). M° Alma-Marceau. **Open** noon-1.45pm, 8-10.45pm Mon-Fri; 8-9.30pm Sat; 8-10.45pm Sun. **Average** €100. **Lunch menu** €45. **Credit** AmEx, MC, V. **Wheelchair access**. **Map** D5.

For Thanksgiving we treated ourselves to lunch at the Maison Blanche as a witty nod towards our American cousins. The Pourcel brothers from Montpellier were seemingly oblivious of the holiday, or was that creamy pumpkin and chestnut appetiser a coded acknowledgement? The sleek rooftop restaurant with its spectacular view over Paris was packed with a business clientele for lunch. Little cheese gougères augured well for our starters of lobster tail salad with violet potatoes, and a winning dish of crayfish and veal sweetbreads with a pot of frothy cappuccino de cèpes. There is rather too much frothing and moussing in the Pourcel world, and asceticism seems to replace strong flavours. A main course of partridge was paintably displayed, but the promised sauce poivrade was thin on the plate. Sole fillets came interleaved with slivers of foie gras, and jambon de boeuf was accompanied by a rich purée of chestnuts – luxury comfort food, but lacking punch. Puddings included delicious raspberry- and chocolate-filled nems. Service was impeccable, as it should be when the bill is well over €100 per person.

Man Ray (Mandalaray)

34 rue Marbeuf, 8th (01.56.88.36.36/www. mandalaray.com). M° Franklin D Roosevelt. **Open** 7pm-midnight daily. Closed 24 Dec. **Average** €46. **Prix fixe** €35. **Credit** AmEx MC, V. **Wheelchair access**. **Map** D4.

Sliding down the snaking staircases of this perennially hip restaurant, one cannot help but feel fabulous. The cavernous space has the look of a 21st-century opium den, glowing with red lights and pumping with house music. A mezzanine bar horseshoes around the whole operation, providing an ideal lookout over the beautiful people below. Perhaps not surprisingly, the food seems a bit of an afterthought. The menu offers some very respectable, if pricey, sushi and sashimi platters, as well as a selection of caviars for the big rollers. The alternative 'seasonal menu', however, dips into the mediocre. We were presented with unremarkable and diminutive portions of sea scallops with

caramelised endives, and steak with a béarnaise sauce that, to all appearances, had been meted out into its little glass cup hours before arriving at our table. Having turned up towards the tail end of dinner service, we watched as the battalion of black-clad servers was replaced by a white-clad battalion, who would guide Man Ray – no longer restaurant, but nightclub – through to the dawn. And this, really, is what this place does best.

Sens par la Compagnie des Comptoirs

23 rue de Ponthieu, 8th (01.42.25.95.00/ www.lacompagniedescomptoirs.com). M° Franklin D Roosevelt. **Open** noon-3pm, 8-11pm Mon-Fri; 8-11pm Sat. Closed three weeks in Aug. **Average** €60. **Lunch menu** €18, €25. **Credit** AmEx, MC, V. **Wheelchair access**. **Map** E4.

Royal watcher and celeb journalist Stéphane Bern was being made up for a TV show as we came in to lunch at Sens, the latest in the Pourcel twins' Compagnie des Comptoirs concept after Montpellier, Avignon, La Grande Motte, Ile Maurice and London. Here their pet designer Imaad Rahmouni has created a sophisticated grey dining room in what used to be Korova, with silver neo-Louis XV chairs, skylit mezzanine bar and a red and silver snooker table. Inspired by French colonial trading posts, the menu features 'southern flavours' and techniques, stretching from the chefs' native Languedoc to Asia. Fashionable fusion may have now become rather familiar, but here we found it combined with refreshing use of seasonal produce. Thus our winter visit included a rich, frothy cep cappuccino with poached egg, while steamed lacquered duck, its skin rubbed with spices, came with a homely pumpkin purée. Among the neat little extras were the delicious tumbler of chocolate ganache and raspberries that accompanied our coffee – more than a substitute for dessert – and, as the Pourcels come from a wine-making family, it's worth trusting their choice of Languedoc wines.

Spoon, Food & Wine ★

14 rue de Marignan, 8th (01.40.76.34.44/ www.spoon.tm.fr). M° Franklin D Roosevelt. **Open** noon-2pm, 7-10.30pm Mon-Fri. Closed end July-end Aug. **Average** €50. **Prix fixe** €45-€85. **Credit** AmEx, DC, MC, V. **Wheelchair access** (with reservation). **Non-smoking**. **Map** E4.

One can be forgiven for being suspicious of any restaurant with a complicated methodology. If you need to come up with a concept, it's usually because your basics are shaky. Right? Wrong – when the chef behind the venture is Alain Ducasse, at least. And the proof is Spoon. The menu here may be so complicated that it requires a maths degree, but it's worth the headache. The idea is that you can add your meal up by moving between different columns, sort of like the food combining diet, but delicious. Theoretically, this means that you can come up with weird concoctions such as steak, curry sauce and cucumber, but as this would be the culinary

Toyko Eat. *See p112.*

equivalent of a novelty tie, we don't recommend it. In reality the wonderful staff guide you through, asking questions about preferred tastes and textures to help you choose. We went with their suggestions and were far from disappointed. A starter of salt cod topped with soft-boiled egg was so delicious that we couldn't stop thinking about it, while scallop ceviche with mandarins and wasabe pearls was inventive and fresh. A main of peanut-coated spare ribs and steak with satay sauce proved thoroughly tasty. An extensive (if expensive) wine list is fun for wine buffs (order a glass of Château Bacchus, England's finest wine, and torment French dinner companions).

Hôtel Amour ★

8 rue Navarin, 9th (01.48.78.31.80). M° St-Georges. **Open** 7pm-midnight daily. **Average** €35. **Credit** AmEx, MC, V. **Map** H2.

Out front, a neon sign shines AMOUR, and that's what this hotel off the happening rue des Martyrs is about. Previously a bordello, it has been reborn as the latest hip Paris hotel under the auspices of André Blackbock, the graffiti artist and nightlife impresario. The restaurant, which also serves as the hotel's reception area and lounge, is a laid-back space with a wood-grain linoleum floor, and flea market Danish modern furniture mixed with retro chairs by Charlotte Perriand and Jean Prouvé. This unique look has an odd-ball charm and provides the perfect backdrop to the groovy young types who pack the place nightly. Rather surprisingly, the French comfort food served here is delicious. You can have a proper meal or just a snack – start with l'assiette verte, a great plate of steamed seasonal organic vegetables in a lemony vinaigrette made with deliciously fruity olive oil, and then go for the grilled tuna with wok-fried vegetables, one of the best cheeseburgers in town, or the excellent steak-frites (including real own-made chips). There is a good cheese course if you want an excuse to have more wine, or you can finish up with fruit tart. The ivy-planted garden out back is a superb spot for al fresco dining, and don't miss the magenta plastic Mickey Mouse with the massive erection on the way down to the toilets.

Le Martel

3 rue Martel, 10th (01.47.70.67.56). M° Château d'Eau. **Open** noon-3pm, 7.30-11.30pm Mon-Fri; 7.30-11.30pm Sat. **Average** €20. **Credit** DC, MC, V. **Wheelchair access**. **Non-smoking room**. **Map** K3.

The 10th arrondissement, which is dominated by two railway stations, has always found it difficult to establish any strongly defined fashion personality, but a visit to Le Martel suggests things may be changing. With its dark tables and cream walls, the room looks great, and the welcome on a Friday evening was unusually warm to our decidedly unstylish figures. The restaurant quickly filled with young men dressed in black and moody-looking yuppie couples. What draws the crowds is the interesting menu, which combines the best of North Africa and France. We decided to try both aspects of these parallel cuisines, beginning with a light chicken pastilla, which was less challenging than the thicker and spicier pigeon version. It almost felt as if we had changed restaurants as we moved on to our French main courses. A sesame-coated rare pavé of tuna was a first-rate version of this popular contemporary dish, accompanied by excellent homemade frites. The ris de veau were simply grilled with a little salt, tender and pure, served with sauté potatoes. On another occasion we might try the couscous royale or one of the handsome-looking tagines. Desserts follow a similar contrast, with sticky oriental pastries face-to-face with plainer traditional French puds.

Le Quinzième

14 rue Cauchy, 15th (01.45.54.43.43). M° Balard.
Open noon-2.30pm, 8-10.30pm Mon-Fri; 8-10.30pm
Sat. Closed one week in Aug. **Average** €75. **Prix
fixe** €95. **Lunch menu** €30, €35. **Credit** AmEx,
MC, V. **Wheelchair access. Map** A8.
This is reality TV territory, but don't let that cloud
your judgement. *Le Quinzieme: Cuisine Attitude* is
the result of a film crew following chef Cyril Lignac's
attempt to recruit a team and open a restaurant in
four months, Jamie Oliver-style. The ubiquitous
dove-grey interior is partnered with soft lighting
to flatter the thirtysomething professionals who
filled the room. A slightly nervous waiter described
the menu in intimate detail, even going so far as to
inform us that the two types of butter on offer were
there to 'accompany the bread'. After such a fanfare,
we were expecting dough heaven – but were
disappointed by a jawbreaker. Much better was a
heavenly chorizo and tomato spread. A roasted sole
fillet topped with a perfect lobe of foie gras was
delicious, while a tender nugget of roast lamb came
with delicately scented carrots with turmeric and a
tasty, if unusual, ham and apple spring roll. We
skipped pudding, which didn't matter as we were
handed a goody bag 'for the morning' on our way
out. We're happy to confirm that the buttery cake
inside was scrumptious… and that we didn't have
the willpower to save it for breakfast.

Café de l'Homme

*Musée de l'Homme, 17 pl du Trocadéro, 16th
(01.44.05.30.15/www.cafedelhomme.com). M°
Trocadéro.* **Open** noon-3pm, 7.45-11.30pm Mon-
Sat; 11am-4pm, 7.45-11.30pm Sun. **Average** €50.
Lunch menu €28 (Mon-Fri only). **Credit** AmEx,
MC, V. **Wheelchair access. Map** B5.
Doing dinner with the beautiful people is always all
about the view, and for that, the Café de l'Homme is
a winner. Forget the glitterati all around and instead
feast your eyes on the Eiffel Tower. Our favourite
phallic symbol rises suggestively right in front
of the huge windows at this restaurant tucked
away inside the Musée de l'Homme. Tearing our
eyes away to the menu was a chore, but choices such
as duck spring rolls, salmon nori, salade niçoise and
chicken Caesar salad reminded us that we were in
standard hip restaurant territory. We went with a
perfectly good asparagus and poached egg and a
tepid but tasty spring roll. For mains, we choose
Colombo chicken with mixed rice that was very
good, if rather mild, and a steak tartare with fries.
Our resident raw meat expert was disturbed by the
overly sloppy texture and even more so by the
accompanying sauce, which tasted like badly made
prawn cocktail gloop. Some people may enjoy Marie
sauce with their raw steak. Not us. We had a better
meal at Sora Lena (18 rue Bayen, 17th, 01.45.74.73.73),
a trendy restaurant under the same management
that serves up memorable Italian fare such as superb
Corsican charcuterie, veal scalopine in lemon sauce
and simple yet delicious desserts like tiramisu.

Le Cristal Room

*8 pl des Etats-Unis, 16th (01.40.22.11.10/
www.baccarat.com). M° Iéna.* **Open** noon-2pm,
7.30-10pm Mon-Sat. **Average** €80. **Credit**
AmEx, MC, V. **Wheelchair access. Map** C4.
Overlooking a tranquil square in the swanky 16th
arrondissement, a sumptuous historic townhouse
has become the glittering headquarters, boutique
and showroom of Baccarat, the venerable French
crystal company. There's also an intimate restaurant,
Le Cristal Room, with stunning decor by Philippe
Starck and a light luxury snack menu by chef
Thierry Burlot of Quinze. What makes this salon
such a giggle is Starck's pastiche of grandeur – he
left the wall spaces where tapestries or paintings had
been hanging empty, exposing the brick walls
behind to create brilliant contrast to the ox-blood red
marble mouldings and huge Baccarat chandeliers
overhead. The expensive menu was definitely
conceived to please puckish rich types, but you can
still eat well here if you have a real appetite. Start
with chestnut soup with white truffles or scallops
with caviar, and then go with risotto with white
truffles or spaghetti with cherry tomatoes, or maybe
something a little meatier such as hare à la royale
with quince or lobster spit-roasted with vanilla bean.
Desserts are excellent, including cocoa soufflé or a
tarte Tatin of quince and pears, but the wine list is
stiffly marked up. Don't miss the most spectacular
bathrooms in Paris, and when you book specify that
you want a table in the main room.

Tokyo Eat

*Palais de Tokyo, 13 av du Président-Wilson,
16th (01.47.20.00.29). M° Alma Marceau or Iéna.*
Open noon-3pm, 8-11.30pm Tue-Sun. **Average**
€35. **Credit** AmEx, MC, V. **Wheelchair access.
Non-smoking room. Map** D5.
Tokyo Eat is normally a fun, sceney place to spend
an evening. The vast dining space in the hangar-like
Palais de Tokyo buzzes with creative types, gossiping
along to the DJ's ever-changing soundtrack. Along
with the menu that features modern brasserie classics
at reasonable prices, the waiter brings a playlist and
you order songs with your supper. Music by artists
as diverse as Scissor Sisters and Stevie Wonder
is then woven into the DJ's set list over the course
of the evening. When the mains for the rest of our
party of four arrived at the same time as the starters
for two and when the waiter didn't want to take an
extra song order, we realised that tonight, the artistic
temperament had spread from the museum to the
kitchen. A sea bream tartare was uninspiring, and the
salmon – an anaemic sliver of fish drowning in a foul-
looking gloop – tasted only marginally better. An
asparagus and parmesan risotto was disturbingly
similar to the tarragon rice that accompanied some
(good) pan-fried cod. However, steak tartare was
excellent and the wine list good value and well chosen.
All in all, though, a little disappointing, but because
we have eaten here on many occasions and normally
thoroughly enjoy the experience, we'll be back.

Le Snacking

The leisurely three-course-lunch, with its obligatory carafe of rouge, is well and truly obsolete, if we are to believe the latest statistics that show Parisians spend an average of no more than 34 minutes on the midday meal. With a ticket déjeuner (the lunch voucher provided by most companies) worth around €7, city folk are increasingly turning to soup and sandwich options, giving rise to a whole new breed of eaterie that is still finding itself. If many quick lunch spots are sadly sterile, with nary a whiff of unpasteurised cheese or garlicky pâté in the air, those listed here serve up 'le snacking' with soul (and occasionally even a glass of wine).

Bioboa

3 rue Danielle-Casanova, 1st (01.42.61.17.67). Mº Pyramides. **Open** 11am-6pm Mon-Sat. **Average** €16.50. **Credit** MC, V. **Non-smoking. Map** H4.

The fact that this place describes itself as a 'food spa' goes a long way to showing how adamantly it embraces the notion of organic ('bio' in French) produce being the province of young style-setters rather than of a bunch of ageing granola-crunching hippies. Everything here has a funky if slightly sterile 21st-century tinge to it: the white designer chairs and tables, the weirdly beautiful bird fresco that winds throughout the eaterie, and the mammoth fridge overflowing with ludicrously expensive spring water, exotic smoothies and colourful takeaway salads for the fabulously busy. We, however, went for the full Bioboa experience. Sharing a big table with a gaggle of snooty French PR chicks, we happily dug into a healthy feast comprised of soft-boiled eggs with sweet roasted autumn vegetables, as well as a big, juicy veggie tofu burger – one of Bioboa's staples. And although we

drew sarcastic comments from our neighbours for drizzling the latter in organic ketchup (a very Anglo faux pas, apparently) we emerged from the 'food spa' feeling suitably virtuous.

La Ferme Opéra

55 rue St-Roch, 1st (01.40.20.12.12). Mº Pyramides. **Open** 8am-8pm daily. **Average** €15. **Credit** MC, V. **Non-smoking room. Map** H4.

This barn-like series of rooms, with a covered courtyard serving as a bar at the back, feels instantly welcoming. Perhaps it's the non-sterile look, with wooden stools at low tables in the smoking section and big wicker armchairs in the non-smoking area (where a morning regular felt it was OK to aim his smoke out the window). Or it could be the food itself: tempting croissants, little Portuguese custard cakes and wholewheat scones (bizarrely, no butter is available) displayed at the front, with refrigerator cases holding produce from the Ile-de-France region (around Paris), healthy desserts such as fromage blanc with fruit, and tempting salads. Our fruit salad

Scoop. *See p114.*

Bioboa. *See p113*.

had been over-chilled to the point of freezing, but staff quickly changed it for us. Health-giving juices are extracted behind the counter, while at lunch there is a choice of hot dishes and quiches. There's also free wireless internet access.

Foody's Brunch Café

26 rue Montorgueil, 1st (01.40.13.01.53). M° Châtelet or Les Halles. **Open** 11.30am-5pm Mon-Sat. Closed first three weeks in Aug. **Average** €9. **Prix fixe** €8-€12.50. **Credit** MC, V. **Wheelchair access. Map** J5.
The salad days never end here at this pioneering New York-style deli, the first in the capital to let you design your own veggie masterpiece. Head over to the buffet and pile your big or small bowl skyscraper high with yummies including everything from red beans, pasta, bulgur and courgette to artichoke hearts. Not exactly a die-hard foodie's paradise, but great for those simply searching for a fresh alternative to boring lunchtime jambon-beurre sandwiches, or calorie-counters wanting to police exactly what goes down their discerning gullet. Be warned, however: the space is incredibly cramped, so eating on the premises is not an especially appealing option. Grab your nifty self-styled salad and a piece of fruit or fromage blanc dessert for afters and go out and enjoy gawping at the real-life, buzzy spectacle that's forever unfolding all along the rue Montorgueil.

Rouge Saint-Honoré

34 pl du Marché-St-Honoré, 1st (01.42.61.16.09). M° Pyramides or Tuileries. **Open** 11.30am-2.30pm, 6.30-11pm daily. **Average** €25. **Prix fixe** €16.50, €21.50. **Credit** AmEx, MC, V. **Non-smoking room. Map** G4.
While this is hardly a red-hot venue, it remains a warm and welcoming one nonetheless. Especially on a wet and despicable May day when you just wish you'd stayed tucked away nice and snug under your duvet instead of trudging off to work. Although the place is filled with equally beleaguered clock-watchers, the dark-panelled walls lined with beautifully packaged Italian delicacies and the

swift and friendly staff make it an ideal spot to momentarily switch off. Until recently it went by the name of Rouge Tomate – but despite its unceremonious rebaptism, the tomato's juicy and fragrant presence is still felt throughout the menu. It makes a subtle cameo in the three-cheese risotto; forms a flavourful trio alongside anchovies and tuna in the Mediterranean-style tagliatelle; and makes a gangbusters star turn in the feisty house Bloody Mary. Luckily, the genial owners have more sense than to try to inject tomatoes willy-nilly in all the dishes just for sheer gimmick's sake. Which means we got to enjoy a rouge-free yet totally scrumptious tarte Tatin, before reluctantly scuttling back to work through the pouring rain.

Scoop ★

154 rue St-Honoré, 1st (01.42.60.31.84/www. scoopcafe.com). M° Palais Royal. **Open** 11am-7pm Mon-Sat; noon-7pm Sun. **Average** €15. **Prix fixe** €10-€14. **Credit** MC, V. **Non-smoking room. Map** J5.
What started out as an American-style ice-cream parlour has taken on a Parisian personality well suited to its fashionable surroundings just behind the Louvre. It's worth coming here for the design alone: downstairs is a long white counter illuminated by globe lights for more functional meals, while upstairs is a loungey area with body-hugging armchairs, perfect for an extended chat with friends. For lunch, choose from healthy wraps, soups such as the delectable pumpkin version served on our most recent visit, savoury tarts and hot dishes, but be sure to save room for the main event – ice-creams in flavours such as chocolate espresso, toasted pecans or Vermont maple syrup or, for an even bigger indulgence, the turtle sundae (vanilla ice-cream with chocolate and caramel sauce and pecans). Service is not ultra-speedy during peak times, so try to arrive early if you're rushed (later on, they run out of wraps and tarts). Delicious pancakes are served for Sunday brunch (noon-4.30pm), along with hot dishes such as salmon and ratatouille for the more conventional eater.

Le Mimosa

44 rue d'Argout, 2nd (01.40.28.15.75). M° Sentier.
Open noon-3.30pm Mon-Fri. **Prix fixe** €12, €14.
Average €14. **Credit** MC, V. **Map** J5.
'Sheer cuteness' is the most spontaneous way to
describe this cheerful little yellow eaterie a stone's
throw from Les Halles. It is also an apt description
of our waitress's gorgeous four-year-old son, who
gazed at us intently as we made our choices from
the two- and three-course menus (€12 and €14
respectively). It surely ranks among the cleverest
hard-sell ploys in all of culinary history. He smiled
mischievously as we finally opted for the ultra-
generous salade de crudités; a nice and flaky filet de
cabillaud (cod) with basmati rice and a delicious
gratin de courgettes (each main comes with a choice
of two sides); as well as a zingy fruit compote. All
chased down beautifully with a sound Burgundy
red. Although the salad was noticeably gritty and
the rice undercooked, on the whole this was as good
and honest a lunchtime experience as you're likely
to get in Paris these days. And of course the pint-
sized male company was a big bonus too.

Bread & Roses

*7 rue de Fleurus, 6th (01.42.22.06.06). M° St-
Placide.* **Open** 8am-8pm Mon-Sat. **Average** €20.
Credit MC, V. **Non-smoking**. **Map** G8.
Come for a morning croissant and you might find
yourself staying for lunch, so tempting are the wares
at this Anglo-influenced boulangerie/épicerie/café.
Nowhere else in Paris have we seen a giant loaf of
English-style brown bread, which is cut into chunks
and sold by weight, or the 'Puissance 10' made with
ten different flours. And that's just the beginning –
in the refrigerated case, big wedges of cheesecake
nestle next to French pastries, while giant
rectangular savoury puff pastry tarts are perched
on the counter. Attention to detail shows even in the
authentically pale tarama, which is matched with
buckwheat-and-seaweed bread. Prices reflect the
quality of the often-organic food, but that doesn't
seem to be a problem for the moneyed locals, who
order birthday cakes here for their offspring. Given

the cheerful setting – pale wood with plenty of
natural light inside and a few pavement tables – it's
a mystery why the staff can't crack a smile.

Delicabar

*1st floor, Bon Marché-Rive Gauche, above the
Grande Epicerie de Paris, 26-38 rue de Sèvres,
7th (01.42.22.10.12/www.delicabar.fr). M° Sèvres
Babylone.* **Open** 9.30am-7pm Mon, Tue, Wed, Fri;
10am-9pm Thur; 9.30am-8pm Sat. **Average** €18.
Credit AmEx, DC, MC, V. **Map** G7.
We were on a mission to find the eye-popping dress
of our dreams. And we were starving. Curved
around the heart of the swish Bon Marché
department store, the Delicabar called out to us like
an oasis does to poor souls in the desert. We
squished on to one of the sorbet-hued banquettes
and speed-read through a menu smugly detailing
chef Sébastien Goudar's desire to blend unorthodox
ingredients in the name of what is pompously
dubbed 'snackchic'. All we cared about was getting
fed. In the end our rather nice salade beige (laden
with chicken and slices of pear) and tartelette salée
surprise (chock-full of grains and sprouts) were so
dinky that you felt that you were at a kiddie tea
party. Yet there were lashings of our dessert, a foul
chocolate roulade streaked with bits of caramelised
red pepper. Maybe the crafty aim is to keep us ladies
off the sweet stuff to ensure we'll be able to fit into
the designer clothes in the nearby women's
department. Well, it worked like a charm for us!

Al-Diwan

*30 av George V, 8th (01.47.20.72.00). M° Alma
Marceau or George V.* **Open** 8am-11.30pm daily.
Average €10. **Credit** AmEx, DC, MC, V. **Non-
smoking**.
This Lebanese deli, rather incongruously slotted
among the avenue George V's ritzy fashion
boutiques and hotels, is certainly a far more cheap
'n' cheerful option than its snooty sister restaurant,
which seems to make it some strange point of
honour to take all the fun out of the Middle Eastern
experience. Stroll into the takeaway around 10pm
on any Saturday evening and you'll see entire

families, complete with grandmas and sleepy toddlers, consuming a late supper of soujouk (spicy sausage) and meat chawarma sandwiches alongside preening teenagers gleefully refuelling before setting out for a late night on the tiles, as a scratchy radio wails in the background. The two chefs doling out the piping-hot fare make for just as arresting a spectacle – rolling out pittas, skewering off the meat and drizzling bitter sesame sauce with such brio that customers reward them by clanging slews of euros into a bowl. Unfortunately, despite its impressive preparation, our houmous concoction was a bland and soggy mess, but other veggie options such as the falafel, halloumi cheese or bata harra (fried aubergines and potatoes with coriander) sandwiches were suitably palate-tingling.

Granterroirs ★

30 rue de Miromesnil, 8th (01.47.42.18.18/ www.granterroirs.com). M° Miromesnil. **Open** 9am-8pm Mon-Fri. **Food served** noon-3pm. Closed three weeks in Aug. **Average** €25. **Credit** MC, V. **Wheelchair access. Non-smoking room. Map** F3.

This épicerie with a difference is the perfect remedy for anyone whom the word 'terroir' fills with sheer unadulterated terror – conjuring up visions of big indigestible helpings of grease-soaked peasant food. Here, the walls heave with more than 600 enticing specialities from southern France, including Périgord foie gras, tapenade from Provence and charcuterie from Aubrac, as well as a fine selection of wines straight from the domaines. Great gift ideas to treat yourself or that special gourmet in your life, but why not sample some of the goodies on display first by enjoying Granterroirs' midday table d'hôte feast? Come in early to ensure that you can choose from the five succulent plats du jour on offer (we were lucky enough to dig into a melt-in-the-mouth piece of marinated salmon with dill on a bed of warm potatoes), plonk yourself at one of the massive communal tables and soak up the laid-back ambience. You'll emerge feeling as if you've just had a delightful, lightning-quick break in the country.

Cojean

17 bd Haussmann, 9th (01.47.70.22.65/ www.cojean.fr). M° Chaussée d'Antin La Fayette. **Open** 8am-7pm Mon-Fri; 10am-7pm Sat. **Average** €14. **Credit** MC, V. **Non-smoking. Map** H4.

Stroll around the boulevard Haussmann during lunchtime and you'll notice that Cojean's pretty powder-blue takeaway bags outnumber those of the famous 'golden arches'. But that's where the similarities end, because as fast food goes the chic French fresh fare franchise is truly the anti-McDonald's. Instead of lethargic teens frying up frozen burgers, you have hunky, model-type waiters helping you pick from a tempting roster of tasty and healthy goodies. We bypassed this luminous restaurant's vast yet noisy terrace for a nice, relaxed indoor picnic among the slickly designed tables and chairs. The toasted Italian sandwich with porchetta,

provolone and tomatoes was richly satisfying, while the unusual quinoa and half-smoked salmon salad with squash and gooseberries tasted like summer, as did the tang-tastic rhubarb, kiwi and strawberry crumble. We left with a spring in our step, feeling ready to run a marathon – or at the very least give our credit cards a good workout over at the nearby Galeries Lafayette department store. For more branches other than the key ones listed below, see the website.

Other locations: 6 rue de Seze, 9th (01.40.06.08.80); 16 rue Clément-Marot, 8th (01.47.20.44.10).

Rose Bakery ★

46 rue des Martyrs, 9th (01.42.82.12.80). M° Notre-Dame-de-Lorette. **Open** 9am-7pm Tue-Sat; 10am-5pm Sun. Food served all day. Closed two weeks in Aug. **Average** €20. **Credit** MC, V. **Wheelchair access. Non-smoking. Map** H3.

Rose Bakery has a knack for making even the humble grated carrot salad look incredibly appetising. This English-themed café run by a Franco-British couple stands out for the quality of its ingredients – organic or from small producers – and too-good-to-be-true puddings, such as carrot cake, sticky toffee pudding and, in winter, an enormous chocolate-chestnut tart. The compose-your-own salad plate is crunchily satisfying, but the thin-crusted pizzettes, daily soups and occasional risottos are equally good choices. Just don't expect much beyond scones in the morning, except on weekends, when brunch is served to a packed-out house (by the time we finally reached the front of the queue, we were almost ready for lunch). Popular with health-conscious locals who love the smoke-free atmosphere and expats who can't believe their luck, the dining room is minimalist but welcoming. Service is friendly, if overwhelmed.

Bar à Soupes

33 rue de Charonne, 11th (01.43.57.53.79). M° Bastille or Ledru-Rollin. **Open** noon-3pm, 6.30-11pm Mon-Sat. Closed last week in July, first week in Aug. **Average** €12. **Lunch menu** €9. **Credit** MC, V. **Non-smoking room. Map** M7.

Slurping away at a big steaming bowl of soup like a five-year-old hardly seems like the pose that any self-respecting French trendoid would want to adopt. But surprisingly enough, over the past few years, Parisians have been embracing their gormless inner child, thanks partly to this place, the city's first bona fide soup bar. This brightly decorated haunt with equally chirpy staff is a godsend for hyperactive workaholics looking for a cheap, quick and tasty way of refuelling throughout the day, as well as keeping warm during the interminable Parisian winter. The daily changing selections range from exotic options such as tomatoes with apples and ricotta, Indian-style yellow lentils and pumpkin with oysters, to more trad ones such as gazpacho. There's also a €9 prix fixe that includes charcuterie, a cheese plate or dessert, plus coffee or a glass of wine. All great reasons to go on and soup up your life in style.

Vegetarian

If you think all Parisians are hedonists, you need only visit one of the city's vegetarian restaurants to see a more earnest style of French person. He/she doesn't smoke, wouldn't touch Pierre Hermé's pâtisseries with a bargepole and considers heaps of shredded raw root veggies a perfectly satisfying lunch. Whether or not you are vegetarian, the best of these restaurants can prove a refreshing change after (far) too much cream sauce. Alternatively, many of the snacking options springing up all over Paris (*see pp113-116*) offer vegetarian choices, and most bistro chefs can improvise something meatless if you ask very nicely.

La Victoire Suprême du Cœur

41 rue des Bourdonnais, 1st (01.40.41.93.95/ www.vscoeur.com). Mº Châtelet. **Open** 11.45am-10pm Mon-Sat. Closed two weeks in Apr and Aug. **Average** €25. **Lunch** €12.50-€15.90. **Prix fixe** €15.30-€19.30. **Wheelchair access. Non-smoking. Credit** AmEx, MC, V. **Map** J6.

It took us a while to catch on to the fact that the 'supreme victory of the heart' in question doesn't refer to the health benefits of a low-cholesterol vegetarian diet, but to guru Sri Chinmoy, whose charming supporters run the restaurant. The smart room with low tables has a new age feel, but we chose to sit on the pleasant terrace in this relatively traffic-free side street near Les Halles – only the aroma of freshly baked pizzas a few doors down dampened our healthy intentions. The food had its high points, and there's a good choice for vegans. A mushroom pâté was totally successful, and a heap of freshly fried frittered onions was less greasy than most Indian pakoras. Avoiding the meat and fish taste-alikes, our mains included a goat's cheese and spinach quiche, whose top had been blackened hard, and a mushroom bake with blackberry sauce that looked unprepossessing but was actually delicious. Accompaniments included a solid but nourishing split pea purée and some chewy, fibrous red rice. Disappointed by an unseasoned lassi, we enjoyed our slightly wicked organic cider, which was a refreshing tipple for our excellent chocolate tart and rather-too-cold red fruit crumble.

Le Potager du Marais ★

22 rue Rambuteau, 3rd (01.42.74.24.66). Mº Rambuteau. **Open** 6.30-10.30pm Mon-Fri; noon-10.30pm Sat; 1-10.30pm Sun. **Average** €25. **Prix fixe** €20. **Non-smoking. Credit** MC, V. **Map** K5.

The Potager du Marais was alive and buzzing with enthusiastic diners when we arrived, so we immediately knew that this is a vegetarian restaurant that must be getting something right. The emphasis here is on organic food, and the place is blessedly free of any proselytising veggie literature. The long railway compartment room feels like a proper restaurant, something confirmed by a delicious red lentil soup, and a plate of well-dressed, squeaky fresh crudités. The good impression was confirmed by an excellent aubergine curry, which was not particularly spicy, but flavoursome and substantial. Our other main was a comforting gratin of leeks, topped with pungent melted comté cheese. All was beginning to feel like a real restaurant until a carrot flan turned up among the puddings; one of those taste-free vegetarian concoctions, which was not saved by some orangey caramel sauce. A happier choice was the excellent chocolate mousse, which was nicely complemented by the carafe of drinkable organic rosé. Two charming staff coped with the crowds effectively, only slightly outraged when someone asked if the restaurant was really non-smoking – a chastened diner had forgotten that this delightful spot really does have your well-being at heart.

Les 5 Saveurs d'Anada

72 rue du Cardinal-Lemoine, 5th (01.43.29.58.54/ www.anada5saveurs.com). Mº Cardinal Lemoine. **Open** noon-2.30pm, 7-10.30pm Tue-Sun. **Prix fixe** €13.50, €26.50. **Credit** AmEx, MC, V. **Non-smoking. Map** K8.

Formerly Les Quatre et Une Saveurs, this wood-beamed restaurant near the top of rue Mouffetard has changed owners and name, but not its earnest approach to macrobiotic, '100 per cent organic' cooking. Like almost every other vegetarian restaurant in Paris, it takes itself just that little bit too seriously. Then again, it's hard to be hedonistic when you eschew meat, eggs, cheese, butter or sugar (the macrobiotic diet) – and it can do anyone good to have a virtuous, cleansing meal. Recovering from a rich French feast the previous night, we were happy to tuck into our assiette garnie and assiette complète, the difference being that the complète adds seaweed and lentils to the mix. One had cod as its main ingredient and the other nutty-tasting seitan (wheat protein), served with a topping of preserved ginger. Our failure to get through the piles of raw grated carrot and beetroot, pickled cabbage, grains and colourful steamed vegetables earned us a bit of a scolding from the owner, and indeed the fresh vegetables deserved more respect. Making a tart without any of the naughtier ingredients – butter, sugar, eggs – creates a challenge, but pear tart with almonds in a pool of dairy-free custard proved surprisingly tender-crusted and tasty. It certainly appealed to us more than a bowl of agar-agar, one of the other choices. To drink, try one of the freshly made juices or a pot of tea prepared with unusual care.

Le Grenier de Notre-Dame

18 rue de la Bûcherie, 5th (01.43.29.98.29/ www.legrenierdenotredame.net). Mº Maubert Mutualité or St-Michel. **Open** *June-Sept* noon-11pm daily. *Jan-May, Oct-Dec* noon-2pm, 6-10.30pm daily. **Average** €25. **Prix fixe** €14.50 (dinner only). **Lunch menu** €12.50. **Credit** MC, V. **Map** J7.

Le Grenier's riot of exterior green picks out the restaurant in its hideaway near the Seine, while an extravagant array of vegetables painted on the outside tables hints at the equally comprehensive range on the menu. The welcome from manager Laurent Boiseau is warm as you settle among an international clientele in the intimacy of playroom-bright decor. Inventive and imaginative are words to describe the fare, which features, typically, long-time Grenier favourite meatless cassoulet, plus vegetarian lasagne and lentil moussaka, complemented by plenty of salad vegetables and an exceptional country bread with sesame seeds. The three-course dinner menu has less zap than à la carte, but for veggie reassurance 80% of the ingredients and all the wines are organic, and the components of the 13 exotic non-alcoholic cocktails are processed as you listen. Special effects are a choice of 22 teas and a lightweight afternoon menu. The only downer was the dodgy FM-radio background music.

La Petite Légume

36 rue des Boulangers, 5th (01.40.46.06.85). Mº Cardinal Lemoine or Jussieu. **Open** noon-3pm, 7-10pm Mon-Sat. **Average** €20. **Non-smoking**. **Credit** MC, V. **Map** K8.

The little vegetable in question grows happily in a side street near Jussieu university. Both thinkers and scholars drop by to appreciate a healthy macrobiotic way of life, which is gently promoted in this charmingly intimate little restaurant with an attractive mezzanine. We went for a couple of assiettes complètes, a bargain at just €14, one topped with a savoury stuffed pepper and the other an unusually tasty smoked tofu and onion tart. The accompanying collection of hot and cold vegetables plus grains followed the usual macro-organic formula of brown rice, carrots, and salad that you dress yourself from the generous condiments on the table. The rice was well cooked and, once topped with some fortifying gomasio (sesame salt), the dish made a filling lunch, served by the adorable owner who radiates a healthy inner calm. Our organic Chinon red wine was a bit rough and cloudy – we reckon we'd have been better served by one of the freshly made vegetable or fruit juices. Own-made puddings

are virtually sugar free, but the grain-based coffee substitute is for fanatics only. Organic products are on sale and a takeaway service is available.

Guenmaï

6 rue Cardinale, 6th (01.43.26.03.24). Mº Mabillon or St-Germain-des-Prés. **Open** 11.45am-3.30pm Mon-Sat. Closed Aug. **Average** €20. **Non-smoking**. **Credit** MC, V. **Map** H7.

Macrobiotic restaurants always overplay the well-being card, and Guenmaï is lined with books promising longevity and good health when freed from the evils of dairy products, sugar and animal fat. The green-trellised room is airy and light and the staff are encouragingly welcoming. We'd recently visited a macrobiotic shrine in south-west France and were able to endear ourselves to the owners by mentioning this fact. Our lunch was simple but tasty. The usual combination of grains and vegetables, both perfectly cooked, had as their centrepiece a daily special of vegetable tempura, or some mini vegetable spring rolls. Both were crisp and delicious (fortunately, macrobiotics have no problem with calorific deep frying). There was also some sinful organic beer, which was a nice concession to everyday cosmopolitan living. A fruit tart of apple purée topped with strawberries showed that good cooking can produce an excellent sugar-free dessert, allowing the flavours of the ingredients to shine in a way often absent from sweeter confections. Many dishes can be bought to take away, and although Guenmaï is hardly a bargain it does achieve its goal with discreet charm.

Aquarius ★

40 rue de Gergovie, 14th (01.45.41.36.88). Mº Pernety or Plaisance. **Open** noon-3pm, 7-10.30pm Mon-Sat. Closed last two weeks in Aug, ten days at Christmas. **Average** €15. **Prix fixe** €15 (dinner only). **Lunch menu** €11. **Credit** MC, V. **Wheelchair access**. **Non-smoking room**. **Map** F10.

Aquarius has won a loyal following of families and fashionable diners alike with its imaginative, homely cuisine and warm-as-toast setting. We felt we were stepping into someone's front room, the atmosphere complemented by an ornamental bubbler and enough art deco window glass to lend class. Mozzarella with a salad of tomato, carrot and sweet beetroot, plus perfectly seasoned creamed vegetable soup, feature on the €15 three-course evening menu. Mushroom loaf, uplifted by a mushroom sauce, or cannelloni stuffed with spinach and ricotta and served with courgettes and lentils, are typical main courses. Helpings are astonishingly generous. Super-prompt service retains charm and efficiency. Of the wines, the organic varieties are pricey, but a carafe of house merlot should satisfy most people. We went for the excellent, no-frills apple crumble instead of cocoa-rich chocolate ice-cream or the naughty gâteau. A la carte 'exotica' include three seaweeds in puff pastry or aubergine caviar. Booking is advisable.

Petit Pain complet 0,70
Bol de riz 4
Soupe miso 6
Potage de légumes 6,90
Salade verte aux fruits secs 6,50
Assiette de crudités 8
Crudités au tofu 9
Tarte salée avec crudités 9,15
Tarte seule 6,20

La Petite Légume

Dietetic Shop

11 rue Delambre, 14th (01.43.35.39.75). M° Vavin.
Open noon-3pm, 7-10.30pm Mon-Fri; noon-3pm
Sat. **Average** €20. **Credit** MC, V. **Non-smoking**.
Map G9.

Even the greediest carnivores are occasionally tempted by the purity of a meat-free diet. Armed with our pre-summer extra pounds, we set off with pioneering spirit to the Dietetic Shop. The name hardly promises gastronomic delights and the alternative therapy health shop decoration reminded us of Damien Hirst's now-defunct Pharmacy restaurant in Notting Hill, London. Our eye was caught by something called elixir de joie, which, despite the name, isn't a Donizetti opera but a cordial for the 'stressed'. Not that stress was much in evidence among the charming ladies-who-lunch, albeit on uncomfortable wooden benches. Moans of pleasure rang out as they tucked into a warm far aux abricots, which seemed to us a glutinous dessert without yumminess of any sort. We preceded this with a plate of seitan gourmet and vegetables, sprinkled with a savoury macrobiotic mix of grilled sesame and salt. High on a list of dishes not to order ever again was the salad of tofu and pasta: undressed ingredients united in silent misery. A couple of glasses of organic rosé cheered us up before we decided to seek our corporal salvation elsewhere, which is a shame as the gastronomically evangelical owners are delightful, and no doubt weight tumbles away if you eat here regularly – along with the will to live.

Au Grain de Folie

24 rue de la Vieuville, 18th (01.42.58.15.57).
M° Abbesses. **Open** 12.30-2.30pm, 7.30-10pm
Tue-Sat; 1-3pm, 7.30-10pm Sun. **Average** €14.
Prix fixe €12, €16. **No credit cards.**
Wheelchair access. **Map** H1.

It may not be the smallest restaurant in Paris, but there can't be too many other places where adult strangers can get this intimate without breaking the law. The menu, like the floor space, is limited but cleverly organised. For starters, the avocat au roquefort was nicely seasoned, the salad leaves crisp and fresh, while the potage de légumes is a warming mini meal in itself. If you want to sample the tzatziki, houmous and guacamole, try sharing the €20 starter selection. Main courses are dominated by salads, but otherwise there's vegetable tart, vegetable pâté and toasted goat's cheese. Everything comes with a generous dollop of lentils, plenty of bulgur wheat and lashings of crudités, and while the food is produced to order in a kitchen the size of a Japanese phone booth, the ingredients are treated with respect and served with almost Zen imperturbability. For dessert, don't miss the apple crumble with hazelnuts. Oh, and if you do need the loo, don't close the outer door before you've opened the inner one.

Restaurant
Le Méchoui
du Prince

'Marhaba'
Welcome

Prepare to discover the finest and most subtle aspects of the orient.
This delicate yet highly perfumed culinary style combines sweet
and savoury ingredients with a range of spices to create harmonious
dishes of 1001 flavours.
Travel with us through the gateway to the East.

Air-conditionned and non smoking rooms – Open daily noon–3pm
and 6pm–12.30am
34–36 rue Monsieur le Prince, 6th – Tel: 01.43.25.09.71 –
Mº Odeon or Cluny-la-Sorbonne, RER Luxembourg

International

AFRICAN & INDIAN OCEAN	122
THE AMERICAS	124
CARIBBEAN	129
EASTERN MEDITERRANEAN	130
FAR EASTERN	132
INDIAN	141
ITALIAN	144
JAPANESE	150
JEWISH	154
NORTH AFRICAN	156
SPANISH	160
OTHER INTERNATIONAL	162

African & Indian Ocean

When the Paris winter starts to seem endlessly grey, these tropical restaurants bring a welcome burst of sunshine. A West African meal typically begins with a potent rum cocktail (or ginger juice), before moving on to hearty stews such as maffé or the Senegalese national dish, thieb'oudjen, a spicy fish stew. Seychelles cooking borrows from India, while you'll find a strong Portuguese influence in Cape Verdean restaurants. Ethiopian food, meanwhile, offers a convivial style of eating that must be experienced. For **North African** restaurants, *see pp156-159*.

International

Chez Dom ★

34 rue de Sambre-et-Meuse, 10th (01.42.01.59.80).
M° Colonel Fabien. **Open** noon-2.30pm, 8pm-2am Tue-Fri; 8pm-2am Sat, Sun. **Average** €25. **Credit** MC, V. **Wheelchair access. Map** M3.
The sisters are still doing it for themselves at this happy little joint run by Dominique Sy. With parents from Senegal and Martinique, she pulls in home-cooking secrets from both continents. The sound and scent of sizzling soul food hits you as you enter through the kitchen, and everyone gets a planter's punch on the house to get things going as they scan the blackboard menu. We loved our starters of aloco (juicy, deep-fried plantain) accompanied by refreshing sauce chien (chopped tomato, onion, garlic, parsley and chives) and avocado salad. The curried pork with coconut is delicious, but then so are all the curries – from mild, lemony yassa to fiery goat colombo spiced with aromatic pepper. The pièce de résistance, though, was the huge chunk of capitaine, crisply grilled and served with rice, aloco and sauce chien. Sexy chocolate lives up to its name but proved mere foreplay when compared to the mango gratin – a must. The wines can be a bit ropey – better to stick to rum or ginger juice. In summer there's a 20-seat terrace on the pavement.

Ile de Gorée

70 rue Jean-Pierre Timbaud, 11th (01.43.38.97.69).
M° Parmentier. **Open** 7pm-midnight daily. Closed Aug. **Average** €26. **Credit** MC, V. **Wheelchair access. Map** M4.
It was a cold and rainy night when we embarked for Ile de Gorée, a Senegalese restaurant in the heart of the Oberkampf bar scene, but potent ginger-rum punches, live kora music and the staff's cheery smiles instantly warmed us up. The decor is reminiscent of a beachcomber's bamboo hut, with rattan lining the walls and the ceiling, soft lighting and splashes of blue and yellow on the walls and tablecloths. The generous starters – tender plantain slices and moist prawn fritters served with a tangy tomato and onion dip – also helped put us in a beach mood. These were followed by hearty Senegalese couscous and stuffed mullet served with a slightly spicy brown sauce, a speciality of the country's former capital, St-Louis. We prolonged our stay on the isle with an exotic fruit salad and some freshly brewed mint tea.

Waly Fay

6 rue Godefroy Cavaignac, 11th (01.40.24.17.79).
M° Charonne or Voltaire. **Open** 8pm-2am Mon-Sat; noon-5pm Sun. **Average** €25. **Sunday brunch** €18-€22. **Credit** MC, V. **Wheelchair access. Map** N7.
Restaurants with interior design concepts that work are rare in Paris, and we were struck on entering Waly Fay by just how well the distressed interior had been managed. Artfully lit by candles, the mixture of exposed walls and perfectly laid tables created an atmosphere that was immediately welcoming, helped no doubt by a tingling ginger and rum cocktail. The cuisine lived up to the chic atmosphere: a shredded cabbage bayou salad with prawns, grapefruit and a touch of blue cheese was perfectly balanced with a pungent dressing, while the crab gratin was a savoury, highly seasoned celebration of the shellfish. The Frenchman in our party played safe with his main course, ordering char-grilled brochettes of tender juicy lamb, chicken and beef served with good rice and a bowl of spicy pepper-based sauce. More adventurous was Senegalese speciality thieb'oudjen, fish in a spicy tomato and vegetable sauce, prepared with real sophistication. We drank a strong organic vacqueras red for €25, which stood up to the spices, and accompanied us through to an exquisite corossol (an exotic fruit) sorbet and ginger ice-cream, both served with raisins doused in old rum. Service was outstandingly friendly.

Chez Céleste

18 rue de Cotte, 12th (01.43.44.15.30). M° Ledru-Rollin. **Open** 11.30am-3pm Mon; 11.30am-3pm, 7-11pm Tue-Sat. Closed 1-15 Aug. **Average** €18. **Lunch menu** €11, €12. **Credit** AmEx, MC, V. **Wheelchair access. Map** N7.
Two steps from the teeming place d'Aligre market just east of Bastille, Chez Céleste is a hole-in-the-wall Cape Verdean resto-cum-nightspot. Reflecting the island nation's polyglot residents, the menu draws

on Portuguese and West African cuisines. We tried the salade bacalhau (a ceviche-like marinated mix of salt cod, red peppers and oil) and the petite assiette sampler of nutmeggy black pudding and lightly fried accras (salt cod fritters). For mains, we had a delicious, sticky pile of barely blackened gambas in a creole sauce and fall-off-the-bone tender chicken colombo. Little Portuguese-inspired custard tarts were scrumptious though tough-crusted; slightly soupy coconut flan was the ultimate cold-weather comfort food. Live music from Thursday to Saturday might bring a mellow guitar duo crooning romantic Brazilian songs or more raucous rhythms; whatever it is, on a packed weekend night it will distract from the wait between courses.

Entoto ★

143-145 rue Léon-Maurice-Nordmann, 13th (01.45.87.08.51). Mº Glacière. **Open** 7-11pm Mon-Sat. **Average** €30. **Credit** MC, V. **Wheelchair access. Non-smoking room. Map** J10.

If Africa has one unmissable cuisine, it's got to be Ethiopian. And Entoto is about as good as it gets. Novice and initiated alike need look no further than the beyayenetou entoto: a platter of seven different specialities, two meat and five lentil/vegetable; there's a vegetarian version as well. The whole lot is served up on a giant disc of injera, an airy, slightly sour pancake made of tef (a sort of millet), which traditionally substitutes for cutlery. Little baskets of it, freshly cooked, are kept topped up. We had zingy ground beef, tender chunks of lamb stewed in a thick hot-sour sauce, unctuous split peas and pink lentils, melting spinach, a delicately spiced bulgur wheat, plus pumpkin berbère. Berber-style refers to the mix of herbs and spices (pink pepper, garlic, ginger, rue, basil, thyme, cinnamon and cloves) that gives so much Ethiopian food its distinctive taste; even spice-phobes will be seduced by its delicacy. If you still have room, finish with a dark slice of alluring reine de Saba chocolate cake.

Le Mono

40 rue Véron, 18th (01.46.06.99.20). Mº Abbesses or Blanche. **Open** 7-11pm Mon, Tue, Thur-Sun. Closed Aug. **Average** €25. **Credit** AmEx, MC, V. **Map** H1.

This family restaurant specialising in Togolese cuisine makes you feel right at home. Starting with a potent rum punch served with a smile, we savoured an interesting assortment of appetisers, including crispy prawn fritters (beware the insipid cocktail sauce), stuffed crab and a wonderful aromatic black pudding with a spicy tomato dipping sauce. For mains, chicken leg in peanut sauce was a fall-off-the-bone, melt-in-your-mouth treat, while beef skewers in tomato sauce, though slightly chewy, had plenty of flavour. The real winners, however, were the crispy, non-greasy fried plantains and the sweet potato chips. Having feasted on them, we could no longer find room for the tempting banana-based desserts. But we're sure to return, both for the exotic delicacies and the smiling Akakpo family.

Rio dos Camarãos

55 rue Marceau, 93100 Montreuil-sous-Bois (01.42.87.34.84/www.riodos.com). Mº Robespierre. **Open** 7.30-11.30pm Tue-Sat. Closed Aug. **Average** €30. **Credit** AmEx, MC, V.

Rio dos Camarãos doesn't focus on a single country. Its pan-African, multi-talented kitchen prepares an extensive menu from Senegal, the Ivory Coast and Cameroon, plus Benin and the Congo. Starters come under the category 'waiting for the bush taxi', while set lunch menus have tongue-in-cheek names like Sans Papiers ('illegal immigrants'). Dishes range from staples such as yassa and n'dole, to a version of a peanut-based maffé kandja with prawns, beef, cod, carrots and okra. Try the two house favourites: attiéké, a braised whole capitaine fish with a spicy tomato-pepper sauce; and Rio dos Camarãos, a gourd seed gumbo with cod and prawns. A warm cinnamon and banana Tatin makes a fine finisher. Expect a short hike from the Métro station.

Rio dos Camarãos

The Americas

One look at Parisian businessmen tucking into hamburgers with a knife and fork and it becomes clear that American food remains very much a novelty in Paris. Breakfast in America has branched out with a second, non-smoking diner in the Marais, and PDG dishes up deluxe burgers and weekend brunch. A new Latin American discovery is Múkura, which serves vividly flavoured Colombian food in a bright, non-smoking setting on the Canal St-Martin.

NORTH AMERICA

Joe Allen

30 rue Pierre Lescot, 1st (01.42.36.70.13/www. joeallenparis.com). Mº Etienne Marcel. **Open** noon-midnight daily. Closed last two weekends in July, first two weeks in Aug. **Average** €30. **Prix fixe** €22.50 (dinner only). **Lunch menu** €13.50. **Credit** AmEx, MC, V. **Wheelchair access. Map** J5.
Joe Allen, with outposts in New York, London, Miami Beach and Maine, takes a more subtle approach than its American counterparts in Paris. The dining room is more sober, with brick walls, dark wood floors that give it a clubby feeling, and brightly starched white tablecloths with linen napkins. You'll find some memorabilia, with tributes to American sport, cinema and theatrical greats. Absent are the bumbag-toting tourists and small children, replaced by a well-heeled Parisian crowd possibly feeling nostalgic for their student days back in the US. The menu seems stuck in the 1970s, with dishes such as Caesar salad and grilled prime rib with baked potato. But what we had was more than satisfying. Buffalo wings, served with a spicy sweet barbecue sauce, were quite good, while quesadillas oozed melted jack cheese and were delicately topped with homemade salsa and better-than-average guacamole. The cheeseburger was one of the best we've had in Paris, with freshly ground beef, aged cheddar cheese and a side of perfectly browned shoestring fries. Desserts included American favourites such as pecan pie, carrot cake and New York-style cheesecake. Our bilingual French waiter was adorable too.

Breakfast in America

4 rue Malher, 4th (01.42.72.40.21/www.breakfast-in-america.com). Mº St-Paul. **Open** 8.30am-10.30pm daily. **Average** €15. **Credit** MC, V. **Wheelchair access. Non-smoking. Map** L6.
Connecticut-born Craig Carlson's dream of opening a chain of American diners across Europe and Asia appears to be coming true. His first Breakfast in America, a brightly coloured mom-and-pop-style diner, complete with laminated countertops, cherry-red booths and bar stools and retro tiling, opened on rue des Ecoles on the Left Bank a few years ago. Now there is a second outlet on the Right Bank in a trendy part of the Marais. While you'll still find a genuine, albeit clichéd, diner atmosphere, this one's a bit more polished (and blessedly tobacco-free). The menu at both locations is the same, with breakfast served all day, and other American fare such as burgers, nachos and club sandwiches, plus a few salads. A recent Sunday breakfast at the Marais location included a heaping stack of blueberry pancakes and the 'deuces wild', two eggs prepared to your liking, two fluffy pancakes with real maple syrup and two strips of crisp bacon. Paired with a bottomless cup of Joe or jus de chaussettes (sock juice, or watery coffee), it almost felt like breakfast back home.
Other locations: 17 rue des Ecoles, 5th (01.43.54.50.28).

PDG ★

20 rue de Ponthieu, 8th (01.42.56.19.10). Mº Franklin D Roosevelt. **Open** noon-2.45pm, 7-10.45pm daily. Closed one week mid-Aug. **Average** €25. **Lunch menu** €20 (Mon-Fri). **Credit** AmEx, DC, MC, V. **Wheelchair access** (on request). **Map** E4.
A reference to the high-powered executives who lurk in this area (PDG means CEO). Small and crowded, with diner-red banquettes and bistro-style wooden tables, it takes a tasteful French approach to Americana with just a few movie posters, cheerful hanging lights and a bar for solo diners. We never thought the day would come when we'd feel happy to pay €15 for a burger, but here the bun is prepared by a 'meilleur ouvrier de France' baker, the meat is thick and juicy and the mustard is French's (as opposed to French). There are ten burgers to choose from, including the extravagant jumbo bacon cheese – a double burger with double bacon and cheddar – and the Mexican, served with guacamole on the side. Depending on which burger you choose (there are chicken and vegetarian versions), it might come with fries, sautéed grenaille potatoes or pan-fried spinach. We also tried a huge pastrami club sandwich – a rather Parisian interpretation with thickly sliced meat, but satisfying nonetheless. The desserts are a let-down after this, so sip a coffee and enjoy the sight of CEOs negotiating a burger – and possibly a deal – with red napkins tucked into their collars.
Other locations: PDG Rive Gauche, 5 rue du Dragon, 6th (01.45.48.94.40).

Blue Bayou

Blue Bayou

111-113 rue St-Maur, 11th (01.43.55.87.21/
www.bluebayou-bluebillard.com). M° Parmentier
or St-Maur. **Open** noon-2pm, 7.30-11.30pm Mon-
Thur; noon-2pm, 7.30pm-1am Fri, Sat; 11am-3.30pm,
7.30-11.30pm Sun. **Average** €27.50. **Prix fixe** €15-
€28. **Credit** AmEx, MC, V. **Wheelchair access**.
Map M5.

Two-step up from the ground-floor billiards room
and enter Louisiana back country, aka a cabin
made of lumber shipped from the sawmills of the
Mississippi, a 3.5m-long embalmed alligator, a whole
lotta bluegrass tunes and plenty of attitude. The
crayfish terrine starter was quickly sidelined when
we began wrestling with the whole-shell blackened
prawns to dip their juicy meat into the rémoulade.
Jambalaya, with chunks of spiced sausage, chicken
and 'dirty rice', needed a good kick of cayenne but
was tasty nonetheless, while the gumbo was chock-
full of seafood and Cajun goodness. After all this, we
needed a hammock, but what we got instead was
grade-A pecan pie and New York cheesecake. Special
nights featuring Cajun dance and an open crawfish
bar burn down the house.

Indiana Café

14 pl de la Bastille, 11th (01.44.75.79.80/www.
indiana.cafe.com). M° Bastille. **Open** 11.30am-
1am Mon-Thur, Sun; 11.30am-3am Fri, Sat.
Average €25. **Credit** MC, V. **Map** L4.

This branch of the Parisian Tex-Mex chain was
packed on an early Friday evening with young chain-
smoking student types, who were surely there to take
advantage of the half-price cocktails on offer from
5-8pm. We found respite upstairs in the dining room,
whose walls were adorned with an odd mix of
American Indian art and flat-screen TVs. The menu
offers a bit of everything: classic American bar food
such as mozzarella sticks and chicken wings, Tex-
Mex specialities such as deep-fried chimichangas and
enchiladas, southern barbequed ribs and fried
chicken, and a section titled 'Indiana Evasion' with
tropical salmon and steak teriyaki. Our drinks,
Margaritas served in a tumbler with a cloyingly
sweet taste and no salt to be found, were the first sign
that this would not be the Tex-Mex we were longing
for. The guacamole lacked zip and the salsa was
equally bland. We had high expectations for the blue
cheese burger, but it ended up being quite ordinary
too. Fries were, thankfully, hot and crisp, though
not hand-cut. We finished with a cheesecake and
drowned our sorrows in another round of Margaritas.

LATIN AMERICA

Anahi ★

49 rue Volta, 3rd (01.48.87.88.24). M° Arts et
Métiers. **Open** 8pm-midnight daily. Closed 25 Dec,
1 Jan, weekend of 15 Aug. **Average** €40. **Credit**
MC, V. **Map** K4.

A rickety old building on a narrow and poorly lit
street in the nether regions of the Marais houses
Paris's trendiest Argentinian restaurant. That's if

FAJITAS

MEXICAN RESTAURANT

"Miguel cooks deliciously fresh northern Mexican dishes with some southern specials among the starters (...). The signature fajitas with beef and chicken are a magnificent main."
Time Out Paris Penguin Guide 2002

OPEN DAILY NOON-11PM
CLOSED MONDAY EXCEPT JULY-AUGUST 6PM-11PM

15 RUE DAUPHINE, 6TH - M° ODEON OR PONT NEUF

TEL: 01.46.34.44.69

WWW.FAJITAS-PARIS.COM

Airline flights are one of the biggest producers of the global warming gas CO_2. But with **The CarbonNeutral Company** you can make your travel a little greener.

Go to **www.carbonneutral.com** to calculate your flight emissions then 'neutralise' them through international projects which save exactly the same amount of carbon dioxide.

CarbonNeutral®flights

Contact us at
shop@carbonneutral.com
or call into the office on
0870 199 99 88
for more details.

customers like Johnny Depp, Quentin Tarantino and Thierry Mugler are any sign of style. It's the slabs of grilled beef fresh (well, vacuum-packed) from the pampas that pull them in, and the cheery welcome from Carmina and Pilat, the sisters who set up Anahi in this old charcuterie some 20 years ago. Surrounded by the original white tiled walls, stylish black and white photos of the sisters and an art deco ceiling that was painted by Albert Camus' brother, you can tuck into spanish fare with onions, or a stand-out ceviche made with sea bass. Mains of skewered chicken breast marinated in lemon and served with apple and pineapple salsa and sweet potato purée, and grilled prawns with peanuts and okra, are satisfying and attractive, but the bif angosto – a tender, juicy fillet served with a simple green salad – is the star. Try to fit in a crème caramel, immersed in sweet caramel sauce, and make sure you try a Chilean red. Delicioso.

Calle 24
13 rue Beautreillis, 4th (01.42.72.38.34). Mº Bastille. **Open** 7.30-11.30pm Mon-Sat. **Average** €26. **Prix fixe** €24. **Credit** MC, V. **Wheelchair access**. **Map** L7.
This tiny Cuban bar-cum-eaterie booms out on a quiet Marais street as the place to be, at least for the noisy thirty- and fortysomethings who pack it nightly and make booking essential. Old Cuban adverts paper the ceiling, so as you crane your neck take care not to topple off the bar stool. Like everyone else you'll be guzzling Hemingway's favourite – mint-packed Mojitos – as you wait for a table. Main courses, such as the marinated grilled chicken or cod-stuffed squid in an inky sauce, are decent and filling; with a choice of three side dishes that include rice, beans, fried plantain and a manioc gratin, you're guaranteed not to leave hungry, and the prix fixe menu won't break the bank, either. Cuban food, as those who have tramped the streets of Havana know only too well, is resolutely non-gourmet, and Calle 24 is no exception. Go instead for atmosphere, cocktails, a large selection of appetite-quenching tapas – such as cod and sweet potato fritters, pork and bean pâté, and lime-zapped perch ceviche – not to mention the wide smile of Mechy, the Cuban expat and one-time dancer who reigns over it all with gusto.

Anahuacalli ★
30 rue des Bernardins, 5th (01.43.26.10.20). Mº Maubert Mutualité. **Open** 7-11pm Mon-Sat; noon-2pm, 7-11pm Sun. **Average** €32. **Credit** AmEx, V. **Map** K7.
Just off the boulevard St-Germain, a few steps away from the Seine, is this lovely Mexican restaurant. The airy dining room, its pale yellow walls adorned with original Latin-influenced art, and wood-beamed ceiling, is a far cry from the tacky Tex-Mex type joints that can be found in any big city. It only took a few sips of our refreshingly tart Margaritas served with a bowl of crunchy tortillas and two wonderful sauces to realise why this restaurant has

been deemed one of the best, if not the best, Mexican restaurant in Paris by just about everyone. We began with the tú y yo, a plate filled with taquitos (crisp tubes of tortillas stuffed with shredded chicken), ceviche, guacamole and nopalitos, a mildly flavoured cactus salad. Turkey with mole, a sauce made with several varieties of chillies and dark chocolate, was rich and complex. The excellent beef fillet was covered in an earthy sauce made with cuitlacoche, a fungus that grows naturally on the ears of corn and is sometimes called Mexican corn truffle. Dessert was the equally good banana flambé, with cajeta, a sweet goat's milk sauce with caramel.

Botequim
1 rue Berthollet, 5th (01.43.37.98.46). Mº Censier Daubenton. **Open** noon-2.30pm, 8-11.30pm Mon-Sat; 8-11.30pm Sun. **Average** €30. **Credit** AmEx, MC, V. **Map** J9.
A botequim, a sort of Brazilian café, is a corner bar, bistro and café, all rolled into one. This Parisian botequim, located on a small street in the 5th arrondissement, with its tropical plants, bright yellow and green colour scheme and a hodgepodge of musical instruments and other Brazilian artefacts, creates a convivial mood. We started off with two powerful caipirinhas, made with lime juice, sugar and cachaça, a potent liqueur made from sugar cane. Next came a satisfying salad of hearts of palm, tomato, corn, avocado, cashews and shrimp and the panaché, an assortment of lightly fried chicken, beef and cheese beignets. Feijoada, a staple of Brazilian cuisine, didn't disappoint, with warm black beans, tender pork, a touch of spice and the traditional accompaniments of farofa (manioc flour), kale and fresh orange slices. For something lighter try the moqueca de peixe, a bahian-style fish stew with coconut milk and coriander. The ample portions didn't leave much room for dessert, but we couldn't resist the creamy manjar, delicious coconut custard.

El Palenque
5 rue de la Montagne-Ste-Geneviève, 5th (01.43.54.08.99). Mº Maubert Mutualité. **Open** 12.30-2.30pm, 7-10pm Mon-Sat. **Average** €30. **No credit cards**. **Non-smoking**. **Map** J8.
El Palenque is an unpretentious eaterie for the unconditional carnivore. For starters try the grilled chorizo criollo, a mild cousin of the Spanish spiced sausage, which is simply served on a wooden platter with chunks of bread. After that, the options are all seriously high in protein. The parillada completa is a two-person challenge, a mountain of meat involving black pudding, sweetbreads, sausages, kidneys and ribs. Less stout souls will find the steaks demanding in their own way, the standard cuts of Argentinian beef looming larger than their European equivalents. Our faux-filet was enormous, tender and perfectly cooked. Green salad and thick corn pancakes (torrejas choclo) are an unbeatable accompaniment. We paired the food with a bottle of Trapiche pinot noir, light in colour but robustly fruity. The dessert list features quince and sweet

potato in various guises, as well as a crème caramel doused in condensed milk. The milico membrillo – sweet potato jelly with a slice of brie – was a surprising success. Dinner is served at 8pm and 10pm: don't be late, as there's generally a queue of hopefuls waiting to pounce – carnivores all.

Múkura ★

79 quai de Valmy, 10th (01.42.01.18.67). M° Jacques Bonsergent. **Open** noon-10pm Tue-Sun. **Average** €25. **Lunch menu** €10, €12. **No credit cards. Non-smoking. Map** L4.

Popping our heads round the door of this cosy, brightly coloured spot on the Canal St-Martin, we inhaled the most wonderful aromas. On returning it became obvious why it smells so good: this is a non-smoking restaurant, and what a difference it makes! Amid the sunny decor of red and yellow walls, hanging baskets of garlic and a dresser bearing an enormous bowl of exotic fruit, the charming Esperanza serves up meat and maize dishes and fruity salads, while through a hole in the wall you can see the chef working in his squeaky-clean kitchen. The Colombian food is like a fruity version of Mexican. The guacamole was excellent, and the delicious marinera combined papaya with prawns and a deep pink sauce a million miles from prawn cocktail. Encantador was chicken stuffed with spinach, potatoes and bacon, while panchita resembled chilli con carne topped with a crisply fried egg and was accompanied by maize triangles and avocado. Desserts included hot chocolate-coated banana, and a fruit fantasia that enabled us to taste a whole fruit family (the passion fruits). The crowd here is not as self-consciously trendy as that of the nearby Canal cafés. Is this because they can't smoke? 'Only imbeciles would be put off!', says Esperanza.

El Paladar

26 bis rue de la Fontaine au Roi, 11th (01.43.57.42.70). M° Goncourt or République. **Open** 7.30pm-midnight Mon-Sat. **Average** €25. **Prix fixe** €20-€30. **Credit** MC, V. **Wheelchair access. Map** M4.

Grafitti-covered pink and aqua walls and wooden tables set the tone at this pleasantly understated Cuban outpost. The outgoing staff were happy to explain the regularly changing menu of Cuban food from the fried and stewed schools of cooking. Yuca con mojo (sautéed manioc with onions and garlic) proved oily but delicious, and tostones (batter-fried plantains) were surprisingly light and crispy. Main dishes include pork, chicken, fish and arroz a la cubana, an impressive load of tomatoes, eggs and rice. We sampled pavo salteado (stewed turkey and potatoes seasoned with bay leaves) and pollo pio-pio (chicken fried in citrus). The pescado guisado fish struck the only false note, with its oddly muddy sauce of tomatoes, garlic, onions, potatoes and peppers. Overall, the dishes had plenty of substance and character. The flan maison, a stupendous sugar-soaked coconut custard, ended the meal on a high, in more ways than one.

El Bodegón de Pancho

8 rue Guy Môquet, 17th (01.53.31.00.73). M° Brochant. **Open** noon-10pm daily. Closed two weeks in July. **Average** €10. **Prix fixe** €10. **Credit** MC, V. **Wheelchair access.**

This little hole-in-the-wall eatery is for Colombians, carnivores and those with a taste for the surreal. You don't have to love Botero's rotund women (check out the prints on the wall) to come here, but you might leave looking like one. Little bottles of sweet and fizzy pink soda – labelled apple on the bottle but tasting like strawberry Frutella – set the mood. Unless you're having the hearty two-course set menu, which includes an excellent, sturdy soup (a meal in itself) and the daily special, skip the starters; you can't afford to take the edge off your appetite. The justly popular bandeja paisa, a peasanty and very porky speciality, is magnificent in proportion and will defy all but the hungriest: a large plate comes heaped with thick strips of crisply roasted pork, a scoop of spiced ground pork and a chunky chorizo sausage, plus rice, black beans, a plantain fritter and a small, hard semolina biscuit. Just in case that's not enough, the whole thing is topped with a fried egg. You won't have room for dessert, of course, but that shouldn't (and won't) stop you from digging into the rich, tasty rice pudding or the more refined guava paste served with slices of tangy Andean cheese. The makeshift stools, plastic tablecloths and adverts for long-distance phone cards are a constant reminder that Pancho is a home away from home for the neighbourhood's Colombian community. If you're lucky, and speak a little Spanish, you might just get invited to play a round of sapo (a local game with metal discs and a frog's mouth) to work up your appetite.

Ay Caramba!

59 rue Mouzaia, 19th (01.42.41.76.30/www. restaurant-aycaramba.com). M° Botzaris, Place des Fêtes or Pré St-Gervais. **Open** 7.30-11.30pm Tue-Thur; 7.30pm-2am Fri-Sun. Closed Christmas, New Year, two weeks in Aug. **Average** €35. **Credit** AmEx, DC, MC, V.

In a quiet residential district on the edge of town, this restaurant stands out with its brightly coloured walls, cacti and Disneyesque decor. Luckily, we had reserved, as the immense dining room was filling up with noisy groups, families with small children and young couples from the surrounding suburbs, another reminder that we were far from the city centre. Sipping a pitcher of frozen Margaritas made with fresh lime juice, we settled on chorizo quesadillas and guacamole to start – both quite good. Mains, though, were a bit of a let-down. Enchiladas with rice and beans did nothing to convince a French friend trying his first Mexican meal that this cuisine is worth exploring, and the fajitas lacked pzazz. The pecan pie and brownie were pleasant enough, if slightly soulless. By that time, however, the Mariachi band was playing and the Margaritas were kicking in, and it was hard not to get into the spirit.

Caribbean

In many ways Antillais cooking is the ultimate fusion food, as French, African, Indian, Spanish, English and other culinary cultures have contributed to the islands' repertoire. However, this cuisine is under-represented in Paris considering the sizeable community of some 200,000 people from the region – it may be that the grey climate is not suited to this sunny, slow-paced style of cooking. High-profile Antillaise chef Babette de Rosières has made a bold statement by moving from the suburbs into the former premises of Jamin, the restaurant that launched the career of superchef Joël Robuchon.

La Créole

122 bd du Montparnasse, 14th (01.43.20.62.12). M° Vavin. **Open** noon-2pm, 8-10pm Tue-Thur; noon-2pm, 8-11pm Fri, Sat. **Average** €35. **Prix fixe** €22.50. **Credit** AmEx, DC, MC, V. **Wheelchair access. Map** G9.

La Créole feels exactly like a typical Martiniquais 'habitation', the residence of a sugar cane plantation owner. Vibrant bouquets of tropical flowers, sunny-natured waitresses clad in colourful, lacy damas, and white wicker furniture can lull even the most stressed-out wannabe holidaymaker into believing he's abroad. Once we'd slipped into 'wish you were here' mode thanks to the complimentary crunchy accras (salt cod fritters) and particularly the warming effects of our luscious but pungent ti'ponch (rum with sugar syrup and a squirt of lime), we were ready to launch into our first course. In our spicy stuffed crabs, the flesh-to-breadcrumb ratio was tipped towards the latter but the tangy chiktaï salad of salty, toasted cod was lip-smackingly good and the christophine squash gratin creamy yet light. The main courses were the star attraction, however, and the diva of them all was the magnificent ouassou: lobster-sized crayfish in a gloriously spicy red sauce that made finger licking imperative. A well-executed classic pork colombo sported plenty of meat and a psychedelic touch of peppers. The thick-cut char-grilled tuna steak proved lighter than it first seemed thanks to the sauce chien, a refreshing lime and garlic vinaigrette. The chocolate, coconut and orange desserts provided a satisfying finale, although a thick white blancmange brought back less-than-fond memories of school canteens.

Le Flamboyant

11 rue Boyer-Barret, 14th (01.45.41.00.22). M° Pernéty. **Open** 8-10.30pm Tue; noon-2pm, 8-10.30pm Wed-Sat; noon-2pm Sun. **Average** €30. **Credit** MC, V. **Map** F10.

Although it's named after a feathery tropical tree with flamboyant flowers that's found in Martinique and Guadeloupe, you wouldn't know that this quiet place with a classic bistro façade and lace panels in the windows was Antillais, or French West Indian, until you went in and opened the menu. Order some crunchy golden accras to nibble while enjoying a ti'ponch, and then go for authentic, carefully cooked main courses such as shark curry, colombo de cabri (goat with colombo, a French Creole spice mixture) or spicy black pudding. A little expensive, but that doesn't prevent it from being very popular with Paris's prosperous Caribbean community.

La Table de Babette

32 rue de Longchamp, 16th (01.45.53.00.07). M° Trocadéro. **Open** noon-2pm, 8-10.30pm Mon-Sat. **Average** €50. **Prix fixe** €39. **Lunch menu** €34. **Credit** AmEx, MC, V. **Wheelchair access. Map** C5.

Babette de Rosières, one of the best-known Antillaise chefs in Paris, is determined to lift Creole cooking out of the ethnic slot it occupies in the Paris culinary landscape. This nuanced and delicious cuisine is not always viewed as serious cooking by the Paris gastronomic establishment, so, as part of her crusade, de Rosières has moved into the former premises of Jamin, the setting in which Joël Robuchon emerged as a world-renowned chef. Clearly, she'd like to follow a similar trajectory, which perhaps explains the painfully mannered service, formal decor and whopping prices. The food has been prettied up – and unfortunately toned down – for this swanky corner of the 16th arrondissement. Also missing is the generosity of Creole cooking and entertaining, the version on offer here having been violently pasteurised. We found just a shred or two of crab in our gratinée of christophine squash and in our féroce (mashed avocado, crab and cayenne pepper), and so were truly hungry when the main courses arrived – John Dory en blaff (a highly seasoned stock) and (superb) slow-braised pork in five-spice powder. Desserts were a bit of a let-down too – sweet potato mousse was bland, while flambéed banana was soggy. The big thumping bill at the end of the meal drives home the point of the evening in case you've missed it – under the name of the restaurant is printed 'gastronomie antillaise' and 'formerly Jamin'.

Eastern Mediterranean

There's more to Middle Eastern cuisine in Paris than the plate-smashing Greeks lining the cobbled streets of the Latin Quarter. New arrival Liza showcases the best of Beirut, while long-established Mavrommatis is renowned for its refined Greek fare. The best Lebanese and Iranian restaurants serve the immigrant communities of the 15th, off the tourist track but not so far from the Eiffel Tower.

Big feeds and authentic Cypriot flavours at super-friendly **Kazaphani**.

Liza ★

*14 rue de la Banque, 2nd (01.55.35.00.66). M°
Bourse.* **Open** noon-2.15pm, 8-10.30pm daily.
Average €38. **Prix fixe** €42 (dinner only). **Lunch
menu** €17-€32. **Credit** AmEx, DC, MC, V. **Map** H4.
Liza Soughayar has created one of the best foreign restaurants to open in Paris for a long time. Her idea was to showcase the chic style and superb food of Beirut, her home town. All of the furniture and table settings here come from Lebanon, and they surprise with their edgy design. White enamelled steel tables are perforated in lacy patterns over a lining of sky-blue enamelled steel, mother-of-pearl screens line the windows, floors are covered with dark parquet or black and white cement tiles, and white lamps with nipped waists hang over the large bar in the front dining room. The menu is also unexpected, including many meze that even those well versed in Lebanese cuisine won't know. Lentil, fried onion and orange salad is a delicious dish, as is the kebbe (minced, seasoned raw lamb) and the grilled halloumi cheese with own-made apricot preserves. Main courses such

as minced lamb with coriander-spiced spinach and rice or a mixed grill of Mediterranean fish are light, flavourful and well presented. Try one of the fine Lebanese wines, and finish up with the halva ice-cream with carob molasses. This place packs out with a young crowd every night, so be sure to book.

Mavrommatis

*5 rue du Marché des Patriarches, 5th (01.43.31.17.17/
www.mavrommatis.fr). M° Censier Daubenton.* **Open**
noon-2.15pm, 7-11pm Tue-Sat. Closed Aug. **Average**
€45. **Prix fixe** €34. **Lunch menu** €22. **Credit**
AmEx, MC, V. **Wheelchair access. Map** J9.
'Kalos orisate,' said our smiling waiter while showing us to our table laid with starched napkins, fine crystal and porcelain. And we indeed felt at home among the old photographs, oriental carpets and traditional oak furniture that grace this aristocratic setting. The authentic yet innovative Greek cuisine echoed the refinement. Starting with the megali pikilia, we nibbled our way through an assortment of traditional cold meze – marinated red

peppers, smooth houmous, taramósalata, garlicky tzatziki, generous octopus salad and delicate stuffed dolmades – as well as heartier hot appetisers such as cinnamon-spiced meatballs, aubergine feta croquettes and Cypriot speciality koupies. Main courses showcased the chef's creativity. Roasted quails with grape leaves, bulgur wheat and a honey pistachio sauce were a successful yet non-traditional sweet and savoury combination, while swordfish on a bed of red and green peppers put a twist on another speciality, spetsofaie. An unusual date and vanilla parfait provided the perfect finale.

Other locations: Les Délices d'Aphrodite, 4 rue de Candolle, 5th (01.43.31.40.39).

Kibele

*12 rue de l'Echiquier, 10th (01.48.24.57.74). M°
Bonne Nouvelle or Strasbourg St-Denis.* **Open** noon-3pm, 7pm-midnight Mon-Sat. **Average** €20. **Prix fixe** €12.50, €14.90 (dinner only). **Lunch menu** €9. **Credit** MC, V. **Wheelchair access. Map** K4.

In a locality filled with kebab shops, Kibele serves more sophisticated Greek and Turkish cuisine at fair prices. The arty photos, contemporary pottery, soft lighting and neo-classical columns provided a modern backdrop to our culinary Mediterranean journey, while Greek red wine from Naoussa added to the mood. Our first stop was an assortment of tasty hot and cold meze, including crisp spinach and feta croquettes, homemade dolmades and funnel-shaped cake-like courgette fritters, accompanied by fluffy warm Turkish bread. Next stop was Anatolia – the minced-meat kebab filled with pistachios and melting Turkish cheese served with bulgur wheat was delightful, but prawns drowning in an ouzo and saffron sauce were sweet and bland. We bypassed the honey-drenched pastries in favour of rose-flavoured loukoumia (Turkish delight) and mint tea, which sadly came in sachets. Before leaving we joined a reggae gig in the basement, where concerts are held every evening.

Kazaphani

*122 av Parmentier, 11th (01.48.07.20.19). M°
Goncourt or Parmentier.* **Open** noon-3pm, 7-11pm Tue-Fri, Sun; 7-11pm Sat. Closed last two weeks in Aug. **Average** €30. **Prix fixe** €18-€35. **Credit** AmEx, MC, V. **Wheelchair access. Map** M5.

The welcome at Kazaphani was so relaxed that we felt as though we had walked into someone's home. But, like everything at this family-run Cypriot restaurant, it warms up slowly and is all the better for it. We opted for the meze menu with three courses for €32. Though there were only two of us, the dishes just kept on coming, and what we gained in choice we did not lose in quality. Of note were the octopus in olive oil, lemon and garlic, wonderfully lemony mushrooms, a tasty paste of broad beans and a taramósalata so pale and creamy it was worlds away from the lurid pink concoction that so often insults the name. Next came plates of massive aniseed-flavoured gambas, calamari and deep-fried whitebait. We were nearly beaten by the meat course

but this was also of excellent quality, particularly the crisp meatballs and stuffed pork. Hatzimichalis or Nemea are good choices for red wines, although we went for retsina. By the time we got on to délice d'Aphrodite (yoghurt, walnuts and honey) and fruit salad with coconut and sorbet, Pavlos was sitting at our table, offering us an alcohol-spiked coffee, talking about boyhood memories. Kazaphani gives nostalgia its true meaning in Greek – longing for home.

Mazeh

*20 rue Marmontel, 15th (01.45.32.40.70). M°
Convention.* **Open** 7-11pm Tue; noon-3pm, 7-11pm Wed-Sun. Closed one week in Aug. **Average** €32. **Prix fixe** €23.80. **Lunch menu** €13. **Credit** MC, V. **Wheelchair access. Map** B8.

What it lacks in decor – stucco walls, heavy pine furniture and lace table runners – this Persian restaurant makes up for in refinement. On a recent visit, starters were all very delicate in flavour, from a chicken and potato purée with capers and saffron to roasted aubergine laced with confit onions. Main courses are mostly variations on the kebab, with the house specialities being elaborate sweet and savoury rice dishes served with grilled meats. The pilaf with cherries and pistachios perfectly complemented the tender marinated lemon cockerels, while buttery saffron rice loaded with raisins and orange zest set off a moist marinated lamb fillet. Although the main course portions are generous, leave room for dessert, including the refreshing rose sorbet with lime juice or the selection of Persian pâtisseries, which include almond brittle and rosewater-flavoured marzipan. Service was friendly and helpful; the only downside was the waiter's lack of knowledge about wine.

Restaurant Al Wady ★

*153-155 rue de Lourmel, 15th (01.45.58.57.18). M°
Lourmel.* **Open** noon-3pm, 7-11.30pm daily. **Average** €25. **Prix fixe** €19. **Lunch menu** €11, €14. **Credit** AmEx, MC, V. **Non-smoking room. Map** B9.

Al Wady is not the type of place we'd take a visiting friend keen for a picture-postcard Parisian dining experience. Unless, that is, said acquaintance had a hankering for a Lebanese feast to rival the best in the Middle East. The heroically long menu makes for an agony of indecision, so we settled on the meze platter. At €38 for two it's a great way to sample house specialities such as garlicky houmous, moist tabouleh and smoky baba ganoush. And that's just for starters. Pastries cooked golden brown hide the perfect bite of delicately spiced lamb, while succulent chicken pieces in a caramelised orange glaze will appeal to those with a sweet palate. Feeling carnivorous, we bypassed salads in favour of the mixed grill: a meatlovers' selection of lamb and chicken charred to perfection and presented alongside a cooling salad of yoghurt tossed with lemon, cucumber and tomato. The yardstick for true greatness in Lebanese kitchens is measured by the falafel – neither too grainy nor too moist, Al Wady's are orbs of herbed wonder. The coffee is strong and the pastries can be bought in boxes to take away.

Far Eastern

Given France's colonial past, you might expect a high standard of Asian food in Paris. Sadly, however, many restaurants (especially the chic ones) opt to dumb down their cooking for the tender French palate and offer prix fixe menus of predictable standards that discourage diners from exploring lesser-known dishes. There is great Chinese and Laotian food to be had in Chinatown (on the outer edge of the 13th arrondissement) and Belleville (in the 20th), but it's hard to find a Thai restaurant capable of wowing a seasoned gastronome. One cuisine that doesn't seem to suffer too much in Paris is Korean, with wonderful restaurants in the 9th and 15th arrondissements.

CAMBODIAN

La Mousson

9 rue Thérèse, 1st (01.42.60.59.46). M° Pyramides. **Open** noon-2.30pm, 7-10.30pm Mon-Sat. Closed three weeks in Aug. **Average** €20. **Prix fixe** €18, €24 (dinner only). **Lunch menu** €14, €18. **Credit** MC, V. **Non-smoking. Map** H5.

Just steps from the cluster of Japanese restaurants on the rue Ste-Anne is this oasis of Cambodian hospitality. Furnished with items that could have come right out of Phnom Penh's colourful street markets – from the mass-manufactured mural of Angkor Wat to the woven cotton scarves that serve as tablecloths – La Mousson still feels welcoming and comfortable, particularly if you begin the meal with the house cocktail, a fragrant concoction of rice wine and lychee juice. The food is equally simple and pleasant. Cold spring rolls, thick with lettuce, mint, vermicelli, shrimp and shredded chicken, satiated any pre-dinner hunger pangs. Caramelised filet mignon was decent, if somewhat overcooked. Amok, a classic Cambodian dish of tender fish fillets steamed in coconut milk within a banana leaf, was much better – soft and exotically perfumed. The best dish, however, was the excellent minced pork with lemongrass, a pungent mix of pork, coconut milk, shrimp paste and shrimp. Wash it all down with the very affordable wine, and your wallet will be pleasantly surprised too.

Le Cambodge

10 av Richerand, 10th (01.44.84.37.70). M° Goncourt or République. **Open** noon-2.30pm, 8-11.30pm Mon-Sat. Closed 1 Aug-15 Sept, 24 Dec-1 Jan. **Average** €16. **Credit** MC, V. **Map** L4.

It doesn't take bookings, it's always full and the tables are so close together you can practically kiss your neighbour's tonsils. This should be enough to put most people off a restaurant. However, with over ten years in business to show for it, the food, service and low prices more than make up for what Le Cambodge lacks in convenience and comfort. The

system here is simple: you write your order on a piece of paper, including personal preferences such as 'no coriander', 'no peanuts' or 'extra rice', and after a short wait the dishes appear. We ordered the bobun special, a hot and cold mix of sautéed beef, noodles, salad, beansprouts and imperial rolls, and banhoy, or the Ankorian picnic, a selection of same ingredients to be wrapped in lettuce and mint leaves and dipped in a sauce. Each cost around €6 and tasted very fresh. Le Cambodge also serves soups, salads and curries including the house speciality natin, stewed pork in a fragrant coconut sauce. If you crave more space, order your food to go and have a summer picnic by the Canal St-Martin.

La Coloniale ★

161 rue de Picpus, 12th (01.43.43.69.10). M° Porte Dorée. **Open** noon-2pm, 7.30-10.30pm Mon-Sat. Closed Aug. **Average** €25. **Lunch menu** €12, €15. **Credit** MC, V. **Wheelchair access. Non-smoking room. Map** Q9.

Chef Thaknol Moeur hails from Cambodia, while his French wife Dominique (who also speaks Khmer) flits about the dining room singing along to 1920s jazz tunes that match the pleasing, Asian-themed bric-a-brac scattered about. We're neighbourhood regulars, drawn again and again by the very reasonable prices and the kitchen's exemplary skill with fresh basil, coriander and hot peppers in its tangy soups and creamy curries that are leagues above the average corner Asian traiteur's pre-fab cuisine. Begin with a ginger chicken soupe de l'Indo, an orange-bright, coconut-based curry, or the chicken beignets – baguette slices fused to breast meat and deep-fried. Then dive into the succulent chicken satay, the loc-lak (beef fried rice) or the seafood noodles sauté – a mix of mussels, squid, scallops and prawns seared in black pepper. The amok is a memorable little soufflé-like steamed salmon, coconut and lemongrass concoction served in a ramekin. Most dishes arrive with superb dipping sauces and cute pickle garnishes carved into

For Cambodian comfort food, you can't go wrong at the perenially popular **Le Cambodge**.

sea creature shapes. For dessert, try the bohbor kthi – jackfruit in squishy tapioca topped with toasted sesame seeds. Ask for one of the tiny non-smoking room's two tables for extra privacy.

CHINESE

Chez Vong ★

10 rue de la Grande Truanderie, 1st (01.40.26.09.36). M° Etienne Marcel. **Open** noon-2.30pm, 7-11.30pm Mon-Sat. **Average** €50. **Lunch menu** €23.50. **Credit** AmEx, DC, MC, V. **Wheelchair access. Non-smoking room. Map** J5.
The staff at this soothingly intimate Chinese restaurant obviously take pride in the excellent cooking here, which covers the great dishes of Canton, Shanghai, Beijing and Sichuan. From the warm greeting at the door to the knowledgeable and trilingual service (Cantonese, Mandarin and French), each phase of the dining experience is thoughtfully orchestrated to showcase the delicious possibilities of China's diverse cuisine. Tables, draped in pink cloth, are widely spaced; low lighting and green ceramic bamboo partitions heighten the sense of intimacy. The atmosphere is such a far cry from the clamour and brusqueness of typical Chinese restaurants that we wondered how authentic the food could be. Any doubts were soon extinguished from the first arrival of the beautifully presented dishes, which are immediately placed on heated stands at the table. Expertly cooked spicy shrimp glistened in a smooth, robust sauce of onions and ginger. Silky ma po tofu melted in the mouth, its spicy and peppery flavours melding with the fine pork mince in synergistic succulence. Very tender pepper beef, served with fresh baby corn, mushroom and carrots, came in a crisp, savoury 'bird's nest', an acknowledgement that garnishes too should be palatable. Ravioli of prawn, bamboo shoots and coriander were divinely delicate, the thin wrapper barely containing the ingredients. This perfect meal came at a price, but it was worth every cent.

Mirama

17 rue St-Jacques, 5th (01.43.54.71.77). M° Cluny La Sorbonne or St-Michel. **Open** noon-10.45pm daily. **Average** €20. **Credit** MC, V. **Non-smoking room. Map** J7.
Serving surprisingly good food at fair value in an area otherwise packed with tourist traps, this tidy little Cantonese is a delightful place to refuel next time you're in St-Michel. Eyeing the lacquered ducks and glazed pork ribs hanging in the open kitchen at the entrance, we chose a table in the front room – a non-smoking area – where we had a clear view of the chef. Start with one of the many soups on offer, such as the noodle soup with chunks of tender braised beef and fresh green onion in a rich beef broth. We devoured a plate piled with sliced roasted duck and pork on rice that easily fed two. We also enjoyed the sweet and sour chicken, replete with pieces of pineapple and green pepper. A side dish of broccoli in oyster sauce was cooked perfectly crisp-tender, but the sauce lacked zing. Portions here are generous and there is a wide selection of classic dishes with (thankfully) no attempt to introduce non-traditional ingredients for the sake of being inventive. Service is pleasant and efficient.

New Nioullaville

32-34 rue de l'Orillon, 11th (01.40.21.96.18). M° Belleville. **Open** 11.45am-3pm, 6.45pm-1am daily. **Average** €20. **Lunch menu** €8.30-€13.50 (Mon-Fri). **Credit** AmEx, MC, V. **Wheelchair access. Map** M4.

The immense dining room, convivial atmosphere, wide selection of dishes from China and Thailand and gentle prices make this one of our favourite places to celebrate with a large group of friends – at the start of Chinese New Year, performers dressed as colourful dragons danced up and down the restaurant's aisles beneath a ceiling hung with bright red lanterns. Arrive hungry and hail down one of the dim sum carts circling the room. We particularly liked the steamed shrimp dumplings, shrimp balls and fried pork dumplings. For main courses, it's hard to go wrong with the Sichuan/ Cantonese specialities. The Genghis Khan beef – tender strips of steak sautéed with ginger, onion, fresh basil and lemongrass – was outstanding. Prawns lightly fried with salt and pepper were plump and fresh. Chop suey was a delicious mixture of more than six vegetables, and cold Tsingtao beer from China hit the spot. Unfortunately, service can be erratic, with some dishes arriving long after others on busy nights. For dessert, there is a large selection of Chinese cakes, plus western-style ice-creams.

Le Président

120-124 rue du Fbg-du-Temple, 11th (01.47.00. 17.18). M° Belleville. **Open** noon-3pm, 7pm-2am daily. **Average** €20. **Lunch menu** €12.50. **Credit** AmEx, MC, V. **Wheelchair access. Non-smoking room. Map** M4.

It's quite a trek through the lobby (porcelain, dried bits of shark, photos of visiting celebs – well, Serge Gainsbourg and Mitterrand – a 1989 award for Asian cuisine, etc) and up the imposing staircase. But, if the place looks a bit tired, the food is fresh and bright, and there's a roaring trade in

Big Fat Asian Weddings (always a good sign) – hence the Imelda Marcos pavilion and sofa in the middle of the dining room, perfect for those happy snaps. At Sunday lunch, we joined cheerful (western) family parties pondering their orders over hot, fresh dim sum from the steam trolley. The kids devoured chicken noodles and ice-cream, grimaced at the lobster tank and took turns on the sofa, while we tackled platters of tender pork with huge smoky-tasting mushrooms, stir-fried squid and chicken with cashews, all colourfully garnished with broccoli, crunchy water chestnuts and neat little stars of carrot. Then came creamy, steamed coconut dumplings on bitter chocolate sauce. We were even treated to a ravishing Chinese bride and much popping of corks.

Wok

23 rue des Taillandiers, 11th (01.55.28.88.77). M° Bastille or Ledru-Rollin. **Open** 7.15-11.15pm daily. **Average** €20. **Prix fixe** €16.50. **Credit** MC, V. **Wheelchair access. Map** M7.

Wok is the epitome of Bastille youth culture. The long central pine refectory table and the decor's Zen-like minimalism is coupled with loud rock music and a food concept that ensures great value and freshness. The idea is to take your bowl, already half-filled with noodles or rice, to a buffet of uncooked vegetables, meat and fish, which you pile on, preferably taking into account what might taste good together. You then present your bowl to the chef, who asks what spices and aromatics you want, then with a sizzle and a crack your selection is tossed into the white-hot wok and returned to you in minutes as an authentic Chinese stir-fry. We were pleased with our efforts of combining

Le Pacifique

squid and Chinese mushrooms with rice noodles, and the food benefits from the short time lapse between wok and mouth. The starters, in this case some ordinary vegetarian nems (spring rolls) and heavy vegetable tempura, were poor, and the sweet nems with chocolate sauce was too hybrid an idea to pull off, but for an excellent stir-fry in a hot ambience look no further.

Likafo ★
39 av de Choisy, 13th (01.45.84.20.45). Mᵒ Porte de Choisy. **Open** noon-midnight daily. **Average** €20. **Credit** MC, V. **Wheelchair access.**

When a Chinese reader first told us about this Hong Kong-style restaurant, he made us promise not to publish the information. Since then, the French press has discovered Likafo and the dining room now fills with a happy mix of Chinese and western diners, all ordering their favourite dishes off the extensive menu. We like this nondescript place on the outer edge of Chinatown so much that we even came here for a family meal on Christmas Eve, but had never taken notes until our most recent visit. The poulet croustillant sauce soja is a must for anyone who loves the tangy taste of Chinese vinegar, matched here with battered and deep-fried chicken strips. Noticing that many around us were ordering hot-pots, we chose one filled with rice and spare ribs in a potent red chilli and black bean sauce. Black beans also appeared in our third dish of green pepper and Chinese mushrooms stuffed with a succulent prawn filling. We always order a plate of seasonal green vegetables, which are reliably fresh and beautifully cooked. For more adventurous palates, there are plenty of dishes featuring ingredients such as tripe and duck's tongues. Whatever you order, though, you can't go wrong.

Tricotin
15 av de Choisy, 13th (01.45.84.74.44). Mᵒ Porte de Choisy. **Open** 11am-11pm daily. **Average** €12. **Credit** MC, V. **Wheelchair access.** **Non-smoking room.**

Tricotin flanks a gloomy passage off the southern end of avenue de Choisy, aka Main Street Chinatown, complete with skyscrapers, exotic supermarkets and Cantonese calligraphy on the McDonald's next door. To the left, a small starched-linen dining room dispenses Thai, Malay and Cambodian cuisine, while the huge, bright canteen to the right is the place for dim sum, giant noodle soups, salads and Chinese standards. After a disappointing visit, we were delighted to find the latter right back on track: the kitchen bustling with a ship-shape crew of white-clad chefs, the tables packed with a multi-generational mix of locals and visitors from uptown. Perfect crispy nems with garden-fresh green salad and mint sprigs were followed by stacked baskets containing some of the finest steamed tit-bits we've had: perfectly textured rice ravioli concealing flavoursome jewel-bright greens and shrimp, and a huge sticky rice dumpling dotted with tender morsels of pork, neatly wrapped

in a giant lotus leaf. Chicken noodles, glazed duck and crispy steamed Thai broccoli were all exemplary, as was a platter of pleasingly large, firm scallop slices with mushrooms and cashews. Less familiar exotica include the drinks – sweet red beans mashed in soya milk, fresh coconut juice with slivers of translucent flesh, mix-it-yourself chocolate syrup with hot condensed milk – and the house dessert, ban dout, a thick, jelly-like substance served with sweet 'n' salty soya milk, caramel and sesame seeds.

Le Pacifique ★
35 rue de Belleville, 20th (01.42.49.66.80). Mᵒ Belleville. **Open** 11am-1.30am daily. **Average** €25. **Prix fixe** €14-€33. **Credit** MC, V. **Wheelchair access.** **Map** N3.

We were expecting all the elements of a typical Sunday dim sum lunch: crowds, queues and surly service. Instead, we were swiftly welcomed into a fairly sedate restaurant partially divided into two rooms. The front – with floor-to-ceiling windows – looked out on to the hubbub of the busy street. No trolleys of food being pushed by gruff old ladies here. The comprehensive selection of dim sum is ordered off the menu and delivered to the table in quick succession, or even all at the same time. From the fluffy steamed pork buns to the plump prawn dumplings and fragrant sticky rice steamed in lotus leaf, every dish that arrived was reassuringly authentic. It might not be the finest dim sum you can get in Paris, but it's good enough. The choice of interesting tea is a further incentive.

INDONESIAN

Djakarta Bali
9 rue Vauvilliers, 1st (01.45.08.83.11/www. djakartabali.com). Mᵒ Louvre Rivoli. **Open** 7pm-midnight Tue-Sun. **Average** €25. **Prix fixe** €20-€45. **Credit** DC, MC, V. **Wheelchair access.** **Non-smoking room.** **Map** J5.

If you have a nut allergy, stay far, far away. Virtually every dish served here is smothered in peanut sauce. Unimaginative, you might think, but the warm surroundings, friendly service and good food will help you forgive the repetition. The menu offers several types of rijsttafel, the Dutch-inspired smörgåsbord of steamed rice served with an indefinite succession of small side dishes. The most comprehensive set was the rijsttafel Bali, which included about eight generously portioned courses and a handful of smaller sides and condiments. The feast kicked off with a clear and tangy chicken soup perfumed with Indonesian herbs. Highlights that followed included deep-fried spring rolls, fried chicken liver and beef brochettes – all dipped, coated or marinated in an intense, dark peanut sauce. Despite the homogenous flavouring, each dish was uniquely delicious. A la carte, a mixed vegetable salad (again dressed with peanut sauce) was pleasantly refreshing, beef rendang could have benefited from a longer simmer, while the

Time Out
Travel Guides

France

Time Out
Paris

Time Out
South of France
Provence & the Côte d'Azur

Time Out
Paris
Eating & Drinking

**Available at all good bookshops
and at timeout.com/shop**

**Time Out
Guides**

giant prawns steamed in banana leaf – though indeed gigantic and fresh – swam in a coconut milk-based curry sauce that was tasty but a tad watery. Still, the dishes are exotically alluring and they are prepared with pride. From the traditional Balinese handicrafts and artwork that adorn the room to the careful selection of dishes on offer, the restaurant – run by the children of a high-ranking Indonesian minister exiled in Paris from the mid-1960s – remains a welcoming showcase of the Spice Islands' fragrant cuisine.

KOREAN

Han Lim

6 rue Blainville, 5th (01.43.54.62.74). M° Cardinal Lemoine or Place Monge. **Open** 7-10.30pm Tue; noon-2.30pm, 7-10.30pm Wed-Sun. Closed Aug. **Average** €25. **Lunch menu** €14. **Credit** MC, V. **Map** J8.

If home-style Korean cuisine is what you're after, this 20-year-old haunt is your place. Koreans and foreigners alike come here for their fix of comfort food and garlic. Bring an appetite, as the portions are plentiful. We started with the deep-fried pork- and vegetable-filled gyoza, which were fresh and well cooked. Vegetarians should sample the hefty but reliable classic Korean pancake with spring onion. The menu is brief, but there's something for everyone. If you have a penchant for beef, try the traditional bulgogi – sweet and juicy marinated strips that you cook yourself, accompanied by an array of homemade side dishes such as hot and spicy daikon, fresh kimchi (cabbage) and the milder spinach with sesame – but mind the garlic. Another speciality to consider sharing is the crispy fried chicken with garlic, big enough to fill you up for the day. We waddled out, doggy bag in hand.

Gin Go Gae ★

28 rue Lamartine, 9th (01.48.78.24.64). M° Cadet. **Open** noon-2.30pm, 7-11pm Mon-Sat. **Average** €20. **Lunch menu** €9.50, €10.50. **Credit** MC, V. **Wheelchair access. Non-smoking room.** **Map** J3.

We had been coming here about once a week for the €9.50 lunch menu, surely one of the best bargains in Paris, but had always been intrigued by the à la carte offerings (after all, who could resist the offer of 'non-spiced soup of cowhead meat'?). One day, in a desperate bid to shake off a vicious cold, we pointed at the kimchi soup, a broth spiked with the fermented spiced cabbage that is perhaps the essence of Korean cooking. Ever kind and discreet, the owner looked at us as if to say, 'are you sure you know what you're doing?' before returning with a lidded bowl brimming with the sinus-clearing stuff. We can't swear that this concoction cured us, but it certainly cheered us up immensely, as does every meal at this modest yet comfortable spot. On an ordinary day, we usually settle for the juicy

fried gyoza or crisp galettes de soja (a sort of vegetable croquette) to start, followed by the raw fish with rice or the bibimbap, a hearty bowl of beef, vegetables and rice tossed together in an invigorating sauce. Every meal comes with several small bowls of vegetables, such as marinated spinach, potatoes and mung beans.

Restaurant Euro

65 rue du Fbg-Montmartre, 9th (01.53.21.07.89). M° Notre-Dame-de-Lorette. **Open** noon-3pm, 7-11pm daily. **Average** €19. **Lunch menu** €10-€25. **Prix fixe** €19-€25. **Credit** MC, V. **Wheelchair access. Map** J3.

Traditional food, as cooked by Madame Oh at Restaurant Euro, rests on a foundation of garlic, ginger, soy sauce, rice vinegar and sesame oil, always accompanied by medium-grained white rice, in a steel bowl to match the metal chopsticks. Begin with a tasty binn dae teok, a type of fried bean pancake, or a kimchi version. The vermicelli noodle starter, chapchae, is fried with tender carrots, mushrooms and pork. Dol sot bibimbap combines beef with lettuce, seaweed, egg, beansprouts, carrots and spinach (there's also a veggie version, oh saek bibimbap), and if you look clueless enough your server will mush it all up for you in true local style. It's also good to try the accompaniments that automatically come with most dishes: kimchi, as well as panchan, various ceramic dishes filled with the likes of pickled ferns, dried fish, seasoned beansprouts and cucumber salad. The at-your-table charcoal barbecues are on the pricey side, but budget diners can fry their own gas wok versions of beef, chicken or seafood, especially excellent value when part of the €19 dinner menu.

Odori

18 rue Letellier, 15th (01.45.77.88.12). M° Emile Zola or La Motte Picquet Grenelle. **Open** noon-2.30pm, 7-10.30pm Tue-Sun. Closed a few days in Dec. **Average** €17.50. **Credit** MC, V. **Wheelchair access. Non-smoking room. Map** C8.

It's out of the way, hidden down an obscure street, yet it's perpetually packed with Korean diners – an encouraging sign of delicious, authentic food, confirmed at the first piquant bite. You might baulk at the thought of steak tartare in an unfamiliar environment, but this sublime starter is worth the gamble. Not that it is one: the ice-cold meat, scented with sesame oil and textured with slivers of Fuji apple, raw garlic and a raw egg, is always fresh and cleanly prepared. Follow this mild dish with a comforting beef and leek soup, a Korean staple that is just hot and spicy enough to be warming rather than blazing. Pork and tofu sautéed with spicy sauce is equally balanced in flavour, although not in ingredients (in our experience the tender slices of pork are all too few). The classic Korean barbecue comes with the usual side dishes of kimchi and various root vegetables, marinated in vinegar or tossed in the same lively chilli paste. Korean beef arrives sizzling on a hot plate

International

surrounded by a moat of sweet but mild stock. Those who prefer to cook over a real charcoal (not gas) grill should choose the Korean short ribs instead. Service is friendly but harried.

MALAYSIAN

Chez Fung
32 rue de Frémicourt, 15th (01.45.67.36.99).
M° Cambronne or La Motte Picquet Grenelle.
Open noon-2.30pm, 7-10.30pm Mon-Sat. Closed Aug.
Average €20. **Prix fixe** €14.50 (dinner only).
Lunch menu €9.90 (Mon-Sat). **Credit** MC, V.
Non-smoking room. Map D8.

One of the rare Malaysian restaurants in Paris, this little place, down an unremarkable side street, is a real gem for the budget-conscious. The charming Regina, who has recently taken over from her uncle, graciously welcomed us at the door and patiently explained the offerings, going as far as to pluck laminated photos from the window to give us a better idea of what was on offer. While munching on coconut milk-roasted peanuts we perused the extensive menu but opted for the prix fixe, unbeatable value at €14.50. The rojak starter, a fruit and vegetable salad in a soy and honey dressing, was simple yet surprising. Less inspired was the main of stewed beef rendang, which proved somewhat stringy, though its velvety sauce was satisfyingly rich. Happily, the delicately spiced salmon steamed in a banana leaf was superb. Desserts of coconut-filled crêpes and a creamy coconut milk mousse hit just the right note after the heat of the curried mains.

THAI AND LAOTIAN

Khun Akorn
8 av de Taillebourg, 11th (01.43.56.20.03).
M° Nation. **Open** noon-2pm, 7.30-11pm Tue-Sun.
Average €40. **Credit** AmEx, MC, V.
Non-smoking room. Map Q7.

As far as Thai restaurants in Paris go, Khun Akorn is the best middle-of-the-road option. It's neither the small neon-lit local canteen nor the fancy high-end hotspot. The big main room is a friendly open space made intimate with carved wooden partitions and the Thai decor is traditional without being over the top. Start with the tongsai platter: a selection of starters including dumplings in banana leaves, crispy tartlets filled with minced prawn and chicken and beef satay. Top it off with the refreshing papaya salad, which has just the right amount of fishiness to it. We followed this with a green chicken curry that was perfect in everything but spiciness, or lack thereof, a common problem in many Asian restaurants here. The grilled squid salad was disappointingly tossed with tasteless winter tomatoes. If not dazzled by our meal, we were still very pleased. The service, while efficient, lacked Thai hospitality. Only brandishing our credit card managed to illicit a smile.

Rouammit & Huong Lan ★
103 av d'Ivry, 13th (01.53.60.00.34). M° Corvisart.
Open 11am-4pm, 7-11pm Tue-Sun. Closed last two weeks in Aug. **Average** €12.50. **Lunch menu** €8.90-€11.90. **Credit** MC, V. **Wheelchair access**.

Fans of South-east Asian food eventually learn to seek out Laotian holes-in-the-wall in Paris rather than splurge on flashier Thai restaurants. A perfect example is this plainly decorated Chinatown joint (bare tables, strips of carved wood here and there), which is easy to spot thanks to the queue out the door. Show up early or be prepared to wait: the food here is cheap and delicious and the service super-efficient and friendly. To sample the full range of flavours – hot, sour, aromatic, sweet – it's best to go in a group. Nine of us initially ordered nine dishes, only to order several of them again: among the repeats were lap neua, a tongue-tickling, chilli-spiked salad made with slivers of beef and tripe; lacquered duck in curry sauce; khao nom kroc, Laotian ravioli filled with shrimp; and sweet, juicy prawns stir-fried with Thai basil. Even the sticky rice was exceptional. If you're in the mood for dessert, try the assortment of gelatins, whose worm-like shapes and fluorescent colours appeal only to the adventurous.

Banyan
24 pl Etienne-Pernet, 15th (01.40.60.09.31).
M° Félix Faure. **Open** noon-3pm, 7.30-11.30pm Mon-Sat. **Average** €35. **Prix fixe** €30, €50.
Credit AmEx, MC, V. **Wheelchair access**.
Map N3.

There is not a carved vegetable or a tinkling fountain in sight at this elegant yet relaxed Thai restaurant. The food, reflecting the tasteful surroundings, arrives artfully stacked on square plates. The set fish or meat menu offers a good selection of dishes, but we took the more expensive route and ordered à la carte. We started with tasty, flower-shaped dumplings stuffed with a fresh prawn filling and beef salad whose fragrant herbs and chillies provided just the right amount of heat. The papaya salad, usually a sure test of a Thai restaurant, proved lacklustre and overpoweringly fishy. Our mains, the chef's specials, made up for this: scallops and prawns in a vivid orange curry sauce and thinly sliced steak with an unusual but pleasant banana sauce. Desserts were similarly inventive and beautifully presented, although fresh pineapple with grapefruit sorbet could have done without the lashings of grenadine syrup.

Lao Siam
49 rue de Belleville, 19th (01.40.40.09.68).
M° Belleville. **Open** noon-3pm, 7-11.30pm daily.
Average €20. **Credit** MC, V. **Wheelchair access**.
Non-smoking room. Map N3.

Lao Siam can be hellish on a weekend evening: on a noisy and crowded Saturday night, the service was harassed and erratic. On a rainy Monday evening, however, the staff were efficient – if not exactly enthusiastic or informative – and we all received our food at the same time. Spring rolls, coconut milk-laced soups, Peking duck and other familiar specialities are perfectly acceptable here, but it's worth straying off the beaten track. The boeuf séché, strips of tender but chewy lemongrass-scented dried beef, makes a great starter and goes down well with a glass of Asian beer. The comforting banana shoot and papaya salad was only slightly beleaguered by the inclusion of two insipid peeled shrimps, one of which remained uneaten. We used balls of sticky rice to greedily mop up the tangy dressing of the salade de couenne de porc (crunchy grilled pork rind), and the juices of the pork spare ribs on a bed of garlic, and washed it down with a pot of jasmine tea, which the waiters replenished willingly if unsmilingly.

TIBETAN

Pema Thang
13 rue de la Montagne Ste-Geneviève, 5th (01.43.54.34.34/www.pemathang.aol.com). Mº Maubert Mutualité. **Open** 7-10.30pm Mon; noon-2.30pm, 7-10.30pm Tue-Sat. **Average** €20. **Prix fixe** €13-€17. **Credit** AmEx, MC, V. **Wheelchair access. Non-smoking. Map** J8.
The Dalai Lama smiles benignly down through his spectacles from a portrait on the wall. There's a bit of light chanting on the hi-fi. The woman who takes your order is as calm and beautiful as the hills and the food she brings is a good introduction to the little-known cooking of Tibet. First-time visitors are well advised to try the set menu that lets you sample the specialities of the three regions of Tibet. These

are shadré (mild lamb curry), dingrul (beef stew) and langsha shemok (steamed beef ravioli served with a coriander sauce). We found them all delicately flavoured and original. Desserts were good too – grilled barley cake with own-made yoghurt and rice pudding with dried fruit. As for the tricky question of what to drink with Tibetan food, we recommend beer. Tibetan tea is probably just what you need after a long morning herding yak but, the rest of the time, tea with butter and salt tastes pretty much what it sounds like: disgusting. Our waitress did warn us it was 'spécial', which is what French people often say when they mean 'really bad'. We should have believed her.

VIETNAMESE

Restaurant Pho
3 rue Volta, 3rd (01.42.78.31.70). Mº Arts et Métiers. **Open** 11am-3pm Mon-Sat. Closed Aug. **Prix fixe** €6.90, €7.70. **No credit cards**. **Non-smoking. Map** K4.
Beef pho, Vietnam's fragrant, herb-infused noodle soup seasoned with chillies, basil, beansprouts and lemon, is the star of the show at this restaurant. Here, what you see is what you get – austere decor and fresh, piping hot soup at reasonable prices. Eating elbow-to-elbow in this tight space is an adventure, and it takes a friendly Asian soup house to bring urbanites this close together. The staff's French is limited, but their smiles are frequent and charming. The menu is straightforward: the choices are beef soup with meatballs or roast pork, or bobun (which

La Tonkinoise: memorable meals in a forgettable setting. *See p140.*

includes vermicelli noodles, sliced beef and chopped nem), and on Mondays you can also try banh canh, the chicken soup alternative. Portions are generous, and all soups are replete with meat, noodles, broth and sprouts. Half the fun is spicing it up – the tables are loaded with hot and exotic sauces. You could go for a body-cleansing touch of black vinegar or fire it up straight with red chilli. Eat in or take away, this is one serious soup-slurping, spoon-scraping, cold-fighting canteen.

Thuy Long

111 rue de Vaugirard, 6th (01.45.49.26.01).
M° Falguière, Montparnasse or St-Placide. **Open** 11.30am-9.30pm Tue-Sat. Closed Aug. **Average** €12. **Lunch menu** €10.90, €12.90. **Non-smoking.** **Credit** MC, V. **Map** G8.
An oasis of calm off the busy rue de Rennes, this Vietnamese eaterie is a great spot for a post-shopping bowl of soup or noodles. It's a small, inexpensive, no-frills place frequented mostly by locals but offering an impressive range of dishes. Some are northern Vietnamese classics such as nems, pho and bobun, while others were dreamed up over the years by the Vietnamese cook who runs the restaurant with her husband. We started with dumplings, nems and the signature autumn roll, a delicious spongy rice pancake filled with beef and vegetables, followed by five-spice chicken and noodles with grilled pork and shredded lettuce. Many similar places use ready-made five-spice mixes but in this case we could really taste that ours was own-made (the cook confirmed that it was). The delicious desserts, a bright green coconut dumpling and a coconut tofu cake, made a pleasant ending. The service was slightly unfriendly to start with but soon warmed up. If you're lucky enough to live nearby, you can get everything to take away too.

Le Lotus Blanc

45 rue de Bourgogne, 7th (01.45.55.18.89).
M° Varenne. **Open** noon-2.30pm, 7-10.30pm Mon-Sat. Closed two weeks in Aug. **Average** €20. **Prix fixe** €18-€32 (dinner only). **Lunch menu** €15-€32. **Credit** AmEx, MC, V. **Wheelchair access. Non-smoking room. Map** F6.
Despite the gentrification of Vietnamese restaurants in recent years, there remain places where nothing seems to have changed for decades. This minuscule restaurant, opened in 1975, is one of them: crimson velveteen banquettes and chairs, faded photos and Vietnamese knick-knacks gathering dust on the exposed stone wall. The owner, who immigrated to France in 1964, also possesses an old-world geniality. Trust his recommendations when ordering off the long menu, which covers all the classics. As we discovered, they were by far the best dishes. Lamb wrapped in mulberry leaf was tender and tasty, moistened with a rich, flavourful sauce. Giant prawns stir-fried in salt, pepper and five-spice with onions and spring onions was equally excellent – piquant and perfectly cooked. Beef with basil, chicken with lemon balm, and pork spare ribs were

also well done, but not extraordinary. Then again, they were not the recommendations of the house. Neither was the hors d'oeuvres platter, which unfortunately contained a medley of chewy dumplings. If you ask him, the owner will happily sit down and regale you with tales of growing up in pre-war Saigon. It will help you appreciate the unfussy cuisine here for what it really is: an authentic home-cooked meal.

Dong Huong ★

14 rue Louis-Bonnet, 11th (01.43.57.18.88).
M° Belleville. **Open** noon-11pm Mon, Wed-Sun. Closed last two weeks in July, first week in Aug. **Average** €11. **Credit** MC, V. **Wheelchair access. Non-smoking room. Map** M4.
If you're puzzled about where to find great Asian food in Belleville, go with a map to locate this hidden treasure, which is no secret to the city's Vietnamese immigrants. Once you've tasted the crunchy nems and steaming pho, you'll find yourself drawn back again and again. On our most recent weekday visit, the dining room – which attracts up to 2,000 customers a day – was as busy as ever. You might start with bành cuôn, steamed Vietnamese ravioli stuffed with minced meat, mushrooms, beansprouts, spring onions and deep-fried onion, or bite into freshly fried nems, wrapped in lettuce leaves with sprigs of mint. The pho, however, is easily a meal in itself – our favourite is the peanutty, spiced-up satay version. Grilled meats such as the com ga lui (chicken with lemongrass) are popular with Asian diners, but we haven't ever got that far. If you're in the mood to forgo wine or beer, try one of the sweet Asian drinks or an iced Vietnamese coffee.

La Tonkinoise

20 rue Philibert Lucot, 13th (01.45.85.98.98).
M° Maison Blanche or Porte de Choisy. **Open** noon-3.30pm, 7-10.30pm Tue-Sun. Closed Aug. **Average** €25. **No credit cards.**
Don't let the bright fluorescent lighting and ordinary surroundings of this restaurant put you off, because La Tonkinoise serves up better-than-average Vietnamese cuisine. On a recent visit we let our waiter choose and weren't disappointed. Lightly fried, crunchy spring rolls, or nems, were among the best we've had in Paris. Paper-thin beef marinated in lemon and served rare with coriander was fragrant and fresh, and piping hot shrimp cakes burst with plump shrimp and shredded potato. A hot-pot of chicken and rice was simple, but quite good; monkfish, a speciality, was served in a well-seasoned sauce perfumed with fresh dill; grilled beef and shrimp were accompanied by generous amounts of mint, romaine lettuce and vermicelli noodles, all to be wrapped together with a quick splash of nuoc cham before being devoured. A glutinous warm coconut cake and a pleasant-enough coconut milk drink swarming with multicoloured gummies rounded out the authentic experience.

Indian

Although Indian restaurants have popped up all over Paris in the last ten years, locals remain wary of strong spices. Expect subtly flavoured dishes, plenty of cream and set menus that cater to the French habit of eating a meal in several courses. A Paris peculiarity is the cheese naan, a wedge of Vache Qui Rit melted inside the tandoori-baked bread. Sharing doesn't come easily to Parisians, so let the waiter know if you would like dishes to be placed in the centre of the table. Few restaurants stray beyond north Indian classics, but you'll find scruffy bastions of south Indian and Sri Lankan authenticity around La Chapelle, where you can enjoy a hearty, boldly spiced meal for a few euros.

Gandhi-Opéra ★

66 rue Ste-Anne, 2nd (01.47.03.41.00/www. gandhi.fr). Mº Quatre Septembre. **Open** noon-2.30pm, 7-11.30pm Mon-Sat; 7-11.30pm Sun. **Average** €40. **Prix fixe** €23, €28, €35. **Lunch menu** €13.50, €17.50. **Credit** AmEx, DC, MC, V. **Wheelchair access. Map** H4.

In a road largely given over to Japanese restaurants, Gandhi does a good job of flying the flag for Indian cuisine. The airy but tacky interior will win no prizes for design concept, but service is charming and after so many disappointing curry house experiences in Paris, the food here came as a welcome surprise. On a recent visit we began our meal with a juicy tandoori quail and a generous helping of prawn pakora. A lamb vindaloo was of course nowhere near up to authentic levels of strength, but at least it was a genuinely spicy dish, as was the well-above-average chicken tikka masala, accompanied by perfect basmati rice. Our addiction to cheese naans was sated by Gandhi's version, which came proudly puffed, straight from the oven. Perhaps one too many chilled Kingfisher beers led us to think a French chocolate pudding might be interesting, when we would have been better off choosing a homemade kulfi, but this restaurant is nevertheless a useful address for anyone in need of a curry fix while they're in Paris.

Yugaraj

14 rue Dauphine, 6th (01.43.26.44.91/www. yugaraj.com). Mº Odéon or Pont Neuf. **Open** noon-2pm, 7-10pm Tue-Sun. **Average** €60. **Prix fixe** €27.70, €37.50, €49.55. **Lunch menu** €22.80. **Credit** AmEx, DC, MC, V. **Map** H6.

Yugaraj welcomes you into a cosy world of antique Hindu statuettes in a plush intimacy that at the time of writing was up for a refit. Staff are charming, and the wordy menu impressed us by listing suppliers and carefully describing the dishes. This is an Indian restaurant that caters for a well-heeled, spice-shy, Left Bank crowd with near-the-Seine prices

to match. Our meal began with a selection of vegetarian starters, and some deliciously crisp beignets de crabe, but the golf ball-sized fritters came in at €11 per putt, which slightly dampened our enthusiasm. Our main course lamb korma and chicken tikka Makhani both contained excellent meat and were expertly cooked, but spicing even in these mild dishes seemed unduly timid. The portions were restrained, and despite two fluffy cheese naans and some fragrant rice, we ordered an extra flaky paratha to bulk out our meal, which is not something we've often had to do in an Indian restaurant. The homemade kulfi was delightful, while the refreshing vin gris helped brace us for the arrival of a bill well in excess of €100.

Kastoori

4 pl Gustave Toudouze, 9th (01.44.53.06.10). Mº St-Georges. **Open** 11.30am-3pm, 6.30pm-midnight daily. **Average** €17.50. **Prix fixe** €15. **Lunch menu** €8, €10 (Mon-Fri only). **Credit** MC, V. **Map** H2.

It's no surprise that Kastoori's terrace, on this delightful 19th-century square, is often full: the friendly, family-run Indian restaurant remains one of the few good-value eateries in the area. We're not talking ubiquitous mass-produced buffets: Kastoori has excellent-value set menus at lunch and dinner, each dish prepared with care and home-mixed spices. Amid lanterns, Indian fabrics and incense inside, or under the hot lamps outside, start by ordering some popadoms to taste the homemade chutneys served in an ornate metal boat, and choose from tangy raita and kaleji (coriander-sprinkled curried lamb liver) for starters, followed by a choice of tandoori chicken, chicken curry, saag paneer or the dish of the day. Each northern Indian dish is delectably different from the others, and is accompanied by a choice of cheese naan or saffron rice. Don't miss out on the delicious lassis and kulfis. Note that you can bring your own wine – and there's no corkage fee.

International

Aux Comptoirs des Indes – fine Indian dining in a laid-back atmosphere.

Bharath Café

67 rue Louis Blanc, 10th (01.58.20.06.20). Mᵒ La Chapelle. **Open** 11am-11pm daily. **Average** €7.50. **Prix fixe** €10, €13. **Credit** AmEx, MC, V. **Map** L2.

For the most authentic south Indian/Sri Lankan food in town, venture out to La Chapelle. Of all its gems, the best we have found is this Sri Lankan eatery. Don't be deterred by the basic decor, brusque service or the throngs of men loitering in and around the café. These Tamil immigrants are fussy about their food. We started with meat rolls – compact deep-fried pancakes stuffed with mutton, potatoes and spices. Tempting as they are, don't have more than two or you will have no room for the tantalising main dishes. One of our favourites is the lamb kotta roti (shredded thick chapatis mixed with tender meat, eggs, green chillies and onions), big enough for two at a laughably low price. Another house speciality is masala dosai (crêpes filled with curry, potatoes and mustard seed), originally a breakfast dish but equally filling for dinner. Braver souls should try the stronger dishes, including the spicy chicken curry with rice and a small helping of lentil curry. You will be mopping your brow while begging for more. From the array of colourful desserts, we opted for the red dodhal (a firm, sweet jelly with nuts) – a bit of an acquired taste.

Ganesha Corner

16 rue Perdonnet, 10th (01.46.07.35.32). Mᵒ La Chapelle. **Open** 9am-11pm daily. **Average** €10. **Lunch menu** €8. **Credit** MC, V. **Map** L2.

The grungiest spot in the heart of the thriving Sri Lankan community is Ganesha Corner, constantly packed with locals in search of a cheap feed or just a silver beaker of creamy lassi and a chat with their mates. It can seem very male dominated and overwhelming, but staff are friendly and patient. The well-made deep-fried street food such as vadai (lentils, chickpeas and vegetables), samosas, patis and rolls are popular as takeaway snacks. If the pings of the microwaves reminded us that this will never be a good way to reheat fried food, they are at least served with an outstandingly fragrant coconut, lime and chilli paste-cum-sauce. Lamb biryani was spicy as requested, but for this bargain price it was hardly surprising that the meat only played a walk-on role. A braver dip into the menu brought an insipid dish of calamari curry, which came with a huge plate of rice and spicy accompaniments, all to be mopped up by piles of own-made parathas. Next time we will try one of the delicious-looking southern Indian dosai, accompanied by Sri Lankan Lion lager.

New Pondichery ★

189 rue du Fbg-St-Denis, 10th (01.40.34.30.70). Mᵒ La Chapelle. **Open** 11am-11pm daily. **Average** €10. **Prix fixe** €6.90, €10.90. **Credit** MC, V. **Wheelchair access. Non-smoking room. Map** K2.

We were hungry, but clearly had not fasted enough for New Pondichery's spread. Enticed by nearly every south Indian dish on the menu (and tempted too by the rock-bottom prices), we went overboard, ordering several starters, breads and mains. The pleasant but non-intrusive waiters first brought over cardamom-flavoured lassi, which we sipped while nibbling a bonda (mustard seed-flecked fried potato dumpling) and an order of idli (steamed rice cakes) – tasty with the coconut chutney, but apparently reheated in the microwave. Then came the breads: a huge, veggie-packed naan, and surely Paris's chewiest, flakiest pan-fried paratha with a dark and spicy onion sauce. A deep breath before the main event: massive crêpe-like brahmane dosai with curried fresh cabbage and potato, tender chicken korma (a refreshingly light version), and a cheesy spinach palak paneer, which we may not have ordered but happily demolished. Our bellies bursting, we tried to avoid dessert, but a slice of semolina-based barfi arrived nonetheless, and we couldn't help but finish it. The modest dining room eschews Indian clichés, but who cares about the no-frills atmosphere when the feast is this irresistibly filling?

Aux Comptoirs des Indes

50 rue de la Fontaine au Roi, 11th (01.48.05.45.76). Mº Goncourt. **Open** noon-2.30pm, 7-11pm Mon-Sat. **Average** €18. **Prix fixe** €11, €15. **Lunch menu** €7, €9.50. **Credit** MC, V. **Wheelchair access. Map** M4.
Silk curtains, hanging lanterns and Hindi pop music create a welcoming, low-key ambience at this unassuming yet ambitious restaurant. The kind owner hails from Pondicherry in the south, but his menu's signature dishes stretch from India's tip to tail. We began with the evening's only sour note: a house lemon-lime drink called nimbu pani that tasted oddly artificial. Otherwise, we had nothing but praise for the expertly cooked fare. The assortment of pakoras and crisp samosas arrived piping hot and seasoned with chopped herbs, and the naan contained pieces of fresh garlic. Chicken korma proved exceptionally chunky and nutty, while jinga prawns in a tomato-coconut sauce had been prepared with whole curry leaves. With a topping of cardamom pods, cloves and fried onions, even the basmati rice demonstrated an uncommon level of care. The frozen kulfi dessert came with colourful candy sprinkles. All in all, Aux Comptoirs des Indes displays a rare attention to detail.

Margoa

7 rue Waldeck Rousseau, 17th (01.45.72.39.41). Mº Porte Maillot. **Open** noon-2.30pm, 7.15-11.30pm Mon-Fri; 8-11.30pm Sat; noon-11.30pm Sun. **Average** €40. **Lunch menu** €13. **Non-smoking room. Credit** AmEx, MC, V.
This kosher Indian restaurant is tucked away in a tiny side street near Porte Maillot. The fusion of kosher methods with Indian recipes results in divine, surprisingly light Indian food. Starters come with a rack of sauces and a waiter explains the taste of each one. To warm up your taste buds, try the aubergine fondue, with its enticing smell of spices and melting texture. The meat samosas were almost as good, though a little too salty. The menu boasts a wide range of chicken, fish and beef dishes, making it virtually impossible to choose. After much deliberation, we finally opted for the chicken tikka

saag and the fish jalfrezi, both of them juicy and well spiced. Also worth a special mention are the naans – the texture was perfect – neither too crisp nor too soggy. We were too stuffed for dessert, but the gasps of our neighbours were enough to vouch for their fine quality. Although expensive, Margoa is a cut above what you're likely to find at your local Indian. It also offers a catering and takeaway service.

Le Nawab ★

174 rue Ordener, 18th (01.46.27.85.28). Mº Guy Môquet. **Open** noon-2.30pm, 7-11.30pm daily. **Average** €30. **Prix fixe** €16.50, €20. **Lunch menu** Mon-Fri €8, €9. **Credit** AmEx, MC, V. **Wheelchair access**.
This excellent little Indian restaurant in a rather dismal street under Montmartre has changed names since the last edition of the guide, but happily the traditional Indian cuisine has remained untouched. We arrived late but were warmly welcomed into a room packed with French spice fans, a rare breed who know when they have found a place that hits the spot. The menu holds few surprises, but our starters included a refreshing prawn chat salad rich in yoghurt and cucumber, a tasty plate of lamb tikka and some heavy vegetable fritters accompanied by a pungent dish of relishes, all served with panache on a platter complete with an impressive carrot sculpture. Winners from the main courses were two freshly cooked, juicy tandoori quails, and a dish of mater paneer, a delicious peas and cheese accompaniment. The butter chicken was creamy and comforting, and the rice and cheese naans were well above average. Some homemade kulfi completed an excellent value-for-money meal. The service was particularly charming and even ran to offering us warming digestifs to help us on our way.

Le Gange

65 rue Manin, 19th (01.42.00.00.80). Mº Laumière. **Open** noon-2.30pm, 7-11.30pm daily. **Average** €32.50. **Prix fixe** €15.50-€25.50. **Lunch menu** €12.50. **Credit** AmEx, MC, V. **Non-smoking room** (Mon-Fri only). **Map** N2.
Indian restaurants are in hot competition around Buttes-Chaumont and Le Gange wears its plaudits loud and clear. Could it live up to its PR? We were not impressed by a single lukewarm popadom, but the decor of carved wood screens, attractive lighting and gentle Indian music quickly warmed things up. Our waiter from Chandigarh was enthusiastic with his recommendations and we were soon tucking into spicy, succulent tandoori quails, and deep-fried aubergines that tasted divine with the accompanying sweet liquid relish. Cheese and garlic naans made a delicious accompaniment. Of our main courses the lamb biryani was the star, wonderfully moist rice with delicate spices and the tenderest lamb. The tangy karahi prawn was slightly overpowered by onion. We then tasted a delectable mango sorbet and one of the best kulfis we'd ever had, and were offered a digestif on the house. Better still, the milky chai with cardamom, served in a pot, is the perfect finish.

International

Italian

Italian authenticity inevitably loses something when it crosses the border into France, be it the pasta's al dente bite, the generosity of the servings or the clever minimalism that makes this cuisine great. But that hasn't stopped pasta from joining sushi and sandwiches as one of the top Paris food crazes of the 21st century. A new Italian opens nearly every week, Mori Venice Bar making the biggest recent splash, but it's often best to seek out tried-and-true addresses that are not simply riding the wave.

International

Vincent et Vincent

60 rue Jean-Jacques Rousseau, 1st (01.40.26.47.63/ www.vetv.fr). M° Les Halles. **Open** noon-2.30pm, 7.30-11pm Mon-Fri; 7.30-11.30pm Sat. Closed last two weeks in Aug. **Average** €25. **Lunch menu** €15. **Credit** MC, V. **Wheelchair access. Map** J5.
It's easy to see why a happy young fashion and design crowd has quickly adopted this Italian on the northern fringe of Les Halles. Aside from that catastrophic French propensity to put cream in absolutely everything, the pasta here is de Cecco, one of the better Italian brands, it's not overcooked and it's offered in a variety of shapes and sauces. Start, though, with the excellent mixed antipasti plate. It's an all-vegetarian affair that includes borlotti beans, broad beans, braised baby onions, grilled peppers, fried aubergines and courgettes dressed with generous shavings of parmesan. To help those who are not completely pasta literate, there's a blackboard with pasta shapes set next to their names. The penne with shrimps in a light tomato sauce and cassarecia in a mixed mushroom sauce were both very good. The Italian wines are pricey, but the Côtes du Ventoux is a fair bet.

La Bocca

59-61 rue Montmartre, 2nd (01.42.36.71.88). M° Sentier. **Open** noon-2.30pm Mon-Wed; noon-2.30pm, 8-11pm Thur; noon-2.30pm, 8pm-midnight Fri, Sat; noon-2.30pm, 7.30-11pm Sun. **Average** €30. **Credit** MC, V. **Wheelchair access. Map** J5.
In the evening this two-floor Italian bistro is one of the most romantic addresses you could choose for dinner, with its mirrors, candles, Murano glass chandeliers and cosy Napoleon III armchairs. Even the waiter, sporting a tight black sweater and two diamond studs, was beautiful. The blackboard menu features various starters followed by one meat, one fish and four pasta dishes, two of which were vegetarian on our visit. It's the vegetables that star here, with a melanzana parmigiano consisting of thin layers of succulent aubergine interspersed with mozzarella, parmesan, tomato purée and fresh basil. The squid and green bean starter was deliciously fresh too, seasoned with parsley on a bed of mesclun,

and both were so generous that we thought we'd ordered mains by mistake. The farfalle with courgettes, tomato and basil was perfectly al dente, but the one false note was the costata with sautéed potatoes – a fatty veal escalope entirely swamped by a bland cream sauce that bore little trace of the promised thyme. Italian wines tend to be expensive in France; we were not terribly impressed by our Il Falcone Reserva 1999 at €36.50, though it was a good match for the food. Stick with the pasta, and finish with the peppermint panna cotta with kiwi fruit coulis and almonds.

Mori Venice Bar

2 rue du Quatre Septembre, 2nd (01.44.55.51.55). M° Bourse. **Open** noon-4pm, 8pm-midnight Mon-Fri; 8pm-midnight Sat. **Average** €50. **Credit** AmEx, MC, V. **Map** H4.
This newly opened place is already proving popular for its Philippe Starck decor and cutting-edge, Venetian-inspired food. The clientele, as one might expect across from the Bourse, consists largely of business folk and beautiful people at lunch, but it's full of locals at night. The breads are several cuts above the Italian standard in Paris, the coffee is Illy and the waiters are professional and charming. You can't go wrong with dried meats such as a divine bresaola, vegetables such as seasonal asparagus, or the daily specials – we had a mouth-watering, if not particularly Italian, veal blanquette and cuttlefish in squid ink sauce that was light yet satisfying. However, both the polenta and potatoes were over-salted. The wines can send the bill into the stratosphere, running all the way up to €480.

Al Filo delle Stagione

8 rue de Beauce, 3rd (01.48.04.52.24). M° Filles du Calvaire. **Open** noon-2.30pm, 8-11pm Mon-Fri; 8-11pm Sat. **Average** €30. **Prix fixe** €33 (dinner only). **Lunch menu** €23. **Seasonal truffle menu** €57. **Credit** AmEx, MC, V. **Map** L5.
Hidden away on a tiny side street in the trendy upper Marais, this small jewel box of an eaterie packs in a local clientele for well-executed Italian cuisine and a relaxed though refined atmosphere. The kitchen,

International

Gli Angeli

run by a young chef who cut his teeth with Christian Constant and Alain Senderens, offers a wide choice of different dishes, with starters such as classic cold cut ham to deep-fried mozzarella balls, and main dishes such as fresh lobster risotto (the rice just a touch undercooked), and fusillotti al formaggio e speck (ham and cheese pasta). Desserts are the usual affair with a selection of sorbets, fondant au chocolat and the ever-present tiramisu. Nice touches include the made-to-measure pizzette and the option of paying only for the wine you consume. Service was attentive and friendly.

Gli Angeli ★

5 rue St-Gilles, 3rd (01.42.71.05.80). M° Bréguet Sabin or Chemin-Vert. **Open** noon-3pm, 7.30-11pm daily. Closed two weeks at Christmas. **Average** €40. **Credit** MC, V. **Map** L6.

Located around the corner from place des Vosges yet somehow off the beaten track, Gli Angeli is that rarity in Paris – a true Italian trattoria. Although the ambience is pleasantly traditional – a big wooden bar backed by hundreds of bottles, old Italian posters and tables so close you can join in the adjacent couple's conversation – the lighting is unusually bright and prices fairly steep. Open since 1996, Gli Angeli is owned by the friendly Alto Adige-born Signor Amadeo, and draws primarily French and Italian customers. The wine selection is ample and well chosen, covering all the major wine-producing regions in Italy. Even better are the reasonably priced carafes, such as the Montepulciano (just €9 for 50cl). The antipasti are

outstanding – don't miss the beignets di carciofi, half artichokes marinated in olive oil and lemon, and deep-fried. The pasta selection offers a smattering of classics, as well as more imaginative creations. While the fish selection is limited, Gli Angeli does offer a good range of meats, including the Milanese speciality vitello tonnato (veal cutlets with a tuna sauce). Finish it off with one of the excellent grappas.

L'Osteria

10 rue de Sévigné, 4th (01.42.71.37.08). M° St-Paul. **Open** 8-10.15pm Mon; noon-2.15pm, 8-10.15pm Tue-Fri. Closed Aug. **Average** €55. **Credit** MC, V. **Wheelchair access. Map** L6.

This railroad car-like dining room in the Marais is a maddening place for a meal. The food is delicious, but it's run like a private club. Risotto, a dish for which L'Osteria is famed, is not listed on the menu, and since they're keen to turn tables you'll be warned off it unless you're a regular. It's so crowded and smoky that it's hard to relax, and the atmosphere is decidedly self-conscious. This doesn't seem to stop a stellar crowd from eating here, though – Claudia Cardinale looked pretty pleased with her tagliolini al ragù the night we came in, and there was a host of TV and movie people as well. This is about as close to real Italian cooking as you'll find in Paris. Starters of mozzarella in carrozza (fried in a light batter) and octopus, both bedded on peppery rocket, were delicious, as were delicate tortelloni stuffed with beef and spinach, and a perfectly cooked tagliolini in cinammon-spiked veal ragù. There are some nice wines too, at reasonable prices.

timeout.com

Over 50 of the world's greatest
cities reviewed in one site.

Chez Bartolo

*7 rue des Canettes, 6th (01.43.26.27.08). M°
Mabillon or St-Germain-des-Prés.* **Open** noon-
2.30pm, 7-11.30pm Tue-Sat; noon-2.30pm Sun.
Average €35. **No credit cards. Map** H7.
The pizza may be excellent here, but be prepared to
have it dished up with an enormous slice of attitude.
Chez Bartolo attracts many local Italians with the
authenticity of its cooking. Spilling through the
entryway, diners find themselves in the middle of
the restaurant, where they are often made to wait for
a table (even with reservations). True to its Italian
heritage, the menu is a guideline, rather than a list
of what is actually available, and it's common to find
that the dish or bottle of wine you have selected has
run out. If you can handle the various irritations,
the food is absolutely delicious. While the pastas
and meat dishes are well above average, it's the
pizza that truly stands out. A perfect balance of
crispy crust, tangy tomato sauce, plus mozzarella,
anchovies and capers, it may just merit the hassle
involved in eating here.

Café Minotti

*33 rue de Verneuil, 7th (01.42.60.04.04). M° Rue
du Bac.* **Open** noon-2.30pm, 7.30-10.30pm Tue-Sat.
Closed three weeks in Aug. **Average** €50. **Lunch
menu** €26, €32. **Credit** AmEx, MC, V. **Non-
smoking room. Map** G6.
Nicolas Vernier, who cooked at the Ducasse-run Il
Cortile, runs this pricey but wonderful restaurant on
the Left Bank. Gorgeous tomato-red Murano
chandeliers create a dramatic atmosphere, and
Vernier is at the top of his game with a brilliant
produce-driven menu that stars superb Tuscan
charcuterie and a perfect tempura of langoustines to
start, followed by wonderfully inventive pasta.
Squid-ink spaghetti came dressed in a discreet
vinaigrette and was generously garnished with
vongole (tiny clams), baby squid and octopus, while
boned guinea hen in a rich reduction sat atop
maltagliati (homemade spinach noodles), which
were then doused with a foamy chestnut cream at
the table to make a splendid winter dish. A trio of
panna cotta flavoured with vanilla, mandarin orange
and liquorice was a perfect dessert for sharing.
Popular with the local publishing crowd, this place
also pulls celebrities in the evening. Food is also
served in the more relaxed low-ceilinged bar area.

Le Perron

*6 rue Perronet, 7th (01.45.44.71.51). M° St-Germain-
des-Prés.* **Open** noon-2.15pm, 7.30-10.45pm Mon-
Sat. Closed Aug. **Average** €40. **Lunch menu**
€25. **Credit** AmEx, MC, V. **Wheelchair access.
Non-smoking room. Map** G6.
If you were to judge an Italian restaurant on looks
alone, you probably wouldn't choose to eat in this
one: dark wood beams and a mish-mash of half-
levels make it look more like an old-fashioned St-
Germain tavern. But the warm welcome is genuinely
Italian and the cuisine, with its range of antipasti,
risottos, pasta and veal dishes, is closer to a true

Italian trattoria than at many of Paris's flashier
places. Enticing first courses include vongole in
umido (lightly sautéed clams), salsicce abruzzese
alla griglia (sausages marinated in wild fennel), and
antipasto del Perron (sun-dried tomatoes, courgettes,
aubergines, mushrooms and chicory baked in olive
oil). Whatever was meant to go with the morels on
the plat du jour had run out, so the kitchen paired
them up with a tender veal escalope instead, and also
concocted a simple ragù for a child. Pièce de
résistance, though, was the zabaglione: hot, highly
alcoholic and frothy, and overflowing down the
sides of the glass.

La Taverna degli Amici ★

*16 rue du Bac, 7th (01.42.60.37.74). M° Assemblée
Nationale or Solférino.* **Open** noon-2.30pm, 7-11pm
Mon-Sat. Closed Aug, two weeks Dec. **Average** €30.
Lunch menu €13-€18. **Credit** MC, V. **Non-
smoking room. Map** G6.
An Italian haven within easy walking distance of
the Musée d'Orsay, La Taverna is the ideal spot for
a quick business lunch or a big, rambunctious dinner
with friends. Divided over two floors, with smokers
on the first floor and a non-smoking ground level,
the yellow-walled rooms are well lit and airy. Run
by the friendly Notaro family, who own, manage and
cook, the restaurant has barely been open a couple
of years, yet it's constantly bustling. It offers a six-
page wine list, and a daily changing menu, featuring
seasonal specialities. Don't miss the mixed
bruschette, including three different outstanding
vegetable toppings, such as grilled courgettes
marinated in olive oil, lemon and parsley. Pastas
come with fresh, tasty toppings, such as the popular
penne with caccioricotta (made with ewe's milk) and
rocket. Most of the regulars finish their meal with
the creamy own-made tiramisu.

Le Bistrot Napolitain ★

*18 av Franklin-D-Roosevelt, 8th (01.45.62.08.37).
M° St-Philippe-du-Roule.* **Open** noon-2.30pm,
7-10.30pm Mon-Fri. Closed Aug. **Average** €20.
Credit AmEx, MC, V. **Wheelchair access.
Map** E4.
This rather chic Italian off the Champs-Elysées is as
far from a tourist joint as it is possible to be. At
lunchtime it is packed with suave Italian-looking
businessmen in modish pinstripes and St-Tropez
types with silicone lips. The decor is plain, the
tablecloths starched white, and the kitchen open
with the pizzaiolo shoving pillowy pizzas in and out
of the oven while orders are shouted over the heads
of diners. Generosity was our overwhelming feeling
about the food – not just big plates, but lashings of
the ingredients that others skimp on, such as the
slices of tangy parmesan piled high over rocket on
the fresh and tender beef carpaccio we shared for a
starter. The pizzas are as good as they say they are.
The Enzo came with milky, almost raw mozzarella
and tip-top tomatoes. For pasta, choose between
dried or fresh with some interesting variations: the
fresh saffron tagliatelle was rich and creamy,

International

La Taverna degli Amici. *See p147.*

enhanced by the flavour and colour of this delicate spice. Helpings are so big that you really have to be Italian to stomach a meat or fish course after this.

Le Stresa

7 rue Chambiges, 8th (01.47.23.51.62). M° Alma-Marceau. **Open** 12.15-2.15pm, 7.30-10.30pm Mon-Fri. Closed Aug. **Average** €80. **Credit** AmEx, DC, MC, V. **Map** D5.

The bizarre funk of white truffles, cigarette smoke and strong perfume on unwashed skin adds real olfactory drama to this snug dining room. Aside from some excellent old-fashioned Italian cooking, one of the other reasons to frequent Stresa is to be reminded of the fact that plastic surgery only rarely succeeds. The red velvet banquettes here are populated by pert and pricey silicone, long tell-tale earlobes and strategically placed Alice bands. In a dining room where everyone watches everyone else with chronometric precision, the game is to secure the extra attentions of the two brothers who run the place. And the food? Beef carpaccio with rocket and parmesan shavings came in a light lemony dressing, while artichokes alla Romana were overcooked. Spaghetti alla Belmondo – tomato sauce in an admirably perfect emulsion, bits of mozzarella, tiny black olives and a nosegay of fresh basil – was excellent, and so it should be for €30. Equally good was saltimbocca – tender veal scallops topped with fried ham and garnished with fresh spinach. At €45, the Pio Cesare Barbera d'Alba was a good buy, too, though very few people actually look at the wine list, ordering without asking the price or what it is. Suffice to say that it's all rather like putting your money in the collection plate at church – you just hope and assume that it will be spent in a useful and honest way. Just about as close to San Marco and an *Ab Fab* scene as you'll find anywhere in Paris.

I Golosi

6 rue de la Grange-Batelière, 9th (01.48.24.18.63). M° Grands Boulevards or Richelieu Drouot. **Open** noon-2.30pm, 7-11.30pm Mon-Fri; noon-2.30pm Sat. Closed last two weeks in Aug, one week in Dec. **Average** €30. **Credit** MC, V. **Wheelchair access. Map** J3.

Not far from the offices of *Le Figaro*, this original and fresh Italian is effervescent with French journalistic talent. Sipping a crisp prosecco, we noted the presence of one recently released reporter-hostage and another notable grand reporteur. Their sources were good on this occasion as the cooking here is high quality and reasonably priced. Drawn by the racy meat-and-fish-in-the-same-plate idea, we went for a shared starter of vitello tonnato, wafers of veal in a tuna and caper sauce – tangy and interesting. We then stuck into suckling pig baked with turnips and artichokes, and a bracing tartare of (raw) veal. We enjoyed fantastic panna cotta with the last of our Rosso di Montalcino Fornacino. Fabulous food with efficient and good-looking service.

Da Mimmo

39 bd de Magenta, 10th (01.42.06.44.47). M° Jacques Bonsergent. **Open** noon-2.30pm, 7-30-11.30pm Tue-Sat. Closed Aug. **Average** €40. **Credit** MC, V. **Map** L4.

Da Mimmo appeared to be just another pizza joint on this noisy boulevard. The first hint that this touch of Naples might be a cut above was the big table of antipasti, unusually fresh and tempting. The menu of pizzas and pasta also seemed mundane, but then our eye caught the list of specials, which included pasta with truffles, funghi porcini, scampi and other original dishes. Warming to our task, we settled down with a bottle of Chianti and a platter of antipasti, served with some wonderful pizza bread. For mains, linguine con scampi was the real thing, perfectly cooked al dente pasta with just a hint of chilli and garlic tossed with a few crustaceans – a genuine Neapolitan taste.

La Madonnina

10 rue Marie et Louise, 10th (01.42.01.25.26). M° Jacques Bonsergent. **Open** noon-2.30pm, 8-11pm Mon-Thur; noon-2.30pm, 8-11.30pm Fri, Sat. Closed two weeks in Aug. **Average** €32.50. **Lunch menu** €11-€15. **Credit** MC, V. **Wheelchair access.** **Map** L4.

La Madonnina toes the edge of kitsch so skilfully that it comes off as cool. With candles, mustard yellow walls and a smattering of red-checked tablecloths, it's the perfect place for a romantic night out or dinner with a small group of friends. The cosy decor is capped off with a pale painting of the Virgin Mary and little hanging angels. Background music ranges from the latest ambient chart toppers to traditional Italian instrumentals. La Madonnina describes itself as a trattoria napoletana but it would be fair to say that most of the dishes are from southern Italy. Start with a kir Madonnina, the restaurant's own take on the traditional French aperitif, made here with sparkling white wine and rose liqueur. The short menu (about five options per category) changes monthly; don't miss the melt-in-your-mouth own-made pastas, such as artichoke and ricotta ravioli, or the authentic cassata, an extremely sweet Sicilian version of cheesecake, not often seen on menus outside Italy. Come early or reserve, as the restaurant only seats about 40. Parents, take note: on Saturday lunchtimes there's a children's menu for €9, and the whole restaurant becomes non-smoking.

Les Amis de Messina

204 rue du Fbg-St-Antoine, 12th (01.43.67.96.01/ www.lesamisdesmessina.fr). M° Faidherbe Chaligny. **Open** noon-2.30pm, 8-10.30pm Mon-Fri; 8-11.30pm Sat. Closed Aug. **Average** €35. **Credit** AmEx, MC, V. **Wheelchair access. Non-smoking room.** **Map** N7.

Sicilian cuisine is one of the finest in Italy and this airy restaurant with its open kitchen features a number of Sicilian specialities, such as pasta alla Norma (named after the opera by Bellini, who was born in Catania, the island's second largest city). Our starters included a classic melanzane alla parmigiana and a more interesting plate of perfectly fried vegetables. Not remarkably original dishes, but prepared with real care and precision. Pasta with funghi porcini topped with a dome of Parma ham was a delicious mixture of the cooked and the raw, and the spaghetti alle vongole had a generous serving of clams and just the right balance of olive oil, garlic and parsley. Puddings included a first-rate tiramisu and that great Sicilian speciality, canoli (sweet tubular cakes). The meal was served by a friendly team who recommended a fine Sicilian red, priced at €24.50, and a couple of limoncellos to see us on our way.

Sardegna a Tavola ★

1 rue de Cotte, 12th (01.44.75.03.28). M° Ledru Rollin. **Open** 7.30-11pm Mon; noon-3pm, 7.30-11pm Tue-Sat. **Average** €40-€50. **Credit** MC, V. **Map** N8.

'I'm from Sardinia. Sardinia and nowhere else!,' responded the gruff owner of this pocket-sized restaurant when asked what part of Italy he was from by a first-time diner. A stone's throw from the boisterous Marché d'Aligre, this is obviously an insider's eaterie with a lot of return customers, evidenced by the packed-to-the-rafters status on a Monday night. We were off to a great start with the amuse-bouche of spicy homemade sausages, parsley-flecked potatoes, and a thin, crunchy olive-oil-drenched flatbread. The appetiser of garlic-and-parsley-marinated clams and mussels was a very messy yet wholesome and fun way to fuel our appetite for what was to come. The main dishes of potato, chèvre and mint-filled ravioli in a rich tomato broth and orange-flavoured langoustines with tagliatelle were copious, and so satisfying we barely had room for the dessert, a vanilla flan with forest berries. Despite the steep prices, and the not-so-central location, fans of Italian – sorry, Sardinian – cuisine should make the pilgrimage here if they're in the mood for the real thing. Decent house reds and whites are available at €13 a pitcher.

Sale e Pepe

30 rue Ramey, 18th (01.46.06.08.01). M° Château Rouge or Jules Joffrin. **Open** noon-2.30pm Mon; noon-2.30pm, 8-11.30pm Tue-Fri; noon-3pm, 8pm-midnight Sat. **Average** €20. **Prix fixe** €20 (dinner only). **Lunch menu** €15. **Credit** MC, V. **Non-smoking room.** **Map** J1.

This little Italian in Montmartre really is worth relaxing your scruples for. The small, marble-walled room is run by a generous, friendly Italian and his young chef, and it's filled with a happy mix of arty locals who love the relatively inexpensive and well-chosen Italian wines and all-in formula for dinner – you get an antipasto, pizza, pasta and dessert for just €20. Everyone eats the same thing, but the menu changes daily and rarely includes anything off-putting. A recent dinner began with rolled aubergine stuffed with cheese and garnished with parmesan shavings and a few leaves of rocket, and continued with a ham and mushroom pizza, salmon penne and a choice of tiramisu or panna cotta. If the pizza was tasty enough, the salmon penne was undercooked rather than al dente, with a rather meagre sauce. But desserts were fine and the coffee and complimentary grappa ended a meal that was enjoyable more due to high spirits (and lots of them) than the cooking. On other occasions, however, the pasta has been much better, so we'll definitely be back.

Japanese

Parisians have developed a real fondness for 'les sushi' over the past decade, although the most commonly found variety comes prepackaged at the supermarket or in one of the ubiquitous Asian traiteurs that have replaced an alarming number of traditional French food shops. Fortunately, a growing number of Japanese restaurants – and not just sushi specialists – cater to the more discriminating diner. Newcomer Isse Tempura & Tapas serves virtually grease-free tempura and other Japanese snacks not far from the Louvre, while Kai has kept up the lofty standard of the restaurant it replaced, Zen. If it's a good sushi fix you're after, it's hard to do better than the functional nine-seat sushi bar Comme des Poissons.

Higuma

*32 bis rue Ste-Anne, 1st (01.47.03.38.59). Mº
Pyramides.* **Open** 11.30am-10pm daily. **Average**
€15. **Prix fixe** €10, €11.50. **Credit** MC, V. **Map** H4.
On a street lined with small, authentic Japanese eateries, Higuma's no-nonsense, satisfying food and service make it one of the area's most popular picks. Customers walking in are greeted by a blast of aromatic steam emanating from the open kitchen-cum-bar, where a small team of cooks ladle out giant bowls of noodle soup piled high with meat, vegetables or seafood. While some solo diners slurped their meals at the counter, we went for a table in the second room, sparsely decorated with laminated, autographed menus yellowing against the humid walls. We began with a plate of gyoza – seven hot and succulent dumplings whose thin skins imparted a particularly refined texture. Next, the kimuchi lamen, a generous bowl of homemade noodles in a spicy soup topped with that piquant Korean staple, kimchi. Nikuyasai itame, a fried noodle dish with pork and vegetables, however, was bulked up with more beansprouts than pork. On the way out, we spotted local celebrity Edouard Baer. The actor was hunched down alone at a table, undisturbed by other diners too preoccupied with the business of eating.

Isse Tempura & Tapas

*45 rue de Richelieu, 1st (01.42.96.26.60). Mº Bourse
or Palais Royal.* **Open** noon-2.30pm, 7-10.30pm Mon-Sat. **Average** €25. **Credit** AmEx, MC, V. **Map** H5.
Isse was once the name of the best sushi restaurant on the rue Ste-Anne, a street lined with Japanese noodle houses and sushi joints (many of which are run by Chinese). That restaurant has become Bizan, and the new Isse (no relation to the old one) is now making a name of its own. Despite the 'tapas' element, this newcomer has no Spanish slant – the speciality is tempura and other nibbly Japanese dishes, with sushi on offer for those who can't do without their fix of raw fish. Tempted by many dishes on the menu, we soon had our table filled with

surprisingly generous servings given the prices – €6 for deliciously tangy prune-stuffed sardine tempura, and €5 for a bowl of silky, cold hiyayakko tofu topped simply with green onion and ginger. A big plate of vegetable tempura for €10 was exemplary, the batter ethereal and crisp with no greasiness. Sushi, presented in perfect rectangles, tasted fresh and delicious, as did a bowl of chirashi. Stuffed by now, we polished off the last drops of our umenishiki saké and vowed to return to this high-ceilinged and brightly lit spot, which has a pleasing modern Japanese feel to it.

Kai ★

*18 rue du Louvre, 1st (01.40.15.01.99). Mº
Louvre Rivoli.* **Open** noon-2pm, 7-10.30pm
Tue-Sat; 7-10.30pm Sun. Closed Aug. **Average**
€60. **Prix fixe** €58-€90. **Lunch menu** €27-€38.
Credit MC, V. **Map** H5.
Occupying the premises of the defunct sushi bar Zen, this new Japanese restaurant has rapidly developed a following among fashionable diners with discriminating tastes. Decor and cuisine both reflect a meticulous attention to aesthetics. Luxurious chocolate leather banquettes line one wall of the dark, harmoniously designed space, while an impressive refectory table in blond wood fills up the other half. Tall sprigs of cherry blossoms lend the only splash of colour in a room that manages to be both minimalist and warm. The 'Kai-style' sushi was a uniquely modern and zesty take on a classic: marinated and lightly grilled yellowtail is pressed on to a roll of shiso-scented rice. Seared tuna with avocado, miso and roasted pine nuts also surprised and delighted, thanks to the ultra-fresh fish and perfect balance of flavours. Not to be outdone, the grilled aubergine with miso, seemingly simple, turned out to be a smoky, luscious experience. For mains, a generous dish of breaded pork lacked the finesse and refinement of the starters, but was nonetheless satisfying. Thoroughly French desserts come from celebrity pastry chef Pierre Hermé.

Kinugawa ★

9 rue du Mont-Thabor, 1st (01.42.60.65.07).
M° Tuileries. **Open** noon-2.30pm, 7-10pm Mon-
Sat. Closed two weeks at Christmas. **Average**
€55. **Prix fixe** €30-€40. **Non-smoking room**
(reservation recommended). **Credit** MC, V. **Map** G5.
Kinugawa is a hushed, plush temple to Japanese
haute cuisine – exquisite and expensive. Aptly
situated on an unassuming street near the posh
shops of rue St-Honoré, this two-storey restaurant
is something of an institution, having served
countless well-heeled Japanese and Parisians for
more than 20 years. Service is discreet and solicitous,
tempting you to almost whisper your order. Not a
problem if you forgo the long list of à la carte items
in favour of the set meals or kaiseki, the most refined
and rarefied form of Japanese cuisine. Essentially a
succession of finely prepared dishes elaborately
crafted from the freshest, most seasonal ingredients,
kaiseki is much more than a meal: it is an experience.
The first course included jewel-like portions of
compressed fish cake, herring roe, grilled slivers
of cuttlefish painted with egg, smoked salmon rolled
in wafer-thin tamago, and a cold poached fig in
sesame sauce. Next came supremely fresh turbot
sashimi; a purifying 'teapot' consommé of shrimp
and field mushrooms that was clean and clear;
chunks of marinated raw beef grilled at the table
over a smouldering charcoal broiler; braised daikon
in a glutinous broth, subtly enhanced by button
mushrooms, shrimp, lime and spring onion; a
refreshing cold salad of wakame, abalone and sea
cucumber; and steamed fish in a scallop broth. The
impressive culinary parade ended with a whimper,
however, in an uninspired plate of sushi that lacked
taste and presentation. Dessert too was the standard
green tea ice-cream with red bean – tasty if
somewhat unoriginal. At Kinugawa, you might not
get the full impact of Japan's mind-blowing kaiseki,
but you will get a very good introduction indeed.
Other locations: 4 rue St-Philippe du Roule, 8th
(01.45.63.08.07).

Laï Laï Ken

7 rue Ste-Anne, 1st (01.40.15.96.90). M° Pyramides.
Open noon-2.45pm, 6-10pm daily. **Prix fixe** (dinner
only) €13.50, €21. **Lunch menu** €9.50. **Credit** MC,
V. **Map** H5.
Just off the north-east end of rue de Rivoli, Laï Laï
Ken is a canteen-style operation catering to the
comfort-food cravings of a thriving Japanese
clientele of students (mostly male) and chain-
smoking, power-dressed execs (mostly female).
Forget Zen and the art of persuading slivers of raw
fish into pale pink rosebud formations on exquisite
lacquered platelets: this place dishes up the oriental
equivalent of shepherd's pie and steamed jam
sponge with custard. Western diners were few on
our visit, as the regulars wolfed down steaming
noodle soups and authentic, well-made stir-fries.
Although the room was packed to capacity on a
freezing weekday lunchtime, the courteous, efficient
staff kept the buzz below a frenzy – lone diners
were never invited to double up, and no one was
rushed. Belly pork strips in a rich, flavoursome broth
were suitably satisfying – complete with large pieces
of uncompromisingly slippery tofu – while a dessert
of steamed sweet red bean dumplings was
disappointingly dry, but helped down by frequent
refills of jasmine tea or sizeable cans of Asahi beer.

Takara ★

14 rue Molière, 1st (01.42.96.08.38). M° Palais
Royal. **Open** 12.30-2.15pm, 7-10.15pm Tue-Fri;
7-10.30pm Sat, Sun. Closed lunchtime in Aug.
Average €25 (lunch), €60 (dinner). **Prix fixe**
€49-€65. **Lunch menu** €23-€26. **Credit** MC, V.
Map H5.
It would be tempting to utter a string of superlatives
to describe the dazzling cooking here. But it would
probably be more effective to state that this is simply

Kai

International

the best Japanese food you'll find anywhere in Paris. An exaggeration, you say? Erase your doubts by kicking off with four plump raw oysters, served out of the shell and in a light vinegar sauce topped with shredded green onions and a pinch of peppery, grated radish. Succumb to the aphrodisiac powers of this seasonal starter then satiate your desire with a quivering morsel of fresh scallop sushi. Follow it with the monkfish liver sushi, an unusual and delightful mélange of cubed, creamy monkfish liver and rice wrapped in crispy nori. Then move on to the fresh turbot sashimi: roll up each translucent sliver with a sprig of chives, a sprinkle of chopped green onion and a dab of grated radish. Dip it into the vinaigrette and chew it slowly. When you open your eyes, rouse yourself back to reality with some bolder flavours: the maguro tuna with blanched leeks in miso paste provides just the right kick. Grilled eel maki with cucumber is melt-in-the-mouth tender; chawanmushi – a seafood and vegetable custard – slips seductively down the throat. Think it's perfect so far? Try the astonishing agedashi tofu: deep-fried cubes of the silkiest tofu coated in a light, subtly elastic batter, delicately softened by a warm mirin-based broth. Beyond perfect, it is ingenious. Takara also specialises in sukiyaki and shabu shabu – a kind of self-serve Japanese hotpot.

Bizan

56 rue Ste-Anne, 2nd (01.42.96.67.76). M°
Pyramides. **Open** noon-2pm, 7-10pm Tue-Fri; 7-10pm Sat. Closed three weeks in Aug. **Average** €80. **Prix fixe** €40, €60. **Lunch menu** €19-€30. **Credit** AmEx, MC, V. **Map** H4.

Isse – whose chef moved back to Japan a couple of years ago – was a hard act to follow, and Bizan's business cards come with the reminder: 'in the style of Isse'. Certainly, on the absolute freshness of the fish, Bizan has held to tradition. Seductively displayed inside individual wooden boxes arranged on top of the tiny sushi bar, the restaurant's ever-changing selection of raw fish comes in a choice of beautiful guises – simply sliced and served as sashimi or sushi, or more unusually or elaborately prepared, as in the delightful sesame-crusted, seared tuna tataki that was offered as a starter on the tasting menu. Available at lunch or dinner, the menu dégustation Bizan offered a generous series of meticulously prepared dishes that tickled the palate in various ways. A main dish of tempura soft shell crab with sweet mustard mayonnaise was a wonderful surprise, not least because of the rarity of this crustacean in Parisian restaurants. A smoke-scented consommé of wild Japanese mushrooms put shame to the miso soup that normally comes with such meals, while the sashimi offering of tuna and yellowtail was predictably fresh. There are also lunch menus, which, though more moderately priced, offer considerably less. Still, the Bizan spécial does have its merits, mainly in the moist tonkatsu – breaded pork fillet served with a rich sweet-and-sour dipping sauce. The minuscule restaurant itself is not

unlike the bento box some of the food is served in: blond wood, clean lines and compartmentalised into three floors seating only a handful of people each.

Isami

4 quai d'Orléans, 4th (01.40.46.06.97). M° Pont
Marie. **Open** noon-2pm, 7-10pm Tue-Sat. Closed three weeks in Aug. **Average** €50. **Credit** MC, V. **Map** K7.

'We serve only raw fish here,' the soft-spoken hostess warned us as we entered this small but perfectly formed restaurant facing the Seine, its pale wood shelves lined with Japanese teapots and crockery. That suited us just fine, as a strong sushi craving had hit us on this blustery mid-winter afternoon. We took a seat at the sushi bar, where we could watch the Zen-like motions of the expert chef, and settled on chirashi sushi – perfectly fresh strips of fish and seafood on a bed of rice with just the right amount of vinegar. An appetiser of fresh tuna and natto – a glutinous, fermented soybean – was satisfyingly well balanced in texture and flavour; another starter of cuttlefish with spicy cod roe was equally appetising. The assorted sashimi platter includes typical fare such as scallop, salmon, tuna, mackerel, snapper, sweet prawn and sea bream. It's not the most mind-blowing raw fish in Paris, but – as the popularity of this restaurant proves – this is definitely as close as you'll come to Tokyo on the Ile St-Louis.

Asia-Tée

47 rue de la Montagne Ste-Geneviève, 5th
(01.43.26.39.90). M° Maubert Mutualité. **Open** noon-2.30pm, 7-10.30pm Tue-Sat. **Average** €30. **Prix fixe** €30-€50. **Lunch menu** €15. **No credit cards. Map** J8.

This is a Japanese restaurant with a difference: the chef, Kenji, also repairs antique watches on the premises, at a little desk in front of the window. His love of antiques extends to the furniture, with an eclectic collection of art deco chairs and a granny-style wooden buffet that avoid any Japanese clichés. Tables are draped in white linen and the atmosphere is laid-back, like the chef himself. But the real surprise here is the originality of the food, which liberally borrows from the French repertoire. The speciality is sakana, small tasting dishes that are also available in full portions and that change with the seasons. Our €30 prix fixe began with amuses-bouches of crunchy little mini spring rolls, a single piece of sushi and a creamy-centered crab croquette before a warming bowl of miso soup. Then came our sakana, starting with a few flawless sushi and beautiful sashimi drizzled with sesame oil. Next up was an equally silky slice of foie gras mi-cuit – nothing very Japanese about it – and the same crab croquettes that had featured in the amuses-bouches. Finally, chunks of slow-cooked pork belly in quince and raisin sauce, and seared scallops with julienne vegetables. The originality continued through to a dessert of poached quince with praline ice-cream. The food itself wasn't especially refined, but that's not the intention of sakana, which in Japan would be eaten as tapas-style snacks in a bar. The third member of our group ordered a selection of sushi, tempura, sashimi and grilled fish (€26), which, though equally delicious, came all at once while our meal unfolded at its unhurried pace.

Azabu ★

3 rue André-Mazet, 6th (01.46.33.72.05). M° Odéon. **Open** noon-2pm, 7.30-10.30pm Tue-Sat; 7.30-10.30pm Sun. **Average** €35 (lunch), €50 (dinner). **Prix fixe** €33, €39. **Lunch menu** €15.50, €18.50. **Credit** AmEx, MC, V. **Non-smoking room. Map** H7.

At Azabu westerners gather on the main floor and Japanese downstairs, but it's by choice. In the compact main room you can watch the teppanyaki chef at work, which is a thrill for those who rarely witness such a performance. This being our first visit, we sat at the counter for a prime view of the confident and unflappable chef. Pre-cooked ingredients are poised around him in pretty Japanese bowls, ready to be thrown on to the grill, sliced or chopped, tossed with other ingredients and drizzled with sweet, gingery sauces. Settling on the €39 menu Azabu, which started with an amuse-bouche of puréed squash and a delicate scallop flan, we chose our appetisers and main courses, some of which come with price supplements. The aubergine miso, prepared in the small kitchen at the back, was the silkiest half-aubergine we have ever tasted, cut into small cubes to be scooped out with a little wooden spoon. Equally juicy were four squares of tofu, topped with minced chicken in a delicious sweet sauce. Razor clams cooked with ginger before our eyes were a rare autumn treat, while scallops, also with a touch of ginger, were fat and beautifully seared – both of these came with a glistening selection of vegetables, pearly rice and a bowl of soup. Saké is the best accompaniment, of course.

Yen

22 rue St-Benoît, 6th (01.45.44.11.18). M° St-Germain-des-Prés. **Open** noon-2pm, 7.30-10.30pm Mon-Sat. **Average** €50. **Prix fixe** €55 (dinner only). **Lunch menu** €30.50. **Credit** AmEx, DC, MC, V. **Wheelchair access. Map** H7.

Like the minimalist, blond decor of this two-storey space, the cooking here is clean, stylishly muted and faultlessly presented. Serving mainly soba – a slender Japanese buckwheat noodle – and tempura, Zen-like Yen is the perfect stop for a satisfying, healthy lunch. The deluxe lunch special arrived in a two-tiered wood bento box, the delicate morsels of each tiny course encased in its own compartment. A cake of compressed rice with taro root; marinated spinach; avocado and fresh tuna in sesame sauce; fried cubes of salmon fillet with marinated cucumber; squishy wedges of flavourful tofu; and a terrine of compressed braised chicken breast all acted as light, appetite-enhancing accompaniments to the main fare of perfectly fried mixed tempura. The excellent, homemade soba – served hot or cold according to preference – came with shredded green onions, a thimble of wasabi and a bowl of mirin-based dipping sauce. We had just enough room to try the dessert, provided by pâtissier Sadaharu Aoki: ginger and white sesame ice-cream topped with black sesame and green tea macaroons.

Comme des Poissons

24 rue de la Tour, 16th (01.45.20.70.37). M° Passy. **Open** 11.30am-3pm, 5.30-9pm Tue-Sat; 5.30-9pm Sun. **Average** €40. **Lunch menu** €13.50. **Credit** MC, V.

The staff at this teeny, bare-bones sushi bar act as if they don't want you there – at a recent lunch the typically grudging service became downright hostile when the chef yelled at a diner for daring to show up 15 minutes late. Alas, they can't help but lure in an ever-swelling parade of regulars seduced by the astonishingly fresh fish and reasonable prices. The undecorated restaurant, if you could even call it that, features nothing but nine stools surrounding a basic sushi counter. Obviously, fish is the only attraction here. And what a star it is. Fresh beyond reproach, basics such as tuna, salmon, yellowtail and eel are sliced, diced or thrown together with the kind of no-nonsense confidence that only top-quality ingredients can command. Judging from fellow diners, a perennial favourite is a salad of barely seared salmon with seaweed and 'special' sauce. The buttery grilled eel sushi satisfies all the prerequisites of the simple classic, while the excellent tuna with natto comes, unusually, with a generous portion of the gooey fermented beans. Many Japanese customers feast on dishes that don't appear on the menu – we learned later that it's just a matter of asking the chef for a surprise. Service is fast, even hurried – probably because there are many others waiting for your seat.

Kifuné

44 rue St-Ferdinand, 17th (01.45.72.11.19). M° Argentine. **Open** 7-9.45pm Mon; noon-2.45pm, 7-9.45pm Tue-Sat. Closed public holidays, three weeks in Aug. **Average** €55. **Lunch menu** €25. **Credit** MC, V. **Map** C3.

This gem of a neighbourhood sushi bar is particularly prize-worthy for its authentic izakaya atmosphere, complete with chain-smoking Japanese businessmen, and surprisingly generous cuts of fresh sushi and sashimi, albeit at Tokyo prices. Sashimi of tuna, tuna belly and salmon arrive like marble slabs, opulently cold and thick – the tuna belly or toro so unctuously dense its flesh was opaque and pearly. Scallop sushi, again, was first rate in freshness and heft, its ivory flesh drooping off the edges of a finely vinegared finger of pressed rice. A starter of slivered raw cuttlefish with uni (sea urchin) was appropriately sublime, although the paltry spoonful of uni wasn't exactly generous. We noticed, however, that the same dish delivered to a Japanese man next to us included much more of the delicacy. A special order? Or preferential treatment to a regular customer? With Japanese clients filling most of the tiny, smoke-filled room, it could well be either or both.

Jewish

Bagel shops may be thin on the ground in Paris, but you will find crunchy falafel, zingy zakouski and tongue-tingling Tunisian salads and couscous. Head to the Marais for Central European and Middle Eastern eats – pastrami, chopped liver, chicken soup – and to multicultural Belleville for North African specialities. There are also significant Jewish communities in the 9th, 17th and 19th arrondissements, where you'll find everything from kosher curry to sushi.

International

L'As du Fallafel ★

24 rue des Rosiers, 4th (01.48.87.63.60). M° St-Paul. **Open** 11am-midnight Mon-Thur, Sun; 11am-sundown Fri. **Average** €12. **Credit** MC, V. **Wheelchair access**. **Map** L6.

This world-famous green and yellow diner feels like downtown Tel Aviv. So adept were the quartet of phone-jugglers next to us that they managed to play cards while each simultaneously talking into theirs. Behind them a man in a kippah continued to do business throughout his meal. Even if you have an aversion to this aural appendage, make an exception for L'As du Fallafel as both the atmosphere and falafels are out of this world. There are other things on the menu – plates of grilled meat and Israeli salads – but we recommend sticking with the falafel special (€6.50), a fat, round pitta filled to bursting with freshly fried falafel, sliced fried aubergine, houmous and fresh green salad. It's served on a paper plate with a fork to break up the falafels. Tasty little condiments made with peppers and gherkins are in small pots on the table. We accompanied ours with fresh carrot juice, which appeared so quickly staff must have telepathically registered the order, and nectar d'Israel, a bottled kosher fruit drink. Serving all day long, this is a great place for a filling bite.

Chez Marianne

2 rue des Hospitalières-St-Gervais, 4th (01.42.72. 18.86). M° St-Paul. **Open** noon-midnight daily. **Prix fixe** €12-€18. **Credit** MC, V. **Map** K6.

With its homespun philosophical statements painted on the windows, Chez Marianne is a popular Marais institution, with Jewish North African dishes combined with Eastern European stalwarts. On a Monday lunchtime, both rooms of the restaurant were bursting with a crowd for the most part familiar with the menu, which allows you to put together your own platter from the various zakouski. Outstanding items on our six-element version (€18) included first-rate chopped liver, a crispy beef-stuffed brik, excellent houmous and some of the best falafel in Paris, which can also be enjoyed in a sensational takeaway sandwich. Choose your items carefully to avoid doubling up on flavours and textures. Our

veteran neighbour was rich in anecdotes of his mother's meatballs, which are apparently moister than Marianne's rather dry version, and his recipe has been noted for future home use. He also gently chastised us for eating too fast and drinking the excellent Fleurie too rapidly, not leaving enough to wash down a substantial mixed fruit strudel and a generous plate of sweet halva. The jolly but haphazard service in part explains the popularity of the place, which is no longer a bargain.

Micky's Deli

23 bis rue des Rosiers, 4th (01.48.04.79.31). M° St-Paul. **Open** 11.30am-3pm, 7-11.30pm Mon-Thur, Sun; 11.30am-2.30pm Fri. **Average** €17. **Credit** AmEx, DC, MC, V. **Map** L6.

The image of a classic New York deli has been superimposed on this old Marais shopfront, and the marriage of stone walls, '50s-style ads and photographs of yellow cabs in the Big Apple makes for a great atmosphere. A largely Jewish clientele is tucking into massive multidecker hamburgers and mountains of chips. Although there are other things on the menu – notably the copious salad plates and grills – the hamburgers are the winning formula. Housed in crisp, lightly toasted baps, they come with a side of creamy aubergine purée, a fried egg and a whole gherkin. The Micky burger comes with pastrami for extra kosher oomph and the turkey burger is just as luscious. Slather your chips with Brooklyn-made Gefen tomato ketchup. All the meat here is Glatt kosher, a super-strict kosher category that insists on animals in peak condition. A small selection of desserts includes the usual brownie.

Pitchi Poï ★

7 rue Carron/9 pl du Marché Ste-Catherine, 4th (01.42.77.46.15/www.pitchipoi.com). M° St-Paul. **Open** noon-11pm daily. **Average** €30. **Prix fixe** €22.50. **Credit** AmEx, MC, V. **Wheelchair access**. **Map** L6.

The all-you-can-eat Sunday brunch buffet is justly famous, but Pitchi Poï deserves a look-in at any time for its hearty Eastern European specialities: beef goulash, tchoulent (duck confit with slow-baked potatoes, Polish giant beans and barley) or klops with mamaliga (veal loaf with polenta). Vegetarians needn't despair as there's also datcha (smoked salmon with baked potatoes, soured cream and herbs) or vegetable strudel with salad. Lighter options include zakouski platters of chopped liver, gefilte fish and real taramasalata, with frequently replenished bread baskets of matzoh, pumpernickel and rye. The decor shows the same careful attention to quality and detail – low on shtetl nostalgia, high on Eastern Med charm (jewel-coloured scatter cushions, hand-decorated stained-glass tea lights). And all on a cobbled, leafy, traffic-free square in the Marais. At lunch on a winter bank holiday the dining room and terrace gradually filled with multi-generational Jewish families and arties, while we devoured osso bucco with fresh pasta, followed by fabulously thick, cinnamon-scented fromage blanc with a compote of baked preserved fruits. Wines include Hungarian Tokaj and Israeli cabernet sauvignon, but in our case an iced goldwasser with our coffee completed a perfect meal.

La Boule Rouge

*1 rue de la Boule Rouge, 9th (01.47.70.43.90). M°
Grands Boulevards.* **Open** noon-3pm, 7pm-midnight
Mon-Sat. Closed Aug. **Average** €35. **Prix fixe** €25.
Credit AmEx, DC, MC, V. **Map** J3.
For our first visit we enjoyed a particularly warm welcome at this family-run Tunisian restaurant where Monsieur is the maître d' and Madame is the cook. It's been here for a good 30 years and has that comfortable feel of a place where the owner and customers know each other well. In the first room, suited rag trade barons kept an eye on the football match on the wide-screen TV, while the main dining room with its camel ceiling fresco was abuzz with conversation. No sooner had we sat down than nine plates of kemia arrived. These light and refreshing vegetable dishes, gently spiced with harissa, included sweet boiled carrots, marinated radishes, cucumber with grapefruit and a baked omelette. Unless you want to flash your cash there is no point in going further than the €25 prix fixe, an incredible deal that includes the kemia, a couscous or grilled main course (with a €3 supplement for fish), cakes, mint tea and a small pitcher of wine. You can try some unusual couscous dishes here, such as the beef and spinach baila, which stains your couscous inky green, or the comforting nikitoucha, chicken in a slightly spicy broth with corn. Saturday is the best night to come for this festive Sephardi atmosphere.

Patrick Goldenberg

69 av Wagram, 17th (01.42.27.34.79). M° Ternes.
Open 9.30am-11pm daily. **Food served** noon-11pm.
Average €30. **Prix fixe** €25. **Credit** AmEx, MC, V.
Map D3.
With the first rays of sunshine music executives were out on the terrace of Goldenberg's. Inside, past the mouth-watering deli counters, with their selection of herrings, gefilte fish, pork-free sausages and vodkas, is a dark and atmospheric realm decorated with all sorts of Ashkenazi memorabilia. Patrick Goldenberg's father opened the restaurant in 1970

and the menu recounts in brief his odyssey from Odessa before bamboozling with a wide choice of specialities. Patrick himself is not short on personality, and there was much banter before we finally ordered. The zakouski allow you to compose your own selection of Russian hors-d'oeuvres, including superb herrings, pirogi (veal or cheese dumplings), stuffed vine leaves and gendarmes (long, rectangular dried sausages). Instead we went for the set menu, which started with herrings served with raw onions and a creamy potato salad, followed by pojarski (veal and chicken fritters), a classic chicken soup and pot-au-feu. The poorly reheated pojarski were a big disappointment, though the pot-au-feu was tender and good. We probably ordered badly – zakouski or bagels are apparently the way to go – but at least the cheesecake was fabulous. The place has charm and we enjoyed the musical selection, which ran seamlessly from klezmer to Chopin.

Maison Benisti

108 bd de Belleville, 20th (no phone). M° Belleville.
Open 9am-10pm daily. **Average** €15. **No credit
cards. Map** N4.
Looking like a launderette that's had its machines ripped out and replaced with serving counters and plastic chairs, Benisti is all you could ever wish for in a Jewish eatery. A man kneads couscous with his bare hands, another grins from behind his sandwich counter, while in the dining room behind him whole families are tucking into steaming bowls of soup and men sit huddled in their anoraks (wrap up in winter as there doesn't seem to be any heating). If you eat in, go to the counters and point to what you want. Couscous comes with delicious, coriander-flavoured meatballs and tender beef floating in its broth; or there are whole pike-perch and tuna steaks baked in an oily tomato sauce. A load of little plates of salads also appeared at our table. But what sets this restaurant apart from other North Africans in Paris is the spicing, which has extra chutzpah. Benisti is first and foremost a pâtisserie, so don't miss out on the sticky cakes dripping with honey.

New York meets Paris at **Micky's Deli**.

International

North African

What curry is to Britain, couscous is to France, so if you're looking for respite from cream sauces, the cooking of Algeria, Tunisia or Morocco would be a good choice. You'll find everything from simple neighbourhood couscous joints serving great hunks of char-grilled meat alongside giant vats of vegetable and chickpea stew to lavish riad-style dining rooms specialising in fragrant Moroccan tagines. Choose a North African wine to accompany your meal and finish with sweet mint tea, which is always ceremoniously poured from a great height. For Jewish Tunisian restaurants, *see p155*.

Chez Omar

47 rue de Bretagne, 3rd (01.42.72.36.26). M° Arts et Métiers or Temple. **Open** noon-2.30pm, 7-11.30pm Mon-Sat; 7-11.30pm Sun. **Average** €40. **No credit cards**. **Map** L5.

As the name implies, Chez Omar combines hearty Maghreb and French staples, in a mildly dilapidated bistro complete with etched glass screens and a zinc bar that oozes atmosphere. The celeb crowd has moved on, but it's still packed at night, so prepare to queue. On a quiet weekday lunchtime, however, we feasted in an atmosphere of expansive calm. Starters were a crisp, not-too-sweet pastilla (crisp brik crêpes stuffed with chicken, almonds, raisins and mixed spice and dusted with icing sugar), and a second brik with melting peppers and egg. We crossed continents for the mains: a vast slab of pan-fried duck breast à la française, and a generous platter of méchoui (lamb basted with spiced butter, traditionally spit-roasted whole over a pit of charcoal). Omar's version is the real thing – roasted in the oven rather than the back yard, but tender and flavoursome with crisp, aromatic skin to die for, plus additional platters of couscous and vegetables in broth. Wine was a half-litre of Boulaouane, a sun-soaked red from Algeria. For dessert, delicate pastries from Paris's legendary North African pâtisserie La Bague de Kenza are served on a huge ceramic cake stand. Be warned – at €2.50 each, the wrappers stack up all too quickly.
Other locations: Café Moderne, 19 rue Keller, 11th (01.47.00.53.62).

404 ★

69 rue des Gravilliers, 3rd (01.42.74.57.81). M° Arts et Métiers. **Open** noon-2.30pm, 8pm-2am Mon-Fri; noon-4pm (brunch), 8pm-2am Sat, Sun. **Average** €40. **Lunch menu** €21. **Brunch** €21. **Credit** AmEx, DC, MC, V. **Wheelchair access**. **Map** K5.

Algerian-born Momo has a secret formula: however much others try to copy, they can't replicate the unique atmosphere of his Paris and London restaurants. It might be the fact that the exquisite lamps are antiques, there's real tadelakt in the bathroom, or that celeb friends like Ozwald Boateng might drop in; most likely it's because the staff in their tastefully decorated T-shirts just can't wait for the party to kick off. Book for the late sitting if you like to dance on the tables: before you've finished your mint cocktails the waiters will already be gyrating on the bar. Through the haze of alcohol, after repeated bottles of a quaffable gris de Guerrouane, we can nevertheless say that the food was richly satisfying. Starters include some more unusual additions to the traditional briks, such as salade méchouia (a refreshing combination of diced tomato, red peppers and garlic), zalouk (aubergine and garlic) and stuffed sardines. Of the mouth-watering tagines the chicken with pear is a winner, but the real revelation of our meal was the fish tagine absolutely bursting with flavour. We also liked the moist pastilla (sugar-dusted brik pastry with a pigeon filling), although by the end it left us digging into others' leftovers to kill the sugar overload. The fruit salads and pistachio pastries seemed more of an afterthought as the soundtrack brought everyone to their feet.

Le Ziryab

L'Institut du Monde Arabe, 1 rue des Fossés St-Bernard, 5th (01.53.10.10.16/www.yara-prestige. com). M° Jussieu. **Open** 11.30am-2.30pm, 7.30-10pm Tue-Sat. **Average** €60. **Prix fixe** €50. **Credit** AmEx, DC, MC, V. **Wheelchair access**. **Map** K7.

Having passed through airport-style security and zoomed to the top floor of the Institut du Monde Arabe in a glass lift, you can't help but feel a little privileged. With a change of chef, Ziryab has returned to doing a superior take on traditional Moroccan cuisine, and after the ubiquitous lanterns and ornate plasterwork of so many North African restaurants, it comes as a refreshing change to enjoy couscous and tagines in a setting where crisp tablecloths, minimalist red lamps and an amazing view, lit up periodically by the passing bateaux-mouches, form the only decor. We settled on a mixed meze to share as a starter. Smoky puréed aubergine, smooth houmous, tabouleh and a selection of hot, stuffed brik pastries were served in individual dishes and accompanied by piping hot pitta bread – each one was sublime. The menu includes quite a few fruity variations on the tagine – we opted for the chicken with pineapple, whose cinnamon aroma was announced with aplomb when the waiter whisked off its terracotta cone in the manner of a silver dome. The couscous méchoui did not disappoint either, with its broth full of tasty vegetables, a hunk of lamb that fell off the bone and the welcome addition of fresh mint. Desserts of crème brûlée delicately flavoured with liquorice and a fruit salad in a minty nage with green tea ice-cream showed finesse. Our only regret was taking the waiter's recommendation of the Coteaux du Mascara red, which made a rather heavy accompaniment to this food. It all feels a bit like being in a swanky hotel and the attentive staff did not make us feel in the least bit rushed when we were the last people there.

Le Méchoui du Prince

34-36 rue Monsieur-le-Prince, 6th (01.43.25.09.71). Mº Odéon or St-Michel. **Open** noon-2.30pm, 6.30pm-midnight Mon-Sat. **Average** €24. **Lunch menu** €12. **Credit** DC, MC, V. **Wheelchair access**. **Map** H7.

The elegant brocade banquettes and gold-embroidered scatter cushions of this smart, friendly restaurant add a touch of class to the familiar panoply of North African bric-a-brac. The menu features an interesting range of tagines and couscous varieties, and the lunchtime prix fixe is excellent value. We started out with a tasty tuna brik and an exceedingly ordinary sardine salad (iceberg lettuce with pale, crunchy tomatoes and acid French vinaigrette, but pleasant enough grilled fish), followed by the Casbah couscous (beef and chicken), and a chicken, almond and prune tagine. The couscous was attractively served with the grains cradled in a deep vase fitted into the top of a tall pitcher holding the vegetables and plenty of flavoursome broth. The grains were so light and fluffy that we couldn't resist repeated dunks of the serving spoon, in sheer wonderment. Sadly, the uninspired meat let the side down: pale, cool meatballs and dry chicken. The tagine scored similarly mixed marks – beautifully presented in its chunky earthenware dish with snug-fitting conical lid, the meat had clearly cooked long and slow in the delicious sauce, but the leg joints of poor-quality chicken left us fishing around for shreds of melting flesh amid a haystack of spindly bones. In addition, we nearly broke a couple of teeth on prune stones, having mistaken them for the wonderful toasted almonds. Desserts included a refreshing duo of melon and plum sorbets doused in powerfully fruity fig liqueur. Not feeling up to a large quantity of heady Maghreb wine, we were disappointed to find nothing by the glass except one red Bordeaux, so we opted for refreshing mint tea instead.

Wally le Saharien

36 rue Rodier, 9th (01.42.85.51.90). Mº Anvers or Notre-Dame-de-Lorette. **Open** noon-2pm, 7.30-10.30pm Tue-Sat. **Average** €30. **Prix fixe** €45. **Credit** MC, V. **Map** J2.

Wally serves fine North African cuisine in an intimate, kitsch-free setting. Kilim cushions soften the ornate wooden armchairs, and exotic fabrics swathe vases of orchids. The menu dégustation delivers the Full Wally – a striking line-up of flavours starting with vegetable broth full of fresh coriander, and a crisp pastilla dusted with icing sugar and stuffed with minced chicken and sweetmeats. Next came a small portion of the house's famous grilled sardine(s), with a pesto-style mix of capers and basil. The centrepiece is the Saharan méchoui and couscous – our grains were light and delicately spicy, but the meat was scarce on a vast length of rib. Finally, the delicate house pastries are a festival of orange flower water, ground almonds and other exotica. A tiny, preserved Chinese apple wrapped in almond pastry intrigued us so much that the waitress brought another for us to dissect. A la carte dishes include tchackhouka (similar to ratatouille) served as a starter with wedges of own-made bread, and tagines served with cracked wheat: lamb or chicken with olives and lemon confit, or sweeter, spicier options with apricots and almonds. Some, such as spiced jumbo prawns, are cooked to order – call ahead to see

Time for tea at **Le Méchoui du Prince**.

what's on offer. Figure-conscious diners will love the refreshing dessert of orange slices dusted with spice and icing sugar. A word on wines: don't miss the vin gris, a delicious Algerian rosé from Medina.

L'Homme Bleu

55 bis rue Jean-Pierre Timbaud, 11th (01.48.07. 05.63). M° Parmentier. **Open** 7pm-1am Tue-Sat. Closed Aug. **Average** €30. **Credit** MC, V. **Wheelchair access. Non-smoking room. Map** M5.

It's best to go with a group to L'Homme Bleu to get to grips with its tempting array of Maghreb specialities, not to mention big portions. Just be sure to arrive by 8pm to secure a table, as the popular restaurant does not take reservations. Our group of five ordered four starters and four mains to share, with the express purpose of saving room for the platter of jewel-like Algerian pastries brought to the table at the end of the feast. The friendly Algerian and Moroccan waiters were happy to oblige and it wasn't long before hot appetisers were circling our table in the cosy stone cellar. Mhadjeb, a flaky pancake filled with sautéed tomato, onions and green peppers; burek, a brik casing oozing mild white cheese; brik s'tmellalt, an envelope of thin pastry stuffed with tuna, egg and coriander; and pastilla, a sugar- and cinnamon-dusted pastry filled with chicken, toasted almonds, onions, egg and orange flower water, all disappeared quickly. Next came the tagines and couscous. Our favourites were tagine s'laxrif, a sizzling stew of lamb, dates, figs, raisins, almonds and cinnamon, and the couscous merguez, featuring a pile of the long, spicy sausages. The bottle of Medea rouge from northern Algeria was very drinkable, though a tiny glass of lemonade wasn't worth €4. Sweet mint tea was the perfect accompaniment to those delicious pastries.

Le Mansouria

11 rue Faidherbe, 11th (01.43.71.00.16). M° Faidherbe Chaligny. **Open** 7.30-11pm Mon, Tue; noon-2pm, 7.30-11pm Wed-Sat. **Average** €45. **Prix fixe** €29, €44. **Credit** MC, V. **Wheelchair access. Non-smoking room. Map** N7.

Owned by outspoken cookery writer Fatema Hal, the Mansouria prices itself as a gourmet alternative to your local couscous joint. Reports have varied wildly, and after our latest visit, we can only concur. This was a meal that began swimmingly, barely kept its head above water during the mains, and sank into the abyss at dessert. Meze-style starters included excellent aubergine caviar, a fresh salad of finely chopped parsely, coriander leaves and mint, another of whole chickpeas lightly flavoured with chopped tomato and herbs, and melting stewed peppers. A sickly-sweet, syrupy tomato chutney, and grated carrot swimming in orange flower water were, however, inedible – the latter much like swallowing a mouthful of perfume mixed with slimy string. Honey-roast lamb turned out to be a tender joint of meat slathered with a sickly, vivid orange sauce in which it had clearly not been cooked (there was no sign of the hoped-for caramelised coating). A chicken, fig and walnut tagine looked OK, but a dig beyond the skin revealed brilliant white, dry meat, with scalding sauce. On to the desserts, and the sorriest assortment of Moroccan pastries. Pastilla au lait was an ice-cold, gelatinous slop tasting of nothing but sugar and orange flower water, sandwiched between crispy brik leaves. Redeeming features? The service, which was friendly, efficient and utterly disarming, and the wine – a fabulous half-bottle of gris (pale rosé) from Gerrouane, near the Moroccan city of Meknès: fruity and freezing, with just a hint of resin.

Wally le Saharien. *See p157.*

Le Tagine

*13 rue de Crussol, 11th (01.47.00.28.67). M°
Oberkampf.* **Open** 7-11.15pm Tue; noon-2.30pm,
7-11.15pm Wed-Sun. **Average** €35. **Credit** AmEx,
V, MC. **Map** M5.

On a side street a stone's throw from the lively
Oberkampf neighbourhood, this unassuming little
restaurant packs in a local crowd for well-executed
Moroccan cuisine. Run by the same husband and
wife team (and surveyed by their wily poodle) for
the past 20 years, Le Tagine offers up tried and true
classics such as starters of shredded carrot salad
flavoured with orange flower water or tomato and
grilled peppers, followed by a daily special couscous
(served piping hot from a traditional wooden bowl),
with spicy meatballs, merguez sausages and juicy
lamb cutlets. The lamb tagine with prunes was as
satisfying for its earthy consistency as it was for the
delicate mix of spices employed in its preparation.
Dessert was a berber crêpe with fresh honey,
followed by mint tea. The limited wine list did offer
a respectable Crozes Hermitage, but the K'sar Beni
2004 that we opted for was unexciting.

Restaurant des Quatre Frères

*127 bd de Ménilmontant, 11th (01.43.55.40.91).
M° Ménilmontant.* **Open** noon-3.30pm, 6-11pm Mon-
Thur, Sat; 6-11pm Fri. **Average** €18. **Credit** MC, V.
Wheelchair access. **Non-smoking room**.
Map N5.

Have you ever wondered what 'family dining' might
be like in Algiers? For less than €10 the four
brothers who run this unassuming local hotspot
(paper cloths on formica tables and help-yourself
soft drinks) will give you a good introduction. A tiny
blackboard menu lists the essentials but regulars
know to ask for the extras (like bottles of olive oil
for dousing the chickpea soup). For starters try the
mhadjeb (a thickish crêpe stuffed with lightly spiced
red peppers) or the tangy chorba soup. Couscous,
the most expensive main, boasts some of the lightest,
fluffiest semolina in Paris, but the daily special is
worth the adventure. On our visit it was a chicken
chakchoukha: a thick crêpe covered in a saucy
portion of potatoes and chickpeas and topped with
a succulent, pan-grilled quarter chicken. What pulls
in the locals, however, is the array of skewered meat
(beef, lamb, turkey, liver and, of course, merguez),
cutlets, chops and herb-filled patties, all laid out
buffet-style. The waiter will whisk them off to the
open grill (fanned inventively with a hairdryer) and
before you know it you'll be chomping away like
everyone else at an Algerian barbecue.
Other locations: 37 bd de la Villette, 19th
(01.42.01.78.86).

Le Souk ★

*1 rue Keller, 11th (01.49.29.05.08). M° Bastille or
Ledru-Rollin.* **Open** 7.30-11.30pm Tue-Fri; noon-
2.30pm, 7.30pm-midnight Sat; noon-2.30pm, 7.30-
11.30pm Sun. **Average** €27. **Prix fixe** €19.50,
€26.50. **Credit** MC, V. **Wheelchair access**.
Non-smoking room. **Map** N7.

Potted olive trees mark an unassuming entrance
where savvy diners push past the battered kilim
covering the doorway into a lively den of Moroccan
cuisine. The swirl of animated conversation, aromas
of incense and cumin and harem-like decor provide
a heady introduction to an authentic dining
experience. We started with pastilla, a savoury
pastry stuffed with duck, raisins and nuts, flavoured
with orange blossom water and sprinkled with
cinnamon and powdered sugar. It made instant
converts of our two uninitiated dining companions,
who were also seduced by the creamy aubergine
scooped up with hunks of fluffy Moroccan bread,
baked on the premises. Don't fill up on starters,
though, as the enormous tagines and couscous are
first rate. Our favourite was tagine canette, duckling
stewed with honey, onions, apricots, figs and
cinnamon then showered with toasted almonds. The
combination of tender meat, sweet plump fruits and
crunchy nuts was also irresistible in the tagine de
palmeraie, made with chicken, dates, onions and
almonds. Couscous bidaoui arrived in handsome
earthenware – a bowl of the semolina atop an urn of
rich broth containing carrots, turnips and cabbage.
A hefty shank of lamb was served on the side, as
were little bowls of chickpeas, harissa and golden
raisins. Cold beer went down very well with the
meal, but we also would have been happy with a
bottle of Algerian or Moroccan red wine, reasonably
priced at €17. For dessert try the excellent
millefeuille with fresh figs. Sweet mint tea poured in
a long stream by a djellaba-clad waiter was the
perfect ending to a terrific meal. Book in advance.

Au P'tit Cahoua

*39 bd St-Marcel, 13th (01.47.07.24.42). M° St-
Marcel.* **Open** noon-2.15pm, 7.30-11pm daily.
Closed several days in Aug, 24-25 Dec. **Average**
€27. **Lunch menu** €12.50. **Credit** MC, V. **Map** K9.

The tented interior packed with North African
earthenware tagines, bowls and lamps gives Au P'tit
Cahoua an intimate souk feel, the word 'cahoua'
being slang for café. On a miserable day, we were
instantly transported to warmer climes. This
couscous haunt has always been one of the best in
town, an impression confirmed by our crispy
courgette fritters and triangular briouates, even if
the fillings seemed to have shrunk somewhat in the
frying process. The pigeon pastilla is a difficult dish
to prepare well; here it was a total success, the sugar
topping contrasting intriguingly with the savoury
pigeon filling. Méchoui was served on a hot cast-iron
plate, a huge melting joint of lamb, served with a
spicy ratatouille of fresh vegetables. The fluffy
grains of the couscous were highly praised by our
office-partying neighbours. Service was extremely
friendly, but one waiter was insufficient for a full
restaurant. Miraculously, though, he still managed
to pour us glasses of deliciously fragrant mint tea
from a gravity-defying height.
Other locations: 24 rue des Taillandiers, 11th
(01.47.00.20.42).

International

Spanish

Although Spanish cuisine remains under-represented in Paris, the few restaurants listed here make up for it in atmosphere and authenticity. The most ambitious of this select bunch is Fogón Saint-Julien, which has moved from cramped Latin Quarter premises to a swish new location facing the Seine. For a French take on tapas-style eating, try Senderens (*see p67*), L'Atelier de Joël Robuchon (*see p55*) or Salon Hélène Darroze (*see p53*).

see p67, *see p55*, *see p53*

Caves Saint Gilles ★

4 rue St-Gilles, 3rd (01.48.87.22.62). M° Chemin Vert. **Open** noon-3.30pm, 7.30-11.30pm Mon-Thur, noon-3.30pm, 7pm-midnight Fri-Sun. Closed Christmas, New Year. **Average** €25. **Credit** MC, V. **Map** L6.

If you dream of tiny boquerones fritos (fried fresh anchovies), the delectable curly bits of chipirones a la plancha (grilled baby squid), pimientos stuffed with bacalao (salt cod), or a steaming zarzuela (fish and seafood stew), then you'll love this place. More Madrid than the Marais, its tiled walls, old bullfight posters and charmingly accented staff draw a devoted clientele of expats, Iberia aficionados and lucky locals eager to soak up its easy ambience, traditional tapas and sturdy specials. Dinner is always crowded (booking is not an option), so if you want elbow room, go for lunch, when a smooth Galician white, paired with calamari, pulpo (octopus) or fried cod – in fact, why not try them all? – will leave you well and truly chilled. Whether you're heading to the nearby Picasso museum or a bench in the place des Vosges, don't forget dessert – we opted for generous slices of manchego with a side of thick membrillo (quince paste) and ogled our neighbour's arroz con leche (rice pudding) that surely must have been made by a resident grandmother, it looked so good. An added bonus: horchata de chufa – a sweet, milky substance made from Valencian chufa nuts – is usually available, if you know to ask.

Fogón Saint-Julien

45 quai des Grands-Augustins, 6th (01.43.54. 31.33). M° St-Michel. **Open** 7pm-midnight Tue-Fri, noon-2.30pm, 7pm-midnight Sat-Sun. Closed last two weeks in Aug, first two weeks in Jan. **Average** €40. **Prix fixe** €35, €40. **Credit** MC, V. **Map** J6.

With its subdued shades of oatmeal, free-form white lamps, sleek designer chairs and bread in stiff linen bags, Alberto Herraiz's newly located oven (fogón) has nothing of Almodóvar or Hemingway about it. While most expats rely on kitsch or bullfighters to draw the sangria crowd, Herraiz is a stylish experimenter with a penchant for minimalist paellas,

designer tapas and hidden cutlery (it's under the table in specially made drawers). The tapas menu offers a succession of poshly presented mouthfuls, savoury and sweet, while the rice menu pairs bite-sized, enigmatic tapas at either end (grilled salmon on horseradish mousse, fine slices of head cheese draped over asparagus spears; lemon-mango compote and yoghurt ice-cream, a pear-topped mini meringue with liquorice mousse) with a paella main. Our langoustine with calamari and vegetables came with perfect, sea-perfumed saffron rice, but the six little langoustines, perched on top, were disappointingly dry (and not worth their €5 supplement). The third member of our party stuck to the nut-fed Iberian charcuterie and struck rich: lip-smacking, lean and fabulously smoky chorizo, plus Catalan bread (which was smothered in crushed tomato, garlic and olive oil), was simply outstanding. In its new location, the Fogón is a magnet for moneyed locals and a good bet for people-watching, especially on Sunday night.

Bellota-Bellota

18 rue Jean-Nicot, 7th (01.53.59.96.96/www. bellota-bellota.com). M° Invalides, Pont de l'Alma or La Tour Maubourg. **Open** 11am-11pm Mon-Fri; 10am-11pm Sat. **Average** €50. **Credit** AmEx, MC, V. **Wheelchair access. Non-smoking room. Map** E6.

Attractively done up with blue and white Spanish tiles, wooden tables, a bar and soft lighting, this is a very pleasant destination for a snack or light supper. Bellota ('acorn' in Spanish) is a reference to the preferred food of the black, free-grazing Iberico race of pig that produces this ham. The restaurant serves five different Bellota-Bellota hams from four different geographical regions of southern and western Spain, and each one is purported to have a slightly different flavour and consistency. As part of various tasting platters, the ham is served with manchego ewe's milk cheese from La Mancha province, anchovies, olives, pickled garlic and pimentos, and tuna, accompanied by excellent bread. A first-rate assortment of Spanish wines, by the bottle or glass, friendly service and reasonable prices make this a very attractive choice.

La Paella

50 rue des Vinaigriers, 10th (01.46.07.28.89/
www.restaurantlapaella.com). M° Gare de l'Est,
Jacques Bonsergent or République. **Open** noon-
2.30pm, 7-11pm Mon-Fri; noon-2.30pm, 7pm-
midnight Sat. **Average** €30. **Prix fixe** €27.
Credit AmEx, DC, MC, V. **Wheelchair access**.
Non-smoking room. Map L3.
Anyone looking for a breather from the relentless
trendiness of the Canal St-Martin should make
tracks to this homely Spanish spot that looks like a
neighbourhood paella place in Valencia – that is,
slightly spare and rather over-lit. Paella, not
surprisingly, is the name of the game here, as it's
cooked to order and served in vast portions, a fact
that makes this place popular with Paris's Spanish
community. Depending on how hungry you are, you
can nibble your way through an assortment of tapas
while waiting the requisite half-hour for paella,
or, knowing that the Iberian rice dish is to arrive
in an imminent avalanche, you might want to share
a platter of excellent Spanish charcuterie and bide
your time. This place really gets jumping on
Saturday nights, when it pulls an intriguingly varied
crowd, so be sure to book. Very friendly service and
a nice wine list are further draws.

La Plancha ★

34 rue Keller, 11th (01.48.05.20.30). M° Bastille
or Ledru-Rollin. **Open** 6pm-1.30am Tue-Sat.
Closed Aug, one week at Christmas. **Average**
€30. **No credit cards. Wheelchair access**.
Non-smoking room. Map M6.
This is a tiny and lively bodega, with Basque flags,
pelota scoops, bullfighting posters, a photo of a
rugby scrum and a couple of Lufthansa life jackets
hanging from the ceiling like jamón. Though the
owner assumes everyone with an accent can't speak
French, we warmed to his patter once a jug of spicy

sangria arrived. 'Take your time, we're open until
2am,' he assures everyone. Don't bother trying to
scrutinise the menu pinned to the wall – just say
whether you prefer meat, fish or vegetables and
leave it to the kitchen. Our trio of tapas comprised
generous portions of marinated red peppers, the
freshest deep-fried squid, and chorizo with a
smattering of patatas bravas. After a pause we
enjoyed seared tuna steaks and gambas from the
plancha (grill) with a crusting of sel de Guérande –
so fresh that we started to wonder whether we were
in San Sebastián. Crème brûlée and gâteau Basque
straight from the oven were of the same standard.
Aside from the great food, the atmosphere here is
killer – the crammed seating and the wine loosen
tongues and by the end of the night it feels like a
great summer party south of the border.

Casa Eusebio

68 av Félix Faure, 15th (01.45.54.11.88).
M° Boucicaut. **Open** noon-2pm, 8-10.30pm
Tue-Sat. Closed Aug, one week at Christmas.
Average €25. **Lunch menu** €12.50. **Credit**
AmEx, MC, V. **Wheelchair access. Map** B9.
This tiny bistro is like many in Spain – simple and
straightforward – despite the full-on French interior
of a former café: huge mirrors and ceramic tiles
depicting 18th-century court scenes at Versailles
are somewhat at odds with the basic, unpretentious
food. The tapas are limited to chorizo, cheese
(manchego), fish or meat empanadas, anchovies,
tortilla and both jabugo and serrano ham. All are
perfectly fine. Mains include a generous serving of
paella and tender small calamari swimming in a
bowl of their own black ink. It's a small, family-run
place (the owner is also the waiter) and it's always
busy. If you find yourself in the nether regions of the
15th and feel like a Spanish fix, this will sate, but it's
not really something you need to cross town for.

International

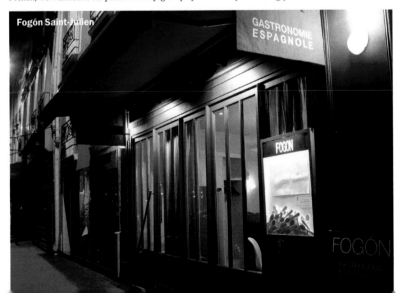

Fogón Saint-Julien

GASTRONOMIE ESPAGNOLE

FOGON

FOGÓN

Other International

The following restaurants are not only fine ambassadors for their countries' cooking, but also the perfect venues for members of the city's international communities to reminisce in like-minded company.

International

AFGHAN

Koutchi

40 rue du Cardinal Lemoine, 5th (01.44.07.20.56). M° Cardinal Lemoine. **Open** noon-2.30pm, 7-10.30pm Mon-Sat. **Average** €17.50. **Prix fixe** €15.50 (dinner only). **Lunch menu** €9.20, €12.50. **Credit** MC, V. **Wheelchair access**. **Map** K8.

There can be few better places to broaden your food horizons in Paris than at this cheerful little blue-painted restaurant in the Latin Quarter, named after the Afghan word for 'nomad'. The wood-panelled and carpet-draped dining room feels especially hospitable on a blustery day, when you can warm up with the gently spiced stews typical of Afghan cooking. Ordering from the two set lunch menus, we started with a well-made Afghan salad and lightly spiced stewed aubergines topped with tangy fresh cheese. Main course dahl with chunks of veal proved subtler than its Indian counterpart, yet was intriguingly aromatic, while the pilawa was a winning mix of savoury and sweet, with a spiced meat sauce for ladling over a plate piled with rice, raisins, almonds and carrot. Dogh, a yoghurt and mint drink, seemed the necessary accompaniment, but there is also a simple wine list. Our bargain menus included a pistachio and rosewater flan – unusual and agreeable. Although Koutchi has been around for some time, the owner's enthusiasm is always evident, hence the loyal following.

HUNGARIAN

Le Paprika

28 av Trudaine, 9th (01.44.63.02.91/www.le-paprika.com). M° Anvers or Pigalle. **Open** noon-11pm Mon-Fri; noon-midnight Sat, Sun. **Average** €35. **Lunch menu** €13.70, €17. **Credit** MC, V. **Wheelchair access**. **Map** J2.

This genteel Hungarian bastion is a charming hybrid of 1950s Mitteleuropa – a home from home for elderly Eastern Europeans, with its interior of glass lamps, cream damask tablecloths and gypsy musicians in the evenings – and a brasserie where younger locals come for a drink and plat du jour by the bar or on the heated terrace. Be prepared: this food is not for the faint of heart. From the no-choice daily Hungarian lunch menu, we had a starter of hortobágyi palacsinta, a crêpe stuffed with a thick, minced veal ragoût in a paprika and cream sauce;

and a bowl of székely gulyás, a mildly spicy, deep-red paprika-stained goulash of tender stewed veal, with a big dollop of sour cream and Transylvanian-style cabbage (sauerkraut in cream). We also tried csáky bélszin, thick beef fillet with a slab of fried foie gras on top, in a cream and morel sauce with a dish of little spaetzle-style noodles, before sharing the menu's apple strudel with nicely crisp filo pastry. The wine list covers both France and Hungary.

POLISH

La Crypte Polska

1 pl Maurice Barrès, 1st (01.42.60.43.33). M° Madeleine. **Open** noon-3pm, 7-10pm Tue-Sun. **Average** €24. **Prix fixe** €14.90-€17.20. **Credit** MC, V. **Map** G4.

Forget any preconceptions about Polish food, because a few steps from costly Chanel and the glamour of the Ritz is one of the capital's culinary bargains. Where else, in spitting distance of the Louvre, can you get a heaving plate of smoked salmon with blinis for €8? Chase it down with a €3.90 shot of hot krupnik and the rue de Rivoli will never be the same. Rib-sticking, traditional mains – duck with apple, polish sausage, roasted pork and various stuffed dumplings – feature prominently and cabbage is, of course, ubiquitous. The three-course 'urban menus' (Poznan, Krakow, Warsaw) are guaranteed fillers. The crypt in question lies beneath the religious heart of Polish Paris, the church of Notre-Dame-de-l'Assomption, which still pulls an impressive Sunday crowd. Don't forget the vodka: the goldwasser, named for its distinctive gilded flakes, provides a pungent buzz of long-marinated herbs and spices.

PORTUGUESE

O Por do Sol

18 rue de la Fontaine-du-But, 18th (01.42.23.90.26). M° Lamarck Caulaincourt. **Open** noon-2pm, 7-10pm Mon, Tue, Thur, Fri, Sun; 7-10pm Sat. Closed Aug. **Average** €25. **Prix fixe** €22. **Credit** MC, V. **Map** H1.

Bacalhau, or salted cod, has been a staple of the Portuguese diet since the 16th century; they call it 'fiel amigo' (faithful friend), and in José and Elesia's tiny dining room you'll find out why. We started by sharing a plate of beignets de morue – fluffy cod fritters that left us fighting for the last bite – followed by two cod mains. Grilled cod, brushed with olive oil and pepper, was thick, moist and the perfect choice for those who like tasty, simple fish. But we were hard pressed to imagine anything better than the morue du chef, cod layered with roasted onion, pepper, tomato and potato in a heaving casserole. Portugal's favourite pasteis de nata, delicious custard tarts, finished the meal and left us swapping memories of remote villages with our convivial hosts. About the wine: vinho verde (young, green wine that has a distinctive fizz) is a perfect, refreshing match for the hearty cuisine. You'll find the white on the menu, but the red is kept secret: chilled, it is an excellent accompaniment for the cod.

Koutchi

ROMANIAN

Athanor

4 rue Crozatier, 12th (01.43.44.49.15). M° Reuilly-Diderot. **Open** noon-2.30pm, 7-11.30pm Tue-Sat. Closed Aug. **Average** €35. **Prix fixe** €23. **Lunch menu** €12. **Credit** AmEx, MC, V. **Wheelchair access. Map** N8.

Initially, Athanor's distressed decor might seem like a sophisticated design concept but, once settled in, you realise that the collection of bric-a-brac – ranging from old carpets to a copy of a Mondrian painting – is just part of the homely atmosphere that extends from the motherly welcome to the delicious Romanian cuisine. We began with a couple of shots of vodka: a sweet Amande céleste and a drier, appetite-inducing number. On paper the mix of cheese terrine, tarama and herring pâté looked mundane, but they were all tasty and homemade, accompanied by one of the many Romanian wines on offer – our Feteascá Albá was an outstandingly supple golden white. A melting, long-cooked pork dish with figs was served on a bed of moreish savoury rice, while the perch (Athanor specialises in freshwater fish) with creamy chilli sauce and triangles of polenta was equally delicious. The puddings, a nut cake and a cherry cake, were unsophisticated but comforting, and needed just a suitable digestif to finish off a delightful lunch. The patronne recommended the 60° Slivovitz pascale, which left us in a haze of happiness for the rest of the day.

RUSSIAN

Dominique

19 rue Bréa, 6th (01.43.27.08.80). M° Vavin. **Open** *Restaurant* 7.30pm-midnight Tue-Sat. *Bar/boutique* noon-midnight Tue-Sat. **Average** €50. **Prix fixe** €40 (dinner only). **Credit** AmEx, DC, MC, V. **Map** G9. Of all the Russian restaurants in Paris, this is the one that has best preserved the ambience of the old émigré haunt. Though it's expensive, it is possible to escape without your wallet getting a KGB-type seeing-to from men in long leather coats. One option is to sit yourself down on one of the stools in the splendid and atmospheric bar with its red walls,

long wooden counter and marble tables. Here you can down glasses of vodka chilled to the consistency of engine oil and snack on zakouski (the herring plate is particularly fine) or a bowl of borscht with pirojki (beef-stuffed pastries). Finish up with a slice of delicious vatrouchka (cheesecake). A tip when it comes to the vodka: order by the glass, even if there are several of you, to sample some of the more wonderful creations. As for the restaurant, it has a warmer feel, with tapestries, samovars and songs from Brezhnev-era protest singer Vladimir Vissotski. A few spoons of caviar, a bottle of Cristall vodka and the 'Prince Potemkin-style' salmon koulibiaka (wrapped in light pastry), and you could soon be feeling like an oligarch on a big night out.

SCANDINAVIAN

Trëma

8 rue de Marseille, 10th (01.42.49.27.67). M° Jacques Bonsergent. **Open** noon-3pm, 7.30pm-1am Mon-Fri; 7.30pm-1am Sat. **Average** €30. **Credit** AmEx, MC, V. **Wheelchair access. Map** L4.

There's nothing like the pop of champagne to fizz a winter night away. Pair it with elegant, white-plated cubes of gravadlax, thin strips of smoked eel on a film of apple purée, crispy endive nests of fruit-laced smoked trout and warm, silky scallops – or indeed any of the 21 other refined Scandinavian tapas on offer here (most in the €8-€10 range) – and you'll wonder where you've been for so long. Sleek and modern (the loos look like they're straight out of the Stockholm design museum), the year-old Trëma, named for the double dots above the 'e', is the product of a pan-Nordic love affair, a Finnish chef and a spot-on sense of style. From first pop to last lick, we were encouraged – by our solicitous waitress, the mellow lights, help-yourself salads, and the heady bubbles of our party-pink Besserat de Bellefont – to settle in for the night. And then we found the 13-strong vodka menu. We chose a shot of Zurawinowka, a bright red cranberry-soaked version, which gave us the kick to get home. Tapas are for sharing; with salad and crispbreads, you really don't need more than two a head. And even champagne starts at an affordable €28.

© Bal du Moulin Rouge 2003/2007 - Moulin Rouge

Kris Guittier

Discover the Show of the Most Famous Cabaret in the World !

Dinner & Show at 7pm from €145 • Show at 9pm : €99 & at 11pm : €89

Montmartre - 82, bd de Clichy - 75018 Paris - Reservations : 01 53 09 82 82
www.moulin-rouge.com

On the Town

CAFES, BARS & PUBS	**166**
TEA ROOMS	**191**
WINE BARS	**196**
EATING WITH ENTERTAINMENT	**203**
SHOPPING & COOKING	**205**

Cafés, Bars & Pubs

Is it a café? Is it a bar? Or is it a restaurant? These questions are becoming ever more difficult to answer in Paris, where a single establishment might start the day as a laid-back place for a coffee and croissant over the newspaper, serve home-cooked bistro food to office workers at lunch and bring out the DJ and tapas as local 'bobos' (bohemian bourgeois) pack the place out at night. Both cafés and bars are likely to serve food of some sort at lunch and dinner, as the French rarely imbibe without some accompanying nosh (there are a few exceptions, especially among the student bars, where drinkers will most likely have lined their stomachs with kebabs). An increasing number of cafés are equipped with wireless internet (WiFi), which is usually indicated by a sticker on the door. Generally, Parisians are not heavy drinkers – even less since a government crackdown on drink driving. If your goal is to get sloshed, however, there are plenty of places that will oblige, particularly along rue Oberkampf and in the studenty Latin Quarter.

A word about coffee: the French expresso, or express, is not to be confused with the more sophisticated Italian espresso. Ask for it 'serré' if you prefer it more concentrated and 'allongé' if you're craving an American-style coffee. A crème is made with milk but good, frothy cappuccino is rare. If you want a little frothy milk in your express, ask for a 'noisette'. Milk on the side will be provided on request (at a price) for either coffee or tea. Be warned, however, that tea in a café usually consists of water in a burning-hot metal pot with a tea bag on the side. Also note that in cafés it's usually cheapest to stand at the bar, and most expensive to sit on the terrace.

1ST ARRONDISSEMENT

Café Marly ★

93 rue de Rivoli, cour Napoléon du Louvre, 1st (01.49.26.06.60). M° Palais Royal. **Open** 8am-2am daily. **Food served** 8am-1am. **Credit** AmEx, DC, MC, V. **Non-smoking room.** **Map** H5.

Some say that you haven't done Paris without sitting at least once on the terrace of the Café Marly, with its sumptuous view of the Louvre's once-controversial glass pyramid. Inside is pure plush elegance where snappily dressed, if somewhat aloof, staff can serve you anything from cod with potato purée to a club sandwich. Desserts are particularly tantalising, such as the mango panna cotta or a Moroccan-inspired orange salad with cinnamon. Breakfast (8am-noon) is the best time to enjoy the view without having to put up with lunch and dinner crowds. But anytime is a good time to sit back and soak up the atmosphere, which feels miles from the frenetic streets beyond the Louvre.

Le Fumoir

6 rue de l'Admiral-de-Coligny, 1st (01.42.92.00.24/ www.lefumoir.com). M° Louvre Rivoli. **Open** 11am-2pm daily. **Food served** noon-3pm, 7.30-11.30pm. Closed two weeks in Aug. **Happy hour** 6-8pm. **Credit** AmEx, MC, V. **Wheelchair access.** **Map** H6.

The location of this café-bar and restaurant is hard to beat. Opposite the Louvre's Cour Carrée but thankfully hidden from the museum's crush of tourists, it attracts a dapper crowd, who lounge on the terrace reading the international newspapers on offer or the Fumoir's own literary review. The interior has a distinct Bogart feel, straight out of a 1930s gentlemen's club – chic colonial elegance, with slow-turning ceiling fans and contemporary oils brightening the taupe brown walls. The bar is a handsome wooden affair imported from a Philadelphia speakeasy and home to a serious, expertly mixed cocktail list, such as the delicious apple Martini or equally refreshing Long Island iced tea. Further inside, Le Fumoir becomes more of a restaurant, ending with a trade library at the back, (give a book, get a book), and it even houses a choice of board games.

Hemingway Bar at the Ritz

Hôtel Ritz, 15 pl Vendôme, 1st (01.43.16.30.31/ www.ritzparis.com). M° Concorde or Madeleine. **Open** 6.30pm-2am Mon-Sat. **Snacks served** 6.30pm-2am. Closed first two weeks in Jan. **Credit** AmEx, DC, MC, V. **Wheelchair access.** **Map** F5.

The Hemingway bar is a tiny haven of old-world stateliness and clubby charm. Wood-panelled and lined with memorabilia and photos in homage to its namesake, this is the perfect spot for an intimate rendezvous. And indeed to be served by the world's greatest bartender (according to *Le Figaro*), Colin Field, who is to mixology what Hemingway was to literature. Tell him what you like and he will invent a cocktail for you on the spot. At €400, the Ritz Sidecar, made with pre-phylloxera Cognac, must be the most expensive cocktail on the planet. Less frighteningly priced are the divine raspberry Martini or the champagne mint-infused Serendipity, always topped with a rose or orchid for the ladies. Pulling in its share of expense-account singles, ageing American divorcees and some beautiful young things, this is certainly the place to do cocktails. Across the corridor is the Cambon Bar: the original Ritz bar, done up as it was back in its 1920s heyday.

Jip's

41 rue St-Denis, 1st (01.42.21.33.93/www.jips cafe.com). M° Châtelet or Les Halles. **Open** noon-2am daily. **Food served** noon-3.30pm, 7-11pm. **Credit** MC, V. **Map** J5.
Located in a desert of commercial dross and chain restaurants, little Jip's bright yellow awning brings life and light to the street. During winter, goblets of spicy vin chaud recharge numbed shoppers while in summer the outside terrace becomes a festival of colours and action. Jip's has an unkempt charm; there are myriad tribal sculptures and grass skirts adorning the walls, but the bar, with its colourful jolly of rum bottles, fairy lights and punch bowls of sangria, remains the focal point of the place. This is a cheery spot for a Latino-inspired drink and nibble, the unfussy atmosphere and good choice of (often live) music attracting a multi-ethnic, multi-generational crowd.

Taverne Henri IV

13 pl du Pont-Neuf, 1st (01.43.54.27.90). M° Pont Neuf. **Open** 11.30am-10pm Mon-Fri; noon-5pm Sat. **Food served** nonstop. **Credit** MC, V. **Wheelchair access**. **Map** H6.
Blink and you'll miss it: the Taverne Henri IV is a delightful little place, smack bang on the tip of the Ile de la Cité. The emphasis here is on simple French fare washed down with a good glass of wine – all at very reasonable prices. The eggs baked with blue cheese and ham are delectable and a glass of white Beaujolais even better. If you are having trouble deciding which wine to pick, the hilarious and chatty barman will be happy to make a few suggestions. For the decor, think 'legal profession' – dark wooden bar, certificates on the wall, wine bottles on display, and a few dusty books thrown in for good measure.

2ND ARRONDISSEMENT

Le Café

62 rue Tiquetonne, 2nd (01.40.39.08.00). M° Etienne Marcel. **Open** 10am-2am Mon-Sat. **Food served** noon-10pm. **Credit** MC, V. **Wheelchair access**. **Map** J5
Decorated with a mix of travel-chest goodies and objects inspired by former colonies, this café is a lively spot. The owner, an avid traveller and collector, just can't help sharing his treasures with his customers. The service is prompt and the wholesome traditional food is made with good ingredients. Try a croque-monsieur and you can choose from a range of different breads, or beat a hangover with l'assiette brunch, a filling mix of bacon and eggs with salad and goat's cheese. Come early on weekend nights as the place gets packed by 8pm with a young, hip crowd. There isn't a resident DJ, but it feels like there is, as the house and techno rhythms start pumping from around 7pm.

Hemingway Bar at the Ritz

On the Town

Le Coeur Fou

55 rue Montmartre, 2nd (01.42.33.91.33).
M° Sentier. **Open** 4pm-2am Mon-Sat. **No
credit cards**. **Map** J4.

Cool and chaotic, this postage stamp-sized bar gets
packed early with local hipsters, loud singles and
lounging bohos, making the vibe feel more London
than Paris. Le Coeur Fou is a flirty, noisy place to
clink Caipirinhas and have a darned good night.
Space is pretty limited, but at the back there is a little
raised sofa section to rest your distressed-denim clad
derrière (although beware the surcharge on drinks).

Footsie

*10-12 rue Daunou, 2nd (01.42.60.07.20). M°
Opéra.* **Open** noon-2.30pm, 6pm-2am Mon-Thur;
noon-2.30pm, 6pm-4am Fri, Sat. **Food served**
noon-2.30pm, 7-11pm. **Credit** AmEx, MC, V.
Map G4.

Otherwise known as the FTSE or the London
Stock Exchange, this bar is based on an original
and successful gimmick: that of drink prices
fluctuating with supply and demand. Sound crazy?
The principle is simple: drinks are grouped into five
main types and each purchase increases the cost of
that drink type while the others decrease in price.
Expect to see after-work suit types alongside others
playing City whizz-kids scanning the screens (with
their count-down clocks) and watching for 'price
crashes' and drink deals. Upstairs a group can book
its own room complete with screen for a private
windfall booze-up.

The Frog & Rosbif

*116 rue St-Denis, 2nd (01.42.36.34.73/
www.frogpubs.com). M° Etienne Marcel.* **Open**
noon-2am daily. **Food served** noon-11pm. Closed
24, 25 Dec. **Happy hour** 6-8pm. **Credit** V. **Map** J5.

Paul Chantler and Thor Gudmundsson must be
delighted with the success of their chain of English
pubs, which started with this one. Their ads call it 'a
quintessential English pub', and it is, with thick
wooden pews, autographed rugby shirts, traditional
pub grub and five screens to broadcast the UK's top
sporting events. The Frogpubs serve their own beers,
all brewed on the premises and available on tap. We
particularly enjoyed the strong bitter Parislytic and
the full-bodied stout Dark de Triomphe. Staff are well
marshalled, and the atmosphere friendly.

Other locations: The Frog & British Library,
114 av de France, 13th (01.45.84.34.26); The Frog
& Princess, 9 rue Princesse, 6th (01.40.51.77.38);
The Frog at Bercy, 25 cour St-Emilion, 12th
(01.43.40.70.71).

Harry's New York Bar

*5 rue Daunou, 2nd (01.42.61.71.14/www.harrys-
bar.fr). M° Opéra.* **Open** 10.30am-4am daily. **Food
served** 11am-3pm Mon-Fri. Closed 24, 25 Dec.
Credit AmEx, DC, MC, V. **Map** G4.

Bars and fashions come and go – and then there's
Harry's. This wood-panelled, pennants-bedecked
hangout is reputed to be both the birthplace of
the Bloody Mary and Hemingway's favourite
haunt. It's a legendary Parisian landmark, beloved

La Tourelle, your own window on the world (or Paris, at least).

of expats, visitors and office locals who loosen their ties on more or less an equal footing as white-coated bartenders mix exactly the right measures, seemingly without trying. For a more intimate atmosphere, sip your superlative concoction in the downstairs piano bar where Gershwin composed *An American in Paris* and listen to some of the live soft jazz played most nights from 10pm.

Le Tambour ★
*41 rue Montmartre, 2nd (01.42.33.06.90). M°
Sentier.* **Open** 6pm-6am Mon, Sun; noon-3pm,
6pm-6am Tue-Sat. **Food served** 7pm-1.30am
Mon, Sun; noon-3pm, 6pm-3.30am Tue-Sat.
Credit MC, V. **Map** J5.
This classic nighthawks' bar is decked out with vintage transport chic, its slatted wooden banquettes and bus stop sign bar stools occupied by chatty regulars who give the 24-hour clock its best shot. Neither tatty nor threatening, Le Tambour comprises a small counter area of friendly banter twixt staff and souses, a busy conservatory and a long dining room memorable for its retro Métro map from station Stalingrad and iconic image of Neil Armstrong. Pride of place is given to a philosophical quotation about this being the perfect match of urban and bucolic. Bang on, Tambour, bang on.

La Tourelle
*43 rue Croix des Petits Champs, 2nd (01.42.61.
35.41). M° Bourse or Palais Royal.* **Open** 7am-
10pm Mon-Fri. **Food served** noon-3pm. Closed
first two weeks in Aug. **Credit** MC, V. **Non-
smoking room**. **Map** H5.
This simple and cosy corner café offers a friendly welcome and a good view on to the street from its generous windows. The interior is dominated by a pristine copper-topped bar around which locals gather giving the impression that everyone knows each other. Chat with the bartender and you'll feel like a regular. A great place on a sunny day for a morning coffee and a piece of the house cake, a delicious fairy-light madeira sponge. Otherwise, pop by at lunchtime and choose from the excellent choice of organic bread-based tartines.

3RD ARRONDISSEMENT

Andy Wahloo ★
*69 rue des Gravilliers, 3rd (01.42.71.20.38). M° Arts
et Métiers.* **Open** 5pm-2am Tue-Sun. **Food served**
8pm-midnight. **Happy hour** 5-8pm. **Credit** AmEx,
MC, V. **Wheelchair access**. **Map** K5.
Proving that size really doesn't matter (this place brings new meaning to the word 'bijou'), a formidably fashionable set crowd in here and fight for a coveted place on an upturned paint can (who needs a divan when you've got Dulux?). In summer, though, the bar expands into the atmospheric courtyard, like a bobo version of the Ritz. Andy Wahloo – created by the people behind its neighbour 404 and London's Momo and Sketch – is Arabic for 'I have nothing'. From head to toe, it's a beautifully

designed venue crammed with Moroccan artefacts, and enough colours to fill a Picasso. There's a surge around 9pm and the atmosphere heats up later on.

L'Apparemment Café
*18 rue des Coutures-St-Gervais, 3rd (01.48.87.
12.22). M° Filles du Calvaire or St-Paul.* **Open** noon-
2am daily. **Food served** noon-3pm, 7.30-11.30pm.
Credit MC, V. **Wheelchair access**. **Map** L5.
Light wood panelling, smooth jazz tunes, velvet lounge chairs and soft lighting make this an irresistible setting for a rendezvous. The atmosphere is casual yet romantic, the waiters young and helpful. The menu has a do-it-yourself attitude: choose the ingredients for a made-to-order salad. Brunch includes seafood, meat and cheese dishes, with choices of drinks and accompaniments. Options might appear confusing at first, but offer you ultimate control. Visitors to the nearby Picasso Museum will find this a convenient place to refuel at.

Le Connétable
*55 rue des Archives, 3rd (01.42.77.41.40). M° Hôtel
de Ville or Rambuteau.* **Open** 11am-3pm, 7pm-3am
Mon-Sat. **Food served** noon-3pm, 7pm-midnight
Mon-Sat. Closed Aug. **Credit** AmEx, MC, V.
Map K6.
Look no further for the ultra-Parisian Piaf-and-pastis bar that you always hope you'll stumble on. Le Connétable is one of those wonderfully rare spots where you can find the much-vaunted joie de vivre and bonhomie the French are supposed to be famous for. Expect old geezers getting hammered on rough red, faded divas holding court in the corner, young couples getting fruity on a stuffing-free sofa and up-for-it locals chatting to anything with a pulse and the ability to slur. Best seen after midnight.

4TH ARRONDISSEMENT

Bubar
*3 rue des Tournelles, 4th (01.40.29.97.72). M°
Bastille.* **Open** 7pm-2am daily. **Snacks served**
nonstop. Closed 13 Feb, 14 July, 24, 25, 31 Dec.
Credit AmEx, MC, V. **Map** L7.
You'll be stunned to find such a relaxed and local atmosphere only steps from the busy Bastille… if you can find it at all, that is. Nearly unmarked, this tiny bar is all red, like the wine to which it is dedicated. It's a special pleasure to sample so many good non-French labels, including reds and whites from Chile, Argentina, Italy, Spain and South Africa, for less than €5 a glass. Little tapas await you at the bar, making you feel like you're having an apero at a friend's.

Chez Richard
*37 rue Vieille-du-Temple, 4th (01.42.74.31.65). M°
St-Paul.* **Open** 6pm-2am Tue-Sat. **Food served** 6pm-
midnight. Closed Aug. **Happy hour** 6-8pm. **Credit**
AmEx, DC, MC, V. **Non-smoking room**. **Map** K6.
A compromise between the style-conscious L'Etoile Manquante across the street and the grunge chic of Les Etages next door, Chez Richard pulls in

On the Town

couples, after-work drinkers and clubbers who are equally comfortable sipping chilled champagne, a well-dosed cocktail or simply a beer. The upstairs restaurant serves up decent no-nonsense food at reasonable prices. Elegant and unpretentious.

L'Escale

1 rue des Deux-Ponts, 4th (01.43.54.94.23).
Mᵒ Pont Marie. **Open** 7am-8pm Mon-Sat. **Food served** noon-3.30pm. Closed two weeks in Aug.
Credit MC, V. **Map** K7.
On a freezing winter's day, this old-fashioned brasserie/wine bar offered a retreat from the windy corridors of the Ile St-Louis and comfort food in the form of chou farci, a divine leek quiche and, that Parisian café rarity, the goldenest, crispiest pile of homemade chips, complete with fluffy interior. Quality wines are reasonably priced, and desserts, including a deliciously eggy clafoutis, are all (thankfully) own-made. The crowd of regulars range from scruffy locals to business types discussing 'le marketing': all are on friendly terms with waiter Colette and as ready to offer you their newspaper as to scrap over the last serving of monkfish.

Les Etages

35 rue Vieille-du-Temple, 4th (01.42.78.72.00).
Mᵒ Hôtel de Ville or St-Paul. **Open** 3.30pm-2am daily. **Snacks served** nonstop. **Happy hour** 3.30-9pm. **Credit** AmEx, DC, MC, V. **Map** K6.
'What's the upstairs like?' 'Like a squat' answered the friend who had been a regular here in her student days. A nose around revealed this to be more true than we had imagined: although the two colourful upstairs floors with red walls and lots of low seating were empty at 6pm, a large notice had been put up declaring that only the smoking of cigarettes was permitted by law. A bit like an Amsterdam coffee house without the weed, then, but there's plenty of atmosphere once it fills up with a backpackerish clientele. On a summer evening we enjoyed our Rose Royals – champagne and rose syrup – from a list of fun cocktails. It's a great place for a Mojito too.

L'Etoile Manquante

34 rue Vieille-du-Temple, 4th (01.42.72.48.34/
www.cafeine.com). Mᵒ Hôtel de Ville or St-Paul.
Open 9am-2am daily. **Food served** 9am-1.15am.
Credit DC, MC, V. **Map** K6.
Xavier Denamur's quirky, very Parisian bars on rue Vieille-du-Temple never seem to go out of fashion. This one, with a vaguely designerish decor of brown and cream circles on the ceiling and photographs on the walls, attracts a genuinely mixed crowd. Gay or straight, wacko hairdos, tousled English weekenders and the quintessential waif-like French gamine – everyone looks relaxed in these surroundings. The terrace is always packed, while inside its Tardis-like, stretching back to the smoochy far end, with its red leather banquettes. Drinks are as you'd expect – five beers on tap from blanche to brune, wines by the glass, cocktails, served with little nibbles at aperitif time. The famous loos were

none too clean when we visited and the little toy train that runs between the ladies and the gents was out of action, but the TV camera that films you as you wash your hands, against a background of twinkling stars was still working.

Le Flore en l'Isle

42 quai d'Orléans, 4th (01.43.29.88.27). Mᵒ Hôtel de Ville or Pont Marie. **Open** 8am-2am daily. **Food served** 11am-1am. **Credit** MC, V. **Wheelchair access**. **Map** K7.
Although the terrace here attracts the summer hordes in search of Berthillon ice-cream, sitting at a window table overlooking the Seine and Notre Dame with a coffee and its accompanying plate of chocolate truffles is a favourite Ile St-Louis pastime. Egg- and seafood-based brunch dishes are popular as are the house desserts, including a truly scrumptious gratin aux poires, but avoid the rest of the menu, which is inexcusably bad. Don't be fobbed off into the usually empty tea room next door.

Grizzli Café ★

7 rue St-Martin, 4th (01.48.87.77.56). Mᵒ Châtelet.
Open 9am-2am daily. **Food served** noon-11pm.
Credit AmEx, MC, V. **Map** K6.
According to legend, this café was home to a dancing bear, whose memory is preserved in a framed sketch opposite the bar. With a welcoming terrace, a main floor with white moulded ceilings, and an upstairs of modern black wood, this outstanding café-restaurant offers a symphony of atmospheres and great service. Half-pitchers of good house wine accompany excellent cuisine with interesting twists. Try the delicate shrimp ravioli or the seared tuna with Asian mushrooms. Convenient to Les Halles and Beaubourg, this place gets its share of tourists, but remains popular with locals too.

Lizard Lounge

18 rue du Bourg-Tibourg, 4th (01.42.72.81.34/
www.hip-bars.com). Mᵒ Hôtel de Ville. **Open** noon-2am daily. **Food served** noon-3am, 7-10.30pm.
Happy hour *Ground floor* 5-9pm. *Basement* 8-10pm. **Credit** MC, V. **Map** K6.
When other bars in the Marais held one or two solitary punters at the end of an evening, the Lizard Lounge was still going strong. Bathed in red light, its stone walls, industrial decor and mirrored bar were warmed by the chatter of a lively crowd over Brazilian lounge music. Forty or so reasonably priced cocktails are chalked on a board and we enjoyed the slightly tart banana Daiquiri and apple Martini served by a waitress who soon dispensed with the 'mercis' and revealed herself to be Irish. Like the other bars in the Cheap Blonde group, this one has a happy hour and inexpensive beer on tap, as well as light food. Downstairs we discovered a whole other realm with funkier music – three candlelit cellar rooms including one where people lounge on cushions like at a private party. It's a fun, anglophone bar with a lot more style than British pub imitators – and a strong crowd of regulars.

Le Petit Fer à Cheval

*30 rue Vieille-du-Temple, 4th (01.42.72.47.47/
www.cafeine.com). Mº St-Paul.* **Open** 9am-2am
daily. **Food served** 9am-1.15am. **Credit** DC,
MC, V. **Map** K6.

The tiny horseshoe-shaped zinc bar, which takes
up most of the front room, ensures cosy chitchat
and quips among last orders folk, and Thursdays
and Sundays' barman, Bouba, has particularly
funky taste in music. During the day it's a little more
touristy and you'll find it hard to get into the back
room to taste the delicious assiettes of charcuterie
and winter warmers such as confit de canard. One
last tip: the Irish coffee here is superb, though the
barmen will not thank us for telling you.

Le Pick-Clops

*16 rue Vieille-du-Temple, 4th (01.40.29.02.18).
Mº Hôtel de Ville or St-Paul.* **Open** 7am-2am Mon-
Sat; 8am-2am Sun. **Food served** noon-11.30pm.
Snacks served 11.30pm-1am. Closed 25 Dec.
Wheelchair access. Credit MC, V. **Map** K6.

This bright and vividly coloured café is ideally
placed at one of the Marais' southern gateways.
Inside, it may be as close as Paris gets to a '50s
diner. The intricately tiled floor, mismatched vinyl
chairs, primary colour formica, mirrors, giant peanut
bin and stainless steel fixtures set the stage for
a retro-ish hangout that welcomes both grimy
construction workers and leather-jacketed locals.
The calm morning coffee and tartine scene becomes
a packed beer-drinking zone by day's end.

Stolly's

*16 rue Cloche-Perce, 4th (01.42.76.06.76/www.hip-
bars.com). Mº Hôtel de Ville or St-Paul.* **Open** 4pm-
2am daily. Closed 24, 25 Dec. **Happy hour** 4-8pm.
Credit MC, V. **Wheelchair access. Map** K6.

This seen-it-all drinking den has been in action since
1991, serving a mainly expat crowd with vodka
tonics and old Velvets tunes for nights immemorial.
The staff make the place, helping you feel like part
of what passes for furniture, and smoothing an easy
passage from arriving sober to sinking them until
you're stotious. A terrace eases libation, as do long
happy hours, but don't expect to faff about with food.

5TH ARRONDISSEMENT

The Bombardier

*2 pl du Panthéon, 5th (01.43.54.79.22). Mº Maubert
Mutualité/RER Luxembourg.* **Open** noon-2am daily.
Food served noon-4pm. Closed 24-26 Dec. **Happy
hour** 4-9pm. **Credit** MC, V. **Wheelchair access.**
Map J8.

Snuck into a niche opposite the Panthéon, the
Bombardier is a convincing re-creation of a Home
Counties pub (minus the retired colonels), with
Bombardier beer on tap from Bedford brewer (and
proprietor) Charles Wells. Despite the swirly glass
and olde-worlde tapestry, it's a lot less hardcore
Anglo than most English pubs in Paris, managing
to pull in healthy measures of pretty young French
things. Great for a pint over the Sunday papers, the
weekend footie or a raucous rugby session.

Grizzli Café

Café Delmas

*2-4 pl de la Contrescarpe, 5th (01.43.26.51.26).
M° Place Monge.* **Open** 7.30am-2am Mon-Thur,
Sun; 7.30am-3am Fri, Sat. **Food served** 11am-
midnight daily. **Credit** MC, V. **Wheelchair
access. Non-smoking room. Map** J8.

Place de la Contrescarpe was one of Hemingway's
numerous stomping grounds and it still retains
an alcoholic theme, with two prominent cafés
dominating either side of the fountain in this cobbled
square. One, Café Delmas, has gone decidedly
upmarket – even more so after recent renovations
that have given the terrace an eye-catching black
and red colour scheme and warmed up the modern
interior. It's shoulder-to-shoulder perma-tanned
style gurus and Gucci-clad fashionistas – deservedly
so, as staff are exceptionally friendly and the food
above average, if pricey. When darkness descends,
things become a little less civilised as students and
tourists stumble out of nearby kebab joints.

Café Léa ★

*5 rue Claude Bernard, 5th (01.43.31.46.30). M°
Censier Daubenton.* **Open** 8.30am-2am Mon-Sat;
10am-2am Sun. **Food served** noon-3.30pm Mon-
Sat; noon-4pm Sun. Closed 31 Dec, 1 Jan. **Credit**
AmEx, MC, V. **Wheelchair access. Map** J9.

A splash of colour and a dash of youth are what this
part of the 5th needed, and market shoppers next
door at rue Mouffetard would do well to step over
and sip at the wellspring of it here. Earthen tones
with a touch of ethnic chic dominate the bright one-
room space, surrounded by windows, with a thin
terrace space for those sunnier days. Simple dishes
during the day and a huge reasonably priced brunch
(€18) make it a favourite, but it's just drinks and
snacks – no dinner – in the evening.

Le Crocodile

*6 rue Royer-Collard, 5th (01.43.54.32.37). RER
Luxembourg.* **Open** 10.30pm-6am Mon-Sat (closing
varies). Closed Aug. **Happy hour** 10.30pm-12.30am
Mon-Thur. **Credit** MC, V. **Map** J8.

It's worth ignoring the apparently boarded-up
windows for a cocktail at Le Crocodile. Young,
friendly regulars line the sides of this small, narrow
bar and try to decide on a drink – we were assured
that there are 267 choices, most of them marginally
less potent than meths. Pen and paper are provided
to note your decision; the pen comes in handy for
point-and-choose decisions when everything gets
hazy. We think we can recommend an Accroche-
Coeur, a supremely '70s mix of champagne and
Goldschläger, served with extra gold leaf.

La Gueuze

*19 rue Soufflot, 5th (01.43.54.63.00/www.la-
gueuze.com). M° St-Michel/RER Luxembourg.*
Open 9am-2am daily. **Food served** 12.30pm-1am.
Happy hour 4-7pm Mon-Thur; 4-7pm, 11pm-2am
Fri-Sun. **Credit** MC, V. **Wheelchair access.
Non-smoking room. Map** J8.

This Belgian boozer is heaven for those who could
murder a pint, and hell for aesthetes. Indeed, La
Gueuze's fabulously tacky mock-abbey decor
would drive anyone to drink – thankfully there
are more than a dozen draft beers on tap as well as
a variety of about 150 international beers, including
your basic Budweiser. Those wanting to live more
dangerously can sample more out-there brews like
Mort Subite, or a tangy raspberry Gueuze Bécasse.
To chase down all those bubbles, tuck into a
steaming plateful of moules-frites or choucroute, and
have a post-guzzle stumble around the nearby Jardin
du Luxembourg.

Café Delmas

Le Pantalon

7 rue Royer-Collard, 5th (no phone). M° St-Michel/RER Luxembourg. **Open** 11am-2am Mon-Sat. **Happy hour** 5.30-7.30pm. **No credit cards. Map** J8.

Mad as a bag of frogs, Le Pantalon is a local café that seems at once deeply familiar and utterly surreal. It features the standard fixtures and fittings you find at your corner caff, including the old piss-artist propping up the bar – plus a strange vacuum-cleaner sculpture, disco-light loos and the world's most prosaic proposal of marriage. But aside from the offbeat decor, it's the regulars and staff who tip the balance firmly into eccentricity. Friendly and very funny French grown-ups and international students chat away in a mish-mash of accents and languages. Happy hours are fantastic, but drinks here are always cheap enough to get enjoyably tipsy without worrying about a cash hangover.

Le Piano Vache

8 rue Laplace, 5th (01.46.33.75.03). M° Maubert Mutualité. **Open** noon-2am daily. **Food served** noon-2.30pm. **Happy hour** noon-9pm. **Credit** MC, V. **Map** J8.

A Left Bank drinking haunt for many a decade, this has all the hallmarks of what any beer-stained smoke hovel should be: dark, cramped, filled with a hardcore drinker/student clientele, the walls covered four times over with posters and indeterminate pub grime, and the greatest hits of alternative '80s synth-pop on the stereo. Note that weekday opening hours switch to evenings only out of term time.

Rhubarb ★

18 rue Laplace, 5th (01.43.25.35.03). M° Maubert Mutualité. **Open** 5pm-2am daily (Sept-June); 7pm-2am daily (July, Aug). **Happy hour** 5-10pm (Sept-June); 7-10pm (July, Aug). **Credit** MC, V. **Map** J8.

A wonderful little spot near the top of rue Mouffetard. Cocktails are excellent – Sean's famous apple Martini is sublime, but there are also fab-sounding watermelon and chocolate versions too. A relaxed vibe abounds and a mixed crowd mingles happily at the bar. The cellar is all crumbling pale stone and high ceilings, and while a quiet corner is ideal seduction territory the space works equally well for gaggles of mates on a big night out.

Six-Huit

quai Montebello, 5th (01.46.34.53.05/www.six-huit.com). **Open** 10am-2am daily (Apr-Sept). **Food served** nonstop. **Credit** AmEx, DC, MC, V. **Map** J-K7.

Of all the péniches on this idyllic, narrow stretch of Seine just across the water from the Ile de la Cité, this one is the least pretentious. No white tablecloths, no cabaret, just a 1930s barge polished to perfection by its down-to-earth owners who serve simple food and drink on the original wooden, heavy-footed tables. Open six months of the year, it's a beautiful setting in which to enjoy a beer and a pause on a walk along the towpath. By night Notre-Dame looms and a cooling breeze crosses the deck as passing bateaux-mouches light up the scene. On our visit, were pleased to find that most clients were French, many of them just drinking, although the salads, grilled salmon or faux-filet are just fine. The waiter, however, was almost laughably incompetent. Downstairs is a lovely ballroom with portholes.

Le Verre à Pied

118 bis rue Mouffetard, 5th (01.43.31.15.72). M° Censier Daubenton. **Open** 9am-9pm daily. **Food served** noon-2.30pm. **Credit** MC, V. **Wheelchair access. Non-smoking room. Map** J9.

When Amélie Poulain retreated here for a steadying Cognac she brought new fame to this slice of old working-class Paris. Le Verre, literally at the *pied* (foot) of the rue Mouffetard, is easy to miss amid the bustle of the market, and perhaps the owners prefer it that way. The tobacconist, narrow bar area and tiny lunch room at the back draw in market workers during the week and, on Sundays, the after-church crowd from St-Médard. Assiettes and sandwiches are inexpensive, and a small pichet of merlot goes for €3.

Le Violon Dingue

46 rue de la Montagne-Ste-Geneviève, 5th (01.43.25.79.93). M° Maubert Mutualité. **Open** 8pm-4.30am Tue-Sat. **Happy hour** 8-10pm. **Credit** MC, V. **Map** J8.

The haunt of many a dodgy dragueur, this stalwart of the American collegian run is perhaps the best bar to go to alone, if you intend to leave accompanied. Alcoholic slush puppies, lethal Long Island iced teas and a generous happy hour help to move things along. If you spend more than half an hour without uttering a chat-up line, it's definitely a very slow night. It's buzziest at the back of the bar; only the very bravest (or most desperate) should venture downstairs.

6TH ARRONDISSEMENT

Le Bar

27 rue de Condé, 6th (01.43.29.06.61). M° Odéon. **Open** 9pm-3am Mon-Sat. Closed two weeks in Aug. **Credit** MC, V. **Map** H7.

Le Bar is one of those strange little places that you only ever visit when it's very, very late and you're very, very drunk. It's almost pitch black, has a shrine-type affair at the back of the bar, gravel on the floor, everyone seems to talk in whispers and they serve very strong drinks (whiskies are a speciality). A few words of warning about this place: once you've been here, you'll find yourself strangely drawn back at inappropriate times when you really should go home to bed, and at least one member of the party always falls asleep on the comfy black leather banquettes. Finally, there's a strange echo effect in the corridor down to the toilet, so if Le Bar is your last-ditch attempt to pull before the sun comes up, don't discuss your strategy too loudly.

On the Town

Le Bar Dix

*10 rue de l'Odéon, 6th (01.43.26.66.83). M°
Odéon.* **Open** 6pm-2am daily. **Happy hour**
6-8pm. **No credit cards. Map** H7.
The decor of this popular and long-running hang
dates back to the previous owners, a Spanish couple
who sold up in 1986, but who left a tradition of
sangria behind. If hearing the name of this fruit-filled
Spanish punch makes you wince, you've never tried
theirs, which hasn't made anyone blind during the
course of almost 20 years of assiduous over-
indulgence by a global pack of punters. As almost
every other café in St-Germain turns into a tacky
version of a lounge bar, it's nice to find a funky place
with a bit of character – the jukebox plays Piaf and
Brassens, and the same Toulouse Lautrec prints
have been on the walls for going on half a century.

Bar du Marché

75 rue de Seine, 6th (01.43.26.55.15). M° Odéon.
Open 8am-2am daily. **Food served** 8am-6pm.
Credit MC, V. **Wheelchair access. Map** H7.
The Bar du Marché must make a killing. It's packed
day and night, the trendy crowd overspills from the
terrace on to the street on warm summer nights. You
might have to yell to get the attention of the jovial,
overall-and beret-clad waiters and put up with
cramped seating, but the frivolity and fun
atmosphere are well worth the hassle. Old liquor ad
posters, clown mosaics and newspaper clippings
lend the café a bit of a theatrical feel. Drinks are
generous and inexpensive, and the food served
during the day is acceptable café fare. A perfect
place to flirt away a summer Parisian afternoon.

Café de Flore

*172 bd St-Germain, 6th (01.45.48.55.26/www.
cafe-de-flore.com). M° St-Germain-des-Prés.* **Open**
7.30am-1.30am daily. **Food served** nonstop. **Credit**
AmEx, DC, MC, V. **Wheelchair access. Map** H7.
This is a St-Germain institution for people-watching
and spotting Left Bank celebrities such as author
Frederic Beigbeder, designer Sonia Rykiel (there is
even a breadless club sandwich bearing her name)
and philosopher Bernard Henri Lévy. One of the
classic Parisian literary cafés – every year it awards
the prestigious Prix de Flore to aspiring young
writers – it is trendier and less touristy than its next-
door rival Les Deux Magots. Food is, of course,
prohibitively expensive for café fare – think €20 for
an omelette – but it's well worth ordering the
deliciously thick hot chocolate from the professional
waiters to watch the fashionable world go by.

Café de la Mairie

8 pl St-Sulpice, 6th (01.43.26.67.82). M° St-Sulpice.
Open 7am-2am Mon-Fri; 8am-2am Sat; 9am-9pm
Sun. **Food served** nonstop. **No credit cards.**
Non-smoking room. Map G7.
Facing the leafy St-Sulpice square, across from its
baroque fountain and next to its imposing church
(of *The Da Vinci Code* fame), this café has an
enviable setting that keeps it busy day and night. A
haunt of Henry Miller and Albert Camus, Café de
la Mairie was a hot literary spot in the early
20th century, and is now, with its buzzing terrace
in the heart of St-Germain, a great place for the
less intellectual pursuit of people-watching. Watch
out for Catherine Deneuve, who is rumoured to take
her morning coffee here. But don't expect fabulous
service or food – on our latest visit both the roast
beef plate and salad niçoise were pretty tasteless,
and the waiters abrupt and impersonal – and be
prepared to ignore the car fumes and the noisy traffic
on the terrace.

Le Comptoir des Canettes

*11 rue des Canettes, 6th (01.43.26.79.15).
M° Mabillon.* **Open** noon-2am Tue-Sat. Closed
Aug, 25 Dec-2 Jan. **Credit** AmEx, MC, V. **Map** H7.
A great mix of people – hip thirtysomethings,
students, locals and tourists – congregates at all
hours in the two small rooms and cellar of this
traditional French bar, also known as Chez Georges.
Although the decor is basic – a run-down wooden
comptoir, cramped tables and peeling mustard
wallpaper – the drinks are cheap, the service
friendly and the clientele merry. On summer days
the crowd at the heaving bar spills onto the
pedestrian rue des Canettes, aperitifs in hand. The
most popular and down-to-earth bar by far in the
otherwise touristy St-Sulpice area.

Rhubarb – cheap at half the price. *See p173.*

Coolin

15 rue Clément, 6th (01.44.07.00.92). M° Mabillon.
Open 11am-2am daily. **Food served** noon-3pm,
7-10pm. **Credit** MC, V. **Wheelchair access.**
Non-smoking room (during the day). **Map** H7.
It's so tempting to slate the Coolin for being some
corny hotchpotch of Oirishness. Yes, it does look
straight out of one of those cheesy Guinness adverts.
And yes, there is a bit of potato overkill on the menu.
Nevertheless, the Coolin remains a likeable oasis of
liveliness, in the middle of the stultifyingly dead
Marché St-Germain. So go on and sup on a cold one
or dig into a lusty slice of Bailey's cheesecake, as you
take in the match on the big telly, and trade some
cheeky banter with the cuties manning the bar.
Mighty cushty, as they say in ole Dub.

Les Deux Magots

6 pl St-Germain-des-Prés, 6th (01.45.48.55.25/
www.lesdeuxmagots.com). M° St-Germain-des-Prés.
Open 7.30am-1am daily. **Food served** nonstop.
Credit AmEx, MC, V. **Map** H7.
Although its literary prize is older (awarded since
1933), its decor more elegant and its terrace better
positioned, Les Deux Magots just fails to draw in the
stars like its neighbour, the Flore. Tourists, however,
still converge from around the world to sit in this
literary café that was once the meeting point for
the likes of Oscar Wilde, Picasso, de Beauvoir,
Sartre and Hemingway. So much so that it has
a boutique offering its signature porcelain, and
has opened copycat cafés in Tokyo and Beirut.
Prices are ridiculous and the food mediocre, but on
a drizzly Paris day you can't go wrong with the
decadent hot chocolate.

La Mezzanine de l'Alcazar ★

62 rue Mazarine, 6th (01.53.10.19.99/
www.alcazar.fr). M° Odéon. **Open** 7pm-2am daily.
Food served 7-11.45pm Mon, Tue, Sun; 7pm-
12.15am Wed; 7pm-12.45am Thur-Sat. **Credit**
AmEx, DC, MC, V. **Map** H7.
One of the few chic yet welcoming cocktail bars in
the Odéon area, the mezzanine bar of this Conran
restaurant has established itself as an enduringly
hip watering hole. The bar is airy and well designed,
with spot lighting in vivid colours, comfy modern
furniture and bright murals. Add some great music
and a range of innovative cocktails, such as the
Casablanca (a coconut milk, Bacardi and pineapple
juice concoction) and you have a recipe for success.
From Wednesday night onwards there is a full
music programme, with guest DJs and concerts, and
the Monday night easy-listening sessions are a must.

Le Nemrod

51 rue du Cherche-Midi, 6th (01.45.48.17.05).
M° Sèvres Babylone or St-Placide. **Open** 6.30am-
2am Mon-Sat. **Food served** noon-3pm, 7-11pm.
Closed two weeks in Aug. **Credit** MC, V. **Map** G7.
A busy café-brasserie in the vicinity of the Bon
Marché department store, this is a main pit stop for
local professionals and worn-out shoppers. Known

for its affordable yet good-quality grub, the café is
usually packed at lunchtime, so come early.
Specialising in the hearty food of the Auvergne in
central France, it offers both brasserie fare –
omelettes and copious salads – and heartier meals
such as grilled sausages with aligot (cheesy mashed
potatoes) or truffade (cheesy fried potatoes). The
service is brisk, the decor dated and the seating
cramped, but the Nemrod is a decent value-for-money
choice in this otherwise obscenely expensive area.

La Palette

43 rue de Seine, 6th (01.43.26.68.15). M°
St-Germain-des-Prés. **Open** 9am-2am Mon-Sat.
Food served noon-3pm. Closed three weeks
in Aug. **Credit** MC, V. **Map** H7.
A favourite hangout for students of the Ecole des
Beaux Arts and some artistic wannabes, this café-
bar surrounded by St-Germain art galleries is lively
at almost any time of day. One room has an old-
fashioned zinc bar while the other is filled with
cramped tables and benches. Both are decorated to
the hilt with slightly amateurish paintings and – you
guessed it – a painter's palette. It's a good place to
sip a coffee in the early afternoon, but as the evening
progresses and the students pile in, it becomes
rowdier and smokier. The terrace is popular with all
age groups on warm summer evenings.

Le Purgatoire

14 rue Hautefeuille, 6th (01.43.54.41.36/
www.lepurgatoire.com). M° St-Michel. **Open** 6pm-
4am Thur; 6pm-5am Fri; 9pm-5am Sat; 8pm-5am

Les Deux Magots

Sun. **Happy hour** 6-10pm Thur; 6-8pm Fri;
8pm-midnight Sun. **Credit** MC, V. **Wheelchair
access**. **Map** J7.
You probably wouldn't find your way into this
happy little den unless someone had told you about
it, since the heavy wooden front door is rather off-
putting. Once inside, though, you'll find yourself in
one of the rare bar-clubs in one of the world's most
touristy neighbourhoods that's actually frequented
by locals. Upstairs is devoted to drinking, while
downstairs in the ancient vaulted stone basement
it's all about dancing from Thursday through
Saturday, when a DJ spins a mix of the puzzling rock
pop that only the French could really enjoy.

Le Rostand
*6 pl Edmond-Rostand, 6th (01.43.54.61.58). M° St-
Michel/RER Luxembourg.* **Open** 8am-midnight daily.
Food served nonstop. **Credit** MC, V. **Wheelchair
access**. **Non-smoking room**. **Map** H6.
As you sit across from the Luxembourg gardens on
a sunny terrace drinking a freshly squeezed orange
juice, you may wonder if life gets any better than
this. Even the colonial-inspired interior, complete
with rattan furniture, teak wood and old photos
framing the walls, draws crowds in the winter
months. And although the food is limited to salads,
sandwiches, omelettes and steak tartare, it is of good
quality, such as the fresh and well-presented
Rostand salad with generous prawns, avocado and
grapefruit. There were some minuses – stale-tasting
bread, unwelcoming staff – but, in such an idyllic
location, it's easy to turn a blind eye to such details.

Au Vieux Colombier
*65 rue de Rennes, 6th (01.45.48.53.81). M° St-
Suplice.* **Open** 8am-1am Mon-Sat; 11am-8pm Sun.
Food served noon-11pm Mon-Sat; noon-5pm Sun.
Credit MC, V. **Map** G7.
An art deco jewel among the mainly modern
brasseries of rue de Rennes, this corner café not only
takes you back to the 1920s, it also offers unusually
good café food at easy-to-swallow prices. With most
dishes ranging from €10 to €12, it's hard not to be
tempted by one of the creative salads – including
the Asian-inspired Thai beef salad – or by the pasta
or meat dishes, such as the well-cooked burger with
chips. Service is efficient, the only minus being the
darkness of the interior, which can be fairly gloomy
on a grey winter's day. Favour a table near the
windows instead, which gives a great vantage point
on the street shopping action outside.

7TH ARRONDISSEMENT
Bar Basile
*34 rue de Grenelle, 7th (01.42.22.59.46). M° Rue
du Bac or Sèvres Babylone.* **Open** 7am-11pm Mon-
Sat. **Food served** noon-10pm. **Credit** MC, V.
Wheelchair access. **Non-smoking room**.
Map G7.
Retro '70s-style decor of bold colours and Formica
tables is the backdrop for serious-looking political
science students from neighbouring Sciences-Po to
engage in erudite repartee or peruse the house copies
of *Le Monde Diplomatique*, while nonchalant waiters

On the Town

float around the café, dispensing to the student populace words of wisdom hewn from the université of life. Things get more hectic at lunchtime as students and their professors sit at banquettes and tables to refuel on salads, club sandwiches and more substantial plats du jour.

Café des Lettres

53 rue de Verneuil, 7th (01.42.22.52.17). M° Rue du Bac. **Open** noon-midnight Mon-Sat; noon-4pm Sun. **Food served** noon-4pm, 7-10pm Mon-Sat; brunch noon-4pm Sun. Closed two weeks at Christmas. **Credit** MC, V. **Map** G6.

Café des Lettres has a moody feel, with dark furniture, deep turquoise and maroon walls, deeply meaningful abstract art and a heavy Gauloise-pervaded atmosphere. There may even be the odd brooding intellectual, as the salon is used by the neighbouring Maison des Ecrivains for high-brow literary discussions and novel-reading sessions. Contrastingly airy, the courtyard is a good place to drop in on for an espresso on a summer's afternoon. Food can be disappointing for the price (about €30 per person), which reflects the swish location.

Le Café du Marché

38 rue Cler, 7th (01.47.05.51.27). M° Ecole Militaire. **Open** 7am-midnight Mon-Sat; 7am-5pm Sun. **Food served** 11am-11pm Mon-Sat; 11am-3.30pm Sun. **Credit** MC, V. **Wheelchair access. Non-smoking room. Map** D6.

For an in-the-action location amid the 7th's most lively market street, you can't do much better than Le Café du Marché, which serves as a hub of neighbourhood activity but is equally comfortable welcoming tourists and the curious. Dozens of tables are spread among interior dining rooms, a canopy and plastic-covered area plus an open-air terrace, so you have your choice of seating depending on the sun-cloud-rain continuum. Big salads at €9.50 and classic French main dishes at €10 (confit de canard, poulet rôti, entrecôte) are bargains, though quality varies depending on the dish (a fish special was fine, but pasta with a mix of both red and green pesto sauces was uneventful). Service had been friendly in the past, but was indifferent on our latest visit.

Café Thoumieux

4 rue de la Comète, 7th (01.45.51.50.40/www. thoumieux.com). M° La Tour Maubourg. **Open** noon-3pm, 5pm-2am Mon-Sat. **Hot food served** noon-3pm. **Snacks served** 5pm-2am. **Happy hour** 5-9pm. **Credit** AmEx, MC, V. **Wheelchair access. Map** E6.

A Spanish-flavoured café-bar for the gilded youth of the 7th, the Thoumieux – a more recent annex of the vintage bistro around the corner – can be a cosy place to meet and have some tapas in the early evening, or a late-night purveyor of that last vanilla vodka you don't need. On our last visit the animated barman was sharpening his impersonation of Tom Cruise in *Cocktail*, tossing liquor bottles high into the air and flipping them over his shoulder to catch

them behind his back, or missing them as they fell to the floor. Quite a cost. Perhaps this explains why the happy 'hour' was surreptitiously truncated?

Le Roussillon

186 rue de Grenelle, 7th (01.45.51.47.53/www.cafe roussillon.com). M° La Tour Maubourg. **Open** 6.30am-2am daily. **Food served** 11am-11.30pm (summer); 11am-11pm (winter). **Happy hour** 6-8pm. **Credit** MC, V. **Wheelchair access. Map** D6.

This schizo little café is nestled beside the rue Cler market. In the morning it's the favoured haunt of grey-suited politicians hashing out their day over brekkie. Come noon they give way to a more colourful fauna – botoxed ladies who lunch, feverishly trading gossip as they tuck into opulent salads. The nights belong to the trustafarians from the nearby American University of Paris, who come in to have a little boogie and study the cocktail list more assiduously than they do for their finals. The potent potions are served up by bartenders as pretty as they are rude – and boy are they ever pretty.

Le Varenne ★

36 rue de Varenne, 7th (01.45.48.62.72). M° Rue du Bac. **Open** 7am-8pm Mon, Fri, Sat; 7am-midnight Tue-Thur. **Food served** noon-3pm Mon, Fri-Sat; noon-3pm, 8-11.30pm Tue-Thur. **Credit** MC, V. **Wheelchair access. Non-smoking room. Map** G6.

The trek down rue de Varenne could be dubbed the 'walk of death', as the endless parade of grey, identical government buildings could sap the will to live in even the sunniest soul. Coming across a place as welcoming as Le Varenne on this bleak stretch is akin to finding an oasis in the Sahara. The couple behind this miracle are Caroline and Francis Tafanel, sticklers for first-rate ingredients from the best local suppliers. So just sit back and watch the be-suited civil servants come alive in the warm surroundings as they dig into the scrumptious offerings from the daily-changing blackboard menu.

8TH ARRONDISSEMENT

Atelier Renault

53 av des Champs-Elysées, 8th (01.49.53.70.00/ www.atelier-renault.com). M° Franklin D Roosevelt. **Open** 8am-2am daily. **Food served** noon-12.30am. **Credit** AmEx, DC, MC, V. **Map** E4.

This place lies above what is essentially the Renault car showroom. At street level it's an ever-changing and diverting display of vehicles, while overlooking it all is the café-style restaurant that's all bridges and walkways. Best to bag a table overlooking the cars or the picture windows that buttress on to the Champs-Elysées. Food is international – chicken Caesar salad, steak tartare and a variety of club sandwiches, tapas and daily specials served alongside good ice-creams, sorbets and cocktails. 'La Formule 1' guarantees three mini starters, three mini mains and three mini desserts presented within a guaranteed 20 minutes for €21 – ideal for anyone

Le Varenne

catching a bite before the cinema. The clientele is office workers, out-of-towners and people with children. While somewhat soulless at night, it's perfect for brunch at weekends. Beats most of the ghastly eateries on Les Champs, and for this we must be grateful.

Bar des Théâtres

6 av Montaigne, 8th (01.47.23.34.63). M° Alma Marceau. **Open** 6am-2am daily. **Food served** nonstop. **Credit** AmEx, MC, V. **Map** D5.
Hardly a destination in itself, but if you find yourself in the pricey environs of avenue Montaigne, this is the place to come for a bite or restorative coffee. It's probably the only place in the area that won't make you feel grubby and badly dressed. That's not to say that you won't find the rich and famous here. You will – as it's sandwiched between Prada and Emmanuel Ungaro's HQ, just opposite the Théâtre des Champs-Elysées. The bar was prominently featured in Danièle Thompson's recent film *Fauteuils d'orchestre* and old-school waiters in well-worn blazers ensure decent charcuterie, grillades, omelettes, salads and oysters are served comme il faut. The decor is somewhat shabby – very Paris 1968 with rust-coloured banquettes – but stopping here won't break the bank.

The Bowler

13 rue d'Artois, 8th (01.45.61.16.60/www.the bowlerpub.com). M° Franklin D Roosevelt or St-Philippe du Roule. **Open** 11am-2am Mon-Fri; 1pm-2am Sat, Sun. **Food served** noon-3pm, 7-10.30pm Mon-Fri. Closed 25 Dec, 1 Jan. **Happy hour** 6-11pm (Sat, Sun). **Credit** AmEx, DC, MC, V. **Map** E3.
Unless you're a very lonely expat, it's hard to know what you would be doing in this unashamedly

English pub. It could be anywhere in Blighty. That said, the Bowler, on a quiet corner of this busy quartier, is one of the best expat bars in Paris. Owned by the Mayday Inns chain, the church-salvage interior hosts a healthy mixture of Brits and Frogs. Newcastle Brown Ale, Beamish Red, Guinness and Kronenbourg are all on draught and a wide selection of wines, spirits and cocktails is available. Food is of the burger and fish'n'chips variety rather than anything 'gastropub'. The Bowler caters for footy fans, screening all important fixtures on three flat screens, and hosts 'a legendary quiz' on Sunday nights. Efficient and friendly French service too.

Hôtel Plaza Athénée

25 av Montaigne, 8th (01.53.67.65.65). M° Alma Marceau. **Open** 6pm-2am daily. **Snacks served** nonstop. **Credit** AmEx, DC, MC, V. **Wheelchair access**. **Map** D5.
When it first opened, this was the place to imbibe. It has gone slightly off the boil and the hotel's management no longer seems sure whether the bar is open to the public or to residents only. A recent Saturday night visit saw us barred (too full apparently) while our friends (already inside) were obliged to finish their drinks and join us on the street. If you're a woman, you'll need to be a size eight, wearing this season's clobber and have a taste for jelly shots or iced alcopops to enjoy yourself here. Decorated by Patrick Jouin, a protégé of Philippe Starck, the main interior feature is an ice-blue bar and long communal tables with low-hanging mini chandeliers. On one side are sofas, warm red lighting and an intriguing video fire. The surprisingly affable staff serve imaginative concoctions, including the now-classic Rose Royale (raspberry coulis and champagne) and drinks that magically light up. The clientele is mainly middle-aged Eastern European gents with bored-looking overdressed women. Over-hyped and not as classy as it would like to think.

Mood

114 av des Champs-Elysées, 8th (01.42.89.98.89). M° George V. **Open** 10am-4am daily. **Food served** noon-2pm, 8-11pm. **Credit** AmEx, DC, MC, V. **Map** D4.
On the site of the seedy old Latina Café, Mood had been open only three weeks when we dropped in for a drink. Arranged on three floors off a courtyard, this is a lounge and French/Asian restaurant and a good address for a peaceful drink or light meal. Soup with prawns, vermicelli noodles, coconut milk and ginger can be followed by Hong Kong-style pork served with sweet mango. Sushi, sashimi and maki are also served. The decor is not so fabulous as to establish Mood in the vanguard of hip new places, but the soft gold furnishings, dark wood floor and blowups of old photographs of geishas are undeniably pleasant. Ideally situated for a tipple following the rigours of a visit to the Louis Vuitton flagship store just opposite. Music is of the Café del Mar variety, but live acts and DJs are promised.

On the Town

Le V ★

Hôtel Four Seasons George V, 31 av George V,
8th (01.49.52.70.00). M° George V. **Open** 9am-
2am daily. **Food served** 11am-midnight. **Snacks**
served nonstop. **Credit** AmEx, DC, MC, V.
Wheelchair access. Map D4.

This is a glorious bar in what may be the city's best
palace hotel. Residents favour it at the weekend, so
it's best to book. The enormously professional
and welcoming staff, oh-so-comfortable seating,
dark wood panelling and roaring fire will make
even the poorest feel like King Croesus. Marvel at the
17th-century tapestries, antiques and Jeff Leatham's
exquisite and influential floral arrangements, and
work out why the leggy lovely at the adjacent table
seems so enamoured of the portly troll accompanying
her. Cocktails (particularly the Martinis) and long
drinks are perfectly executed and are priced at
around €25. This is what supping at a grand hotel
is all about.

9TH ARRONDISSEMENT

Café de la Paix

place de l'Opéra, 9th (01.40.07.36.36). M° Opéra.
Open 7am-11.30pm daily. **Food served** 7.30am-
11am (terrace only), noon-3pm, 6-11pm. **Credit**
AmEx, DC, MC, V. **Wheelchair access.**
Non-smoking room. Map G4.

Constructed by Charles Garnier and inaugurated
by Princess Eugenie in 1892, this opulent café is
a Parisian institution that barely needs introducing.
Anybody who is anybody has passed through
these hallowed doors over the years – among them
Wilde, Zola, Maupassant, er, John Travolta – and
nowadays you too can rub shoulders with the
glitterati as long as you are willing to pay for the
pleasure (just to give you an idea, the plat du jour
costs €40). Why not pop in for afternoon tea on the
terrace and order what is arguably the best
millefeuille in Paris? Alternatively, wander past
marble columns and stucco walls towards the
adjoining Grand Hôtel for a glass of bubbly in
the breathtaking winter garden. If eating a meal,
lone travellers can sit at the 'table d'hôtes', an area
reserved for wealthy souls wishing to share their
meal with similarly wealthy souls. What better way
to hook up with a millionaire?

Général Lafayette

52 rue Lafayette, 9th (01.47.7.59.08). M° Cadet.
Open 10am-4am daily. **Food served** nonstop.
Credit AmEx, DC, MC, V. **Map** J3.

This smart, belle époque brasserie has not only been
feeding hungry Parisians for the last 100 years, it
has also been plying them with beer – over 40 beers
to be exact, including several Belgian abbey brews
and a myriad of bottled brews. Wine is also on the
list of attractions and many bottles have been
handpicked from small, regional producers. The
fun continues in the kitchen, where delights such
as Lyon sausage stuffed with pistachios and a

heavenly crème brûlée (perfect every time) ensure a
constant stream of customers (anyone from bankers
to seasoned theatre-goers) from morning to night.

P'tit Creux du Faubourg

66 rue du Fbg-Montmartre, 9th (01.48.78.20.57).
M° Notre-Dame-de-Lorette. **Open** 8am-8pm Mon-Sat.
Food served nonstop. **Credit** MC, V. **Map** H3.

If you're looking for a quick fix in the grub
department and happen to be passing by, a pit
stop in this modest café will fill a hole and leave you
with enough dosh for a spending spree along nearby
rue des Martyrs. At €12.50 for three courses,
including 25cl of wine, it's not a banquet (and don't
be surprised if the waiter takes your bread and gives
it to another table), but you can look forward to
staple choices such as pâté, burgers, roast chicken,
crispy salads, ripe cheeses and homemade apple
tarts. Service here is quick and friendly, the clientele
distinctly local and once inside no one can escape
the owner's lively banter.

World Bar

Fifth floor, Printemps de l'Homme, 64 bd
Haussmann, 9th (01.42.82.78.02). **Open** 9.30am-
7pm Mon-Wed, Fri, Sat; 9.30am-10pm Thur. **Food**
served 11.30am-3.30pm. **Credit** AmEx, MC, V.
Map G3.

The Paul Smith-designed World Bar is a strange
concept at first sight: breezeblock walls covered in
yellowing newspapers, a zinc bar, plastic coated
furniture that looks as if it has been stolen from an
adult crèche, waiters who appear to have stepped
out of a Toni & Guy ad and all this at the top of a
department store! The whole effect could be coined
'canteen chic'. The food is certainly an upmarket
take on fusion pub grub (think salmon with coconut
milk noodles); but for fashion-conscious shoppers
this is a must, and a welcome alternative to the belle
époque-style equivalent in Galeries Lafayette.

10TH ARRONDISSEMENT

L'Atmosphère

49 rue Lucien-Sampaix, 10th (01.40.38.09.21).
M° Gare de l'Est or Jacques Bonsergent. **Open**
10am-2am daily. **Food served** noon-3pm.
No credit cards. Wheelchair access. Map L3.

So you're probably wondering what exactly makes
the atmosphere at L'Atmosphère so very special.
Well, there didn't seem to be anything particularly
worthy of note when we initially popped around
there on a late hazy Sunday afternoon. Sure, there
were a few punters dotted on the terrace overlooking
the 'so trendy it hurts' Canal St-Martin, but inside
there was nary a soul, just quaint pub decor (with
lacy doily curtains, and unvarnished wooden
furniture) that could be straight out of *Coronation
Street*. However, a few potent and cheap gin and
tonics later, we set out to liven things up: the boys
started flailing around madly like flabby
Chippendales, while us girls sang along to Prince's
greatest pumping out of the sound system…

turning ourselves into a rather ad-hoc, and worrisome, opening act for the experimental music slots usually showcased here on Sunday nights.

Chez Adel

10 rue de la Grange-aux-Belles, 10th (01.42.08.24.61). M° Colonel Fabien or Jacques Bonsergent. **Open** noon-2pm, 5pm-2am Tue-Fri; noon-2am Sat, Sun. **Food served** noon-2pm. **Credit** MC, V. **Map** L3.
Syrian-born Adel has conjured up a universe as charming and gregarious as he is. In the daytime his café plays coy, welcoming neighbourhood families looking for an unpretentious spot to tuck into trad fare such as salade Vosgienne, roast beef with mash or oeufs mayonnaise. Yet when dusk falls the place really lets its hair down, as live music spots (Tue-Sat from 8pm) electrify crowds of dirty pretty young things, and Sunday nights showcase slightly anarchist theatre performances. Proof positive that culture is still alive and kicking in the wicked 10th.

Chez Prune

71 quai de Valmy, 10th (01.42.41.30.47). M° République. **Open** 8am-2am Mon-Sat; 10am-2am Sun. **Hot food served** noon-3pm. **Snacks served** 7-11pm. Sunday brunch noon-4pm. **Credit** MC, V. **Wheelchair access**. **Map** L4.
This tried-and-tested hipster haunt seemed like a safe bet for a lunch date with an über-trendy graphic artist. But this was not taking into account that when noon strikes the Prune seems to fall into the thrall of some weird, kinetic energy. All of the neighbourhood's (numerous) cool young things mash into here for their midday feed, while the staff veer from scary ferociousness to all-out amiability with silly schizoid zeal. In an hour and a half we witnessed no fewer than three waiter-induced crashes resulting in spectacular smashing of plates and glasses. Great impromptu dinner theatre to accompany our copious and rather good-value dishes of salmon with thyme cream sauce and squid-ink fettuccini, as well as a virile hunk of entrecôte with gratin dauphinois, accompanied by not-very-fresh sangria. We escaped the mad hurly burly by migrating to the café's now-legendary terrace for coffee, where we took in views of the Canal St-Martin and agreed that the Prune is for couples who've been together forever, have nothing left to talk about and just want to sit back and enjoy the show.

De La Ville Café ★

34 bd Bonne-Nouvelle, 10th (01.48.24.48.09/ www.delavillecafe.com). M° Bonne Nouvelle. **Open** 11am-2am daily. **Food served** noon-3pm, 7pm-midnight Mon-Sat; noon-5pm Sun. **Credit** MC, V. **Wheelchair access**. **Non-smoking room**. **Map** J4.
There is something delightfully schizophrenic about this former brothel turned vibrant hipster venue. By day its vast terrace is crammed with thirtysomethings taking advantage of the free wireless internet to pretend they are working away

How the other half live: **Hôtel Plaza Athénée**. *See p179.*

On the Town

like dervishes when they are really just topping off their tan, drinking in the buzzy atmosphere and watching the pretty young things flitting by. By night, things take an edgier turn, with the action moving indoors as style-setters and hardcore club-heads convene in the bar's disparate chill-out areas (including a back room that seems straight out of a David Lynch film and a mad gilt mirrored affair that is a remnant of the bar's racy past). DJs play Thursday to Saturday, so go on and unwind to some excellent disco, house or electro beats while quaffing lethal cocktails, before finishing off the evening with a sweaty boogie over at the nearby Pulp or Rex.

E-Dune

18 av Claude Vellefaux, 10th (01.42.06.22.14/www. e-dune.com). Mº Colonel Fabien or Goncourt. **Open** 10am-2am Mon-Fri; 2pm-2am Sat; noon-8pm Sun. **Food served** noon-4pm, 8-10pm Mon-Sat; 1-8pm Sunday brunch. **Credit** MC, V. **Map** M3.

A *Friends*-style atmosphere imbues this new multimedia café in the bobo Goncourt area. Frédéric painted the 1960s psychedelia-influenced murals, Jean-Michel (alias DJ Choum) programmes the music and Laurence looks after the food. By day you can lunch on light and healthy dishes such as aubergine 'millefeuille' and a smoked salmon assiette, or use one of three internet stations or wireless internet (free with a drink). By night it has a lounge atmosphere and on certain days collectives are invited in to host evenings of music, art and video work, programmed from laptops at the back. As E-Dune only has a licence for alcohol with food you get fabulous tapenade munchies with every drink, and the non-alcoholic cocktails are wicked.

Le Jemmapes

82 quai de Jemmapes, 10th (01.40.40.02.35). Mº Jacques Bonsergent or République. **Open** 11am-2am Mon, Wed-Sun; 7pm-2am Tue. **Food served** noon-3pm, 7.30-11.30pm Mon, Wed-Sun; 7.30-11.30pm Tue. **No credit cards. Wheelchair access. Map** L4.

As soon as the mercury rises in the capital even the slightest nano-inch, this boho haunt nuzzling the Canal St-Martin is so packed out that slews of trendies are forced to strike their best bar poses on the outside pavement. This sudden gush of customers hardly rankles the waiters, who seem more preoccupied with what killer tune is playing on the stereo than with schlepping drinks. Yet it's worth the hellish wait if only because the cocktails – including a potent Cuba Libre and Mojito – rank among the tastiest in town. The same could be said about some of the young groovers squished alongside you.

Le Patache

60 rue de Lancry, 10th (01.42.08.14.35). Mº Jacques Bonsergent. **Open** 6pm-2am daily. **Snacks served** nonstop. **No credit cards. Wheelchair access. Map** L4.

This slightly barking bistro was one of the first in the Canal St-Martin area to encourage live performances – a tradition that lives on today with eager bobo-types

huddling around the authentic 1900s coal-fuelled stove to watch the show on Thursday, Friday and Saturday nights. But don't expect anything in the Molière or Racine vein. Here they specialise in improvised street scenes torn straight out of real life, which can be rather confusing if you're unaware that the ranting nutter next to you is actually a thespian. The result can be a mixed bag, but it nearly always comes from the heart. The taciturn owner's fantastic mood swings can be highly entertaining too.

Le Petit Château d'Eau

34 rue du Château d'Eau, 10th (01.42.08.72.81). Mº Château d'Eau or Jacques Bonsergent. **Open** 9am-11pm Mon-Fri. **Food served** noon-3pm. Closed Aug. **Credit** MC, V. **Map** K-L4.

Robert, the owner of this place, must be the world's biggest chatterbox. During the hour we spent on the terrace, he spun an endless flow of upbeat verbiage. His amiable volubility reflects the easy, slightly eccentric charm of this no-thrills café, where you check your attitude at the door in exchange for cheap reds, hearty grub and pretty riotous company. On our way out Robert waved us goodbye before resuming his talkathon. Pop by and you'll see he's probably still at it.

Le Réveil du 10ème ★

35 rue du Château d'Eau, 10th (01.42.41.77.59). Mº Château d'Eau or Jacques Bonsergent. **Open** 8am-11.30pm Mon-Fri; 7.30am-3.30pm Sat. **Food served** noon-3pm, 7.30-9.30pm Mon-Fri; noon-3.30pm Sat. **Credit** MC, V. **Wheelchair access. Map** K4.

The perfect old-fashioned Parisian lunch? This snug corner café-cum-bistro à vins decorated with faded photos chronicling the place's history has tables packed with regulars, including the couple in the corner who've been coming once a week for the past 50 years. Mouth-watering portions of meaty food (chunky saucisse d'Auvergne, juicy rib steak, crispy confit de canard) are quickly delivered by the attentive staff, and cheese and dessert boards are irresistible. It's all washed down with an extensive wine list that specialises in thirst-quenching Beaujolais. In a word, perfect.

Le Sainte Marthe

32 rue Ste-Marthe, 10th (01.44.84.36.96). Mº Belleville or Goncourt. **Open** 7.30pm-2am Tue; noon-2am Wed-Sun. Closed 25 Dec. **Food served** 7.30-11.30pm Tue; noon-3.30pm, 7.30-11.30pm Wed-Sun. **Happy hour** 5-9pm. **Credit** MC, V. **Wheelchair access. Map** M3.

Have you ever wished that you could escape the smug 'we're so cool' vibe prevailing down by the quai Valmy or Oberkampf way, just for a night? Do you have a secret fiendish penchant for moleskin, patina, absurd night-time conversations that lurch into the wee hours of the morning, luscious glasses of wine and gloriously cool pints of suds? If your answer to the above is a big resounding yes, then your bliss definitely lies a short stroll away, at the picture-perfect place Ste-Marthe. Go now. Enjoy.

11TH ARRONDISSEMENT

La Bonne Franquette
151 rue de la Roquette, 11th (01.43.48.85.88).
Mº Père Lachaise or Voltaire. **Open** 10am-
midnight Mon-Sat. **Food served** noon-2.30pm,
7.30-10.30pm. **Credit** MC, V. **Wheelchair access**.
Map P6.
This fantastic family-run expo-bar is the antithesis
of its name ('bonne franquette' means rough-and-
ready food), serving delicious couscous dishes and
oriental pastries to hungry crowds of bohemians,
TV types and faithful locals. On a sunny day the
giant terrace is a godsend, but when it's full, and in
winter, the interior holds its own delights with its
cool urban-chic decor and North African-influenced
detail (check out the handmade rugs on the benches).
Monthly art exhibitions also cover the walls and the
waiters won't hesitate to talk to you about the
paintings. Possibly the friendliest bar in Paris.

Le Fanfaron
6 rue de la Main-d'Or, 11th (01.49.23.41.14).
Mº Ledru-Rollin. **Open** 6pm-2am Tue-Sat. **Happy
hour** 6-8pm. Closed two weeks in Aug. **Credit** MC,
V. **Map** N7.
Le Fanfaron (named after Dino Risi's cult 1962 movie)
is a haunt for musically inclined retro-dudes. Envious
buffs come from far and wide to listen to owner
Xavier's personal collection of rare film soundtracks.
The decor is an ode to kitsch-cool with Rolling Stones
and Iggy Pop memorabilia, second-hand furniture,
1960s film posters and Lucy the legless mannequin
who reveals all on one side of the bar. At weekends
MR Raw whacks on LPs way into the wee hours, and
if the inexpensive booze gets the stomach acids rising,
try Xavier's chèvre à ma façon (goat's cheese my way)
or an entire saucisson for a measly €4.

Le Bistrot du Peintre ★
116 av Ledru-Rollin, 11th (01.47.00.34.39).
Mº Ledru-Rollin. **Open** 7am-2am daily. **Food
served** noon-midnight daily. Closed 24, 25 Dec.
Credit MC, V. **Map** N7.
The Pause Café across the street gets more hype, but
if you love cafés Le Bistrot du Peintre is the real
classic in this area. Not only is the 1907 art nouveau
interior a gem, but the food is unusually good for
a café, if a little inconsistent (the plats du jour
and meatier dishes such as confit de canard are
usually reliable bets, and the salads are good too).
The upstairs dining room, though less historic, is
appealing in its own way, with a more spacious feel
(that's relative here) and view of the plane trees
outside. The noisy terrace doesn't get much sun, but
wherever you sit this café has undeniable romance.

Café de l'Industrie
16-17 rue St-Sabin, 11th (01.47.00.13.53).
Mº Bastille. **Open** 10am-2am daily. **Food
served** noon-1am. **Credit** DC, MC, V.
Non-smoking room. **Map** M6.
This popular hangout of the turtleneck and thick-
rimmed eyeglasses crowd has engulfed a former

Moroccan restaurant across the street, bringing its
total seating capacity to 350 and adding frequent jazz
concerts. But the flea-market-chic decor remains the
same in both locales, an exceptionally pleasing
combination of vintage furniture and eclectic
paintings. Food is reasonably priced (mains €10-€12)
and quality seems on the up – our crispy confits with
homemade sautéed potatoes were above average,
and the puds even better. We also love the industrial-
themed steel saucers and holders for the clear glass
coffee cups. Quiet in the off-hours between meals, at
lunch and late nights the place is positively buzzing.

Pause Café
41 rue de Charonne, 11th (01.48.06.80.33).
Mº Ledru-Rollin. **Open** 7.30am-2am Mon-Sat;
9am-8pm Sun. **Food served** noon-midnight
Mon-Sat; noon-5pm Sun. Closed 25 Dec.
Credit AmEx, MC, V. **Map** M7.
We've suspected for some time now that the Pause
Café has been resting on its *Chacun cherche son chat*-
induced cinematic fame. The unusually large terrace
with a dominating corner position is a perfect
location for people-watching and its proximity to the
rue Keller's gay nightspots gives the place a
fascinating mix of regulars. Probably best to avoid
eating the rather dull, irregular food and stick to just
a drink and a baffled gaze.

Planète Mars
*21 rue Keller, 11th (01.43.14.24.44). Mº Ledru-
Rollin.* **Open** 6.30pm-2am Mon-Sat. **Happy hour**
7-10pm. Closed two weeks in Aug. **Credit** MC, V.
Map M6.
From the dour grey of a Bastille backstreet, enter a
world of colour. Shimmery disco balls and bright red
walls tell you straight off that, yes, you are in retro
heaven. Kitsch objects line the walls, a space-age bar
is buttressed by impatient queue jumpers, funky
cocktails abound (top Mojitos), and drink prices defy
inflation so much you'd half suspect them to still be
using old francs. Add to this DJs in a little corner
spinning everything from funk to Northern Soul to
1980s disco and back again, and what have you got?
A red planet full of fun, that's what.

Polichinelle Café
64-66 rue de Charonne, 11th (01.58.30.63.52).
Mº Ledru-Rollin. **Open** 10am-1am daily. **Food
served** noon-3.30pm, 7.30-11.30pm daily.
Credit MC, V. **Map** N7.
This colourful café not far from the Bastille has
many moods, from morning coffee at the bar and
louche summer lunches on the terrace to cosy winter
dinners on the banquettes inside. We returned after
a long absence to be greeted as always by motherly
Hélène. The place looks a tatty now, with a
rather over-conspicuous DJ corner and some half-
hearted cinema posters, but happily there is still a
good atmosphere and some drinkable house wine.
The above-average food is one of Hélène's ways of
keeping the regulars happy, and a juicy magret or
some occasional live jazz make for a surefire success.

On the Town

Oberkampf bar crawl

Despite its nickname, the Oberkampf Strip is not a secret initiation ritual performed by newcomers to the 11th arrondissement in a bid to be accepted by the local bobo (bohemian bourgeois) brigade. Nor does it relate to the strips of fabric made by Christophe-Philippe Oberkampf, Louis XVI's textile genius, after whom the area is named. In fact, 'the Strip' refers to three very boozy streets – rue Oberkampf, rue Jean-Pierre Timbaud and rue St Maur – home to the cheapest happy hours in the capital and the perfect destination for an all-night, kebab-fuelled bar crawl. Developing liver cirrhosis here is a local sport, so if you fancy joining in, follow this guide and you should fall down with flair around 6.30am.

Most happy hours run from 6pm to 9pm, so we started bright and early in rue Jean-Pierre Timbaud at **Café Cannibale** (No.93, 01.49.29.95.59). As yet unscathed by the diminishing effects of dipsomania, we enjoyed the intellectual atmosphere inside. The traditional decor, with its zinc bar and red-topped tables, was as easy on the eye as the cheap beer was on the gullet (just €2.50) and we prepared our bellies for the battle ahead with a large plate of charcuterie.

Next stop, **Le Chat Noir** (No.76, 01.48.06.98.22) is a favourite known for its weekend jazz and Monday night chess tournaments. But don't be put off by the pseudo-civilised agenda: we soon discovered that the artists who hang out here are as much party animals as they are boozers, and quickly got into the swing of things with the house cocktail (€6.50) of Kahlua, Grand Marnier and flambéed Baileys. Over the road, **La Marquise** (No.74, no phone), with its brown walls, old tiled bar and metal chairs, is another reputed drinking temple. Doubling up as a restaurant, it attracts a mixed crowd of trendies, all well versed in the art of liquor consumption. It also holds occasional music concerts (we loved the funky mix of African jazz), and the beer is lip-smackingly good value at €2.50.

The next stint was on rue St Maur, where the **Newport** pub (No.114) pumps out reggae into the wee hours and practically gives away beer (just €1.50 a half) from 6-10pm. If you prefer wine and can show up before 9pm, **A Nouveau Nez** at No.112 (01.43.55.02.30) is a minuscule bar-à-vins that serves wine by the glass (€3) and flogs bottles at shop price. Next door in the **Nun's Café** (No.112 bis, 01.58.30.65.48), alcohol – and copious amounts of it – is consumed by an eclectic party crowd with religious devotion. We plumped for **Les Couleurs** (No.117, 01.43.57.95.61) opposite, a calmer base in which to measure how many alcohol units we entered our bloodstream. The beer here costs less than water.

Next up was rue Oberkampf. For the last decade, former belle époque dancehall, **Café Charbon** (No.109, 01.43.57.55.13) has been hailed the hippest hangout on the Strip. We squeezed into the cramped bar area to rub elbows with the (well)dressed-down revellers around us and slurp on one of the best Margaritas to be had in Paris. Over the road, grungy **La Mercerie** (No.98, 01.43.38.81.30) is a shabby-chic haunt for groups of friends and an infallible find for Mojito fans. At No.115, the trashy **Les Abats Jour à Coudre** bar is decorated in graffiti and holds excellent music concerts; and further down the road, the **Quartier Général** (No.103, 01.43.14.65.78), featuring industrial chic decor, stays open until dawn on Friday and Saturday nights. We opted for new kid on the block **Oxyd'Bar** (corner of rue Oberkampf/ 26 avenue Jean Aicard, 01.48.06.21.81), whose wacky loft-style decor provided a chilled-out backdrop for the funky flow of live jazz and cheap Martinis.

Our night ended at **Cithéa** (No.114, 01.40.21.70.95), a dark boudoir that has given extra oomph to the term 'all-nighter', with its stream of trendy DJs who keep the energy pumping until sunrise. We rolled out of the doors at 6.30am with severe hunger pangs and rejoiced, knowing that it wouldn't be long until the Café Cannibale reopened its door at 8am for brekkie – hurrah!

Pop In

105 rue Amelot, 11th (01.48.05.56.11). M° St-Sébastien-Froissart. **Open** 6.30pm-1.30am Tue-Sun. Closed two weeks in Dec, Aug. **Happy hour** 6.30-9pm. **Credit** MC, V. **Wheelchair access**. **Map** L5.

The Pop In seems to be a contradiction in terms, or at the very least an exercise in postmodern irony. A bar so uncool that it is in fact cutting edge, a place that is so hip it seems tragic. Since it hosted a Christian Dior after-show party and was subsequently colonised by fashion hangers-on, the Pop In has won a reputation as a place that doesn't care, doesn't try, but manages to be cool anyway. It's scruffy, cheap and the staff are genuinely nice. Throw in a cellar bar that alternates between an open-mike night and a club for DJs and you have a recipe for a top night out.

Le Zéro Zéro

89 rue Amelot, 11th (01.49.23.51.00). M° St-Sébastien Froissart. **Open** 6pm-2am daily. Closed two weeks in Dec. **Happy hour** 6-8.30pm. **Credit** MC, V. **Wheelchair access**. **Map** L5.

Revolutionary when it opened in 1999, the ZZ still has a chip on its shoulder. It's as wee as a wardrobe, it drinks like a fish and its music kicks like a mule, so there. And many – menfolk, invariably – rally to the cause. They gather round the minuscule L-shaped bar and utter musings, so profound at the time, so pitiful when chalked up in bare white and black over the counter. Attention should be drawn, however, to the cocktail blackboard, which is extensive and potent, incorporating a Zéro Zéro of dark rum, ginger and lime. And even the ZZ has had to succumb to happy hour discounts despite a more than reasonable pricing structure. Oh, and the decorators haven't touched it since the day it opened.

12TH ARRONDISSEMENT

Barrio Latino

46 rue du Fbg-St-Antoine, 12th (01.55.78.84.75). M° Bastille or Ledru-Rollin. **Open** 11.30am-2am daily. **Credit** AmEx, MC, V. **Map** M7.

If salsa is your cup of tea(quila), this Latino paradise will get your hips swaying on the dancefloor before you can say 'la vida loca'. Decked out in bordello oranges, reds and yellows, the theatrical decor (picture a Spanish hacienda-cum-Parisian boudoir) is a lavish, four-floor affair, with a majestic, wrought-iron staircase designed by Gustave Eiffel, velvet banquettes and giant mirrors. Dine on tasty but overpriced tapas before joining the ground-floor fiesta where Rio-types strut their stuff like Shakira on speed. Good fun – especially the Sunday salsa classes (€10). What a shame the staff have turned snobbery into an art form.

Chez Gudule

58 bd de Picpus, 12th (01.43.40.08.28). M° Picpus. **Open** 8am-2am Mon-Sat. **Food served** noon-3pm, 7-11pm. Closed Aug. **Credit** MC, V. **Map** Q8.

In this bourgeois, residential neighbourhood, Chez Gudule (named after owner Christophe Hueget's grandmother) serves up quality nosh and lashings of alcohol to an unexpected mix of rebellious rockers and well-to-do locals. With old bicycles and an upside-down table hanging off the ceiling, it's a pleasantly odd affair, and simply Christophe's eccentric homage to his former life as a Belgian cycling champion. Summer days here are whiled away on the sunny terrace, but make sure you have time to kill – the waiter certainly has and you'd best follow his example.

China Club ★

50 rue de Charenton, 12th (01.43.43.82.02/ www.chinaclub.cc). M° Bastille or Ledru-Rollin. **Open** 7pm-2am Mon-Thur, Sun; 7pm-3am Fri, Sat. **Food served** 7pm-12.30am. Closed Aug. **Happy hour** 7-9pm Mon-Sat; 7pm-2am Sun. **Credit** AmEx, MC, V. **Map** M7.

Step out of working-class rue de Charenton into this anachronistic eating venue whose sexy take on a 1930s Shanghai gentlemen's club has rare panache. If you're looking for a touch of glamour, relaxed conversation and a sneaky tipple, sink into a leather Chesterfield with a cocktail in hand (there are 62 to choose from) and tantalise your taste buds with some of the best Cantonese cuisine in town (the Shanghai chicken is wonderful). The cigar bar upstairs provides an intimate quarter for romantic escapades and the downstairs cellar holds weekly jazz and world music concerts (see website for details).

La Liberté

196 rue du Fbg-St-Antoine, 12th (01.43.72.11.18). M° Faidherbe Chaligny. **Open** 9am-2am daily. **Food served** noon-3pm. **Credit** MC, V. **Wheelchair access**. **Non-smoking room**. **Map** N7.

By day La Lib is a relaxed spot to muse over a plat du jour. The decor is a little primitive, and rubbing elbows is inevitable, but it's pleasant in a convivial way. Good food too, a notch above the average bar grub and a notch cheaper. By night, though, it's a different story. If you're bored with twee bobonia elsewhere in Paris and are in need of a little edge, La Lib will provide. Attracting drunks of every stripe, it comprises a small terrace and a narrow bar area dangling with knick-knacks – and invariably choc-a-block. The back room is used for groups who actually want to talk to each other. The rest guzzle (house punch or decent Belgian brews by the bottle), and at some point everyone gets a turn to dance like a maniac on the bar counter. The music is always right: African beats, Burning Spear or Little Richard howling 'Lucille', it's just there. Reliably raucous.

Viaduc Café

43 av Daumesnil, 12th (01.44.74.70.70/www.viaduc-cafe.fr). M° Gare de Lyon or Ledru-Rollin. **Open** 8am-2am daily. **Food served** noon-3pm, 7-11pm. **Credit** MC, V. **Map** M8.

The Viaduc Café has come a long way since our last visit, when we witnessed an old lady sharing

On the Town

Chez Gudule. *See p185.*

her chocolate cake and spoon with a Dalmatian. Nowadays a somewhat more stylish clientele arrives in strongly perfumed droves to soak up the friendly atmosphere and tuck into sophisticated comfort food beneath the café's great stone arches. The Viaduc burger was succulent and came with a generous pile of crunchy fries. Equally scrumptious was the tomato risotto served with tender caramelised scallops. On Mondays the fortune-telling evenings (soirées tarologie) are a favourite with the girls (so get down there boys) and the jazz-themed Sunday brunch is excellent value at €26.

13TH ARRONDISSEMENT

Chez Lili et Marcel
1 quai d'Austerlitz, 13th (01.45.85.00.08). Mº Quai de la Gare. **Open** 6am-11.30pm Mon-Fri; 8am-11.30pm Sat, Sun. **Food served** noon-11.30pm. **Average** €13. **Credit** MC, V. **Wheelchair access**. **Non-smoking room**. **Map** M9.
This large revamped bar-resto guards the entrance to the north-east corner of the equally revamped 13th, its yellow awnings pointing towards the river and Bercy opposite as you step down from Quai de la Gare Métro station high above. Done out like an old grocery, with packets of post-war Omo and the like on display, L&M's offers genuine cuisine de famille along with pâtisserie to boot. The sunlit terrace is as lovely as you'll find along this stretch of the Seine, and all in all this is the nicest of the options before catching a film at the MK2 cinema around the corner.

Le Couvent
69 rue Broca, 13th (01.43.31.28.28). Mº Les Gobelins. **Open** 9am-2am Mon-Fri; 6pm-2am Sat. **Food served** 11.30am-3pm, 6.30-11.30pm. **Happy**

hour 5-7pm. **Credit** MC, V. **Wheelchair access**. **Map** J10.
For an address in the middle of nowhere, this heavily beamed bar, a delightful hideaway, is hard to beat. It first appeared in Pierre Gripari's novel *Contes de la rue Broca*, which was published in 1967 but enjoyed renewed success in the 1980s, but has come a long way since those dingy days. Today it's the chouchou of students and thirtysomething couples, especially at concert time, when live chords get feet tapping.

La Folie en Tête
33 rue de la Butte-aux-Cailles, 13th (01.45.80.65.99). Mº Les Gobelins. **Open** 6pm-2am Mon-Sat. Closed 25 Dec-2 Jan. **Happy hour** 6-8pm. **Credit** MC, V. **Wheelchair access**.
The happy-hour aperos for only €1.50 are a bargain even among the deflated pricing of the bucolic Butte-aux-Cailles. There's a laid-back feel in the evening as couples and friends gather around the low tables, sitting on little wooden footstools, which, though convivial, can numb the bum rather quickly. This is less of a problem as the night progresses, as live music or a DJ gets people on their feet. The walls are covered with bruised violins, horns, and organs that look as if they've been retired after long careers of Métro busking. Very down to earth and friendly.

14TH ARRONDISSEMENT

L'Entrepôt
7-9 rue Francis-de-Pressensé, 14th (01.45.40.60.70/ www.lentrepot.fr). Mº Pernety. **Open** noon-2am daily. **Food served** noon-3pm, 7.45-10pm. **Credit** MC, V. **Wheelchair access**. **Non-smoking room**. **Map** F10.
This converted paper warehouse has something for every taste: a bar, a restaurant with leafy outdoor

courtyard and an independent, three-screen arts cinema. Chill out and listen to music (jazz on Thursday, world music on Friday and Saturday) for a mere €5 or just drop in and see what's going down.

Le Plomb du Cantal ★

3 rue de la Gaîté, 14th (01.43.35.16.92). M° Edgar Quinet or Gaîté. **Open** noon-midnight daily. **Food served** nonstop. **Credit** MC, V. **Wheelchair access. Map** G9.

This lively homage to the Auvergne, bravely holding its own between the sex shops of the rue de la Gaîté, may suffer from its 1980s decor, but with food like this, who cares? Aligot and truffade come by the plateful, the house-made shoestring fries arrive by the saucepan-load, and the omelettes are made with three eggs, 300g of potatoes, and if you're really hungry, a supplement of tomme cheese. The roast chestnut-based salade corrézienne is delicious and, like all salads here, too enormous to finish. Wines are generally good, and speedy service and low prices mean that Le Plomb is always packed. Definitely the pick of the street for a post-theatre – or strip show – late-night meal.

Les Tontons

38 rue Raymond Losserand, 14th (01.43.21.69.45). M° Pernety. **Open** 7.30am-2am Mon-Sat. **Food served** noon-3pm, 7pm-midnight. **Credit** MC, V. **Wheelchair access. Map** F10.

Taking its name from a 1960s gangster comedy, this classic-looking café complete with zinc bar is popular for dinner with friends or a late-night drink. Inspired by the south-west, the offerings include a rich duck in foie gras sauce with mushrooms, or, for the serious meat lover, ten different types of tartare. Giant salads, amply decorated with physillis (a house signature), help to balance things out, although vegetarians are fobbed off with the usual bizarre concoctions. Wines are excellent but can be pricey, so choose with care. Be sure to try the crème brûlée, flavoured with pistachio, pear or vanilla.

Le Tournesol

9 rue de la Gaîté, 14th (01.43.27.65.72). M° Edgar Quinet. **Open** 8am-2am daily. **Food served** noon-3pm, 6.30-11pm. **Credit** MC, V. **Wheelchair access. Map** G9.

With theatres and sex shops for neighbours, this sibling of La Fourmi was always going to draw an unstuffy crowd – it's just a shame the staff don't have the same attitude. Apart from the eponymous sunflowers behind the bar, it's industrial chic all the way, with rope-wrapped ducts and raw concrete walls. Food runs to brasserie standards, salads and tartines. Cocktails are well-made classics, though the large drinking area is packed at most times, so chances are you'll be nursing that gin fizz at the bar.

15TH ARRONDISSEMENT

Le Bréguet

72 rue Falguière, 15th (01.42.79.97.00). M° Pasteur. **Open** 5pm-4am Mon-Sat. **Food served** 7pm-midnight. **Happy hour** 5-8pm. **Credit** MC, V. **Map** E9.

OK, so it's in the middle of nowhere and the decor is nondescript, so why bother? Well, aside from the fact that it's rare to find somewhere with this much atmosphere in the fun-free 15th, it's worth the Métro journey for the eclectic drinks list. As well as the usual beers on tap, there is Strongbow cider, commendably smooth Guinness, vodkas and exotic quaffs like Limoncello. Work your way down the list – go on, you know you want to.

Au Dernier Métro ★

70 bd de Grenelle, 15th (01.45.75.01.23/ www.auderniermetro.com). M° Dupleix. **Open** 6.30am-2am daily. **Food served** 11am-1am. **Happy hour** 5.30-7.30pm. **Credit** AmEx, MC, V. **Wheelchair access. Map** C7.

This adorable café makes you feel at home. The walls are covered with colourful memorabilia and a football game plays on the small TV behind the bar.

Le Tournesol

Settle in at **Café Le Passy**.

Lots of the Basque-influenced dishes tempt – we tried the juicy fish brochettes served with saffron rice and one of the big salads, both made with care. There's a bit of pavement seating and the big windows open right up. Beer is a bargain for the neighbourhood. Service could not have been friendlier or more attentive – where else might the waiter address two diners as 'my angels'?

16TH ARRONDISSEMENT
Bar Panoramique
Hôtel Concorde La Fayette, 3 pl du Général-Koenig, 17th (01.40.68.51.31). M° Porte Maillot. **Open** 4pm-3am daily. **Credit** AmEx, DC, MC, V. **Map** B3.
Not everyone will get it, but if your irony glasses are firmly in place, this bar becomes a super-glamorous step back in time. On the 33rd floor of the hotel that stands opposite the car park for buses arriving from Beauvais Airport, it's an unreconstructed fantasy from the heyday of disco – affording spectacular views of the Périphérique, the Eiffel Tower and the Arc de Triomphe. With a glittering brass interior and booths all facing outwards, you can imagine you're at the opening party of what became *The Towering Inferno*. First, order cocktails are €20, €19.50 thereafter. Rousing Billy Joel classics are thumped out on the ivories after 9pm. The clientele is nondescript, but this has the potential to become one of the most chic places in Paris. A real find. Go!

Café Le Passy ★
2 rue de Passy, 16th (01.42.88.31.02). M° Passy. **Open** 6.30am-1.30am Mon-Sat. **Food served** noon-3pm, 7.30-11pm. **Credit** MC, V. **Map** B6.
Passy is one of the livelier parts of this otherwise sedate arrondissement, which helps explain the good-looking clientele at this stylish cream-and-brown corner café designed by Hubert de Givenchy, nephew of the fashion designer. Well-dressed men cluster around the bar at the front while couples and groups gather on high-backed banquettes in the candlelit dining room to sip the house cocktail, Le Passy (champagne, Campari and mandarin imperial) or tuck into cuisine inspired by the rugged Auvergne region in central France. Quite a find in this area.

Le Village d'Auteuil
48 rue d'Auteuil, 16th (01.42.88.00.18). M° Michel-Ange Auteuil. **Open** 7am-10.30pm Mon-Sat; 8am-10.30pm Sun. **Food served** noon-3pm, 7-10.30pm. **Credit** MC, V. **Wheelchair access**.
Le Village is just a local caff, but this is Auteuil, so it's permanently stocked with gilded youth, little old ladies with small dogs, women of a certain age with Chanel shades hiding recent eye-jobs and dapper chaps reading *Le Figaro*. This is a quintessential posh Parisian café: all-heated terrace, brushed zinc bar (complete with huge champagne bucket – no one drinks demis here), moustachioed waiters, strong coffee, decent wine and excellent food. A planche nordique comes complete with good smoked salmon, potato salad that's thankfully not drowned in mayonnaise, chopped eggs, cod roe and Poilâne toast; anything served with the amazing aligot is comfort food heaven and the charcuterie platters are a carnivore's fantasy. Surprisingly for such a posh place, the staff are fantastically friendly.

17TH ARRONDISSEMENT
Le Dada
12 av des Ternes, 17th (01.43.80.60.12). M° Ternes. **Open** 6am-2am Mon-Sat; 6am-midnight Sun. **Food served** noon-11pm. **Credit** AmEx, MC, V. **Map** C3.
A chic café in the swanky but ultra-dull part of the 17th, Dada is a good bet for weekend people-watching. The vast pavement terrace offers almost clichéd views of posh Parisians shopping at the rue Poncelet market or on the avenue des Ternes, and on Saturday afternoons this place is packed with thirtysomethings sipping Diet Coke after a gruelling grocery shop at Daily Monop over the road. The slightly odd Dada-inspired interior provides an interesting backdrop to proceedings.

Lush
16 rue des Dames, 17th (01.43.87.49.46/ www.lushbars.com). M° Place de Clichy. **Open** 5pm-2am daily. Closed 25-28 Dec. **Happy hour** 6-8pm Mon-Fri. **Credit** MC, V. **Map** G1.
When we pitched up to Lush on a bank holiday Monday we were the only people in there, apart from the barmaid and her two mates at the end of the bar. However, she assures us that they have a regular crowd of up-for-it expats and French locals. Presumably of the bobo variety – this is Batignolles, after all. And we could definitely see why people would want to come and drink here. With restful

On the Town

grape-coloured walls, squashy vinyl banquettes and arty photos of the Emerald Isle, it's a nice little spot, a world away from trad smelly boozers. Ideal for a quiet pint or a gossip over a bottle of reasonably priced wine.

Trois Pièces Cuisine ★

101 rue des Dames, 17th (01.44.90.85.10).
M° Rome or Villiers. **Open** 8am-2am Mon-Fri;
9.30am-2am Sat, Sun. **Food served** noon-3.30pm,
8-11.15pm. **Credit** MC, V. **Wheelchair access.**
Non-smoking room (during the day). **Map** G1.
We took a friend who is normally allergic to all things bobo and can happily declare that Trois Pièces Cuisine has won a convert to the cause. All formica bar, 1970s tiling, ironic bad-taste wallpaper and rickety kitchen chairs, it looks just like all the other shabby-chic joints scattered across the city. The difference? Atmosphere. Everyone seemed to be having a great time, the staff were super-smiley, the bar area was crowded and there was a noticeable lack of cooler-than-thou froideur. Despite immense amounts of eavesdropping, we didn't hear anybody talking about their screenplay.

18TH ARRONDISSEMENT

Le Café Arrosé ★

123 rue Caulaincourt, 18th (01.42.57.14.30).
M° Lamarck Caulaincourt. **Open** 8am-2am Mon-
Sat; 8am-7pm Sun. **Average** €20. **Food served**
noon-midnight. **Credit** MC, V. **Map** J1.
Le Café Arrosé may not have anything quantifiably different from a whole host of other café-bistros (red banquettes, menus on blackboards, 1930s tiled floor, a traditional wooden bar and contemporary art hanging on the walls), but there is something inexplicably intoxicating about the ambience of this brand new resto-café. Perhaps it's the smiley staff, the decent wine list and the mouth-watering food (our confit of duck was a sheer delight and the strawberry cappuccino dessert went down without touching the sides); or maybe it's the friendly crowd that piles in around 10pm for a late bite and a carafe of vin rouge. Either way, this new kid on the block looks set to stay.

La Cave Café

*134 rue Marcadet, 18th (01.4606.29.17). M° Jules
Joffrin.* **Open** 8am-1.30am Mon-Sat; 10am-1.30am
Sun and holidays. **Food served** noon-3pm, 8-11pm.
Credit MC, V.
Do you want to know what Montmartre is really like, eat, drink and smoke with the locals and have a genuine Paris experience? If so, this is the place. And, hard to believe, the owner is American, one Arthur Jordan, whose day job is as an architect. Why is that hard to believe? Because it is so French, so Parisian, so Montmartrois. Start with a terrine of rabbit or ceviche of sardines, both served with plenty of green salad in a tangy vinaigrette. Follow with an equally generous meat or fish dish, such as the flavourful tuna. There are many wines to choose

from, most of them 'natural' and sold by the glass, carafe or bottle. Make sure you don't miss the crème renversée for dessert.

La Fourmi

74 rue des Martyrs, 18th (01.42.64.70.35).
M° Pigalle. **Open** 8am-2am Mon-Thur; 8am-
4am Fri, Sat; 10am-2am Sun. **Food served**
noon-3pm, 7-11pm. **Average** €15. **Credit** MC, V.
Map H2.
Set near Pigalle, on the cusp of the 9th and 18th, La Fourmi attracts fun-loving retro-dudes on their way up and down the steep slopes of Montmartre. Thirsty concert-goers from the nearby Elysées-Montmartre and the funky Divan du Monde opposite also pile in for a pre-show pick-me-up, while other hipsters cross the city just to soak up the atmosphere or sift through the endless piles of entertainment flyers. The decor is a successful take on industrial chic, with a huge wine-bottle chandelier and an enormous zinc bar, but the real star is the beer: at just €2.60, every man and his chien can afford to indulge.

Ice Kube

*7 passage Ruelle, 18th (01.42.05.20.00). M° La
Chapelle.* **Open** 6.30pm-1.30am daily. **Credit**
AmEx, DC, MC, V. **Non-smoking. Map** K1.
The team behind the Murano Urban Resort has taken a gamble on the gritty neighbourhood behind Gare du Nord by setting the trendy new hotel Kube in one of its more desolate streets. Reached through a glass cube in the cobbled courtyard, the industrial-chic hotel could not feel less Parisian – so why not complete the bizarre experience with a visit to the ice bar? Forget whatever look you have been cultivating as you don a down-filled jacket and mittens to protect you from the -20° C temperature in the narrow, neon-lit room sculpted from ice. And then, as the chatty bartender pours one shot of flavoured vodka after another into square glasses made of ice, you'll understand why Russians are so fond of this particular drink. After our allotted 30 minutes (€38 for all the vodka you can down), a warm glow came over us as we melted into the cushy armchairs in the lounge. An hour later, we hadn't budged and were still giggling.

Le Sancerre

35 rue des Abbesses, 18th (01.42.58.08.20).
M° Abbesses. **Open** 7am-2am Mon-Thur; 7am-
4am Fri-Sat; 9am-2am Sun. **Food served** 9am-
11pm. **Credit** MC, V. **Map** H1.
This popular Montmartre institution (still with its original zinc bar) is home to a frenzied melting pot of alcohol-fuelled transvestites, tourists, lovers and bobo locals who all come for the cheap beer (less than €3), trashy music and thronging terrace. The decor inside is dark and scruffy, the service undeniably slow and the food (think omelettes and steak-frites) nothing to shout about, yet there is something irresistibly refreshing about the no-frills approach that makes this bar stand out from the

multitude of try-hard cafés dotted around the rest of the Butte. There's live jazz and blues on Sunday evenings (6-10pm).

Les 3 Frères

14 rue Léon, 18th (01.42.64.91.73/www.les3 freres.net). M° Château Rouge. **Open** 8am-2am Mon, Tue, Thur-Sun. **Food served** noon-3pm, 7pm-midnight. **Credit** MC, V. **Map** K1.
From Friday to Tuesday Les 3 Frères is a low-key restaurant where arty types choose between traditional French dishes and spicy Moroccan specialities. Come Thursday, it's a different story. After 8pm, free couscous is doled out in large portions to the owner's friends, friends of the owner's friends, and friends of the owner's friends' friends – which means you and the rest of the neighbourhood! A must for anyone wishing to save money and make friends at the same time. There's live music some evenings (check the website).

19TH ARRONDISSEMENT

Café Chéri(e)

44 bd de la Villette, 19th (01.42.02.02.05). M° Belleville. **Open** 8am-2am daily. **Food served** noon-2am. **Credit** MC, V. **Map** M3.
If Notre-Dame is officially the centre of Paris, then Café Cheri(e) is officially the centre of Belleville. *The* meeting spot in this increasingly hip part of town,

it attracts everyone worth their nocturnal salt. Studiously run-down with mismatched chairs and tables, paint chipping in all the right places and muted red lighting lending a somewhat dodgy atmosphere (in the best possible way), this place offers a nightly line-up of live music and DJs, playing everything from electro to hip hop, with plenty in between. Grab a seat on the terrace if it gets too hot inside and knock back one of the rums. Lethal.

Rendez-Vous des Quais

10-14 quai de Seine, 19th (01.40.37.02.81). M° Stalingrad. **Open** 9am-1am daily. **Food served** noon-1am. **Credit** AmEx, DC, MC, V. **Wheelchair access**. **Map** M2.
Movie buffs, and anyone else looking to escape the noise of the city for an hour or so, linger at this café on the edge of the Bassin de la Villette. Part of the movie theatre next door, this spot, also known as the MK2 Café, offers a pleasant and unobstructed view of the canal from its large, heated terrace. While you can kill two birds with one stone with the 'cinéma' deal, which includes dinner and a movie ticket, the food looks better on the menu than it does on the plate. Best to stick to a beer or a cocktail and watch the tourist boats drift by at sunset.

20TH ARRONDISSEMENT

Entrepot's

2 rue Sorbier, 20th (01.43.49.59.17). M° Ménilmontant. **Open** 8am-1am daily. **Food served** noon-2.30pm, 7-11pm. **Credit** MC, V. **Map** P5.
Tired of the same-old same-old along rue Oberkampf? Then head up rue de Ménilmontant to this quiet tree-lined street. Here you'll find a sunny terrace and a friendly welcome at Entrepot's, a place whose good nature is evident even in its name, a play on words meaning at once 'between friends' and 'the storehouse'. Indeed, this is the ideal spot to enjoy an aperitif with your mates on a summer afternoon, order a modestly priced bistro meal, then continue the evening inside as the locals from this arty neighbourhood descend to chat and listen to live jazz or a little reggae.

Lou Pascalou

14 rue des Panoyaux, 20th (01.46.36.78.10). M° Ménilmontant. **Open** 9am-2am daily. **Food served** nonstop. **No credit cards**. **Map** N4.
Ménilmontant remains relatively undiscovered by tourists, still resolutely working class and with an increasing number of artists moving in and opening up their studios to the public. Catering to this off-the-beaten-track crowd, by day Lou Pascalou attracts a motley crew of writers, students and musicians sipping pastis on the quiet terrace while playing a mean game of chess. Come nightfall, the place is packed, inside and out, with the über-cool from all over the city, here as much to take in the monthly art exhibits and listen to a bit of live music as to see and be seen.

Endearingly low-key **Le Sancerre**. *See p189.*

Tea Rooms

In Paris, tea is often just an excuse to indulge in delectable cakes, from the famed meringue and chestnut Mont Blanc at Angelina's to a homely crumble at Le Loir dans la Théière. Due perhaps to the influence of Mariage Frères, a plain cup of tea can prove rather elusive, with many Parisians preferring perfumed versions. Serious tea lovers head to one of the city's palace hotels, which serve perfect brews with great pomp, or to a tea room specialising in rare Japanese or Chinese leaves.

Angelina's

Angelina's

226 rue de Rivoli, 1st (01.42.60.82.00). M° Tuileries.
Open 9.30am-6.45pm Mon-Fri; 9am-7pm Sat, Sun.
Tea €6. **Pâtisseries** €4-€6. **Credit** AmEx, MC, V.
Map G5.

Surrounded by souvenir shops, Angelina's provides a tasteful haven for tourists and Parisians alike. For more than 100 years this elegant tea room has served some of the richest hot chocolate in town (the chocolat à l'africain, which is also available as a mix for those who wish to relive the moment at home), and under new ownership all that has changed is the slightly spiffed-up decor of leather armchairs, green marble tables and murals. The Mont Blanc, an extraordinary cream-filled meringue topped with chestnut, never disappoints, but on this occasion the lemon and strawberry tarts proved more than worthy competitors. Less entrancing was the rum baba, but that couldn't dampen our enthusiasm for this oh-so-Parisian place.

Jean-Paul Hévin

231 rue St-Honoré, 1st (01.55.35.35.96/www. jphevin.com). M° Tuileries. **Open** noon-6.30pm Mon-Sat. Closed Aug. **Tea** €6. **Pâtisseries** €4.50-€8. **Credit** AmEx, DC, MC, V. **Map** G5.

One of the city's finest chocolatiers runs this elegant and rather minimalist tea room, which is just as suitable for a tête-à-tête as a gossip with friends. Teas, in particular the Marco Polo, are brewed to perfection, bringing out their subtle mélange of scents. Pastries also rely on understated flavours that stand up to the richness of the chocolate. The malzatov, an incredibly light cheesecake promising zero per cent fat, makes a surprisingly satisfying choice for slim shoppers whose next stop is the Chanel store nearby, although it can hardly compete with more intense chocolate creations such as the Turin (sweet pastry topped with chestnut cream mousse, almonds and chocolate) and the tartelette chocolat croustillant.

The art of tea

For those who like to meditate over their cuppa, Paris has an outstanding selection of Far East-influenced tea rooms, many of them run by acknowledged experts. You'll find a range of styles, from the simple setting at **T'cha** (6 rue du Pont de Lodi, 6th, 01.43.29.61.31) – a Chinese tea room with tasty but no-frills sweets such as apple loaf and ginger cookies – to the elaborate spread at **Toraya** (10 rue St-Florentin, 1st, 01.42.60.13.48), a Japanese tea room with groovy decor and modern, artistic revisions of classic Japanese desserts.

L'Empire des Thés (101 av d'Ivry, 13th, 01.45.85.66.33), an upmarket Chinese establishment, has drawn a predominantly French crowd to the heart of Chinatown since it opened a few years ago. The shop serves 160 teas at four miniature tables in its earthy but elegant, butter-beige sitting area. You can also play chess while munching on a pastry provided by Sadaharu Aoki. Green teas sell best, along with grand jasmin impérial – rolled tea leaves resembling miniature pearls.

Neophytes also frequent **La Maison de la Chine**'s tea house (76 rue Bonaparte, 6th, 01.40.51.95.00, www.lamaisondelachine.fr). The regularly changing menu includes some intriguing names for the house-created blends: felicity, prosperity and serenity, for instance. Our 'pledge of love', a semi-green with peony petals, which is often shared by a couple on the verge of marriage, came with a tiny, dried rosebud floating in the teacup; pastries are by superstar Pierre Hermé, whose boutique is a few doors down.

For serious connoisseurs, **La Maison des Trois Thés** (33 rue Gracieuse, 5th, 01.43.36.93.84) is a must. With one of the largest tea cellars in the world, boasting more than 1,000 blends, the tea house is decorated with some 700 canisters of tea, suspended on the main wall of the unique brick-and-iron interior. Two menus list the vintage (as far back as 1890) and more humble brews, but a peek at the second-tier menu must be pre-approved by Madame Tseng. A soft-spoken waiter presents the cryptic menu before bringing boiling water to the chunky, high-rising tables carved from old Chinese doors, and then meticulously explains the infusion process (it's all very solemn and intimidating).

Nestled among the Japanese noodle shops of the neighbourhood between Bourse and Opéra is **Zenzoo** (13 rue Chabanais, 2nd, 01.42.96.27.28), a Taiwanese tea room that will change the way you look at tea forever. Here the speciality is zenzoo, a 'liberal transcription' of zhenzhu naicha, meaning pearl in Chinese. Bobbing within the cold teas are big, amber-coloured tapioca pearls, which you slurp up with the giant straw provided. You can order your zenzoo to go, or you can sit in the sleek and cosy tea room and enjoy the French or Asian lunch special of the day.

A Priori Thé

35-37 galerie Vivienne, 2nd (01.42.97.48.75).
Mº *Bourse.* **Open** 9am-6pm Mon-Sat; 12.30-6.30pm Sun. **Tea** €4.50. **Pâtisseries** €6-€7. **Credit** MC, V. **Wheelchair access**. **Non-smoking room.** **Map** H4.

American Peggy Ancock knew exactly what the capital's creatures of comfort were lacking when she opened A Priori Thé in 1980. The tea room inhabits one of Paris's glitziest covered passages, but its charm comes from its frumpy insouciance towards the gilded surroundings – and the comfort food. Alongside 25 staple brews such as orange pekoe and Darjeeling, Ancock serves up a blissfully fluffy cheesecake with raspberry coulis, intense chocolate brownies and deep-dish fruit crumbles, all in colossal portions. Although the tables under the arcade afford ample people-watching, regulars always fill up the cushioned wicker chairs in the dining room first.

La Charlotte en l'Ile

*24 rue St-Louis-en-l'Ile, 4th (01.43.54.25.83). M°
Pont Marie.* **Open** noon-8pm Thur-Sun. Wed tea
and puppet show by reservation only; Fri 6-8pm
piano tea. Closed July, Aug. **Tea** €4. **Pâtisseries**
€2.50-€4.50. **Credit** MC, V. **Map** K7.

This tiny tea shop is full of the stuff of fairy tales
– pictures of witches on broomsticks, lanterns,
carnival masks and so on. The only thing lacking is
gingerbread. Quirky poetess and chocolatier par
excellence Sylvie Langlet has been spinning her
sweet fantasies here for more than 25 years. In the
minuscule front room she sells her superb dark
chocolate and candied fruit sticks, while at six
tightly packed round tables she offers no less than
36 teas of a quality that would put some five-star
hotels to shame. Our violet and apricot teas were
served in simple blue and yellow bowls from dinky
cast-iron teapots; their aroma alone perked us up.
The desserts, likewise, are magic, and the hot
chocolate is probably the most potent in Paris.
Highly recommended.

Le Loir dans la Théière

3 rue des Rosiers, 4th (01.42.72.90.61). M° St-Paul.
Open 11.30am-7pm Mon-Fri; 10am-7pm Sat, Sun.
Tea €4. **Pâtisseries** €5-€6. **Credit** MC, V. **Non-
smoking room.** **Map** L6.

Decorated with scenes from *Alice in Wonderland*,
among many other bits and pieces, Le Loir is the
kind of place where you could easily while away an
afternoon (and many people do, making it hard to
nab a seat towards 4pm). Comfortable mismatched
furniture complements the decor and the food also
reflects this kitsch homely cool. Cakes have a
through-the-looking-glass quality, particularly the
heap of apple crumble with Chantilly and a truly
towering lemon meringue pie. Our choice of vanilla
tea was a let-down – slightly flavourless and served
in a cool (but big) teapot.

Mariage Frères

*30-32 rue du Bourg-Tibourg, 4th (01.42.72.
28.11). M° Hôtel de Ville.* **Open** *Tea* noon-6.30pm
daily. Closed 1 May, 25 Dec, 1 Jan. **Tea** €7-€25.
Pâtisseries €8-€10. **Brunch** €28-€39 (Sat, Sun).
Credit AmEx, MC, V. **Non-smoking room.**
Map K6.

Established in 1854, Mariage Frères is one of
France's oldest tea importers. When we walked
inside, the old-fashioned elegance and perfume of
more than 500 teas made us think we'd stepped back
into colonial times. Past the crowded tea shop, we
were seated at a white-clothed table in the rather
opulent salon by a white-suited waiter. Here it's all
about 'the art of tea', and it shows – the tea is brewed
to perfection. Ever since Mariage came out with a
tea/chocolate combination in 1860, the company has
specialised in blends – try the Marco Polo or the
thé des poètes solitaires (tea of solitary poets),
accompanied by unusual yet delicious tea-scented
jelly. There is a range of pastries and, on the weekend
(if you can get a table), a decadent brunch.

Other locations: 260 rue du Fbg-St-Honoré, 8th
(01.46.22.18.54); 13 rue des Grands-Augustins, 6th
(01.40.51.82.50).

Café Maure de la Mosquée de Paris

*39 rue Geoffroy St-Hilaire, 5th (01.43.31.38.20).
M° Place Monge.* **Open** 9am-midnight daily. **Tea**
€2. **Pâtisseries** €2. **Credit** MC, V. **Wheelchair
access. Map** K8.

Blue tiles, brass tables and a stunning coffered
ceiling combine with a shaded outdoor terrace to
transport you to a much more exotic location than
this quiet street facing the Jardin des Plantes. No
need for a menu: you order pastries from the counter
on the way in and the sweet mint tea in tiny glasses
from the quick-footed waiters. The honey-fig and
pistachio-almond cakes provide a sugar rush that is
only enhanced by the tea. The Mosquée also houses
a steam room and massage parlour, although check
ahead to see if it's a men's or a women's day in the
hammam. A pleasant change from the stresses of
life in a fast-paced city.

L'Artisan de Saveurs ★

*72 rue du Cherche-Midi, 6th (01.42.22.46.64).
M° St-Placide.* **Open** *Tea* noon-2.30pm, 3.30-6.30pm
Mon-Fri. *Brunch* 11.30am-3.30pm Sat, Sun. **Tea**
€5.60-€6.60. **Pâtisseries** €6.50-€7.90. **Brunch**
€27 (Sat, Sun). **Credit** MC, V. **Wheelchair access.
Non-smoking. Map** F8.

You can't blame L'Artisan for banning smoking in
its butter-yellow tea room, as the slightest speck of
ash would mar the delightful provincial feel here.
Linen tablecloths, tasteful paper napkins and ivory-
coloured tea sets stoke up country-home elegance.
The selection of teas and pastries, meanwhile,
surpasses urban sophistication. L'Artisan's menu
eloquently explains 40 teas – from the standard
Darjeeling to the more exotic Marco Polo varieties –
while a long list of innovative pastries, prepared to
order, defies description. In winter, warm up with a
frothy pineapple gratin spiked with kaffir lime.

Chez les Filles

*64 rue du Cherche-Midi, 6th (01.45.48.61.54).
M° Rennes or St-Placide.* **Open** 11.30am-4.30pm
daily. Closed public holidays. **Tea** €4. **Pâtisseries**
€5. **Brunch** €17 (Sat, Sun). **Credit** MC, V. **Map** G7.

In the heart of bourgeois Paris, near the Bon Marché,
this family-run Berber café is just the place to set
down your shopping bags, put your feet up
(metaphorically speaking, of course) and sip a glass
of mint tea or a rich chocolat à l'ancienne. Owned by
Patricia Oiknine since 1995, Chez les Filles has an
easygoing, motherly warmth. At the back of the
room the cook, framed by silver Moroccan teapots,
prepares overflowing plates of semolina, vegetables,
lentils and salad – a prelude to own-made apple
strudel, North African pastries and thinly sliced
oranges sprinkled with cinnamon. If you're torn
between sweet and savoury, don't fret: you can
sample it all at the weekend brunch.

On the Town

Forêt Noire

Forêt Noire

9 rue de l'Eperon, 6th (01.44.41.00.09). Mº Odéon or St-Michel. **Open** noon-7pm Tue-Sun. **Tea** €5-€6. **Pâtisseries** €6-€7. **Credit** DC, MC, V. **Map** H7.

Although it's more of a small restaurant than a tea room in the early afternoon, Forêt Noire proved itself capable on both fronts on our last visit. The light and airy surroundings complement the beamed ceilings and smart decor. While the plat du jour of lasagne bolognaise could have been more exciting, an excellent lemon tart alongside mandarin tea more than made up for it. The waiter was incredibly friendly and accommodating. One word of warning, though: avoid the table facing the kitchen entrance, as you might find the chef's constant scrutiny somewhat unnerving.

Ladurée

21 rue Bonaparte, 6th (01.44.07.64.87). Mº St-Germain-des-Prés. **Open** 8.30am-7.30pm Mon-Sat; 7.30pm Sun. **Tea** €5-€8.50. **Credit** AmEx, MC, V. **Non-smoking room. Map** H7.

A famed salon de thé and pâtissier, Ladurée was the official pastry consultant (!) on Sofia Coppola's *Marie Antoinette*. Once you've made a pilgrimage to the original 1862 Ladurée in rue Royale and soaked up the splendour of the faux Second Empire Champs-Elysées branch, it's worth stopping into this jewel of a tea room in St-Germain. The salon, crowded with Parisian families and couples having têtes-à-têtes, is all feminine charm and style, with light streaming in and walls covered in a tropical fresco. The main attraction for us was the pastries and after much deliberation we settled on a delectable religieuse chocolat (a sinful variation on the éclair), helped along by the mélange spécial Ladurée, a fragrant tea of citrus, rose, vanilla and cinnamon. We couldn't leave without buying some of Ladurée's famous macaroons – try the rose, bitter chocolate or pistachio. In winter, don't forget the room upstairs, equipped with an open fire – the perfect retreat with a book and a potent hot chocolate.

Other locations: 75 av des Champs-Elysées, 8th (01.40.75.08.75); 16 rue Royale, 8th (01.42.60.21.79); Au Grand Magasin du Printemps, 64 bd Haussmann, 9th.

Les Deux Abeilles

189 rue de l'Université, 7th (01.45.55.64.04). Mº Ecole Militaire or Pont de l'Alma. **Open** 9am-7pm Mon-Sat; 10am-7pm Sun. **Tea** €4.50. **Pâtisseries** €6. **Credit** MC, V. **Map** E5.

The capital's fashionistas still swan here in droves for some very chic tea and sympathy. Helmed by a slightly eccentric mother and daughter duo, this is an enticing cross between grandma's cosy front room and an elegant colonial-era gazebo. Nostalgia is also literally on the menu – the olde-style cakes, scones and brioches are so gorgeous that you'll feel guilty about actually tucking in. But remember, looks aren't everything – discovering that your ever-so-dainty pear tart has been brutally nuked within an inch of its life is definitely enough to break the spell.

Le Bristol

112 rue du Fbg-St-Honoré, 8th (01.53.43.43.00/ www.lebristolparis.com). Mº Miromesnil. **Open** 3-6pm daily. **Tea** €9. **Pâtisseries** €11. **Credit** AmEx, DC, MC, V. **Wheelchair access. Map** E4.

Cross the apricot marble foyer and trip down the steps to the right to a vast lounge complete with marble columns, magnificent bouquets and a view across the lawns. The hotel's teas appear to have been picked by a connoisseur, as confirmed by our choice of the excellent grand foochow fumé pointes blanches and Assam doomou. The accompanying little sandwiches of tuna, smoked salmon and cheese were deliciously buttery, although the absence of cucumber was a tad disappointing.

Hôtel Plaza Athénée ★

25 av Montaigne, 8th (01.53.67.66.65/www.plaza-athenee-paris.com). Mº Alma-Marceau. **Open** 8am-midnight daily. **Tea** €8. **Pâtisseries** €12. **Credit** AmEx, DC, MC, V. **Wheelchair access. Map** D5.

In the 18th century-style Galerie des Gobelins, you can watch the wealthy mingle. On our visit, the Iranian royal family had gathered for tea, next to them a famous opera singer and further down an eminent statesman. People-gazing, however, is a very minor pleasure compared to the Plaza's superb teas and dessert trolley. It's hard to single anything out, but we'd recommend the fraisier, a strawberry and pistachio cream cake that is close to perfection. As for the teas, don't miss the mélange Plaza, a masterly blend of fig, hazelnut, quince and grape. Listening to the harpist and pouring another cup from the armoury of silverware, we felt part of it all. Even the head waiter played the game, slipping us some juicy celebrity gossip.

Les Cakes de Bertrand

7 rue Bourdaloue, 9th (01.40.16.16.28/ www.lescakesdebertrand.com). M° Notre-Dame-de-Lorette. **Open** *Mid-Apr to mid-Oct* noon-3.30pm daily. *Mid-Oct to mid-Apr* 9am-7pm daily. Closed Aug. **Tea** €4-€7. **Pâtisseries** €4-€4.50. **Credit** MC, V. **Wheelchair access. Map** H3.
With its baby blue cabinetry, tapestry-covered chairs and crystal chandeliers, Les Cakes de Bertrand feels like a collector's-item doll's house. Dainty porcelain tea sets and fairytale placemats heighten the tea-taking experience here. Alongside cheesecake, fondant au chocolat and fromage blanc with a fruit

coulis, Bertrand's famous cakes – fruit and nut loaves, or one version with green tea – make a lighter complement for a South African red or Assam tea. With chai, a robust Indian blend spiked with cardamom, we enjoyed a plate of mini cakes in a variety of flavours. The tea room seats 18, who are served, at tea time, by just one person.

L'Oisive Thé

1 rue Jean-Marie Jego, 13th (01.53.80.31.33/ www.loisivethe.free.fr). M° Place d'Italie. **Open** *Brunch* noon-6pm Tue-Sun. **Tea** €4.40-€5. *Tea* noon-7pm Tue-Thur; noon-8pm Fri-Sun. **Pâtisseries** €3-€5. **Credit** MC, V. **Wheelchair access** (reservation recommended). **Non-smoking**.
L'Oisive Thé maintains a French country-Zen feel in a friendly and intimate setting with plenty of natural light. While bright yellow walls, Japanese tea sets and straw floor mats create the distinctive ambience, the fresh feel in the room probably comes from the air purifiers quietly ridding the room of the smoke that pervades other Parisian establishments. From the extensive tea menu (with, laudably, more than 50 to choose from), we chose the aromatic fleur de geisha, a green tea with cherry blossoms, and the corromondel, a not-too-sweet blend of caramel and vanilla, and were disappointed by neither. Daily specials included a mediocre crème caramel and one of the best chocolate cakes we had ever tasted.

Cold comfort

Spoiled by too many spectacular pastries, Parisians don't give frozen desserts their due. Yet, using the finest ingredients, a select group of glaciers churn out what must surely be some of the world's most intense ice-creams and sorbets.

Leading the way is **Berthillon** (31 rue St-Louis-en-l'Ile, 4th, 01.43.54.31.61), which sets the standard. Pop in for a takeaway cone; flavours change according to the seasons (don't miss the fraises des bois in summer). Unfortunately for us, Berthillon must be against using ice-cream to combat the heat – hence the summer closing.

Just as strategically located is **Le Bac à Glaces** (109 rue du Bac, 7th, 01.45.48.87.65, www.bacaglaces.com), up the street from the Bon Marché department store. In its cramped, café-like setting, you can treat yourself to a selection of homemade ice-creams served in something like a giant escargot dish, or have an adult float of sorbet in a glass of Perrier. Flavours range from the classic (bourbon vanilla) to the wacky (mango with Sichuan pepper).

Intense French ice-creams are facing stiff competition from ambitious Italian-style upstarts such as **Amorino** (47 rue St-Louis-en-l'Ile, 4th, 01.44.07.48.08 and several other branches) and **Gelati d'Alberto** (45 rue Mouffetard, 5th, 01.43.37.88.07). The former looks set to conquer Paris with its fluffy, fresh-tasting gelati in flavours such as limone or marron glacé, while Alberto is more of an iconoclast with his lovingly sculpted gelato roses (shame about the grumpy staff).

La Butte Glacée (14 rue Norvins, 18th, 01.42.23.91.58) is an unpretentious gelateria near the Sacré-Coeur. After the long climb up, reward yourself with a stracciatella and banana yoghurt sorbet or a jaw-crunching crocante.

Further off the beaten track, **Raimo** (61 bd de Reuilly, 12th, 01.43.43.70.17) has been in the business since 1947. Although the white-shirted waiters are not overly attentive, the ice-cream more than makes up for it. The fleur de lait is heavenly, as is the woody Vermont maple.

Cheaper scoops are available at out-of-the-way **La Tropicale** (180 bd Vincent-Auriol, 13th, 01.42.16.87.27), which offers jazz music, friendly service and fabulous curaçao and mango sorbets.

On the Town

Wine Bars

Wine is considered an everyday drink in France, which explains why Paris wine bars have so few pretensions. Don't expect fancy tasting glasses or long-winded descriptions – instead, sit back, enjoy a plate of farmer's cheese, rustic charcuterie or a hearty bistro dish, and simply savour the wine. A growing number of wine bars focus on organic wines (French, bien sûr), and with not many organic producers to choose from you might run into the same names again and again – surprising in a country that has over 100,000 vineyards. On the trend-setting Right Bank, many wine bars go one step further and favour biodynamic wines – turning some vintners into bobo (bourgeois bohemian) superstars. The Languedoc features heavily on most lists these days, while the New World is still having trouble making inroads.

Juvénile's

47 rue de Richelieu, 1st (01.42.97.46.49). M° Palais Royal or Pyramides. **Open** 6-11pm Mon; noon-11pm Tue-Sat. **Food served** nonstop. **Glass** €3-€10. **Bottle** €14-€400. **Credit** AmEx, MC, V. **Map** H4.
Situated near the Palais-Royal and the Bourse, in a tiny oh-so-Parisian setting, this wine bar is a classic. Its many peculiarities account for its charm, starting with the quirky Scottish owner, Tim Johnston, and the lovely Scottish waitress. Then there are the wines, served in beautiful glasses and decanters. In terms of clientele, the proximity of the Stock Exchange makes it a key destination for French business people at lunch, who occasionally indulge in – shocking! – New World wines; at night expect a large majority of anglophones. The only downside is the bill, which can add up quickly, but the Juvénile's experience is nonetheless a delightful one.

Le Père Fouettard

9 rue Pierre Lescot, 1st (01.42.33.74.17). M° Etienne Marcel or Les Halles. **Open** 7.30am-2am daily. **Food served** noon-1am. **Glass** €3-€5.50. **Bottle** €16-€60. **Credit** AmEx, MC, V. **Wheelchair access**. **Non-smoking room. Map** J5.
This is a useful address in the heart of Les Halles, decorated in traditional style with the obligatory shiny zinc bar, a small dining room and a large terrace. The pumping soundtrack is slightly at odds with the junky decor, but it wasn't discouraging a steady flow of youngish customers on a freezing night. The selection of wines by the glass threw up a Rasteau 2000 from Trapidis; a good flinty Sancerre, Domaine Cherrier 1998; and a delicious, rich Vin de Pays des Bouches du Rhône 2001 from Château Roquefort. A Brouilly 2000 from Descombes was disappointingly dusty, but swiftly replaced by the accommodating barman with a more interesting Morgon from Flache. We didn't have dinner, preferring just to nibble a little platter of saucisson sec served with cornichons, but reassuring signs

such as Duval charcuterie and Berthillon ice-cream suggest there was no reason not to. Meaty mains – steaks, duck confit, etc – were on offer at around €15, plus a welcome 'coin végétarien' for herbivores.

Au Sans Souci

183 rue St-Denis, 2nd (01.42.36.09.39). M° Réaumur Sébastopol. **Open** 7.30am-midnight Mon-Fri. **Food served** noon-3pm. **Glass** €1.60-€3. **Bottle** €15. **Credit** MC, V. **Wheelchair access. Map** K5.
Michel Godon, the charming, sparkly-eyed owner, has been holding the fort amid the quartier's sex shops for more than three decades, although it was only in 1998 that he revamped this former café and concentrated on the wine. Slightly incongruous for your average wine bar are the pinball, TV and a fantastic jukebox full of French hits from the 1970s. One lone regular was so moved he drained his glass, took out his air guitar and really went for it. Not so frivolous was the careful selection of the wines by the glass, with everything served in 7cl tasters at mad student prices. We were suitably impressed by a very respectable gewürztraminer, a crisp white Sancerre from Philip Raimbault and a sound Vire Clesse. Then things got even better – we were blown away by the superb raspberry fruit of a St-Chinian, Marquise des Mûres. You can have tartines and charcuterie at the bar, and lunch is served upstairs.

Les Enfants Rouges

9 rue de Beauce, 3rd (01.48.87.80.61). M° Temple. **Open** noon-2.30pm Tue, Wed; noon-3pm, 7.30pm-12.30am Thur-Sat. Closed three weeks in Aug. **Glass** €4-€6. **Bottle** €18-€100. **Credit** MC, V. **Map** L5.
Dany Bertin-Denis knows her wines – and we're glad of it. There had to be something special going on in this tiny bistro that's bursting at the seams in a quiet little street. And the special thing here is twofold. First, a beautiful wine list with no false notes. The finest winemakers from most French wine regions and a few rising stars too. Second, warm and cheerful service from a team of women –

not that frequent in a Parisian wine bar. The only drawback to be found in this charming and homely place is the food, which was – on the day we visited – mediocre. Overall, however, Les Enfants Rouges is well worth visiting if you're in the northern part of the Marais.

L'Estaminet ★

Marché des Enfants Rouges, 39 rue de Bretagne, 3rd (01.42.72.34.85/www.aromes-et-cepages.fr). Mº Temple. **Open** 9am-2pm, 4-8pm Tue-Thur; 9am-8pm Fri, Sat; 9am-2pm Sun. **Food served** noon-2.30pm Tue-Fri; nonstop Sat; 10am-2pm Sun. **Glass** €3. **Bottle** €10-€20. **Wheelchair access**. **Credit** MC, V. **Map** L5.

Picture a hidden wine bar in a hidden Parisian market – welcome to L'Estaminet. Its concept is quite simple: after shopping at the charming Marché des Enfants Rouges, you stop at the wine stand and admire its broad selection of decently priced French wines. Then, simply take the bottle you have just bought and drink it at the bar. The owner (of both the wine stand and the wine bar) will ask you for a €5 corkage fee to sit at one of the big wooden tables and enjoy your wine (and potentially his simple yet well-executed cuisine). L'Estaminet offers good-value wines, a warm atmosphere and one of the best opportunities to make new friends in this oh-so-bobo neighbourhood. But beware: as it is located within the covered market, it closes at 8pm (2pm on a Sunday).

La Belle Hortense

31 rue Vieille-du-Temple, 4th (01.48.04.71.60/ www.cafeine.com). Mº Hôtel de Ville or St-Paul. **Open** 5pm-2am daily. **Food served** 7pm-1am. **Glass** €3-€7. **Bottle** €5-€700. **Credit** MC, V. **Wheelchair access**. **Non-smoking room**. **Map** L6.

Take a bookshop, a literary salon and a wine bar. Put it in a small space. Shake. And just drop the outcome on rue Vieille-du-Temple, in the heart of the Marais: that's La Belle Hortense. So many things to do in so little space: buy a book or a bottle of wine (emphasis on the Rhône Valley), have a glass of wine while reading a book in the tiny (non-smoking) salon or at the bar. All in all, a peaceful place to stop for an hour or two and relax in the midst of a tiring Parisian day, and it's still buzzing late at night after other cafés have closed.

L'Enoteca

25 rue Charles V, 4th (01.42.78.91.44). Mº Bastille or St-Paul. **Open** noon-6pm, 7.30-11pm daily. **Food served** noon-2.30pm, 7-11.30pm. Closed one week mid-Aug. **Glass** €3-€8. **Bottle** €15-€455. **Credit** MC, V. **Wheelchair access**. **Map** L7.

If you like Italian wine, then this classy Marais trattoria is a must. The list is astounding, with plenty of hard-to-find wines from all the best producers: Gaja, Aldo Conterno, Vajra, Felsina Berardenga and a stack of vintages. And what a pleasure to taste by the glass – we tried Moscato d'Asti and barbera from Piedmont, and Sant'Agata dei Goti from Campania

(the selection changes weekly). The food is generally delicious too, with antipasti such as porchetta alla romana, generous portions of pappardelle al ragù salsiccie, plus a few reliable meat and fish mains. Booking is advised.

Le Rouge Gorge

8 rue St-Paul, 4th (01.48.04.75.89). Mº St-Paul or Sully Morland. **Open** noon-11.30pm Mon-Sat. **Food served** noon-3pm, 7-11pm. Closed one week in Aug. **Glass** €3.50-€5. **Bottle** €19-€30. **Credit** AmEx, MC, V. **Wheelchair access**. **Map** L7.

The charming façade is as much an incitement to a visit as the attractive but slightly pricey wine list. At the heart of the old antique dealers' quarter, this small wine bar, all wooden beams and exposed stone, exudes Parisian charm. François Briclot makes each and every client feel like part of the family as he lines up sample bottles on your table. Wine themes change every three weeks; on our last visit we tried a succession of succulent Corsican whites and reds, something of a speciality here as Briclot has close links with many winemakers on the 'Ile de Beauté'. The female Moroccan chef, Elhamraoui Touria, logically offers a fine, fragrant couscous rendered even more colourful than usual with the addition of pumpkin, but the Jura speciality of chicken with morels was slightly dry. Wines are also available to take away.

Caves La Bourgogne

144 rue Mouffetard, 5th (01.47.07.82.80). Mº Censier Daubenton. **Open** 7am-2am Mon-Sat. **Food served** noon-11pm. **Glass** €2.50-€4.50. **Bottle** €18-€40. **Credit** MC, V. **Wheelchair access** (on the terrace). **Non-smoking room**. **Map** J9.

This wine bistro is about as Parisian as it gets. Located at the very bottom of rue Mouffetard, it is not one of the horrible tourist traps of the upper section of the street. On the contrary: friendly staff, a young French clientele, authentic bistro cuisine and a tempting wine list all guarantee a relaxing and tasty experience. Burgundy (Bourgogne in French) is the star here. The wine list is not the most comprehensive but the wines are well selected and fairly decently priced. In warm weather, sip a Gevrey Chambertin on the terrace overlooking the place St-Médard and its beautiful Gothic church.

Les Papilles ★

30 rue Gay-Lussac, 5th (01.43.25.20.79). Mº Cluny La Sorbonne/RER Luxembourg. **Open** 8.30am-12.30am Mon-Sat. **Food served** noon-2pm, 7.30-10pm. Closed three weeks in Aug. **Glass** €3.90. **Bottle** €6-€300. **Credit** MC, V. **Wheelchair access**. **Map** J8.

Les Papilles takes the Parisian concept of hybrid wine shop and bar to the next level. Not only will you have the fun of selecting your wine from the shelves of this gourmet épicerie – helped in this by the owner – but you will have to trust the chef, because what you're going to eat is not up to you. The well-priced fixed menu (four courses for €28.50) differs every night but is never disappointing. Haute cuisine trained chef Bertrand Bluy turns this wine journey into a gastronomic experience with dishes such as beetroot gazpacho, roast cod with olive oil mash, fourme d'ambert cheese with a single wine-soaked prune and a chocolate and coffee pudding. All in a very convivial atmosphere, especially if a rugby match is showing in the private room downstairs. Excellent food, delightful wine and friendly service. One of the treasures of the Latin Quarter.

Caves Miard
9 rue des Quatre-Vents, 6th (01.43.54.99.30). M° Odéon. **Open** 10am-10pm Tue-Sat. **Food served** noon-3pm. **Glass** €3-€6. **Bottle** €15-€40. **Non-smoking**. **Credit** MC, V. **Map** H7.
By reading this, you have already overcome difficulty number one: finding out about this place. This former crèmerie blends into a quiet St-Germain street around the corner from Odéon, giving few hints as to what's going on inside. Now for difficulty number two: squeezing in. If you're lucky enough to find a seat at one of the six little tables, you will have the privilege of discovering some delightful organic French wines. All the clients seem to be old friends. The young owner's enthusiastic recommendations will probably lead you to buying a bottle or two to take away. You won't regret it. Food is simple but well made, cheeses are stunning and the surprising wines are terroir-focused.

Fish ★
69 rue de Seine, 6th (01.43.54.34.69). M° Mabillon or Odéon. **Open** noon-2pm, 7-10.45pm Tue-Sun. **Food served** nonstop. Closed first two weeks in Aug, two weeks at Christmas. **Glass** €4-€10. **Bottle** €15-€200. **Credit** MC, V. **Wheelchair access. Non-smoking. Map** H6.
This former poissonnerie (poisson meaning fish) has been turned into a boissonnerie (boisson meaning drink) and in doing so has become the official wine bar of the Odéon/St-Germain area. Expect to find a charming Parisian setting and a great French wine list with an emphasis on powerful, hearty southern wines in a very anglophone atmosphere (the owners, who run the wine shop La Dernière Goutte nearby, are from New Zealand). The food is delicious and service quite professional. Whether you prefer to sit at the bar (funnily enough, this is one of the few Paris wine bars that actually has a bar) or at a table, you will feel comfortable in this informal and ultra-friendly atmosphere. Last detail: Fish is – thank God – totally non-smoking.

L'Ecluse Madeleine
15 pl de la Madeleine, 8th (01.42.65.34.69/ www.leclusebaravin.com). M° Madeleine. **Open** 8.30am-1am daily. **Food served** 11.30am-1am. **Glass** €4-€15. **Bottle** €25-€1,227. **Credit** AmEx, DC, MC, V. **Wheelchair access. Non-smoking room. Map** F4.

Les Papilles. *See p197.*

If you're not too keen on Bordeaux wines, don't bother with this Paris mini chain dedicated to the country's best-known wine region. Bordeaux lovers can choose from a list of wines by the glass or from a selection of about 70 bottles for all budgets. Food is tasty and the service is very professional. One of L'Ecluse's great assets is that it is open until 1am, which makes it the perfect after-dinner spot for a last glass of wine. **Other locations**: throughout Paris.

Le Coin de Verre

38 rue de Sambre-et-Meuse, 10th (01.42.45.31.82). M° Belleville. **Open** 8pm-1am Mon-Sat. **Food served** nonstop. **Glass** €3-€4. **Bottle** €12-€20. **No credit cards. Map** M3.

A very special, rather secret destination, Le Coin de Verre is identifiable only by a single strip light over the door. It's cloak-and-dagger stuff – reservations are imperative and you ring the doorbell to be admitted. So we rang, then we rang again, and then we called by mobile phone to explain we were outside. Following this eccentric rigmarole we were greeted with extraordinary warmth by Michel, who led us past boxes and cases of wine, through to the rustic back room where a log fire was roaring. Here, Hugues set about us with paternal cordiality at a beautifully leisurely pace. The blackboard (all seriously cheap, nothing over €11.50) offered simple charcuterie and cheese plates; we were advised to go for the daily specials (simple blanquette de veau or

grilled andouillette) before they ran out. From a small selection of carefully chosen producers' wines with nothing over €20, he selected a Coteaux du Languedoc, Domaine de la Perrière 2000, which was fruity and smooth. Hugues smiled almost ruefully when challenged about their current success with a steady stream of bohemian insiders – not exactly what they'd set out for, but inevitable.

Le Verre Volé

67 rue de Lancry, 10th (01.48.03.17.34). M° Jacques Bonsergent or République. **Open** 10am-11pm Mon-Sat. **Food served** 12.30am-2.30pm, 7.30-10.30pm. Closed Aug. **Glass** €3-€5. **Bottle** €11-€100. **Credit** MC, V. **Map** L4.

Wines offered at this tiny wine bar are all 'vins naturels' – made using as few pesticides, herbicides and sulfites as possible. You'll find a few famous winemakers but mainly lesser-known, younger generation vintners from all of France's wine regions. Just pick the wine you like on the wall and add a €6 corkage fee. Food is mostly charcuterie and meat-based – it's nothing fancy, but the ingredients are carefully sourced. The atmosphere is cosy and intimate for lunch and surprisingly vibrant and bursting at night. Overall, this is definitely a place to visit if you're in the up-and-coming Canal St-Martin area for the authentic and charming French decor, but also for its uncompromising collection of organic French wines.

Le Clown Bar ★

114 rue Amelot, 11th (01.43.55.87.35). Mº Filles du Calvaire. **Open** noon-3.30pm, 7pm-1am Mon-Sat; 7pm-midnight Sun. **Food served** noon-2.30pm, 7pm-midnight Mon-Sat; 7pm-midnight Sun. **Glass** €3.50-€5. **Bottle** €15-€75. **No credit cards. Map** L5.

If clowns scare you, this isn't the place to go. Clowns are all you see in this traditional little wine bar/bistro, with its listed 1900s decor of clown-themed tiles and painted glass ceiling. If they don't scare you, and if you're looking for a place to eat good food while drinking decently priced wines in a cosy atmosphere, then book a table here. Food is surprisingly well executed. The wine list is classic but vast, with an emphasis on strong, masculine southern France wines. The most adventurous Frenchmen may even indulge in the nice selection of New World wines. The place comes alive again later at night when a hungry crowd from the Cirque d'Hiver next door comes to chat and mingle after the show.

Jacques Mélac

42 rue Léon-Frot, 11th (01.43.70.59.27/ www.melac.fr). Mº Charonne. **Open** 9am-3.30pm, 7.45pm-midnight Tue-Sat. **Food served** noon-2.30pm, 8-10.30pm. Closed Aug, one week at Christmas. **Glass** €3.70. **Bottle** €15-€32. **Credit** MC, V. **Wheelchair access. Map** P6.

The welcome at this long-established wine bar is as warm and broad as the proprietor's handlebar moustache. Just don't try ordering water – which, a sign posted above the bar cautions, is reserved for cooking potatoes. Instead, start with a pelou, a kind of Auvergnat kir made with chestnut liqueur, before diving into a plate of first-rate charcuterie; or, if you're feeling up to it, a meaty and satisfying plat du jour. One of the well-seasoned servers will gladly help you choose from among the selection of hardy young wines from the south-west. If you ask nicely, Jacques will bring out his Barbary organ (a beautiful contraption, like an accordion-sized music box) and regale you with classic French songs, with which all the locals in the room will inevitably join in.

Le Melting Potes

16 rue des Trois-Bornes, 11th (01.43.38.61.75). Mº Parmentier. **Open** 11am-3pm, 7.30-11pm Mon-Thur; 11am-3pm, 7.30pm-midnight Fri; 7.30pm-midnight Sat; 7.30-11pm Sun. Closed Aug. **Glass** €2.50-€4.70. **Bottle** €13-€25. **Credit** MC, V. **Wheelchair access. Map** M4.

Spend a bit of time at Le Melting Potes and you'll be surprised at how quickly Richard and Audrey, the thirtysomething couple that runs this place, start to feel like old potes (pals) of yours. And not just because of the wine you've imbibed. Here, it's the warm atmosphere that makes you feel at home. Wines are carefully selected and very affordable, and tartines are simple and tasty (at night let Richard surprise you with his ever-changing dishes). At this place, wine is not a matter of snobbery, it's just an excuse to have a good time. Definitely *the* wine bar of the Oberkampf area.

La Muse Vin

101 rue de Charonne, 11th (01.40.09.93.05). Mº Charonne. **Open** 11.30am-2.30pm, 6-11pm Mon-Fri; 6-11pm Sat. **Glass** €3-€10. **Bottle** €15-€200. **Credit** MC, V. **Wheelchair access. Map** N7.

Since Guillaume Dubois and Guillaume Dupré opened this wine bar a few years ago, it has been a success. As at most wine bars in the 'bobo' (bohemian bourgeois) 10th and 11th arrondissements, the list focuses on organic wines. A good-value menu is served at lunchtime, while at night chef Guillaume whips up inventive and beautifully presented food. Meanwhile, the other Guillaume wittily guides you through the vast wine list. If you fancy the wine you had, you can even buy a few bottles to go on your way out. Good wine, good food, friendly staff, attractive decor: can you really expect more of a wine bar?

Le Baron Bouge

1 rue Théophile-Roussel, 12th (01.43.43.14.32). Mº Ledru-Rollin. **Open** 10am-2pm, 5-10pm Tue-Thur; 10am-10pm Fri, Sat; 10am-3pm Sun. **Food served** nonstop. **Glass** €1.40-€3.30. **Bottle** €14-€23. **Credit** MC, V. **Wheelchair access. Map** N7.

Le Baron Bouge, next to the boisterous place d'Aligre market, may appear rather rough and ready, but the wines – including varied Loire selections, small châteaux from Bordeaux and Condrieu from the Rhône – are chosen with an eye for quality. There's a bit of bar food – charcuterie and some good goat's cheese (no hot meals) – but few tables, so stand at one of the casks and try to act as insouciant as the regulars. Don't bother with the wine sold from these same casks, though.

Couleurs de Vigne

2 rue Marmontel, 15th (01.45.33.32.96). Mº Convention or Vaugirard. **Open** noon-2pm, 8-11pm Mon-Fri. **Glass** €2-€3.50. **Bottle** €6-€40. **Credit** MC, V. **Wheelchair access. Map** D9.

This wine bar in a neighbourhood you wouldn't visit by accident has become hugely popular for the warm welcome of owner Alain Touchard and the excellent bottles he has selected from all over France. The viniferous offerings are wonderfully idiosyncratic, meaning that it's fun to come here on a regular basis, as you can easily deepen your knowledge of wine without having it feel like a scholarly chore. The decor is appealing as well, with olive green walls, cork-coloured floors and open bins stocked with bottles to take away, and the food is simple and appealing. The meat and cheese plate – which is generous enough to feed two – is a real winner, featuring good Auvergnat products, including cantal and bleu des causses, cured sausage and ham from the Laguiole region, plus country terrine.

Le Vin dans les Voiles

8 rue Chapu, 16th (01.46.47.83.98/www.vindansles voiles.com). Mº Exelmans. **Open** noon-2.30pm Mon; noon-2.30pm, 7-10.30pm Tue-Fri; 7-10.30pm Sat. **Glass** €4.50-€5.50. **Bottle** €19-€200. **Credit** AmEx, MC, V. **Wheelchair access.**

On the Town

Say cheese!

Only the heartiest eaters can do justice to the cheese course – which falls between the main course and dessert – during a full French meal. No wonder, then, that so many chefs prefer to offer a single ripe cheese rather than a selection. Short of keeping a stash on your hotel windowsill, a good way to sample a variety of cheeses is to visit one of the city's cheese bars.

Pain, Vin, Fromages (3 rue Geoffroy l'Angevin, 4th, 01.42.74.07.52), which was established in the 1980s, was taken over in 2005 by a friendly young couple who offer rather pricey compose-your-own cheese plates alongside raclettes, fondues and vacherin (a creamy seasonal cheese available around Christmas). Both wines and breads are carefully selected to match the cheeses.

Across town, the lovely sun-filled **Fil'O'Fromage** (12 rue Neuve Tolbiac,

13th, 01.53.79.13.35), located near the Bibliothèque François Mitterrand, takes a similar approach, with assiettes froides (three cheeses, three cold meats and salad) and tempting poêlons (cooked cheese dishes). Friendly staff provide a torrent of advice in order to help you achieve the ultimate 'alchemic explosion', showing that here both food and customers are taken seriously. Don't miss the Fontainebleau (fromage blanc with whipped cream) or the expertly made coffee.

Fromagerie 31 (64 rue de Seine, 6th, 01.43.26.50.31) has its own modern cheese and wine bar behind a glass partition, and a small terrace in summer. You can order plates of five, seven or nine cheeses, arranged from mildest to strongest, or opt for cheese-themed salads in summer or warm cheese tarts in winter, followed by cheesecake or fromage blanc.

Occupying a weeny space, this engaging bistro à vins has won a neighbourhood following for its warm welcome, easygoing atmosphere, great cooking and nice selection of wines. Sporting a generous moustache and usually wearing a red apron, the jovial proprietor obviously enjoys reciting the brief menu, while encouraging you to discover the unusual bottles he has come across. The menu changes often, but our pressée of rabbit with tarragon, provençal-style squid in tomato sauce, risotto with peas and asparagus, and strawberry-rhubarb crumble were all delicious. You can also pop by for a quick sip with a plate of cheeses or charcuterie, and here again the quality is impressive. One way or another, this is a charming hideaway for a tête-à-tête or a good-value lunch (€24). Just be advised that it's a bit of a trek from central Paris.

Caves Pétrissans

30 bis av Niel, 17th (01.42.27.52.03). M° Pereire. **Open** 12.30-2.15pm, 7.30-10.30pm Mon-Fri. Closed Aug. **Glass** €4. **Credit** AmEx, MC, V. **Non-smoking room. Wheelchair access. Map** C2.
Caves Pétrissans is so authentically French it's a must-visit. A classic turn-of-the-20th-century wine merchant-cum-restaurant, coyly shielded by dingy net curtains from the avenue Niel, it's split into three: the main dining room, slightly overlit but rich with cornicing, zinc bar and mosaic tiles; another smaller room, which serves as the shop; and a tiny, booth-like corner room. Happily, we were seated in the main room where we could best observe the bourgeois crowd of epicurean locals getting down to some serious eating and drinking. Tables are so tightly packed that conversation with the neighbours is inevitable, and enthusiastically taken up by the

patronne. A three-course menu of robust classics was available at €34, but we chose from the more expensive carte. We shared a generous slab of foie gras to start, with a rich oeuf en meurette as a main. Steamed chicken with a creamy tarragon sauce came with perfect basmati rice. Weekly changing wines by the glass were irreproachable: interesting Arbois chardonnay from Tissot; zingy Quincy 2001 from Jerôme de la Chaise; supple Côtes de Brouilly 2001 from Domaine Pavillon. You can also choose from hundreds of bottles at shop price (this is one of the few restaurants in Paris with a well-preserved wine cellar stocked with vintage bottles, so make the most of it), but bear in mind the €16 corkage charge.

Le Petit Chavignol

78 rue de Tocqueville, 17th (01.42.27.95.97). M° Malesherbes or Villiers. **Open** 8am-1am Mon-Sat. **Food served** noon-3.30pm, 7-11.45pm. **Glass** €2.50-€7.50. **Bottle** €12-€100. **Credit** MC, V. **Map** E2.
There's a rustic feel to this popular little bistro, with its copper bar and warm welcome from the woman behind it. We were soon chomping delicious saucisson sec from the Maison Conquet, accompanied by a glass of rather banal Sancerre, which had seemed the obvious aperitif in a bar of this name. Throughout our visit it was all go: the bearded boss in his leather waistcoat was taking orders from a swelling crowd of locals, including a wonderful greying Jean-Paul Belmondo lookalike with a fluffy lapdog. The lure is simple: a good selection of artisanal charcuterie and hearty, generous hot dishes. We felt obliged to try the crottin de chavignol, which was suitably crumbly and served warm with salad. A handwritten wine list covering most regions includes some lesser-known small producers.

On the Town

Eating with Entertainment

From a brashly lit cruise along the Seine to a racy cabaret, there is no end of ways to spice up your dinner in the city of light.

Le Kiosque Flottant 2

BAWDY SONGS

Chez Michou ★

80 rue des Martyrs, 18th (01.46.06.16.04/ www.michou.com). M° Pigalle. **Dinner** 8.30pm-12.30am daily. **Show** 11pm daily. Closed Aug. **Admission** with dinner €97; show & drink €35. **Credit** MC, V. **Map** H2.

Drag queens romp through a whirlwind of Charles Aznavour, Tina Turner and Brigitte Bardot impersonations. Look out for Michou himself, who always wears blue. Book ahead if you want to dine.

BOATS

La Balle au Bond

(01.40.46.85.12/www.laballeaubond.fr). Oct-Apr: facing 55 quai de la Tournelle, 5th. M° Maubert Mutualité. Apr-Oct: quai Malaquais, 6th. M°

Pont Neuf. **Restaurant** noon-7.30pm daily. Closed May-Sept. **Average** €36. **Prix fixe** €20, €38. **Lunch menu** €18. **Concerts** 9pm. **Admission** €5-€6. **Credit** AmEx, MC, V. **Map** K7.

From its prime mooring position, this concert-hall barge provides a good spot from which to soak up sunnier days on the Seine. Depending on when you visit, you will also be able to enjoy a range of concerts, plays and food.

Bateaux Parisiens

Port de La Bourdonnais, 7th (01.44.11.33.44/ meal reservations 01.44.11.33.55/www.bateaux parisiens.com). M° Bir-Hakeim/RER Champ de Mars. **Dinner cruise** 8.30-11pm daily (boarding from 7-8.15pm). **Prix fixe** €92-€140. **Credit** DC, MC, V. **Non-smoking**. **Map** C6.

Expect to be herded in with the multitudes to a vast and overcrowded dining area by waiters who have their small talk (in English, of course) down to a T. The food itself is pleasant enough. As you cruise down the River Seine, the huge glass windows offer stunning scenery by day and night; however, the onboard musical entertainment and running commentary can be intrusive, to put it mildly.

Bateaux-Mouches

Pont de l'Alma, rive droite, 8th (01.42.25.96.10/ recorded information 01.40.76.99.99/www.bateaux-mouches.fr). M° Alma Marceau. **Lunch cruise** 1-2.45pm daily (boarding from 12.15pm). **Dinner cruise** 8.30-10.45pm daily (boarding 7.30-8.15pm). **Lunch** €50. **Dinner** €125. **Credit** DC, MC, V. **Map** D5.

A dinner cruise with Bateaux-Mouches allows you to dine in peace while taking in the floodlit sights along the Seine. The set menu was hit or miss on our visit, but covered a range of French classics. English-speaking waiters were friendly and efficient. Dress smartly (jacket and tie required for men).

Le Kiosque Flottant 2

quai de Montebello, 5th (01.43.54.19.51). M° St-Michel. **Open** 10am-2am daily. Closed Oct-Mar. **Food served** noon-2.30pm, 7-10.30pm. **Average** €40. **Concerts** 9pm Mon, Wed-Sat; noon Sun. **Admission** free with dinner or drink. **Credit** MC, V. **Map** K7.

Of the three Kiosques Flottants, this one has the most magical location, with its full-on view of Notre-Dame's flying buttresses. A romantic destination for a pre- or post-dinner drink, the boat hosts concerts of various styles (jazz, bossa nova, reggae) most nights, and gitane artists at noon on Sundays. **Other locations**: Le Kiosque Flottant 1, quai François-Mauriac, 13th (01.44.67.75.21); Le Kiosque Flottant 3, quai Anatole France, 7th (01.44.67.75.21).

CAFE-THEATRE

Au Bec Fin

6 rue Thérèse, 1st (01.42.96.29.35). M° Pyramides. **Shows** 7pm, 9pm daily; matinées for children 11am, 3pm, 4.30pm during school holidays. Closed Aug. **Tickets** €15; €12 students; €9 children. **Dinner** €18, €25. **Credit** MC, V. **Map** H5.
Dine downstairs on traditional French cuisine such as frogs' legs and snails (watch out for the strong garlic butter), before heading up the rickety staircase to see anything from Oscar Wilde in French to a modern-day *Cinderella* for the kids.

L'Ane Rouge

3 rue Laugier, 17th (01.47.64.45.77). M° Ternes. **Shows** 10pm daily. **Dinner** 8pm. **Tickets** €50-€85. **Credit** MC, V. **Map** C2.
Each evening true comic cabaret combines with a great atmosphere in this glittery café-théâtre. Dine on interesting regional dishes, then sit back and listen to comedians new and old let rip with all the mirth they can muster.

CLASSICAL

Bel Canto ★

72 quai de l'Hôtel de Ville, 4th (01.42.78.30.18/ www.lebelcanto.com). M° Hôtel-de-Ville. **Open** from 8pm daily. Closed Mon and Sun in Aug. **Prix fixe** €68. **Credit** AmEx, MC, V. **Non-smoking**. **Map** K6.
As the first note on the piano is played, the waitress, who only two minutes before was serving your crab tagliatelle, starts to sing a favourite aria from great operas by Verdi, Mozart, Puccini or Rossini. The compulsory set menu is a little on the pricey side (as is the wine list), but this seems irrelevant as you're shouting 'bravo!'

Le Lido

116 bis av des Champs-Elysées, 1st (01.40.76.56.10/ www.lido.fr). M° George V. **Open** daily. **Admission** with dinner 7.30pm €140-€210 (children €30); with champagne 9.30pm €100 (children €20); with champagne 11.30pm €80 (children free). **Credit** AmEx, DC, MC, V. **Wheelchair access**. **Non-smoking**. **Map** D4.
The current revue Bonheur is aptly named – that is, as long as your definition of 'happiness' involves impressively choreographed song and dance numbers executed by a whole host of near-naked, dancing, prancing girls and boys.

Le Moulin Rouge

82 bd de Clichy, 18th (01.53.09.82.82/www.moulin-rouge.com). M° Blanche. **Dinner** 7pm daily. **Shows** 9pm, 11pm daily (for matinées, phone for details). **Admission** with dinner €140-€170; show €97 (9pm), €87 (11pm) with champagne. **Credit** AmEx, DC, MC, V. **Wheelchair access**. **Non-smoking**. **Map** G2.
The Moulin Rouge, with its revue Féerie, is the most traditional glamour revue and the only place with French can-can. Glittery lamp-posts and fake trees lend a tacky charm to the hall, while the dancers cover the stage with faultless synchronisation.

GUINGUETTE & DANCING

Chez Gégène

162 bis quai de Polangis, allée des Guinguettes, 94340 Joinville-le-Pont (01.48.83.29.43/www.chez-gegene.fr). RER Joinville-le-Pont. Restaurant open noon-2.30pm, 7-10pm Tue-Sun. Closed Jan-Mar. **Admission** for Sat night dance €16 with a drink, €38 with dinner; Sun afternoon dance €15 with a drink, €45 with lunch. **Credit** MC, V. **Wheelchair access**.
Typically French and thoroughly un-Parisian, Chez Gégène attracts dance addicts, grannies and urban hipsters. The band (Friday, Saturday nights, Sunday afternoons) sprinkles tango, foxtrot and musette with disco, so those less sure of foot don't feel left out.

JAZZ

Le Caveau des Oubliettes ★

52 rue Galande, 5th (01.46.34.23.09). M° Maubert-Mutualité. **Open** 5pm-4am daily. **Jazz concert** 10pm-2am. **Happy hour** 5-9pm. **Credit** MC, V. **Map** J7.
This historically themed brick bar of Irish character attracts a good Franco-Euro mix of punters to its street-level pub. Come 10pm, they venture down the staircase to the cellar, with its small stage and bar.

Le Franc Pinot

1 quai de Bourbon, 4th (01.46.33.60.64). M° Pont Marie. **Open** 7pm-midnight Tue-Sat. Closed Aug. **Admission** €10-€15 (free Tue). **Concerts** 9pm. **Prix fixe** €35-€55. **Credit** MC, V. **Map** K7.
Set in the centuries-old cellars of the Ile St-Louis, this intimate jazz den serves up a warming mix of rhythm and French comfort food. Loved-up couples, friends and jazz enthusiasts rub shoulders in the shadows.

Autour de Midi-Minuit

11 rue Lepic, 18th (01.55.79.16.48). M° Blanche. **Open** noon-2.30pm, 7pm-2am Tue-Sun. **Food served** until 11pm. Closed Aug. **Admission** €10 (free Tues), €5 when eating. **Concerts** 10pm Fri, Sat. **Jam session** 9.30pm Tue. **Average** €22-€35. **Credit** AmEx, DC, MC, V. **Map** H2.
This Montmartre institution is perhaps the best-value jazz venue in the city thanks to its top acts and copious French cuisine. On concert nights everyone heads down to the jazz lair, where names big and small bop and swing into the wee hours.

Shopping & Cooking

Rare is the Paris neighbourhood that lacks a selection of traditional food shops, from the proud baker who turns out crisp-crusted baguettes à l'ancienne to the charcutier who lets no part of the pig go to waste. St-Germain is a sweet-lover's paradise, with some of the best pâtissiers in town and seemingly a chic chocolatier on every corner. For more down-to-earth shopping, avoid the better-known street markets and head to the open-air ones in the outer arrondissements (see *p210* **Market forces**).

BAKERIES

Le Boulanger de Monge
123 rue Monge, 5th (01.43.37.54.20/www.boulanger demonge.com). Mº Censier Daubenton. **Open** 7am-8.30pm Tue-Sun. **Credit** MC, V. **Map** K9.
Dominique Saibron uses spices to give inimitable flavour to his organic sourdough boule. About 2,000 bread-lovers a day join the queue at his boutique, which also produces one of the city's best baguettes and delicious sweet 'escargots' flavoured with chocolate, cinnamon or lemon.

Kayser
8 & 14 rue Monge, 5th (01.44.07.01.42/ 01.44.07.17.81/www.maisonkayser.com). Mº Maubert Mutualité. **Open** 6.45am-8.30pm Mon-Fri; 6.30am-8.30pm Sat, Sun. **Credit** MC, V. **Map** J7.
In a few years Eric Kayser has established himself as one of the city's star bakers, thanks in large part to his outstanding baguette. The organic bakery, at 14 rue Monge, is less busy than the main shop. **Other locations**: 5 rue Basse des Carmes, 5th (01.44.07.31.61).

Poilâne
8 rue du Cherche-Midi, 6th (01.45.48.42.59/ www.poilane.com). Mº Sèvres Babylone or St-Sulpice. **Open** 7.15am-8.15pm Mon-Sat. **Credit** MC, V. **Map** G7.
Apollonia Poilâne has run this world-famous bakery since her parents' death in 2002. Nothing has changed in the tiny shop, where locals queue for freshly baked country miches, flaky-crusted apple tarts and buttery shortbread biscuits. **Other locations**: 49 bd de Grenelle, 15th (01.45.79.11.49).

Arnaud Delmontel
39 rue des Martyrs, 9th (01.48.78.29.33/ www.arnaud-delmontel.com). Mº St-Georges. **Open** 7am-8.30pm Mon, Wed-Sun. Closed first two weeks in Aug. **No credit cards**. **Map** H2.
With its crisp crust and chewy dough scattered with irregular holes, Delmontel's Renaissance baguette is easily one of the finest in Paris. Luckily, he injects the same skill and perfectionism into his pastries. **Other locations**: 57 rue de Damrémont, 18th (01.42.64.59.63).

L'Autre Boulange
43 rue de Montreuil, 11th (01.43.72.86.04). Mº Faidherbe Chaligny or Nation. **Open** 7.30am-1.30pm, 3.30-7.30pm Mon-Fri; 7.30am-12.30pm Sat. Closed Aug. **Credit** MC, V. **Map** P7.
Michel Cousin rustles up 23 kinds of organic loaf in his wood-fired oven, such as the flutiot (rye bread with raisins, walnuts and hazelnuts), the sarment de Bourgogne (sourdough and a little rye) and a spiced cornmeal bread that's ideal for foie gras. Great croissants and chaussons too.

Le Moulin de la Vierge
166 av de Suffren, 15th (01.47.83.45.55/ www.lemoulindelavierge.com). Mº Sèvres Lecourbe. **Open** 7am-8.30pm Mon-Wed, Fri-Sun. **No credit cards**. **Map** E8.
Basile Kamir learnt breadmaking after falling in love with an old abandoned bakery. Each of his branches has an irresistible fragrance, matched by the quality of his sourdough breads. **Other locations**: 82 rue Daguerre, 14th (01.43.22.50.55); 105 rue Vercingétorix, 14th (01.45.43.09.84).

CHEESE
The sign 'maître fromager affineur' is used to denote merchants who buy young cheeses from farms and age them on their premises; 'fromage fermier' and 'fromage au lait cru' signify farm-produced and raw milk cheeses respectively.

Fromagerie Quatrehomme
62 rue de Sèvres, 7th (01.47.34.33.45). Mº Vaneau. **Open** 8.45am-1pm, 4-7.45pm Tue-Thur; 8.45am-7.45pm Fri, Sat. **Credit** MC, V. **Map** F8.
The award-winning Marie Quatrehomme is behind this inviting fromagerie. Justly famous for classics such as comté fruité, beaufort and the squishy st-marcellin, it sells more unusual specialities such as goat's cheese with pesto and truffle-flavoured brie.

Fromagerie Dubois et Fils

Marie-Anne Cantin
12 rue du Champ-de-Mars, 7th (01.45.50.43.94).
Mᵒ Ecole Militaire. **Open** 8.30am-7.30pm Mon-Sat.
Credit AmEx, MC, V (minimum €15). **Map** D6.
Cantin, a vigorous defender of unpasteurised cheese, is justifiably proud of her dreamily creamy st-marcellins, aged chèvres and roquefort réserve.

Alléosse
13 rue Poncelet, 17th (01.46.22.50.45/www.fromage-alleosse.com). Mᵒ Ternes. **Open** 9am-1pm, 4-7pm
Tue-Thur; 9am-1pm, 3.30-7pm Fri, Sat; 9am-1pm
Sun. **Credit** MC, V. **Map** C2.
People cross town for these cheeses, and you can see why – wonderful farmhouse camemberts, delicate st-marcellins, a choice of chèvres and several rarities.

Fromagerie Dubois et Fils
80 rue de Tocqueville, 17th (01.42.27.11.38).
Mᵒ Malesherbes or Villiers. **Open** 9am-1pm,
4-7.45pm Tue-Fri; 9am-7.30pm Sat. Closed first three
weeks in Aug. **Credit** AmEx, MC, V. **Map** E2.
Superchef darling Dubois stocks 80 types of goat's cheese, plus prized, aged st-marcellin and st-félicien.
Other locations: 79 rue de Courcelles, 17th
(01.43.80.36.42).

CHOCOLATE

Patrick Roger
108 bd St-Germain, 6th
*(01.43.29.38.42/www.patrickroger.com). Mᵒ Cluny La
Sorbonne or Odéon.* **Open** 10.30am-7.30pm Tue-Sat.
Closed three weeks in Aug. **Credit** MC, V. **Map** H7.
This young chocolatier, who worked in the suburb of Sceaux before opening this branch in

the heart of Paris, could best be described as a chocolate sculptor. His whimsical creations include chocolate hens with a brushed-cocoa finish and tins of chocolate sardines. Ingredients are top-notch.

Jean-Charles Rochoux
16 rue d'Assas, 6th (01.42.84.29.45).
Mᵒ Sèvres Babylone. **Open** 2.30-7.30pm Mon;
10.30am-7.30pm Tue-Sat. Closed Mon in Aug.
Credit MC, V. **Map** G7.
Working in a small laboratory downstairs, this passionate young newcomer turns out intense ganaches and little square truffles to rival the best in Paris.

Jean-Paul Hévin
3 rue Vavin, 6th (01.43.54.09.85/www.jphevin.com).
Mᵒ Vavin. **Open** 10am-7pm Tue-Sat. Closed Aug.
Credit MC, V. **Map** G8.
Jean-Paul Hévin dares to fill his chocolates with potent cheeses, which can be served with wine as an aperitif. Even more risqué are his aphrodisiac chocolates, while his chocolate Eiffel Tower is undeniably a classic.
Other locations: 231 rue St-Honoré, 1st
(01.55.35.35.96); 16 av de La Motte-Picquet, 7th
(01.45.51.77.48).

Richart
*258 bd St-Germain, 7th (01.45.55.66.00/
www.richart.com). Mᵒ Solférino.* **Open** 10am-
7pm Mon-Sat. **Credit** AmEx, MC, V. **Map** F6.
At Richart, each chocolate ganache has an intricate design, packages look like jewellery boxes and your purchase comes complete with a tract on how best to savour chocolate.

La Maison du Chocolat

*89 av Raymond-Poincaré, 16th
(01.40.67.77.83/www.lamaisonduchocolat.com).
M° Victor Hugo.* **Open** 10am-7pm Mon-Sat. Closed
Mon in Aug. **Credit** AmEx, MC, V. **Map** B4.
Robert Linxe opened his first Paris shop in 1977
and has been inventing new chocolates ever
since. Don't miss his caramel and chocolate
éclairs, which are surely the best in Paris. See
website for branches.

GLOBAL

Kioko

*46 rue des Petits-Champs, 2nd (01.42.61.33.65).
M° Pyramides.* **Open** 10am-8pm Tue-Sat; 11am-7pm
Sun. **Credit** MC, V. **Map** H4.
This supermarket has everything fans of Japanese
cooking might crave – including ready-made sushi
and koshi hikari rice.

Izraël

*30 rue François-Miron, 4th (01.42.72.66.23).
M° Hôtel de Ville.* **Open** 9.30am-1pm, 2.30-7pm
Tue-Fri; 9.30am-7pm Sat. Closed last week in July,
all Aug. **Credit** MC, V. **Map** K6.
A Marais fixture, this narrow shop stocks spices and
other delights from Mexico, Turkey and India.

Pasta Linea

9 rue de Turenne, 4th (01.42.77.62.54). M° St-Paul.
Open noon-8pm Tue-Sat; 1-8pm Sun. Closed Aug.
Credit AmEx, MC, V. **Map** L6.
Artichoke ravioli with truffle cream sauce or fresh
linguine with tomato and rocket are among
the heavenly hot pastas you might find here, plus
quality dried pastas and prepared sauces to
eat at home.

Mexi & Co

*10 rue Dante, 5th (01.46.34.14.12/http://
mexiandco.fr). M° Cluny La Sorbonne.*
Open 9am-2pm daily. **No credit cards**. **Map** J7.
All you need for a fiesta: marinades for fajitas, dried
chillies, Latin American beers, cachaça and tequilas.

Petrossian

*18 bd de la Tour-Maubourg, 7th (01.44.11.32.32/
www.petrossian.fr). M° Invalides.* **Open** 12.15-2pm,
7.30-10.30pm Tue-Sat. Closed Aug. **Credit** AmEx,
DC, MC, V. **Map** E6.
This is a Russian-themed delicatessen offering silky
smoked salmon, Iranian caviar and gift boxes with
little drawers that will impress even the most jaded
of the jet set.

Jabugo Ibérico & Co

*11 rue Clément-Marot, 8th (01.47.20.03.13).
M° Alma Marceau or Franklin D Roosevelt.*
Open 10am-8.30pm Mon-Sat. **Credit** AmEx, DC,
MC, V. **Map** D4.
This shop specialises in Spanish hams with the
Bellota-Bellota label, meaning the pigs have
feasted on acorns.

Sarl Velan Stores

*87 passage Brady, 10th (01.42.46.06.06/
www.e-velan.com). M° Château d'Eau.* **Open** 10am-
8.30pm Mon-Sat. **Credit** AmEx, MC, V. **Map** K4.
In a crumbling arcade lined with Indian restaurants,
this is a prime source of spices and Indian produce.

Tang Frères

48 av d'Ivry, 13th (01.45.70.80.00). M° Porte d'Ivry.
Open 9am-7.30pm Tue-Sun. **Credit** AmEx, MC, V.
Leading supplier to local restaurants in Chinatown,
this is the best one-stop shop for a stir-fry.

Les Délices d'Orient

*52 av Emile-Zola, 15th (01.45.79.10.00).
M° Charles Michels.* **Open** 8.30am-9pm Tue-Sun.
Credit MC, V. **Map** B8.
Shelves here brim with Lebanese bread, falafel,
olives and all manner of Middle Eastern delicacies.
Other locations: 14 rue des Quatre-Frères-Peignot,
15th (01.45.77.82.93).

Merry Monk

*87 rue de la Convention, 15th (01.40.60.79.54).
M° Boucicaut.* **Open** 10am-7pm Mon-Sat. Closed
Aug. **Credit** MC, V. **Map** B9.
Expat essentials such as ginger biscuits and loose
tea, with a section dedicated to South Africa.

PATISSERIES

Finkelsztajn

27 rue des Rosiers, 4th (01.42.72.78.91). M° St-Paul.
Open 10am-7pm Wed-Sun. Closed 15 July-15 Aug.
No credit cards. **Map** L6.
This motherly shop stocks dense Jewish cakes filled
with poppy seeds, apples or cream cheese.

Gérard Mulot

*76 rue de Seine, 6th (01.43.26.85.77/www.gerard-
mulot.com). M° Odéon.* **Open** 10.45am-8pm Mon,
Tue, Thur-Sun. Closed last week in July, first three
weeks in Aug. **No credit cards**. **Map** H7.
Mulot rustles up some truly stunning pastries,
savoury treats and breads. Typical is the mabillon
– caramel mousse with apricot marmalade.
Other locations: 93 rue de la Glacière, 13th
(01.45.81.39.09).

Pierre Hermé

*72 rue Bonaparte, 6th (01.43.54.47.77). M° St-
Sulpice.* **Open** 10am-7pm Tue-Fri, Sun; 10am-7.30pm
Sat. **Credit** AmEx, DC, MC, V. **Map** G7.
Pastry superstar Hermé attracts the connoisseurs of
St-Germain with his ever-changing collections,
including the trademark Ispahan (strawberry, rose
and lychee tart).
Other locations: 185 rue de Vaugirard, 15th
(01.47.83.29.72).

Sadaharu Aoki

*35 rue de Vaugirard, 6th (01.45.44.48.90/
www.sadaharuaoki.com). M° St-Placide.* **Open**
11am-7pm daily. **Credit** MC, V. **Map** G8.

This skilled Japanese pastry chef combines French techniques to produce original (and pristine) pastries, such as the green tea éclair.
Other locations: 56 bd de Port-Royal, 5th (01.45.35.36.80).

Arnaud Larher
53 rue Caulaincourt, 18th (01.42.57.68.08/ www.arnaud-larher.com). Mº Lamarck Caulaincourt. **Open** 9am-7.30pm Mon-Sat. Closed Aug, one week in Feb. **Credit** MC, V. **Map** H1.
Behind the Sacré Coeur lies a new star in the Paris pastry galaxy. Look out for the all-chocolate Toulouse-Lautrec or the 'baba du moment', punched up with pistachio and cherry or passion fruit.

TREATS & TRAITEURS

Torréfacteur Verlet
256 rue St-Honoré, 1st (01.42.60.67.39/ www.cafesverlet.com). **Open** *Shop* 9.30am-7pm Mon-Sat. *Tea shop* 9.30am-6.30pm Mon-Sat. **Credit** MC, V. **Map** G5.
The freshly roasted coffee here smells as heavenly as the priciest perfume. Eric Duchaussoy roasts rare beans to perfection – sip a p'tit noir at a wooden table, or take home some of the city's finest coffee.

Goumanyat
3 rue Dupuis, 3rd (01.44.78.96.74/www.goumanyat. com). Mº Temple. **Open** 2-7pm Tue-Fri; 11am-7pm Sat. **Credit** AmEx, DC, MC, V. **Map** L5.
Jean-Marie Thiercelin's family has been in the spice industry since 1809, and his spacious, rather secretive shop (buzzer entry) is a treasure trove of super-fresh flavourings. Star chefs come here for Indonesian cubebe pepper, gleaming fresh nutmeg, long pepper (an Indian variety) and Spanish and Iranian saffron.

L'Epicerie
51 rue St-Louis-en-l'Ile, 4th (01.43.25.20.14). Mº Pont Marie. **Open** 11am-8pm daily. **Credit** MC, V. **Map** K7.
This perfect gift shop is crammed with beautiful bottles of blackcurrant vinegar, five-spice mustard, tiny pots of jam, orange sauce, honey with figs and indulgent boxes of chocolate snails.

Jean-Paul Gardil
44 rue St-Louis en l'Ile, 4th (01.43.54.97.15). Mº Pont Marie. **Open** 9am-1pm, 4-7.30pm Tue-Sat; 8.30am-12.30pm Sun. Closed last week in July, first three weeks in Aug. **Credit** MC, V. **Map** K7.
Rarely has meat looked so beautiful – geese hang in the window and a multitude of plaques confirm the butcher's skill in selecting the finest meats, such as milk-fed veal and lamb, coucou de Rennes chickens, Barbary ducklings and Bresse poulard and geese.

Da Rosa
62 rue de Seine, 6th (01.40.51.00.09). Mº Odéon. **Open** 10am-10pm daily. **Credit** AmEx, MC, V. **Map** H7.
José da Rosa sought ingredients for top Paris restaurants before opening his own shop, designed by Jacques Garcia: expect to find Spanish hams, spices from Breton chef Olivier Roellinger, truffles from the Luberon.

Huilerie Artisanale Leblanc
6 rue Jacob, 6th (01.46.34.61.55/www.huile-leblanc.com). Mº St-Germain-des-Prés. **Open** 2-7pm Mon; noon-7pm Tue-Fri; 10am-7pm Sat. Closed two weeks in Aug. **No credit cards. Map** H6.
The Leblanc family started out making walnut oil from its family tree in Burgundy before branching out (so to speak) to press pure oils from hazelnuts, almonds, pine nuts, peanuts, pistachios and olives.

Fauchon
26-30 pl de la Madeleine, 8th (01.47.42.60.11/ www.fauchon.com). Mº Madeleine. **Open** *Shop* 9am-9pm Mon-Sat. *Tea room* 8am-7pm Mon-Sat. *Bakery* 8am-9pm Mon-Sat. **Credit** AmEx, DC, MC, V. **Map** F4.
The latest revamp has breathed new life into grande old dame Fauchon, with a pink and white colour scheme and some of the most tempting savoury goods in town, by Fumiko Kono.

Hédiard
21 pl de la Madeleine, 8th (01.43.12.88.88/ www.hediard.fr). Mº Madeleine. **Open** 9am-9pm Mon-Sat. **Credit** AmEx, DC, MC, V. **Map** F4.
The first establishment to introduce exotic foods to Paris, Hédiard specialises in rare teas and coffees, spices, jams and candied fruits. The original shop, dating from 1880, has a posh tea room upstairs. See the website for other addresses.

Terre de Truffes
21 rue Vignon, 8th (01.53.43.80.44/http://terre detruffes.coreis.fr). Mº Madeleine. **Open** 10am-2.30pm, 6-10pm Mon-Sat. **Credit** AmEx, MC, V. **Map** G4.
Famous for his truffle-based cuisine, Provençal chef Clément Bruno recently opened this truffle boutique and bistro where the tuber's powerful aroma hits your nostrils as you enter. Indulge in a fresh truffle for your cooking or more accessible truffle products, such as an almond truffle cream.

Allicante
26 bd Beaumarchais, 11th (01.43.55.13.02). Mº Bastille. **Open** 10am-1pm, 2-7pm Mon-Sat. **Credit** AmEx, DC, MC, V. **Map** M6.
A trove of oily delights, including rare olive oils from Liguria, Sicily and Greece; fragrant pine nut, pistachio and almond varieties; oils extracted from apricot, peach and avocado pits; even pricey argan oil, pounded by hand by Berber women in Morocco.

Poissonnerie du Dôme
4 rue Delambre, 14th (01.43.35.23.95). Mº Vavin. **Open** 8am-1pm, 4-7.30pm Tue-Sat; 8am-12.30pm Sun. Closed Aug. **Credit** MC, V. **Map** G9.

On the Town

Market forces

There may be no better way to experience Paris than to queue (or, rather, jostle) at an open-air market on a weekend morning, when busy young bobos compete with sharp-elbowed elder folk for farmers' eggs, just-pulled carrots, rare apple varieties and squeaky fresh fish. Only a small percentage of vendors produce what they grow, so look for the sign 'producteur' or 'maraîcher' to support small-scale farming.

The 66 roving markets in Paris have retained their atmosphere and variety, while street and covered markets can be a bit of a let-down, with clothing stores and chains replacing traditional food shops. Here is a selection of the best roving markets, open from 8am to 2pm unless otherwise specified.

Saxe-Breteuil (av de Saxe, 7th, Thur, Sat) has an unrivalled setting facing the Eiffel Tower, as well as the city's most chic produce. Look for farmers' goat's cheese, rare apple varieties, Armenian specialities, abundant oysters and a handful of dedicated small producers.

Marché Square d'Anvers (9th, 3-8pm Fri) is a new afternoon market, adding to the village atmosphere of a peaceful quartier down the hill from Montmartre. Among its highlights are untreated vegetables, hams from the Auvergne, cheeses and award-winning honey.

Marché Bastille (bd Richard-Lenoir, 11th, Thur, Sun) is one of the biggest and most boisterous in Paris. A favourite of political campaigners, it's also a great source of local cheeses, farmer's chicken and excellent affordable fish.

Marché d'Aligre (rue d'Aligre, 12th, Tue-Sun), next to a covered market, is proudly working-class. Stallholders out-shout each other while price-conscious shoppers don't compromise on quality.

Marché Président-Wilson (av Président-Wilson, 16th, Wed, Sat) is a classy market attracting the city's top chefs, who snap up ancient vegetable varietiesfrom star producer Joël Thiébault. Genuine Breton crêpes and buckwheat galettes are available as you shop.

Marché Batignolles (bd des Batignolles, 17th, Sat) is more down-to-earth than the Raspail organic market, with a quirky selection of stallholders. Prices are higher than at ordinary markets, but worth it.

Fine wines, professional expertise and friendly service at **Les Caves Taillevent**.

The fish here are individually selected, many coming straight from small boats off the Breton coast. Among the ones to try are the drool-inducing (but bank-breaking) turbot, the giant crabs and the scallops (when in season).

Beau et Bon

81 rue Lecourbe, 15th (01.43.06.06.53/www. beauetbon.com). M° Volontaires. **Open** 10.30am-1.30pm, 3-7.30pm Tue-Sat; 10.30am-1pm Sun. **Credit** AmEx, DC, MC, V. **Map** D8.

The aptly named Valérie Gentil has transformed her passion for an épicerie. Come here for dried fruit chutneys from Brittany, cardamom jelly, saffron vinegar, puzzle-shaped cake trays and fantasy decorations for kids' birthday cakes.

WINE, BEER & SPIRITS

Legrand Filles et Fils

1 rue de la Banque, 2nd (01.42.60.07.12/ www.caves-legrand.com). M° Bourse. **Open** 11am-7pm Mon; 10am-7.30pm Tue-Fri; 10am-7pm Sat. Closed Mon in Aug. **Credit** AmEx, MC, V. **Map** H4.

Opposite this old-fashioned shop, which offers fine wines and brandies and teas, is a showroom displaying its glasses and gadgets. Wine tastings take place on Thursdays.

Julien, Caviste

50 rue Charlot, 3rd (01.42.72.00.94). M° Filles du Calvaire. **Open** 9.30am-1.30pm, 3.30-8.30pm Tue-Sat; 10.30am-1.30pm Sun. **Credit** AmEx, MC, V. **Map** L5.

The tireless Julien overflows with enthusiasm for the small producers he has discovered, and often holds free wine tastings on Saturdays.

Ryst Dupeyron

79 rue du Bac, 7th (01.45.48.80.93/ www.vintageandco.com). M° Rue du Bac. **Open** 12.30-7.30pm Mon; 10.30am-7.30pm Tue-Sat. Closed two weeks in Aug. **Credit** AmEx, MC, V. **Map** F7.

The Dupeyron family has sold Armagnac for four generations, and has bottles dating from 1868. Treasures include some 200 fine Bordeaux.

Les Caves Augé

116 bd Haussmann, 8th (01.45.22.16.97). M° St-Augustin. **Open** 1-7.30pm Mon; 9am-7.30pm Tue-Sat. **Credit** AmEx, MC, V. **Map** E3.

The oldest wine shop in Paris – Marcel Proust was a regular customer – is serious and professional.

Les Caves Taillevent

199 rue du Fbg-St-Honoré, 8th (01.45.61.14.09/ www.taillevent.com). M° Charles de Gaulle Etoile or Ternes. **Open** 9am-7.30pm Tue-Sat. Closed three weeks in Aug, public holidays. **Credit** AmEx, DC, MC, V. **Map** D3.

Linked to the famed restaurant of the same name, this modern and very professional wine shop makes customers feel welcome whatever their budget.

La Maison du Whisky

20 rue d'Anjou, 8th (01.42.65.03.16/www.whisky.fr). M° Madeleine. **Open** 9.30am-7pm Mon, Sat; 9.30am-8pm Tue-Fri. **Credit** AmEx, MC, V. **Map** F4.

Jean-Marc Bellier explains which whisky matches which food, and also hosts a whisky club.

On the Town

The best guides to enjoying London li

(but don't just take our word for it)

'More than 700 places where you can eat out for less than £20 a head… a mass of useful information in a geuinely pocket–sized guide'

Mail on Sunday

'Armed with a tube map and this guide there is no excuse to find yourself in a duff bar again'

Evening Standard

'I'm always asked ho up to date with shopp and services in a city as London. This guide the answer'

Red Magazine

'Get the inside track on the capital's neighbourhoods'

Independent on Sunday

'A treasure trove of treats that lists the best the capital has to offer'

The People

Rated 'Best Restaurant Gui

Sunday Times

Available at all good bookshops and imeout.com/shop from £6.99

100% Indepen

Learning and tasting

The seemingly inborn French passion for food might lead you to believe that any Parisian can whip up a soufflé at a moment's notice. Not so. Such has been the decline in culinary skill since 1968, when feminists cast off their aprons and embraced the frozen dinner, that a new breed of school is catering to the baffled thirtysomething for whom cooking remains a complete mystery.

Since opening in 2004, **L'Atelier des Chefs** (10 rue de Penthièvre, 8th, 01.53.30.05.82, www.atelierdeschefs. com, fees €15-€130) has been a roaring success among Parisians who make the most of the lunch hour by honing their knife skills and sharing the results of their efforts. The half-hour lunchtime class (in French) – wok-fried pork with diced pumpkin and mace during our visit – takes place at breakneck speed, but the chef is full of useful tips and the atmosphere is friendly. More involved workshops on French or foreign cuisines take place in the mornings and afternoons, some of them in English. A second branch in the Lafayette Maison store is like a goldfish bowl in the kitchen department. For all classes, it's best to book several weeks ahead on the website.

Nestling romantically at the end of a Parisian courtyard, **L'Atelier des Sens** (40 rue Sedaine, 11th, 01.40.21.08.50, www.atelier-des-sens.com, fees €34-€85) is the antithesis of an intimidating cooking school. Here, the atmosphere created by director Natacha Burtinovic in the smart demonstration kitchen is relaxed and informal. Covering all aspects of French and international cuisine (in French), courses normally last two or three hours, but there also the attractive option of a one-hour course at lunchtime or suppertime, where a main course is prepared and then eaten in the atelier or packed up as a takeaway. Moroccan chef Mohamed showed us all about making a designer tagine, in which he treated his own recipe with endearing flexibility, making for lots of note-taking from the amusingly diverse seven people.

L'Atelier de Fred (6 rue des Vertus, 3rd, 01.40.29.46.04, www.latelierdefred.com, fees €35-€60) has generated a great deal of publicity with his Cook-Date workshops, in which three women and three men (or same-sex on gay nights) gamble on meeting a soul-mate as they toy with a whisk. But the author of *Epatez vos amis* offers real

substance in his compact kitchen, with inventive recipes and pâtisserie classes for kids (he will teach in English on request).

If you prefer a class that caters to foreigners, **Promenades Gourmandes** (187 rue du Temple, 3rd, 01.48.04.56.84, www.promenadesgourmandes.com, fees from €215) offers a cultural experience as well as a culinary one. Long-time teacher Paule Caillat's classes begin at the market, where she will show you how to select the finest seasonal ingredients before tackling a typically French three-course menu at her custom-designed Marais apartment. 'All the necessary steps and no unnecessary ones' is the philosophy that has made her classes so popular with visiting Americans, Brits and Australians (the lively Paule is bilingual and teaches in English).

Greeting her students warmly with a cup of coffee and an apron, **Françoise Meunier** (7 rue Paul Lelong, 2nd, 01.40.26.14.00, www.fmeunier.com, fee €90) plays host to a calm and convivial cooking school in her spacious kitchen. A well-travelled Ecole Hôtelière graduate, she covers everything from seasoning to silverware as a mix of students prepares a balanced three-course meal. The highlight of our class was a juicy, perfectly cooked rôti de porc à la dijonnaise, although menus are designed according to students' preferences. Classes are in French, but English translations are available with advance notice.

For a more old-school experience, sign up at **Le Cordon Bleu** (8 rue Léon, Delhomme, 15th, 01.53.68.22.50, www.cordonbleu.edu, fees from €40) for a half-day demonstration or a one-week class. The daily demonstrations, designed for the long-term students attending the school, can be somewhat rushed and impersonal, but are a good way of observing techniques. Also serious is the **Ritz Escoffier Ecole de Gastronomie Française** (38 rue Cambon, 1st, 01.43.16.30.50, www.ritz.paris, fees from €47). Across from the world-famous kitchen and deep in the hotel's bowels, students work with state-of-the-art equipment and experienced chefs who are willing to answer any question. Similarly, a warm welcome awaits at the **Ecole Lenôtre** (Pavillon Elysée, 10 av des Champs-Elysées, 8th, 01.42.65.97.60, www.lenotre.fr, fees from €46), where master chefs reveal their culinary secrets in a relaxed and friendly environment.

ÉCOLE SUPÉRIEURE DE CUISINE FRANÇAISE – FERRANDI

You don't have to speak French to learn French cuisine !

Opt for an intensive, total-immersion training and acquire the skills to start your own successful business :

• Professional bilingual program in the Art and technique of French cuisine (September to June – 1,200 hours)

• Professional program in Classic French Pastry and Bread Baking (October to April – 1,092 hours)

International admissions : Stéphane Curtis

Tel : 33-1 45 27 09 09

www.escf.ccip.fr

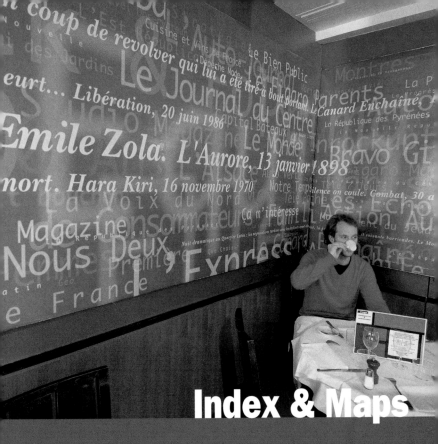

Index & Maps

INDEX	216
LEXICON	234
ARRONDISSEMENT MAP	240
RIGHT BANK MAPS	242
LEFT BANK MAPS	246
AREA MAPS	250
METRO MAP	256

A-Z Index

Le 144 Petrossian p54
18 bd de La Tour-
Maubourg, 7th
(01.44.11.32.32). French

404 p156
69 rue des Gravilliers,
3rd (01.42.74.57.81).
North African

A

**Al Filo delle
Stagione** p144
8 rue de Beauce, 3rd
(01.48.04.52.24). Italian

Al-Diwan p115
30 av George V, 8th
(01.47.20.72.00).
Le Snacking

**Alain Ducasse
au Plaza Athénée** p60
Hôtel Plaza Athénée,
25 av Montaigne, 8th
(01.53.67.65.00/
www.alain-ducasse.com).
French

Alcazar p43
62 rue Mazarine, 6th
(01.53.10.19.99/
www.alcazar.fr). French

L'Alivi p31
27 rue du Roi-de-Sicile,
4th (01.48.87.90.20/
www.restaurant-alivi.com).
French

Allard p44
41 rue St-André-des-Arts,
6th (01.43.26.48.23/
www.allard-restaurant.com).
French

Alléosse p206
13 rue Poncelet, 17th
(01.46.22.50.45/
www.fromage-
alleosse.com).
Shopping & Cooking

Allicante p209
26 bd Beaumarchais,
11th (01.43.55.13.02).
Shopping & Cooking

Altitude 95 p54
1st level, Eiffel Tower,
Champ de Mars, 7th
(01.45.55.20.04).
French

**L'Ambassade
d'Auvergne** p29
22 rue du Grenier
St-Lazare, 3rd
(01.42.72.31.22/
www.ambassade-
auvergne.com). French

Les Ambassadeurs p60
Hôtel de Crillon, 10
pl de la Concorde, 8th
(01.44.71.16.17/
www.crillon.com). French

L'Ambroisie p32
9 pl des Vosges, 4th
(01.42.78.51.45).
French

L'Ami Louis p29
32 rue du Vertbois,
3rd (01.48.87.77.48).
French

**Les Amis
de Messina** p149
204 rue du Fbg-St-Antoine,
12th (01.43.67.96.01/
www.lesamisdes
messina.fr). Italian

Anahi p125
49 rue Volta, 3rd
(01.48.87.88.24).
The Americas

Anahuacalli p127
30 rue des Bernadins,
5th (01.43.26.10.20).
The Americas

Andy Wahloo p169
69 rue des Gravilliers,
3rd (01.42.71.20.38).
Cafés, Bars & Pubs

L'Ane Rouge p204
3 rue Laugier, 17th
(01.47.64.45.77).
Eating with Entertainment

Angelina's p191
226 rue de Rivoli,
1st (01.42.60.82.00).
Tea Rooms

Angl'Opéra p24
39 av de l'Opéra,
2nd (01.42.61.86.25/
www.anglopera.com).
French

L'Angle du Faubourg p61
195 rue du Fbg-St-Honoré,
8th (01.40.74.20.20/
www.taillevent.com).
French

L'AOC p37
14 rue des Fossés-
St-Bernard, 5th
(01.43.54.22.52/
www.restoaoc.com).
French

Apollo p85
3 pl Denfert-Rochereau,
14th (01.45.38.76.77/
www.restaurant-
apollo.com). French

**L'Apparement
Café** p169
18 rue des Coutures-
St-Gervais, 3rd
(01.48.87.12.22).
Cafés, Bars & Pubs

Aquarius p118
40 rue de Gergovie,
14th (01.45.41.36.88).
Vegetarian

L'Ardoise p20
28 rue du Mont-Thabor,
1st (01.42.96.28.18).
French

Arnaud Delmontel p205
39 rue des Martyrs,
9th (01.48.78.29.33/
www.arnaud-
delmontel.com).
Shopping & Cooking

Arnaud Larher p209
53 rue Caulaincourt,
18th (01.42.57.68.08/
www.arnaud-larher.com).
Shopping & Cooking

L'Arpège p54
84 rue de Varenne,
7th (01.45.51.47.33/
www.alain-passard.com).
French

**L'Artisan
de Saveurs** p193
72 rue du Cherche-Midi,
6th (01.42.22.46.64).
Tea Rooms

L'As du Fallafel p154
24 rue des Rosiers,
4th (01.48.87.63.60).
Jewish

Asia-Tée p152
47 rue de la Montagne
Ste-Geneviève, 5th
(01.43.26.39.90).
Japanese

L'Assiette p86
181 rue du Château,
14th (01.43.22.64.86/
www.chezlulu.fr).
French

Astier p74
44 rue Jean-Pierre-
Timbaud, 11th
(01.43.57.16.35/
www.restaurant-
astier.com). French

Astrance p91
4 rue Beethoven, 16th
(01.40.50.84.40).
French

**L'Atelier de Joël
Robuchon** p55
5 rue de Montalembert,
7th (01.42.22.56.56).
French

Atelier Renault p178
53 av des Champs-Elysées,
8th (01.49.53.70.00/
www.atelier-renault.com).
Cafés, Bars & Pubs

Athanor p163
4 rue Crozatier, 12th
(01.43.44.49.15).
Other International

L'Atmosphère p180
49 rue Lucien-Sampaix,
10th (01.40.38.09.21).
Cafés, Bars & Pubs

Au Bec Fin p204
6 rue Thérèse, 1st
(01.42.96.29.35).
Eating with Entertainment

Au Dernier Métro p187
70 bd de Grenelle,
15th (01.45.75.01.23/
www.auderniermetro.com).
Cafés, Bars & Pubs

Au Pied de Cochon p23
6 rue Coquillière, 1st
(01.40.13.77.00/
www.pieddecochon.com).
French

**Au Vieux
Colombier** p177
65 rue de Rennes,
6th (01.45.48.53.81).
Cafés, Bars & Pubs

**Autour de
Midi-Minuit** p204
11 rue Lepic, 18th
(01.55.79.16.48).
Eating with
Entertainment

Au Boeuf Couronné p104
188 av Jean-Jaurès,
19th (01.42.39.54.54).
French

Au Bon Accueil p55
14 rue Monttessuy,
7th (01.47.05.46.11).
French

**Au Bon
Saint-Pourçain** p44
10 bis rue Servandoni,
6th (01.43.54.93.63).
French

Au Grain de Folie p119
24 rue de la Vieuville,
18th (01.42.58.15.57).
Vegetarian

Au P'tit Cahoua p159
39 bd St-Marcel, 13th
(01.47.07.24.42).
North African

Au Petit Marguery p84
9 bd du Port-Royal,
13th (01.43.31.58.59/
www.petitmarguery.fr).
French

Au Sans Souci p196
183 rue St-Denis,
2nd (01.42.36.09.39).
Wine Bars

Au Trou Gascon p82
40 rue Taine, 12th
(01.43.44.34.26/
www.autrougascon.fr).
French

Au Vieux Chêne p79
7 rue du Dahomey,
11th (01.43.71.67.69).
French

L'Auberge du Clou p68
30 av Trudaine, 9th
(01.48.78.22.48/
www.aubergeduclou.
wanadoo.fr). French

Auberge le Quincy p79
28 av Ledru-Rollin,
12th (01.46.28.46.76/
www.lequincy.fr). French

L'Autre Boulange p205
43 rue de Montreuil,
11th (01.43.72.86.04).
Shopping & Cooking

Aux Charpentiers p46
10 rue Mabillon, 6th
(01.43.26.30.05). French

**Aux Comptoirs
des Indes** p143
50 rue de la Fontaine
au Roi, 11th
(01.48.05.45.76). Indian

Aux Lyonnais **p26**
32 rue St-Marc, 2nd
(01.42.96.65.04). French
Aux Négociants **p103**
27 rue Lambert, 18th
(01.46.06.15.11). French
Aux Saveurs
de Claude **p53**
12 rue Stanislas, 6th
(01.45.44.41.74/
www.auxsaveurs
declaude.fr). French
L'Avant-Goût **p83**
26 rue Bobillot, 13th
(01.53.80.24.00).
French
Ay Caramba! **p128**
59 rue Mouzaia, 19th
(01.42.41.76.30/
www.restaurant-
aycaramba.com).
The Americas
Azabu **p153**
3 rue André-Mazet,
6th (01.46.33.72.05).
Japanese

B

La Balle au Bond **p203**
(01.40.46.85.12/
www.laballeaubond.fr).
Eating with Entertainment
Ballon &
Coquillages **p97**
71 bd Gouvion-St-Cyr,
17th (01.45.74.17.98).
French
Le Balzar **p37**
49 rue des Ecoles,
5th (01.43.54.13.67/
www.groupflo.fr). French
Banyan **p138**
24 pl Etienne-Pernet,
15th (01.40.60.09.31).
Far Eastern
Le Bar **p173**
27 rue de Condé,
6th (01.43.29.06.61).
Cafés, Bars & Pubs
Bar Basile **p177**
34 rue de Grenelle,
7th (01.42.22.59.46).
Cafés, Bars & Pubs
Le Bar Dix **p175**
10 rue de l'Odéon,
6th (01.43.26.66.83).
Cafés, Bars & Pubs
Bar du Marché **p175**
75 rue de Seine, 6th
(01.43.26.55.15).
Cafés, Bars & Pubs
Bar Panoramique **p188**
Hôtel Concorde La Fayette,
3 pl du Général-Koenig,
17th (01.40.68.51.31).
Cafés, Bars & Pubs
Bar à Soupes **p116**
33 rue de Charonne,
11th (01.43.57.53.79).
Le Snacking
Bar des Théâtres **p179**
6 av Montaigne, 8th
(01.47.23.34.63).
Cafés, Bars & Pubs
Le Baratin **p106**
3 rue Jouye Rouve,
20th (01.43.49.39.70).
French

Le Baron Bouge **p200**
1 rue Théophile-Roussel,
12th (01.43.43.14.32).
Wine Bars
Barrio Latino **p185**
46 rue du Fbg-St-Antoine,
12th (01.55.78.84.75).
Cafés, Bars & Pubs
La Bastide Odéon **p44**
7 rue Corneille, 6th
(01.43.26.03.65/
www.bastide-odeon.com).
French
Bateaux Parisiens **p203**
Port de La Bourdonnais,
7th (01.44.11.33.44/
www.bateauxparisiens.
com). Eating with
Entertainment
Bateaux-Mouches **p203**
Pont de l'Alma, rive droite,
8th (01.42.25.96.10/
www.bateaux-mouches.fr).
Eating with Entertainment
Beau et Bon **p211**
81 rue Lecourbe,
15th (01.43.06.06.53).
Shopping & Cooking
Bel Canto **p204**
72 quai de l'Hôtel de Ville,
4th (01.42.78.30.18/
www.lebelcanto.com).
Eating with Entertainment
La Belle Hortense **p197**
31 rue Vieille-du-Temple,
4th (01.48.04.71.60/
www.cafeine.com).
Wine Bars
Bellota-Bellota **p160**
18 rue Jean-Nicot,
7th (01.53.59.96.96/
www.bellota-bellota.com).
Spanish
Benoît **p32**
20 rue St-Martin, 4th
(01.42.72.25.76/
www.alain-ducasse.com).
French
Bharath Café **p142**
67 rue Louis Blanc,
10th (01.58.20.06.20).
Indian
A la Biche au Bois **p80**
45 av Ledru Rollin, 12th
(01.43.43.34.38). French
A la Bière **p104**
103 av Simon Bolivar, 19th
(01.42.39.83.25). French
Bioboa **p113**
3 rue Danielle-Casanova,
1st (01.42.61.17.67).
Le Snacking
Le Bis de Severo **p86**
16 rue des Plantes,
14th (01.40.44.73.09).
French
Le Bistral **p97**
80 rue Lemercier, 17th
(01.42.63.59.61). French
Le Bistro de Marius **p61**
6 av George V, 8th
(01.40.70.11.76).
French
Le Bistrot
d'à Côté Flaubert **p97**
10 rue Gustave-Flaubert,
17th (01.42.67.05.81/
www.michelrostang.com).
French

Bistrot d'Hubert **p88**
41 bd Pasteur, 15th
(01.47.34.15.50/
www.bistrodhubert.com).
French
Le Bistrot
Napolitain **p147**
18 av Franklin-D-Roosevelt,
8th (01.45.62.08.37).
Italian
Le Bistrot Paul Bert **p75**
18 rue Paul Bert, 11th
(01.43.72.24.01). French
Le Bistrot
du Peintre **p183**
116 av Ledru-Rollin,
11th (01.47.00.34.39).
Cafés, Bars & Pubs
Le Bistrot
du Sommelier **p62**
97 bdaussmann, 8th
(01.42.65.24.85). French
Le Bistrot
des Vignes **p92**
1 rue Jean-Bologne, 16th
(01.45.27.76.64). French
Bizan **p152**
56 rue Ste-Anne, 2nd
(01.42.96.67.76).
Japanese
Black Calvados **p109**
40 av Pierre 1er de Serbie,
8th (01.47.20.77.77/
www.bc-paris.fr). Fashion
Blue Bayou **p125**
111-113 rue St-Maur,
11th (01.43.55.87.21).
The Americas
La Bocca **p144**
59-61 rue Montmartre, 2nd
(01.42.36.71.88). Italian
El Bodegón de
Pancho **p128**
8 rue Guy Môquet,
17th (01.53.31.00.73).
The Americas
Le Boeuf sur le Toit **p62**
34 rue du Colisée,
8th (01.53.93.65.55).
French
Bofinger **p32**
5-7 rue de la Bastille,
4th (01.42.72.87.82/
www.bofingerparis.com).
French
The Bombardier **p171**
2 pl du Panthéon,
5th (01.43.54.79.22).
Cafés, Bars & Pubs
La Bonne
Franquette **p183**
151 rue de la Roquette,
11th (01.43.48.85.88).
Cafés, Bars & Pubs
Botequim **p127**
1 rue Berthollet, 5th
(01.43.37.98.46).
The Americas
Boucherie Roulière **p44**
24 rue des Canettes, 6th
(01.43.26.25.70). French
Le Bouclard **p101**
1 rue Cavalotti, 18th
(01.45.22.60.01/
www.bouclard.com). French
Bouillon Racine **p46**
3 rue Racine, 6th
(01.44.32.15.60/www.
bouillon-racine.com). French

Le Boulanger
de Monge **p205**
123 rue Monge, 5th
(01.43.37.54.20).
Shopping & Cooking
La Boulangerie **p106**
15 rue des Panoyaux,
20th (01.43.58.45.45).
French
La Boule Rouge **p155**
1 rue de la Boule Rouge,
9th (01.47.70.43.90).
Jewish
Les Bouquinistes **p46**
53 quai des Grands-
Augustins, 6th
(01.43.25.45.94). French
La Bourse ou la Vie **p24**
12 rue Vivienne, 2nd
(01.42.60.08.83).
French
The Bowler **p179**
13 rue d'Artois, 8th
(01.45.61.16.60).
Cafés, Bars & Pubs
La Braisière **p97**
54 rue Cardinet, 17th
(01.47.63.40.37). French
Brasserie de
l'Isle St Louis **p33**
55 quai de Bourbon, 4th
(01.43.54.02.59). French
Brasserie
de la Poste **p92**
54 rue de Longchamp,
16th (01.47.55.01.31).
French
Brasserie Flo **p72**
7 rue des Petites-Ecuries,
10th (01.47.70.13.59/
www.floparis.com).
French
Brasserie Lipp **p46**
151 bd St-Germain,
6th (01.45.48.53.91/
www.brasserielipp.com).
French
Bread & Roses **p115**
7 rue de Fleurus, 6th
(01.42.22.06.06).
Le Snacking
Breakfast
in America **p124**
4 rue Malher, 4th
(01.42.72.40.21).
The Americas
Le Bréguet **p187**
72 rue Falguière,
15th (01.42.79.97.00).
Cafés, Bars & Pubs
Le Bristol **p194**
112 rue du Fbg-St-Honoré,
8th (01.53.43.43.00/
www.lebristolparis.com).
Tea Rooms
Le Bristol **p62**
Hôtel Bristol, 112 rue
du Fbg-St-Honoré, 8th
(01.53.43.43.00/
www.lebristolparis.com).
French
Bubar **p169**
3 rue des Tournelles,
4th (01.40.29.97.72).
Cafés, Bars & Pubs
Le Buddha Bar **p109**
8 rue Boissy d'Anglas,
8th (01.53.05.90.00).
Fashion

C

Le Café p167
62 rue Tiquetonne,
2nd (01.40.39.08.00).
Cafés, Bars & Pubs

Le Café Arrosé p189
123 rue Caulaincourt,
18th (01.42.57.14.30).
Cafés, Bars & Pubs

Café Burq p102
6 rue Burq, 18th
(01.42.52.81.27).
French

Café Chéri(e) p190
44 bd de la Villette,
19th (01.42.02.02.05).
Cafés, Bars & Pubs

Café du Commerce p88
51 rue du Commerce,
15th (01.45.75.03.27/
www.lecafeducommerce.
com). French

Le Café Constant p55
139 rue St-Dominique,
7th (01.47.53.73.34).
French

Café de Flore p175
172 bd St-Germain,
6th (01.45.48.55.26/
www.cafe-de-flore.com).
Cafés, Bars & Pubs

Café de l'Homme p112
Musée de l'Homme,
17 pl du Trocadéro,
16th (01.44.05.30.15/
www.cafedelhomme.com).
Fashion

Café de l'Industrie p183
16-17 rue St-Sabin,
11th (01.47.00.13.53).
Cafés, Bars & Pubs

Café de la Mairie p175
8 pl St-Sulpice, 6th
(01.43.26.67.82).
Cafés, Bars & Pubs

Café Maure de la
Mosquée de Paris p193
39 rue Geoffroy St-Hilaire,
5th (01.43.31.38.20).
Tea Rooms

Café Minotti p147
33 rue de Verneuil,
7th (01.42.60.04.04).
Italian

Café de la Paix p180
place de l'Opéra,
9th (01.40.07.36.36).
Cafés, Bars & Pubs

Café de la Poste p33
13 rue Castex, 4th
(01.42.72.95.35). French

Café Delmas p172
2-4 pl de la Contrescarpe,
5th (01.43.26.51.26).
Cafés, Bars & Pubs

Café des Lettres p178
53 rue de Verneuil,
7th (01.42.22.52.17).
Cafés, Bars & Pubs

Le Café
du Marché p178
38 rue Cler, 7th
(01.47.05.51.27).
Cafés, Bars & Pubs

Café Le Passy p188
2 rue de Passy, 16th
(01.42.88.31.02).
Cafés, Bars & Pubs

Café Léa p172
5 rue Claude Bernard,
5th (01.43.31.46.30).
Cafés, Bars & Pubs

Café Marly p166
93 rue de Rivoli, cour
Napoléon du Louvre,
1st (01.49.26.06.60).
Cafés, Bars & Pubs

Café Thoumieux p178
4 rue de la Comète,
7th (01.45.51.50.40/
www.thoumieux.com).
Cafés, Bars & Pubs

La Cagouille p86
10 pl Constantin Brancusi,
14th (01.43.22.09.01/
www.la-cagouille.fr).
French

Les Cakes
de Bertrand p195
7 rue Bourdaloue,
9th (01.40.16.16.28/
www.lescakesdebertrand.
com). Tea Rooms

Calle 24 p127
13 rue Beautreillis,
4th (01.42.72.38.34).
The Americas

Le Cambodge p132
10 av Richerand, 10th
(01.44.84.37.70).
Far Eastern

Camille p29
24 rue des Francs-
Bourgeois, 3rd
(01.42.72.20.50).
French

Le Carré
des Feuillants p20
14 rue de Castiglione,
1st (01.42.86.82.82/
www.carredesfeuillants.fr).
French

Casa Eusebio p161
68 av Félix Faure,
15th (01.45.54.11.88).
Spanish

Casa Olympe p69
48 rue St-Georges,
9th (01.42.85.26.01).
French

Le Casque d'Or p107
pl Maurice Chevalier,
20th (01.43.58.37.09).
French

La Cave Café p189
134 rue Marcadet,
18th (01.4606.29.17).
Cafés, Bars & Pubs

La Cave
Gourmande p106
10 rue du Général Brunet,
19th (01.40.40.03.30).
French

Le Caveau
des Oubliettes p204
52 rue Galande, 5th
(01.46.34.23.09).
Eating with Entertainment

Les Caves Augé p211
116 bdaussmann,
8th (01.45.22.16.97).
Shopping & Cooking

Caves La
Bourgogne p197
144 rue Mouffetard,
5th (01.47.07.82.80).
Wine Bars

Caves Miard p198
9 rue des Quatre-Vents,
6th (01.43.54.99.30).
Wine Bars

Caves Pétrissans p201
30 bis av Niel, 17th
(01.42.27.52.03).
Wine Bars

Caves Saint Gilles p160
4 rue St-Gilles, 3rd
(01.48.87.22.62). Spanish

Les Caves
Taillevent p211
199 rue du Fbg-St-Honoré,
8th (01.45.61.14.09/
www.taillevent.com).
Shopping & Cooking

La Cerisaie p86
70 bd Edgar Quinet,
14th (01.43.20.98.98).
French

Le Ch'ti Catalan p69
4 rue Navarin, 9th
(01.44.63.04.33).
French

Le Chalet des Iles p93
carrefour des Cascades,
Lac Inférieur du Bois
de Boulogne, 16th
(01.42.88.04.69/
www.lechaletdesiles.net).
French

Le Chamarré p55
13 bd de la Tour-Maubourg,
7th (01.47.05.50.18/
www.lechamarre.com).
French

Charlot, Roi des
Coquillages p69
81 bd de Clichy, 9th
(01.53.20.48.00/
www.charlot_paris.com).
French

Chartier p69
7 rue du Fbg-Montmartre,
9th (01.47.70.86.29/
www.restaurant.chartier.
com). French

Le Chateaubriand p75
129 av Parmentier, 11th
(01.43.57.45.95). French

Chez Adel p181
10 rue de la Grange-
aux-Belles, 10th
(01.42.08.24.61).
Cafés, Bars & Pubs

Chez l'Ami Jean p56
27 rue Malar, 7th
(01.47.05.86.89).
French

Chez les Anges p56
54 bd La Tour-Maubourg,
7th (01.47.05.89.86/
www.chezlesanges.com).
French

Chez Arthur p56
25 rue du Fbg-St-Martin,
10th (01.42.08.34.33).
French

Chez Bartolo p147
7 rue des Canettes, 6th
(01.43.26.27.08). Italian

Chez Casimir p72
6 rue du Belzunce, 10th
(01.48.78.28.80). French

Chez Cecile: La Ferme
des Mathurins p62
17 rue Vignon, 8th
(01.42.66.46.39). French

Chez Céleste p122
18 rue de Cotte, 12th
(01.43.44.15.30).
African & Indian Ocean

Chez Corto p69
47 rue Rodier, 9th
(01.49.95.96.80). French

Chez Dom p122
34 rue de Sambre-
et-Meuse, 10th
(01.42.01.59.80).
African & Indian Ocean

Chez les Filles p193
64 rue du Cherche-Midi,
6th (01.45.48.61.54).
Tea Rooms

Chez Fred p98
190 bis bd Pereire, 17th
(01.45.74.20.48). French

Chez Fung p138
32 rue de Frémicourt,
15th (01.45.67.36.99).
Far Eastern

Chez Gégène p204
162 bis quai de Polangis,
allée des Guinguettes,
94340 Joinville-le-Pont
(01.48.83.29.43). Eating
with Entertainment

Chez Germaine p56
30 rue Pierre-Leroux,
7th (01.42.73.28.34).
French

Chez Gladines p84
30 rue des Cinq Diamants,
13th (01.45.80.70.10).
French

Chez Gudule p185
58 bd de Picpus, 12th
(01.43.40.08.28).
Cafés, Bars & Pubs

Chez Jenny p29
39 bd du Temple,
3rd (01.44.54.39.00/
www.chez-jenny.com).
French

Chez Léna et Mimile p37
32 rue Tournefort, 5th
(01.47.07.72.47/
www.chezlenaetmimile.
com). French

Chez Léon p98
32 rue Legendre, 17th
(01.42.27.06.82). French

Chez Lili et
Marcel p186
1 quai d'Austerlitz,
13th (01.45.85.00.08).
Cafés, Bars & Pubs

Chez Maître Paul p47
12 rue Monsieur-le-Prince,
6th (01.43.54.74.59/
www.chezmaitrepaul.com).
French

Chez Marcel p47
7 rue Stanislas, 6th
(01.45.48.29.94). French

Chez Marianne p154
2 rue desospitalières-
St-Gervais, 4th
(01.42.72.18.86). Jewish

Chez Michel p72
10 rue de Belzunce, 10th
(01.44.53.06.20). French

Chez Michou p203
80 rue des Martyrs,
18th (01.46.06.16.04/
www.michou.com).
Eating with Entertainment

Chez Omar p156
47 rue de Bretagne,
3rd (01.42.72.36.26).
North African
Chez Paul p84
22 rue de la Butte-
aux-Cailles, 13th
(01.45.89.22.11). French
Chez Prune p181
71 quai de Valmy,
10th (01.42.41.30.47).
Cafés, Bars & Pubs
Chez Ramulaud p75
269 rue du Fbg-St-Antoine,
11th (01.43.72.23.29).
French
Chez René p38
14 bd St-Germain,
5th (01.43.54.30.23).
French
Chez Richard p169
37 rue Vieille-du-Temple,
4th (01.42.74.31.65).
Cafés, Bars & Pubs
Chez Toinette p102
20 rue Germain-Pilon,
18th (01.42.54.44.36/
www.chez-toinette.com).
French
Chez La Vieille p21
1 rue Bailleul/37 rue
de l'Arbre-Sec, 1st
(01.42.60.15.78). French
Chez Vong p133
10 rue de la Grande
Truanderie, 1st
(01.40.26.09.36).
Far Eastern
China Club p185
50 rue de Charenton,
12th (01.43.43.82.02/
www.chinaclub.cc).
Cafés, Bars & Pubs
Les Chineurs p30
55 rue de Bretagne, 3rd
(01.42.78.64.50). French
Christophe p38
8 rue Descartes,
5th (01.43.26.72.49).
French
Cinq Mars p58
51 rue de Verneuil,
7th (01.45.44.69.13).
French
A la Cloche d'Or p70
3 rue Mansart, 9th
(01.48.74.48.88/
www.alaclochedor).
French
**Le Clos
des Gourmets** p58
16 av Rapp, 7th
(01.45.51.75.61/
www.closdesgourmets.
com). French
La Closerie des Lilas p47
171 bd du Montparnasse,
6th (01.43.54.50/
www.closeriedeslilas.fr).
French
Le Clou p98
132 rue Cardinet,
17th (01.42.27.36.78/
www.restaurant-leclou.fr).
French
Le Clown Bar p200
114 rue Amelot, 11th
(01.43.55.87.35).
Wine Bars

Coconnas p33
2 bis place des Vosges,
4th (01.42.78.58.16).
French
Le Coeur Fou p168
55 rue Montmartre,
2nd (01.42.33.91.33).
Cafés, Bars & Pubs
Le Coin de Verre p199
38 rue de Sambre-
et-Meuse, 10th
(01.42.45.31.82).
Wine Bars
Cojean p116
17 bd aussmann, 9th
(01.47.70.22.65/
www.cojean.fr).
Le Snacking
La Coloniale p132
161 rue de Picpus,
12th (01.43.43.69.10).
Far Eastern
Comme Cochons p80
135 rue Charenton,
12th (01.43.42.43.36).
French
**Comme
des Poissons** p153
24 rue de la Tour,
16th (01.45.20.70.37).
Japanese
**Le Comptoir
des Canettes** p175
11 rue des Canettes,
6th (01.43.26.79.15).
Cafés, Bars & Pubs
**Le Comptoir
du Relais** p47
9 carrefour de l'Odéon,
6th (01.44.27.07.50).
French
Le Connétable p169
55 rue des Archives,
3rd (01.42.77.41.40).
Cafés, Bars & Pubs
La Connivence p80
1 rue de Cotte, 12th
(01.46.28.46.17). French
La Contre-Allée p87
83 av Denfert-Rochereau,
14th (01.43.54.99.86).
French
Coolin p176
15 rue Clément, 6th
(01.44.07.00.92).
Cafés, Bars & Pubs
Le Cosi p38
9 rue Cujas, 5th
(01.43.29.20.20). French
Le Cou de la Girafe p63
7 rue Paul Baudry,
8th (01.56.88.29.55).
French
Couleurs de Vigne p200
2 rue Marmontel, 15th
(01.45.33.32.96).
Wine Bars
La Coupole p87
102 bd du Montparnasse,
14th (01.43.20.14.20).
French
Le Couvent p186
69 rue Broca, 13th
(01.43.31.28.28).
Cafés, Bars & Pubs
La Créole p129
122 bd du Montparnasse,
14th (01.43.20.62.12).
Caribbean

**Crêperie Bretonne
Fleurie** p77
67 rue de Charonne, 11th
(01.43.55.62.29). French
Le Cristal Room p112
8 pl des Etats-Unis,
16th (01.40.22.11.10).
Fashion
Le Crocodile p172
6 rue Royer-Collard,
5th (01.43.54.32.37).
Cafés, Bars & Pubs
La Crypte Polska p162
1 pl Maurice Barrès,
1st (01.42.60.43.33).
Other International
**Curieux
Spaghetti Bar** p108
14 rue St-Merri, 4th
(01.42.72.75.97). Fashion

D

Le Dada p188
12 av des Ternes,
17th (01.43.80.60.12).
Cafés, Bars & Pubs
Da Mimmo p148
39 bd de Magenta,
10th (01.42.06.44.47).
Italian
Da Rosa p209
62 rue de Seine, 6th
(01.40.51.00.09).
Shopping & Cooking
D'Chez Eux p56
2 av de Lowendal, 7th
(01.47.05.52.55). French
De La Ville Café p181
34 bd Bonne-Nouvelle,
10th (01.48.24.48.09).
Cafés, Bars & Pubs
Delicabar p115
1st floor, Bon Marché-
Rive Gauche, 26-38
rue de Sèvres, 7th
(01.42.22.10.12/www.
delicabar.fr). Le Snacking
**Les Délices
d'Orient** p207
52 av Emile-Zola,
15th (01.45.79.10.00).
Shopping & Cooking
Les Deux Abeilles p194
189 rue de l'Université,
7th (01.45.55.64.04).
Tea Rooms
Les Deux Magots p176
6 pl St-Germain-des-Prés,
6th (01.45.48.55.25/
www.lesdeuxmagots.com).
Cafés, Bars & Pubs
Dietetic Shop p119
11 rue Delambre,
14th (01.43.35.39.75).
Vegetarian
Djakarta Bali p135
9 rue Vauvilliers, 1st
(01.45.08.83.11/
www.djakartabali.com).
Far Eastern
Le Dôme p87
108 bd du Montparnasse,
14th (01.43.35.25.81).
French
Le Dôme du Marais p33
53 bis rue des Francs-
Bourgeois, 4th
(01.42.74.54.17). French

Dominique p163
19 rue Bréa, 6th
(01.43.27.08.80).
Other International
Dong Huong p140
14 rue Louis-Bonnet,
11th (01.43.57.18.88).
Far Eastern
Drouant p26
18 rue Gaillon, 2nd
(01.42.65.15.16/
www.drouant.com). French
Le Duc de Richelieu p81
5 rue Parrot, 12th
(01.43.43.05.64). French

E

E-Dune p182
18 av Claude Vellefaux,
10th (01.42.06.22.14/
www.e-dune.com).
Cafés, Bars & Pubs
**L'Ecluse
Madeleine** p198
15 pl de la Madeleine,
8th (01.42.65.34.69/
www.leclusebaravin.com).
Wine Bars
L'Ecurie p38
2 rue Laplace, 5th
(01.46.33.68.49). French
**En Colimaçon
(Ma Pomme)** p107
107 rue de Ménilmontant,
20th (01.40.33.10.40/
www.encolimacon.com).
French
L'Encrier p81
55 rue Traversière, 12th
(01.44.68.08.16). French
**Les Enfants
Rouges** p196
9 rue de Beauce,
3rd (01.48.87.80.61).
Wine Bars
L'Enoteca p197
25 rue Charles V, 4th
(01.42.78.91.44).
Wine Bars
Entoto p123
143-145 rue Léon-
Maurice-Nordmann,
13th (01.45.87.08.51).
African & Indian Ocean
L'Entracte p102
44 rue d'Orsel, 18th
(01.46.06.93.41). French
L'Entrepôt p186
7-9 rue Francis-de-
Pressensé, 14th
(01.45.40.60.70).
Cafés, Bars & Pubs
Entrepot's p190
2 rue Sorbier, 20th
(01.43.49.59.17).
Cafés, Bars & Pubs
L'Epi Dupin p49
11 rue Dupin, 6th
(01.42.22.64.56). French
L'Epicerie p209
51 rue St-Louis-en-l'Ile,
4th (01.43.25.20.14).
Shopping & Cooking
L'Equitable p38
1 rue des Fossés-
St-Marcel, 5th
(01.43.31.69.20).
French

L'Escale p170
1 rue des Deux-Ponts,
4th (01.43.54.94.23).
Cafés, Bars & Pubs
L'Espadon p21
Hôtel Ritz, 15 pl Vendôme,
1st (01.43.16.30.80/
www.ritzparis.com). French
L'Estaminet p197
Marché des Enfants
Rouges, 39 rue de
Bretagne, 3rd
(01.42.72.34.85).
Wine Bars
Les Etages p170
35 rue Vieille-du-Temple,
4th (01.42.78.72.00).
Cafés, Bars & Pubs
L'Etoile Manquante p170
34 rue Vieille-du-Temple,
4th (01.42.72.48.34).
Cafés, Bars & Pubs

F

**Les Fables
de la Fontaine** p58
131 rue St-Dominique, 7th
(01.44.18.37.55). French
La Famille p103
41 rue des Trois-Frères,
18th (01.42.52.11.12).
French
Le Fanfaron p183
6 rue de la Main-d'Or, 11th
(01.49.23.41.14). Cafés,
Bars & Pubs
Fauchon p209
26-30 pl de la Madeleine,
8th (01.47.42.60.11/
www.fauchon.com).
Shopping & Cooking
La Ferme Opéra p113
55 rue St-Roch, 1st
(01.40.20.12.12).
Le Snacking
**Fermette
Marbeuf 1900** p63
5 rue Marbeuf, 8th
(01.53.23.08.00). French
La Ferrandaise p49
8 rue de Vaugirard,
6th (01.43.26.36.36).
French
Finkelsztajn p207
27 rue des Rosiers,
4th (01.42.72.78.91).
Shopping & Cooking
Fish p198
69 rue de Seine, 6th
(01.43.54.34.69).
Wine Bars
Le Flamboyant p129
11 rue Boyer-Barret,
14th (01.45.41.00.22).
Caribbean
Flora p63
36 av George V, 8th
(01.40.70.10.49).
French
Le Flore en l'Isle p170
42 quai d'Orléans,
4th (01.43.29.88.27).
Cafés, Bars & Pubs
Fogón Saint-Julien p160
45 quai des Grands-
Augustins, 6th
(01.43.54.31.33).
Spanish

La Folie en Tête p186
33 rue de la Butte-
aux-Cailles, 13th
(01.45.80.65.99).
Cafés, Bars & Pubs
La Fontaine Gaillon p26
pl Gaillon, 2nd
(01.47.42.63.22/
www.la-fontaine-
gaillon.com). French
**Foody's
Brunch Café** p114
26 rue Montorgueil,
1st (01.40.13.01.53).
Le Snacking
Footsie p168
10-12 rue Daunou,
2nd (01.42.60.07.20).
Cafés, Bars & Pubs
Forêt Noire p194
9 rue de l'Eperon,
6th (01.44.41.00.09).
Tea Rooms
Fouquet's p64
99 av des Champs-Elysées,
8th (01.47.23.70.60/
www.lucienbarriere.com).
French
La Fourmi p189
74 rue des Martyrs,
18th (01.42.64.70.35).
Cafés, Bars & Pubs
Le Franc Pinot p204
1 quai de Bourbon,
4th (01.46.33.60.64).
Eating with Entertainment
La Fresque p21
100 rue Rambuteau,
1st (01.42.33.17.56).
French
The Frog & Rosbif p168
116 rue St-Denis,
2nd (01.42.36.34.73/
www.frogpubs.com).
Cafés, Bars & Pubs
**Fromagerie
Dubois et Fils** p206
80 rue de Tocqueville,
17th (01.42.27.11.38).
Shopping & Cooking
**Fromagerie
Quatrehomme** p205
62 rue de Sèvres,
7th (01.47.34.33.45).
Shopping & Cooking
Le Fumoir p166
6 rue de l'Admiral-
de-Coligny, 1st
(01.42.92.00.24/
www.lefumoir.com).
Cafés, Bars & Pubs

G

Gandhi-Opéra p141
66 rue Ste-Anne,
2nd (01.47.03.41.00).
Indian
Ganesha Corner p142
16 rue Perdonnet,
10th (01.46.07.35.32).
Indian
Le Gange p143
65 rue Manin, 19th
(01.42.00.00.80). Indian
La Gare p93
19 chaussée de la Muette,
16th (01.42.15.15.31).
French

Garnier p64
111 rue St-Lazare, 8th
(01.43.87.50.40). French
Gaya Rive Gauche p58
44 rue du Bac, 7th
(01.45.44.73.73). French
Général Lafayette p180
52 rue Lafayette, 9th
(01.47.7.59.08).
Cafés, Bars & Pubs
Georges p109
Centre Pompidou, 6th
floor, rue Rambuteau,
4th (01.44.78.47.99).
Fashion
**Georget
(Robert et Louise)** p30
64 rue Vieille-du-Temple,
3rd (01.42.78.55.89).
French
Georgette p70
29 rue St-Georges, 9th
(01.42.80.39.13). French
Gérard Mulot p207
76 rue de Seine, 6th
(01.43.26.85.77/
www.gerard-mulot.com).
Shopping & Cooking
Gin Go Gae p137
28 rue Lamartine,
9th (01.48.78.24.64).
Far Eastern
Gli Angeli p145
5 rue St-Gilles, 3rd
(01.42.71.05.80).
Italian
I Golosi p148
6 rue de la Grange-
Batelière, 9th
(01.48.24.18.63). Italian
Goumanyat p209
3 rue Dupuis, 3rd
(01.44.78.96.74/
www.goumanyat.com).
Shopping & Cooking
Goupil le Bistro p99
4 rue Claude Debussy,
17th (01.45.75.83.25).
French
Graindorge p99
15 rue de l'Arc de
Triomphe, 17th
(01.47.54.99.28/
www.legraindorge.free.fr).
French
Le Grand Colbert p26
2-4 rue Vivienne, 2nd
(01.42.86.87.88).
French
Le Grand Véfour p22
17 rue de Beaujolais,
1st (01.42.96.56.27).
French
La Grande Armée p94
3 av de la Grande-Armée,
16th (01.45.00.24.77).
French
La Grande Cascade p94
Pavillon de la Grande
Cascade, allée de
Longchamp, Bois
de Boulogne, 16th
(01.45.27.33.51).
French
**A la Grange
Batelière** p71
16 rue de la Grange
Batelière, 9th
(01.47.70.85.15). French

Granterroirs p116
30 rue de Miromesnil,
8th (01.47.42.18.18/
www.granterroirs.com).
Le Snacking
**Le Grenier
de Notre-Dame** p118
18 rue de la Bûcherie,
5th (01.43.29.98.29/
www.legrenierdenotre
dame.net). Vegetarian
Grizzli Café p170
7 rue St-Martin, 4th
(01.48.87.77.56).
Cafés, Bars & Pubs
Guenmai p118
6 rue Cardinale, 6th
(01.43.26.03.24).
Vegetarian
La Gueuze p172
19 rue Soufflot, 5th
(01.43.54.63.00/
www.la-gueuze.com).
Cafés, Bars & Pubs
Guy Savoy p99
18 rue Troyon, 17th
(01.43.80.40.61/
www.guysavoy.com). French

H

Han Lim p137
6 rue Blainville, 5th
(01.43.54.62.74).
Far Eastern
Le Hangar p31
12 impasse Berthaud, 3rd
(01.42.74.55.44). French
**Harry's New
York Bar** p168
5 rue Daunou, 2nd
(01.42.61.71.14/
www.harrys-bar.fr).
Cafés, Bars & Pubs
Hédiard p209
21 pl de la Madeleine,
8th (01.43.12.88.88/
www.hediard.fr).
Shopping & Cooking
**Hemingway Bar
at the Ritz** p166
Hôtel Ritz, 15 pl Vendôme,
1st (01.43.16.30.31/
www.ritzparis.com).
Cafés, Bars & Pubs
L'Hermitage p73
5 bd de Denain, 10th
(01.48.78.77.09). French
Higuma p150
32 bis rue Ste-Anne,
1st (01.47.03.38.59).
Japanese
Hiramatsu p94
52 rue de Longchamp,
16th (01.56.81.08.80/
www.hiramatsu.co.jp).
French
Histoire 2 p103
14 rue Ferdinand Flocon,
18th (01.42.52.24.60).
French
L'Homme Bleu p158
55 bis rue Jean-Pierre
Timbaud, 11th
(01.48.07.05.63).
North African
Hôtel Amour p111
8 rue Navarin, 9th
(01.48.78.31.80). Fashion

Hôtel Costes p108
239 rue St-Honoré,
1st (01.42.44.50.25/
www.hotelcostes.com).
Fashion

**Hôtel Plaza
Athénée** p179
25 av Montaigne, 8th
(01.53.67.65.65).
Cafés, Bars & Pubs

**Hôtel Plaza
Athénée** p194
25 av Montaigne, 8th
(01.53.67.66.65/www.
plaza-athenee-paris.com).
Tea Rooms

**Huilerie Artisanale
Leblanc** p209
6 rue Jacob, 6th
(01.46.34.61.55/
www.huile-leblanc.com).
Shopping & Cooking

Huîtrerie Régis p49
3 rue de Montfaucon, 6th
(01.44.41.10.07). French

L'Huîtrier p99
16 rue Saussier-Leroy,
17th (01.40.54.83.44).
French

I

Ice Kube p189
7 passage Ruelle,
18th (01.42.05.20.00).
Cafés, Bars & Pubs

Ile de Gorée p122
70 rue Jean-Pierre
Timbaud, 11th
(01.43.38.97.69).
African & Indian Ocean

Indiana Café p125
14 pl de la Bastille,
11th (01.44.75.79.80/
www.indiana.cafe.com).
The Americas

Isami p152
4 quai d'Orléans,
4th (01.40.46.06.97).
Japanese

**Isse Tempura
& Tapas** p150
45 rue de Richelieu,
1st (01.42.96.26.60).
Japanese

Izraël p207
30 rue François-Miron,
4th (01.42.72.66.23).
Shopping & Cooking

J

**Jabugo Ibérico
& Co** p207
11 rue Clément-Marot,
8th (01.47.20.03.13).
Shopping & Cooking

Jacques Mélac p200
42 rue Léon-Frot, 11th
(01.43.70.59.27/
www.melac.fr). Wine Bars

Jean p71
8 rue St-Lazare, 9th
(01.48.78.62.73). French

**Jean-Charles
Rochoux** p206
16 rue d'Assas, 6th
(01.42.84.29.45).
Shopping & Cooking

Jean-Paul Gardil p209
44 rue St-Louis en l'Ile,
4th (01.43.54.97.15).
Shopping & Cooking

Jean-Paul Hévin p191
231 rue St-Honoré,
1st (01.55.35.35.96).
Tea Rooms

Jean-Paul Hévin p206
3 rue Vavin, 6th
(01.43.54.09.85).
Shopping & Cooking

Le Jemmapes p182
82 quai de Jemmapes,
10th (01.40.40.02.35).
Cafés, Bars & Pubs

Jip's p167
41 rue St-Denis,
1st (01.42.21.33.93).
Cafés, Bars & Pubs

Joe Allen p124
30 rue Pierre Lescot,
1st (01.42.36.70.13/
www.joeallenparis.com).
The Americas

**Josephine
'Chez Dumonet'** p49
117 rue du Cherche-Midi,
6th (01.45.48.52.40).
French

Juan et Juanita p77
82 rue Jean-Pierre
Timbaud, 11th
(01.43.57.60.15). French

Le Jules Verne p58
2nd level, Eiffel Tower,
Champ de Mars, 7th
(01.45.55.61.44). French

Julien p73
16 rue du Fbg-St-Denis,
10th (01.47.70.12.06/
www.julienparis.com).
French

Julien, Caviste p211
50 rue Charlot, 3rd
(01.42.72.00.94).
Shopping & Cooking

Juvénile's p196
47 rue de Richelieu,
1st (01.42.97.46.49).
Wine Bars

K

Kai p150
18 rue du Louvre,
1st (01.40.15.01.99).
Japanese

Kastoori p141
4 pl Gustave Toudouze,
9th (01.44.53.06.10).
Indian

Kayser p205
8 & 14 rue Monge,
5th (01.44.07.01.42/
www.maisonkayser.com).
Shopping & Cooking

Kazaphani p131
122 av Parmentier,
11th (01.48.07.20.19).
Eastern Mediterranean

Khun Akorn p138
8 av de Taillebourg,
11th (01.43.56.20.03).
Far Eastern

Kibele p131
12 rue de l'Echiquier,
10th (01.48.24.57.74).
Eastern Mediterranean

Kifuné p153
44 rue St-Ferdinand,
17th (01.45.72.11.19).
Japanese

Kinugawa p151
9 rue du Mont-Thabor,
1st (01.42.60.65.07).
Japanese

Kioko p207
46 rue des Petits-Champs,
2nd (01.42.61.33.65).
Shopping & Cooking

Le Kiosque p95
1 pl de Mexico, 16th
(01.47.27.96.98). French

**Le Kiosque
Flottant 2** p203
quai de Montebello, 5th
(01.43.54.19.51). Eating
with Entertainment

Koutchi p162
40 rue du Cardinal
Lemoine, 5th
(01.44.07.20.56).
Other International

L

Ladurée p194
21 rue Bonaparte,
6th (01.44.07.64.87).
Tea Rooms

Laï Laï Ken p151
7 rue Ste-Anne, 1st
(01.40.15.96.90).
Japanese

Lao Siam p138
49 rue de Belleville,
19th (01.40.40.09.68).
Far Eastern

Lapérouse p49
51 quai des Grands-
Augustins, 6th
(01.43.26.68.04). French

Lasserre p64
17 av Franklin D Roosevelt,
8th (01.43.59.53.43/
www.lasserre.com).
French

Ledoyen p64
1 av Dutuit, 8th
(01.53.05.10.01). French

**Legrand Filles
et Fils** p211
1 rue de la Banque,
2nd (01.42.60.07.12/
www.caves-legrand.com).
Shopping & Cooking

Les 3 Frères p190
14 rue Léon, 18th
(01.42.64.91.73/
www.les3freres.net).
Cafés, Bars & Pubs

**Les 5 Saveurs
d'Anada** p117
72 rue du Cardinal-
Lemoine, 5th
(01.43.29.58.54).
Vegetarian

La Liberté p185
196 rue du Fbg-St-Antoine,
12th (01.43.72.11.18).
Cafés, Bars & Pubs

Le Lido p204
116 bis av des
Champs-Elysées, 1st
(01.40.76.56.10/
www.lido.fr). Eating
with Entertainment

Likafo p135
39 av de Choisy, 13th
(01.45.84.20.45).
Far Eastern

Liza p130
14 rue de la Banque,
2nd (01.55.35.00.66).
Eastern Mediterranean

Lizard Lounge p170
18 rue du Bourg-Tibourg,
4th (01.42.72.81.34).
Cafés, Bars & Pubs

**Le Loir
dans la Théière** p193
3 rue des Rosiers,
4th (01.42.72.90.61).
Tea Rooms

Le Lotus Blanc p140
45 rue de Bourgogne,
7th (01.45.55.18.89).
Far Eastern

Lou Pascalou p190
14 rue des Panoyaux,
20th (01.46.36.78.10).
Cafés, Bars & Pubs

Lush p188
16 rue des Dames,
17th (01.43.87.49.46/
www.lushbars.com).
Cafés, Bars & Pubs

M

Ma Bourgogne p34
19 pl des Vosges, 4th
(01.42.78.44.64). French

Macéo p22
15 rue des Petits-Champs,
1st (01.42.97.53.85/
www.maceorestaurant.
com). French

Le Mâchon d'Henri p50
8 rue Guisarde, 6th
(01.43.29.08.70). French

La Madonnina p149
10 rue Marie et Louise,
10th (01.42.01.25.26).
Italian

Maison Benisti p155
108 bd de Belleville,
20th (no phone). Jewish

Maison Blanche p110
15 av Montaigne,
8th (01.47.23.55.99).
Fashion

**La Maison
de la Lozère** p50
4 rueautefeuille, 6th
(01.43.54.26.64/
www.lozere-a-paris.com).
French

**La Maison
du Chocolat** p207
89 av Raymond-Poincaré,
16th (01.40.67.77.83/
www.lamaisonduchocolat.
com). Shopping & Cooking

**La Maison
du Whisky** p211
20 rue d'Anjou, 8th
(01.42.65.03.16/
www.whisky.fr).
Shopping & Cooking

**Man Ray
(Mandalaray)** p110
34 rue Marbeuf, 8th
(01.56.88.36.36/
www.mandalaray.com).
Fashion

Le Mansouria p158
11 rue Faidherbe,
11th (01.43.71.00.16).
North African

La Marée p65
1 rue Daru, 8th
(01.43.80.20.00/
www.lamaree.fr).
French

Margoa p143
7 rue Waldeck Rousseau,
17th (01.45.72.39.41).
Indian

Mariage Frères p193
30-32 rue du Bourg-
Tibourg, 4th
(01.42.72.28.11).
Tea Rooms

Marie-Anne Cantin p206
12 rue du Champ-de-Mars,
7th (01.45.50.43.94).
Shopping & Cooking

Le Marsangy p77
73 av Parmentier,
11th (01.47.00.94.25).
French

Le Martel p111
3 rue Martel, 10th
(01.47.70.67.56). Fashion

La Mascotte p103
52 rue des Abbesses,
18th (01.46.06.28.15/
www.la-mascotte-
montmartre.com). French

Mavrommatis p130
5 rue du Marché
des Patriarches, 5th
(01.43.31.17.17/
www.mavrommatis.fr).
Eastern Mediterranean

Mazeh p131
20 rue Marmontel,
15th (01.45.32.40.70).
Eastern Mediterranean

**Le Méchoui
du Prince** p157
34-36 rue Monsieur-
le-Prince, 6th
(01.43.25.09.71).
North African

La Méditérranée p51
2 pl de l'Odéon, 6th
(01.43.26.02.30/
www.la-mediterranee.com).
French

Le Melting Potes p200
16 rue des Trois-Bornes,
11th (01.43.38.61.75).
Wine Bars

Merry Monk p207
87 rue de la Convention,
15th (01.40.60.79.54).
Shopping & Cooking

Le Mesturet p27
77 rue de Richelieu,
2nd (01.42.97.40.68/
www.mesturet.com).
French

Le Meurice p22
Hôtel Meurice, 228
rue de Rivoli, 1st
(01.44.58.10.10/
www.lemeurice.fr). French

Mexi & Co p207
10 rue Dante, 5th
(01.46.34.14.12/
http://mexiandco.com).
Shopping & Cooking

**La Mezzanine
de l'Alcazar** p176
62 rue Mazarine, 6th
(01.53.10.19.99/
www.alcazar.fr).
Cafés, Bars & Pubs

Michel Rostang p100
20 rue Rennequin,
17th (01.47.63.40.77/
www.michelrostang.com).
French

Micky's Deli p154
23 bis rue des Rosiers, 4th
(01.48.04.79.31). Jewish

Le Mimosa p115
44 rue d'Argout, 2nd
(01.40.28.15.75).
Le Snacking

Mirama p133
17 rue St-Jacques,
5th (01.43.54.71.77).
Far Eastern

Moissonnier p41
28 rue des Fossés-St-
Bernard, 5th
(01.43.29.87.65). French

Mon Vieil Ami p34
69 rue St-Louis-en-l'Ile, 4th
(01.40.46.01.35). French

Le Mono p123
40 rue Véron, 18th
(01.46.06.99.20).
African & Indian Ocean

Mood p179
114 av des Champs-
Elysées, 8th
(01.42.89.98.89).
Cafés, Bars & Pubs

Mori Venice Bar p144
2 rue du Quatre
Septembre, 2nd
(01.44.55.51.55). Italian

Le Moulin à Vent p41
20 rue des Fossés-St-
Bernard, 5th
(01.43.54.99.37. French

**Le Moulin
de la Vierge** p205
166 av de Suffren, 15th
(01.47.83.45.55/
www.lemoulindelavierge.
com). Shopping & Cooking

Le Moulin Rouge p204
82 bd de Clichy,
18th (01.53.09.82.82/
www.moulin-rouge.com).
Eating with Entertainment

La Mousson p132
9 rue Thérèse, 1st
(01.42.60.59.46).
Far Eastern

Múkura p128
79 quai de Valmy,
10th (01.42.01.18.67).
The Americas

Le Murano p108
13 bd du Temple,
3rd (01.42.71.20.00).
Fashion

La Muse Vin p200
101 rue de Charonne,
11th (01.40.09.93.05).
Wine Bars

Nabuchodonosor p59
6 av Bosquet, 7th
(01.45.56.97.26). French

Natacha p87
17 bis rue Campagne-
Première, 14th
(01.43.20.79.27).
French

Le Nawab p143
174 rue Ordener,
18th (01.46.27.85.28).
Indian

Le Nemrod p176
51 rue du Cherche-Midi,
6th (01.45.48.17.05).
Cafés, Bars & Pubs

New Nioullaville p133
32-34 rue de l'Orillon,
11th (01.40.21.96.18).
Far Eastern

New Pondichery p142
189 rue du Fbg-St-Denis,
10th (01.40.34.30.70).
Indian

Odori p137
18 rue Letellier, 15th
(01.45.77.88.12).
Far Eastern

L'Oisive Thé p195
1 rue Jean-Marie Jego,
13th (01.53.80.31.33).
Tea Rooms

L'Opportun p88
64 bd Edgar Quinet, 14th
(01.43.20.26.29). French

L'Os à Moelle p89
3 rue Vasco-de-Gama,
15th (01.45.57.27.27).
French

L'Osteria p145
10 rue de Sévigné, 4th
(01.42.71.37.08). Italian

L'Oulette p81
15 pl Lachambeaudie,
12th (01.40.02.02.12/
www.l-oulette.com). French

L'Ourcine p84
92 rue Broca, 13th
(01.47.07.13.65). French

**P'tit Creux
du Faubourg** p180
66 rue du Fbg-Montmartre,
9th (01.48.78.20.57).
Cafés, Bars & Pubs

Le Pacifique p135
35 rue de Belleville,
20th (01.42.49.66.80).
Far Eastern

La Paella p161
50 rue des Vinaigriers,
10th (01.46.07.28.89).
Spanish

El Paladar p128
26 bis rue de la
Fontaine au Roi,
11th (01.43.57.42.70).
The Americas

El Palenque p127
5 rue de la Montagne-
Ste-Geneviève, 5th
(01.43.54.08.99).
The Americas

La Palette p176
43 rue de Seine, 6th
(01.43.26.68.15).
Cafés, Bars & Pubs

Le Pamphlet p31
38 rue Debelleyme, 3rd
(01.42.72.39.24). French

Le Pantalon p173
7 rue Royer-Collard,
5th (no phone). Cafés,
Bars & Pubs

Les Papilles p197
30 rue Gay-Lussac,
5th (01.43.25.20.79).
Wine Bars

Le Paprika p162
28 av Trudaine, 9th
(01.44.63.02.91).
Other International

Le Parc aux Cerfs p51
50 rue Vavin, 6th
(01.43.54.87.83). French

Paris Main d'Or p77
133 rue du Fbg-St-Antoine,
11th (01.44.68.04.68).
French

**Le Passage des
Carmagnoles** p78
18 passage de la
Bonne-Graine, 11th
(01.47.00.73.30). French

Le Passiflore p95
33 rue de Longchamp,
16th (01.47.04.96.81).
French

Pasta Linea p207
9 rue de Turenne, 4th
(01.42.77.62.54).
Shopping & Cooking

Le Patache p182
60 rue de Lancry,
10th (01.42.08.14.35).
Cafés, Bars & Pubs

Patrick Goldenberg p155
69 av Wagram, 17th
(01.42.27.34.79). Jewish

Patrick Roger p206
108 bd St-Germain,
6th (01.43.29.38.42).
Shopping & Cooking

Pause Café p183
41 rue de Charonne,
11th (01.48.06.80.33).
Cafés, Bars & Pubs

PDG p124
20 rue de Ponthieu,
8th (01.42.56.19.10).
The Americas

Pema Thang p139
13 rue de la Montagne
Ste-Geneviève, 5th
(01.43.54.34.34).
Far Eastern

Le Père Claude p89
51 av de la Motte-Picquet,
15th (01.47.34.03.05).
French

Le Père Fouettard p196
9 rue Pierre Lescot,
1st (01.42.33.74.17).
Wine Bars

Perraudin p41
157 rue St-Jacques,
5th (01.46.33.15.75).
French

Le Perron p147
6 rue Perronet, 7th
(01.45.44.71.51). Italian

**Le Petit
Château d'Eau** p182
34 rue du Château d'Eau,
10th (01.42.08.72.81).
Cafés, Bars & Pubs

Le Petit Chavignol   p201
78 rue de Tocqueville,
17th (01.42.27.95.97).
Wine Bars
**Le Petit Fer
à Cheval   p171**
30 rue Vieille-du-Temple,
4th (01.42.72.47.47).
Cafés, Bars & Pubs
Le Petit Marché   p31
9 rue de Béarn, 3rd
(01.42.72.06.67). French
Le Petit Pontoise   p41
9 rue de Pontoise, 5th
(01.43.29.25.20). French
Le Petit Saint-Benoît p51
4 rue St-Benoît, 6th
(01.42.60.27.92). French
La Petite Légume   p118
36 rue des Boulangers,
5th (01.40.46.06.85).
Vegetarian
Pétrelle   p71
34 rue Pétrelle, 9th
(01.42.82 11.02). French
Petrossian   p207
18 bd de la Tour-Maubourg,
7th (01.44.11.32.32).
Shopping & Cooking
Le Piano Vache   p173
8 rue Laplace, 5th
(01.46.33.75.03).
Cafés, Bars & Pubs
Le Pick-Clops   p171
16 rue Vieille-du-Temple,
4th (01.40.29.02.18).
Cafés, Bars & Pubs
Pierre Gagnaire   p65
6 rue Balzac, 8th
(01.58.36.12.50). French
Pierre Hermé   p207
72 rue Bonaparte,
6th (01.43.54.47.77).
Shopping & Cooking
Pitchi Poï   p154
7 rue Carron/9 pl du
Marché Ste-Catherine,
4th (01.42.77.46.15/
www.pitchipoi.com).
Jewish
La Plancha   p161
34 rue Keller, 11th
(01.48.05.20.30). Spanish
Planète Mars   p183
21 rue Keller, 11th
(01.43.14.24.44).
Cafés, Bars & Pubs
Le Plomb du Cantal p187
3 rue de la Gaîté, 14th
(01.43.35.16.92).
Cafés, Bars & Pubs
Poilâne   p205
8 rue du Cherche-Midi,
6th (01.45.48.42.59/
www.poilane.com).
Shopping & Cooking
**Poissonnerie
du Dôme   p209**
4 rue Delambre, 14th
(01.43.35.23.95).
Shopping & Cooking
Polichinelle Café   p183
64-66 rue de Charonne,
11th (01.58.30.63.52).
Cafés, Bars & Pubs
Le Polidor   p52
41 rue Monsieur-le-Prince,
6th (01.43.26.95.34).
French

Pomze   p65
109 bdaussman, 8th
(01.42.65.65.83). French
Pop In   p185
105 rue Amelot, 11th
(01.48.05.56.11).
Cafés, Bars & Pubs
O Por do Sol   p162
18 rue de la Fontaine-du-
But, 18th (01.42.23.90.26).
Other International
**Le Potager
du Marais   p117**
22 rue Rambuteau,
3rd (01.42.74.24.66).
Vegetarian
Le Pré Catelan   p95
rte de Suresnes,
Bois de Boulogne,
16th (01.44.14.41.14/
www.lenotre.fr). French
Le Pré Verre   p42
8 rue Thénard, 5th
(01.43.54.59.47). French
Le Président   p134
120-124 rue du Fbg-
du-Temple, 11th
(01.47.00.17.18).
Far Eastern
A Priori Thé   p192
35-37 galerie Vivienne,
2nd (01.42.97.48.75).
Tea Rooms
Le Purgatoire   p176
14 rueauteuille, 6th
(01.43.54.41.36).
Cafés, Bars & Pubs

Q

Le Quinzième   p112
14 rue Cauchy, 15th
(01.45.54.43.43). Fashion

R

Le Réconfort   p31
37 rue de Poitou, 3rd
(01.49.96.09.60). French
La Régalade   p88
49 av Jean-Moulin, 14th
(01.45.45.68.58). French
Le Reminet   p42
3 rue des Grands-Degrés,
5th (01.44.07.04.24).
French
**Rendez-Vous
des Quais   p190**
10-14 quai de Seine,
19th (01.40.37.02.81).
Cafés, Bars & Pubs
**Le Repaire
de Cartouche   p78**
99 rue Amelot/8 bd des
Filles-du-Calvaire, 11th
(01.47.00.25.86). French
Restaurant Al Wady p131
153-155 rue de Lourmel,
15th (01.45.58.57.18).
Eastern Mediterranean
**Restaurant
Cap Vernet   p66**
82 av Marceau, 8th
(01.47.20.20.40). French
**Restaurant
des Quatre Frères   p159**
127 bd de Ménilmontant,
11th (01.43.55.40.91).
North African

**Restaurant
du Palais-Royal   p23**
110 galerie Valois,
1st (01.40.20.00.27).
French
Restaurant Euro   p137
65 rue du Fbg-Montmartre,
9th (01.53.21.07.89).
Far Eastern
Restaurant GR5   p95
19 rue Gustave Courbet,
16th (01.47.27.09.84).
French
**Restaurant
Hélène Darroze   p52**
4 rue d'Assas, 6th
(01.42.22.00.11). French
**Restaurant
L'Entredgeu   p101**
83 rue Laugier, 17th
(01.40.54.97.24). French
**Restaurant
L'Hermès   p106**
23 rue Mélingue, 19th
(01.42.39.94.70). French
Restaurant Marty   p42
20 av des Gobelins, 5th
(01.43.31.39.51). French
Restaurant Pho   p139
3 rue Volta, 3rd
(01.42.78.31.70).
Far Eastern
**Restaurant Stéphane
Martin   p90**
67 rue des Entrepreneurs,
15th (01.45.79.03.31).
French
**Restaurant
Thierry Burlot   p90**
8 rue Nicolas-Charlet,
15th (01.42.19.08.59).
French
Restaurant Wadja   p53
10 rue de la Grande-
Chaumière, 6th
(01.46.33.02.02). French
Le Réveil du 10ème p182
35 rue du Château d'Eau,
10th (01.42.41.77.59).
Cafés, Bars & Pubs
Rhubarb   p173
18 rue Laplace, 5th
(01.43.25.35.03).
Cafés, Bars & Pubs
Ribouldingue   p42
10 rue St Julien le Pauvre,
5th (01.46.33.98.80).
French
Richart   p206
258 bd St-Germain,
7th (01.45.55.66.00).
Shopping & Cooking
Rio dos Camarãos p123
55 rue Marceau, 93100
Montreuil-sous-Bois
(01.42.87.34.84).
African & Indian Ocean
Ripaille   p101
69 rue des Dames,
17th (01.45.22.03.03).
French
Rose Bakery   p116
46 rue des Martyrs,
9th (01.42.82.12.80).
Le Snacking
Le Rostand   p177
6 pl Edmond-Rostand,
6th (01.43.54.61.58).
Cafés, Bars & Pubs

**La Rôtisserie
de Beaujolais   p43**
19 quai de la Tournelle, 5th
(01.43.54.17.47). French
**Rôtisserie
Ste-Marthe   p73**
4 rue Ste-Marthe, 10th
(01.40.03.08.30). French
**Rouammit
& Huong Lan   p138**
103 av d'Ivry, 13th
(01.53.60.00.34).
Far Eastern
Le Rouge Gorge   p197
8 rue St-Paul, 4th
(01.48.04.75.89).
Wine Bars
**Rouge
Saint-Honoré   p114**
34 pl du Marché-St-Honoré,
1st (01.42.61.16.09).
Le Snacking
Le Roussillon   p178
186 rue de Grenelle,
7th (01.45.51.47.53).
Cafés, Bars & Pubs
Ryst Dupeyron   p211
79 rue du Bac, 7th
(01.45.48.80.93).
Shopping & Cooking

S

Sadaharu Aoki   p207
35 rue de Vaugirard,
6th (01.45.44.48.90).
Shopping & Cooking
Le Sainte Marthe   p182
32 rue Ste-Marthe,
10th (01.44.84.36.96).
Cafés, Bars & Pubs
Sale e Pepe   p149
30 rue Ramey, 18th
(01.46.06.08.01). Italian
**Salon
Hélène Darroze   p53**
4 rue d'Assas, 6th
(01.42.22.00.11). French
Le Sancerre   p189
35 rue des Abbesses,
18th (01.42.58.08.20).
Cafés, Bars & Pubs
Sardegna a Tavola   p149
1 rue de Cotte, 12th
(01.44.75.03.28). Italian
Sarl Velan Stores   p207
87 passage Brady,
10th (01.42.46.06.06).
Shopping & Cooking
Savy   p66
23 rue Bayard, 8th
(01.47.23.46.98).
French
Scoop   p114
154 rue St-Honoré,
1st (01.42.60.31.84).
Le Snacking
Senderens   p67
9 pl de la Madeleine,
8th (01.42.65.22.90).
French
**Sens par la Compagnie
des Comptoirs   p110**
23 rue de Ponthieu,
8th (01.42.25.95.00).
Fashion
Le Sept/Quinze   p90
29 av Lowendal, 15th
(01.43.06.23.06). French

Index

Six-Huit p173
quai Montebello, 5th
(01.46.34.53.05).
Cafés, Bars & Pubs
Le Soufflé p23
36 rue du Mont-Thabor,
1st (01.42.60.27.19).
French
Le Souk p159
1 rue Keller, 11th
(01.49.29.05.08).
North African
La Soupière p101
154 av de Wagram,
17th (01.42.27.00.73).
French
**Spoon, Food
& Wine** p110
14 rue de Marignan,
8th (01.40.76.34.44).
Fashion
**Le Square
Trousseau** p81
1 rue Antoine-Vollon, 12th
(01.43.43.06.00). French
Le Stella p96
133 av Victorugo, 16th
(01.56.90.56.00). French
Stella Maris p67
4 rue Arsène-Houssaye, 8th
(01.42.89.16.22). French
Stolly's p171
16 rue Cloche-Perce,
4th (01.42.76.06.76).
Cafés, Bars & Pubs
Le Stresa p148
7 rue Chambiges, 8th
(01.47.23.51.62). Italian
Le Suffren p90
84 av de Suffren, 15th
(01.45.66.97.86). French

T

**Table d'Hôte
du Palais Royal** p23
8 rue du Beaujolais, 1st
(01.42.61.25.30). French
La Table Dancourt p103
4 rue Dancourt, 18th
(01.42.52.03.98). French
La Table de Babette p129
32 rue de Longchamp,
16th (01.45.53.00.07).
Caribbean
La Table de Fabrice p43
13 quai de la Tournelle, 5th
(01.44.07.17.57). French
**La Table
de Lauriston** p96
129 rue de Lauriston,
16th (01.47.27.00.07).
French
**La Table
de Robuchon** p96
16 av Bugeaud, 16th
(01.56.28.16.16). French
**La Table
du Lancaster** p68
Hôtel Lancaster, 7 rue de
Berri, 8th (01.40.76.40.18).
French
Le Tagine p159
13 rue de Crussol,
11th (01.47.00.28.67).
North African
Taillevent p68
15 rue Lamennais, 8th
(01.44.95.15.01). French

Takara p151
14 rue Molière, 1st
(01.42.96.08.38).
Japanese
Le Tambour p169
41 rue Montmartre,
2nd (01.42.33.06.90).
Cafés, Bars & Pubs
Tang Frères p207
48 av d'Ivry, 13th
(01.45.70.80.00).
Shopping & Cooking
**La Taverna
degli Amici** p147
16 rue du Bac, 7th
(01.42.60.37.74).
Italian
Taverne Henri IV p167
13 pl du Pont-Neuf,
1st (01.43.54.27.90).
Cafés, Bars & Pubs
Le Temps au Temps p78
13 rue Paul Bert, 11th
(01.43.79.63.40). French
**Le Temps
des Cerises** p34
31 rue de la Cerisaie, 4th
(01.42.72.08.63). French
Terminus Nord p74
23 rue de Dunkerque, 10th
(01.42.85.05.15). French
Terre de Truffes p209
21 rue Vignon, 8th
(01.53.43.80.44).
Shopping & Cooking
Thoumieux p59
79 rue St-Dominique, 7th
(01.47.05.49.75). French
Thuy Long p140
111 rue de Vaugirard,
6th (01.45.49.26.01).
Far Eastern
Le Timbre p53
3 rue Ste-Beuve, 6th
(01.45.49.10.40). French
Tokyo Eat p112
Palais de Tokyo, 13 av
du Président-Wilson, 16th
(01.47.20.00.29). Fashion
La Tonkinoise p140
20 rue Philibert Lucot,
13th (01.45.85.98.98).
Far Eastern
Les Tontons p187
38 rue Raymond
Losserand, 14th
(01.43.21.69.45).
Cafés, Bars & Pubs
Torréfacteur Verlet p209
256 rue St-Honoré,
1st (01.42.60.67.39).
Shopping & Cooking
La Tour d'Argent p43
15-17 quai de la Tournelle,
5th (01.43.54.23.31).
French
**La Tour de Montlhéry
(Chez Denise)** p24
5 rue des Prouvaires, 1st
(01.42.36.21.82). French
La Tourelle p169
43 rue Croix des
Petits Champs, 2nd
(01.42.61.35.41).
Cafés, Bars & Pubs
Le Tournesol p187
9 rue de la Gaîté, 14th
(01.43.27.65.72).
Cafés, Bars & Pubs

Le Train Bleu p82
Gare de Lyon, pl
Louis-Armand, 12th
(01.43.43.09.06). French
Trëma p163
8 rue de Marseille,
10th (01.42.49.27.67).
Other International
Tricotin p135
15 av de Choisy, 13th
(01.45.84.74.44).
Far Eastern
**Trois Pièces
Cuisine** p189
101 rue des Dames,
17th (01.44.90.85.10).
Cafés, Bars & Pubs
Le Troquet p91
21 rue François-Bonvin,
15th (01.45.66.89.00).
French
Le Trumilou p34
84 quai de l'Hôtel de Ville,
4th (01.42.77.63.98).
French

U

L'Uitr p91
1 pl Falguière, 15th
(01.47.34.12.24).
French
Un Jour à Peyrassol p27
13 rue Vivienne, 2nd
(01.42.60.12.92). French

V

Le V p63, p180
Hôtel Four Seasons
George V, 31 av George V,
8th (01.49.52.70.00).
French, Cafés, Bars & Pubs
Le Varenne p178
36 rue de Varenne,
7th (01.45.48.62.72).
Cafés, Bars & Pubs
Le Vaudeville p27
29 rue Vivienne, 2nd
(01.40.20.04.62. French
Velly p71
52 rue Lamartine, 9th
(01.48.78.60.05). French
Le Verre à Pied p173
118 bis rue Mouffetard,
5th (01.43.31.15.72).
Cafés, Bars & Pubs
Le Verre Volé p199
67 rue de Lancry,
10th (01.48.03.17.34).
Wine Bars
Viaduc Café p185
43 av Daumesnil,
12th (01.44.74.70.70).
Cafés, Bars & Pubs
**La Victoire Suprême
du Cœur** p117
41 rue des Bourdonnais,
1st (01.40.41.93.95).
Vegetarian
Le Vieux Bistro p37
14 rue du Cloître-
Notre-Dame, 4th
(01.43.54.18.95). French
**Le Village
d'Auteuil** p188
48 rue d'Auteuil, 16th
(01.42.88.00.18).
Cafés, Bars & Pubs

**Le Vin dans
les Voiles** p200
8 rue Chapu, 16th
(01.46.47.83.98).
Wine Bars
Vincent et Vincent p144
60 rue Jean-Jacques
Rousseau, 1st
(01.40.26.47.63). Italian
Le Violon d'Ingres p59
135 rue St-Dominique, 7th
(01.45.55.15.05). French
Le Violon Dingue p173
46 rue de la Montagne-
Ste-Geneviève, 5th
(01.43.25.79.93).
Cafés, Bars & Pubs
Le Voltaire p59
27 quai Voltaire, 7th
(01.42.61.17.49). French

W

Wally le Saharien p157
36 rue Rodier, 9th
(01.42.85.51.90).
North African
Waly Fay p122
6 rue Godefroy Cavaignac,
11th (01.40.24.17.79).
African & Indian Ocean
Le Wepler p104
14 pl de Clichy, 18th
(01.45.22.53.24).
Cafés, Bars & Pubs
Willi's Wine Bar p24
13 rue des Petits-Champs,
1st (01.42.61.05.09).
French
Wok p134
23 rue des Taillandiers,
11th (01.55.28.88.77).
Far Eastern
World Bar p180
64 bdaussmann, 9th
(01.42.82.78.02).
Cafés, Bars & Pubs

Y

Yen p153
22 rue St-Benoît, 6th
(01.45.44.11.18).
Japanese
Yugaraj p141
14 rue Dauphine, 6th
(01.43.26.44.91). Indian

Z

Ze Kitchen Galerie p54
4 rue des Grands-
Augustins, 6th
(01.44.32.00.32). French
Zébra Square p96
3 pl Clément Ader, 16th
(01.44.14.91.91). French
Le Zéphyr p107
1 rue du Jourdain, 20th
(01.46.36.65.81). French
Le Zéro Zéro p185
89 rue Amelot, 11th
(01.49.23.51.00). Cafés
Le Ziryab p156
L'Institut du Monde Arabe, 1
rue des Fossés St-Bernard,
5th (01.53.10.10.16).
North African
Les Zygomates p83
7 rue de Capri, 12th
(01.40.19.93.04). French

Arrondissement Index

1st arrondissement

The Americas

Joe Allen p124
30 rue Pierre Lescot,
1st (01.42.36.70.13/
www.joeallenparis.com)

Cafés, Bars & Pubs

Café Marly p166
93 rue de Rivoli, cour
Napoléon du Louvre,
1st (01.49.26.06.60)

Le Fumoir p166
6 rue de l'Admiral-de-
Coligny, 1st
(01.42.92.00.24/
www.lefumoir.com)

**Hemingway Bar
at the Ritz** p166
Hôtel Ritz, 15 pl Vendôme,
1st (01.43.16.30.31/
www.ritzparis.com)

Jip's p167
41 rue St-Denis, 1st
(01.42.21.33.93/
www.jipscafe.com)

Taverne Henri IV p167
13 pl du Pont-Neuf, 1st
(01.43.54.27.90)

Eating with Entertainment

Au Bec Fin p204
6 rue Thérèse, 1st
(01.42.96.29.35)

Le Lido p204
116 bis av des Champs-
Elysées, 1st
(01.40.76.56.10/
www.lido.fr)

Far Eastern

Chez Vong p133
10 rue de la Grande
Truanderie, 1st
(01.40.26.09.36)

Djakarta Bali p135
9 rue Vauvilliers, 1st
(01.45.08.83.11/
www.djakartabali.com)

La Mousson p132
9 rue Thérèse, 1st
(01.42.60.59.46)

Fashion

Hôtel Costes p108
239 rue St-Honoré,
1st (01.42.44.50.25)

French

L'Ardoise p20
28 rue du Mont-Thabor,
1st (01.42.96.28.18)

Au Pied de Cochon p23
6 rue Coquillière, 1st
(01.40.13.77.00/
www.pieddecochon.
com)

**Le Carré
des Feuillants** p20
14 rue de Castiglione,
1st (01.42.86.82.82/
www.carredesfeuillants.fr)

Chez La Vieille p21
1 rue Bailleul/37 rue
de l'Arbre-Sec, 1st
(01.42.60.15.78)

L'Espadon p21
Hôtel Ritz, 15 pl Vendôme,
1st (01.43.16.30.80/
www.ritzparis.com)

La Fresque p21
100 rue Rambuteau,
1st (01.42.33.17.56)

Le Grand Véfour p22
17 rue de Beaujolais,
1st (01.42.96.56.27)

Macéo p22
15 rue des Petits-Champs,
1st (01.42.97.53.85)

Le Meurice p22
Hôtel Meurice, 228
rue de Rivoli, 1st
(01.44.58.10.10/
www.lemeurice.fr)

**Restaurant
du Palais-Royal** p23
110 galerie Valois,
1st (01.40.20.00.27/
www.restaurantdu
palaisroyal.com)

Le Soufflé p23
36 rue du Mont-Thabor,
1st (01.42.60.27.19)

**Table d'Hôte du Palais
Royal** p23
8 rue du Beaujolais,
1st (01.42.61.25.30/
www.carollsinclair.com)

**La Tour de Montlhéry
(Chez Denise)** p24
5 rue des Prouvaires,
1st (01.42.36.21.82)

Willi's Wine Bar p24
13 rue des Petits-Champs,
1st (01.42.61.05.09/
www.williswinebar.com)

Italian

Vincent et Vincent p144
60 rue Jean-Jacques
Rousseau, 1st
(01.40.26.47.63/
www.vetv.fr)

Japanese

Higuma p150
32 bis rue Ste-Anne,
1st (01.47.03.38.59)

**Isse Tempura
& Tapas** p150
45 rue de Richelieu,
1st (01.42.96.26.60)

Kai p150
18 rue du Louvre, 1st
(01.40.15.01.99)

Kinugawa p151
9 rue du Mont-Thabor,
1st (01.42.60.65.07)

Laï Laï Ken p151
7 rue Ste-Anne, 1st
(01.40.15.96.90)

Takara p151
14 rue Molière, 1st
(01.42.96.08.38)

Other International

La Crypte Polska p162
1 pl Maurice Barrès,
1st (01.42.60.43.33)

Shopping & Cooking

Torréfacteur Verlet p209
256 rue St-Honoré,
1st (01.42.60.67.39)

Le Snacking

Bioboa p113
3 rue Danielle-Casanova,
1st (01.42.61.17.67)

La Ferme Opéra p113
55 rue St-Roch, 1st
(01.40.20.12.12)

Foody's Brunch Café p114
26 rue Montorgeuil,
1st (01.40.13.01.53)

Rouge Saint-Honoré p114
34 pl du Marché-St-Honoré,
1st (01.42.61.16.09)

Scoop p114
154 rue St-Honoré,
1st (01.42.60.31.84/
www.scoopcafe.com)

Tea Rooms

Angelina's p191
226 rue de Rivoli, 1st
(01.42.60.82.00)

Jean-Paul Hévin p191
231 rue St-Honoré, 1st
(01.55.35.35.96)

Vegetarian

**La Victoire
Suprême du Cœur** p117
41 rue des Bourdonnais,
1st (01.40.41.93.95)

Wine Bars

Juvénile's p196
47 rue de Richelieu,
1st (01.42.97.46.49)

Le Père Fouettard p196
9 rue Pierre Lescot,
1st (01.42.33.74.17)

2nd arrondissement

Cafés, Bars & Pubs

Le Café p167
62 rue Tiquetonne,
2nd (01.39.09.08.00)

Le Coeur Fou p168
55 rue Montmartre,
2nd (01.42.33.91.33)

Footsie p168
10-12 rue Daunou,
2nd (01.42.60.07.20)

The Frog & Rosbif p168
116 rue St-Denis,
2nd (01.42.36.34.73)

**Harry's New
York Bar** p168
5 rue Daunou, 2nd
(01.42.61.71.14/
www.harrys-bar.fr)

Le Tambour p169
41 rue Montmartre,
2nd (01.42.33.06.90)

La Tourelle p169
43 rue Croix des
Petits Champs, 2nd
(01.42.61.35.41)

Eastern Mediterranean

Liza p130
14 rue de la Banque,
2nd (01.55.35.00.66)

French

Angl'Opéra p24
39 av de l'Opéra, 2nd
(01.42.61.86.25/
www.anglopera.com)

Aux Lyonnais p26
32 rue St-Marc, 2nd
(01.42.96.65.04)

La Bourse ou la Vie p24
12 rue Vivienne, 2nd
(01.42.60.08.83)

Drouant p26
18 rue Gaillon, 2nd
(01.42.65.15.16/
www.drouant.com)

La Fontaine Gaillon p26
pl Gaillon, 2nd
(01.47.42.63.22/
www.la-fontaine-
gaillon.com)

Le Grand Colbert p26
2-4 rue Vivienne, 2nd
(01.42.86.87.88)

Le Mesturet p27
77 rue de Richelieu,
2nd (01.42.97.40.68)

Un Jour à Peyrassol p27
13 rue Vivienne, 2nd
(01.42.60.12.92/
www.peyrassol.com)

Le Vaudeville p27
29 rue Vivienne, 2nd
(01.40.20.04.62)

Indian

Gandhi-Opéra p141
66 rue Ste-Anne, 2nd
(01.47.03.41.00)

Italian

La Bocca p144
59-61 rue Montmartre,
2nd (01.42.36.71.88)

Index

Mori Venice Bar p144
2 rue du Quatre
Septembre, 2nd
(01.44.55.51.55)

Japanese

Bizan p152
56 rue Ste-Anne, 2nd
(01.42.96.67.76)

Shopping & Cooking

Kioko p207
46 rue des Petits-Champs,
2nd (01.42.61.33.65)

Legrand Filles et Fils p211
1 rue de la Banque, 2nd
(01.42.60.07.12/
www.caves-legrand.com)

Le Snacking

Le Mimosa p115
44 rue d'Argout, 2nd
(01.40.28.15.75)

Tea Rooms

A Priori Thé p192
35-37 galerie Vivienne,
2nd (01.42.97.48.75)

Wine Bars

Au Sans Souci p196
183 rue St-Denis, 2nd
(01.42.36.09.39)

3rd arrondissement

The Americas

Anahi p125
49 rue Volta, 3rd
(01.48.87.88.24)

Cafés, Bars & Pubs

Andy Wahloo p169
69 rue des Gravilliers,
3rd (01.42.71.20.38)

L'Apparemment
Café p169
18 rue des Coutures-St-
Gervais, 3rd (01.48.87.
12.22)

Le Connétable p169
55 rue des Archives,
3rd (01.42.77.41.40)

Far Eastern

Restaurant Pho p139
3 rue Volta, 3rd
(01.42.78.31.70)

Fashion

Le Murano p108
13 bd du Temple, 3rd
(01.42.71.20.00/
www.muranoresort.com)

French

L'Ambassade
d'Auvergne p29
22 rue du Grenier
St-Lazare, 3rd
(01.42.72.31.22)

L'Ami Louis p29
32 rue du Vertbois,
3rd (01.48.87.77.48)

Camille p29
24 rue des Francs-
Bourgeois, 3rd
(01.42.72.20.50)

Chez Jenny p29
39 bd du Temple,
3rd (01.44.54.39.00/
www.chez-jenny.com)

Les Chineurs p30
55 rue de Bretagne,
3rd (01.42.78.64.50)

Georget
(Robert et Louise) p30
64 rue Vieille-du-Temple,
3rd (01.42.78.55.89)

Le Hangar p31
12 impasse Berthaud,
3rd (01.42.74.55.44)

Le Pamphlet p31
38 rue Debelleyme,
3rd (01.42.72.39.24)

Le Petit Marché p31
9 rue de Béarn, 3rd
(01.42.72.06.67)

Le Réconfort p31
37 rue de Poitou, 3rd
(01.49.96.09.60)

Italian

Al Filo delle Stagione p144
8 rue de Beauce, 3rd
(01.48.04.52.24)

Gli Angeli p145
5 rue St-Gilles, 3rd
(01.42.71.05.80)

North African

404 p156
69 rue des Gravilliers,
3rd (01.42.74.57.81)

Chez Omar p156
47 rue de Bretagne,
3rd (01.42.72.36.26)

Shopping & Cooking

Goumanyat p209
3 rue Dupuis, 3rd
(01.44.78.96.74)

Julien, Caviste p211
50 rue Charlot, 3rd
(01.42.72.00.94)

Spanish

Caves Saint Gilles p160
4 rue St-Gilles, 3rd
(01.48.87.22.62)

Vegetarian

Le Potager
du Marais p117
22 rue Rambuteau,
3rd (01.42.74.24.66)

Wine Bars

Les Enfants Rouges p196
9 rue de Beauce, 3rd
(01.48.87.80.61)

L'Estaminet p197
Marché des Enfants
Rouges, 39 rue de
Bretagne, 3rd
(01.42.72.34.85/
www.aromes-et-cepages.fr)

4th arrondissement

The Americas

Breakfast in America p124
4 rue Malher, 4th
(01.42.72.40.21)

Calle 24 p127
13 rue Beautreillis,
4th (01.42.72.38.34)

Cafés, Bars & Pubs

Bubar p169
3 rue des Tournelles,
4th (01.40.29.97.72)

Chez Richard p169
37 rue Vieille-du-Temple,
4th (01.42.74.31.65)

L'Escale p170
1 rue des Deux-Ponts,
4th (01.43.54.94.23)

Les Etages p170
35 rue Vieille-du-Temple,
4th (01.42.78.72.00)

L'Etoile Manquante p170
34 rue Vieille-du-Temple,
4th (01.42.72.48.34/
www.cafeine.com)

Le Flore en l'Isle p170
42 quai d'Orléans,
4th (01.43.29.88.27)

Grizzli Café p170
7 rue St-Martin, 4th
(01.48.87.77.56)

Lizard Lounge p170
18 rue du Bourg-Tibourg,
4th (01.42.72.81.34/
www.hip-bars.com)

Le Petit Fer à Cheval p171
30 rue Vieille-du-Temple,
4th (01.42.72.47.47/
www.cafeine.com)

Le Pick-Clops p171
16 rue Vieille-du-Temple,
4th (01.40.29.02.18)

Stolly's p171
16 rue Cloche-Perce,
4th (01.42.76.06.76/
www.hip-bars.com)

**Eating with
Entertainment**

Bel Canto p204
72 quai de l'Hôtel de Ville,
4th (01.42.78.30.18/
www.lebelcanto.com)

Le Franc Pinot p204
1 quai de Bourbon,
4th (01.46.33.60.64)

Fashion

Curieux
Spaghetti Bar p108
14 rue St-Merri, 4th
(01.42.72.75.97)

Georges p109
Centre Pompidou, 6th floor,
rue Rambuteau, 4th
(01.44.78.47.99)

French

L'Alivi p31
27 rue du Roi-de-Sicile,
4th (01.48.87.90.20/
www.restaurant-alivi.com)

L'Ambroisie p32
9 pl des Vosges, 4th
(01.42.78.51.45)

Benoît p32
20 rue St-Martin, 4th
(01.42.72.25.76/
www.alain-ducasse.com)

Bofinger p32
5-7 rue de la Bastille,
4th (01.42.72.87.82/
www.bofingerparis.com)

Brasserie de
l'Isle St Louis p33
55 quai de Bourbon,
4th (01.43.54.02.59)

Café de la Poste p33
13 rue Castex, 4th
(01.42.72.95.35)

Coconnas p33
2 bis place des Vosges,
4th (01.42.78.58.16)

Le Dôme du Marais p33
53 bis rue des Francs-
Bourgeois, 4th
(01.42.74.54.17)

Ma Bourgogne p34
19 pl des Vosges, 4th
(01.42.78.44.64)

Mon Vieil Ami p34
69 rue St-Louis-en-l'Ile,
4th (01.40.46.01.35)

Le Temps des Cerises p34
31 rue de la Cerisaie,
4th (01.42.72.08.63)

Le Trumilou p34
84 quai de l'Hôtel de Ville,
4th (01.42.77.63.98)

Le Vieux Bistro p37
14 rue du Cloître-
Notre-Dame, 4th
(01.43.54.18.95/
www.lamaree.fr)

Italian

L'Osteria p145
10 rue de Sévigné,
4th (01.42.71.37.08)

Japanese

Isami p152
4 quai d'Orléans, 4th
(01.40.46.06.97)

Jewish

L'As du Fallafel p154
24 rue des Rosiers,
4th (01.48.87.63.60)

Chez Marianne p154
2 rue desospitalières-
St-Gervais, 4th
(01.42.72.18.86)

Micky's Deli p154
23 bis rue des Rosiers,
4th (01.48.04.79.31)

Pitchi Poï p154
7 rue Caron/9 pl du
Marché Ste-Catherine,
4th (01.42.77.46.15)

Shopping & Cooking

L'Epicerie p209
51 rue St-Louis-en-l'Ile,
4th (01.43.25.20.14)

Finkelsztajn p207
27 rue des Rosiers,
4th (01.42.72.78.91)

Izraël p207
30 rue François-Miron,
4th (01.42.72.66.23)

Jean-Paul Gardil p209
44 rue St-Louis en l'Ile,
4th (01.43.54.97.15)

Pasta Linea **p207**
9 rue de Turenne, 4th
(01.42.77.62.54)

Tea Rooms

Le Loir
dans la Théière **p193**
3 rue des Rosiers,
4th (01.42.72.90.61)

Mariage Frères **p193**
30-32 rue du Bourg-
Tibourg, 4th
(01.42.72.28.11)

Wine Bars

La Belle
Hortense **p197**
31 rue Vieille-du-Temple,
4th (01.48.04.71.60/
www.cafeine.com)

L'Enoteca **p197**
25 rue Charles V, 4th
(01.42.78.91.44)

Le Rouge Gorge **p197**
8 rue St-Paul, 4th
(01.48.04.75.89)

5th arrondissement

The Americas

Anahuacalli **p127**
30 rue des Bernadins,
5th (01.43.26.10.20)

Botequim **p127**
1 rue Berthollet, 5th
(01.43.37.98.46)

El Palenque **p127**
5 rue de la Montagne-
Ste-Geneviève, 5th
(01.43.54.08.99)

Cafés, Bars & Pubs

The Bombardier **p171**
2 pl du Panthéon, 5th
(01.43.54.79.22)

Café Delmas **p172**
2-4 pl de la Contrescarpe,
5th (01.43.26.51.26)

Café Léa **p172**
5 rue Claude Bernard,
5th (01.43.31.46.30)

Le Crocodile **p172**
6 rue Royer-Collard,
5th (01.43.54.32.37)

La Gueuze **p172**
19 rue Soufflot, 5th
(01.43.54.63.00/
www.la-gueuze.com)

Le Pantalon **p173**
7 rue Royer-Collard,
5th (no phone)

Le Piano Vache **p173**
8 rue Laplace, 5th
(01.46.33.75.03)

Rhubarb **p173**
18 rue Laplace, 5th
(01.43.25.35.03)

Six-Huit **p173**
quai Montebello, 5th
(01.46.34.53.05/
www.six-huit.com)

Le Verre à
Pied **p173**
118 bis rue Mouffetard,
5th (01.43.31.15.72)

Le Violon Dingue **p173**
46 rue de la Montagne-
Ste-Geneviève, 5th
(01.43.25.79.93)

**Eastern
Mediterranean**

Mavrommatis **p130**
5 rue du Marché
des Patriarches, 5th
(01.43.31.17.17/
www.mavrommatis.fr)

**Eating with
Entertainment**

La Balle au Bond **p203**
(01.40.46.85.12/
www.laballeaubond.fr)

Le Caveau
des Oubliettes **p204**
52 rue Galande, 5th
(01.46.34.23.09)

Le Kiosque
Flottant 2 **p203**
quai de Montebello,
5th (01.43.54.19.51)

Far Eastern

Han Lim **p137**
6 rue Blainville, 5th
(01.43.54.62.74)

Mirama **p133**
17 rue St-Jacques, 5th
(01.43.54.71.77)

Pema Thang **p139**
13 rue de la Montagne
Ste-Geneviève, 5th
(01.43.54.34.34/
www.pemathang.
aol.com)

French

L'AOC **p37**
14 rue des Fossés-
St-Bernard, 5th
(01.43.54.22.52/
www.restoaoc.com)

Le Balzar **p37**
49 rue des Ecoles,
5th (01.43.54.13.67/
www.groupflo.fr)

Chez Léna et Mimile **p37**
32 rue Tournefort, 5th
(01.47.07.72.47/
www.chezlenaet
mimile.com)

Chez René **p38**
14 bd St-Germain,
5th (01.43.54.30.23)

Christophe **p38**
8 rue Descartes,
5th (01.43.26.72.49)

Le Cosi **p38**
9 rue Cujas, 5th
(01.43.29.20.20)

L'Ecurie **p38**
2 rue Laplace, 5th
(01.46.33.68.49)

L'Equitable **p38**
1 rue des Fossés-
St-Marcel, 5th
(01.43.31.69.20)

Moissonnier **p41**
28 rue des Fossés-
St-Bernard, 5th
(01.43.29.87.65)

Le Moulin à Vent **p41**
20 rue des Fossés-
St-Bernard, 5th
(01.43.54.99.37/
www.au-moulinavent.com)

Perraudin **p41**
157 rue St-Jacques,
5th (01.46.33.15.75)

Le Petit Pontoise **p41**
9 rue de Pontoise,
5th (01.43.29.25.20)

Le Pré Verre **p42**
8 rue Thénard, 5th
(01.43.54.59.47)

Le Reminet **p42**
3 rue des Grands-Degrés,
5th (01.44.07.04.24)

Restaurant Marty **p42**
20 av des Gobelins,
5th (01.43.31.39.51)

Ribouldingue **p42**
10 rue St Julien le Pauvre,
5th (01.46.33.98.80)

La Rôtisserie
de Beaujolais **p43**
19 quai de la Tournelle,
5th (01.43.54.17.47)

La Table de Fabrice **p43**
13 quai de la Tournelle,
5th (01.44.07.17.57/
www.latabledefabrice.fr)

La Tour d'Argent **p43**
15-17 quai de la Tournelle,
5th (01.43.54.23.31/
www.tourdargent.com)

Japanese

Asia-Tée **p152**
47 rue de la Montagne
Ste-Geneviève, 5th
(01.43.26.39.90)

North African

Le Ziryab **p156**
L'Institut du Monde
Arabe, 1 rue des Fossés
St-Bernard, 5th
(01.53.10.10.16)

Other International

Koutchi **p162**
40 rue du Cardinal
Lemoine, 5th
(01.44.07.20.56)

Shopping & Cooking

Le Boulanger
de Monge **p205**
123 rue Monge, 5th
(01.43.37.54.20/
www.boulanger
demonge.com)

Kayser **p205**
8 & 14 rue Monge, 5th
(01.44.07.01.42/
01.44.07.17.18/
www.maisonkayser.com)

Mexi & Co **p207**
10 rue Dante, 5th
(01.46.34.14.12)

Tea Rooms

Café Maure de la
Mosquée de Paris **p193**
39 rue Geoffroy St-Hilaire,
5th (01.43.31.38.20)

Vegetarian

Les 5 Saveurs
d'Anada **p117**
72 rue du Cardinal-
Lemoine, 5th
(01.43.29.58.54/
www.anada5saveurs.com)

Le Grenier de
Notre-Dame **p118**
18 rue de la Bûcherie,
5th (01.43.29.98.29/
www.legrenierdenotre
dame.net)

La Petite Légume **p118**
36 rue des Boulangers,
5th (01.40.46.06.85)

Wine Bars

Caves La Bourgogne **p197**
144 rue Mouffetard,
5th (01.47.07.82.80)

Les Papilles **p197**
30 rue Gay-Lussac,
5th (01.43.25.20.79)

6th arrondissement

Cafés, Bars & Pubs

Au Vieux Colombier **p177**
65 rue de Rennes,
6th (01.45.48.53.81)

Le Bar **p173**
27 rue de Condé, 6th
(01.43.29.06.61)

Le Bar Dix **p175**
10 rue de l'Odéon, 6th
(01.43.26.66.83)

Bar du Marché **p175**
75 rue de Seine, 6th
(01.43.26.55.15)

Café de Flore **p175**
172 bd St-Germain,
6th (01.45.48.55.26/
www.cafe-de-flore.com)

Café de la Mairie **p175**
8 pl St-Sulpice, 6th
(01.43.26.67.82)

Le Comptoir
des Canettes **p175**
11 rue des Canettes,
6th (01.43.26.79.15)

Coolin **p176**
15 rue Clément, 6th
(01.44.07.00.92)

Les Deux Magots **p176**
6 pl St-Germain-des-Prés,
6th (01.45.48.55.25/
www.lesdeuxmagots.
com)

La Mezzanine
de l'Alcazar **p176**
62 rue Mazarine, 6th
(01.53.10.19.99/
www.alcazar.fr)

Le Nemrod **p176**
51 rue du Cherche-Midi,
6th (01.45.48.17.05)

La Palette **p176**
43 rue de Seine, 6th
(01.43.26.68.15)

Le Purgatoire **p176**
14 rueautefeuille, 6th
(01.43.54.41.36/
www.lepurgatoire.com)

Le Rostand p177
6 pl Edmond-Rostand,
6th (01.43.54.61.58)

Far Eastern

Thuy Long p140
111 rue de Vaugirard,
6th (01.45.49.26.01)

French

Alcazar p43
62 rue Mazarine, 6th
(01.53.10.19.99/
www.alcazar.fr)

Allard p44
41 rue St-André-des-Arts,
6th (01.43.26.48.23)

Au Bon Saint-Pourçain p44
10 bis rue Servandoni,
6th (01.43.54.93.63)

Aux Charpentiers p46
10 rue Mabillon, 6th
(01.43.26.30.05)

Aux Saveurs
de Claude p53
12 rue Stanislas,
6th (01.45.44.41.74/
www.auxsaveursde
claude.fr)

La Bastide Odéon p44
7 rue Corneille, 6th
(01.43.26.03.65/
www.bastide-odeon.com)

Les Bouquinistes p46
53 quai des Grands-
Augustins, 6th
(01.43.25.45.94/
www.lesbouquinistes.com)

Boucherie Roulière p44
24 rue des Canettes,
6th (01.43.26.25.70)

Bouillon Racine p46
3 rue Racine, 6th
(01.44.32.15.60/
www.bouillon-racine.com)

Brasserie Lipp p46
151 bd St-Germain, 6th
(01.45.48.53.91/
www.brasserielipp.com)

Chez Maître Paul p47
12 rue Monsieur-le-Prince,
6th (01.43.54.74.59/
www.chezmaitrepaul.com)

Chez Marcel p47
7 rue Stanislas, 6th
(01.45.48.29.94)

La Closerie des Lilas p47
171 bd du Montparnasse,
6th (01.40.51.34.50)

Le Comptoir du Relais p47
9 carrefour de l'Odéon,
6th (01.44.27.07.50)

L'Epi Dupin p49
11 rue Dupin, 6th
(01.42.22.64.56)

La Ferrandaise p49
8 rue de Vaugirard, 6th
(01.43.26.36.36)

Huîtrerie Régis p49
3 rue de Montfaucon,
6th (01.44.41.10.07)

Josephine
'Chez Dumonet' p49
117 rue du Cherche-Midi,
6th (01.45.48.52.40)

Lapérouse p49
51 quai des Grands-
Augustins, 6th
(01.43.26.68.04)

Le Mâchon d'Henri p50
8 rue Guisarde, 6th
(01.43.29.08.70)

La Maison
de la Lozère p50
4 rueautefeuille, 6th
(01.43.54.26.64/
www.lozere-a-paris.com)

La MédItérranée p51
2 pl de l'Odéon, 6th
(01.43.26.02.30/
www.la-mediterranee.com)

Le Parc aux Cerfs p51
50 rue Vavin, 6th
(01.43.54.87.83)

Le Petit Saint-Benoît p51
4 rue St-Benoît, 6th
(01.42.60.27.92)

Le Polidor p52
41 rue Monsieur-le-Prince,
6th (01.43.26.95.34)

Restaurant
Hélène Darroze p52
4 rue d'Assas, 6th
(01.42.22.00.11)

Restaurant Wadja p53
10 rue de la Grande-
Chaumière, 6th
(01.46.33.02.02)

Salon Hélène
Darroze p53
4 rue d'Assas, 6th
(01.42.22.00.11)

Le Timbre p53
3 rue Ste-Beuve, 6th
(01.45.49.10.40)

Ze Kitchen Galerie p54
4 des Grands-
Augustins, 6th
(01.44.32.00.32/
www.zekitchengalerie.fr)

Indian

Yugaraj p141
14 rue Dauphine, 6th
(01.43.26.44.91/
www.yugaraj.com)

Italian

Chez Bartolo p147
7 rue des Canettes,
6th (01.43.26.27.08)

Japanese

Azabu p153
3 rue André-Mazet,
6th (01.46.33.72.05)

Yen p153
22 rue St-Benoît, 6th
(01.45.44.11.18)

North African

Le Méchoui du Prince p157
34-36 rue Monsieur-le-
Prince, 6th
(01.43.25.09.71)

Other International

Dominique p163
19 rue Bréa, 6th
(01.43.27.08.80)

Shopping & Cooking

Da Rosa p209
62 rue de Seine, 6th
(01.40.51.00.09)

Gérard Mulot p207
76 rue de Seine, 6th
(01.43.26.85.77/
www.gerard-mulot.com)

Huilerie
Artisanale Leblanc p209
6 rue Jacob, 6th
(01.46.34.61.55/
www.huile-leblanc.com)

Jean-Charles
Rochoux p206
16 rue d'Assas, 6th
(01.42.84.29.45)

Jean-Paul Hévin p206
3 rue Vavin, 6th
(01.43.54.09.85/
www.jphevin.com)

Patrick Roger p206
108 bd St-Germain,
6th (01.43.29.38.42/
www.patrickroger.com)

Pierre Hermé p207
72 rue Bonaparte, 6th
(01.43.54.47.77)

Poilâne p205
8 rue du Cherche-Midi,
6th (01.45.48.42.59/
www.poilane.com)

Sadaharu Aoki p207
35 rue de Vaugirard,
6th (01.45.44.48.90/
www.sadaharuaoki.
com)

Le Snacking

Bread & Roses p115
7 rue de Fleurus, 6th
(01.42.22.06.06)

Spanish

Fogón Saint-Julien p160
45 quai des Grands-
Augustins, 6th
(01.43.54.31.33)

Tea Rooms

L'Artisan de
Saveurs p193
72 rue du Cherche-Midi,
6th (01.42.22.46.64)

Chez les Filles p193
64 rue du Cherche-Midi,
6th (01.45.48.61.54)

Forêt Noire p194
9 rue de l'Eperon, 6th
(01.44.41.00.09)

Ladurée p194
21 rue Bonaparte, 6th
(01.44.07.64.87)

Vegetarian

Guenmaï p118
6 rue Cardinale, 6th
(01.43.26.03.24)

Wine Bars

Caves Miard p198
9 rue des Quatre-Vents,
6th (01.43.54.99.30)

Fish p198
69 rue de Seine, 6th
(01.43.54.34.69)

7th arrondissement

Cafés, Bars & Pubs

Bar Basile p177
34 rue de Grenelle,
7th (01.42.22.59.46)

Café des Lettres p178
53 rue de Verneuil,
7th (01.42.22.52.17)

Le Café du Marché p178
38 rue Cler, 7th
(01.47.05.51.27)

Café Thoumieux p178
4 rue de la Comète,
7th (01.45.51.50.40/
www.thoumieux.com)

Le Roussillon p178
186 rue de Grenelle,
7th (01.45.51.47.53/
www.caferoussillon.com)

Le Varenne p178
36 rue de Varenne,
7th (01.45.48.62.72)

**Eating with
Entertainment**

Bateaux Parisiens p203
Port de La Bourdonnais,
7th (01.44.11.33.44/
meal reservations
01.44.11.33.55/
www.bateauxparisiens.com)

Far Eastern

Le Lotus Blanc p140
45 rue de Bourgogne,
7th (01.45.55.18.89)

French

Le 144 Petrossian p54
18 bd de La Tour-
Maubourg, 7th
(01.44.11.32.32)

Altitude 95 p54
1st level, Eiffel Tower,
Champ de Mars, 7th
(01.45.55.20.04/
www.altitude-95eleor.com)

L'Arpège p54
84 rue de Varenne,
7th (01.45.51.47.33/
www.alain-passard.com)

L'Atelier de Joël Robuchon
p55
5 rue de Montalembert,
7th (01.42.22.56.56)

Au Bon Accueil p55
14 rue Monttessuy,
7th (01.47.05.46.11)

Le Café Constant p55
139 rue St-Dominique,
7th (01.47.53.73.34)

Le Chamarré p55
13 bd de La Tour-Maubourg,
7th (01.47.05.50.18)

Chez Germaine p56
30 rue Pierre-Leroux,
7th (01.42.73.28.34)

Chez l'Ami Jean p56
27 rue Malar, 7th
(01.47.05.86.89)

Chez les Anges p56
54 bd La Tour-Maubourg,
7th (01.47.05.89.86/
www.chezlesanges.com)

Index

Cinq Mars p58
51 rue de Verneuil,
7th (01.45.44.69.13)

Le Clos des Gourmets p58
16 av Rapp, 7th
(01.45.51.75.61)

D'Chez Eux p56
2 av de Lowendal,
7th (01.47.05.52.55)

**Les Fables
de la Fontaine** p58
131 rue St-Dominique,
7th (01.44.18.37.55)

Gaya Rive Gauche p58
44 rue du Bac, 7th
(01.45.44.73.73)

Le Jules Verne p58
2nd level, Eiffel Tower,
Champ de Mars, 7th
(01.45.55.61.44)

Nabuchodonosor p59
6 av Bosquet, 7th
(01.45.56.97.26)

Thoumieux p59
79 rue St-Dominique,
7th (01.47.05.49.75/
www.thoumieux.com)

Le Violon d'Ingres p59
135 rue St-Dominique,
7th (01.45.55.15.05/
www.leviolondingres.com)

Le Voltaire p59
27 quai Voltaire, 7th
(01.42.61.17.49)

Italian

Café Minotti p147
33 rue de Verneuil,
7th (01.42.60.04.04)

Le Perron p147
6 rue Perronet, 7th
(01.45.44.71.51)

**La Taverna
degli Amici** p147
16 rue du Bac, 7th
(01.42.60.37.74)

Shopping & Cooking

**Fromagerie
Quatrehomme** p205
62 rue de Sèvres, 7th
(01.47.34.33.45)

Marie-Anne Cantin p206
12 rue du Champ-de-Mars,
7th (01.45.50.43.94)

Petrossian p207
18 bd de la Tour-Maubourg,
7th (01.44.11.32.32/
www.petrossian.fr)

Richart p206
258 bd St-Germain,
7th (01.45.55.66.00/
www.richart.com)

Ryst Dupeyron p211
79 rue du Bac, 7th
(01.45.48.80.93)

Le Snacking

Delicabar p115
1st floor, Bon Marché-Rive
Gauche, above the
Grande Epicerie de Paris,
26-38 rue de Sèvres,
7th (01.42.22.10.12/
www.delicabar.fr)

Spanish

Bellota-Bellota p160
18 rue Jean-Nicot, 7th
(01.53.59.96.96/
www.bellota-bellota.com)

Tea Rooms

Les Deux Abeilles p194
189 rue de l'Université,
7th (01.45.55.64.04)

8th arrondissement

The Americas

PDG p124
20 rue de Ponthieu,
8th (01.42.56.19.10)

Cafés, Bars & Pubs

Atelier Renault p178
53 av des Champs-Elysées,
8th (01.49.53.70.00/
www.atelier-renault.com)

Bar des Théâtres p179
6 av Montaigne, 8th
(01.47.23.34.63)

The Bowler p179
13 rue d'Artois, 8th
(01.45.61.16.60/
www.thebowlerpub.com)

Hôtel Plaza Athénée p179
25 av Montaigne, 8th
(01.53.67.65.65)

Mood p179
114 av des Champs-
Elysées, 8th
(01.42.89.98.89)

Le V p180
Hôtel Four Seasons
George V, 31 av George V,
8th (01.49.52.70.00)

**Eating with
Entertainment**

Bateaux-Mouches p203
Pont de l'Alma, rive droite,
8th (01.42.25.96.10/
recorded information
01.40.76.99.99/
www.bateaux-mouches.fr)

Fashion

Black Calvados p109
40 rue Pierre 1er de Serbie,
8th (01.47.20.77.77/
www.bc-paris.fr)

Le Buddha Bar p109
8 rue Boissy d'Anglas,
8th (01.53.05.90.00/
www.buddha-bar.com)

Maison Blanche p110
15 av Montaigne,
8th (01.47.23.55.99/
www.maison-blanche.fr).
Fashion

**Man Ray
(Mandalaray)** p110
34 rue Marbeuf, 8th
(01.56.88.36.36/
www.mandalaray.com)

**Sens par la Compagnie
des Comptoirs** p110
23 rue de Ponthieu, 8th
(01.42.25.95.00/
www.lacompagniedes
comptoirs)

Spoon, Food & Wine p110
14 rue de Marignan,
8th (01.40.76.34.44)

French

**Alain Ducasse
au Plaza Athénée** p43
Hôtel Plaza Athénée,
25 av Montaigne, 8th
(01.53.67.65.00/
www.alain-ducasse.com).

Les Ambassadeurs p60
Hôtel de Crillon,
10 pl de la Concorde,
8th (01.44.71.16.17/
www.crillon.com)

L'Angle du Faubourg p61
195 rue du Fbg-St-Honoré,
8th (01.40.74.20.20/
www.taillevent.com)

Le Bistro de Marius p61
6 av George V, 8th
(01.40.70.11.76)

**Le Bistrot
du Sommelier** p62
97 bdaussmann, 8th
(01.42.65.24.85)

Le Boeuf sur le Toit p62
34 rue du Colisée, 8th
(01.53.93.65.55/
www.boeufsurletoit.com)

Le Bristol p62
Hôtel Bristol, 112 rue
du Fbg-St-Honoré,
8th (01.53.43.43.00/
www.lebristolparis.com)

**Chez Cecile:
La Ferme
des Mathurins** p62
17 rue Vignon, 8th
(01.42.66.46.39)

Le Cou de la Girafe p63
7 rue Paul Baudry, 8th
(01.56.88.29.55)

**Fermette
Marbeuf 1900** p63
5 rue Marbeuf, 8th
(01.53.23.08.00/
www.fermettemarbeuf.com)

Flora p63
36 av George V, 8th
(01.40.70.10.49)

Fouquet's p64
99 av des Champs-Elysées,
8th (01.47.23.70.60/
www.lucienbarriere.com)

Garnier p64
111 rue St-Lazare, 8th
(01.43.87.50.40)

Lasserre p64
17 av Franklin D Roosevelt,
8th (01.43.59.53.43/
www.lasserre.com)

Ledoyen p64
1 av Dutuit, 8th
(01.53.05.10.01)

La Marée p65
1 rue Daru, 8th
(01.43.80.20.00/
www.lamaree.fr)

Pierre Gagnaire p65
6 rue Balzac, 8th
(01.58.36.12.50/
www.pierre-gagnaire.com)

Pomze p65
109 bdaussman, 8th
(01.42.65.65.83/
www.pomze.com)

**Restaurant
Cap Vernet** p66
82 av Marceau, 8th
(01.47.20.20.40)

Savy p66
23 rue Bayard, 8th
(01.47.23.46.98)

Senderens p67
9 pl de la Madeleine,
8th (01.42.65.22.90)

Stella Maris p67
4 rue Arsène-Houssaye,
8th (01.42.89.16.22/
www.stellamarisparis.com)

La Table du Lancaster p68
Hôtel Lancaster,
7 rue de Berri, 8th
(01.40.76.40.18/
www.hotel-lancaster.fr)

Taillevent p68
15 rue Lamennais,
8th (01.44.95.15.01/
www.taillevent.com)

Le V p63
Hôtel Four Seasons George
V, 31 av George V, 8th
(01.49.52.70.00/
www.fourseasons.com)

Italian

Le Bistrot Napolitain p147
18 av Franklin-D-Roosevelt,
8th (01.45.62.08.37)

Le Stresa p148
7 rue Chambiges, 8th
(01.47.23.51.62)

Shopping & Cooking

Fauchon p209
26-30 pl de la Madeleine,
8th (01.47.42.60.11/
www.fauchon.com)

Hédiard p209
21 pl de la Madeleine,
8th (01.43.12.88.88/
www.hediard.fr)

Jabugo Ibérico & Co p207
11 rue Clément-Marot,
8th (01.47.20.03.13)

Les Caves Augé p211
116 bdaussmann,
8th (01.45.22.16.97)

Les Caves Taillevent p211
199 rue du Fbg-St-Honoré,
8th (01.45.61.14.09/
www.taillevent.com)

**La Maison
du Whisky** p211
20 rue d'Anjou, 8th
(01.42.65.03.16/
www.whisky.fr)

Terre de Truffes p209
21 rue Vignon, 8th
(01.53.43.80.44/
http://terredetruffes.
coreis.fr)

Le Snacking

Al-Diwan p115
30 av George V, 8th
(01.47.20.72.00)

Index

Granterroirs p116
30 rue de Miromesnil,
8th (01.47.42.18.18/
www.granterroirs.com)

Tea Rooms

Le Bristol p194
112 rue du Fbg-St-Honoré,
8th (01.53.43.43.00/
www.lebristolparis.com)

Hôtel Plaza Athénée p194
25 av Montaigne, 8th
(01.53.67.66.65/
www.plaza-athenee-
paris.com)

Wine Bars

L'Ecluse Madeleine p198
15 pl de la Madeleine,
8th (01.42.65.34.69/
www.leclusebaravin.com)

9th arrondissement

Cafés, Bars & Pubs

Café de la Paix p180
place de l'Opéra, 9th
(01.40.07.36.36)

Général Lafayette p180
52 rue Lafayette, 9th
(01.47.7.59.08)

P'tit Creux
du Faubourg p180
66 rue du Fbg-Montmartre,
9th (01.48.78.20.57)

World Bar p180
Fifth floor, Printemps de
l'Homme, 64 bdaussmann,
9th (01.42.82.78.02)

Far Eastern

Gin Go Gae p137
28 rue Lamartine, 9th
(01.48.78.24.64)

Restaurant Euro p137
65 rue du Fbg-Montmartre,
9th (01.53.21.07.89)

Fashion

Hôtel Amour p111
8 rue Navarin, 9th
(01.48.78.31.80)

French

L'Auberge du Clou p68
30 av Trudaine, 9th
(01.48.78.22.48)

Casa Olympe p69
48 rue St-Georges, 9th
(01.42.85.26.01)

Le Ch'ti Catalan p69
4 rue Navarin, 9th
(01.44.63.04.33)

Charlot, Roi des
Coquillages p69
81 bd de Clichy, 9th
(01.53.20.48.00)

Chartier p69
7 rue du Fbg-Montmartre,
9th (01.47.70.86.29)

Chez Corto p69
47 rue Rodier, 9th
(01.49.95.96.80)

Georgette p70
29 rue St-Georges, 9th
(01.42.80.39.13)

Jean p71
8 rue St-Lazare, 9th
(01.48.78.62.73)

A la Cloche d'Or p70
3 rue Mansart, 9th
(01.48.74.48.88/
www.alacloche
dor.com)

A la Grange Batelière p71
16 rue de la Grange
Batelière, 9th
(01.47.70.85.15)

Pétrelle p71
34 rue Pétrelle, 9th
(01.42.82 11.02)

Velly p71
52 rue Lamartine, 9th
(01.48.78.60.05)

Indian

Kastoori p141
4 pl Gustave Toudouze,
9th (01.44.53.06.10)

Italian

I Golosi p148
6 rue de la Grange-
Batelière, 9th
(01.48.24.18.63)

Jewish

La Boule Rouge p155
1 rue de la Boule Rouge,
9th (01.47.70.43.90)

North African

Wally le Saharien p157
36 rue Rodier, 9th
(01.42.85.51.90)

Other International

Le Paprika p162
28 av Trudaine, 9th
(01.44.63.02.91/
www.le-paprika.com)

Shopping & Cooking

Arnaud Delmontel p205
39 rue des Martyrs,
9th (01.48.78.29.33/
www.arnaud-
delmontel.com)

Le Snacking

Cojean p116
17 bdaussmann,
9th (01.47.70.22.65/
www.cojean.fr)

Rose Bakery p116
46 rue des Martyrs,
9th (01.42.82.12.80)

Tea Rooms

Les Cakes
de Bertrand p195
7 rue Bourdaloue, 9th
(01.40.16.16.28/
www.lescakesde
bertrand.com)

10th arrondissement

**African & Indian
Ocean**

Chez Dom p122
34 rue de Sambre-et-
Meuse, 10th
(01.42.01.59.80)

The Americas

Múkura p128
79 quai de Valmy, 10th
(01.42.01.18.67)

Cafés, Bars & Pubs

L'Atmosphère p180
49 rue Lucien-Sampaix,
10th (01.40.38.09.21)

Chez Adel p181
10 rue de la Grange-
aux-Belles, 10th
(01.42.08.24.61)

Chez Prune p181
71 quai de Valmy,
10th (01.42.41.30.47)

De La Ville Café p181
34 bd Bonne-Nouvelle,
10th (01.48.24.48.09/
www.delavillecafe.
com)

E-Dune p182
18 av Claude Vellefaux,
10th (01.42.06.22.14/
www.e-dune.com)

Le Jemmapes p182
82 quai de Jemmapes,
10th (01.40.40.02.35)

Le Patache p182
60 rue de Lancry, 10th
(01.42.08.14.35)

Le Petit
Château d'Eau p182
34 rue du Château d'Eau,
10th (01.42.08.72.81)

Le Réveil du 10ème p182
35 rue du Château d'Eau,
10th (01.42.41.77.59)

Le Sainte Marthe p182
32 rue Ste-Marthe, 10th
(01.44.84.36.96)

**Eastern
Mediterranean**

Kibele p131
12 rue de l'Echiquier,
10th (01.48.24.57.74)

Far Eastern

Le Cambodge p132
10 av Richerand, 10th
(01.44.84.37.70)

Fashion

Le Martel p111
3 rue Martel, 10th
(01.47.70.67.56)

French

Brasserie Flo p72
7 rue des Petites-Ecuries,
10th (01.47.70.13.59/
www.floparis.com)

Chez Arthur p72
25 rue du Fbg-St-Martin,
10th (01.42.08.34.33)

Chez Casimir p72
6 rue du Belzunce, 10th
(01.48.78.28.80)

Chez Michel p72
10 rue de Belzunce, 10th
(01.44.53.06.20)

L'Hermitage p73
5 bd de Denain, 10th
(01.48.78.77.09)

Julien p73
16 rue du Fbg-St-Denis,
10th (01.47.70.12.06/
www.julienparis.com)

Rôtisserie
Ste-Marthe p73
4 rue Ste-Marthe, 10th
(01.40.03.08.30)

Terminus Nord p74
23 rue de Dunkerque,
10th (01.42.85.05.15/
www.terminusnord.com)

Indian

Bharath Café p142
67 rue Louis Blanc,
10th (01.58.20.06.20)

Ganesha Corner p142
16 rue Perdonnet, 10th
(01.46.07.35.32)

New Pondichery p142
189 rue du Fbg-St-Denis,
10th (01.40.34.30.70)

Italian

Da Mimmo p148
39 bd de Magenta,
10th (01.42.06.44.47)

La Madonnina p149
10 rue Marie et Louise,
10th (01.42.01.25.26)

Other International

Trëma p163
8 rue de Marseille, 10th
(01.42.49.27.67)

Shopping & Cooking

Sarl Velan Stores p207
87 passage Brady,
10th (01.42.46.06.06/
www.e-velan.com)

Spanish

La Paella p161
50 rue des Vinaigriers,
10th (01.46.07.28.89/
www.restaurantla
paella.com)

Wine Bars

Le Coin de Verre p199
38 rue de Sambre-
et-Meuse, 10th
(01.42.45.31.82)

Le Verre Volé p199
67 rue de Lancry,
10th (01.48.03.17.34)

11th arrondissement

**African & Indian
Ocean**

Ile de Gorée p122
70 rue Jean-Pierre
Timbaud, 11th
(01.43.38.97.69)

Waly Fay p122
6 rue Godefroy Cavaignac,
11th (01.40.24.17.79)

The Americas

Blue Bayou p125
111-113 rue St-Maur,
11th (01.43.55.87.21/
www.bluebayou-
bluebillard.com)

Index

El Paladar p128
26 bis rue de la
Fontaine au Roi, 11th
(01.43.57.42.70)

Indiana Café p125
14 pl de la Bastille, 11th
(01.44.75.79.80)

Cafés, Bars & Pubs

Le Bistrot du Peintre p183
116 av Ledru-Rollin, 11th
(01.47.00.34.39)

La Bonne Franquette p183
151 rue de la Roquette,
11th (01.43.48.85.88)

Café de l'Industrie p183
16-17 rue St-Sabin, 11th
(01.47.00.13.53)

Le Fanfaron p183
6 rue de la Main-d'Or, 11th
(01.49.23.41.14)

Pause Café p183
41 rue de Charonne,
11th (01.48.06.80.33)

Planète Mars p183
21 rue Keller, 11th
(01.43.14.24.44)

Polichinelle Café p183
64-66 rue de Charonne,
11th (01.58.30.63.52)

Pop In p185
105 rue Amelot, 11th
(01.48.05.56.11)

Le Zéro Zéro p185
89 rue Amelot, 11th
(01.49.23.51.00)

**Eastern
Mediterranean**

Kazaphani p131
122 av Parmentier, 11th
(01.48.07.20.19)

Far Eastern

Dong Huong p140
14 rue Louis-Bonnet,
11th (01.43.57.18.88)

Khun Akorn p138
8 av de Taillebourg,
11th (01.43.56.20.03)

New Nioullaville p133
32-34 rue de l'Orillon,
11th (01.40.21.96.18)

Le Président p134
120-124 rue du Fbg-du-
Temple, 11th
(01.47.00.17.18)

Wok p134
23 rue des Taillandiers,
11th (01.55.28.88.77)

French

Astier p74
44 rue Jean-Pierre-
Timbaud, 11th
(01.43.57.16.35)

Au Vieux Chêne p79
7 rue du Dahomey,
11th (01.43.71.67.69)

Le Bistrot Paul Bert p75
18 rue Paul Bert, 11th
(01.43.72.24.01)

Le Chateaubriand p75
129 av Parmentier,
11th (01.43.57.45.95)

Chez Ramulaud p75
269 rue du Fbg-St-Antoine,
11th (01.43.72.23.29)

**Crêperie
Bretonne Fleurie** p77
67 rue de Charonne,
11th (01.43.55.62.29)

Juan et Juanita p77
82 rue Jean-Pierre
Timbaud, 11th
(01.43.57.60.15)

Le Marsangy p77
73 av Parmentier,
11th (01.47.00.94.25)

**Paris Main
d'Or** p77
133 rue du Fbg-St-Antoine,
11th (01.44.68.04.68)

**Le Passage des
Carmagnoles** p78
18 passage de la
Bonne-Graine, 11th
(01.47.00.73.30)

**Le Repaire
de Cartouche** p78
99 rue Amelot/8 bd
des Filles-du-Calvaire,
11th (01.47.00.25.86)

Le Temps au Temps p78
13 rue Paul Bert, 11th
(01.43.79.63.40)

Indian

**Aux Comptoirs
des Indes** p143
50 rue de la Fontaine
au Roi, 11th
(01.48.05.45.76)

North African

L'Homme Bleu p158
55 bis rue Jean-Pierre
Timbaud, 11th
(01.48.07.05.63)

Le Mansouria p158
11 rue Faidherbe, 11th
(01.43.71.00.16)

**Restaurant
des Quatre Frères** p159
127 bd de Ménilmontant,
11th (01.43.55.40.91)

Le Souk p159
1 rue Keller, 11th
(01.49.29.05.08)

Le Tagine p159
13 rue de Crussol, 11th
(01.47.00.28.67)

Shopping & Cooking

Allicante p209
26 bd Beaumarchais,
11th (01.43.55.13.02)

**L'Autre
Boulange** p205
43 rue de Montreuil,
11th (01.43.72.86.04)

Le Snacking

Bar à Soupes p116
33 rue de Charonne,
11th (01.43.57.53.79)

Spanish

La Plancha p161
34 rue Keller, 11th
(01.48.05.20.30)

Wine Bars

Le Clown Bar p200
114 rue Amelot, 11th
(01.43.55.87.35)

Jacques Mélac p200
42 rue Léon-Frot, 11th
(01.43.70.59.27/
www.melac.fr)

Le Melting Potes p200
16 rue des Trois-Bornes,
11th (01.43.38.61.75)

La Muse Vin p200
101 rue de Charonne,
11th (01.40.09.93.05)

12th arrondissement

**African & Indian
Ocean**

Chez Céleste p122
18 rue de Cotte, 12th
(01.43.44.15.30)

Cafés, Bars & Pubs

Barrio Latino p185
46 rue du Fbg-St-Antoine,
12th (01.55.78.84.75)

Chez Gudule p185
58 bd de Picpus,
12th (01.43.40.08.28)

China Club p185
50 rue de Charenton,
12th (01.43.43.82.02/
www.chinaclub.cc)

La Liberté p185
196 rue du Fbg-St-Antoine,
12th (01.43.72.11.18)

Viaduc Café p185
43 av Daumesnil, 12th
(01.44.74.70.70/
www.viaduc-cafe.fr)

Far Eastern

La Coloniale p132
161 rue de Picpus,
12th (01.43.43.69.10)

French

Au Trou Gascon p82
40 rue Taine, 12th
(01.43.44.34.26/
www.autrougascon.fr)

Auberge le Quincy p79
28 av Ledru-Rollin,
12th (01.46.28.46.76/
www.lequincy.fr)

Comme Cochons p80
135 rue Charenton,
12th (01.43.42.43.36)

La Connivence p80
1 rue de Cotte, 12th
(01.46.28.46.17)

Le Duc de Richelieu p81
5 rue Parrot, 12th
(01.43.43.05.64)

L'Encrier p81
55 rue Traversière,
12th (01.44.68.08.16)

A la Biche au Bois p80
45 av Ledru Rollin,
12th (01.43.43.34.38)

L'Oulette p81
15 pl Lachambeaudie,
12th (01.40.02.02.12/
www.l-oulette.com)

Le Square Trousseau p81
1 rue Antoine-Vollon,
12th (01.43.43.06.00)

Le Train Bleu p82
Gare de Lyon, pl Louis-
Armand, 12th
(01.43.09.06/
www.le-train-bleu.com)

Les Zygomates p83
7 rue de Capri, 12th
(01.40.19.93.04)

Italian

Les Amis de Messina p149
204 rue du Fbg-St-Antoine,
12th (01.43.67.96.01/
www.lesamisdes
messina.fr)

Sardegna a Tavola p149
1 rue de Cotte, 12th
(01.44.75.03.28)

Other International

Athanor p163
4 rue Crozatier, 12th
(01.43.44.49.15)

Wine Bars

Le Baron Bouge p200
1 rue Théophile-Roussel,
12th (01.43.43.14.32)

13th arrondissement

**African & Indian
Ocean**

Entoto p123
143-145 rue Léon-Maurice-
Nordmann, 13th
(01.45.87.08.51)

Cafés, Bars & Pubs

Chez Lili et Marcel p186
1 quai d'Austerlitz,
13th (01.45.85.00.08)

Le Couvent p186
69 rue Broca, 13th
(01.43.31.28.28)

La Folie en Tête p186
33 rue de la Butte-
aux-Cailles, 13th
(01.45.80.65.99)

Far Eastern

Likafo p135
39 av de Choisy, 13th
(01.45.84.20.45)

**Rouammit
& Huong Lan** p138
103 av d'Ivry, 13th
(01.53.60.00.34)

La Tonkinoise p140
20 rue Philibert Lucot,
13th (01.45.85.98.98)

Tricotin p135
15 av de Choisy, 13th
(01.45.84.74.44)

French

Au Petit Marguery p84
9 bd du Port-Royal, 13th
(01.43.31.58.59/
www.petitmarguery.fr)

L'Avant-Goût p83
26 rue Bobillot, 13th
(01.53.80.24.00)

Index

Chez Gladines p84
30 rue des Cinq Diamants,
13th (01.45.80.70.10)

Chez Paul p84
22 rue de la Butte-aux-
Cailles, 13th
(01.45.89.22.11)

L'Ourcine p84
92 rue Broca, 13th
(01.47.07.13.65)

North African
Au P'tit Cahoua p159
39 bd St-Marcel, 13th
(01.47.07.24.42)

Shopping & Cooking
Tang Frères p207
48 av d'Ivry, 13th
(01.45.70.80.00)

Tea Rooms
L'Oisive Thé p195
1 rue Jean-Marie Jego,
13th (01.53.80.31.33/
www.loisivethe.free.fr)

14th arrondissement
Cafés, Bars & Pubs
L'Entrepôt p186
7-9 rue Francis-de-
Pressensé, 14th
(01.45.40.60.70/
www.lentrepot.fr)

Le Plomb du Cantal p187
3 rue de la Gaîté, 14th
(01.43.35.16.92)

Les Tontons p187
38 rue Raymond
Losserand, 14th
(01.43.21.69.45)

Le Tournesol p187
9 rue de la Gaîté, 14th
(01.43.27.65.72)

Caribbean
La Créole p129
122 bd du Montparnasse,
14th (01.43.20.62.12)

Le Flamboyant p129
11 rue Boyer-Barret,
14th (01.45.41.00.22)

French
Apollo p85
3 pl Denfert-Rochereau,
14th (01.45.38.76.77/
www.restaurant-apollo.com)

L'Assiette p86
181 rue du Château,
14th (01.43.22.64.86/
www.chezlulu.fr)

Le Bis de Severo p86
16 rue des Plantes, 14th
(01.40.44.73.09)

La Cagouille p86
10 pl Constantin Brancusi,
14th (01.43.22.09.01/
www.la-cagouille.fr)

La Cerisaie p86
70 bd Edgar Quinet, 14th
(01.43.20.98.98)

La Contre-Allée p87
83 av Denfert-Rochereau,
14th (01.43.54.99.86)

La Coupole p87
102 bd du Montparnasse,
14th (01.43.20.14.20/
www.flobrasseries.com/
coupoleparis)

Le Dôme p87
108 bd du Montparnasse,
14th (01.43.35.25.81)

Natacha p87
17 bis rue Campagne-
Première, 14th
(01.43.20.79.27)

L'Opportun p88
64 bd Edgar Quinet,
14th (01.43.20.26.29)

La Régalade p88
49 av Jean-Moulin,
14th (01.45.45.68.58)

Shopping & Cooking
Poissonnerie du Dôme p209
4 rue Delambre, 14th
(01.43.35.23.95)

Vegetarian
Aquarius p118
40 rue de Gergovie,
14th (01.45.41.36.88)

Dietetic Shop p119
11 rue Delambre, 14th
(01.43.35.39.75)

15th arrondissement
Cafés, Bars & Pubs
Au Dernier Métro p187
70 bd de Grenelle,
15th (01.45.75.01.23/
www.auderniermetro.com)

Le Bréguet p187
72 rue Falguière,
15th (01.42.79.97.00)

Eastern
Mediterranean
Mazeh p131
20 rue Marmontel, 15th
(01.45.32.40.70)

Restaurant Al Wady p131
153-155 rue de Lourmel,
15th (01.45.58.57.18)

Far Eastern
Banyan p138
24 pl Etienne-Pernet,
15th (01.40.60.09.31)

Chez Fung p138
32 rue de Frémicourt,
15th (01.45.67.36.99)

Odori p137
18 rue Letellier, 15th
(01.45.77.88.12)

Fashion
Le Quinzième p112
14 rue Cauchy, 15th
(01.45.54.43.43)

French
Bistrot d'Hubert p88
41 bd Pasteur, 15th
(01.47.34.15.50). French
Café du Commerce p88
51 rue du Commerce, 15th
(01.45.75.03.27)

L'Os à Moelle p89
3 rue Vasco-de-Gama,
15th (01.45.57.27.27)

Le Père Claude p89
51 av de la Motte-Picquet,
15th (01.47.34.03.05)

**Restaurant
Stéphane Martin** p90
67 rue des Entrepreneurs,
15th (01.45.79.03.31)

**Restaurant
Thierry Burlot** p90
8 rue Nicolas-Charlet, 15th
(01.42.19.08.59)

Le Sept/Quinze p90
29 av Lowendal, 15th
(01.43.06.23.06)

Le Suffren p90
84 av de Suffren, 15th
(01.45.66.97.86)

Le Troquet p91
21 rue François-Bonvin,
15th (01.45.66.89.00)

L'Ultr p91
1 pl Falguière, 15th
(01.47.34.12.24)

Shopping & Cooking
Beau et Bon p211
81 rue Lecourbe, 15th
(01.43.06.06.53/
www.beauetbon.com)

**Les Délices
d'Orient** p207
52 av Emile-Zola, 15th
(01.45.79.10.00)

Merry Monk p207
87 rue de la Convention,
15th (01.40.60.79.54)

**Le Moulin
de la Vierge** p205
166 av de Suffren, 15th
(01.47.83.45.55/
www.lemoulinde
lavierge.com)

Spanish
Casa Eusebio p161
68 av Félix Faure, 15th
(01.45.54.11.88)

Wine Bars
Couleurs de Vigne p200
2 rue Marmontel, 15th
(01.45.33.32.96)

16th arrondissement
Cafés, Bars & Pubs
Bar Panoramique p188
Hôtel Concorde La Fayette,
3 pl du Général-Koenig,
17th (01.40.68.51.31)

Café Le Passy p188
2 rue de Passy, 16th
(01.42.88.31.02)

Le Village d'Auteuil p188
48 rue d'Auteuil, 16th
(01.42.88.00.18)

Caribbean
**La Table
de Babette** p129
32 rue de Longchamp,
16th (01.45.53.00.07)

Fashion
Café de l'Homme p112
Musée de l'Homme,
17 pl du Trocadéro,
16th (01.44.05.30.15)

Le Cristal Room p112
8 pl des Etats-Unis,
16th (01.40.22.11.10)

Tokyo Eat p112
Palais de Tokyo, 13
av du Président-Wilson,
16th (01.47.20.00.29)

French
Astrance p91
4 rue Beethoven, 16th
(01.40.50.84.40)

Le Bistrot des Vignes p92
1 rue Jean-Bologne,
16th (01.45.27.76.64)

Brasserie de la Poste p92
54 rue de Longchamp,
16th (01.47.55.01.31)

Le Chalet des Iles p93
carrefour des Cascades,
Lac Inférieur du Bois de
Boulogne, 16th
(01.42.88.04.69)

La Gare p93
19 chaussée de la Muette,
16th (01.42.15.15.31)

La Grande Armée p94
3 av de la Grande-Armée,
16th (01.45.00.24.77)

La Grande Cascade p94
Pavillon de la Grande
Cascade, allée de
Longchamp, Bois
de Boulogne, 16th
(01.45.27.33.51)

Hiramatsu p94
52 rue de Longchamp,
16th (01.56.81.08.80/
www.hiramatsu.co.jp)

Le Kiosque p95
1 pl de Mexico, 16th
(01.47.27.96.98)

Le Passiflore p95
33 rue de Longchamp,
16th (01.47.04.96.81)

Le Pré Catelan p95
rte de Suresnes, Bois
de Boulogne, 16th
(01.44.14.41.14)

Restaurant GR5 p95
19 rue Gustave Courbet,
16th (01.47.27.09.84)

Le Stella p96
133 av Victorugo, 16th
(01.56.90.56.00)

La Table de Lauriston p96
129 rue de Lauriston, 16th
(01.47.27.00.07)

La Table de Robuchon p96
16 av Bugeaud, 16th
(01.56.28.16.16)

Zébra Square p96
3 pl Clément Ader,
16th (01.44.14.91.91)

Japanese
Comme des Poissons p153
24 rue de la Tour, 16th
(01.45.20.70.37)

Index

Shopping & Cooking

**La Maison
du Chocolat** p207
89 av Raymond-Poincaré,
16th (01.40.67.77.83/
www.lamaisondu
chocolat.com)

Wine Bars

**Le Vin dans
les Voiles** p200
8 rue Chapu, 16th
(01.46.47.83.98/
www.vindanslesvoiles.com)

17th arrondissement
The Americas

**El Bodegón
de Pancho** p128
8 rue Guy Môquet,
17th (01.53.31.00.73)

Cafés, Bars & Pubs

Le Dada p188
12 av des Ternes,
17th (01.43.80.60.12)

Lush p188
16 rue des Dames,
17th (01.43.87.49.46/
www.lushbars.com)

Trois Pièces Cuisine p189
101 rue des Dames,
17th (01.44.90.85.10)

Eating with
Entertainment

L'Ane Rouge p204
3 rue Laugier, 17th
(01.47.64.45.77)

French

Ballon & Coquillages p97
71 bd Gouvion-St-Cyr,
17th (01.45.74.17.98)

Le Bistral p97
80 rue Lemercier, 17th
(01.42.63.59.61)

**Le Bistrot d'à Côté
Flaubert** p97
10 rue Gustave-Flaubert,
17th (01.42.67.05.81/
www.michelrostang.com)

La Braisière p97
54 rue Cardinet, 17th
(01.47.63.40.37)

Chez Fred p98
190 bis bd Pereire,
17th (01.45.74.20.48)

Chez Léon p98
32 rue Legendre,
17th (01.42.27.06.82)

Le Clou p98
132 rue Cardinet, 17th
(01.42.27.36.78)

Goupil le Bistro p98
4 rue Claude Debussy,
17th (01.45.75.83.25)

Graindorge p99
15 rue de l'Arc de
Triomphe, 17th
(01.47.54.99.28)

Guy Savoy p99
18 rue Troyon, 17th
(01.43.80.40.61)

L'Huîtrier p99
16 rue Saussier-Leroy,
17th (01.40.54.83.44)

Michel Rostang p100
20 rue Rennequin,
17th (01.47.63.40.77/
www.michelrostang.com)

**Restaurant
L'Entredgeu** p101
83 rue Laugier, 17th
(01.40.54.97.24)

Ripaille p101
69 rue des Dames,
17th (01.45.22.03.03)

La Soupière p101
154 av de Wagram,
17th (01.42.27.00.73)

Indian

Margoa p143
7 rue Waldeck Rousseau,
17th (01.45.72.39.41)

Japanese

Kifuné p153
44 rue St-Ferdinand,
17th (01.45.72.11.19)

Jewish

Patrick Goldenberg p155
69 av Wagram, 17th
(01.42.27.34.79)

Shopping & Cooking

Alléosse p206
13 rue Poncelet, 17th
(01.46.22.50.45/
www.fromage-alleosse.com)

**Fromagerie
Dubois et Fils** p206
80 rue de Tocqueville,
17th (01.42.27.11.38)

Wine Bars

Caves Pétrissans p201
30 bis av Niel, 17th
(01.42.27.52.03)

Le Petit Chavignol p201
78 rue de Tocqueville,
17th (01.42.27.95.97)

18th arrondissement
African & Indian
Ocean

Le Mono p123
40 rue Véron, 18th
(01.46.06.99.20)

Cafés, Bars & Pubs

Les 3 Frères p190
14 rue Léon, 18th
(01.42.64.91.73/
www.les3freres.net)

Le Café Arrosé p189
123 rue Caulaincourt,
18th (01.42.57.14.30)

La Cave Café p189
134 rue Marcadet,
18th (01.4606.29.17)

La Fourmi p189
74 rue des Martyrs,
18th (01.42.64.70.35)

Ice Kube p189
7 passage Ruelle,
18th (01.42.05.20.00)

Le Sancerre p189
35 rue des Abbesses,
18th (01.42.58.08.20)

Eating with
Entertainment

**Autour de
Midi-Minuit** p204
11 rue Lepic, 18th
(01.55.79.16.48)

Chez Michou p203
80 rue des Martyrs,
18th (01.46.06.16.04)

Le Moulin Rouge p204
82 bd de Clichy, 18th
(01.53.09.82.82)

French

Aux Négociants p103
27 rue Lambert, 18th
(01.46.06.15.11)

Le Bouclard p101
1 rue Cavalotti, 18th
(01.45.22.60.01)

Café Burq p102
6 rue Burq, 18th
(01.42.52.81.27)

Chez Toinette p102
20 rue Germain-Pilon,
18th (01.42.54.44.36)

L'Entracte p102
44 rue d'Orsel, 18th
(01.46.06.93.41)

La Famille p103
41 rue des Trois-Frères,
18th (01.42.52.11.12)

Histoire De p103
14 rue Ferdinand Flocon,
18th (01.42.52.24.60)

La Mascotte p103
52 rue des Abbesses,
18th (01.46.06.28.15/
www.la-mascotte-
montmartre.com)

La Table Dancourt p103
4 rue Dancourt, 18th
(01.42.52.03.98)

Le Wepler p104
14 pl de Clichy, 18th
(01.45.22.53.24)

Indian

Le Nawab p143
174 rue Ordener, 18th
(01.46.27.85.28)

Italian

Sale e Pepe p149
30 rue Ramey, 18th
(01.46.06.08.01)

Other International

O Por do Sol p162
18 rue de la Fontaine-
du-But, 18th
(01.42.23.90.26)

Shopping & Cooking

Arnaud Larher p209
53 rue Caulaincourt,
18th (01.42.57.68.08)

Vegetarian

Au Grain de Folie p119
24 rue de la Vieuville,
18th (01.42.58.15.57)

19th arrondissement
The Americas

Ay Caramba! p128
59 rue Mouzaia, 19th
(01.42.41.76.30)

Cafés, Bars & Pubs

Café Chéri(e) p190
44 bd de la Villette,
19th (01.42.02.02.05)

**Rendez-Vous
des Quais** p190
10-14 quai de Seine,
19th (01.40.37.02.81)

Far Eastern

Lao Siam p138
49 rue de Belleville,
19th (01.40.40.09.68)

French

Au Boeuf Couronné p104
188 av Jean-Jaurès,
19th (01.42.39.54.54)

La Cave Gourmande p106
10 rue du Général Brunet,
19th (01.40.40.03.30)

A la Bière p104
103 av Simon Bolivar,
19th (01.42.39.83.25)

Restaurant L'Hermès p106
23 rue Mélingue, 19th
(01.42.39.94.70)

Indian

Le Gange p143
65 rue Manin, 19th
(01.42.00.00.80)

20th arrondissement
Cafés, Bars & Pubs

Entrepot's p190
2 rue Sorbier, 20th
(01.43.49.59.17)

Lou Pascalou p190
14 rue des Panoyaux,
20th (01.46.36.78.10)

Far Eastern

Le Pacifique p135
35 rue de Belleville,
20th (01.42.49.66.80)

French

Le Baratin p106
3 rue Jouye Rouve,
20th (01.43.49.39.70)

La Boulangerie p106
15 rue des Panoyaux,
20th (01.43.58.45.45)

Le Casque d'Or p107
pl Maurice Chevalier,
20th (01.43.58.37.09)

**En Colimaçon
(Ma Pomme)** p107
107 rue de Ménilmontant,
20th (01.40.33.10.40)

Le Zéphyr p107
1 rue du Jourdain, 20th
(01.46.36.65.81)

Jewish

Maison Benisti p155
108 bd de Belleville, 20th

Index

Lexicon

Food

A point medium-rare (meat).
Abats offal.
Accra salt-cod fritter.
Acidulé tart (adjective).
Agneau lamb.
Aiglefin haddock.
Aiguillettes thin slices.
Ail garlic.
Aile wing.
Aïoli garlic mayonnaise.
Airelle cranberry.
Algues seaweed.
Aligot mashed potatoes with cheese and garlic.
Aloyau beef loin.
Amande almond; – **de mer** small clam.
Amer/amère bitter.
Ananas pineapple.
Anchoïade anchovy dip.
Anchois anchovy.
Andouille pig's offal sausage, served cold.
Andouillette grilled chitterling (offal) sausage.
Aneth dill.
Anguille eel.
Anis aniseed.
Araignée de mer spider crab.
Artichaut artichoke.
Asperge asparagus.
Assiette plate.
Aubergine aubergine (GB), eggplant (US).
Avocat avocado.
Axoa Basque veal stew.

Baies roses pink peppercorns.
Ballotine stuffed, rolled-up piece of boned fish or meat.
Bar sea bass.
Barbue brill.
Basilic basil.
Bavarois moulded cream dessert.
Bavette beef flank steak.
Béarnaise hollandaise sauce with tarragon and shallots.
Belon flat, round oyster.
Betterave beetroot.

Beurre butter; – **blanc** butter sauce with white wine and shallots; – **noir** browned butter.
Beignet fritter or doughnut.
Biche deer, venison.
Bien cuit well done (for meat).
Bifteck steak.
Bigorneau periwinkle.
Biologique organic.
Blanc white; – **de poulet** chicken breast.
Blanquette a 'white' stew (with eggs and cream).
Blette Swiss chard.
Boeuf beef; – **bourguignon** beef stew with red wine; – **du charolais** charolais beef (a breed); – **gros sel** boiled beef with vegetables; – **miroton** sliced boiled beef in onion sauce; – **de salers** salers beef (a breed).
Bordelaise sauce with red wine, shallots and marrow.
Boudin blanc white veal, chicken or pork sausage.
Boudin noir black (blood) pudding.
Bouillabaisse Mediterranean fish and shellfish stew.
Bouillon stock.
Boulettes de viande meatballs.
Bourride fish stew.
Brandade de morue salt cod puréed with olive oil.
Brebis sheep's milk cheese.
Brik North African filo pastry package.
Brochet pike.
Brochette kebab.
Brouillé(s) scrambled (egg).
Brûlé(e) literally, burned, usually caramelised.
Bulot whelk.

Cabillaud fresh cod.
Cabri young goat.
Caille quail.
Calamar squid.
Campagne/campagnard country-style.
Canard duck.
Canette duckling.

Cannelle cinnamon.
Carbonnade beef stew with onions and beer.
Carré d'agneau rack or loin of lamb.
Carrelet plaice.
Cassolette small casserole.
Cassis blackcurrants, also blackcurrant liqueur in kir.
Cassoulet stew of haricot beans, sausage and preserved duck.
Céleri celery.
Céleri rave celeriac.
Céleri rémoulade grated celeriac in mustard mayonnaise.
Cèpe cep or porcini mushroom.
Cerfeuil chervil.
Cerise cherry.
Cervelas garlicky Alsatian pork sausage.
Cervelle brains.
Champignon mushroom; – **de Paris** cultivated button mushroom.
Chantilly whipped cream.
Chapon capon.
Charcuterie cured meat, such as saucisson or pâté.
Charlotte moulded cream dessert with a biscuit edge.
Chasseur sauce with white wine, mushrooms, shallots and tomato.
Châtaigne chestnut.
Chateaubriand fillet steak.
Chaud(e) hot.
Chaud-froid glazing sauce with gelatine or aspic.
Chausson pastry turnover.
Cheval horse.
A cheval with egg on top.
Chèvre goat's cheese.
Chevreuil young roe deer.
Chicorée frisée, or curly endive (GB), chicory (US).
Chiffonade shredded herbs and vegetables.
Chipiron squid.
Choron béarnaise sauce with tomato purée.
Chou cabbage; – **de Bruxelles** Brussels sprout; – **frisé** kale; – **rouge** red cabbage; – **fleur** cauliflower.

Choucroute sauerkraut (**garnie** if topped with cured ham and sausages).
Ciboulette chive.
Citron lemon.
Citron vert lime.
Citronelle lemongrass.
Citrouille pumpkin.
Civet game stew in blood-thickened sauce.
Clafoutis thick batter (usually baked with fruit).
Cochon pig; – **de lait** suckling pig.
Cochonnailles cured pig parts (ears, snout, cheeks...).
Coco a type of white bean.
Coeur heart.
Coing quince.
Colin hake.
Colombo Antillais spice mix.
Concombre cucumber.
Confit slow-cooked, usually in fat.
Confiture jam.
Congre conger eel.
Contre-filet sirloin.
Coq rooster.
à la Coque in its shell.
Coquelet baby rooster.
Coquillages shellfish.
Coquille shell; – **St-Jacques** scallop.
Cornichon pickled gherkin.
Côte/côtelette rib or chop.
Côte de boeuf rib.
Cotriade Breton fish stew.
Coulis thick sauce or purée.
Courge vegetable marrow (GB), squash (US).
Courgette courgette (GB), zucchini (US).
Crème anglaise custard.
Crème brûlée caramelised custard dessert.
Crème fraîche thick, slightly soured cream.
Crêpe pancake.
Crépinette small, flattish sausage, often grilled.
Cresson watercress.
Creuse oyster with long, crinkly shell.
Crevette prawn (GB), shrimp (US); – **grise** grey shrimp.
Croque-madame croque-monsieur topped with an egg.
Croque-monsieur toasted cheese and ham sandwich.

Crottin small, round goat's cheese (literally, turd).
Croustade bread or pastry case, deep-fried.
en croûte in a pastry case.
Crudités raw vegetables.
Crustacé shellfish.
Cuisse leg (poultry).
Curcuma turmeric.

Darne fish steak.
Datte date.
Daube meat braised slowly in red wine.
Daurade/dorade sea bream.
Demi-glace meat glaze.
Demi-sel slightly salted.
Désossé(e) boned.
Diable demi-glace with cayenne and white wine.
Dinde turkey.
Duxelles chopped, sautéed mushrooms with shallots.

Echalote shallot.
Ecrémé skimmed (milk).
Ecrevisse crayfish.
Emincé fine slice.
Encornet squid.
Encre de seiche squid ink.
Endive chicory (GB), Belgian endive (US).
Entrecôte beef rib steak.
Entremets cream or milk-based dessert.
Epeautre spelt.
Eperlan smelt; whitebait.
Epicé(e) spicy.
Epices spices.
Epinards spinach.
Escabèche fish fried, marinated and served cold.
Escalope cutlet.
Escarole slightly bitter, slightly curly salad leaves.
Espadon swordfish.
Espelette small, hot Basque pepper.
Estouffade meat stew.
Estragon tarragon.
Etrille small crab.

Façon in the style of.
Faisan pheasant.
Farci(e) stuffed.
Faux-filet sirloin steak.

Fenouil fennel.
Feuille de chêne oak leaf lettuce.
Feuilleté puff pastry.
Fève broad bean.
Figue fig.
Filet mignon tenderloin.
Financier small rectangular cake.
Fines de claire crinkle-shelled oysters.
Fines herbes mixed herbs.
Flambé(e) sprinkled with alcohol, then set alight.
Flet flounder.
Flétan halibut.
Florentine with spinach.
Foie liver.
Foie gras fattened liver of goose or duck; – **cru** raw foie gras; – **entier** whole foie gras; – **mi-cuit** barely cooked (also called frais or nature); **pâté de** – liver pâté with a foie gras base; **poêlée** pan-fried.
Fondu(e) melted.
Fondue savoyarde bread dipped into melted cheese.
Fondue bourguignonne beef dipped in heated oil.
Forestière with mushrooms.
au four oven-baked.
Fourré(e) filled or stuffed.
Frais/fraîche fresh.
Fraise strawberry; – **des bois** wild strawberry; – **de veau** part of the calf's intestine.
Framboise raspberry.
Frappé(e) iced or chilled.
Frisée curly endive (GB), chicory (US).
Frit(e) fried.
Frites chips (UK), French fries (US).
Friture tiny fried fish.
Froid(e) cold.
Fromage cheese; – **blanc** smooth cream cheese.
Fruits secs dried fruit and nuts.
Fruits de mer seafood, especially shellfish.
Fumé(e) smoked.
Fumet fish stock.

Galantine pressed meat or fish, usually stuffed.
Galette flat cake of savoury pastry, potato pancake or buckwheat crêpe.
Garbure thick vegetable and meat soup.

Garni(e) garnished.
Gelée jelly or aspic.
Genièvre juniper berry.
Gésiers gizzards.
Gibier game.
Gigot d'agneau leg of lamb.
Gigue haunch of game, usually venison or boar.
Gingembre ginger.
Girofle clove.
Girolle wild mushroom.
Gîte shin of beef.
Gîte à la noix topside or silverside of beef.
Glace ice, also ice-cream.
Glacé(e) frozen; ice-cold; iced (as in cake).
Glaçon ice cube.
Gombo okra.
Gougère choux pastry and cheese mixture in a ring.
Goujon breaded, fried strip of fish; also a small catfish.
Goût taste.
Goûter to taste, or snack.
Graisse fat, grease.
Granité water-ice.
Gras(se) fatty.
Gratin dauphinois sliced potatoes baked with milk, cheese and garlic.
Gratiné(e) browned with breadcrumbs or cheese.
Grattons pork crackling.
à la Grecque served cold in olive oil and lemon juice.
Grenade pomegranate.
Grenadier delicate, white-fleshed sea fish.
Grenoblois sauce with cream, capers and lemon.
Grenouille frog.
Gribiche sauce of vinegar, capers, gherkins and egg.
Grillade grilled food, often mixed grill.
Grillé(e) grilled.
Griotte morello cherry.
Gros(se) large.
Groseille redcurrant.
Groseille à maquereau gooseberry.
Gros sel rock salt.

Haché(e) chopped, minced (GB), ground (US).
Hachis minced meat (hash); – **Parmentier** minced meat with mashed potato topping.

Haddock smoked haddock.
Hareng herring; – **à l'huile** marinated herring.
Haricot bean; – **vert** green bean.
Herbe herb; grass.
HO fashionable abbreviation for olive oil.
Hollandaise sauce of egg, butter, vinegar and lemon.
Homard lobster.
Huile oil.
Huître oyster.
Hure cold sausage made from boar's or pig's head.

Ile flottante poached, whipped-egg white 'island' in vanilla custard.

Jambon ham; – **de Paris** cooked ham; – **cru** raw, cured ham; – **fumé** smoked ham; – **de pays** cured country ham.
Jambonneau ham hock; – **de canard** stuffed duck drumstick.
Jardinière with vegetables.
Jarret shin or knuckle.
Joue cheek or jowl.
Julienne finely cut vegetables; also ling (fish).
Jus juice.

Lait milk; **(agneau/cochon) de lait** milk-fed lamb/ suckling pig.
Laitue lettuce.
Lamproie lamprey eel.
Landaise in goose fat with garlic, onion and ham.
Langue tongue.
Langouste spiny lobster or crawfish.
Langoustine Dublin Bay prawns or scampi.
Lapereau young rabbit.
Lapin rabbit.
Lard bacon.
Lardon cubed bacon bit.
Légume vegetable.
Lentille lentil.
Lièvre hare.
Liégoise coffee or chocolate ice-cream sundae.
Lieu jaune pollack.
Limande lemon sole.

Lisette small mackerel.
Litchi lychee.
Lotte monkfish.
Loup sea bass.
Lyonnais served with onions or sautéed potatoes.

Mâche lamb's lettuce.
Magret de canard duck breast.
Maïs maize, corn.
Maison homemade, or house special.
Mangue mango.
Maquereau mackerel.
Marcassin young wild boar.
Mariné(e) marinated.
Marjolaine marjoram.
Marmite small cooking pot, or a stew served in one; – **dieppoise** Normandy fish stew.
Marquise mousse-like cake.
Marron chestnut.
Matelote freshwater fish stew cooked in wine.
Mélange mixture.
Ménagère home-style.
Menthe mint.
Merguez spicy lamb or lamb and beef sausage.
Merlan whiting.
Mesclun mixed young salad leaves.
Meunière fish with browned butter and lemon.
Meurette red wine and stock used for poaching.
Mi-cuit(e) half/semi-cooked.
Miel honey.
Mignon small meat fillet.
Millefeuille puff pastry with vanilla cream; also used to describe layered vegetables.
Minute fried quickly.
Mirabelle tiny yellow plum.
Mirepoix chopped carrots, onion and celery.
Moelle bone marrow.
Moelleux au chocolat runny-centred chocolate cake.
Morille morel mushroom.
Mornay béchamel sauce with cheese.
Morue cod, usually salt cod.
Moules mussels; – **marinières** cooked in white wine with shallots.
Moulu(e) ground, milled.

Mousseline hollandaise sauce with whipped cream.
Mousseron type of wild mushroom.
Moutarde mustard.
Mouton mutton.
Mulet grey mullet.
Mûre blackberry.
Muscade nutmeg.
Myrtille bilberry/blueberry.

Nage poaching liquid.
Nantua crayfish sauce.
Nature plain, ungarnished.
Navarin lamb stew.
Navet turnip.
Nem Vietnamese-style imperial (spring) roll.
Nid nest.
Noisette hazelnut, or small, round piece of meat, or coffee with a little milk.
Noix walnut.
Nouilles noodles.

Oeuf egg; – **à la coque** soft-boiled; – **cocotte** baked with cream; – **dur** hard-boiled; – **en meurette** poached in red wine; – **à la neige** *see île flottante*.
Oie goose.
Oignon onion.

Onglet similar to bavette.
Oreille ear, usually pig's.
Orge barley.
Ortie nettle, used in soup.
Os bone; – **à moelle** marrow bone.
Oseille sorrel.
Oursin sea urchin.

Pain bread; – **d'épices** honey gingerbread; – **grillé** toast; – **perdu** French toast.
Palombe wood pigeon.
Palourde a type of clam.
Pamplemousse grapefruit.
en papillote steamed in foil or paper packet.
Panaché mixture.
Panais parsnip.
Pané(e) breaded.
Parfait sweet or savoury mousse-like mixture.
Parmentier with potato.
Pastèque watermelon.
Pâte pastry.
Pâté meat or fish pâté; – **en croûte** in a pastry case (similar to pork pie).
Pâtes pasta or noodles.
Paupiette meat or fish rolled up and tied, usually stuffed.
Pavé thick, square steak.
Pêcheur based on fish.

Perdreau young partridge.
Perdrix partridge.
Persil parsley.
Petit gris small snail.
Petit pois pea.
Petit salé salt pork.
Pétoncle queen scallop.
Pets de nonne ('nun's farts') light puffy fritters.
Pied foot (or trotter).
Pigeonneau young pigeon, squab.
Pignon pine kernel.
Piment pepper or chilli; – **d'Espelette** from the French Basque country.
Pimenté(e) spicy.
Pince claw.
Pintade/pintadeau guinea fowl.
Pipérade Basque egg, pepper, tomato, onion and ham mixture.
Pissaladière caramelised onion and anchovy tart.
Pistache pistachio nut.
Pistou Provençal basil and garlic pesto, without pine nuts.
Plat dish; main course.
Plate flat-shelled oyster.
Pleurotte oyster mushroom.
Poché(e) poached.
Poêlé(e) pan-fried.
Poire pear.

Saved by a phrase

How to get out of sticky situations in Paris restaurants…

Is there any raw shellfish in this dish?
Y-a-t'il des fruits de mer crus dans ce plat?

I'm allergic to… peanuts/seafood.
Je suis allergique aux… arachides/ fruits de mer.

I can't eat anything that contains… milk/wheat/fat.
Je ne peux rien manger qui contient… du lait/du blé/de la graisse.

I'm a vegetarian – no white or red meat, no fish.
Je suis végétarien – je ne mange ni viande blanche, ni viande rouge, ni poisson.

Will you ask the chef not to put too much salt in it, please?
Pourriez-vous demander au chef de mettre très peu de sel, s'il vous plaît?

I'm on a diet, what do you recommend?
Je suis au régime. Pourriez-vous me conseiller un plat diététique?

Does the special include any pork/offal?
Est-ce que le plat du jour contient du porc/ des abats?

What can you recommend for children?
Que pouvez-vous conseiller pour les enfants?

Do you have any less fragrant cheeses?
Avez-vous des fromages moins forts?

Which of the desserts is the lightest?
Quel est le plus léger des desserts?

Do you have any sandwiches without mayonnaise?
Avez-vous des sandwichs sans mayonnaise?

I liked it very much, but I have a small appetite.
C'était très bon, mais j'ai un petit appétit.

Index & Maps

Poireau leek.
Poisson fish.
Poitrine breast cut.
Poivrade peppery brown sauce served with meat.
Poivre pepper.
Poivron red or green pepper.
Pomme apple.
Pomme de terre potato (often referred to as pomme); – **allumettes** shoestring French fries; – **à l'huile** cold, boiled potatoes in oil; – **au four** baked potato; – **dauphines** deep-fried croquettes of puréed potato; – **gratin dauphinois** baked with cream; – **Pont Neuf** thick-cut chips; – **sarladaises** fried in goose fat with parsley and garlic.
Porc pork.
Porcelet suckling pig.
Potage thick soup.
Pot-au-feu boiled beef with vegetables.
Potée meat and vegetable stew.
Potiron pumpkin.
Poudre powder or granules.
Poularde chicken or hen.
Poule hen; – **au pot** stewed with vegetables and broth.
Poulet chicken
Poulpe octopus.
Poussin small chicken.
Praire small clam.
Pressé(e) squeezed.
Primeur early or young, of fruit, vegetables or wine.
Printanière springtime; served with vegetables.
Profiterole ice-cream filled pastry puff, served with melted chocolate.
Provençal(e) with garlic and tomatoes, and often onions, anchovies or olives.
Prune plum.
Pruneau prune.

Quenelle poached dumplings, usually pike.
Quetsch damson plum.
Queue tail; – **de boeuf** oxtail.

Râble saddle.
Racine root.
Raclette melted cheese served with boiled potatoes.

Radis radish.
Ragoût meat stew.
Raie skate.
Raifort horseradish.
Raisin grape.
Râpé(e) grated.
Rascasse scorpion fish.
Ratte small, firm potato.
Ravigote thick vinaigrette.
Ravioles de Royans tiny cheese ravioli.
Recette recipe.
Récolte harvest.
Régime diet.
Réglisse liquorice.
à la Reine with chicken.
Reine-claude greengage (plum).
Reinette dessert apple.
Rémoulade mayonnaise with mustard, chopped herbs, capers and gherkins.
Rillettes potted meat, usually pork and/or goose.
Rillons crispy chunks of pork belly.
Riquette wild rocket.
Ris sweetbreads.
Riz rice; – **sauvage** wild rice.
Rognon kidney.
Romarin rosemary.
Roquette rocket.
Rosbif roast beef.
Rosette dry, salami-like pork sausage from Lyon.
Rôti roast.
Rouget red mullet.
Roulade rolled-up portion.
Rouille red, cayenne-seasoned mayonnaise.
Roussette rock salmon (dogfish).
Roux flour- and butter-based sauce.
Rumsteck rump steak.

Sabayon frothy sauce made with wine and egg yolks, sometimes a dessert.
Sablé shortbread biscuit.
Saignant rare (for meat).
Safran saffron.
St-Pierre John Dory.
Saisonnier or **de saison** seasonal.
Salé(e) salted.
Salmis game or poultry stew.
Sandre pike-perch.
Sang blood.

Sanglier wild boar.
Sarrasin buckwheat.
Sarriette savoury (herb).
Saucisse fresh sausage.
Saucisson small sausage.
Saucisson sec dried sausage, eaten cold.
Sauge sage.
Saumon salmon.
Saumonette sea eel.
Sauvage wild.
Gratin Savoyard potatoes baked in stock with cheese.
Scarole see escarole.
Sec/sèche dry.
Seiche squid.
Sel salt.
Selle saddle or back.
Sirop syrup.
Soisson white bean.
Soja soya.
Soubise béchamel sauce with rice and cream.
Souper supper.
Souris d'agneau lamb knuckle.
Speck Italian smoked ham.
Sucre sugar.
Sucré(e) sweet.
Supion small cuttlefish.
Suprême breast; – **de volaille** fowl in a white roux with cream and meat juice.
crêpe Suzette pancake flambéed in orange liqueur.

Tagine (or **tajine**) Moroccan meat stew served in a conical dish.
Tapenade Provençal olive and caper paste, usually with anchovies.
Tartare raw minced steak (also tuna or salmon).
Tarte Tatin caramelised upside-down apple tart.
Tartine buttered baguette or open sandwich.
Tendron de veau veal rib.
Tête head.
Thon tuna.
Thym thyme.
Tian Provençal gratin cooked in an earthenware dish.
Tiède tepid or warm.
Tigre qui pleure Thai-style sautéed beef (weeping tiger).
Timbale rounded mould, or food cooked in one.

Tomate tomato; – **de mer** sea anemone.
Topinambour Jerusalem artichoke.
Toulouse large sausage.
Tournedos thick slices taken from a fillet of beef; – **Rossini** with foie gras and truffle.
Tournesol sunflower.
Tourte covered tart or pie, usually savoury.
Tourteau large crab.
Tranche slice.
Travers de porc spare ribs.
Trénels lamb's tripe.
Tripes tripe.
Tripoux Auvergnat dish of sheep's tripe and feet.
Trompette de la mort horn of plenty mushroom.
Truffade fried potato cake or mashed potato with cheese.
Truffe truffle, the ultimate fungus, **blanche** (white) or **noire** (black); chocolate truffle.
Truffé(e) stuffed or garnished with truffles.
Truite trout; – **de mer/ saumonée** salmon trout.

Vacherin a meringue, fruit and ice-cream cake; or soft, cow's milk cheese.
Vapeur steam.
Veau veal; – **élevé sous la mère** milk-fed veal.
Velouté sauce made with white roux and bouillon; creamy soup.
Ventre belly, breast or stomach.
Vénus American clam.
Verdurette vinaigrette with herbs and egg.
Verrine served in a clear glass.
Viande meat.
Vichyssoise cold leek and potato soup.
Volaille poultry.

Yaourt yoghurt.

Zeste zest or peel.

Drink

Appellation d'Origine Contrôlée (AOC) wine (or food) conforming to specific strict quality rules.
Bière beer.
Bock 12cl of beer.
Boire to drink.
Boisson a drink.
Blanche pale wheat beer.
Blonde lager (GB), beer (US).
Brune dark beer.
Café small espresso coffee; – **allongé** 'lengthened' (twice the water); – **au lait** milky coffee; – **crème** coffee with steamed milk; – **serré** strong espresso (half the water);
Carafe d'eau jug of tap water.
Calvados apple brandy.
Cardinal kir with red wine.
Chocolat (chaud) (hot) chocolate; – **à l'ancienne** thick hot chocolate.
Chope tankard.
Citron pressé freshly squeezed lemon juice.
Décaféiné/déca decaffeinated coffee.
Demi (demi-pression) 25cl of draught beer; – **ordinaire** 25cl of the least-expensive lager.
Demi-litre half a litre (50cl).
Express espresso; **double** – double espresso.
Fillette Loire Valley term for 50cl carafe of wine.
Gazeuse fizzy/carbonated.
Grand cru top-quality wine.
Infusion herbal or fruit tea.
Jus de fruits fruit juice.
Kir crème de cassis and dry white wine – **royal** crème de cassis and champagne.
Lait milk.
Lillet old-fashioned aperitif.
Marc clear brandy made from grape residues.
Mirabelle plum brandy.
Noisette espresso with a drop of milk.
Orange pressée freshly squeezed orange juice.
Panaché beer and lemonade shandy.
Pastis anise aperitif.
Pichet jug or carafe.
Plat(e) still, non-carbonated.

Poire Williams pear brandy.
Porto port.
Pot lyonnais 46cl carafe.
Pression draught lager.
Quart quarter litre (25cl).
Thé tea; – **à la menthe** green tea with dried or fresh mint.
Tilleul linden flower tea.
Tisane herbal tea.
Verveine verbena tea.
Vieille Prune plum brandy.
Xérès sherry.

Savoir faire

A volonté all you can eat (or drink).
Addition bill.
Amuse-gueule (or amuse-bouche) appetiser or hors d'oeuvre.
Assiette plate.
A la carte ordered separately (ie not on the fixed-price menu or formule).
Bobo bohemian bourgeois.
Carte des vins wine list.
Cendrier ashtray.
Commande order.
Commander to order.
Compris(e) included.
Comptoir counter.
Couvert cutlery, also used to express the number of diners.
Couteau knife.
Cuillère spoon.
Dégustation tasting.
Eau du robinet tap water.
Entrée starter.
Espace non-fumeur non-smoking area.
Formule set-price menu.
Fourchette fork.
Majoration price increase.
Menu set-price selection, also called a formule or prix fixe.
Menu dégustation tasting menu, sampling several different dishes.
Monnaie change.
Offert complimentary.
Plat main course.
Pourboire tip.
Prix fixe set-price menu.
Rince-doigts finger bowl.
Serveur/serveuse waiter/waitress.
Table d'hôtes refectory table.
Verre glass.
Zinc bar counter.

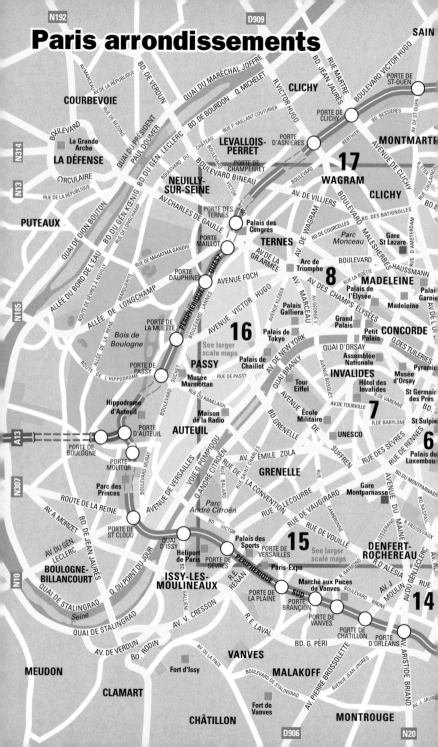

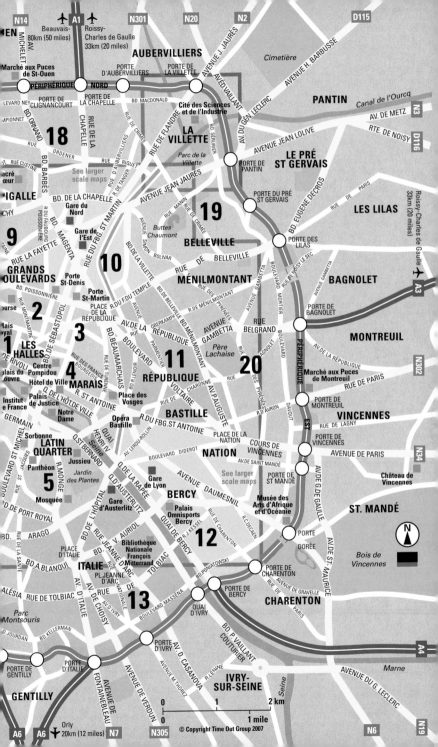

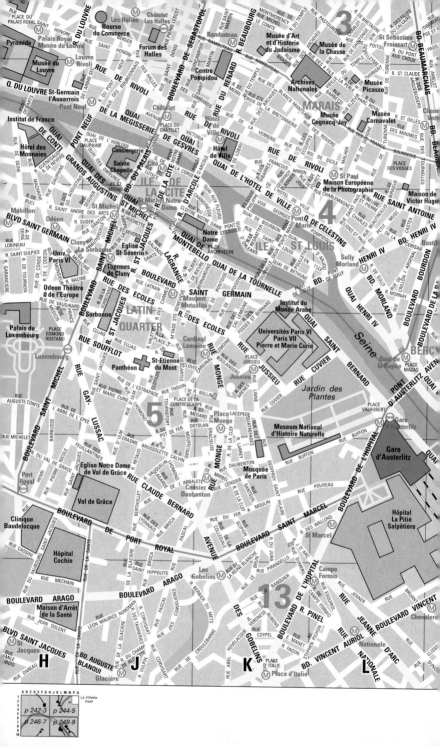

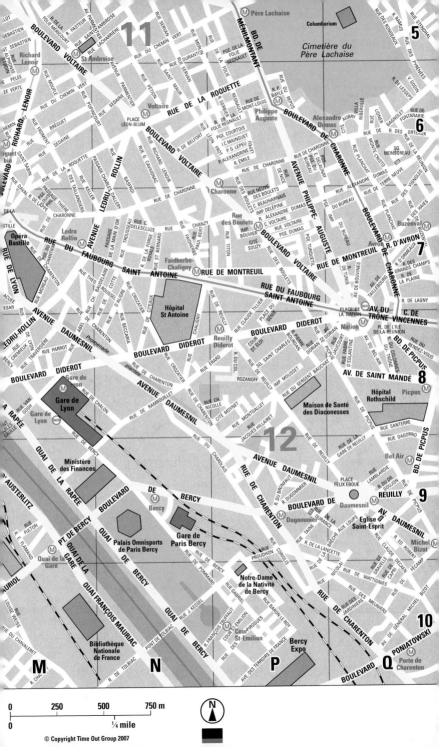

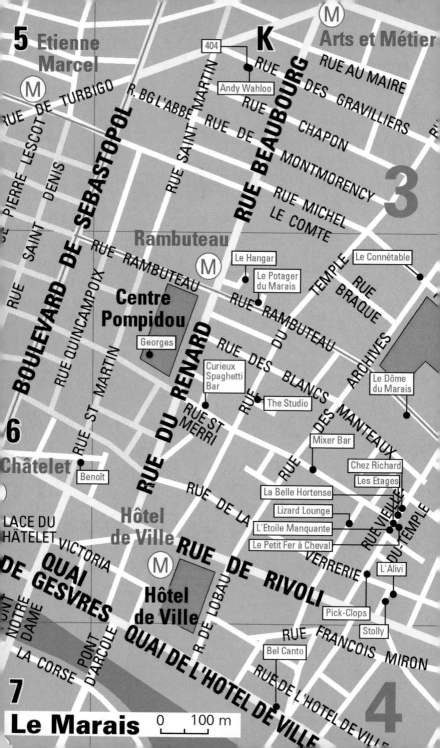